PUBLIC SECTOR LABOR RELATIONS:
ANALYSIS AND READINGS

Second Edition

DAVID LEWIN
Graduate School of Business
Columbia University

PETER FEUILLE
Institute of Labor and Industrial Relations
University of Illinois

THOMAS KOCHAN
Sloan School of Management
Massachusetts Institute of Technology

THOMAS HORTON AND DAUGHTERS

26662 South New Town Drive, Sun Lakes, Arizona 85224

Soc
HD
8005.6
U5
L48
1981

Library of Congress Cataloging in Publication Data

Lewin, David, 1943-
    Public sector labor relations.

    1. Collective bargaining—Government employees—
United States—Case studies.   2. Trade unions—Government
employees—United States—Case studies.   3. Employee-
management relations in government—United States—
Case studies.   I. Feuille, Peter, joint author.   II. Kochan,
Thomas A., joint author.   III. Title.

HD8005.6U5L48   331.89′01′353   82-3021
ISBN 0-913878-23-5

Contents

Preface to the Second Edition

The second edition of *Public Sector Labor Relations: Analysis and Readings* has been substantially revised. The volume now contains thirty separate reading selections (compared to thirty-seven in the first edition), sixteen of which are new. Three of these sixteen articles were written specifically for this volume, while the others together with those retained from the first edition were originally published elsewhere—in scholarly and professional journals and as portions of books and monographs. Each of the chapter introductions has been rewritten to take account of new developments, issues, research and public policies. Part IV now contains two collective bargaining exercises, one set in local police service, the other in local public education.

As was noted in the preface to the first edition, we are well aware that a common complaint about books of readings is that they rarely are constructed in such a way as to provide teachers and students with a coherent perspective on the subject matter at hand. Another of the alleged shortcomings of readings books is that they often feature the overcondensation or editing of reading selections, thereby offering only bits or snatches of the relevant material to the reader. We have sought to avoid these deficiencies in several ways. First, by attempting to integrate (a) the topics chosen for inclusion, (b) the textual material and reading selections, and (c) the readings contained in each chapter and subdivision thereof. Second, by in most cases reprinting as full a version as possible of the author or authors' original paper, article, monograph or book chapter. Third, by organizing the materials into three major sections: background and overview, collective bargaining processes and collective bargaining outcomes. These correspond to what we believe are the key dimensions of public sector labor relations, namely, setting, process and outcome. Fourth, by integrating, to the extent possible, research on public sector labor relations with research drawn from the private sector. This is most clearly apparent in the editors' introduction to each chapter. Fifth, by including collective bargaining exercises drawn from real-world public sector labor-management relationships that permit the student to apply and observe experientially some of the concepts and processes discussed in this book.

As before, the undertaking and completion of this edition of the book reflects a fully collaborative effort. Each author prepared the written material for and edited the reading selections in the chapters for which he was responsible. These were then reviewed and modified as required, by one or, in most cases, both of the other authors. Lewin bore primary responsibility for Chapters 2, 3, and 6, Kochan for Chapters 4 and 7, and Feuille for Chapter 5 and the collective bargaining exercises (Part IV). Chapters 1 and 8 reflect contributions from and a blending of the views of the three authors.

The reader will note that we have contributed considerably more written material to some chapters than to others, and also that the material and readings are arranged according to topical subdivision in some but not all chapters. This results from our conscious strategy in writing and organizing the materials to overcome gaps in the literature. In some topic areas, the gaps were substantial (though less so than in 1977 when the first edition was published), while in others the gaps were relatively small and/or the existing literature hung together reasonably well. Hence, we purposely chose to be responsive to such diversity in our own writing and editorial efforts rather than designing an artificially uniform organizational format for the book.

We believe that this book is well suited to courses in public sector labor relations, where it can serve as a basic textbook, and to courses in private sector collective bargaining and labor-management relations, where it can serve as a companion volume to other textbooks. However, by drawing from a broad base of public sector labor relations research, including three articles that deal with aspects of the Canadian experience in this area, we hope to broaden the appeal of this volume beyond those who are particularly interested in governmental collective bargaining. Specifically, the concepts, analytical frameworks, research designs, empirical findings and policy implications contained in the following pages, together with the explicit recognition throughout of the economic, political, legal and organizational forces that affect public sector bargaining processes and outcomes, commend the book to those interested in public management and administration, urban studies, labor economics, personnel and human resource management, organizational behavior and, of course, industrial relations.

Publication of this work would not have been possible without the gracious permission of many individuals and organizations to reprint the reading selections contained herein. In addition to the authors who are specifically identified in the Table of Contents and in the readings, we wish explicitly to acknowledge our appreciation to the following: *The Arbitration Journal,* The Association of Labor Mediation Agencies, The Brookings Institution, D.C. Heath and Company, *Industrial and Labor Relations Review, Industrial Relations,* Industrial Relations Research Association, New York State School of Industrial and Labor Relations, Cornell University, Princeton University Press, The Rand Corporation, *The Review of Economics and Statistics* and the *Yale Law Journal.* We also wish to thank our publisher, Thomas Horton and Daughters, for encouraging us to prepare a revised edition of this book.

In sum, we hope that the second edition of *Public Sector Labor Relations: Analysis and Readings* serves the purpose of pulling together in one volume the key issues, concepts and research findings pertaining to contemporary public sector labor relations. It was the absence of such a volume that motivated us to prepare the first edition of the book; the reactions of teachers and students to that volume were important to our decision to produce a second edition. We will feel that this was a wise decision if teachers and students find the book to be a useful learning tool.

February 1981   David Lewin
Peter Feuille
Thomas Kochan

PART I

BACKGROUND AND OVERVIEW

1

Introduction

OBJECTIVES AND FOCUS OF THE BOOK

The practice of collective bargaining in the United States is constantly changing, and nowhere is this more clearly visible than in the American public sector. Unionism first emerged in the public sector on a large scale in the early 1960s. Throughout the remainder of the 1960s and the first half of the 1970s, collective bargaining spread at a rapid and consistent pace to the point where, by 1976, approximately 39 percent of all public employees were members of bargaining organizations.[1] Thus, in the space of less than twenty years, public sector unionism developed to the point where it surpassed the level of penetration achieved by unions in the private sector (currently around 20 percent).

In introducing the first edition of this book in 1977, we argued that the door was then closing on the first generation of public sector bargaining. In contrast to the initial experiences of the 1960s, the transition to a second generation was taking place in a more austere economic and resistant political environment and was being guided by more experienced and sophisticated union, management, and neutral professionals. The early years of this second generation were dominated by efforts of the parties to adjust and adapt to the effects of the bargains struck in the earlier years. Management, in particular, sought to counterbalance some of the early contract gains of unions by taking a harder stand at the bargaining table. In those states with a number of years of bargaining experience, unions sought to modify and strengthen the impasse procedures under which they operated. All parties—unions, public employers, and third party neutrals—continued to experiment with and form strong opinions about the merits of the expanding array of alternatives for resolving disputes. Finally, the policies, practices, and events of the first generation of bargaining were evaluated and interpreted by a large number of academic researchers and other interested parties.

As we prepared this second edition, a hiatus in the development of public sector bargaining seemed to be occurring. Union growth in the public sector has slowed. In the past five years, few states have enacted new laws providing bargaining rights for public employees; instead, most legislative activity has focused on amending existing laws in those states that passed

1

their initial legislation in earlier years. The question before us, and one which will be filtered into our discussions throughout the book, is whether we are merely witnessing the calm before the storm of a new decade of rapid change, or whether we are beginning to settle into a semi-stable equilibrium where future changes are more incremental than dramatic in nature.

Our central objectives in this second edition are to present and assess the state of knowledge concerning the key issues and problems of public sector bargaining by drawing on some of the research completed to date. In addition, we will propose a number of unanswered questions that we believe will confront policy makers and practitioners in the years ahead and that, therefore, need additional attention from researchers. Our approach is based on the premise that in order to make accurate judgments and recommendations about labor relations phenomena, we must first understand the variables shaping labor relations events and the implications of altering one or more of these variables. We therefore stress the need to have an overall conceptual framework in mind for analyzing, interpreting, and placing in perspective the myriad of interrelated aspects of a collective bargaining system. The material in each of the following chapters is organized in a way that allows the reader to apply this premise, while also being introduced to collective bargaining in government.

In introducing each chapter, we first try to outline the central issues of interest that have been identified either by researchers or practitioners. In a research sense, this amounts to identifying the central dependent variables in each area. Second, we attempt to specify, where appropriate or possible, the underlying factors which shape these events; that is, we outline the explanatory or independent variables that have been identified in the area. Third, we attempt to identify important public policy issues in each area. Fourth, we address the key decisions that unions and employers must make in meeting the challenges facing them in each of the areas. Finally, we offer a summary assessment of the current state of knowledge and research in each area along with a suggested agenda for future research and discussion. Thus, while a rich blend of conceptual, policy, and descriptive material is included in this volume in order to give the reader a balanced exposure to the field, the text and readings also reflect our goal of advancing the state of research and thinking about public sector collective bargaining.

The three core concepts in the framework used to organize the material in this book are the environment or context of union-management relations, the nature of the bargaining process, and the outcomes or impacts of the bargaining process. This general conceptual framework is portrayed in Figure 1. We will briefly outline the substance of these concepts in order to set the stage for the chapters to follow. Before doing so, however, we should note that the present volume is not intended to serve as a basic collective bargaining text. We have included very little material dealing with private sector labor relations practices, union history, administration, and so on. The reader will find more comprehensive treatments of American collective bargaining in other volumes.[2]

We begin by examining the environmental contexts of the bargaining process. In the private sector, the role of the economic environment has been extensively discussed, both theoretically and empirically. Product and

Fig. 1 The general framework.

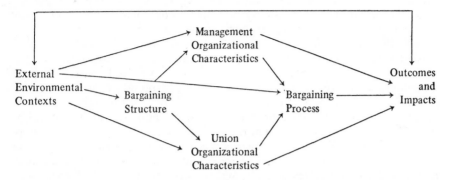

labor market constraints, employer ability to pay, labor costs as a percentage of total costs, demand elasticities, and so on, have all played a prominent role in explaining the behavior of the parties in bargaining and the outcomes of the process. Consequently, it behooves us to examine the nature of the economic context of bargaining in the public sector.

The legal environment also has been assigned an important role in the development of the study of collective bargaining in the private sector. However, the role of public policy has received a more prominent role in public sector research because of the diversity of federal, state, and local policies in this area. This diversity provides a potential laboratory for debate, experimentation, and evaluation of alternative policy options. Consequently, we will examine the nature and the development of the diversity of policy frameworks and attempt to place the role of policy in perspective.

The evolution of bargaining in the public sector has forced both researchers and practitioners to pay greater attention to the role of the political environment in which bargaining takes place. Although the notion that the political context plays a role in shaping the behavior of the parties in bargaining is certainly not new, the fact that the public employer is primarily a political institution—in contrast to the private employer—has markedly increased the attention given to this aspect of the environment. We believe that the political nature of government is the key feature from which flow most of the important differences between public and private sector labor relations. Hence, the readings throughout the book reflect our belief in the centrality of this aspect of the bargaining environment.

In the past few years, labor and management professionals have become increasingly aware of the impacts that shifts in the demographic makeup of society exert on their bargaining relationships. The declining enrollments in public schools, the shrinking tax bases of communities in the North that are affected by the movement of industry and population to the Sunbelt, and the changing racial and ethnic composition of urban areas have altered the demand for public services, reduced the resources available for collective bargaining, and increased the importance of the human resource provisions found in bargaining agreements. Therefore, we will treat these demographic characteristics as an additional dimension of the environment and discuss their impacts on collective bargaining.

3

From our treatment of the environmental contexts, we move inward to the structural and organizational factors which are important to understanding the nature of bargaining process and bargaining outcomes in the public sector. The concept of bargaining structure has generally been treated in private sector research by addressing the question of the appropriate bargaining unit. This overall policy issue can be broken down into the following questions: (1) What is the impact of centralized or decentralized bargaining structures? (2) What is the impact of broad versus narrow bargaining units? and (3) What is the appropriate bargaining status for supervisory and/or managerial employees? Most of the research in the public sector has ignored the first question, since there has been very little experience in state and local governments with centralized (multi-employer or coalitional) bargaining structures. The second question is especially relevant, however, for those states and cities that have multiple sets of bargaining units and personnel and budget-making policies which cut across these units. Consequently, we will examine the advantages and disadvantages of alternative ways of structuring bargaining relationships. Because of the feeling that supervisors in the public sector differ in their functions and responsibilities from their private sector counterparts, a great deal of controversy has erupted over the appropriate bargaining rights for public sector supervisors. We will examine these arguments and again seek to identify the relevance of alternative policy options for the process and outcomes of bargaining.

The importance of organizational characteristics of the employer in shaping the process and outcomes of bargaining has received more attention in the public than in the private sector. Most of the literature has focused on the difficult problem of adapting governmental structures and decision-making processes to the requirements of collective bargaining. Although this is a problem that faces all employers when bargaining arrives on the scene, the political nature of public employers and the traditions of separation of powers, representative government, and multiple points of access to decision makers increase the magnitude of the problem for the public employer. For example, there is no objective formula by which a city government can decide how much of a voice in labor relations matters shall be given to the mayor, the city council, the city attorney, the civil service commission, and so on. In fact, for many public jurisdictions during the initial period of bargaining, the most important problem may be deciding who is the employer for labor relations purposes. Experience has also shown that this is not just a transitory problem that withers away as the bargaining relationship "matures." Instead, the question of who has the power to speak for and commit management to a decision in public sector bargaining continues to be a "normal" part of the politics of the decision-making process. Consequently, most of our material dealing with management as an actor in collective bargaining focuses on these types of problems and their impacts upon bargaining processes and outcomes.

The labor relations context and bargaining structure materials in Chapters 2 and 3 set the stage for analyzing the more visible of our three core concepts: the characteristics of the bargaining process itself, including the resolution of negotiating impasses and the outcomes or impacts of bargain-

4

ing. We will introduce the material on the interaction process in Chapter 4 by reviewing some of the bargaining process concepts that are found in the private sector literature and then suggesting how some of these notions need to be adapted to be consistent with the bargaining process that is evolving in American public jurisdictions. Specifically, we will focus on the notion that, in contrast to the bilateral paradigm of the private sector, bargaining in the public sector tends to take on multilateral characteristics because of the multiplicity of management interests involved in and the political nature of the public employer. Then we will examine how the bargaining process becomes transformed as the scope of issues discussed broadens to include those of interest not only to public employees and their employers, but to other groups in the community.

Since the function of the negotiation process is to resolve differences between employers and employees, we will devote a good portion of our analysis of the bargaining process to the means used in the public sector to accomplish this end. Thus, in Chapter 5, we will examine the legal status and the normative arguments regarding the right to strike as well as the procedural mechanisms—mediation, factfinding, and the various forms of arbitration—that have been used to resolve negotiating disputes. In particular, we will focus on the compatibility—or lack of it—between the incentives to engage in good faith bargaining and the availability of various impasse procedures.

The research on alternatives for resolving negotiation impasses provides a logical link to an analysis of the final set of dependent variables in our framework, namely, the outcomes and impacts of bargaining. Ultimately, the two general questions that policymakers, union and management practitioners, and researchers must struggle with in this area are: (1) What determines the kinds of outcomes that are achieved in bargaining in the public sector? and (2) What are the impacts of these outcomes on the goals of the parties and the larger society? In this section we will not only examine the traditional impact-of-unions-on-wages research, but we will also discuss and include in the text studies that attempt to isolate the determinants of outcomes within a unionized context. This second approach essentially investigates the environmental, structural, organizational, and procedural factors which determine variations in outcomes under collective bargaining. The material in Chapters 6 and 7 will further illuminate the diversity of impacts and outcomes across thousands of bargaining relationships and will underscore the difficulty of assigning proof of causality to particular independent variables.

Our final chapter will feature a look backward at the earlier chapters with an eye toward evaluating the state of public sector bargaining research. In this final chapter we will ask what we have learned from all of this research, what we have yet to learn, and how we can narrow the gaps in existing knowledge. We close our reading material by discussing the implications that public sector research and practice may have for the study and practice of collective bargaining in general.

In the supplementary material at the end of this volume, we have attempted to go beyond the usual book of text and readings by providing readers with opportunities for getting their feet wet. Specifically, we have included two negotiation exercises, one between a city and a police union and the other between a school district and a teacher union. The participants' objective is to apply some of the conceptual material presented in this volume to the experience of negotiating a public sector labor contract.

THE AUTHORS' PERCEPTIONS

Since our interpretation and analysis of the issues examined in this book will be affected by our values and by our views of the current stage of development of public sector collective bargaining, we owe the reader a sketch of how we perceive the governmental labor relations arena, circa 1981. At a basic level, we are committed to the right of public employees to form, join, and participate in unions in order to participate via collective bargaining and other political processes in decisions which affect their work lives. For more than forty years, the bedrock principle of our national labor policy has been that private sector employees have the right to participate in an organized manner in the decisions which affect their employment. We have yet to encounter any compelling reasons why public employees should not also enjoy similar rights. Operationally, this value premise means that this volume will contain very little material dealing with the appropriateness of collective bargaining for public employees,[3] but will contain a great deal of material dealing with the appropriate shape of collective bargaining systems.

We currently see bargaining continuing in its second phase or generation that began in the mid-1970s. Compared to its initial or developmental phase, this second generation is characterized by five interrelated factors: (1) a more difficult, less expansive economic environment for collective bargaining; (2) less political influence by public sector unions and an increased aggressiveness by public sector management; (3) increased challenges to the effectiveness of dispute settlement procedures; (4) an eroding real wage position of public employees; and (5) an increasingly assertive "public" that wants more efficiency in government and input into key decision-making processes and is less willing to support public services with increased tax burdens. The first four conditions have been apparent since at least the mid-1970s; the fifth factor is perhaps of more recent vintage.

The Economic Environment of Collective Bargaining

The most important development affecting the environment of collective bargaining in the public sector since the early 1970s has been the severe economic and financial problems of state and local governments. The tightening economic constraints are partly a function of the prolonged and deep recession accompanied by high levels of inflation that the American economy experienced in the 1970s, and partly a function of the longer-term economic and social decline of many American cities. The cyclical downturn follows a decade of expanding employment in state and local governments and a period of "catch-up" wage increases. While the impact of these economic pressures has been illustrated most visibly by the near default of New York City in 1975 and Cleveland in 1979, their impact has been felt in almost every major city in the northeastern part of the United States and many other cities located elsewhere. These recent developments have speeded the pace of the longer-term decline of these cities.[4] Large industrial centers of the Northeast have been losing jobs to both their surrounding suburbs and to the lower tax and faster growing "Sunbelt" states. This has meant that the cities that experienced the greatest degree of militancy among public employees in the 1960s and early 1970s are now faced not only with declining or at best constant tax bases, but also with highly sophisticated collective bargaining relationships with their employees. Thus, those cities with the most severe financial difficulties are also the ones that must deal with the most militant and effective public sector labor unions in the country. While the magnitude of their economic problems varies considerably, few local or state governments have been immune to the twin pressures of economic stagnation and high inflation.

Changing Structures of Political Influence

The changes in the economic environment of the 1970s led to a changed political climate for public sector collective bargaining. One important result of the deteriorating economic position of state and local governments has been that the political influence of public sector labor unions appears to have declined relative to that of other interest groups. Even politicians who have been elected with labor support have found it possible to take a hardline, fiscally conservative approach to collective bargaining with their public employees. In different ways, the Democratic governors of the states of California, New York, Connecticut, and Massachusetts and the mayors of such cities as New York, Seattle, and Boston have all adopted positions which effectively reduce the political access or influence of the public sector unions that helped put them in office.[5]

We believe that the bargaining processes which evolved during the first generation of governmental collective bargaining accurately have been described as "multilateral" in nature, that is, involving the interplay of diverse interest groups rather than simply conforming to the bilateral dichotomy of labor versus management. Some observers have argued that a bilateral decision-making structure and process based on the private sector bargaining model would so insulate the process from the "public interest" and from the "normal political process" (one characterized by the interplay of multiple interest groups and multiple access points) that the democratic principles upon which government is based would be inherently destroyed or weakened (see, for example, the Wellington and Winter reading in Chapter 2). Other observers, however, have argued that the political process infringed on the integrity of the collective bargaining process because power within the management structure was shared among diverse and often conflicting interest groups in a way that provided an incentive for labor unions to play one interest off against another. The result of this situation of dispersed management power and internal management conflict was that much of the bargaining between union representatives and those management officials that held the critical decision-making power went on away from the formal negotiating table. A whole new vernacular grew up for this

7

practice—end runs, backdoor deals, two bites at the apple, double-decking, and so on.

In practice, it appears that while the bilateral negotiations process grew in importance throughout the first generation of public sector bargaining, enough potential for multilateral bargaining was maintained to preserve the ability of politicians to intervene in the process when their critical interests were perceived to be at stake. Since labor costs are the biggest single controllable item in state and local government budgets, politicians have turned to a hard-line bargaining policy as one means of dealing with their economic problems. This strategy partly reflects economic necessity and partly a reaction or backlash to the perceived excesses of bargaining settlements that were negotiated during the first generation, especially in the areas of pensions and other fringe benefits. During the 1960s and the early 1970s, it was politically expedient and sometimes necessary for elected officials to agree to wage and fringe benefit improvements without regard for the funding consequences of these agreements. Since employment levels were expanding at a rapid rate during that period, the full financial implications of settlements negotiated during the first generation have only recently begun to be felt. In addition, the harder-line stance toward public employees that is currently popular among elected officials partly reflects simple political expediency. Whether the actual budgetary conditions necessitate a hold-the-line approach or not, it is clear that many politicians can now benefit politically from publicly endorsing a hardline strategy.[6] In other words, although the formal bargaining process continues to be the dominant mechanism for the exchanges between public unions and public employers, the economic pressures and public opinion changes just discussed have caused many politicians to become more actively involved in labor relations matters in ways which have reduced union influence. In turn, these stiffening managerial postures have, in some instances, resulted in increased bargaining turmoil (see the material in Chapter 5).

Challenges to Dispute Resolution Procedures

The first generation of collective bargaining was marked by great expectations of finding effective ways to structure a good faith bargaining process without the right to strike—an arrangement which directly contradicted private sector practice and conventional wisdom. Public policymakers created impasse procedures as alternatives to the strike, and these procedural experiments generally were acclaimed as successful.[7] Such claims by both practitioners and researchers continue, by and large, into the second generation of bargaining, and the empirical evidence from the first generation largely supports some of these claims. In most jurisdictions that have been studied, the empirical data show that a majority of disputes were settled by the parties without relying on impasse procedures. Furthermore, the studies tend to show that most of the disputes that went to impasse resulted in settlement at some nonbinding step—mediation or factfinding, as examples. The remaining disputes tended to get resolved through some combination of further negotiations, arbitration, employer unilateral determination, or strike.

Although the strike was outlawed in most jurisdictions, strikes did occur; however, the time lost due to strikes was much lower in the public than in the private sector. Those public sector strikes which did occur tended to be short.

There are some ominous signs beginning to appear on the horizon, though, that may ultimately upset the early favorable predictions of the effectiveness of these dispute resolution procedures. First, we have witnessed a progression from mild forms of third-party intervention to stronger forms of third-party determination. For example, most of the early statutes provided for mediation, perhaps followed by factfinding with recommendations. In the late 1960s and early 1970s, however, a number of states amended their procedures to provide for various forms of compulsory arbitration for police and firefighters. Most of the legislative choices were for conventional binding arbitration, though more recently a number of states have opted for an even stronger form of third-party determination that has been labeled "final offer" arbitration. Second, there is some evidence of a growing reliance on mediation and factfinding by other employee groups, especially teachers. Data from New York State, for instance, indicate that the parties have gone further into impasse procedures in a larger proportion of negotiations in recent than in earlier years.[8] A third development that may suggest trouble is that the parties to the most experienced and professional bargaining relationships and the ones in the most difficult bargaining environments are the heaviest users of impasse procedures. In effect, they have experienced the "narcotic effects" that were predicted by the critics, that is, that the parties will become addicted to using the impasse procedures as a painless means of avoiding the hard bargaining necessary to reach direct agreement. The parties in the largest cities with the most politicized union-management relationships and the most difficult economic problems have a much higher rate of reliance on impasse procedures than do the smaller jurisdictions, and thus the former appear to be dependent upon these procedures as part and parcel of their negotiations processes. These developments have raised an important and difficult question: Is there some sort of natural half-life for dispute resolution procedures after which the parties learn how to incorporate the procedures into their bargaining strategies and ultimately cause the procedures to become less effective over time?

In general, these procedures performed reasonably well during the first generation of public sector bargaining when the environment was such that unions were able to make strong economic gains, the political incentives for management to resist union pressure were low, and the economic position of employees was one of catching up with the economic position of their private sector counterparts. The early years of the second generation saw more states enact stronger dispute resolution systems (i.e., ones ending in arbitration). The early experience with these "severe" systems has once again been generally (but not uniformly) favorable, especially when the environmental pressures impinging on the public sector during this time period are taken into account. Whether these procedures will continue to meet the challenges posed by the increasingly difficult environments that appear to be ahead remains an important question for future observation and research.

Moderation of Economic Gains and the Emergence of Relative and Real Wage Losses

As suggested above, during the first generation of bargaining the average pubic employee experienced "catch-up" wage increases that in many cases put him or her on the favorable side of a comparison with private sector counterparts doing comparable work (though, as the Chapter 6 readings suggest, it is not clear that unionism and collective bargaining were exclusively or even primarily responsible for these relative wage gains).[9] At the same time, the fringe benefit packages of public employees also expanded at a faster rate than seemed to be the case in the private sector. So far during the second generation of public sector bargaining, the gains of the early days have proved difficult to match.[10] The economic and political environments have made it more difficult to improve wage and fringe levels at a rate that the rank-and-file public employee union member had come to expect. Public management learned that it could successfully resist union demands in bargaining and became increasingly willing to do so. Although we lack the longitudinal data needed to assess the wage gains over time in a precise manner, it appears that the early gains have been somewhat eroded by the high rates of inflation of recent years (see Chapter 6 for some data on this issue). Given the current political climate and the austere economic environment on the one hand, and the pressures that normally build up within unions as real wages decline on the other, we can anticipate considerable tension and conflict in the public sector in the next several years.

The challenge to governmental wage-setting processes in the near future will be to provide equitable rates of wage increase that neither tax governments into bankruptcy nor allow the wage gains of the earlier years to be eroded to their pre-bargaining levels. The long-run problem to be faced is one of finding a workable basis for financing public (especially municipal) employees' salaries while improving the services provided to the community —or, in other words, balancing equity and efficiency considerations in public sector wage determination.

The Assertive Public

The inherent nature of public sector bargaining gives the "public," or more realistically, various public interest groups, the right to exert their influence over bargaining issues that are perceived to affect their vital interests. The economic and political trends summarized above, along with the growing public sentiment against big government, high taxes, and poor services, have increased the desire of a number of these interest groups to assert themselves in collective bargaining decision making. Some of these efforts have been indirect, as, for example, through sponsorship of state referenda to limit or reduce the size of property taxes. Others have taken the form of general efforts to pass and/or enforce open meeting or "sunshine" laws that require bargaining sessions and dispute resolution procedures to be open to the public. Still others have taken a more direct approach, including requests for public seats at the bargaining table.

In addition to the role of community or taxpayer interest groups, various federal agencies and the judicial branch of government have asserted their roles as enforcers of equal employment opportunity and affirmative action statutes and rules. As we will see in Chapter 7, federal and state efforts to desegregate public schools have heightened our sensitivities to the conflicts between the collective bargaining principle of seniority and the public policy objective of affirmative action.

Finally, in the past decade state and federal governments have become increasingly important sources of revenue for (or bankrollers of) our major cities. While the growing federal role is most visible in the case of New York City, where the federal government has guaranteed since 1975 the loans used to guide the city through its financial crisis, the proportion of the revenues of the largest cities in the United States that come from one or another state or federal source has been consistently increasing over the past decade. At a minimum, the increased dependence of local governments on outside revenue sources leads to more complex bargaining. Over the longer run, if this trend continues, we may see the state and/or federal governments demanding greater control over wage setting practices as the quid pro quo for their financial aid.

In short, the combined effects of these various external forces that are impinging on the traditional parties to the public sector bargaining process have produced an era where the potential for "third-party" interests to influence the process and outcomes of bargaining is indeed quite high. Whether, or how, this potential is realized in the years ahead remains to be seen.

LABOR RELATIONS RESEARCH, PERSONAL PREFERENCES, AND POLICY IMPLICATIONS

One of the purposes of this volume is to assess some of the research into governmental labor relations. Accordingly, we close this introductory chapter by offering some suggestions to assist the reader in evaluating the material in this book—including, of course, our own writing—with a more critical eye.

Research Considerations

In this volume, the reader will encounter a large number and variety of evaluative statements which assess the shape of relationships among labor relations variables. For example, in Chapter 2, Wellington and Winter argue that the full transplant of private sector collective bargaining into the public sector will give government unions too much power vis-a-vis other interest groups. As another example, in Chapter 5, Feuille argues that final offer arbitration has less of a chilling effect upon the incentive to bargain than does conventional arbitration.

The reader should assess these types of evaluative statements along several dimensions. First, how carefully specified are the variables being researched? For instance, are such workhorse phrases as "too much power" or "the chilling effect" given some reasonably precise meaning, or are they stated in vague and general language? Precise definition and specification permit more careful measurement and stronger conclusions than do the use of open-ended concepts, but such precision may run the risk of abstracting away from operational issues and problems. Second, it is necessary to distinguish between associational and causal relationships. For example, the fact that a high wage level coexists with an aggressive union does not necessarily mean that the union is responsible for the high wage. This causality may exist, but first it is necessary to control for the other variables that influence wage rates. Further, research into social phenomena—especially those connected with power-based adversarial interactions—usually cannot be accomplished via controlled experiments (as chemists might perform in their laboratories), and as a result it is very difficult to isolate the effect of one variable (say, conventional arbitration) upon another (say, wage rates).[11]

Third, one of the recurring themes in this volume is the need for the reader to be aware of the diversity across thousands of public sector union-management relationships. This diversity necessarily limits the validity of sweeping generalizations about labor relations phenomena, and is especially true when one considers negotiating and impasse practices and bargaining outcomes.[12] Similarly, the research process itself is constrained by time, effort, and financial scarcity and hence is based upon informal or formal *sampling* of the entire population of such phenomena. Therefore, the reader needs to consider the scope of the data that are presented and the extent to which the data support generalizations. Researchers are always faced with the temptation to expand the scope of their conclusions, and the reader should pay careful attention to possible inconsistencies between an author's conclusionary reach and the limits of his or her data.

Fourth, the reader should consider the relationship between the research issue being investigated and the data that are used. Because research is a costly process, there is a tendency for researchers to rely upon readily available data in their investigations. We have witnessed, for example, more "chilling effect" studies which compare the proportions of arbitrated and negotiated settlements than studies which directly measure the parties' movement or compromising behavior in negotiations. Thus, the reader may profitably inquire if the kind of data that are used are sufficient to answer the research issues being addressed and, further, what other kinds of information might provide better answers.

Personal Preferences

A fifth dimension involves the interpretive latitude which exists in most of the writing in this area. The public sector labor relations literature continues to contain authoritative opinions, conventional wisdom, logical arguments, case studies, classification studies, and "ad hoc" surveys. The research methods used often are more informal and implicit than formal and explicit. Substantively, this literature consists of writings about various facets of human interactions over scarce resources in adversarial contexts where the outcomes of these interactions may be valued quite differently by different writers. And the literature is replete with such conclusions as "arbitration (or factfinding or supervisory bargaining, etc.) is working well" but unaccompanied by any comparison standard, thereby leaving the reader to ask "working well compared to what?"

12

We make these points not to condemn the authors of the existing literature but instead to caution the reader that there is considerable room for personal preferences to influence conclusions. For instance, there are no precise formulae by which one can conclude that unions have "too much" or "too little" power or that the parties rely "too heavily" on arbitration. This means that a given body of information may be interpreted in contrary fashion (i.e., one person's unit fragmentation is another person's employee democracy). Similarly, it is the very rare researcher/writer who can be totally divorced from any normative opinion on these research topics, given that most of the topics are related to the allocation of scarce resources which may have a substantial impact upon human welfare. In sum, most writers have considerable latitude to interpret the data they report, and their interpretations can be affected by their own preferences or values.[13]

Policy Implications

Public sector collective bargaining tends to increase the visibility and societal impact of government acting in its government-as-employer role relative to its government-as-regulator role. This is because public sector bargaining is a process of governmental decision making which allocates a variety of scarce public resources. The importance of the bargaining process to the government-as-employer role has resulted in considerable policy attention to the shape of the bargaining process—as can be seen most clearly in the attempts of various jurisdictions to regulate carefully the resolution of negotiating impasses. In general, we can say that the structure, process, and outcomes of public sector bargaining are closely connected with expressions of public labor relations policy.

The close connection between practices and policy creates an incentive for researchers/writers in the field to discuss the "policy implications" of their research. This is a wholesome tendency to the extent that their research is germane to policy issues. However, we urge the reader to evaluate carefully any policy implications or conclusions encountered in these (and other) readings. As we have noted, it is difficult to isolate the effect on bargaining of a single policy variable. In addition, it is often difficult to specify policy recommendations without some rank ordering of societal or policy makers' preferences (avoiding strikes, encouraging the incentive to bargain, etc.). As a result, the reader should check to see if a writer's public policy implications (where offered) are supported by his or her data or if these implications appear to be based on criteria other than empirical research (such as conventional wisdom, logical argument or personal preference). In sum, we encourage the reader to be cognizant of the limits as well as the contributions of research to public sector labor relations policy.

FOOTNOTES

1. For an analysis of public sector union growth and membership see John F. Burton, Jr., "The Extent of Collective Bargaining in the Public Sector," in

Benjamin Aaron, Joseph R. Grodin, and James L. Stern (eds.), *Public-Sector Bargaining* (Washington, D.C.: Bureau of National Affairs, 1979), pp. 1-43.

2. Three such volumes are D. Quinn Mills, *Labor Management Relations* (New York: McGraw-Hill, 1978); John Fossum, *Labor Relations* (Dallas: Business Publications Inc., 1979); and Thomas A. Kochan, *Collective Bargaining and Industrial Relations: From Theory to Policy and Practice* (Homewood, IL: Richard D. Irwin, 1980).

3. Three works which do question the appropriateness of "compulsory collective bargaining" in government are Sylvester Petro, "Sovereignty and Compulsory Public-Sector Bargaining," *Wake Forest Law Review*, 10, 1 (March 1974), 25-165; Ralph de Toledano, *Let Our Cities Burn* (New Rochelle, NY: Arlington House, 1975); and Robert S. Summers, *Collective Bargaining and Public Benefit Conferral: A Jurisprudential Critique* (Ithaca, NY: New York State School of Industrial and Labor Relations, 1976).

4. See, for example, Thomas Muller, *Growing and Declining Urban Areas: A Fiscal Comparison* (Washington, D.C.: The Urban Institute, 1975).

5. For example, the governor of New York proposed in 1976 that his obligation to bargain with state employees be "suspended" for one year, for he felt this was necessary to show investors that the state was holding the line on wages while it began to pull itself out of its economic malaise. Although his idea never was seriously pursued within the state legislature, it symbolizes the declining influence that public unions have with many elected officials. A more concrete example comes from Seattle, where in 1975 the local firefighters' union tried to have Mayor Wes Uhlman removed from office after he dismissed the city fire chief. In the recall election, the mayor amassed a far larger victory margin than he did in his 1973 reelection—when he had the active support of the firefighters' union. See Bureau of National Affairs (BNA), *Government Employee Relations Report*, No. 613, (July 6, 1975), B4-5, for a report on the Seattle situation. Finally, in 1978, California governor Jerry Brown embraced the property tax cuts and spending limitations required by Proposition 13, which was approved by the state's voters in June of that year. Brown's reversal of his initial anti-Proposition 13 stance was bitterly opposed by public sector union leaders, who had endorsed and otherwise strongly supported him in the 1974 California gubernatorial campaign.

6. See BNA, *Government Employee Relations Report*, No. 626, (October 6, 1975), Z1-5, for a special report on the shift in public opinion regarding government unions. For more widely available reports, see "Strike of San Francisco City Craft Unions Fails to Win the Support of Public or Labor," *Wall Street Journal*, April 15, 1976, p. 30; "Public Employees Lose Leverage," *Business Week*, December 22, 1975, p. 15; "Public Employees Hit Tough Going as Strikes, New York's Ills Stir Opposition," *Wall Street Journal*, December 12, 1975, p. 34; and "The Public Disdain of Public Employees," *New York Times*, June 27, 1976, section 4, p. 3. A more recent case in point is found in the strike by the Chicago firefighters in the spring of 1980. This was largely a dispute between the Democratic mayor of Chicago and the leadership of the firefighters' union.

7. For a review of the early impasse procedure studies, see Thomas P. Gilroy and Anthony V. Sinicropi, "Impasse Resolution in Public Employment: A Current Assessment," *Industrial and Labor Relations Review*, 25 (July 1972), 496-511.

8. New York State Public Employment Relations Board, *PERB News*, 9 (March 1976), 1.

9. Nor is it clear when public employees in various jurisdictions achieved parity with or surpassed their private sector counterparts. Some literature suggests that the catch up occurred prior to unionization and especially formal collective

bargaining in government. See Walter Fogel and David Lewin, "Wage Determination in the Public Sector," *Industrial and Labor Relations Review*, 27 (April 1974), 410-31; Sharon P. Smith, "Pay Differentials Between Federal Government and Private Sector Workers," *Industrial and Labor Relations Review*, 29 (January 1976), 179-197; and Economic Development Council of New York City, Inc., *Looking Ahead in New York City: Reducing the 1975-76 Budget Gap in New York City* (New York: EDC, April 1975).

10. For evidence on this point, see the discussion in Chapter 6 and the sources of data cited therein.

11. For a critical appraisal of public sector bargaining literature, especially the "union power" thesis, see David Lewin, "Public Employment Relations: Confronting the Issues," *Industrial Relations*, 12 (October 1973), 309-21.

12. For further elaboration of the diversity thesis, see David Lewin, Raymond D. Horton, and James W. Kuhn, *Collective Bargaining and Manpower Utilization in Big City Governments* (Montclair, NJ: Allenheld Osmun, 1979). Note that the diversity of private sector labor relations is considerably greater than is generally recognized.

13. See, for example, Peter Feuille, "Analyzing Compulsory Arbitration Experiences: The Role of Personal Preferences, Comment," *Industrial and Labor Relations Review*, 28 (April 1975), 432-435; and Mark Thompson and Jaimes Cairnie, "Reply," in the same issue of this journal, pp. 435-438.

PART II

COLLECTIVE BARGAINING PROCESSES

2

Labor Relations Contexts

THE ECONOMIC-FINANCIAL CONTEXT

The purpose of the introduction and readings included in the opening section of this chapter are to provide an overview of the economic and financial context of public sector labor relations. We begin by discussing some of the economic sources of power that private sector unions draw upon to achieve gains through collective bargaining, and then assess the relevance of these factors to the public sector. Next, we examine the sources of and trends in revenue available to state and local governments. Finally, we close by looking ahead at the longer term financial prospects for local government, posing some questions that researchers and policy makers will have to struggle with in the future.

Most theories of the economic sources of power of private sector labor unions rely primarily on Alfred Marshall's four principles of the derived demand for labor. According to Marshall, unions will be most powerful when the following conditions are present:

1. the demand for the final product is inelastic,
2. labor is a strategic factor in the "production" process,
3. labor costs are a small percentage of total costs, and
4. the supply of alternative factors of production is inelastic, i.e., the price of alternatives to union labor in the production process, e.g. capital or non-union labor, rises rapidly as more of these factors are used.[1]

The public sector presents a mixed picture for labor on the above dimensions. From one perspective, the demand for public sector labor is often asserted to be more inelastic than in the private sector. That position is forcefully stated by Wellington and Winter in the initial reading selection of this chapter, and is in part supported empirically by Ashenfelter and Ehrenberg in their analysis of the demand for labor in the American public sector over the 1958-1969 period. However, the latter's results also show that the degree of labor elasticity in government, that is, the extent to which employment levels decline when wages are increased, varies considerably among public services and is greater in high than in low density states. On balance, it might appear that this characteristic of the governmental economy acted

17

to increase the economic power of unions during the first generation of public sector bargaining. Two additional concerns must be raised, however, before generalizing from these conclusions.

First, the finding that a stronger tradeoff between wage increases and employment existed in the governments of high density than low density states suggests that a stronger employment response was emerging in those environments that have experienced the longest and strongest union pressure for public sector wage increases. In a sense, then, these data contain some insights into economic confrontations that the large industrialized cities of the Northeast have been experiencing with their public employees, particularly since the mid-1970s. Second, the estimates of the employment response to wage increases included in Ashenfelter and Ehrenberg's paper are based on data from years when the demand for labor in the public sector was expanding at a rapid rate. Between 1959 and 1969, all public employment in the United States increased by just under 50 percent, with the increases in state government, 80 percent, and local government, 53 percent, dwarfing that in the federal sector, 24 percent.[2] In contrast, between 1969 and 1977, (the last year for which complete data are available), all public employment increased by only 21 percent, with the rates of increase slowing dramatically in state and local governments, 33 and 28 percent, respectively, and the federal sector actually experiencing a 4 percent employment decline. Moreover, for the first time since collective bargaining emerged on a broad scale in government, some public employers have initiated substantial personnel layoffs and some others are facing such a prospect. This is particularly true of governments located in agriculture and energy poor states, where the phenomenon of public employee layoffs first began to be noticed in the mid-1970s.[3] Thus, while the "inelasticity of demand" as a source of union power may have been important in the first generation of public sector bargaining, more recently it has been less important and in the near future it appears that it will not provide public sector labor organizations with insulation from the adverse effects of negotiated wage increases.

Whether the public sector is experiencing a short-term employment adjustment to the rapid growth and wage increases of the recent past, or whether, as is seemingly more apparent, a structural shift in the elasticity of demand for public labor is taking place, is an important question for future research. What is clear, though, is that the fact of employment slowdowns and cutbacks and the threat of future cutbacks have been incorporated into the rhetoric and strategy of management negotiators in many—perhaps even most—public jurisdictions. These facts and this threat, combined with the demonstration effects of especially large reductions of municipal employment, as occurred, for example, in New York City in the mid-to-late 1970s, may be enough to neutralize this source of power for public sector unions, both in the near and longer term future.

The strategic position of labor as a factor of production obviously is an important source of power in the "essential" public sector services. However, it is difficult to generalize about the overall degree of essentiality of labor in the public sector, since the functions performed by public sector employees are so very diverse. Thus, while the services performed by police, firefighters, and perhaps transit and sanitation workers are highly essential and therefore provide a source of power to their unions, the services of library workers, college faculty or teaching assistants, and many general categories of white collar workers are less essential. Teachers, snow plow drivers (essential in January but dispensable in June?) and many other occupations fall somewhere in the middle range of essentiality. Consequently, this source of power is likely to vary widely across different public sector bargaining units.

Perhaps the most important long run economic constraint on the bargaining power of public employees is the high percentage of total government expenditures accounted for by labor costs. Specifically, payroll costs account for approximately 62 percent of local government expenditures and 40 percent of state government expenditures.[4] More important, within local government, those employee groups that have been most militant and most highly organized, namely, police, firefighters, teachers and sanitation workers, are in the most labor intensive services. This means that wage increases for these groups have relatively large impacts on the total costs of the functions in which they are employed. Over time, therefore, as the public becomes even more resistant to further tax increases, management's strongest incentive to hold down negotiated wage increases will exist in especially labor intensive functions. Reductions of services in these functions inevitably require cutbacks in employment levels or reductions in wage and benefit costs in the main occupations associated with them. Consequently, this source of power should, in the long run, act to hold down rates of increases in wage and benefit levels for public employees.[5] (Evidence of the effects of unions on public sector pay and benefits will be presented in Chapter 6).

The fourth Marshallian condition involves the case of replacing union labor with capital or other factors of production (e.g. non-union workers). The service orientation of the public sector makes it very difficult to reduce the wage bill through technological change, so that this is not as important a constraint on union power as in the private manufacturing sector. The converse of this, however, is that productivity growth in public employment is also lower than the average productivity growth in manufacturing. Therefore, wage improvements based on productivity are also constrained in government. In short, while the threat of technological change is not much of an impediment to public employee unions in the short run, the returns from technological change are also less available to public employees over the long run.

A final economic characteristic that has received a good deal of attention as a source of union power in the private sector is the degree of concentration or market power that employers enjoy. The theoretical argument for concentration as a source of power is that large employers in concentrated industries have considerable discretion in wage determination and, therefore, provide more "bargaining room" for the union. In the public sector this range-of-discretion argument is also made on the basis that (1) governmental employers are often monopolists in providing public services, and (2) there is no economic market clearing price for the services provided by government. Following this reasoning, the power that some unions in the private sector gain from dealing with large employers in concentrated industries may also be available to organized public employees. However, others have argued on theoretical grounds that unions obtain no special advantages in bargaining with a monopolist, and also that governments do not necessarily possess the characteristics of a monopolist.[6] Indeed, the growing use of the private sector to provide services that have traditionally been regarded as the exclusive or predominant domain of government is additional evidence against the government-as-monopolist thesis.

Overall, then, the economic characteristics of public employment present a mixed prognosis for the long term strength that public employee unions will be able to exercise in collective bargaining with their employers. While the inelastic demand for services, the monopoly power of employers, and the essentiality of some services performed by government employees should act in unions' long run favor, these advantageous economic characteristics are offset by the labor intensity of public services, the productivity constraints inherent in public employment and changing conceptions of service essentiality and the scope of governmental activity. While experience and research to date do not allow us to predict with precision the relative strengths of these opposing forces, we believe and propose to the reader that the long term economic outlook is more problematic than has often been suggested. This view will be reinforced by an analysis of the more specific financial problems of state and local governments.

Financial Contexts of State and Local Governments

Analysis of the impact of specific financial conditions of state and local governments on the public sector collective bargaining process requires that the sources of revenue available to these governments be understood. Table 1 presents an overall picture of the sources of revenue for state and local government for the fiscal year 1977.[7] Among the major points to be noted from these data is that state governments rely most heavily on sales taxes, federal aid, and individual income taxes (these are sources of general revenues as opposed, for example, to insurance trust funds, which derive from legally mandated payroll and/or employer taxes and which are expended on specific line items such as retirement, disability and unemployment benefits). Local governments obtain the highest percentage of their revenues from property taxes and state aid (just under 31 percent in each case). Over the last several years, local governments have become somewhat less dependent on property taxes as a revenue source, but somewhat more dependent on state aid. Federal aid to local governments (but not state governments) rose especially rapidly during the 1970s, following the expansion of revenue sharing (under the doctrine of the "new federalism"). However, in 1977, federal monies accounted for only between 6 and 12 percent of local government budgets and were 8.5 percent of the total. Still, this was more than twice the proportion of local government revenues than federal aid represented in 1970.

In addition to the revenues that can be obtained from taxes and from higher levels of goverment, local and state officials can generate funds from various user charges as well as from short and long term borrowing. User charges increased markedly during the 1970s, accounting for about 14

TABLE 1
Sources of Revenue for State and Local Governments, Fiscal 1977

Source	State Government $ (Millions)	%	Local Government $ (Millions)	%
TOTAL	204,475	100.0	196,321	100.0
Federal aid	45,938	22.5	16,637	8.5
State aid	—	—	60,311	30.7
Local aid	2,737	1.3	—	—
Property taxes	2,260	1.1	60,275	30.7
INCOME TAXES:				
Individual	25,493	12.5	3,752	1.9
Corporation	9,174	4.5	—	—
Sales taxes	52,362	4.5	8,232	4.2
Charges and miscellaneous	20,106	9.8	27,237	13.9
Insurance trust	32,365	15.8	2,783	1.4
Other revenue	14,040	6.9	17,093	8.7

Source: Adapted from The Tax Foundation, Inc., *Facts and Figures on Government Finance,* 20th Biennial Edition (New York: The Tax Foundation, Inc., 1979), p. 19, Table 7.

percent of local government revenues and 10 percent of state government revenues in 1977, while borrowing increased rapidly during the expansionary 1960s but slowed markedly in the cyclical 1970s. However, we do not propose to present here a comprehensive analysis of these specific sources of funds or of governmental finance generally. Instead, we will attempt to highlight some of the general financial characteristics that affect labor relations at the local level, since this is where the financial problems of government are presently having their strongest impact on collective bargaining.

The major constraints on local government revenues come from the (1) tax base of the community, (2) the willingness of the public or politicians to vote for tax rate increases, (3) constitutional or other legal restraints imposed by state governments of the revenue raising powers of local governments, and (4) constraints on the borrowing capacity of governments based on their credit ratings.

The key to the strength of the tax base in a community is that employment affects the revenue generating potential of property taxes. According to a study of the New York City tax base, for example, industries can be rank ordered as follows according to the criterion of the amount of revenue generated per employee:

1. finance, insurance, and real estate,
2. wholesale trade,
3. manufacturing,
4. retail trade,
5. transportation and communications
6. services.[8]

Unfortunately, the number of jobs has been declining in many of the large old central cities of the United States, particularly in the Northeast where public employee unionism is strongest. The flight of jobs from old central cities in the Northeast to the suburbs and to the Southern and Western parts of the country is a long term problem resulting from a complex set of social and economic factors. This decline of jobs has a two-pronged effect. On the one hand, the tax base declines reduce the revenue available to the central cities. On the other hand, since the population does not contract as rapidly as the numbers of jobs decline and because the population shifts that follow job losses are such that those who leave have higher average income than those who remain behind, the need for services in the city does not diminish at a corresponding rate. The net result of these effects is to leave those who remain in the city with a higher need for public services but a smaller tax base to finance such services.

Together with the long term decline of the large cities, the short run effects of the business cycle have further exacerbated the financial problems of local governments in the past several years. The 1969-70 recession acted to accelerate the decline of jobs in large cities, and some of these cities had not fully recovered from that event before the effects of the deep recession of 1974-75 and the milder 1979-80 recession began to be felt. The basic problem facing local governments during economic downturns is that, while their revenues are cyclically sensitive (especially sales and income taxes, and, to a lesser extent, state aid), the demand for their services is not. In fact, the demand for some services, such as police protection and social welfare, increases during recessions. Recent recessions, moreover, were further complicated by the high rates of inflation that persisted over several years. One study, for example, estimates that between 1972 and 1974, the net purchasing power of the tax base of local governments declined by about $3.3 billion.[9]

In summary, economic problems of the cities are partly a function of the long term social and economic decline of the central cities and partly a function of the short run effects of the recessionary and inflationary pressures of the 1970s—pressures which appear likely to continue in the 1980s. The problems are most severe in those cities that are oldest and most highly unionized. Hence, these cities are likely to continue to experience a difficult economic environment for public sector bargaining even if and when economic expansion occurs.

Although there are no systematic data available to evaluate the trend in tax rates across cities over the past several years or the extent to which cities around the country are pushing up against their tax and debt limits, it is probably fair to say that these problems are particularly serious in the Northeastern part of the country, particularly in the State of New York. For example, if one excludes New York City and Yonkers on the ground that they were placed in forms of state receivership during the 1970s to oversee governmental decision-making so as to avoid default,[10] the next five largest cities—Buffalo, Rochester, Syracuse, Albany, and Binghamton—are all either at, or very close to, their constitutional tax limits. But by no means have these problems been confined to the Northeast or to governments in New York State. In the late 1970s, the municipal government of Cleveland was in default, the local governments of Memphis and New Orleans experienced severe financial difficulties (and well-publicized municipal employee strikes), and the city of Los Angeles was planning measures to meet an anticipated fiscal crisis.[11] While the tax rates in these and other cities vary considerably, it is clear that, in recent years, American taxpayers have become increasingly unwilling to accept tax increases. In fact, as the passage of Proposition 13 by California voters in June 1978 and the initiatives to sponsor similar referenda in other states make evident, taxpayers are seeking tax reductions, not just budget caps or slowdowns in tax hikes. Thus, the alternatives available to local government officials largely have been constrained to seeking increased state and federal aid, increasing the debt financing of operating expenditures and reducing the level of services. None of these alternatives are very attractive at any time and certainly do not appear to be feasible long term solutions to the problems that the cities have faced and will continue to face in financing equitable wage and benefit adjustments for their employees.

To conclude, all of the financial characteristics reviewed above reinforce the view that was advanced after summarizing the longer term economic sources of power available to public sector employees; namely, that the economic-financial environment of government is not likely to be conducive to large wage and fringe benefit increases in the near future, and perhaps beyond, unless alternative means are found for financing public expenditures or unless the central cities experience some unanticipated economic and social renaissance. In such an environment, substantial constraints will exist on public sector collective bargaining, in contrast to the expansionary economic context within which such bargaining first emerged and developed.

FOOTNOTES

1. The Marshallian conditions are summarized in Albert Rees, *The Economics of Trade Unions*, rev. ed. (Chicago: University of Chicago Press, 1977), pp. 66-69.
2. The data in this section were derived from the Tax Foundation, Inc., *Facts and Figures on Government Finance*, 20th biennial edition (New York: The Tax Foundation, Inc., 1979), p. 16, Table 4. Also see *Economic Report of the President, January 1980* (Washington, D.C.: Government Printing Office, 1980), p. 291, Table B-75.
3. See, for example Ralph Schlosstein, "State and Local Government Finances During Recession," *Challenge*, 18 (July-August 1975), 47-50.
4. See Roy W. Bahl, David Greytak, Alan K. Campbell, and Michael S. Wasylenko, "Intergovernmental and Functional Aspects of Trends in Public Employment in the United States," *Public Administration Review*, 32 (November-December 1972), 815-32.
5. Without getting deeply into the issue, the reader should note that there is much controversy about the relationship between labor's proportion of total production cost and its relative bargaining power. This is the most controversial of the Marshallian conditions outlined above. On this point, see Rees, *op. cit.*, p. 68, especially note 1.
6. See, for example, *Ibid.*, pp. 86-89.

7. The data in this section are from the Tax Foundation, Inc., *op. cit.*, p. 19, Table 7. Note that some data on public employee pay changes during the 1970s are presented in Chapter 6.
8. Roy W. Bahl, et. al., *Taxes, Expenditures and the Economic Base* (New York: Praeger, 1974).
9. Alan K. Campbell, "The Economic Impact on Urban Society in 1976," speech delivered to a Conference on Public Sector Labor Relations in a Troubled Economy, sponsored by the Labor Management Relations Service and the American Arbitration Association. Reprinted in Bureau of National Affairs, *Government Employee Relations Report*, (Washington, D.C.: BNA, January 19, 1976), pp. E1-E3. Also, see Charles 4. Levine (ed.), *Managing Fiscal Stress: The Crisis In The Public Sector* (Chatham, NJ: Chatham House, 1980).
10. The financial affairs of both these cities are overseen by the New York State Financial Control Board, which was established by the state legislature.
11. See Bureau of National Affairs (BNA), *Government Employee Relations Report*, (Washington, D.C.: BNA), various issues in 1978, 1979 and 1980.

The Limits of Collective Bargaining in Public Employment

Harry H. Wellington and Ralph K. Winter, Jr.*

In the area of public employment the claims upon public policy made by the need for industrial peace, industrial democracy, and effective political representation point toward collective bargaining. This is to say that three of the four arguments that support bargaining in the private sector—to some extent, at least—press for similar arrangements in the public sector.

Government is a growth industry, particularly state and municipal government. With size comes bureaucracy, and with bureaucracy comes the sense of isolation of the individual worker. His manhood, like that of his industrial counterpart, seems threatened. Lengthening chains of command necessarily depersonalize the employment relationship and contribute to a sense of powerlessness on the part of the worker. If he is to share in the governance of his employment relationship as he does in the private sector, it must be through the device of representation, which means unionization.[1] Accordingly, just as the increase in the size of economic units in private industry fostered unionism, so the enlarging of governmental bureaucracy has encouraged public employees to look to collective action for a sense of control over their employment destiny. The number of government employees, moreover, makes it plain that those employees are members of an interest group that can organize for political representation as well as for job participation.[2]

The pressures thus generated by size and bureaucracy lead inescapably to disruption—to labor unrest—unless these pressures are recognized and

*Yale University Law School. Reprinted from Harry Wellington and Ralph K. Winter, Jr., *The Unions and the Cities* (Washington, D.C.: The Brookings Institution, 1971), pp. 12-32.

unless existing decision-making procedures are accommodated to them. Peace in government employment too, the argument runs, can best be established by making union recognition and collective bargaining accepted public policy.[3]

Much less clearly analogous to the private model, however, is the unequal bargaining power argument. In the private sector that argument really has two aspects. The first is affirmative in nature. Monopsony[4] is believed sometimes to result in unfair individual contracts of employment. The unfairness may be reflected in wages, which are less than they would be if the market were more nearly perfect, or in working arrangements that may lodge arbitrary power in a foreman, that is, power to hire, fire, promote, assign, or discipline without respect to substantive or procedural rules. A persistent assertion, generating much heat, relates to the arbitrary exercise of managerial power in individual cases. This assertion goes far to explain the insistence of unions on the establishment in the labor contract of rules, with an accompanying adjudictory procedure, to govern industrial life.[5]

The second, or negative, aspect of the unequal bargaining power argument relates to the social costs of collective bargaining. As has been seen, the social costs of collective bargaining in the private sector are principally economic and seem inherently limited by market forces. In the public sector, however, the costs seem economic only in a very narrow sense and are on the whole political. It further seems that, to the extent union power is delimited by market or other forces in the public sector, these constraints do not come into play nearly as quickly as in the private. An understanding of why this is so requires further comparison between collective bargaining in the two sectors.

The Private Sector Model

Although the private sector is, of course, extraordinarily diverse, the paradigm is an industry that produces a product that is not particularly essential to those who buy it and for which dissimilar products can be substituted. Within the market or markets for this product, most—but not all—of the producers must bargain with a union representing their employees, and this union is generally the same throughout the industry. A price rise of this product relative to others will result in a decrease in the number of units of the product sold. This in turn will result in a cutback in employment. And an increase in price would be dictated by an increase in labor cost relative to output, at least in most situations.[6] Thus, the union is faced with some sort of rough trade-off between, on the one hand, larger benefits for some employees and unemployment for others, and on the other hand, smaller benefits and more employment. Because unions are political organizations, with a legal duty to represent all employees fairly,[7] and with a treasury that comes from per capita dues, there is pressure on the union to avoid the road that leads to unemployment.[8]

This picture of the restraints that the market imposes on collective bargaining settlements undergoes change as the variables change. On the one hand, to the extent that there are nonunion firms within a product market, the impact of union pressure will be diminished by the ability of consumers to purchase identical products from nonunion and, presumably, less expensive sources. On the other hand, to the extent that union organization of competitors within the product market is complete, there will be no such restraint and the principal barriers to union bargaining goals will be the ability of a number of consumers to react to a price change by turning to dissimilar but nevertheless substitutable products.

Two additional variables must be noted. First, where the demand for an industry's product is rather insensitive to price—that is, relatively inelastic—and where all the firms in a product market are organized, the union need fear less the employment-benefit trade-off, for the employer is less concerned about raising prices in response to increased costs. By hypothesis, a price rise affects unit sales of such an employer only minimally. Second, in an expanding industry, wage settlements that exceed increases in productivity may not reduce union employment. They will reduce expansion, hence the employment effect will be experienced only by workers who do not belong to the union. This means that in the short run the politics of the employment-benefit trade-off do not restrain the union in its bargaining demands.

In both of these cases, however, there are at least two restraints on the union. One is the employer's increased incentive to substitute machines for labor, a factor present in the paradigm and all other cases as well. The other restraint stems from the fact that large sections of the nation are unorganized and highly resistant to unionization.[9] Accordingly, capital will seek nonunion labor, and in this way the market will discipline the organized sector.

The employer, in the paradigm and in all variations of it, is motivated primarily by the necessity to maximize profits (and this is so no matter how political a corporation may seem to be). He therefore is not inclined (absent an increase in demand for his product) to raise prices and thereby suffer a loss in profits, and he is organized to transmit and represent the market pressures described above. Generally he will resist, and resist hard, union demands that exceed increases in productivity, for if he accepts such demands he may be forced to raise prices. Should he be unsuccessful in his resistance too often, and should it or the bargain cost him too much, he can be expected to put his money and energy elsewhere.[10]

What all this means is that the social costs imposed by collective bargaining are economic costs; that usually they are limited by powerful market restraints; and that these restraints are visible to anyone who is able to see the forest for the trees.[11]

The Public Sector Model: Monetary Issues

The paradigm in the public sector is a municipality with an elected city council and an elected mayor who bargains (through others) with unions representing the employees of the city. He bargains also, of course, with other permanent and ad hoc interest groups making claims upon government (business groups, save-the-park committees, neighborhood groups, and so forth). Indeed, the decisions that are made may be thought of roughly as a result of interactions and accommodations among these interest groups, as influenced by perceptions about the attitudes of the electorate and by the goals and programs of the mayor and his city council.[12]

Decisions that cost the city money are generally paid for from taxes and, less often, by borrowing. Not only are there many types of taxes but also there are several layers of government that may make tax revenue available to the city; federal and state as well as local funds may be employed for some purposes. Formal allocation of money for particular uses is made through the city's budget, which may have within it considerable room for adjustments.[13] Thus, a union will bargain hard for as large a share of the budget as it thinks it possibly can obtain, and even try to force a tax increase if it deems that possible.

In the public sector, too, the market operates. In the long run, the supply of labor is a function of the price paid for labor by the public employer relative to what workers earn elsewhere.[14] This is some assurance that public employees in the aggregate—with or without collective bargaining—are not paid too little. The case for employer monopsony, moreover, may be much weaker in the public sector than it is in the private. First, to the extent that most public employees work in urban areas, as they probably do, there may often be a number of substitutable and competing private and public employers in the labor market. When that is the case, there can be little monopsony power.[15] Second, even if public employers occasionally have monopsony power, governmental policy is determined only in part by economic criteria, and there is no assurance, as there is in the private sector where the profit motive prevails, that the power will be exploited.

As noted, market-imposed unemployment is an important restraint on unions in the private sector. In the public sector, the trade-off between benefits and employment seems much less important. Government does not generally sell a product the demand for which is closely related to price. There usually are not close substitutes for the products and services provided by government and the demand for them is relatively inelastic. Such market conditions are favorable to unions in the private sector because they permit the acquisition of benefits without the penalty of unemployment, subject to the restraint of nonunion competitors, actual or potential. But no such restraint limits the demands of public employee unions. Because much government activity is, and must be, a monopoly, product competition, nonunion or otherwise, does not exert a downward pressure on prices and wages. Nor will the existence of a pool of labor ready to work for a wage below union scale attract new capital and create a new, and competitively less expensive, governmental enterprise.

Even if a close relationship between increased economic benefits and unemployment does not exist as a significant deterrent to unions in the public sector, might not the argument be made that in some sense the taxpayer is the public sector's functional equivalent of the consumer? If taxes become too high the taxpayer can move to another community. While it is generally much easier for a consumer to substitute products than for a taxpayer to substitute communities, is it not fair to say that, at the point at which a tax increase will cause so many taxpayers to move that it will produce less total revenue, the market disciplines or restrains union and public employer in the same way and for the same reasons that the market disciplines parties in the private sector? Moreover, does not the analogy to the private sector suggest that it is legitimate in an economic sense for unions to push government to the point of substitutability?

Several factors suggest that the answer to this latter question is at best indeterminate, and that the question of legitimacy must be judged not by economic but by political criteria.

In the first place, there is no theoretical reason—economic or political—to suppose that it is desirable for a governmental entity to liquidate its taxing power, to tax up to the point where another tax increase will produce less revenue because of the number of people it drives to different communities. In the private area, profit maximization is a complex concept, but its approximation generally is both a legal requirement and socially useful as a means of allocating resources.[16] The liquidation of taxing power seems neither imperative nor useful.

Second, consider the complexity of the tax structure and the way in which different kinds of taxes (property, sales, income) fall differently upon a given population. Consider, moreover, that the taxing authority of a particular governmental entity may be limited (a municipality may not have the power to impose an income tax). What is necessarily involved, then, is principally the redistribution of income by government rather than resource allocation,[17] and questions of income redistribution surely are essentially political questions.[18]

For his part, the mayor in our paradigm will be disciplined not by a desire to maximize profits but by a desire, in some cases at least, to do a good job (to implement his programs), and in virtually all cases by a wish either to be reelected or to move to a better elective office. What he gives to the union must be taken from some other interest group or from taxpayers. His is the job of coordinating these competing claims while remaining politically viable. And that coordination will be governed by the relative power of the competing interest groups. Coordination, moreover, is not limited to issues involving the level of taxes and the way in which tax moneys are spent. Nonfinancial issues also require coordination, and here too the outcome turns upon the relative power of interest groups. And relative power is affected importantly by the scope of collective bargaining.

The Public Sector Model: Nonmonetary Issues

In the private sector, unions have pushed to expand the scope of bargaining in response to the desires of their members for a variety of new benefits (pension rights, supplementary unemployment payments, merit increases). These benefits generally impose a monetary cost on the employer. And because employers are restrained by the market, an expanded bargaining agenda means that, if a union negotiates an agreement over more subjects, it generally trades off more of less or less of more.

From the consumer's point of view this in turn means that the price of the product he purchases is not significantly related to the scope of bargaining. And since unions rarely bargain about the nature of the product produced,[19] the consumer can be relatively indifferent as to how many or how few subjects are covered in any collective agreement.[20] Nor need the consumer be concerned about union demands that would not impose a financial cost on the employer, for example, the design of a grievance procedure. While such demands are not subject to the same kind of trade-off as are financial demands, they are unlikely, if granted, to have any impact on the consumer. Their effect is on the quality of life of the parties to the agreement.

In the public sector the cluster of problems that surround the scope of bargaining are much more troublesome than they are in the private sector. The problems have several dimensions.

First, the trade-off between subjects of bargaining in the public sector is less of a protection to the consumer (public) than it is in the private. Where political leaders view the costs of union demands as essentially budgetary, a trade-off can occur. Thus, a demand for higher teacher salaries and a demand for reduced class size may be treated as part of one package. But where a demand, although it has a budgetary effect, is viewed as involving essentially political costs, trade-offs are more difficult. Our paradigmatic mayor, for example, may be under great pressure to make a large monetary settlement with a teachers' union whether or not it is joined to demands for special training programs for disadvantaged children. Interest groups tend to exert pressure against union demands only when they are directly affected. Otherwise, they are apt to join that large constituency (the general public) that wants to avoid labor trouble. Trade-offs can occur only when several demands are resisted by roughly the same groups. Thus, pure budgetary demands can be traded off when they are opposed by taxpayers. But when the identity of the resisting group changes with each demand, political leaders may find it expedient to strike a balance on each issue individually, rather than as part of a total package, by measuring the political power of each interest group involved against the political power of the constituency pressing for labor peace. To put it another way, as important as financial factors are to a mayor, political factors may be even more important. The market allows the businessman no such discretionary choice.

Second, public employees do not generally produce a product. They perform a service. The way in which a service is performed may become a subject of bargaining. As a result, the nature of that service may be changed. Some of these services—police protection, teaching, health care—involve questions that are politically, socially, or ideologically sensitive. In part this is because government is involved and alternatives to governmentally provided services are relatively dear. In part, government is involved because of society's perception about the nature of the service and society's need for it. This suggests that decisions affecting the nature of a governmentally provided service are much more likely to be challenged and are more urgent than generally is the case with services that are offered privately.

Third, some of the services government provides are performed by professionals—teachers, social workers, and so forth—who are keenly interested in the underlying philosophy that informs their work. To them, theirs is not merely a job to be done for a salary. They may be educators or other "change agents" of society. And this may mean that these employees are concerned with more than incrementally altering a governmental service or its method of delivery. They may be advocates of bold departures that will radically transform the service itself.

The issue is not a threshold one of whether professional public employees should participate in decisions about the nature of the services they provide. Any properly run governmental agency should be interested in, and heavily reliant upon, the judgment of its professional staff. The issue rather is the method of that participation.

The Theory Summarized

Collective bargaining in public employment, then, seems distinguishable from that in the private sector. To begin with, it imposes on society more than a potential misallocation of resources through restrictions on economic output, the principal cost imposed by private sector unions. Collective bargaining by public employees and the political process cannot be separated. The costs of such bargaining, therefore, cannot be fully measured without taking into account the impact on the allocation of political power in the typical municipality. If one assumes, as here, that municipal political processes should be structured to ensure "a high probability that an active and legitimate group in the population can make itself heard effectively at some crucial stage in the process of decision,"[21] then the issue is how powerful unions will be in the typical political process if a full transplant of collective bargaining is carried out.

The conclusion is that such a transplant would, in many cases, institutionalize the power of public employee unions in a way that would leave competing groups in the political process at a permanent and substantial disadvantage. There are three reasons for this, and each is related to the type of services typically performed by public employees.

First, some of these services are such that any prolonged disruption would entail an actual danger to health and safety.

Second, the demand for numerous governmental services is relatively inelastic, that is, relatively insensitive to changes in price. Indeed, the lack of close substitutes is typical of many governmental endeavors.[22] And, since at least the time of Marshall's *Principles of Economics*, the elasticity of demand for the final service or product has been considered a major determinant of union power.[23] Because the demand for labor is derived from the demand for the product, inelasticity on the product side tends to reduce the employment-benefit trade-off unions face. This is as much the case in the private as in the public sector. But in the private sector, product inelasticity is not typical. Moreover, there is the further restraint on union power created by the real possibility of nonunion entrants into the product market. In the public sector, inelasticity of demand seems more the rule than the exception, and nonunion rivals are not generally a serious problem.

The final reason for fearing a full transplant is the extent to which the disruption of a government service inconveniences municipal voters. A teachers' strike may not endanger public health or welfare. It may, however, seriously inconvenience parents and other citizens who, as voters, have the power to punish one of the parties—and always the same party, the political leadership—to the dispute.

All this may seem to suggest a sharper distinction between the public and private sectors than actually exists. The discussion here has dealt with models, one for private collective bargaining, the other for public. Each model is located at the core of its sector. But the difference in the impact of collective bargaining in the two sectors should be seen as a continuum. Thus, for example, it may be that market restraints do not sufficiently discipline strike settlements in some regulated industries or in industries that rely mainly on government contracts. Indeed, collective bargaining in such industries has been under steady and insistent attack.

In the public sector, it may be that in any given municipality—but particularly a small one—at any given time, taxpayer resistance or the determination of municipal government, or both, will substantially offset union power even under existing political structures. These plainly are exceptions, however. They do not invalidate the public-private distinction as an analytical tool, for that distinction rests on the very real differences that exist in the vast bulk of situations, situations exemplified by these models.

Footnotes

1. See *Final Report of the Industrial Commission*, p. 805; C. Summers, "American Legislation for Union Democracy," 25 *Mod. L. Rev.* 273, 275 (1962).
2. For the "early" history, see S. Spero, *Government as Employer* (Remsen, 1948).
3. See, for example, *Governor's Committee on Public Employee Relations, Final Report* (State of New York, 1966), pp. 9-14.
4. Defined by the authors as a buyer's monopoly in which the terms and conditions of employment are generally below those that would exist under perfect competition (eds.).
5. See N. Chamberlain, *The Union Challenge to Management Control* (Harper, 1948), p. 94.
6. The cost increase may, of course, take some time to work through and appear as a price increase. See Rees, *The Economics of Trade Unions*, pp. 107-09. In some oligopolistic situations the firm may be able to raise prices after a wage increase without suffering a significant decrease in sales.
7. *Steele v. Louisville & Nashville Railroad Co.*, 323 U.S. 192 (1944).
8. The pressure is sometimes resisted. Indeed, the United Mine Workers has chosen more benefits for less employment. See generally M. Baratz, *The Union and the Coal Industry* (Yale University Press, 1955).
9. See H. Cohany, "Trends and Changes in Union Membership," 89 *Monthly Lab. Rev.* 510-13 (1966); I. Bernstein, "The Growth of American Unions, 1945-1960," 2 *Labor History* 131-57 (1961).
10. And the law would protect him in this. Indeed, it would protect him if he were moved by an antiunion animus as well as by valid economic considerations. See *Textile Workers Union of America v. Darlington Manufacturing Co.*, 380 U.S. 263 (1965). Of course, where fixed costs are large relative to variable costs, it may be difficult for an employer to extricate himself.
11. This does not mean that collective bargaining in the private sector is free of social costs. It means only that the costs are necessarily limited by the discipline of the market.
12. See generally R. Dahl, *Who Governs? Democracy and Power in an American City* (Yale University Press, 1961). On interest group theory generally, see D. Truman, *The Government Process: Political Interests and Public Opinion* (3d printing; Alfred A. Knopf, 1955).
13. See, for example, W. Sayre and H. Kaufman, *Governing New York City: Politics in the Metropolis* (Russell Sage, 1960), pp. 366-72.

14. See M. Moskow, *Teachers and Unions* (University of Pennsylvania, Wharton School of Finance and Commerce, Industrial Research Unit, 1966), pp. 79-86.
15. This is based on the reasonable but not unchallengeable assumption that the number of significant employers in a labor market is related to the existence of monopsony. See R. Bunting, *Employer Concentration in Local Labor Markets*, pp. 3-14. The greater the number of such employers in a labor market, the greater the departure from the classic case of the monopsony of a single employer. The number of employers would clearly seem to affect their ability to make and enforce a collusive wage agreement.
16. See generally R. Dorfman, *Prices and Markets* (Prentice-Hall, 1967).
17. In the private sector what is involved is principally resource allocation rather than income redistribution. Income redistribution occurs to the extent that unions are able to increase wages at the expense of profits, but the extent to which this actually happens would seem to be limited. It also occurs if unions, by limiting employment in the union sector through maintenance of wages above a competitive level, increase the supply of labor in the nonunion sector and thereby depress wages there.
18. In the private sector the political question was answered when the National Labor Relations Act was passed: the benefits of collective bargaining (with the strike) outweigh the social costs.
19. The fact that American unions and management are generally economically oriented is a source of great freedom to us all. If either the unions or management decided to make decisions about the nature of services provided or products manufactured on the basis of their own ideological convictions, we would all, as consumers, be less free. Although unions may misallocate resources, consumers are still generally able to satisfy strong desires for particular products by paying more for them and sacrificing less valued items. This is because unions and management generally make no attempt to adjust to anything but economic considerations. Were it otherwise, and the unions—or management—insisted that no products of a certain kind be manufactured, consumers would have much less choice.
20. The major qualification to these generalizations is that sometimes unions can generate more support from the membership for certain demands than for others (more for the size of the work crew, less for wage increases). Just how extensive this phenomenon is, and how it balances out over time, is difficult to say; however, it would not seem to be of great importance in the overall picture.
21. R. Dahl, *A Preface to Democratic Theory* (University of Chicago Press, 1956), p. 145.
22. Sometimes this is so because of the nature of the endeavor—national defense, for example—and sometimes because the existence of the governmental operation necessarily inhibits entry by private entities, as in the case of elementary education.
23. A. Marshall, *Principles of Economics* (8th ed.; Macmillan, 1920), pp. 383-86.

The Demand for Labor in the Public Sector

Orley C. Ashenfelter and Ronald G. Ehrenberg*†

The rapid growth of collective bargaining in the state and local sector has produced substantial controversy over the legal treatment of unions and collective negotiations in the sector. A part of the controversy revolves around the relative magnitudes of the wage elasticities of demand for labor in the public and private sectors. If the public sector has a lower elasticity, unionists there face a smaller potential decrease in employment from a given wage increase than do unionists in the private sector, and market forces consequently impose a smaller constraint on unions negotiating in the public sector. In this case a theoretical framework is required both to define formally the "wage elasticity of demand for labor in the public sector" and to provide estimates of it for comparison with the private sector. Our purpose in this paper is the *exposition* of the empirical implications of a theory of the demand for labor by state and local governments based on the classical theory of consumer choice.[1]

I. Theoretical Framework

The basic building blocks in our analysis of the demand for public sector workers are: (1) a well-behaved utility function that orders the satisfaction received by some "effective" decision maker from the services of workers employed in the various functional categories of the nonfederal *public* sector and from the quantities of goods and services purchased from the *private* sector; and (2) the budget constraint on total resources faced by this effective decision maker. The assumption that our effective decision maker chooses both employment levels in each governmental category and quantities of each privately purchased good to maximize his satisfaction, given the constraint imposed by the wage rates, prices, and income that he faces, leads immediately to an extensive set of familiar implications about the effects of exogenous changes in the latter on the optimum quantities of the former. Set up in this way, the problem is a straightforward application of the classical theory of consumer choice to a case where the inputs of labor to the public sector are also subjects for decision. With one additional maintained hypothesis it is precisely these implications that we attempt to test.

Unfortunately, the interpretation of the demand functions for labor that we derive from the above assumptions remains cloudly untill three further issues are resolved. First, since the choices that we describe in the public sector require a collective decision, it is appropriate to ask whose preferences

*Department of Economics, Princeton University, and New York State School of Industrial and Labor Relations, Cornell University, respectively. Reprinted from Daniel Hamermesh, editor, *Labor in the Public and Nonprofit Sectors* (Princeton, N.J.: Princeton University Press, 1975), pp. 55-78.
†We are deeply indebted to David A. Smith for his extensive assistance. We are also grateful to Burton Weisbrod and Hirschel Kasper for their comments on an earlier version of the paper.

are described by the utility function that it is presumed to be maximized. As is well known, there are plausible conditions under which we may be assured that an open, democratic political system will make the preferences of the median voter on an issue into those of the effective decision maker.[2] Under those conditions, the effective decision maker *is* the "typical" voter, whose wishes are carried out by elected officials chosen because their positions coincide with those of the typical voter. Although this description of the process of collective choice seems more realistic than others, it should be clear that successful empirical tests of the hypotheses we set out below do not constitute strong evidence of the existence of such a process if there are other contenders that give rise to a stable, well-behaved utility function.

Second, we must consider the rationale for including the services of labor, rather than the quantity of the public service produced and then consumed, as subject to choice in the public sector. Although public services rendered are no doubt what provide satisfaction to the typical consumer, it is often impossible to measure the quantity of public services, and it is generally impossible for the decision maker to change the quantity produced without changing the quantity of factor inputs set aside for their provision. Consequently, we may deal interchangeably with the satisfaction from the quantity of a municipal service produced and, so long as there exists a stable relationship between factor inputs and the quantity of service produced, the satisfaction from the services provided by the inputs set aside to produce a particular municipal service. In addition, we are forced by data limitations to assume that for the period of our analysis the per capita stock of factor inputs other than labor is fixed, so that changes in the per capita quantity of labor input are the only *short-run* method for changing the quantity of public services. Since we take the year as our period of analysis, we are therefore assuming that the *year-to-year* change in the service flow received by the individual from a particular public service is a function only of the change in the per capita employment level. The change in the price of a unit of each public service is a function only of the change in the wage.

Finally, we must note that, in addition to the direct production of public services, governments have the option of purchasing services from the private sector. It is the sum of the public services provided in both manners that should enter our representative consumer's utility function. To the extent that the proportion of a public service provided by each method varies either across states or over time (other than by a trend factor), our parameter estimates of the demand for state and local government *employees* may be biased.

II. Empirical Results

Our basic data source is a set of annual first differences of employment, wage rates, and income for individual states over the years 1958-1969 excluding 1964.[3] Before we can turn to estimation, however, a number of preliminary considerations must be examined. In most investigations of the demand for public services, a large number of variables in addition to those reflecting income and prices that we have discussed thus far are examined for their explanatory power. These additional variables are generally taken

34

to measure differences or variations in "tastes" for various types of public services. The most natural procedure for integrating such variables into the classical demand theory framework is to assume that satisfaction is derived from the quantity consumed per capita and to allow the weights in the population deflator to differ and thus reflect the age distribution of the population, the urban-rural location of the population, etc. Unfortunately, however, the time series data for individual states are far too small to follow this procedure; we will be forced to pool our time series for the various states. In view of this we have tried to increase the homogeneity of the sample by arbitrarily splitting it into two subsamples according to whether or not a state was one of the twenty-five states with the highest density (in persons per square mile).[4] As a practical matter, the high-density states also tend to be the most urbanized and are concentrated in the northeast region of the United States. Though it is crude, this procedure does allow us to test whether there are systematic differences in the behavioral responses to wage and income changes according to one plausible criterion.

Our most fundamental empirical results [based on data for ten noneducational categories of public services] appear in Table 1.[5] We have tabulated here the estimated price elasticity of demand for each category of labor (evaluated at the means), holding the real employment budget constant. These elasticities indicate the percentage change in employment in a category per percentage change in its wage rate, holding all other wages constant and making a simultaneous compensation adjustment that keeps the overall real employment budget constant. They thus represent substitution of labor among functional categories within a constant real employment budget. As we have already noted, if they are negative they imply that the compensated substitution effect of a wage change on employment demand is negative; this is the most fundamental implication of the utility maximization theory. As can be seen from Table 1, all of these demand elasticities are negative in the high-density sample of states, and they are significant at conventional test levels in all but one of the ten employment categories. The results for the low-density sample of states are slightly less favorable. While nine of the ten elasticities are negative and eight significantly so, it is disturbing that the elasticity for hospital employees in the low-density states not only has a positive sign, but a coefficient nearly six times its standard error. On balance, these results provide strong support for the utility-maximization theory from the data for the high-density states and weaker support from the data for the low-density states.

We can only speculate at this point about the reasons for the different empirical results in the high- and low-density states. Clearly, more analysis that explicitly incorporates demographic and other factors into the analytical framework would be fruitful. At this point we are inclined to ascribe the difference to the much more homogeneous character of the high-density states compared to the low-density states.[6] Even so, perhaps we need not be too disturbed for the accuracy of the results that follow, since over 75 percent of all state and local government employment is in the high-density group of states. Nevertheless, in order to see what additional light we can shed on this issue, we have tabulated in Table 2 our estimates of the marginal expenditures on labor services resulting from an increase in the real employ-

TABLE 1
Elasticities of Demand for Labor Holding the Real Employment Budget Constant[a]

Category of Labor Services:	High Density States	Low Density States
1) Streets and Highway	−.018	−.099
	(.2)	(1.3)
2) Public Welfare	−.279	−.371
	(2.7)	(4.8)
3) Hospitals	−.291	.194
	(7.7)	(5.6)
4) Public Health	−.100	−.440
	(2.1)	(2.4)
5) Police Protection	−:218	−.255
	(3.2)	(3.2)
6) Fire Protection	−.665	−.700
	(5.1)	(6.5)
7) Sanitation and Sewerage	−.247	−.460
	(2.8)	(3.4)
8) Natural Resources	−.353	−.424
	(4.2)	(4.3)
9) General Control and Financial Administration	−.189	−.161
	(2.6)	(2.2)
10) Other Noneducational Services	−.468	−.317
	(8.9)	(3.5)

[a]Absolute value of t-statistics in parentheses.

ment budget for the ten categories of labor services in the two samples. As can be seen from the table, the main differences are substantially smaller marginal expenditure shares for streets and highways in the high-density states and substantially higher shares for public health, police and fire protection, sanitation, and other noneducational services (e.g., libraries) in them. The latter services tend to be more important in urban or dense areas than the former, and these results seem plausible enough.[7]

III. Implications and Conclusions

We may compare our estimated demand elasticities for labor in the public sector with plausible estimates of demand elasticities for labor in the private sector in order to determine whether market forces have a stronger or weaker effect on bargaining in the public sector than in the private sector. Unfortunately, there seem to be even fewer estimates of labor-demand elasticities (as opposed to marginal productivity relations) for the private sector than there are for the public sector. It is possible, however, to make some plausible, rough estimates for labor demand elasticities in the typical

TABLE 2
Estimates of the Marginal Expenditures on Labor Services from an Increase in the Real Employment Budget

Category of Labor Services:	High Density States	Low Density States
Streets and Highways	.120	.347
	(34.5)	(14.7)
Public Welfare	.018	.015
	(15.4)	(4.4)
Hospitals	.125	.171
	(37.5)	(10.9)
Public Health	.046	−.007
	(36.1)	(1.2)
Police Protection	.092	.032
	(55.7)	(7.3)
Fire Protection	.060	.021
	(32.2)	(3.0)
Sanitation and Sewerage	.042	.015
	(28.3)	(1.1)
Natural Resources	.076	.065
	(44.4)	(6.7)
General Control and Financial	.174	.170
Administration	(63.4)	(14.7)
Other Noneducational Services	.247	.170
	(59.5)	(8.2)

[a] Absolute values of t-statistics in parentheses.

industry (which we take to be the bargaining unit) by using the classical Hicksian formula for the elasticity of derived demand.[8] Our calculations lead to the conclusion that private-sector demand elasticities are in the neighborhood of −.5 to −1.0, though perhaps as large as −1.5 for some durable goods.[9] The estimates of the comparable demand elasticities derived in this paper are −.4 for non-educational labor. Although there is more variability in the plausible values one might attach to labor demand elasticities in the private sector than we are comfortable with, it does not seem likely that comparable demand elasticities in the private sector are as much as twice the aggregate values observed in the public sector. Even if we take this extreme assumption and suppose 10 percent to be a reasonable estimate for the average union/nonunion wage differential in the private economy,[10] it would take only a 20 percent union/nonunion wage differential to produce the same disemployment effects in the public sector as the existing union/nonunion wage differential might produce in the private sector. More plausible estimates of private-sector elasticities imply union/nonunion wage differentials that are even lower. To carry this line of reasoning much further, however, would require an explicit model of union behavior.

References

Ashenfelter, O., 1972. "Racial Discrimination and Trade Unionism," *Journal of Political Economy* 80 (May/June), 435-464.

Barten, A.P., 1968. "Estimating Demand Functions," *Econometrica* 36 (April), 213-251.

Bergstrom, T., and Goodman, R., 1973. "Private Demand for Public Goods," *American Economic Review* 63 (June), 280-297.

Downs, A., 1957. *An Economic Theory of Democracy*. New York: Harper and Row.

Ehrenberg, R., 1972. *The Demand for State and Local Government Employees: An Economic Analysis*. Lexington, Mass.: D.C. Heath.

Hicks, J.R., 1932. *The Theory of Wages* (original edition), 2nd edition. New York: Macmillan, 1964.

Kaspar, H., 1971. "On Political Competition, Economic Policy and Income Maintenance Programs," *Public Choice* 10 (Spring), 1-21.

Theil, H., 1967. *Economics and Information Theory*. Chicago: Rand McNally.

Tullock, G., 1967. *Towards a Mathematics of Politics*. Ann Arbor: University of Michigan Press.

Waud, R., 1968. "Manhour Behavior in U.S. Manufacturing: A Neoclassical Interpretation," *Journal of Political Economy* 76 (May/June), 407-428.

Footnotes

1. Only an attenuated version of the authors' theoretical framework is presented here. Readers interested in the full model and the demand equations to which it gives rise should consult the original source of the paper [editors].

2. See Downs (1957) and Tullock (1967). These conditions have recently been spelled out in detail by Bergstrom and Goodman (1973).

3. These data have been described in detail in Ehrenberg (1972, Chapter 3). They are time series of ten observations for each of fifty states, though sporadic errors in the published Bureau of the Census sources reduce the total number of data points to slightly less than 500. Employment is for full-time equivalent workers, and the wage rate is average monthly payroll costs per man, obtained as the ratio of total monthly payroll to full-time equivalent employment. All employment and income data are expressed in per capita terms.

4. The twenty-five high-density states (ranked in order of density from highest to lowest) are:

1. Rhode Island	10. Illinois	18. Tennessee
2. New Jersey	11. Michigan	19. South Carolina
3. Massachusetts	12. Indiana	20. West Virginia
4. Connecticut	13. Virginia	21. Kentucky
5. New York	14. California	22. Wisconsin
6. Maryland	15. Hawaii	23. Louisiana
7. Pennsylvania	16. North Carolina	24. Georgia
8. Ohio	17. Florida	25. New Hampshire
9. Delaware		

The twenty-five low-density states (ranked in order of density from highest to lowest) are:

1. Alabama	6. Washington	11. Maine
2. Missouri	7. Vermont	12. Kansas
3. Iowa	8. Texas	13. Nebraska
4. Mississippi	9. Oklahoma	14. Oregon
5. Minnesota	10. Arkansas	15. Colorado

16. Arizona	20. Idaho	23. Nevada
17. Utah	21. New Mexico	24. Wyoming
18. South Dakota	22. Montana	25. Alaska
19. North Dakota		

5. Though we do not go into the details in the text, our estimation scheme is a variant on the so-called "Rotterdam" model for estimating complete systems of demand functions. See Barten (1968) and Theil (1967, esp. pp. 233-237).

6. An alternative hypothesis suggested to us by Hirschel Kasper is that in the high-density states there is more political competition that forces decision-makers in these states to conform more closely to the preferences of the median voter than do decision-makers elsewhere. For an alternative test of this hypothesis see Kasper (1971).

7. The authors also provide, in a more limited way, an estimate of the demand for labor in public educational services. Interested readers should consult their original paper [editors].

8. For the case where the supply of capital to an industry is taken to be perfectly elastic, the elasticity of demand for labor is a weighted average of the elasticity of demand for the product and the elasticity of substitution between capital and labor. The weights equal the share of labor in the value of output and one minus that share. (See Hicks (1966, p. 244).) Our impression is that the elasticity of substitution is often estimated at near or below unity in most industries. With labor's share between .5 and .7 and most estimated product demand functions taken to be inelastic, this implies labor demand elasticities between $-.5$ and -1.0, though perhaps as high (in absolute value) as $-.1.5$ for some durable goods where product demand functions may be elastic.

9. Waud (1968) directly estimated wage elasticities of demand for various two-digit manufacturing industries and obtained mean elasticities of $-.405$ and -1.507 respectively for the nondurable and durable industries. His estimates, however, were obtained holding real GNP constant and consequently are biased towards zero.

10. Ashenfelter (1972) estimates an average union/nonunion wage differential in the private sector of 10 percent for 1967.

THE POLITICAL CONTEXT

In his classic book, *The Government Process: Political Interests and Public Opinion*,[1] David Truman pointed out that political interest group access is the predominant mode of influence in the decision-making processes of government. He suggested that for any interest group in the public sector to have an impact, it must develop effective political access to key decision makers and then use that access effectively. This analysis seems to contain clear and direct implications for the process of public sector bargaining.

However, a different view was posited by George Hildebrand at the time that public sector bargaining was just beginning to spread in the United States.[2] Hildebrand proposed that the application of pressure to elected officials through multiple channels of access threatens the "integrity" of the formal bargaining process. He believed that the use of such a strategy would eventually transform the bargaining process into a form of "machine politics."

For Truman, the building and utilization of political access are natural and legitimate tactics that historically have been the means by which interest groups pursue their objectives in public policy making processes. This implies that the pressure for union and management officials to follow the interest group pattern during bargaining is quite strong and that the parties will not automatically conform to the accepted bargaining behavior found in the private sector. The fundamental lesson here is that the political structure and environment shape the behavior of the bargainers. The reason that these types of behavior are perhaps not as common in the private sector is not that some unwritten code of ethics is more predominant there but, rather, that the opportunity for such behavior may occur less frequently in that context.

The differing interpretations of Truman and Hildebrand underscore the inherent conflict that exists between the two highly valued goals of (1) developing an efficient bilateral negotiations process in which management acts as a unified team and the union applies pressure through formal negotiations, and (2) the goal of maintaining multiple points of access required for an effective democratic decision-making process. The conflict between these two goals is one of the most difficult dilemmas in public sector bargaining and lies at the heart of most discussions of the role of "politics" in bargaining.

The first article in this section, by Summers, builds on the arguments presented above and suggests that the critical policy issue for practitioners in the public sector is to find a way of achieving both of the aforementioned goals in a way that sacrifices neither. His major contributions, however, are in his analysis of the implications of political power for the outcomes of collective bargaining in the public sector. Summers argues that without collective bargaining, employee interests would not be strong enough to overcome the opposing interest group pressure of taxpayers and consumers of public services. While he believes that collective bargaining will increase the political strength of unions and thereby result in large wage increases, he does not envision this political strength increasing to a proportion beyond the legitimate right of public employees to have greater access to or influence over their wages, hours, and working conditions. However, Summers also feels that there is little natural economic basis for employee alliances with other community interest groups. Indeed, he goes further and sees a conflict between organized employee groups and other community groups. Thus, for Summers, the problem is to design a structure which provides enough influence for employees to affect issues where their vital interests are at stake while, at the same time, not precluding community (countervailing) interest groups from pursuing their own vital interests in the policymaking process.

In the second article in this section, Cohen takes issue with Summers' analysis and also with that offered by Wellington and Winter (a portion of which appeared earlier).[3] Cohen does not judge public employee unionism and bargaining necessarily to reduce a preexisting democratic condition or to retard a potential rise in the level of democracy. He cautions that, in the absence of public employee bargaining, the governmental decision-making process does not ineluctably operate according to the pure democratic ideal. There are a variety of possible distortions of this process, as reflected in one-party dominance, low voter turnout in elections to public office, and the superior power position that one or another interest group may occupy in the political process. Further, he observes, the evidence from the late 1970s demonstrates that public officials and various interest groups are effectively able to counter the demands and ostensible dominance of public employee unions. From this perspective, the rise of organized public employees and the spread of collective bargaining in the public sector may indeed be countervailed by the public will, as expressed through political channels. Therefore, he contends, unionized public workers do not pose as substantial a threat to political democracy as others have claimed.

Together, these two pieces provide a lucid and lively contrast of major points of view on this controversial issue. Additionally, since they were written several years apart—Summers' article in 1974, Cohen's in 1979—they provide the reader with an opportunity to compare conclusions that were reached under different political (*and* economic) conditions for public sector bargaining.

FOOTNOTES

1. Published by Alfred A. Knopf, New York, 1955.
2. George H. Hildebrand, "The Public Sector," in John T. Dunlop and Neil W. Chamberlain (eds.), *Frontiers of Collective Bargaining* (New York: McGraw-Hill, 1967), pp. 125-154. For a somewhat different analysis, see Paul F. Gerhart, *Political Activity by Public Employee Organizations at the Local Level: Threat or Promise?* (Chicago: International Personnel Management Association, 1974).
3. Harry H. Wellington and Ralph K. Winter, Jr., *The Unions and the Cities* (Washington, D.C.: The Brookings Institution, 1971). See also Wellington and Winter, "Structuring Collective Bargaining in Public Employment," *Yale Law Journal,* 79 (April 1970), 805-870. Cohen attacks even more frontally the analysis contained in Robert S. Summers, *Collective Bargaining and Public Benefit Conferral: A Jurisprudential Critique* (Ithaca, N.Y.: Institute of Public Employment, New York State School of Industrial and Labor Relations, 1976).

Public Employee Bargaining: A Political Perspective

Clyde W. Summers*

Collective bargaining in public employment is different from collective bargaining in private employment, for "government is not just another industry." This proposition I consider self-evident, for in private employment collective bargaining is a process of private decisionmaking shaped primarily by market forces, while in public employment it is a process of governmental decisionmaking shaped ultimately by political forces. The introduction of collective bargaining in the private sector restructures the labor market, while in the public sector it also restructures the political process.

*Yale University Law School. Reprinted from *Yale Law Journal,* Vol. 83 (1974), pp. 1156-1200.

However, it does not follow from the proposition that collective bargaining in the public and private sectors is different, that collective bargaining in the public sector is inappropriate or that practices in the private sector cannot be transplanted to the public sector. Collective bargaining in both sectors is a process for determining terms and conditions of employment and it might serve both the private and public decisionmaking processes equally well in similar, or even quite different, ways. What does follow from this proposition is that public sector bargaining must be examined as a part of the governmental process. The appropriateness of collective bargaining practices in the public sector cannot be judged by analogies to the private sector but only by inquiries into how those practices fit within and affect the decisionmaking processes of government.

Basic Characteristics of Public Employment

Before attempting to analyze how collective bargaining fits within the political process, it is essential to articulate certain basic characteristics of public employment and the process for deciding terms and conditions of employment. These characteristics are present whether there is collective bargaining or not. All are obvious, but too easily overlooked.

First, decisions as to terms and conditions of employment for public employees are governmental decisions made through the political process. Market forces influence those decisions by determining the availability of workers to fill public jobs, by affecting the value placed on public services by voters and their elected officials, and by altering the willingness or ability of taxpayers to pay for those services. But the influence of market forces is filtered through the political process, where they conjoin with noneconomic forces and considerations to produce a political decision. The decision is responsive not only to economic but also to political forces and this is true whether terms and conditions of employment are declared unilaterally by public officials or determined bilaterally by collective agreement. Although collective bargaining requires new structures and procedures and may lead to different substantive results, the decisionmaking process nevertheless remains political.

Second, in public employment the employer is the public—in ultimate political terms, the voters to whom the public officials are responsible. The voters, however, consist largely of two overlapping groups whose interests differ: first, those who use the employees' services and, second, those who pay for those services through taxes. The public employer, when seen not as an abstraction but as a collectivity of individuals, is made up of purchasers and users of the employees' services. Members of the public, as purchasers and users, are motivated by economic considerations; they want to maximize services and minimize costs. The public employees' interest in lighter work load and higher wages conflicts with their employers' interest in more service and lower taxes. As in private employment, the economic interests of the employer and his employees are adverse. This opposition of economic interests between the public employer and public employee is present regardless of whether there is collective bargaining.

Third, the voters who share the employers' economic interests far outnumber those who share the employees' economic interest. Almost every voter uses, in one way or another, the services of public employees and almost every voter also pays for those services through taxes, directly or indirectly. Public employees of a governmental unit and their families make up only a small proportion of the voting population in that governmental unit—substantially less than 10 percent. At the local level some public employees are not residents and cannot vote in the governmental unit by which they are employed. This does not mean that public employees are politically helpless, but it does mean that, to the extent people vote their pocketbooks, public employees are at a significant disadvantage when their terms and conditions of employment are decided through a process responsive to majority will.

Fourth, public employees, even without collective bargaining, vote and normally do participate in determining the terms and conditions of employment. Many can vote and all can support candidates, organize pressure groups, and present arguments in the public forum. Because their terms and conditions of employment are decided through the political process, they have the right as citizens to participate in those decisions which affect their employment. Such a right is not enjoyed by employees in the private sector. That participation can be meaningful and effective in obtaining better wages, shorter hours, and many other benefits, as the experience of many public employee organizations demonstrates. In part, this is because people do not always vote their pocketbooks; appeals to fairness or altruism can influence political decisionmaking.

From these four characteristics of public employment there emerges more clearly the central significance of public employee bargaining. Introduction of collective bargaining into the public sector alters the governmental process, creating within that process special procedures for making decisions about the wages and working conditions the public will give its employees. This is, of course, no argument against public employee bargaining, unless there is some predisposition against innovations in government. There is no immediate evident reason for assuming that customary or preexisting processes are best, or even adequate, when the decision to be made by the public is the special one of how much the public will pay its servants. On the contrary, the fact that the economic interests of the voting public, both as taxpayers and as users of public services, run directly counter to the economic interests of public employees in wages and working conditions suggests that public employees may need special procedures to insure that their interests receive adquate consideration in the political process.

Clear recognition that public employee bargaining alters the political process helps us frame what I believe is the central question: How can the political process best be structured for determining the terms and conditions of public employment? The issue is not whether bargaining in the public sector is like bargaining in the private sector, or whether the practices of private sector bargaining can be transplanted to the public sector, but rather what practices in the public sector will improve the political process. . . . How can the political process best be structured for mediating the adverse interests of the voting public and its employees? Collective bargaining should be evaluated in terms of its impact on and contribution to that political process.

We must now confront the question of whether the change worked by collective bargaining in the political process can be justified. Can we properly give public employees a special procedure that enables them to bargain separately from, and in some respects prior to, other interest groups in the budget-making process? Certainly giving one of several competing interest groups such a special status and role in governmental decisionmaking is not in the pattern of our "normal" political processes and might be considered inappropriate in a democratic society. However, closer examination of the interplay of interest groups in budget-making reveals that the position of public employees in that process is quite different from that of other interest groups. Because of that difference collective bargaining may be an appropriate means of placing public employees on more nearly equal footing with other interest groups in the budget-making process.

The special position of public employees, which provides the basis for their claim to a special procedure, has three major elements. First, payroll costs in most cities constitute 60 to 70 percent of the total operating budget. Any significant general wage increase leads almost inescapably to a budget increase. The employees, in lobbying for increases, cannot persuasively argue that the necessary funds can be obtained by reductions in other expenditures, nor will they willingly argue that increased wage rates can be paid by reduction in the number of employees. They must, therefore, attempt to overcome opposition to an increased budget and this casts them in direct opposition to the taxpayers as an interest group. Moreover, among all of the interest groups seeking larger budget allocations, the employees are the most visible and the most susceptible to focused resistance. A modest percentage increase adds to the budget a massive dollar amount—often the largest single increase in the entire budget—on which the taxpayer opposition can focus. No other increase can be so readily attacked with such great savings for the taxpayer. The only budget item of comparable magnitude is the allocation for education, but again salaries and fringe benefits account for 65 percent of school expenditures. Opposition to increases in the school budget focuses most strongly on increases in teachers' salaries since the other increases are made up of many small amounts, none of which alone has any substantial impact on the total budget.

Second, in the political bargaining among competing interest groups seeking shares of the total budget, the employees are not simply one group among many bargaining on the same basis. On the contrary, the employees' demands run directly against the demands of each other interest group. Other interest groups are concerned ultimately, not with budget dollars, but with levels of service and they make budget demands in order to obtain a desired level of service. Voters urging increased appropriations for the police want more and better police protection; motorists urging larger allocations for streets want better snow removal and fewer potholes; and parents pressing for larger school budgets want more teachers, smaller classes, and better facilities. But if the employees obtain higher salaries and better fringe benefits, the budget dollars available will provide fewer police patrols, less snow removal and street repair, and fewer teachers in more crowded classrooms. Groups interested in the levels of different governmental services compete and bargain with each other for relative shares of the total budget, but employees must compete and bargain for a larger portion of each group's share. The employees' demand for a general wage increase is thus directly adverse to every other group's interest in the level of services.

Third, in the political process of budget-making public employees seeking general increases have few natural allies and only limited ability to form coalitions. The budget cost of a general wage increase is normally too great, and the employees have too few votes, to make the employee group an attractive political partner to other interest groups. Several interest groups seeking improved services and willing to pay increased taxes may combine to overcome the opposition of other taxpayers to increased taxes. But such coalitions will seldom support a general wage increase, for it would greatly increase the budget cost and reduce the improvement in services which they seek. Many voters may be persuaded that higher teachers' salaries may buy better education for the same money and that higher policemen's salaries may provide more police protection, but few will be persuaded that a general increase for all public employees will buy more service for the budget dollar. The public employees' only natural ally is organized labor, which in some cities has considerable political influence. Even that support is often more official than effective when public employees make demands on the budget, for most union members are also taxpayers and have less than wholehearted enthusiasm for higher taxes to pay higher wages to their own employees.

Because of these three elements, public employees are at a unique disadvantage in the complex political bargaining process of budget-making. They are not one interest group among many in multilateral bargaining, but rather stand alone confronting the combined opposition of all the other interest groups. They must contend with both those groups opposing increased taxes and those seeking increased services. Because labor costs make up such a large portion of the budget, the employees' claims are highly visible to the other interest groups and thus vulnerable to their concerted attack.

In the absence of collective bargaining, the budget-making process, I believe, leaves public employees unable to protect their interests adequately against those whose interests are opposed. Collective bargaining creates a structure which is responsive to the political reality and gives the employees a more effective voice in the political process. The union confronts across the bargaining table a public official who represents the summarized and consolidated interest of the groups opposing the employees' interest. That public official is forced to consider the employees' interests and negotiate the extent to which their claims will exert pressures for an increased budget or for decreased services. Because the bargaining process gives the union a special opportunity to present evidence and argument and because bargaining requires the public official to give answers with reasons, the union is able to substitute, in some measure, rational discussion for political pressure. This special procedure, and the more effective voice it gives public employees in budget-making, seems an appropriate and necessary modification of the political process.

Determination of Goals and Methods

Not all potential subjects of bargaining involve budgetary considerations. Professional employees, in particular, may want to participate in determining the goals to be achieved by the agency and the methods to be used in achieving those goals.

When teachers seek greater control over choice of textbooks or student discipline policies, budget costs and levels of service are not in question; the only issues are the purposes of the school and the means of their accomplishment. Similarly, when teachers seek curriculum changes or support for certain extra-curricular activities, there may be cost implications, but the dominant issue is one of educational goals and the worthwhileness of what is being proposed as against what is being done. Such demands present a totally different political configuration than demands for increased salaries or smaller class size, for they raise no resistance from taxpayers as a group or from others who seek a larger share of the budget for other purposes. The only interest groups directly concerned—and they may be deeply concerned —are the parents and the students. Furthermore, their interests are not necessarily opposed to those of the teachers. Unlike the situation in which wages or other benefits with budget costs are sought, there is no combination of interest groups opposing the teachers' demands. The imbalance of political pressures, which is the underlying justification for collective bargaining as a method of giving employees special access to the political process, is not present.

In addition, disputes over the goals and methods of a public agency may create interest groups which cut across the interest groups concerned with budget costs. Some parents may favor strict student discipline, some may favor lenience and toleration, and some may favor leaving wide discretion in the individual teacher. Similarly, parents may disagree as to what subjects in the curriculum should be emphasized or what extra-curricular activities should be supported. The interest groups shift from issue to issue, each issue presenting a potentially different alignment.

Teachers, too, often disagree among themselves on such issues, sometimes with diametrically opposed and strongly held views. Though the union may speak for the majority, it is less likely to represent a consensus when making demands on such issues than when making demands for increased benefits or decreased work loads.

Collective bargaining on such subjects enables the union to speak with a single voice as representative of those holding opposing views and gives the union increased political effectiveness when it is confronted not by a coalition but by a fragmented opposition. More important, the union does not bargain with the representative of those holding an opposing view on "goal" issues; it bargains with the representative of those who seek lower taxes and more services. The government representative is thus under pressure to accept the union's demands on nonbudget items in return for union concessions which will keep down the cost of the agreement.

Collective bargaining in the public sector, from the perspective of this inquiry, is a specially structured political process for making certain governmental decisions. The primary justification for this special process is that it gives the employees increased political effectiveness to help balance the massed political resistance of taxpayers and users of public services. One consequence of public employee bargaining is at least partial preclusion of public discussion of those subjects being bargained. And the effect of an agreement is to foreclose any change in matters agreed upon during the term of the agreement. Because it constitutes something of a derogation from traditional democratic principles, collective bargaining should be limited to those areas in which public employees do indeed encounter massed resistance. In other areas, disputes by public employees should be resolved through the customary channels of political decisionmaking.

Does Public Employee Unionism Diminish Democracy?

Sanford Cohen*

Current pessimistic evaluations of public sector unionism are reminiscent of the earlier criticisms of private sector unionism, bluntly summarized in Lindblom's assertion that unions were destroying the competitive price system.[1] The ensuing debate over the economic impact of private sector unions produced no obvious consensus at the time, but many students of the subject were apparently satisfied with a rebuttal that posited the impossibility of showing that unionism was responsible for a diminution of price competition in a market already far removed from the competitive model. Judging from the journal literature, however, one now senses a general acceptance of the proposition that there is some incompatibility between collective wage determination and a condition of continuing price stability: union wage policy may not have destroyed the competitive price system, but it certainly is viewed as being troublesome.

Contemporary criticism of public sector unions is focused more on their political than their economic consequences, the general thesis being that a private power center operating inside the government skews the results of the normal political process and thereby diminishes democracy. These criticisms have caused some unease among students of industrial relations who, by and large, had not previously questioned the wisdom of the spread of collective bargaining to the public sector. When those criticisms are carefully examined, however, I believe one must conclude that, as in the earlier controversy over private sector unionism, today's critics of public sector unionism have a point but there is something more to be said. This comment represents an effort to suggest the character of the "something more."

*Department of Economics, University of New Mexico. Reprinted from *Industrial and Labor Relations Review*, Vol. 32 (January 1979), pp. 189-195.

The Criticisms

In the literature considering the consequences of unionism, it is possible to identify two distinct analytical traditions. One, along the approaches of such scholars as Selig Perlman and Frank Tannenbaum, examines the philosophy, psychology, and broad goals of union members and leaders to determine where a particular union movement should be placed along a spectrum of ideologies.[2] The other, with roots that reach back at least to Henry Simons, is preoccupied with the labor market behavior of union organizations and, on the basis of that behavior, decides whether unions contribute to or interfere with a proper functioning of markets.[3]

With only slight modification, that description can apply to the contemporary contention over the consequences of public sector unions. On the one hand, those unions can be analyzed in terms of a broad family of variables that shed light on where the unions might be placed on some prodemocracy-antidemocracy scale. On the other hand, the analysis might be limited to the question of whether the quantum of power that now rests with public sector unions changes the pre-union distribution of power to the extent that certain public decision-making processes (especially those at local levels of government) are less democratic than heretofore.

The differentiation suggested above is significant in that conclusions about the consequences of unionism are obviously conditioned by the selection of an analytical approach. The more prominent attacks upon public sector unions fall into the second of the two analytical traditions, and it is important to note at the outset the limited perspective of that analysis and to express a caution concerning policy inferences drawn from that perspective. In the private sector, for example, one might conclude from a purely economic analysis that union wage behavior has contributed to price inflation and, consequently, that union bargaining power should be limited by appropriate policy measures. A more comprehensive analysis might suggest, however, that on balance labor organizations have been stabilizing institutions in an era of considerable social instability. Although the latter conclusion does not directly rebut the former, it does suggest an important consideration for policy makers, who should consider the full consequences of their determinations.

The most cogent of the arguments that question the compatibility of public sector bargaining and the democratic process are those by Wellington and Winter and by Summers.[4] Following Dahl,[5] Wellington and Winter describe the normal American political process as one with a high probability that an active, legitimate group can effectively make itself heard at some crucial stage in the process of decision making. They conclude that public sector unions, able to combine the power to withhold labor with the usual methods of political pressure, possess a disproportionate share of effective power in the decision-making process and thus "skew the results of the 'normal' political process."[6] This conclusion is derived from a series of propositions: (1) Citizen consumers, faced with a public employee strike, are likely to be seriously inconvenienced given the absence of any substitute for most government services; (2) The citizenry, consequently, will place enormous pressure upon a mayor for a strike settlement; (3) Under these circumstances, it is difficult if not impossible for a mayor to give weight to the longer run fiscal implications of union demands; (4) The mayor will, then, defer to the general pressure for a settlement, a politically safe course since "few citizens can decipher a municipal budget or trace the relationship between today's labor settlement and next year's increase in the mill rate."[7] Furthermore, the cost of a settlement may be borne by a constituency—the state or nation—much larger than that represented by the mayor; (5) Given these considerations, the union's fear of a long strike, which is the major check on union power in the private sector, is not a factor in the public sector.

On the basis of the scenario traced above, Wellington and Winter conclude that the political process has been radically altered and that interest groups with priorities different from unions are apt to be less successful in their pursuit of government revenues than are the unions with power to interrupt services.

Summers also concludes that "public sector employee bargaining is, on balance, probably not good for society, and especially not good in a field such as public school education. . . ."[8] But while the general thrust of his contention is similar to that of Wellington and Winter, his position rests less on the assumption of union strength derived from the strike or the threat to strike. The mere existence of public employee bargaining is sufficient proof of a diminution of democracy for Summers, because such bargaining requires the sharing of public authority with private bodies.[9] This is particularly true when public sector bargaining occurs pursuant to statute, since public employing bodies are then obliged by law to share decisional authority with entities not subject to the control of or accountable to the public for the positions they take.[10] Thus, Summers contends, even when the outcomes under bargaining do not differ significantly from those reached in the absence of bargaining, there is an adverse impact on the democratic process, which is intended to afford opportunities for "process values" such as public participation as well as for public control of decisional processes. Insofar as bargaining short circuits, blocks off, or diminishes public participation, it limits the realization of process values.[11]

While Wellington and Winter and Summers do not explicitly exclude federal level collective bargaining from their analyses, their references to the federal area are sparse and apparently they are not seriously exercised about what occurs at that level. In fact, the federal model would seem to answer the larger portion of their objections to public employee bargaining. The strong proscription of strikes, the delimitation of the negotiable issues, and the final authority of the government to determine disputes over negotiability reduce the scope of bargaining in the federal sector to boundaries compatible with what Wellington and Winter and Summers would recommend.[12] Given those limits on bargaining in the federal service and the prevailing processes of decision making with the federal bureaucracy, it would be difficult to argue that collective bargaining for federal employees has had a significant effect on democratic processes, and the writers under review here do not do so.

It is more difficult to explain the absence in their works of direct references to state employees, for a number of the points made about local bargaining would appear to apply at the state level. One can only speculate about this gap, but clearly it is the public employee strike these writers find most objectionable and perhaps the relative rarity of strikes by state employees accounts for their preoccupation with bargaining in local government.

Wellington and Winter further limit their analysis by distinguishing between strikes over monetary issues and those involving nonmonetary matters, and they describe their analysis as valid for the former but not necessarily for the latter. They maintain that in disputes over nonmonetary issues, intense concern on the part of well-organized interest groups opposed to a union would buttress a mayor in his resistance to union demands; yet, even in this situation, when rank-and-file back their union leadership, pressures for a settlement from the general public would, in time, become irresistible.

Summers does not make the monetary-nonmonetary distinction. His analysis is focused on the public schools, in which nonmonetary personnel issues are actually most likely to touch sensitive policy questions: class size, preparation periods, tenure, and teaching loads, for example, are matters of both working conditions and educational policy. Furthermore, although not monetary subjects in the sense of having a direct relationship to wages and fringe benefits, such issues usually have significant cost implications.

Vulnerable Assumptions

Conclusions about the relationship between collective bargaining by public employees and the condition of democracy generally rest upon assumptions about the nature of union power, public attitudes, and the behavior of public officials in impasse situations. The validity of the conclusions expressed obviously depends on the accuracy of the assumptions made. Considering first the issue of union power, we may ask whether unions operating in the public sector are, in fact, the power juggernauts described by Wellington and Winter and Summers. To the extent that they have overstated the case, their arguments lose force.[13]

These writers admit that public employee unions do not always win their strikes or achieve all their demands. Yet, the reasons for the union failures are not clear from their arguments. If, like their private sector counterparts, public sector unions win some and lose some, there must exist some limits on their power that are not identified in the analyses summarized above. In short, the Wellington-Winter and Summers arguments *per se* are unable to accommodate the experience of union defeat or retreat or, more generally, any instance of unions settling for less than what they would prefer. As examples of union defeats in the public sector accumulate, the picture of these unions as an irresistible force becomes flawed and the logic of an inherent inconsistency between public sector bargaining and the expression of public preferences through democratic processes becomes less persuasive. The Wellington-Winter position is especially vulnerable on this score since one is not led inevitably to the conclusion that the political process has been skewed when one finds that there *are* mayors concerned more about future budget integrity than current labor peace.

Although relatively recent in vintage, the Wellington-Winter and Summers arguments are oddly archaic in tone, perhaps because they present paradigms that were more relevant during the heady times of the 1960s and early 1970s than they are today. There have now been several examples of public officials in major metropolitan centers—New York, Seattle, San Francisco, and Atlanta, for example—standing firm against what they considered excessive union demands. Adding to these the numerous examples of industrial relations confrontations in smaller communities with results that do not confirm the Wellington-Winter and Summers hypotheses on union power, we find a variegated pattern of union power, which is not easily summarized in simple expressions of union dominance.[14]

According to the Wellington-Winter model, the public is concerned exclusively with a restoration of interrupted services regardless of settlement cost. Summers sees the public more as a blackmail victim with no choice but to pay up when essential services are cut off by work stoppages. Similarly, both analyses represent public officers as inevitably bucking under to union power plays on the basis of their reading of public preferences.

The Wellington-Winter and Summers assumptions are defensible in describing a particular period in the history of public sector unionism, although even for that period they may have neglected some important considerations. On the basis of more recent history, however, the longer run validity of their assumptions must be questioned.

During the large-scale emergence of municipal employee unionism in the 1960s, illegal strikes were frequent, essential services were interrupted with unpleasant consequences for the public, and many of the settlements reached were fiscally unsound. The unions—at least some of them—appeared to have acquired a type of power that did indeed skew the results of the normal political process. But can these experiences from the formative period of a new system of municipal industrial relations be extrapolated as a continuing pattern? If not, current conclusions about the long-run impact of public employee unions on the democratic process become conjectural.

Historically, union thrusts into new territory (industrial, geographical, or occupational) have been attended by conflict manifested through strikes and general disorder. Thus, some of the disruption that occurred can be attributed to the normal turmoil of a new union penetration. However, this turmoil touched the public more directly than does the typical labor-management impasse. Unaccustomed to seeing garbage pile up, the schools closed, and uniformed officers on picket lines, the public understandably pressured its elected officials to deal effectively with what it perceived as emergencies—in other words, to settle the strike. Concurrent with much of the rise of the public employee unions, furthermore, the state of the economy facilitated such settlements in that municipalities and school districts enjoyed, or at least thought they enjoyed, some play in their budgets.

The situation has changed, of course. Almost everywhere, local governments are in financial straits, the public is much less likely to panic in the face of service interruptions, and public officials are less reluctant to take tough bargaining stances than they were only a few years ago. Public and official reaction to a particular union action, consequently, is less predictable than Wellington and Winter suggest, and the ultimate effect of public employee bargaining on democracy is less discernible.

The Summers Model

On the basis of the general tenor of his arguments, the response Summers would likely make to the considerations expressed above can be anticipated: the fact that unions in the public sector do not always prevail is not significant. So long as private groups not accountable to the public share in decisional authority, democracy has been diminished.

In so arguing, Summers assumes a clear-cut dichotomy between democratic procedures before and after the onset of collective bargaining. Prior to collective bargaining, public employing bodies are considered broadly democratic; when bargaining begins, this condition is diminished.

The situation, of course, is not as neat as this and Summers admits as much when he notes that "in prebargaining days, local, state and federal bureaucracies were sometimes unresponsive to the public will, and in some law-making processes at some of these levels, powerful interest groups frequently had (and continue to have) disproportionate say."[15] In such circumstances, however, Summers argues that the remedy is not to create still more powerful interest groups such as unions to diminish democracy even further.

The argument at this point, however, has taken a subtle turn. It is one thing to contend that public employee unions have diminished a pre-existing democratic condition and another to presume that they inhibit a potential rise in the level of democracy in situations where the democratic will is otherwise stifled. In the case of unionization of employees within an insensitive bureaucracy, the appearance of a union does not necessarily make the unresponsive bureaucracy more unresponsive. What it necessarily does, according to Summers, is to diminish the possibility for improvement by piling a new layer of insensitivity to public interest on top of an existing one.

This conclusion requires the assumption that unionization of a group of employees affects no variables in an institutional power structure other than that of employee power. It is not difficult, however, to conceive of situations in which an organizing process breaks the bureaucratic shield so as to enlarge the possibilities of general public influence.[16] In such cases, unionization will have improved the democratic condition. Summers's error on this point is that of treating possibilities as certainties.

It is clear, however, that the main concern of Summers is with those situations in which a union enters a public institution that is sensitive to and affected by close and frequent public contact. His model is public education, which he visualizes as reflecting the public will through various types of public participation in decision making and frequent elections of school board members. In his vision, the unionization of teachers reduces democracy in the schools by limiting the reach of the general public voice.

To the extent that democracy is measured by its conformity to the populistic model described by Summers, public employee bargaining does indeed limit democracy since such bargaining inevitably will determine some matters outside the arena subject to direct and immediate public influence. The validity of Summers's conclusions, however, depends upon the realism of both his model and his concept of democracy. If either can be tenably questioned, his conclusions must be adjudged to be possibilities rather than inevitable results.

First, a question of fact. In the typical school district, is there a flourishing town-hall democracy that monitors and controls the operations of the schools in a significant way? Summers provides no supporting evidence on this point and contrary evidence exists: school board meetings, although tumultuous on occasion, ordinarily play to empty halls. In addition, the 7 percent voter turnout in the 1977 New York City community school board elections does not bespeak a vigorous grass-roots democracy in a city afflicted with severe problems in public education. Although 7 percent may be a low turnout for this type of election, the percentages achieved elsewhere are not impressive.[17]

Even if we assume an active citizenry at the school district level, is it not necessary to acknowledge the constraints on their influence from sources other than unions? Consider, for example, the role of the state legislature in local school finance and the towering influence of the colleges of education in determining what is taught and how it is taught. The political condition modified by the appearance of unionism is more complex than Summers's model suggests.

Waiving these considerations, we are left with the fundamental question of how to determine whether a specific institutional change—the unionization of public employees—has affected the democratic process so as to make it less democratic. If, as Summers presumes, union-management negotiations preempt the exercise of effective public influence on significant matters of public policy, there should be little objection to his conclusions. It is necessary to ask, however, following Dahl's formulation, whether collective bargaining in public agencies reduces the probability that active and legitimate groups can make themselves effectively heard at some crucial stage in the decision-making process.[18] Clearly, public employee bargaining may force changes in the processes through which nonunion groups express themselves, and the direct town-hall type of participation that Summers sees in the area of public education may have suffered from the advent of public employee unions. Democracy is diminished, however, only if alternative avenues for effective influence by nonunion groups are not available. Since alternative avenues for political action obviously are available,[19] the residual question goes to the matter of their effectiveness, leading us full circle to the Wellington-Winter argument of why public sector bargaining diminishes democracy—not because the general public is unable to express itself politically, but because unions in that sector possess a disproportionate share of political influence.

Conclusions

Experience will provide the ultimate test of the Wellington-Winter hypothesis. The record to date, however, while not conclusive, provides some basis for challenging their position. Writing in a popular magazine that has not been unfriendly to public sector unions, one observer concludes 'For the past few years . . . the challenge for the public employee unions has been to cope with a backlash against their continued success and public be damned attitudes. . . . In many . . . cities, municipal unions have been settling for little or no increase in wages and benefits. In some localities, an anti-union stance has measurably enhanced the popularity of politicians."[20]

In short, the public has been expressing itself on the matter of public sector unions in ways Wellington and Winter and Summers would approve, and it appears to be doing so effectively. If it is the public will, expressed through one political channel or another, that ultimately determines how much and in what ways public sector bargaining affects the general processes of democracy, the problem presented by such scholars as Wellington and Winter and Summers need not be especially worrisome.

Footnotes

1. Charles E. Lindblom, *Unions and Capitalism* (New Haven: Yale University Press, 1949), p. 4.
2. Selig Perlman, *A Theory of the Labor Movement* (New York: Augustus M. Kelley, 1949), and Frank Tannenbaum, *The Labor Movement: Its Conservative Functions and Social Consequences* (New York: G. P. Putnam's Sons, 1921).
3. Henry Simons, *Economic Policy for a Free Society* (Chicago: The University of Chicago Press, 1948), ch. 6.
4. Harry H. Wellington and Ralph K. Winter, "The Limits of Collective Bargaining in Public Employment," *Yale Law Journal.* Vol. 78, No. 7 (June 1969), pp. 1123-27; Wellington and Winter, *The Unions and the Cities* (Washington, D.C.: The Brookings Institution, 1971); and Robert S. Summers, *Collective Bargaining and Public Benefit Conferral: A Jurisprudential Critique* (Ithaca, New York: Institute of Public Employment, New York State School of Industrial and Labor Relations, 1976).

   Given the volume of literature on the politics of public employee bargaining, it is surprising that so little meets the arguments of Wellington and Winter and of Summers head-on. The lack of response to Summers's thesis is especially surprising in view of the uncompromising character of his attack against public sector bargaining. Studies that raise doubts about the significance of the union impact on public sector wages, although not directed explicitly at Wellington and Winter or at Summers, can be interpreted as a challenge to their conclusions about the power of unions in that sector. Such studies, however, do not deal directly with the question that clearly preoccupies Wellington and Winter and Summers: the question of the power of unions to prevail in their contests with public employers. In any event, public sector wage impact studies present an inconclusive picture. See David Lewin, "Public Sector Labor Relations: A Review Essay," in Lewin, Peter Feuille, and Thomas A. Kochan, eds., *Public Sector Labor Relations: Analysis and Readings* (Glen Ridge, N.J.: Thomas Horton and Daughters, 1977), p. 375.

   Although there are many references in the literature to a possible collision between public sector bargaining and democratic processes, very few writers appear to be exercised about the possibility. In his essay, "Public Employee Bargaining: A Political Perspective," Clyde Summers, for example, admits that collective bargaining in the public sector "constitutes something of a derogation from traditional democratic principles" (Lewin, Feuille, and Kochan, *Public Sector Labor Relations,* p. 49). Nevertheless, he concludes that basic characteristics of public employment justify a specially structured political process such as collective bargaining for making certain government decisions.

The explicit issue of whether public sector collective bargaining diminishes democracy can—Wellington and Winter and Summers would say "should"—be examined independently of questions about the economic impact and general desirability of public sector unionism.

5. Robert A. Dahl, *A Preface to Democratic Theory* (Chicago: The University of Chicago Press, 1956), p. 145.
6. Wellington and Winter, "The Limits of Collective Bargaining," p. 1123.
7. Ibid., p. 1125.
8. Summers, *Collective Bargaining*. xi.
9. Ibid., p. 4.
10. Ibid.
11. Ibid., p. 7.
12. "Labor-Management Relations in the Federal Service," Executive Order 11491, as amended, 1975.
13. Although Summers does not base his case primarily on the power of unions to interrupt services, the union-led strike is by no means insignificant in his analysis. His monograph is laced, for example, with references to the "extraordinary leverage" of the union (p. 47) which has and knows it has the public "over a barrel" (p. 7). For Wellington and Winter, union power expressed through the strike is important in a critical way given their assumptions of the behavior of municipal officers in the face of a strike or strike threat.
14. A 1976 police strike in Las Cruces, New Mexico, for example, is noteworthy in that the strike, which ended disastrously for the union, was followed shortly thereafter by an unsuccessful union effort to influence the outcome of a municipal election. The point, of course, is that unions operating both within and outside of the government may be ineffectual in both locations. See Sanford Cohen and Christian Eaby, "The Beginnings of Public Employee Unionism in New Mexico," unpublished manuscript (available on request).
15. Summers, *Collective Bargaining*, p. 2.
16. My point here is that the organizing process is something of a public event which exposes a bureaucracy to general view, with the possible result that it appears to be more within the reach of public pressures for basic changes. In a way, Wellington and Winter suggest this in their conclusions about the generation of pressure on a mayor in the course of a work stoppage. If such pressure is as irresistible as Wellington and Winter suggest, why would it not be effective when applied for other purposes?
17. The *New York Times*, June 5, 1977, IV, p. 6. Comprehensive studies of voter participation in school board elections are rare. All writers who refer to the matter, however, state that the turnout is usually low. See, for example, Frederick Wirt and Michael Kirst, *The Political Web of American Schools* (Waltham, MA.: Little, Brown and Co., 1972), p. 63; Thomas Eliot, *Governing America, The Politics of a Free People* (New York: Dodd, Mead and Co., 1946), p. 895; Thomas Dye, *Politics in States and Communities* (Englewood Cliffs, N.J.: Prentice-Hall, Inc., 1973), p. 438. Dye, who makes reference to "that small band of voters who turn out for school elections," estimates that, on the average, less than one-third of the eligible voters bother to cast ballots in school elections.
18. Dahl, *A Preface to Democratic Theory*, p. 145.
19. Such avenues would include direct appeal to the appropriate political and administrative officials, expressions of preference through referenda on tax levies, support of anti-union candidates in school board and other elections, lobbying at budget hearings in the state legislature, and appeal through the media for support of particular positions. Summers, incidentally, appears to

have given no consideration to the possibility that, in a particular union-public-management impasse, public sympathy might be with the union and that the impasse could open possibilities for a democratic expression of grass roots opinion that might not otherwise exist. This, of course, has occurred. See Robert U. Anderson, *et al.*, "Support Your Local Police—On Strike?" *Journal of Police Science and Administration*, Vol. 4, No. 1 (March 1976), pp. 1-8.

20. Roger M. Williams, "The Clamor over Municipal Unions," *Saturday Review* (March 5, 1977), p. 14.

THE LEGAL CONTEXT

Unlike private sector labor relations, public sector unionism and bargaining are not presently subject to regulation at the national level. Instead, each state of the United States is free to regulate the public sector bargaining that occurs within its borders. The first state law supporting public employee unionism and bargaining was adopted in Wisconsin in 1959. From the mid-1960s to the early 1970s, numerous states enacted public sector bargaining laws, largely in response to the demands of newly organized public workers. Thereafter, the pace of new legislation slowed markedly, and recent legislative activity in the area of public sector bargaining has focused on experimentation with various forms of dispute resolution procedures (which will be treated in Chapter 5). As of this writing, about half the states have enacted public sector bargaining laws and another 15 or so maintain more limited "meet and confer" statutes.[1] There are few remaining state legislative prohibitions on public employee unionism, though such prohibitions were common, indeed pervasive, less than a quarter-century ago.

What factors determine the propensity of a state to enact public sector bargaining legislation? This question has been addressed by Thomas Kochan, who employed scaling, correlation, and regression techniques to analyze the relationship between, on the one hand, the economic, political, and industrial relations environments of the 50 states, and, on the other, the comprehensiveness of their public sector bargaining statutes.[2] Kochan showed that the states that have passed the most comprehensive legislation tend to be more highly industrialized, have higher levels of per capita income, spend more per capita on public services, and have a longer history of innovating with legislation in other policy areas than other states. Consequently, there were some systematic environmental pressures which led to the passage of public sector bargaining laws during the 1960s and early 1970s. However, as Kochan himself notes, the quantitative analysis seemed to explain only about one-third of the variation among the states in the comprehensiveness of their statutes regulating public sector labor relations. A more complete explanation of this phenomenon awaits further research which, if undertaken, would permit replication of Kochan's study design and empirical testing under environmental conditions which seem quite different from those that prevailed a decade or more ago.

Other researchers have sought to explain the emergence and development of one or another specific bargaining statute in a particular state or local government. The first article in this section, by Staudohar, serves as a leading example of this type of study. Staudohar describes the passage of the 1970 Hawaii state statute which provides the right to strike and, as the author states, is "one of the most extensive in terms of employee rights." His article highlights the intensive forms of lobbying, pressure group bargaining, and legislative maneuvering that go on in the process of negotiating a public sector bargaining statute through a state legislature. His paper illustrates the importance of having cohesive interest groups that are effectively organized to represent the interests of their constituencies regarding the detailed aspects of such a statute. Interested readers may compare the Staudohar article with others in the literature in order to understand the impact of differences in the social and political environment and the strength of different interest groups on the final outcome of legislative battles relative to public sector laws. Clearly a complex range of decisions confront policymakers and administrators who attempt to adapt a comprehensive statute to the unique political, legal, and economic context of a state. The Staudohar piece also nicely complements quantitative research, such as that conducted by Kochan, into the determinants of public sector bargaining laws.

Once public sector bargaining legislation comes into being, it is subject to alteration via the political process. This is particularly true of the statutory provisions that deal with impasse procedures. The second article in this section, by Kochan, describes the interplay of political forces at work in New York State during the late 1970s which resulted in an amendment to that state's Taylor Law that, among other things, eliminated factfinding but renewed the provision authorizing compulsory interest arbitration of police and firefighter labor disputes. Kochan shows how the various union and mangement organizations used the results of an independent research study of the effectiveness of the Taylor Law's impasse procedures selectively to support their own respective positions and oppose those of others with regard to amending the law. In particular, Kochan concludes that "it was the political power of the police and firefighters that provided the votes needed to insure that some form of arbitration would be extended."

It should be further noted that one often needs to look beyond bargaining legislation to understand the full force of the legal constraints affecting state and local government labor negotiations. These constraints include constitutional limits on state and local taxing authority, tax rates and tax composition; civil service systems operated by commissions that typically claim broad authority over terms and conditions of governmental employment; and legislative controls on certain pension benefits, insurance plans, working hours, and union security arrangements, to name but a few items. Some of these constraints are eased (formally or otherwise) as collective bargaining develops in government, but others are not and still others may be hardened. More important, perhaps, the myriad constraints vary from state to state and even among local governments within a state so that a student of this subject must look to the governmental entity in question and to its relations with other levels of government to gain specific understanding of how these constraints impinge upon the bargaining process.[3]

An important consideration in the legal context of public sector bargaining involves the possibility of federal legislation governing unionism and bargaining rights of state and local employees. Several bills concerned with this issue have been introduced into recent sessions of Congress, but none have gotten out of committee in either the Senate or the House of Representatives. Basically, three alternative policy approaches have been embodied in these bills: (1) extension of the National Labor Relations Act and the jurisdiction of the National Labor Relations Board to employees of state and local governments, (2) specific comprehensive bargaining legislation for public employees, or (3) the establishment of minimum standards of collective bargaining rights for state and local employees, with the specific form of legislation left to the states for enactment and administration.

One of the reasons that these bills have not been translated into law is that there was no consensus within the major interest groups affected by potential legislation regarding the options or the particulars within each option. For example, a heated debate developed within the labor movement over whether any legislation should provide for compulsory arbitration as a means of resolving bargaining impasses for public employees. Another dispute arose within the labor movement regarding whether the states that have public sector legislation ought to be able to preempt federal legislation, or vice versa. The issue of preemption is perhaps one of the most complex problems facing policymakers when considering any type of federal legislation for public sector labor relations.

There is something of a dilemma involved in the issue of federal bargaining legislation for government workers in the United States. The longer we permit the states to settle this issue individually, the more difficult it will be to find a way to develop a workable federal law. Thus, the longer federal legislation is delayed, the more powerful the minimum standards approach becomes. If this is the case, however, each state will have to carry a heavy administrative burden. While that would be expensive and perhaps confusing, it would preserve the "laboratory environment" that allows us to learn more about the impact of various policy options on the public sector bargaining process. Not surprisingly, the Association of Labor Mediation Agencies has forcefully endorsed the minimum standards approach, since this option does the least harm to the constituent agencies' jurisdictions.

In addition to the above problems, there is an overriding concern over the constitutionality of federal legislation designed to regulate the labor relations of state and local governments. An indirect test of the probable fate of federal collective bargaining legislation for state and local employees was provided by the U.S. Supreme Court in its 1976 decision that ruled unconstitutional the extension of the national Fair Labor Standards Act to municipal governments.[4] The Supreme Court's decision has generally been interpreted to imply that any type of federal collective bargaining law for state and local governments would likewise be ruled unconstitutional. Thus, there is a difficult constitutional hurdle that must be overcome before any form of federal legislation in this area can become a reality.

Our discussion so far has dealt only with the legal framework for collective bargaining in state and local governments. We would be amiss, however, if we failed to include a description of the legal context for employees of the federal government. The first limited endorsement of bargaining rights for federal employees came with the signing of Federal

Executive Order 10988 by President Kennedy in 1962. Seven years later, this original order was replaced by Executive Order 11491, which was in turn amended on several occasions during the 1970s. In late 1978, Congress passed the Civil Service Reform Act, which superseded Executive Order 11491 and for the first time provided a statutory basis for federal sector labor relations.[5] In brief, the act:

1. protects the rights of employees to join or not join labor organizations;
2. establishes (a) the Federal Labor Relations Authority (FLRA), a three-member body appointed by the president, to administer the law's provisions dealing with organization, representation, and bargaining rights; (b) the Federal Services Impasse Panel, a seven-member entity within and appointed by the FLRA, to resolve negotiating impasses by taking "whatever action is necessary" (usually mediation, followed by factfinding with recommendations); and (c) assigns to the Assistant Secretary of Labor for Labor-Management Relations responsibility for administering standards of conduct for federal labor organizations, particularly in the areas of internal democracy and financial integrity;
3. provides procedures for exclusive representation and national consultation rights for employee organizations (to consult on agency-wide personnel policies);
4. specifies the scope of bargaining and enumerates management rights;
5. requires the negotiation of grievance procedures;
6. requires the approval of all labor agreements by the top agency administrator; and
7. enumerates a list of unfair labor practices for employee and employer organizations.

One of the key differences between the federal system and most state and local statutes or the National Labor Relations Act is that wages, fringe benefits, civil service provisions, and many agency personnel and other policies and regulations are excluded from the scope of federal sector bargaining. Despite these limitations, unionization and collective bargaining have spread to approximately 50 percent of all General Schedule (white-collar) employees and to over 80 percent of all Wage Grade (blue-collar) employees in the federal service. (Employees of the quasi-public U.S. Postal Service bargain under separate statutory authority and are about 90 percent organized).

Not surprisingly, the most controversial issue regarding the legal framework for bargaining in the federal sector centers on the restrictions on the scope of bargaining that were built into the executive order system. A variety of direct and indirect constraints exist on the scope of federal employee bargaining; some of these, but only some, are addressed by the Federal Civil Service Reform Act. We do not have space to consider further the provisions of the act that pertain to labor relations, but the reader should be aware of the continuing debate among policymakers, agency administrators, neutrals, and union officials that is shaping the evolution of collective bargaining in the federal sector.[6] Developments in this sector may be among the most important that occur in the area of governmental labor relations during the 1970s (see Chapter 8 for further discussion of this point).

FOOTNOTES

1. See U.S. Department of Labor, *Summary of State Policy Regulations for Public Sector Labor Relations: Statutes, Attorney Generals' Opinions and Selected Court Decisions* (Washington, D.C.: Government Printing Office, 1977), and B.V.H. Schneider, "Public-Sector Labor Legislation, An Evolutionary Analysis," in Benjamin Aaron, Joseph R. Grodin, and James L. Stern (eds.), *Public-Sector Bargaining* (Washington, D.C.: Bureau of National Affairs, 1979), pp. 191-233.
2. "Correlates of State Public Employee Bargaining Laws," *Industrial Relations* 12 (October 1973), 322-337.
3. For an early but still relevant anaysis of these constraints in Michigan jurisdictions, see Charles M. Rehmus, "Constraints on Local Governments in Public Employee Bargaining," *Michigan Law Review* 67 (March 1969), 919-930.
4. See *National League of Cities* v. *Usury,* 96 S. Ct. 2465, 426 v.s. 833 (1976).
5. See Bureau of National Affairs, "The Civil Service Reform Act," *Government Employee Relations Report,* Reference File-171 (Washington, D.C.: Bureau of National Affairs, December 4, 1978), pp. 21:1001-21:1059, especially 21:1041-21:1055.
6. See Bureau of National Affairs, "Civil Service Commission's Analysis of the Civil Service Reform Act of 1978," *Government Employee Relations Report* no. 781 (Washington, D.C.: Bureau of National Affairs, October 16, 1978), pp. 73-78.

The Emergence of Hawaii's Public Employment Law

Paul D. Staudohar*

The Hawaii legislature in 1970 passed a public employment bargaining law which is one of the most extensive in terms of employee rights yet produced. The theoretical foundation of this law, like that of much recent legislation in this area, includes an important assumption of the private sector's National Labor Relations Act: that a policy guaranteeing the right to organize and to bargain collectively will work to reduce conflict engendered by an inequality of bargaining power. The Hawaii law went further than most, however, in that it allowed concerted activities by public employees for their mutual aid and protection. Provision of the right to strike has drawn national attention to the law, although it has other distinctive features which are being carefully observed as well. Thus, the Hawaii law may be a forerunner of future state and federal labor legislation, and its evolution warrants examination.

This paper[1] explores the dynamics of the 1970 law[2] from the standpoint of how and why its key provisions came about, particularly those dealing

*College of Business Administration, California State University, Hayward. Reprinted from *Industrial Relations* 12 (October 1973), pp. 338-351.

with (1) the scope of bargaining, (2) union security, (3) appropriate bargaining units, and (4) the right to strike. Each of these has its own legislative-lobbying history and rationale for adoption, and, therefore, it should be useful to analyze them separately.

Earlier Legislation

Government employees in Hawaii were denied the right to strike and picket by a 1949 statute.[3] In the following year, the first Hawaii Constitution provided that public employees had the right to organize and to present grievances and proposals. The Constitution, however, was only an expression of legislative sentiment since it was not made effective until 1959 when Hawaii became a state. The next important event was in 1965 when a bill was introduced into the state legislature to give state and local government employees limited bargaining rights. Sponsored by the United Public Workers union, it was patterned after federal Executive Order 10988 and provided for informal, formal, and exclusive recognition, while excluding wages from the scope of bargaining. Lacking widespread support, the bill failed passage. In 1967, the legislature passed a law that required departments to consult with employees or employee organizations on matters affecting working conditions and when formulating and implementing personnel policies and practices. Also, prior to making major policy or operational changes, departments were required to notify employees of the proposed changes and, when employees so requested, to discuss them. The 1967 legislation added to the earlier statutory strike ban the condition that employees had the right to join those organizations which did not assert the right to strike against government or propose to assist in one.[4]

A major step toward passage of a comprehensive public employment bargaining law was taken when the present state constitution was adopted in 1968. Article XII of the constitution mandated a collective bargaining law by providing that, "Persons in public employment shall have the right to organize for the purpose of collective bargaining as prescribed by law." Besides being important as an impetus to the law that was ultimately passed, the mandate is significant in that the constitutional convention from which it sprang had a broad representation directly responsible for initially proposing and then reviewing constitutional provisions. This afforded opportunity for reflection on the question of whether a collective bargaining law was appropriate for Hawaii in a forum representative of society and apart from the state legislature as such.

The 1970 Law

Pursuant to the constitutional mandate, at the 1969 session of the state legislature various interest groups, including three major labor organizations —the Hawaii Government Employees Association (HGEA),[5] the United Public Workers (UPW),[6] and the Hawaii Education Association (HEA)[7] —introduced public employment bargaining bills. In hearings on the bills, conducted by the Senate Public Employment Committee, testimony focused on the issues of unit determination, who should bargain for the public employer, the right to strike, and impasse resolution. Some of the positions taken by interest groups at the hearings differed from those generally taken by their counterpart organizations on the Mainland. For example, the Department of Civil Service of the City and County of Honolulu and the Director of Personnel Services for the County of Hawaii favored the right to strike, and the Hawaii Employers Council[k] and the State Department of Personnel Services supported compulsory arbitration. The labor organizations generally advocated the right to strike, while opposing compulsory arbitration.

It became apparent from the testimony of the concerned organizations that, although there was bipartisan support for passage of a law providing more extensive public employee bargaining rights, insufficient evidence and study existed to understand and press for specific provisions. Some unions had pushed hard for passage of a law in the 1969 session, but there was a lack of firm commitment on the part of most. It was recognized that public employee bargaining was a complex subject with potentially far-reaching implications, making it prudent to investigate the issues more thoroughly before acting.

Shortly after the realization that legislation was unlikely in 1969, the first public employee strike in Hawaii's history took place in May. It was largely an attempt by 1,600 blue-collar workers, the most essential of whom were garbage collectors, to pressure the legislature into granting a pay increase. Unions representing the workers included UPW and HGEA. At issue was complete reinstatement of a bill passed by the house which raised wages for all government employees. Upon being sent to the senate, committee action had eliminated a 5 per cent increase for long-service employees from the house's bill. With the indication that their demands would be seriously considered (although the increment was not reinstated), the workers returned to their jobs after a two-day stoppage. The strike illustrated an increasing militancy among Hawaii's public employees, corresponding to rising unrest on the Mainland, and caused more thought to be given to the collective bargaining process as a way of determining wages and other employment conditions.

The formal 1969 session of the legislature ended without a law being passed. Later in the year, during the interim period between sessions, the house appointed a 17-person group called the Ad Hoc Committee on Collective Bargaining for Public Employees to study the issues and come up with recommendations for consideration by the lawmakers. The committee included representatives of the major employee organizations and of large private industrial firms. Chairman of the group was Arthur J. Dalton, chief of employee relations of the Federal Aviation Administration, Pacific Region. There was limited representation from other branches of government, but no legislators were on the committee.

In January 1970, the Ad Hoc Committee issued its report to the house which was incorporated into a bill introduced as H.B. 1353. The proposed bill sought to establish bargaining units as broad as possible, cutting across departmental and jurisdictional lines. Teachers, instructors at the university, policemen, firefighters, and professional employees, among others, were to be in separate statewide units. The bill was silent on the right to strike, but it cited the continuance of application of existing state law, including (by inference) that banning strikes by government employees. Wages, salaries, and job classification were not within the scope of bargaining. Bargaining impasses were directed to mediation, fact-finding, and, if still not resolved, the administering board set up under the bill would make a binding decision, thus making it a form of compulsory arbitration.

Scope of bargaining. Only three members of the committee, including the chairman, signed the report in full concurrence. The main source of controversy was over the scope of bargaining. Representatives of private business on the committee were against the idea of bargaining over wages, as was the Hawaii Employers Council which favored a prevailing wage rate statute. There was also a difference of opinion among the union representatives. Although HGEA had originally supported a bill providing for bargaining over wages in 1969, it repudiated this position and instead recommended tying wages of public employees to prevailing rates in the private sector. The International Longshoremen's & Warehousemen's Union (ILWU — the dominant union in Hawaii) representative on the committee took the same stand.[9] The position of these unions was dictated by a realization that the legislature was not likely to relinquish its control over spending and that, even after negotiation, ultimate ratification would have to come from the legislature. This being the case, a separate prevailing wage rate statute was thought to be a less arbitrary way of determining wages and probably of more benefit to employees. Other unions with representation on the committee — the Hawaii Federal of Teachers, UPW, and HEA — favored bargaining over wages, but because their counterparts from HGEA and the ILWU disagreed, along with the committee members from private industry, it was excluded from the committee's report and the bill.

The 1970 legislative session had before it the bills carried over from the 1969 session plus four additional bills, for a total of eight. By the end of March it began to appear that the legislature would not get a law passed because of the inability of the unions to agree among themselves on certain issues, notably bargaining over wages. The chairmen of key committees in the senate and house favored including wages in bargaining, but HGEA and the ILWU remained adamantly inclined toward tying wages to private sector rates. It was the chairman of the Senate Committee on Public Employment, Sakae Takahashi, who was most responsible for getting the unions and the legislature over the impasse and moving rapidly in the direction of compromise. Takahashi, in consultation with the state's Legislative Reference Bureau, put together a modified bill, combining provisions from earlier bills, which was introduced into both houses in early April. At the hearings on the bill, employee organizations indicated their general support, having by then come to the conclusion that unless they made some compromise among themselves passage was improbable. The new bill closely resembled the law that was finally adopted with regard to powers of the public employment relations board, bargaining units, scope of bargaining, distinction between cost and noncost bargaining items, management rights, impasse resolution procedure (including voluntary binding arbitration), and the right to strike.

Union security. A vexing problem for the legislators was union security. A senate committee recommended a mandatory agency shop. Beyond this, the senate committee also recommended that a union shop provision be made a negotiable item. However a house committee disagreed on the union shop issue. Compromise was reached by dropping the union shop recommendation and accepting the mandatory agency shop, a feature which an important management spokesman had earlier indicated would be acceptable.[10]

Appropriate bargaining units. Considering the uniqueness of Hawaii's governmental structure, the establishment of predetermined statewide units[11] appeared to be innovative and logical. Many of the functions performed by county governments elsewhere are conducted at the state level in Hawaii, such as school administration, welfare, property tax assessment, and administration of the system of lower courts. On the other hand, services such as police and fire protection, public works, and sanitation—ordinarily within the purview of city government on the Mainland—are handled by county governments in Hawaii. The four counties, Hawaii, Kauai, Maui, and the City and County of Honolulu, provide the local government service.

Legislative approval was required for cost items under the law ultimately passed. If employees involved were employed by the state, cost items had to be approved by the state legislature. Where employees in a statewide unit were in an occupational category employed by the counties, legislative approval was required by the state and the four counties. This was thought to have the result of enabling each of the legislative bodies to consider fund appropriate for a collective bargaining agreement in conjunction with other competing demands for money. The rationale was to get away from numerous requests for implementing collective bargaining agreements, each of which would require consideration, and the difficulty of allocating funds properly when requests for appropriations are coming in at various times during the legislative session. (Accordingly, the parties to bargaining were encouraged in the law to conclude negotiations at the time the legislative bodies are acting on the operating budget.)

Following the pattern in other states, the legislature determined, without much debate, that bargaining would take place between the executive branch of government and the representative employee organizations. A question arose, however, over the role, if any, that the legislative branch would play in the bargaining process. Was the legislature to be put in a position of merely providing an official sanction to the bargain reached by the executive branch, with effective decision-making power and authority lodged in that branch of government? Or should the legislature be more of a review body which would make final determination on money items, not unlike its existing role, but with some pressure to sanction what had been tentatively agreed upon by representatives of the executive branch? The law adopted the latter role for the legislature, making it the final arbiter on bargaining items involving costs. The legislature previously had control over money as the tax-levying authority, and there was overall sentiment among the interest groups and key members of the legislature for retaining some control. As indicated above, HGEA and the ILWU had foreseen the likelihood of final determination by the legislature of matters involving expenditure, and for that reason had favored a prevailing wage rate statute in lieu of bargaining over wages. However, confronted with the choice of no legislation in 1970 versus a law which sanctioned bargaining over wages but with final legislative determination on expenditures, these labor organizations acquiesced in the latter alternative. Thus, resistance to the feature of legislative determination on expenditures was overcome.

The right to strike. Perhaps the most sensitive issue for the legislature to resolve was that of the right to strike. Similar to the manner in which industrial warfare in Hawaii's private sector tends to be more explosive than on the Mainland because of the concentration of economic power, strike action in Hawaii's public sector can easily sweep through the entire state. At the local level, since there are only four counties performing the functions normally handled by cities on the Mainland, the chance of a strike spreading across Hawaii's counties is more probable than a strike spreading from city to city in most states. Teacher strikes, on the other hand, are more likely to be statewide because teachers are employed by the state. Thus, adoption of features in a labor relations system which would minimize these conflicts became essential. Evidence from other jurisdictions of the effects of allowing strikes was nonexistent; most jurisdictions which had outlawed strikes had found that the strike ban did little, if anything, to prevent them. The two houses of the legislature had differing views on the right to strike question. When it came to reconciling the issue between them the senate viewpoint prevailed, probably representing the majority opinion on the issue. Early in 1970 several key members of the executive branch, including the mayor of the county of Hawaii, and the lieutenant governor and governor of the state, came out publicly in favor of the right to strike by some or all public employees.

The public employment collective bargaining law was passed on May 6. An event took place on that day which may have given encouragement to the legislators, all of whom were up for re-election in 1970, to pass the law. The United Public Workers union called a statewide strike protesting the inaction of a senate committee on a 5 per cent wage increase that had been approved by the house. This bill had been originally intended to provide an adjustment for blue-collar workers, but, after house approval, the senate added various white-collar workers to the bill raising its costs and casting doubt on its approval. Initially involved in the strike were nurses, hospital maintenance employees, and several categories of blue-collar workers. HGEA, with its mostly white-collar workers, joined the strike during the second day, and about 13,500 workers in all were active in the stoppage; an estimated 7,000 marched on the state capitol. Lack of custodial services and cafeteria workers closed schools. After three days the strike ended with the legislature granting the blue-collar raise and increasing the wages of about half the white-collar workers. High-ranking public officials publicly regarded the strike as more of a "demonstration," ducking the issue of its illegality. It was a clear victory for the strikers and underscored the need for a bargaining law.

Summary and Conclusions

Comparison of the law passed by the legislature with the bills supported by interest groups shows some accommodation to each of the groups. From the HEA-sponsored legislation (H.B. 727) was taken part of the strike policy (involving injunctions where public health or safety was endangered or impasse procedures were not followed), the mandatory agency shop, and binding grievance arbitration. H.B. 755, supported by UPW, contained the distinction between cost and noncost bargaining items, with the former requiring approval by the legislature. The proposal backed by HGEA (H.B. 1353) had provisions for specified statewide bargaining units, management rights, and unfair practices by labor and management. The Department of Civil Service, City and County of Honolulu, had supported H.B. 1529, which excluded position classification and retirement benefits from the scope of bargaining and was influential on the right to strike. The bills promoted by the State AFL-CIO (H.B. 1839) and the Hawaii Federation of Teachers (H.B. 1947) were the same except for provisions having to do with the size and selection of the state board. From these bills the rights of employees, scope of bargaining, and the grievance arbitration sections of the law were taken.

While the law is far reaching and liberal in many respects, apparently adequate safeguards are built into it. What seems to be a broad scope of bargaining that includes wages, hours, and other terms and conditions of employment is tempered by specific exclusions as well as a potentially strong management rights provision. The legislature, having retained the right to approve cost items negotiated between the parties, has what should be an effective restraint on settlements under most circumstances. The right to strike is also not unqualified, as it requires utilization of dispute settlement procedures and a cooling-off period as prior conditions to striking and stipulates that a strike (or impending strike) must not endanger public health or safety.

Examination of (1) the processes leading to passage of the law and (2) the legislative rationale with regard to its key provisions, suggests that some of the factors at work were unique to Hawaii, while others apply more generally elsewhere. Conditions peculiar to Hawaii result primarily from a governmental structure which has no overlapping jurisdictions and which centralizes functions in the state and only four counties. Since decision making over provision and administration of government service is uniquely placed and greatly concentrated, certain provisions of the Hawaii law (e.g., predetermined statewide bargaining units) are not likely to be duplicated elsewhere.

The legislative process differed from that in most other jurisdictions in being preceded by a constitutional convention in 1968 with broad public representation. One of the resulting changes in the state constitution mandated collective bargaining for public employees, and this was an important incentive to legislative action. Apart from the mandate, the legislative process was more familiar. Interest groups brought forth and lobbied for passage of bills representing the interests of leadership and constituencies. It was the responsibility of the politicians to reconcile and accommodate these interests, along with those of the larger constituency they represented and with the constraints of Hawaii governmental organization. Group pressures partially offset each other, as the legislature aggregated the interests by selecting provisions from various bills. Public hearings and appointment of a study commission outside the legislature were helpful in shaping the legal framework and generating consensus. Strikes were used to spur the law's adoption, first in 1969 when it became apparent that no bill would be passed in that session, and again in 1970 on the same day that legislators voted on passage.

Footnotes

1. The author wishes to acknowledge the helpful criticisms and suggestions of Joel Seidman, B. V. H. Schneider, John B. Ferguson, Edwin C. Pendleton, Thomas Q. Gilson, and Joyce M. Najita.
2. Hawaii Revised Statutes, 1970, Ch. 89; *Government Employee Relations Report,* No. 389, May 18, 1970, pp. F-1 to F-9.
3. Act 42, Special Session Laws, 1959.
4. Act 50, Revised Laws of Hawaii, 1967. See also Act 287, Revised Laws of Hawaii, 1967, which permitted employees to attend certain informational and educational meetings conducted during working hours by duly recognized representatives of employee organizations.
5. HGEA, which has about 20,000 members, all of whom are state and county employees in Hawaii, became affiliated with the American Federation of State, County, and Municipal Employees (AFSCME) as Local 152 in 1971.
6. UPW, with 8,000 members in Hawaii state and county government, affiliated with AFSCME as Local 646 in 1971.
7. HEA, which has about 6,500 active members, split in 1971 into three organizations for bargaining purposes: the Hawaii State Teachers Association, the College and University Professional Association, and the Hawaii Educational Officers Association.
8. HEC is open to all employees in Hawaii and represents a large portion, mostly in the private sector. Its services include collective bargaining, administration of contracts, research, and technical advice on personnel and industrial relations matters.
9. It should be noted that the ILWU played a relatively small role in the drive for public employment legislation. Response to the containerization problem and competition for local hotel and restaurant worker jurisdiction had priority on the union's resources.
10. Testimony of Robert R. Grunsky, President, Hawaii Employers Council, presented to the Senate Public Employment Committee, November 14, 1969, located in the State of Hawaii Public Archives.
11. Precedents for statewide bargaining in Hawaii had been established in the longshore, sugar, and pineapple industries.

The Politics of Interest Arbitration

Thomas A. Kochan*

An amendment to Section 209 of the New York State Public Employees Fair Employment Act (commonly known as the Taylor Law) extending compulsory interest arbitration for police officers and firefighters until July 1, 1979, was signed into law by Governor Hugh Carey on June 7, 1977.

The amendment eliminated fact-finding; required a record of the hearing, if requested by the parties; and stipulated that the arbitration panel consider statutory criteria and specify the basis for its findings in interest arbitration cases. Judicial review of the award was also provided for in the amendment.

Three years before the passage of the amendment, Dr. Thomas A. Kochan of the New York State School of Industrial and Labor Relations at Cornell University began a study, sponsored by the National Science Foundation, to evaluate the relative merits of fact-finding and arbitration as dispute settlement techniques. The conclusions and recommendations of that study were presented to policy makers and union and management officials in New York State in December 1976 at a symposium organized by the New York State Public Employment Relations Board.

In the following months, the study became the focal point for debate among police and firefighter unions, public officials, and neutral groups over the pending legislation. Several parties relied on the report in an attempt to influence the final form of the amendment.

The following is an account of the events leading up to the passage of the legislation, in which the research study played a central role. The author describes the positions of the unions and such organizations as the New York Conference of Mayors and the New York State Public Employer Labor Relations Association, as well as of the New York State Public Employment Relations Board and the governor, in the debate.

This article is part of a larger study, "Dispute Resolution under Fact-finding and Arbitration: An Empirical Evaluation," which was published by the American Arbitration Association in 1978.

When discussions began about the possibility of amending Section 209 of the New York State Public Employees Fair Employment Act, both the police and firefighter unions in New York State took the initial position that the arbitration statute should be extended for an additional experimental period without alterations. In a memorandum outlining its position, the New York State Fire Fighters Association presented four arguments in support of extension without modification.[1] First, the firefighters argued that there was a better chance of preserving labor peace with arbitration than without it. To support this position, they pointed to the report on interest arbitration that had been presented to them at the New York State Public Employment Relations Board Symposium in December 1976. They cited the finding in

---

*Reprinted from *The Arbitration Journal*. 33 (March 1978). pp. 5-9.

that report that no strikes had occurred under the arbitration statute, along with the more qualitative statement that strike pressures had been building up prior to the enactment of the arbitration amendment. Information that no firefighter strikes had occurred up to that time in 13 states with binding arbitration compared to a number of strikes in states without arbitration over the last three years was also used to support this argument.

Second, the union cited the report's finding that there were no significant increases or decreases in the size of wage settlements due to the arbitration statute. Third, the firefighters pointed out that the research showed that 60 percent of the arbitration awards were unanimous and that, where arbitration broke down, it was mainly due to a lack of commitment on the part of city governments to collective bargaining and arbitration. Fourth, the union emphasized the finding that arbitration had no more of a chilling or a narcotic effect than there had been under procedures before the passage of the arbitration statute.

The positions of the police and firefighters were probably best summarized in the comments made at the PERB symposium by the presidents of the New York State Fire Fighters Association and the New York State Police Conference. Robert Gollnick of the firefighters said,

> We concur with the use of binding arbitration for one simple reason: it's a terminal point, something we've never had before, something we desperately need. . . . We're already meeting, selecting committees of the New York State Professional Fire Fighters, looking into select strike plans in the event the arbitration laws are not renewed. We're also going to be sitting down with our brothers in the Police Conference and maybe having a joint select committee in select cities for strikes in the event the arbitration laws are not renewed. It's our only alternative. Without arbitration we have to have the right to strike. If we don't have the right to strike we're going to violate the law and do it anyway.[2]

Similarly, Al Scaglione of the Police Conference summarized his organization's position as follows:

> . . . if you take away binding arbitration and do not give us the right to strike, let me tell you the leadership of our State organization, the leadership of our locals, will not be able to contain their membership. There will be a revolt regardless of what direction the leadership goes. And the only thing that can keep peace is the continuance of binding arbitration.[3]

The New York Conference of Mayors

In contrast, the official position adopted by the New York Conference of Mayors was that the arbitration amendment should be allowed to expire. The Conference of Mayors also referred to the report and used many of its conclusions to support its arguments. For example, the conference's major comment on the report was that:

> While the findings [of the report] are notable, some recommendations are questionable. The major conclusion is that compulsory arbitration should be continued with some modifications. The Conference of Mayors does not agree. Nor do we believe that the study's findings sustain that conclusion.[4]

Like the New York State Fire Fighter Association's position paper, the Conference of Mayors' paper cited the report's conclusions regarding the lack of strikes under the arbitration statute and the comment in the report that the return to fact-finding might result in the eruption of pressures that were building up prior to the passage of the arbitration amendment. Unlike the firefighters, however, the Conference of Mayors noted the report's statement that the potential for work disruptions was based on a subjective interpretation of interview data which was not documented by any quantitative evidence. The conference concluded:

> *In other words, the author acknowledges that his recommendations to continue the arbitration statute for police and firefighters cannot be documented by any statistical evidence. The people of this state would hope that the legislature would not make a judgment upon such a limited finding.*[5]

In addition to the police and firefighters' unions and the Conference of Mayors, many other individuals and groups that used the report focused on this single finding and interpretation regarding the likely impact on labor peace of alternative procedures. This was perhaps one of the least significant findings of the research since, as the Conference of Mayors' paper pointed out, it was a subjective or qualitative interpretation of comments based on conversations with union and management representatives interviewed in the project rather than a fact based on quantitative evidence. Almost every group used this statement in the report to support whatever position it advocated. Those who were in favor of extending arbitration used it to argue that the arbitration statute in fact deterred strikes. Those who advocated going back to the fact-finding procedure used it to argue that there was no evidence one way or the other that the two procedures differed in their effectiveness as a strike deterrent.

The Conference of Mayors' paper went on to make seven other points in support of its position, most of which were either based on data contained in the report or were rebuttals or criticisms of the report's conclusions and recommendations. Specifically, the conference (1) questioned the importance of the finding that negotiated settlements were not significantly different from settlements achieved through arbitrated awards, (2) suggested that arbitration had not been effective as a dispute resolution procedure because the rate of impasses had increased, (3) argued that the lack of deviation between fact-finding recommendations and arbitration awards raises the question about the worth of arbitration "in light of the invasion of both home rule and authority of elected officials to establish budgets and set local real property taxes," (4) questioned whether the added costs of arbitration were worthwhile, given the fact that the report had found that there were no significant differences in wage settlements due to arbitration, (5) suggested that it was improper to take away the right of labor and management to say no in collective bargaining and turn this right over to generally inexperienced neutrals, (6) questioned whether the previous record under fact-finding was bad enough to warrant changing the statute, and (7) pointed to the lack of any analysis of the effects of police and fire arbitrated wage levels on the economic costs of other city employee settlements.[6]

New York State Public Employer Labor Relations Association

The most severe criticism of the report's recommendations was contained in the position paper prepared by the New York State Public Employer Labor Relations Association (NYSPELRA). Like the Conference of Mayors, this group advocated allowing the arbitration amendment to expire.

> Some observations were made [in the report] which NYSPELRA fully support. However, on the more substantive and crucial question of interest arbitration, we believe the study has some major deficiencies. . . . Despite the fact that the . . . study found a 13 to 18% increase in the number of impasses with the new procedure, [it] recommends continuing some form of arbitration. This type of reasoning (or lack thereof) is not, unfortunately, an isolated instance in the report.
>
> The report cites ineffective collective bargaining in some jurisdictions prior to the arbitration amendment and states that this ineffectiveness continued in these jurisdictions under arbitration. It then says that this problem can not be attributed to arbitration; it omits pointing out that it cannot be attributed to fact-finding/legislative hearing either, and provides no evidence that it can be. Yet, [the report] says that returning to fact-finding/legislative hearing appears to be inadvisable. There is absolutely no concrete evidence anywhere in the report to substantiate that opinion.[7]

The group went on to take issue with a number of other conclusions contained in the report. Again, it focused on the paragraph discussing strikes. It also disagreed with the conclusion that there was not a greater chilling effect under the arbitration statute than had been present under fact-finding. It relied on its own experiences to substantiate its claim.

> The members of NYSPELRA work "in the trenches" daily. We have had to work within the impasse procedures. That experience had led us to the inevitable conclusion that binding arbitration has been a deterrent to good faith collective bargaining rather than an encouragement to it.
>
> We believe that the arbitration process has not only had a chilling effect upon bargaining, but that chilling effect has in many instances spilled over into the bargaining with other units who have said there is no point in settling (bargaining) until their brothers in police and/or fire get their arbitration award. . . . For these reasons, we strongly urge PERB to recommend that the 1974 amendment relating to binding interest arbitration be allowed to expire with the consequent restoration of a fair, consistent, impasse procedure which recognizes and honors the democratic system within which that procedure must take place and which is an encouragement to collective bargaining rather than a deterrent.[8]

The Governor's Proposal

The director of the Office of Employee Relations for the State of New York, Donald Wollett, outlined the position of the governor at the PERB Symposium. His recommendation was to maintain the tripartite arbitration system with one very fundamental change. The arbitration decision would only be binding on the union, while the legislative body in the municipality would have the option of reviewing the arbitration decision and either approving or rejecting it. The position developed by the governor's representative was based partly on a general philosophical opposition to interest arbitration and partly in response to the dilemma identified in the report due to the role of judicial review of tripartite arbitration decisions. For example, at the PERB symposium Wollett said that

> *Three or four weeks ago I was in Chicago for a meeting sponsored by the American Bar Association on public sector labor relations. And there was a good deal of talk about binding interest arbitration, which is the focus of this conference. And one of the experts, a law professor from the University of Wisconsin, described people who do not have any doubts, serious doubt, about the constitutional legitimacy and the political wisdom of binding arbitration as "thoughtful, enlightened, and emancipated." And I suppose that means that people who do have those doubts are "thoughtless, unenlightened, and unemancipated." So I want to identify for you at the outset where I'm coming from; I'm a member of that "thoughtless, unenlightened, and unemancipated" group, because I do have serious doubts about the constitutional legitimacy and, more importantly, the wisdom of binding arbitration, whether it involves the uniformed services or whether it involves other kinds of occupational groups in the public sector.*[9]

Wollett went on to comment on a number of the report's research findings. His principal focus was on the discussion of the problems a court has in judging the reasonableness of an arbitration award arrived at through negotiation in a tripartite arbitration panel. While he indicated that he had no objections to the mediation-negotiation-arbitration process that was identified as being common to this statute, he agreed that courts not only would have a difficult time reviewing these decisions, but went one step further by arguing that since these arbitration decisions are essentially political decisions, the courts should not be reviewing them. Instead, he felt that the appropriate body to review political decisions was the legislative body in the community.

PERB's Recommendation

After the symposium was completed, the New York State PERB also made public its recommendation on the statute. Following considerable debate by the three members of the PERB board, the board unanimously recommended continuation of the arbitration statute without modification. The following quote from PERB's recommendation summarizes the reasons underlying its position.

> *1. The three year experiment was really more limited than the passage of three years would imply. The first year was largely used in litigation of the constitutionality question and the cut off date for the [study] was about a year before the experiment's scheduled expiration date of June 30, 1977. In addition, the time during which the experiment took place occurred in one of the most difficult periods of New York State financial history—a period when voluntary settlement was most difficult and any dispute resolution system would have*

been severely tested. This was not a good time for any kind of experiment with a new system.

2. In spite of a few difficult situations in controversial awards: a. The system provided finality of resolution; b. The arbitration wage awards were, generally speaking, in line with negotiated settlements. In fact, the wage awards averaged about one and one-half percent less than the negotiated agreements: c. Although there were three minor instances of slow down, there were no police or fire work stoppages; d. Judicial review, albeit limited, has been declared to be available.

3. The experiment should be permitted to continue for a longer period in order to provide a more representative experience base.[10]

The Legislative Process

After each of the above groups formulated its initial positions, the governor introduced a bill to implement his proposal for revising the arbitration statute. The police and firefighters, in turn, introduced a bill into the legislature that called for continuation of the statute without modification. These bills were referred to various committees. No public hearings, however, were held on either. Instead, the various interest groups began an intensive lobbying campaign with individual members of the state legislature. Meanwhile, additional summaries of the report were furnished to members of the legislature and their staffs. Several months before the June 30, 1977, expiration date, intensive negotiations began between representatives of the governor's office and several key legislative leaders after it became clear to the legislators and to the governor that the police and firefighters had sufficient votes in both houses of the legislature to pass their bill providing an extension of the arbitration amendment without modifications.

The governor, however, was still publicly committed to vetoing an extension and was still advocating his proposed revisions. After several meetings between representatives of the governor and legislative leaders, a compromise bill emerged. This bill provided for continuation of the arbitration statute for two years, eliminated fact-finding as an intermediate step in the impasse procedure, provided that the parties share the costs of arbitration, and added a statement to the section dealing with the criteria for arbitration decisions that required the arbitrators to consider not only comparability of wages, but also the level of such fringe benefits as health insurance, leave policies, pensions, and holidays. The proposed bill also tightened the language on how these criteria were to be used by replacing the phrase "arbitrators may consider the following criteria" with language indicating that arbitrators "shall" consider these criteria. Furthermore, the initial compromise stipulated that the decisions of the State Court of Appeals on judicial review of the arbitration statute would be considered to be the appropriate scope of judicial review under the new amendment. Finally, this compromise bill required that a transcript of arbitration proceedings be kept and required the neutral arbitrators to appear in court if the award was subjected to judicial review.

This compromise proved to be unacceptable to several parties. The major objections came from PERB. Specifically, PERB objected to having the neutral arbitrator appear in court to defend his or her award under judicial review. Therefore, this draft proposal was further amended by dropping the requirement for a transcript and the provision providing for arbitrators to appear in court. This compromise bill was then introduced into the legislature and was passed by an overwhelming margin in both houses.

After the bill was passed by the legislature, but before the governor had signed it into law, the New York State Court of Appeals, the highest court in the state, issued a decision that upheld an arbitration award rendered in the case involving the City of Buffalo and the Buffalo police.[11]

This award had been overturned by a lower court in the state and thus the Court of Appeals reversed the lower court's decision. In its decision, the Court of Appeals made the statement that even though it felt that the legislation was less than well conceived, the court could not find evidence in the record presented to it that the decision did not have a substantial basis in the record or was arbitrary or capricious. Therefore, even though it was clear from the language used in the decision that the court felt that, given the economic problems of the City of Buffalo, the arbitration award was too high, it had no recourse but to uphold the award. This decision caused the governor to have some last-minute reservations about signing the bill. After considerable additional pressure was applied by the police and firefighter unions, however, the governor signed the bill into law. It called for a two-year extension, with modifications in the language on the decision criteria, the elimination of fact-finding, and cost sharing by the parties.[12]

In the message accompanying his signature, the governor made the following comments to indicate the reasons why he signed the bill. Essentially, the intent of these comments was to provide some legislative history for future consideration in interpreting the intent of the arbitration amendments.

In my Annual Message to the Legislature, I proposed the enactment of legislation subjecting these arbitration determinations to legislative review, in order to assure appropriate political accountability. Legislation to require such review was included in my Budget Bill dealing generally with public employee labor relations (S.1337/A.1637). That bill did not receive favorable consideration by the Legislature.

This bill before me is the product of discussions between Donald H. Wollett, Director of Employee Relations, and the Legislative Leaders, the purpose of which was to consider alternatives to the mere extension of existing provisions of law, in the absence of some requirement that arbitration determinations be subject to meaningful judicial, if not legislative, review.

This bill tightens the standards and procedures in the compulsory arbitration process, so that the review of arbitration determinations by the courts henceforth will be meaningful.

Just yesterday, the Court of Appeals, in City of Buffalo v. Rinaldo, *noted two defects in the present law. According to the Court: "The source of judicial power to review findings . . . is not to be found in the statute which itself is completely silent on the matter, but rather in the requirements of due process."*

The Court also stated: "The statute, the wisdom of which it is for others to decide, vests broad authority in the arbitration panel to determine municipal fiscal priorities within existing revenues [and to] determine that a particular increase in compensation should take precedence over other calls on existing or even diminishing municipal revenues."

The bill before me corrects both of these defects.

First, the standard for judicial review that was developed by the Court of Appeals in the case of Caso v. Coffey, i.e., that the arbitrators' awards "are to be measured according to whether they are rational or arbitrary and capricious" remains unchanged. However, the source of judicial power to review arbitral findings and arbitral awards no longer generates solely from the requirements of due process; the statute itself now requires judicial review.

Second, the question of whether the arbitrators' work was rational or arbitrary and capricious is to be answered in terms of how well they carried out the statutory mandate to consider, among other things, the financial ability of the public employer and the comparative levels of compensation (including fringe and retirement benefits) currently enjoyed by the employee affected, and, where the statutory criteria point in different directions, to specify the basis for choosing one over the other.

These changes impart to the Courts the wisdom of the Legislature that judicial review must be strengthened so that it operates as an effective safeguard against arbitral abuses. This bill is intended to narrow the expansive authority accorded to arbitrators by the Court of Appeals in City of Buffalo v. Rinaldo *and to make it clear that arbitrators must make findings with respect to each statutory criterion which the parties put in issue, that each such finding must have an evidentiary basis in the record, and that the arbitrators must specify in their final determination what weight was given to each finding and why.*

I am aware of the concern of local government officials, many of whom have expressed opposition to any extension of compulsory arbitration, that compulsory arbitration may operate so as to place unreasonable financial burdens on local governments. Legislative review of arbitration determinations would, I believe, directly address that concern.

I am persuaded, however, that the enactment of this bill constitutes an improvement in the statutory provisions for compulsory arbitration. I am not convinced that a statutory structure such as the Taylor Law, which envisions a collective bargaining system for public employees, should mandate compulsory arbitration. For that reason, and in light of the fact that this bill provides for additional experimentation for just two years, I expect that there will be a continuation study of how the system actually works, so that we will have as complete a picture as possible before 1979 when we will again be faced with the decision of whether to continue, modify or eliminate the experimental arbitration procedures.[13]

Impact of the Research

Did this research have a significant impact on the legislative debate and its final outcome? Readers will have to draw their own conclusions. It is clear, however, that the research did stimulate and focus the debate over the statute around the report's findings, conclusions, and recommendations. In the final analysis, however, it was the political power of the police and fire-fighters that provided the votes needed to insure that some form of arbitration would be extended. Once the political balance of power was clarified, the negotiations among the critical parties revolved around the question of what shape the arbitration procedures would take. It was at this point that the report's recommendations had their greatest substantive impact on the future of the law.

Overall, the most accurate assessment of the short-run effects of the report was that each interested party felt compelled to rationalize its public position on the policy issue in terms of the findings of this research. Either the parties used findings that were favorable to their position to document support for their views or they challenged the findings and conclusions and recommendations of the study where their position differed from those contained in the report. Thus, this research did not change any of the positions of the interest groups in any significant way. Rather, the interest groups used the research to support positions that reflected their philosophical and partisan viewpoints.

Almost all the attention given to the report during the legislative debate focused on specific conclusions and recommendations concerning the effects of the change from fact-finding to arbitration and on the changes that the report advocated in the arbitration procedure. Very little attention was given to the latter half of the report in which there was a discussion of the longer-run deterioration in the performance of collective bargaining since the passage of the Taylor Act. In many respects, these longer-run findings were more important than were specific findings regarding the marginal effects of the change from fact-finding to arbitration. It remains to be seen whether some of the longer-run concerns raised in the report are given any attention in the future.

Footnotes

1. "Memorandum in Support of Extending Compulsory Arbitration for Fire and Police" (unpublished document, no date). See also *The Proceedings of the Symposium on Police and Firefighter Arbitration in New York State, December 1-3, 1976* (Albany: New York State Public Employment Relations Board, 1976), pp. 29-32.
2. *Symposium Proceedings,* pp. 29-30.
3. *Symposium Proceedings,* p. 41.
4. New York Conference of Mayors and Municipal Officials, "Position Paper— Compulsory Arbitration," March 1977 (unpublished document), p. 1.
5. *Ibid.,* p. 2.
6. *Ibid.,* p. 2-6.
7. *Symposium Proceedings,* pp. 221-222.
8. *Symposium Proceedings,* pp. 223-224.
9. *Symposium Proceedings,* p. 129.
10. *Symposium Proceedings,* p. 213.
11. City of Buffalo v. Rinaldo, No. 414 (New York Court of Appeals, June 6, 1977).
12. Senate Bill S-5859 and Assembly Bill A-8466, signed June 7, 1977.
13. "Memorandum filed with Senate Bill No. 5859-A." Governor Hugh Carey, State of New York Executive Chamber, June 7, 1977, pp. 1-2.

3
Labor Relations Structure

BARGAINING UNITS

By and large, the American industrial relations system features decentralized collective bargaining. This is especially so in the public sector, where multi-employer bargaining is virtually unknown (except for the single case reported by Feuille, Juris, Jones, and Jedel later in this chapter), and where government employees enroll in and are represented by a wide variety of labor organizations. At this point in the development of public sector labor relations in the United States, collective bargaining agreements are negotiated between single employers and single unions, with several and sometimes many such agreements in force in a specific government at any point in time. This is not to deny the existence, and in some cases pervasiveness, of pattern-setting or information exchanges with respect to collective bargaining within and among governments. Rather, it is to affirm the reality that the structure of public sector collective bargaining is at present highly decentralized.

At the same time, the reader should recognize that the growth of unionism and bargaining in government is a recent phenomenon, that only a decade and a half ago there existed few laws regulating public sector labor relations, and that, from a historical perspective, the parties to bargaining have had but a limited experience. As was noted earlier, it is even more recently that public employers and organized public workers entered into a second generation of collective bargaining, one that features more constrained economic and political environments than existed at an earlier time. If the economic and political climates become even more restrictive, public employers and public employees may attempt to structure new relationships, both with their counterparts and with each other, and this may alter the structure of public sector bargaining. Such an outcome is far from certain, though, for it would require individual governments and unions to subordinate their particular interests to a larger joint interest, something which they may be unwilling to do or legally prohibited from doing. Nevertheless, this discussion underscores the limited experiential base of bargaining in government, especially in comparison with the private sector, and reinforces the notion that the structure of bargaining is not an immutable characteristic of public sector labor relations.

Like other aspects of governmental labor relations, the structure of bargaining is dependent upon the interests, preferences, and characteristics of labor and management, which are, in turn, influenced by the economic, political, and legal characteristics of the immediate environment (recall Figure 1 in Chapter 1). As the latter continue to change over time, they should give rise to modifications of some dimensions of bargaining structure in government. These changes may then be chronicled and analyzed by interested observers and members of the research community.

Despite the relative recency and comparatively short history of public sector collective bargaining in the United States, important issues have emerged that are germane to the topic of bargaining structure. It is to these issues that the materials in this chapter are addressed. Perhaps the key issue in this regard is the determination of the bargaining unit and, relatedly, the role of supervisory personnel in public organizations.

The bargaining unit is that entity to which a specific group of employees belongs for purposes of representation in negotiations with management. The public sector, like the private, overwhelmingly follows the principle of exclusive representation in the determination of bargaining units. This means that one and only one labor organization may represent an employee group for purposes of collective bargaining, provided that the group has in fact voted for (or otherwise convinced the employer of the efficacy of) such representation. The principle of exclusive representation, which imposes on labor organizations the duty to represent all employees in the bargaining unit whether or not they are members of the union, is a peculiarly American institution, a cornerstone of public and private sector labor laws.[1]

Decisions as to the composition of bargaining units typically are made by administrative agencies that are statutorily created to administer one or another bargaining statute. The National Labor Relations Board has jurisdiction over the private sector in this regard, while comparable agencies occupy equivalent roles in state and local governments. (The Federal Labor Relations Authority performs this function in the federal sector.) Those states that authorize collective bargaining for public employees usually invest a public employment relations board or commission with the power to determine bargaining units. In making such decisions, the administrative agencies establish a fundamental characteristic of—a direct influence on—subsequent bargaining relationships. Hence, these agencies must carefully consider their decisions in determining bargaining units, especially the criteria used to make such decisions.

How broad or narrow should public sector bargaining units be? There is no simple—or single—answer to this question. A 1979 study of seven public jurisdictions and the federal sector found that "the 'community of interest' standard is the most widely used in unit determination," but also that this standard is the one "most open to differing interpretation."[2] As an example, the Michigan Labor Mediation Board found that:

Community of interest is determined by a number of factors and criteria, some of which are as follows: similarity of duties, skills and working conditions, job classifications, employee benefits, the amount of interchange, a transfer of employees, the integration of the employer's physical operations, the centraliza-

tion of administrative and managerial functions, the degree of central control of operations including labor relations, promotional ladders used by employees, and supervisory hierarchy and common supervision.[3]

In a court case involving a local school district and teachers' union in New Jersey, the Supreme Court of that state added to the considerations that may be encompassed under the community of interest standard:

" . . . the possible effect on employee-employer relations if the employees involved are admitted to one unit. They decide whether the group involved will operate cohesively as a unit; whether the unit will probably be effective in the public quest for labor peace. Community of interest has been regarded as identity of interest. An important consideration is whether the employee sought to be included in the unit is one from whom the other employees may need protection; whether his inclusion will involve a potential conflict of interest."[4]

It is generally the case that, for purposes of representation and bargaining, the professional worker's community of interest is not shared with that of the nonprofessional. Similarly, white-collar workers typically do not regard themselves as sharing common interests with blue-collar workers. In both the public and private sectors, these differing interests often give rise to separate, narrow bargaining units, even when blue-collar and white-collar workers or professionals and nonprofessionals are represented by the same union.

More specific distinctions between employee groups may be made, of course, especially in the public sector where individual governments usually employ a more diverse, heterogeneous work force, occupationally speaking, than even the largest private employers. And, while some public employee unions might wish to represent the widest possible array of government workers, they may be prevented from doing so by the distinct, often conflicting interests that exist among employees of the public work force and members of individual unions and associations. For example, Stieber has pointed out that the American Federation of State, County and Municipal Employees (AFSCME), the largest public employee union in the United States with some 1.1 million members who are employed in a wide variety of occupations, prefers a city- or countywide unit of nonuniformed blue-collar workers, with a separate unit for white-collar personnel.[5] The AFSCME has such an arrangment with the City of Philadelphia, but in New York City, owing to the local bargaining statute and decisions of the Office of Collective Bargaining (OCB) which administers the law, this union has many units of nonuniformed blue-collar and white-collar employees.

Unions that have members in both the public and private sectors (known as "mixed" unions), such as the Service Employees International Union (SEIU), the Laborers' International Union (LIU), and the International Brotherhood of Teamsters, are much less likely than AFSCME to be designated as the exclusive representative in city- and countywide bargaining units. SEIU typically has units composed of custodial and janitorial workers, hospital and other institutional workers, and social workers; the LIU generally represents unskilled employees in, for example, street and highway maintenance; and the Teamsters union has been interested primarily in representing truck drivers, equipment operators, and equipment maintenance workers.[6] In the uniformed services, the trend has been for separate labor organizations to represent police, fire, and sanitation personnel, with superior officers in the police and fire services represented in bargaining by other organizations. This results in narrow or single-occupation bargaining units. The same is generally true of nurses' labor organizations, such as the American Nurses Association (ANA), and teachers' labor organizations, such as the American Federation of Teachers (AFT) and the National Education Association (NEA), although the ANA and AFT in particular have been involved in disputes over the inclusion of paraprofessional nurse and teacher aides, respectively, in their bargaining units.

The diversity of views displayed by these various labor organizations, reflecting a multiplicity of relatively narrow communities of interest, suggests that a public employer will negotiate with at least several distinct unions and bargaining units, rather than an all-encompassing organization or unit. As labor relationships develop further in the public sector, smaller bargaining units may merge with larger ones and employers may be more readily able to achieve their commonly articulated goal of dealing with broader units. A leading example of such a development occurred in New York City municipal government, where the number of bargaining units declined dramatically, from 405 to 80, between 1968 and 1979 (see the Lewin-McCormick paper later in this chapter).[7] At present, however, the wide variety of unions and bargaining units found in most American governments is a major characteristic and determinant of the decentralized structure of collective bargaining in the public sector.[8]

A key issue in the structuring of public sector collective bargaining is addressed in the first reading in this section, by Hayford and Sinicropi; namely, the bargaining status of supervisory personnel. In the private sector, supervisors are excluded from coverage of the Taft-Hartley Act. Employers need not recognize organizations of supervisors or bargain with them, though they may choose to do so voluntarily. Consequently, few labor agreements are negotiated between supervisors and private employers.

In contrast, supervisory personnel in the public sector frequently bargain on a formal basis with the governments that employ them. This occurs, in part, because "the demarcation between various functions, supervisory responsibilities, and management and employee rights is more obscure (in government) than in conventional manufacturing employment."[9] In other words, public sector supervisors, even more than their private sector counterparts, are the proverbial "men [and women] in the middle."[10] Often they perceive themselves as supervisors in name only and therefore seek more explicitly to define their positions and job rights through unionism and collective bargaining. On this issue, as on many others, public sector labor organizations display a diversity of views and attitudes. Some employee associations, including in the federal service (for example, the American Federation of Government Employees), prefer supervisors to be included with nonsupervisory personnel in the largest possible bargaining unit.[11] Others, such as the AFSCME and SEIU, seek and often do represent supervisory personnel, but in units separate from those for nonsupervisory employees. Still other labor organizations of teachers, patrol officers, firefighters, and sanitation and disposal personnel generally prefer not to represent supervisors. In a few instances, as in the case of the ANA, unionists oppose management attempts to identify supervisors and exclude them from a bargaining unit, on the grounds that such personnel do not really perform supervisory functions and the underlying motivation of management is to reduce union power.

The relative newness of public sector unionism and bargaining also must be considered in analyzing the presence of supervisor-employer labor negotiations in government. Once again, comparison with the private economy is instructive. There, supervisors were accorded full representation and bargaining rights under the Wagner Act of 1935 and retained those rights for 12 years. Only with the passage in 1947 of the Taft-Hartley amendments to the Wagner Act were supervisors excluded from coverage of federal labor legislation. As collective bargaining develops further in government, as labor relationships mature, and as or if the economy of the public sector becomes more restrictive, further pressures may develop for the restriction, if not elimination, of supervisory bargaining rights.

Finally, the phenomenon of supervisory bargaining in government is also due in part to supportive public policy statutes. As the article by Hayford and Sinicropi points out, supervisors are accorded at least some bargaining rights in almost all of the state and local public jurisdictions that they examined. Among those states, only Iowa explicitly excludes supervisors from coverage of its public sector bargaining law. The rest generally authorize supervisory bargaining, with the common proviso that supervisors be in separate bargaining units (but not separate unions) from nonsupervisory personnel. A few state laws exclude "bona fide" supervisors from collective bargaining coverage.[12] Hayford and Sinicropi's discussion of this issue illuminates some of the problems encountered in structuring public sector labor relations when large numbers of government employees hold supervisory job titles but do not actually perform supervisory work. Finally, the authors contrast the permissive policies of state and local governments in relation to supervisory bargaining rights with the considerably more restrictive practices of the federal government that developed under Executive Order #11491 and which were subsequently codified by the Civil Service Reform Act of 1978.

FOOTNOTES

1. See Derek C. Bok, "Reflections on the Distinctive Character of American Labor Laws," *Harvard Law Review*, 84 (April 1971), 1394-1463.
2. Richard S. Rubin, *Public Sector Unit Determination, Administrative Procedures and Case Law* (Washington, D.C.: U.S. Department of Labor, Labor-Management Services Administration, 1979), p. 8.
3. As quoted in *ibid.*, p. 3. See *City of Warren*, Michigan Labor Median Board Case No. R65-H30, January 18, 1966, p. 37.
4. As quoted in Rubin, *op. cit.*, p. 9. See *Board of Education, Town of West Orange v. Wilton*, 57 NJ 404, 273 A. 2d 44 (1971).
5. Jack Stieber, *Public Employee Unionism: Structure, Growth, Policy* (Washington, D.C.: The Brookings Institution, 1973), pp. 140-141.
6. *Ibid.*, pp. 141-142.

7. New York City Office of Collective Bargaining, "OCB News," February 6, 1980, p. 3. Note also that when forming new public sector bargaining laws or when facing newly organized public workers, policymakers and management officials may attempt to structure a few broad bargaining units. For an example in higher education, see David Lewin, "The Politics of Collective Bargaining Legislation for Public Higher Education in California," *Proceedings of the Thirty-Second Annual Winter Meeting of the Industrial Relations Research Association* (Madison, Wis.: IRRA, 1980), pp. 145-154.

8. For some recent data on the size, composition, and distribution of bargaining units in state and local government, see U.S. Bureau of the Census, *Labor-Management Relations in State and Local Governments: 1978,* Series 655 No. 95 (Washington, D.C.: Government Printing Office, 1980), pp. 142-175, Tables 9-13.

9. David Lewin, "Public Employment Relations: Confronting the Issues," *Industrial Relations,* 12 (October 1973), 319.

10. On this point, see a classic article by Fritz J. Roethlisberger, "The Foreman: Master and Victim of Double Talk," *Harvard Business Review,* 23 (Spring 1945), 283-98.

11. See Steiber, *op. cit.,* pp. 142-143. For a discussion of federal sector policy in this area, see Rubin, *op. cit.,* pp. 28-29.

12. Steiber, *op. cit.,* pp. 138-148, and Rubin, *op. cit.,* p. 29.

Bargaining Rights Status of Public Sector Supervisors

Stephen L. Hayford and Anthony V. Sinicropi*

One of the most significant problems in public sector labor relations concerns the status and role of supervisors in the collective bargaining structure. This problem does not exist in the private sector, where supervisors possess no right to join bargaining units with other employees or to form units of their own for bargaining purposes. However, supervisors in the public sector have not been subject to uniform and predictable treatment, a condition explained by several factors:

1. The public sector is not regulated by a singular pre-emptive federal statute, but by a patchwork of state laws, Governors' executive orders, Attorney General opinions, municipal ordinances, and a federal executive order—all of which offer variations reflective of the peculiarities of each jurisdiction.

2. Public sector bargaining, a relatively new phenomenon, has yet to achieve the stability of the private sector's nearly four decades of experience. Indeed, public sector bargaining, no more than 15 years old, is only now gaining widespread acceptance and understanding.

*College of Business Administration, Virginia Polytechnic Institute and State University and Department of Business Administration, University of Iowa. Reprinted from *Industrial Relations,* 15 (February, 1976), 44-61.

3. Perhaps most important is the matter of the definition of supervisor, the rights granted such an employee, and the manner in which provisions are interpreted and applied. In the private sector, the definition is delineated in one statute—The Labor Management Relations Act (LMRA). Supervisors are excluded from coverage,[1] and a single administrative agency, the National Labor Relations Board (NLRB), is left to determine whether a class of workers and/or a group of jobs is supervisory. In the public sector, each state which has enacted public employee bargaining legislation and the federal government, through Executive Order 11491, have their own definition of supervisor (if such a definition is specified).

While there are some marked differences between state statutes, as they relate to the definition of supervisor, there is a general and overriding consistency in such definitions—with some exception they resemble the one found in the LMRA. The real distinction in treatment seems to result from the addition of qualifying language and from interpretation by administering agencies. It is these differences upon which our investigation will focus.

Analytical Framework

Our analytical framework allows for concise categories within which policies toward supervisors in selected jurisdictions can be placed. Four major categories were chosen:

(1) Exclusion—All Supervisors: jurisdictions where all supervisors are excluded from any form of statutory[2] bargaining rights protection;

(2) Exclusion—Bona Fide Supervisors:[3] jurisdictions where only bona fide supervisors are excluded from bargaining—in these governmental units many employees who have been classified by the public employer as "supervisors" have not been so categorized by the respective administrative agencies for the purpose of the statutes;

(3) Full Bargaining Rights—Autonomous Units: jurisdictions where supervisors have statutory rights comparable to rank-and-file employees but are separated into autonomous bargaining units; and

(4) Meet and Confer—Autonomous Units: jurisdictions where there is statutory protection for supervisors in units separate from rank-and-file employees but without an employer obligation to bargain with them.

Table 1 represents a compilation of the statutory treatments afforded supervisors in each jurisdiction discussed in this study. The information there will serve as the basis for discussion.

Federal Government Policy

Although federal collective bargaining under Executive Order 11491, as amended, has no binding authority on state and local jurisdictions, it has influenced state and local policy. It is therefore important to analyze the federal government's policy towards supervisors and collective bargaining.

The Assistant Secretary of Labor for Labor Management Relations is responsible for the interpretation and application of the Executive Order.[4] His decisions are subject to review by the Federal Labor Relations Council

TABLE 1
Bargaining Rights Status of Supervisors in Selected Jurisdictions

Jurisdiction	Statutory definition of supervisor	Bargaining rights status of supervisors	Unit placement of supervisors	Additional statutory provisions
Private sector	Sec. 2(11) – Labor Management Relations Act[a]	None	–	–
Federal government	Sec. 2(c) Executive Order 11491, consistent with LMRA definition	None	–	Sec. 24 – Executive Order 11491 "Savings Clause"
Iowa	Sec. 4(2) Public Employment Relations Act, consistent with LMRA definition[b]	None	–	–
Wisconsin	Sec. 111.81(19) – State Employment Relations Act[c]; Sec. 111.70(1)(a)– Municipal Employment Relations Act, consistent with LMRA definition	Only bona fide supervisors excluded from coverage	Less than bona fide supervisors in rank-and-file units	Sec. 111.81(3)(d) State Employment Relations Act[d]
Oregon	Sec. 243.650(14)– Public Employee Collective Bargaining Law, consistent with LMRA definition[e]	Only bona fide supervisors excluded from coverage	Less than bona fide supervisors in rank-and-file units	–
Connecticut	Sec. 7-471(2)– Municipal Employee Relations Act[f]	Only bona fide supervisors excluded from coverage	Less than bona fide supervisors in rank-and-file units	–
Hawaii	Sec. 89-2(18)– Collective Bargaining in Public Employment Law, consistent with LMRA definitions	Full bargaining rights	Autonomous units; less than bona fide supervisors in rank-and-file units	–
Minnesota	Sec. 179.63(9)– Public Employee: Labor Relations Act, consistent with LMRA definition[g]	Full bargaining rights	Autonomous units; less than bona fide supervisors in rank-and-file units	Sec. 179.71(3) Public Employee Labor Relations Act
Massachusetts	No definition in statute	Full bargaining rights	Autonomous units; less than bona fide supervisors in rank-and-file units	–

State	Statutory definition	Bargaining rights	Unit	
New York	No definition in statute	Full bargaining rights	Autonomous units; less than bona fide supervisors in rank-and-file units	—
Michigan	No definition in statute	Full bargaining rights	Autonomous units; less than bona fide supervisors in rank-and-file units	—
Pennsylvania	Sec. 301(6) – Public Employee Relations Act, consistent with LMRA definition	Meet and confer rights	Autonomous units; less than bona fide supervisors in rank-and-file units	—

a". . . any individual having authority, in the interest of the employer, to hire, transfer, suspend, layoff, recall, promote, discharge, assign, reward, or discipline other employees, or responsibly to direct them, or to adjust their grievances, or effectively to recommend such action, if in connection with the foregoing the exercise of such authority is not of a merely routine or clerical nature, but requires the use of independent judgment."

bThis section also excludes as supervisory employees all school superintendents, assistant superintendents, principals, and assistant principals.

cIn this section the definition of supervisor is prefaced by the phrase ". . . any individual whose principal work is different from that of his subordinates. . . ."

dThis section allows WERC to consider petitions for the formation of two statewide units of supervisors (professional and nonprofessional).

eIn this section the definition of supervisory employee is followed by the phrase, "However, the exercise of any function of authority enumerated in this subsection shall not necessarily require the conclusion that the individual so exercising that function is a supervisor. . . ."

fThis section stipulates that in making a determination of supervisory status the board shall consider, among other criteria, whether the principal functions of the position are characterized by not fewer than two of the following: (a) certain management control duties; (b) duties that are distinct and dissimilar from those of subordinates; (c) exercising judgment in grievance adjustment and personnel and contract administration; and (d) participating in the establishment and implementation of performance standards. (paraphrased)

gSection 179.63(9a) defines "supervisory employee" as "the administrative head and his assistant" when it refers to "a municipality, municipal utility, police or fire department."

(FLRC) when major policy issues are presented or where in the Council's judgment it appears that a "capricious or arbitrary decision" has been made.[5] The Assistant Secretary and the FLRC have often been concerned with the question of supervisory bargaining rights. While the Council considers the uniqueness of each federal employment relationship under Executive Order 11491, it nevertheless has shown an inclination to act consistent with NLRB policies.

Section 2(b) of Executive Order 11491 excludes from the definition of employee anyone serving as a "supervisor."[6] An exhaustive review of recent decisions by the Assistant Secretary and the FLRC discloses a restrictive approach to the issue of supervisory bargaining rights. This restrictive approach is based upon an expansive interpretation of the Executive Order's definition of "supervisor."

In the leading case on the supervisory issue, *China Lake Naval Weapons Center,* the FLRC chose to take a "disjunctive" view of the Section 2(c) definition of supervisor. Under the policy established in this case, an individual is a supervisor if he possesses the authority to perform *any* of the functions enumerated in Section 2(c) in a manner requiring independent judgment.[7] The presence of higher level review of a supervisor's decisions does not detract from the authority that supervisor possesses.[8] This disjunctive interpretation of the supervisor definition is identical to the policy position of the NLRB and the federal courts under the Labor Management Relations Act.[9]

In related cases the Council has held that: (1) in the determination of supervisory status under Section 2(c), it is immaterial whether the employee in question carries out his function(s) in a formal or informal manner;[10] (2) *the duties of the employee,* not the number of subordinates, determine supervisory authority;[11] and (3) it is not necessary that an individual's subordinates be "employees" under the Executive Order for he/she to be deemed a supervisor.[12]

It is evident from this account that the FLRC has adopted an expansive interpretation of the supervisory definition contained in Executive Order 11491 and thereby has placed considerable constraints on the bargaining rights of all supervisors. These findings demonstrate that supervisors in federal employment face the continued prospect of a highly constrained bargaining rights status. Thus, in the context of our analytical framework, federal government treatment of supervisory personnel can be placed, with only very minor exception, in the category, Exclusion—All Supervisors.

Supervisors in State and Local Employment

In contrast to the uniform policy enforced under the Federal Executive Order, the comprehensive public employee bargaining statutes enacted by the several states present varying standards for determining the bargaining rights status of supervisors. The four categories noted are utilized in analyzing these statutes and their application. While all comprehensive state statutes are not fully considered, a sampling of those typifying each category is reviewed.

Exclusion—All Supervisors. Of the 16 states (by the authors' count) which have enacted comprehensive public employee bargaining legislation,[13] only Iowa's Public Employment Relations Act of 1974 appears to exclude completely supervisors from its coverage, without any modifying qualifications or additional related statutory language. Section 4(2) of the Iowa law provides that, among other groups, "any supervisory employees" are to be excluded from coverage. The Act's definition of "supervisory employee" parallels the definition of supervisor found in the LMRA.

The Iowa statute's definitions section also enumerates specific supervisory positions excluded from bargaining. Section 4(2) includes the proviso that "all school superintendents, assistant superintendents, principals, and assistant principals shall be deemed to be supervisory employees." This "enumeration" approach is at variance with the majority of state statutes in that it relies upon job titles rather than on job content or responsibilities to determine bargaining rights status. Interestingly enough, reference in the Iowa statute to specific job titles (other than agency chief executive officers) is limited to public education positions. Iowa, by virtue of the language of its Public Employment Relations Act, clearly falls in the category, Exclusion—All Supervisors.

Exclusion—Bona Fide Supervisors. The policy approaches developed by Wisconsin, Connecticut, and Oregon best exemplify the treatment that excludes from bargaining rights protection only bona fide supervisors. Wisconsin's State Employment Relations Act of 1971 removes from the definition of "employee" those "employees who are performing in a supervisory capacity."[14] The Act utilizes the standard definition of supervisor derived from the LMRA with the addition of the phrase ". . . any individual whose principal work is different from that of his subordinates. . . ."[15] The Wisconsin Municipal Employment Relations Act of 1971 does not exclude supervisors from its coverage;[16] it also permits "law enforcement and firefighting supervisors" to form separate units for bargaining purposes.[17] Despite these differences in language, the Wisconsin Employment Relations Commission (WERC) has interpreted and applied both of these statutes in a consistent manner.

In recent decisions dealing with the supervisory issue WERC has frequently drawn a distinction between "working foremen"[18] or "lead workers,"[19] who are not excluded from the statutes' protection, and "supervisors," who are excluded. The WERC has held that to be deemed a supervisor for the purposes of the state's bargaining laws, an employee must exercise sufficient supervisory authority (essentially the requirement of authority to hire, discharge, discipline, etc., in a manner requiring independent judgment) over people, rather than directing an activity (e.g., a nursing care plan) or performing administrative duties.[20] In addition, the Commission, in making this delineation between "working foremen" and "supervisors," has relied heavily on the statutory requirement that a supervisor's principal work must differ from that of his subordinates. Finally, the Commission has held that the frequency with which an employee performs the requisite supervisory functions enumerated in the Act will not be a major consideration in determining such an employee's status.[21]

Both Oregon and Connecticut's public employee bargaining laws allow the administrative agencies to exercise a great deal of discretion in determining whether supervisory employees should be allowed to bargain collectively. Oregon's statute, revised in 1973, specifically excludes supervisors from its definition of "employee."[22] However (in addition to the standard definition), the Oregon law defines "supervisory employee" further with the phrase, ". . . the exercise of any function of authority enumerated in this subsection shall not necessarily require the conclusion that the individual so exercising that function is a supervisor within the meaning of (this 1973 Act)."[23]

Connecticut's Municipal Employee Relations Act (MERA) of 1965, as amended in 1975, does not explicitly exclude supervisors from its coverage. Section 7-471(2) of that statute grants to the State Board of Labor Relations the power to determine whether a supervisory position is covered by the Act. In making the determination of whether a supervisory position should be excluded from coverage, the Board is instructed to consider, among other criteria, whether the principal functions of the position are characterized by not fewer than two of the following: performing of certain management control duties, performing such duties as are distinct and dissimilar from subordinates' work, exercising judgment in grievance adjustment and personnel and contract administration, and participating in the establishment and implementation of performance standards for subordinates.

The Connecticut Board has made it clear that supervisors who do not meet at least two of the criteria established by Section 7-471(2) will, in most cases, not be excluded from MERA coverage. The trend in Connecticut is clearly toward inclusion of many individuals with supervisory titles under the state's public employee bargaining statute.[24]

It appears that both the Wisconsin Commission and the Connecticut Board have consistently required definitive evidence that the statutory definitions of supervisor are satisfied before deeming an employee to be a supervisor. The frequent appearance of the terms "working foremen," "lead man," and "lead workers" and the inclusion of such individuals in rank-and-file bargaining units in both WERC and Board decisions indicates that neither automatically concludes that an employee classified as a supervisor by title or otherwise is a supervisor for the purpose of the states' public employee bargaining statutes. Therefore, the practice seems to indicate that several much less than bona fide supervisors have been placed in the same classification with rank-and-file employees and granted bargaining rights protection. The operative statutory provisions in Wisconsin, Oregon, and Connecticut and the interpretation and application of these provisions acts to place those states in the category, Exclusion—Bona Fide Supervisors.

Full Bargaining Rights—Autonomous Units. The states of Hawaii, Minnesota, Massachusetts, New York, and Michigan, through either explicit statutory language or through the interpretative decisions of their administrative agencies, grant full bargaining rights to supervisors in autonomous bargaining units. Hawaii and Minnesota specifically provide for bargaining units made up exclusively of supervisors. Hawaii's public employee statute

88

1970, as amended 1975, divides all covered public employees into 13 state-wide units, including units of "supervisory employees in blue collar positions," "supervisory employees in white collar positions," and "educational officers and other personnel of the department of education under the same salary schedule."[25] The statute incorporates the prototype definition of "supervisory employees."[26] These provisions have been implemented with few clarifying interpretations by the Hawaii Public Employment Relations Board (PERB), and one prescribed supervisory unit is reported formed and engaged in bargaining with the state.[27]

Minnesota's Public Employee Labor Relations Act states that "supervisory and confidential employees, principals and assistant principals may form their own organizations."[28] Section 179.63.(9) defines "supervisory employee" in the standard manner. Section 179.63.(9a) defines "supervisory employee" as "the administrative head and his assistant" when it refers to "a municipality, municipal utility, police or fire department." Finally, Section 179.71(3) requires that for the Director of Mediation Services (who makes the initial unit determination decisions under the Act) to deem an employee to be a supervisor, he must find that such employee "may perform or effectively recommend a majority of the functions referred to in Section 179.63, subdivisions 9 or 9a. . . ." Therefore, one can conclude that under the Minnesota statute a broad range of supervisory personnel, bona fide and otherwise, are granted full collective bargaining rights. Further, the decisions of the Minnesota Public Employment Relations Board (PERB) indicate that Minnesota follows a policy of including less than bona fide supervisors in units of rank-and-file employees.

The New York and Massachusetts public employee bargaining laws make no reference to supervisory employees. However, both statutes do exempt "managerial employees" from coverage by bargaining rights provisions. The Massachusetts and New York statutes exclude from coverage employees who: participate in policy formulation, or are required on behalf of the public employer to assist in preparation for or conduct of collective bargaining, or have a major role in either personnel management or contract administration.[29]

The Massachusetts law became effective on July 1, 1974; hence, there are few interpretative decisions by the Massachusetts Labor Relations Commission (MLRC). In its major decision involving the supervisory issue, the Commission indicated a "strong preference" for placing bona fide supervisors in autonomous bargaining units.[30] In the same manner as Minnesota's PERB, the MLRC has established a policy of placing less than bona fide supervisors in the same units with rank-and-file employees.

The New York Public Employee Relations Board (PERB) has interpreted the "managerial employee" exclusion contained in the Taylor Law 1967, as amended 1974, so as to bar from collective bargaining only employees who have an important role in one of the three areas mentioned (i.e., only "managerial" employees are excluded from the Taylor Law's coverage). As to policy formulation provisions, the New York PERB, in upholding a decision by the Director of Public Employment Practices and Representation, has held that, "To be meaningful, the concept of policy formulation must be applied not at the lowest operating unit of the employer . . . but at a level of responsibility sufficiently high to encompass a discrete department or agency. . . ."[31] Thus, much of the supervisory activity that might arguably be characterized as policy-making does not necessarily exclude a supervisor from the statute's grant of bargaining rights if that activity occurs on a sub-agency or sub-departmental level. This policy position, along with a PERB ruling that the Taylor Act's definition of "employee" does not exclude supervisors, appears to grant bona fide supervisors collective bargaining rights identical to those of rank-and-file employees.

The New York PERB's policy as to the unit placement of supervisors is essentially the same as that established in Minnesota and Massachusetts. Bona fide supervisors are placed in autonomous bargaining units, while less than bona fide supervisors are included in the same units with rank-and-file employees.[32]

The Michigan Public Employment Relations Act 1965, as amended 1973, which does not cover state civil service employees, has been interpreted by the Michigan Employment Relations Commission (MERC) and the Michigan Court of Appeals so as to include supervisors under its statutory protection.[33] In a manner similar to its counterparts in New York and Massachusetts, MERC has held (in accordance with Section 423.213 of the Act) that only public employees in policy-making "executive" positions are excluded from bargaining.[34] A long line of consistent decisions by MERC in unit determination cases reflects a policy of establishing exclusive supervisory units based on the appropriate unit criteria contained in the Act.

Thus, the Hawaii and Minnesota statutes afford supervisors bargaining rights that act to place those states in the category, Full Bargaining Rights— Autonomous Units. Michigan, Massachusetts, and New York, by virtue of interpretative decisions by their respective administrative agencies, fall into the same category.

Meet and Confer—Autonomous Units. Pennsylvania's Public Employee Relations Act 1970 is unique. While it sanctions formation of "separate, homogenous units" of supervisory employees, it obligates the public employer only "to meet and discuss" with organizations of supervisors.[35] The statutory definition of supervisor parallels that in LMRA and in many other state bargaining laws.[36] In determining supervisory status, the Pennsylvania Labor Relations Board (PLRB) has relied heavily upon job descriptions. The PLRB has held that ". . . it is the existence of the power (to hire, discharge, etc.) and not past exercise of the power which constitutes supervisory status."[37]

The PLRB has also formulated a rigorous test of the "effectively recommend" portion of the definition of supervisor. The mere offering of "suggestions which may or may not be acted upon" without further investigation by superior officials does not act to designate an employee as a supervisor.[38] Finally, PLRB decisions have reflected the opinion that the Pennsylvania Act requires that the requisite functions performed by a supervisory employee must be of a nonroutine nature and must involve the supervision of people, not of things.[39] Thus, it appears that many less than bona fide supervisors are not considered supervisors for purposes of the Pennsylvania Act.

Pennsylvania, unlike others, falls in the category, Meet and Confer—Autonomous Units, by statutory language. However, it must be noted that the various tests utilized by the PLRB to determine bona fide supervisory status act to grant full bargaining rights to many employees who are supervisors in name only.

The remaining states. Although 16 states (again, by our count) have enacted comprehensive public employee bargaining legislation, we have focused upon 10. The experience under these 10 statutes provides the most comprehensive basis for thorough analysis in light of the length of their enactment and the volume of interpretative decisions handed down by the respective administrative agencies charged with their implementation. However, the six remaining statutes—those of Maine, New Hampshire, New Jersey, Alaska, Vermont, and Washington—do warrant mention; for one thing, none contains a specific definition of the term supervisor or supervisory employee.

Five statutes have been interpreted as allowing some form of supervisory collective bargaining. Maine and New Hampshire allow inclusion of supervisors in mixed units. The Executive Director of the Maine Public Employee Relations Board is authorized to exclude supervisors from bargaining, upon the public employer's request, if that position is characterized by certain "management control duties." New Jersey also permits mixed units where "established practice, prior agreement, or special circumstances" prevail; otherwise, New Jersey sanctions separate supervisor-only units. Under the regulations of the Alaska Department of Labor and the state personnel board, supervisors are placed in separate units. Section 908 of the Vermont Labor Relations Law, in language somewhat analogous to the Massachusetts and New York laws, allows "management level employees" below a major policy-making level to form autonomous units for the purposes of bargaining collectively. Finally, the Washington State Personnel Board has promulgated a rule (Section 366-42-010(2)) that excludes "supervisors" from any form of bargaining rights. Thus, under the Public Employees' Collective Bargaining Act 1967, as amended 1973, and Executive Order 71-04, supervisory employees in Washington are without representational status.[40]

Summary and Conclusions

The bargaining rights status of public sector supervisors is far from being settled. While it is clear that a federal employment experience has paralleled that of the private sector, several state legislatures and/or administrative agencies have chosen a more expansive approach, which has taken two principal forms.

The first approach is reflected by Wisconsin, Oregon, and Connecticut which have chosen to exclude only bona fide supervisors from the coverage of their public employee collective bargaining laws. This has been accomplished by the application of a rigorous test of the statutory definition of "supervisor." Thus, many individuals with supervisory titles are not held to be supervisors for statutory purposes. This policy is founded upon the often cited contention that many public employees in supervisory positions are not really managers. As a rule these "less than bona fide supervisors" are placed in the same bargaining units with rank-and-file employees.

The second view is exemplified by the actions of five states: Hawaii, Minnesota, New York, Massachusetts, and Michigan. They have elected to grant full bargaining rights protection to all supervisory employees. The policy makers in these states apparently do not see any conflict of interest (between the supervisor's role as a member of management and their participation in collective bargaining with management) when bona fide supervisors are allowed to bargain collectively. In these jurisdictions bona fide supervisors are placed in autonomous bargaining units, while less than bona fide supervisors are included in rank-and-file units. This approach is analogous to the final position adopted by the National Labor Relations Board prior to enactment of the Taft-Hartley amendments.[41]

Several factors have contributed to the divergent direction taken by the states vis-a-vis the private sector and the federal government. Perhaps foremost among them is the desire of the supervisors themselves. In several jurisdictions public sector supervisors have demonstrated a strong desire to be included in the bargaining process. This desire is manifested in elections and unit determination petitions and also was no doubt felt through lobbying activities when much of the legislation was developed. This activity, coupled with the questionable managerial status of many supervisors in public employment, has undoubtedly weighed heavily upon the decisions of the various state legislatures and administrative agencies.

The early stage of development of public sector collective bargaining must also be considered a critical factor. In many public sector bargaining relationships the major emphasis has yet to shift from contract negotiation to contract administration. In the private sector, the grievance procedure is well institutionalized, and the supervisor's key role in contract administration is widely recognized. Since successful contract administration has not yet become the focus of the labor relations programs in the majority of public sector jurisdictions, the role of the supervisor in those labor relations structures has not been clearly delineated. Therefore, the role ambivalence felt by public sector supervisors has not yet emerged as a major concern which their superiors have considered in depth.

Footnotes

1. Labor-Management Relations Act (Taft-Hartley Act), Section 2(3), 61 Stat. 156 (1947). The authors wish to express their appreciation to the following individuals who assisted in the preparation of this article: Robert E. Doherty, Director, Institute of Public Employment, New York State School of Labor and Industrial Relations, Cornell University; Donald R. Crowell II, Special Assistant to the Secretary of Labor, and Thomas P. Gilroy and Richard E. Pegnetter of the University of Iowa.
2. The term, "statutory," refers to Executive Order 11491 and municipal ordinances, as well as to state public employee bargaining statutes.
3. For purposes of this study, bona fide supervisors are defined as employees with supervisory titles who possess consequential managerial responsibility and exercise consequential managment authority. Less than bona fide supervisors are defined as employees with supervisory titles who neither possess consequential

managerial responsibility nor exercise consequential management authority.

4. Executive Order 11491, Section 6(1).
5. Regulations of the Federal Labor Relations Council, Section 411.12. Considerations governing review 37 F.R. 20668, October 3, 1972.
6. The section 24 "Savings Clause" of Executive Order 11491 does grant bargaining rights to a very limited group of supervisory personnel in occupations where supervisors have traditionally bargained collectively in the private sector. This "grandfather" clause has had the effect of permitting the recognition of a few supervisory units in the maritime trades.
7. *Department of the Navy, United States Naval Weapons Center China Lake, California* (A/SLMR No. 128, FLCR No. 7aA-11, May 25 1973).
8. *Ibid.*
9. *Ohio Power v. NLRB* (6th Cir., 1949), 24 LRRM 2350. See also *NLRB v. Edward G. Budd Manufacturing Company,* 322 U.S. 840 (December, 1947) and *Corn Products Refining Company v. Plant and Grain Processors, AFL,* 87 *NLRB* 187 (1949).
10. *Department of the Navy, Mare Island Naval Shipyard* (A/SLMR No. 129, FLRC 72A-12, May, 25, 1973). Thus, such qualifiers as *sufficient* authority, *formal* disciplining, or *permanent* transfers are not to be used in making determinations of supervisory status under the Executive Order.
11. *USDA—Northern Marketing and Nutrition Research Division, Peoria, Illinois.* A/SLMR No. 120, FLRC No. 72A-4 (April 17, 1973).
12. *McConnell Air Force Base, Kansas,* A/SLMR No. 134, FLRC No. 72A-15 (April 17, 1973).
13. The 16 states are Alaska, Connecticut, Hawaii, Iowa, Maine, Massachusetts, Michigan, Minnesota, New Hampshire, New Jersey, New York, Oregon, Pennsylvania, Vermont, Washington, and Wisconsin.
14. Wisconsin *Statutes,* Chapter III, Sub. Chapter V; L. 1971, Chapter 270, effective April 30, 1972, Section 111.83(15).
15. *Ibid.,* Section 111.81(19).
16. *Ibid.,* Sub Chapter IV; L. 1959, Chapter 509, as amended; Law 1971, Chapter 124, Section 111.70 (1)(b).
17. *Ibid.,* Section 11.70(3)(d).
18. Wisconsin Employment Relations Commission, *AFSCME Local 2, District Council 48 and Greenfield School District No. 6,* Case XIII, No. 15041 MC-718, Decision No. 10788 (February 14, 1972).
19. Wisconsin Employment Relations Commission, *Stanley Boyd Area School, Joint District No. 4,* Case III, No. 16162 ME-854, Decision No. 11589-A (July 19, 1973).
20. Wisconsin Employment Relations Commission, *Washington County Sheriff's Association and Washington County,* Case X, No. 15386 ME-764, Division No. 10845-A (April 18, 1972).
21. Wisconsin Employment Relations Commission, *Stanley Boyd Area School. . . .*
22. Oregon, *Revised Statutes,* Sections 243.711-243.795, as last amended L. 1973, Chapter 536, effective October 5, 1973, Section 243.650(17).
23. *Ibid.,* Section 243.650(14).
24. Connecticut State Board of Labor Relations, *Clifford W. Beers Guidance Clinic and AFSCME Local 1303.* Case No. E-2358, Decision No. 1104 (January 12, 1973).
25. Hawaii *Revised Statutes,* Chapter 89, Laws of 1970, c. 171 as amended, Section 89-6(a). This section also provides that supervisors may be included with nonsupervisory employees in units of registered nurses; nonprofessional hospital and institutional employees; firemen; policemen; and professional and scientific employees, if both supervisors and nonsupervisors mutually agree to such a unit.

26. *Ibid..* Section 89-2(18).
27. *Government Employee Relations Report* (Washington, D.C.: Bureau of National Affairs, Inc.), No. 518, August 27, 1973, p. B-18.
28. Minnesota *Statutes,* Sections 179.61-179.76; L. 1971, Chapter 33; effective July 1, 1972, as amended, Section 179.65(6). Note that the "essential employee" reference in this section appears to be of little practical significance.
29. McKinney's Consolidated Laws of New York, Civil Service Law, Sections 200-214; L. 1967, Chapter 392 as amended, Section 201(7)(a); Annotated Laws of Massachusetts, L. 1973, Chapter 1078, Sections 2-2B, 4-8, effective July 1, 1974, Section 1.
30. Massachusetts Labor Relations Commission, *City of Chicopee, School Committee and Chicopee Federation of Teachers, Local 2416, AFT, AFL-CIO and Chicopee Teachers Association,* Case No. MCR-1228 (November 18, 1974).
31. New York State Public Employment Relations Board, *Matter of Copiague Public Schools,* PERB Cases No. E-0025, E-0026, and C-0709 (January 3, 1973), and information in a letter to the authors from Robert E. Doherty, Director, Institute of Public Employment, New York State School of Labor and Industrial Relations, Cornell University, November 25, 1974.
32. New York State Public Employment Relations Board, *Matter of Board of Education . . . and Matter of Copiague Public Schools.*
33. *School District of the City of Dearborn v. Labor Mediation Board of the State of Michigan* (now MERC) and *Dearborn Schools Operating Engineers Association,* Michigan Court of Appeals, Division 1, No. 6550 (filed February 25, 1970), and Michigan Employment Relations Commission, *Wayne County Sheriff Department and Metropolitan Council 23, AFSCME and Service Employees Local 502-M,* MERC Case Nos. R710-187 and R71F-246 (February 4, 1972).
34. *Ibid.*
35. Pennsylvania *Statutes, Annotated,* Chapter 19; L. 1970, No. 195, Section 604(5).
36. *Ibid.,* Section 301(6).
37. Pennsylvania Labor Relations Board, *Bellefonte Area School District,* Case No. PERA-R-2372-C (March 1, 1973).
38. Pennsylvania Labor Relations Board, *Altoona Area School District,* Case No. PERA-U-2571-C (April 4, 1973).
39. Pennsylvania Labor Relations Board, *City of Jeannette,* Case No. PERA-U-2227-W (December 15, 1972).
40. Information in a letter to the authors from Donald R. Crowell II, Special Assistant to the Secretary of Labor, August 19, 1974.
41. *Packard Motor Car Company,* 61 NLRB 4 (1945). The NLRB held that supervisors were "employees" for purposes of the NLRA and that when organized in autonomous units they could constitute appropriate bargaining units.

STRUCTURING THE EMPLOYMENT RELATIONSHIP

In focusing on bargaining units and supervisory representation, the previous material emphasized the role of employee preferences and union behavior in structuring public sector collective bargaining relationships. The discussion and article in this section explore from different perspectives the internal dynamics of management as a component of bargaining structure. Particular emphasis is given to the establishment of a collective bargaining function in government, to the behavior of management representatives in negotiations and to the role of management's labor negotiator as a mediator of internal, conflicting interests.

When faced with the imperative of public employee unionism, public employers must decide how to organize themselves for collective bargaining—even if something less than full-blown bargaining is required of or desired by them. The dominant practice among American governments, especially large ones, has been to establish a formal labor relations staff function, headed by a director of labor relations who usually serves as management's chief negotiator.[1] This was the dominant pattern of management organization found by Burton in his survey of 40 American local governments reported in the single reading contained in this section. More recently, Derber observed that "centralization of management responsibility in [governmental] collective bargaining was fostered by a mounting recognition that the bargaining process demands professional skills, specialized knowledge, quick access to relevant data, and quantities of time and energy."[2] Such a pinpointing of management responsibility for labor negotiations is strongly advocated by most writers on this subject, who base their views and recommendations heavily on private sector labor relations practices.

It should not be assumed, however, that a labor relations staff function is easily formed or implemented in government. As Burton demonstrates, in the process of establishing such a function, there occurs a transfer of responsibility (i.e., power) from the legislative to the executive branch, and, within the executive branch, from the chief administrative officer, budget director, civil service commission, department heads, and/or other management actors to the chief executive. Such transfers of power are resisted, of course, both before and after the fact, so that end runs, lobbying, and other political tactics of public labor organizations, which typically precede the formalization of bargaining in government and are the principal outlet of such organizations' energies prior to bargaining, do not quickly dissipate upon the creation by management of a labor relations function. In the long run, however, according to Burton, the need to coordinate management's bargaining position outweighs other considerations, thereby "resolving" these internal management conflicts. Indeed, Burton argues that, in the clash between collective bargaining and the civil service system in government, the latter "seems doomed."[3] This is consistent with his view that public employee unionism challenges governments to overcome their fractionalized management structures, and that the establishment of a formal labor relations function centralizes management's authority for and position in collective bargaining.

Similar views have been expressed by others. For example, Shaw and Clark cite the lack of labor relations expertise among public officials and managers as the major rationale for their belief that management's authority for bargaining should be centralized in a formal labor relations function and for their judgment that the "end run" must be eliminated for collective bargaining to operate effectively in government.[4] They further contend that government officials must follow the lead of the private sector, not only in structuring their labor relations functions, but also in motivating public managers. From this perspective, public managers, especially negotiators, must be convinced of the need to represent government agencies' interests in bargaining and to retain management's decision-making prerogatives; supervisors should be considered part of management and the management bargaining team; and governmental compensation schemes should be revised to reward outstanding—and punish poor—performance. Moreover, note Shaw and Clark, public management should view itself as the acting rather than the reacting party in collective bargaining specifically and in the employment relationship generally. A strong management rights clause in collective agreements presumably expresses this concept of management. Finally, these authors argue that public managers must reexamine their virtual total opposition to public employee strikes, weighing the costs and benefits of work stoppages in relation to other bargaining outcomes. As Shaw and Clark put it, "a [public employee] strike may reduce . . . employee demands and . . . may well be a good investment in the future."[5]

Whether these policy prescriptions would, if followed by governments, fundamentally alter the nature of public sector collective bargaining is questionable. On the surface, they appear to move government closer to the dominant model and negotiating practices of the private sector. But they do not eradicate some of the special characteristics of government or some of the differences between the public and private sectors which Shaw and Clark, Wellington and Winter and others have identified.[6] These include the lack of a profit motive in government, the political component of decision making in public entities, and the lack of clear distinctions between managerial and nonmanagerial employees. In such circumstances, it may not be possible fully to centralize authority and overcome a fractionalized management structure, to eliminate a multiplicity of managerial interests, or to subsume diverse interests under and invest policymaking responsibility in a chief labor negotiator. In other words, efforts to centralize formally public management's authority for labor relations in a manner analogous to the private sector, as reported here by Burton and as advocated by many others, may have only limited impact in terms of altering the internal dynamics of governmental management as well as collective bargaining.

This conclusion is reinforced by the findings of a study conducted by Thomas Kochan in which he examined the role and functions of the management negotiator in public sector collective bargaining. This study was based upon an analysis of survey data concerning fire department labor relations in some 221 American municipalities.[7] In this work, Kochan found that power is broadly dispersed within the managements of city governments; that the broader the dispersion the more internal conflicts that occur; and that conflicts revolve around differences in the goals and interests of various management officials, including city council members, labor negotiators, fire chiefs, mayors, city managers, and civil service commissioners. The more conflicts that occur among city officials, the more bargaining takes on a multilateral rather than a bilateral character, that is, negotiations involve more than two distinct parties and operate in such a way that no clear separation exists between the employee and management organizations.[8] In this context, it is not possible to confine bargaining to the formal negotiations process in as much as various city officials bargain informally with each other as well as with organized employees. Hence, management is faced with the problem of coordinating these multiple interests prior to the advent of and during formal negotiations.

This is the principal task facing management's negotiator in public sector labor relations. Specifically, to coordinate management's diverse interests, Kochan proposes a dual role for the negotiator, on the one hand as a mediator of internal management disputes, on the other hand as an external bargaining representative in negotiations. This is not the conventional concept of the governmental labor negotiator's role, especially among negotiators, who tend to see themselves as policymakers and dominant management actors. The latter view, however, overlooks the distribution of power among municipal officials and the legitimate interests that such officials have within the political decision-making processes of government. Unless the management negotiator is prepared to deal openly with and coordinate these often conflicting internal interests, he or she is unlikely to represent the public employer effectively in external bargaining. Thus, Kochan's analysis of the manner in which the negotiator's behavior is affected by internal management dynamics indicates that fractionalized, multiparty management cannot simply be done away with merely by formally centralizing management's authority for governmental labor relations in the executive branch of government.

FOOTNOTES

1. In small governments or units of government, a common practice is ". . . to hire a lawyer or industrial relations specialist on an ad hoc basis to represent management at the bargaining table." See Milton Derber, "Management Organization for Collective Bargaining in the Public Sector," in Benjamin Aaron, Joseph R. Grodin, and James L. Stern, editors, *Public-Sector Bargaining* (Washington, D.C.: Bureau of National Affairs, 1979), p. 95.
2. *Ibid.*, pp. 94-95.
3. This conclusion is questioned in an article by David Lewin and Raymond D. Horton, "The Impact of Collective Bargaining on the Merit System in Government," *The Arbitration Journal*, 30 (September, 1975), 199-211.
4. Lee C. Shaw and R. Theodore Clark, Jr., "The Practical Differences Between Public and Private Sector Collective Bargaining," *UCLA Law Review*, 19 (August 1972), 867-886.
5. *Ibid.*, p. 883.
6. See Harry Wellington and Ralph K. Winter, Jr., *The Unions and the Cities* (Washington, D.C.: The Brookings Institution, 1971), and David Lewin, Raymond

D. Horton, and James W. Kuhn, *Collective Bargaining and Manpower Utilization in Big City Governments* (Montclair, N.J.: Allanheld Osmun, 1979).
7. Thomas A. Kochan, *Resolving Internal Management Conflicts for Labor Negotiations* (Chicago: International Personnel Management Association, 1973).
8. See the reading by Kochan in Chapter 4 of this volume for a fuller definition and an empirical test of the concept of multilateral bargaining.

Local Government Bargaining and Management Structure

John F. Burton, Jr.*

This paper deals with the impact of bargaining on the administration of personnel relations.[1] The primary focus is on the management side, and my comments catalogue the changes in management structure that can be expected as the bargaining relationship matures. This paper is based on field work in about 40 cities and other local government units for the Brookings Institution *Studies of Unionism in Government*.[2] The article will primarily consist of generalizations based on this field work, although I will include some specific examples of the practices about which I am generalizing.[3]

My discussion consists of three parts: (1) a brief overview of how cities decide personnel issues in the absence of unions; (2) the initial impact of collective bargaining on management structure; and (3) the impact of a mature bargaining relationship on management structure.

The central thesis of this paper is that bargaining forces a centralization of authority within management which overcomes the fragmentation of control over various issues typical in a nonunionized unit of local government.

Management Structure before Collective Bargaining

By the term "management structure," I primarily mean the location within the local government of the authority to decide management's position on personnel issues. There are two primary types of personnel issues: budget issues and nonbudget issues.

Budget issues. Authority over personnel issues which require budget appropriations, primarily wage rates and fringe benefits, is typically a joint responsibility of the chief executive and the local legislature. The city manager or mayor, in cooperation with his budget director, prepares wage and fringe recommendations for the city council as a part of his preparation of an annual city budget. However, the mayor's proposed executive budget is only a recommendation to the city council, which can amend, reject, or

*New York State School of Industrial and Labor Relations, Cornell University. Reprinted from *Industrial Relations*, 11 (May 1972), 123-140.

accept the recommendation. Authority over budget issues, then, is shared by the chief executive and the local legislature. Which branch of government is the dominant partner varies from city to city. The dominance to some extent depends on whether the city has a mayor-council, council-manager, commission, or other form of government.[4] Within each of these forms, variations in the relative power of the executive and legislature are also found. In Chicago, which has a mayor-council form of government, the mayor is in practice able to dominate the entire budgetary process, while in Los Angeles the city council has primary authority over employee wages and salaries, and the mayor has only a minimal role.[5]

The basic authority of the chief executive and legislature over budget issues is complicated by legal or charter restrictions and the existence of intermediate agencies which also participate in the setting of wage rates and fringe benefits. First, either the state or the local city charter may limit the discretion of local officials on appropriations for wages. Also, nonwage aspects of employee compensation may be set either by state law, as in the case of police and fire pensions in Wisconsin, or by city charter, as in the case of vacation and sick leave benefits in San Francisco. Municipalities may also be restricted as to sources of revenue. Chicago, for example, may not increase its sales tax without the approval of the state legislature, and state law in Washington permits municipal budgets to increase by only 6 per cent per year.

Second, there can be intermediate agencies between the mayor and the council, and even semi-autonomous departments which are not dependent on the city for financing, which have an impact on budget issues. In numerous cities, such as San Francisco, the civil service commission is responsible for preparing salary recommendations for the city council, and these recommendations need not be coordinated with the mayor's proposed budget. In much of New England, independent boards of finance, which are appointed by the mayor for fixed terms, have full legal responsibility for preparing municipal budgets for submission to the city council, leaving the elected mayor or appointed city manager with only an indirect control over his budget.

Authority for budget issues is further fragmented by the existence of semi-independent departments which have considerable discretion on wage rates and fringe benefits. Such departments are most common in counties and in municipalities with the commission form of government, but are also found in other cities. These departments either have their own taxing power or are the beneficiaries of earmarked funds from the state or city. In either instance, they are often under no legal compulsion to coordinate their wage strategies with other city departments or to take guidance from the mayor or city council. Los Angeles, which has six independent salary-setting authorities, exemplifies this point. The mayor and the council set salaries for less than 60 per cent of the city employees. Clearly, there is no one central salary-setting authority in Los Angeles, and there is a similar diffusion of authority in many large cities.

Nonbudget issues. The "standard" method for resolving issues related to the selection of employees, the allocation or definition of jobs, and the resolution of job-related disputes is to delegate authority for the issues to a civil service commission which makes decisions on the basis of the merit principle. Because many of the cities in our survey deviated from this standard method, an elaboration of the civil service merit system is necessary.

A merit system may be defined as "a personnel system in which comparative merit or achievement governs each individual's selection and progress in the service. . . ."[6] As an alternative to the merit system, selection and progress can be based on factors such as seniority, party affiliation, union membership, race, and sex. The merit principle can be used for various personnel isues: (1) narrow scope—recruitment of new personnel; (2) intermediate scope—recruitment, retention, promotion, training, and classification of positions on the basis of objective analysis; or (3) broad scope—all previous issues, plus salary administration based on objective standards.[7]

The scope of the merit principle can vary, and so can the role of the civil service commission. The commission can be: (1) independent—with full legal authority to make unilateral decisions without the approval of the mayor or council, and the legal authority is not infringed upon by other agents of the government; (2) dominated—where the ostensible autonomy of the commission is illusory because elected officials are able to appoint commissioners who are subject to political influence and manipulation; or (3) nonexistent.

When the term "civil service merit system" is used, or shorter terms such as "civil service system," the reference is usually to an independent civil service commission which applies the merit principle to a broad or intermediate scope of issues and which also serves as an appeals board for grievances filed by employees because of disciplinary actions taken by the city. This model of a civil service system was found in many cities in our sample, including Milwaukee and St. Louis, but several cities did not fit the model. For example, in Chicago, the civil service commission is neither independent nor a defender of the merit principle, but is just one component of a flourishing partronage system. And in Bloomington, Illinois, there is no civil service commission, but the city manager uses the merit principle for all non-wage personnel issues, such as recruitment and promotion. These examples demonstrate that any discussions of the civil service merit system must carefully distinguish between the civil service commission as an institution and the merit principle as a basis for resolving personnel issues.

Conclusion. Prior to the emergence of collective bargaining, the major characteristic of management structure is the bewildering fragmentation of authority for personnel issues among numerous management officials. Depending on the issue being considered, a newly formed union might be required to negotiate with the chief executive officer, the finance committee of the legislative body, the civil service commission, the personnel director, the departmental manager, the budget director, the controller, the city attorney, and others. I stress this fragmentation, not only because it is a necessary background for understanding the balance of this paper, but because it is one of the factors which distinguish public and private sector bargaining. In the private sector, authority for personnel issues is more likely to be concentrated at a particular point within the management structure, and that point is more likely to be obvious to a new union.

The Initial Impact of Bargaining on Management Structure

How does management at the local government level alter its structure in response to the emergence of bargaining? This section discusses the early stages of bargaining, which could be either informal bargaining or rudimentary formal bargaining. In informal bargaining, the end result of the negotiations is not a written contract, but some other evidence of union influence such as an amended city ordinance, a revised personnel manual, or an oral agreement. In formal bargaining, the parties negotiate a written contract.

Initial patterns. A common initial response of local governments is to impose a system of collective bargaining on the existing structure of authority with little or no modification. Primary responsibility for negotiations can be assigned to either the executive or legislative branch, but no pre-existing center of authority is subordinated or greatly diminished in influence.

In municipalities with executive budgets, the chief executive or his fiscal officer (budget director) will normally meet informally with employee organizations prior to the formulation of a final budget. Employee organizations are permitted to petition or to meet and confer with city officials and make proposals on pending wage and fringe benefit increases. Since the employee organizations are primarily interested in economic issues, the budget director represents the city in these informal discussions. The same individual may initially attempt to retain this responsibility after the establishment of formal collective bargaining.

In Chicago, which is still largely characterized by informal bargaining, the employee organizations submit all requests to the budget director, and after conferring with him may meet directly with the mayor on any outstanding problems. A similar procedure was used in Seattle until 1967 when a transition to formal bargaining was made. Since Seattle has an executive budget, the mayor assumed initial responsibility for negotiations and appointed his budget director, along with the budget consultant of the city council, to represent the city in negotiations. In other cities, the personnel director, or solicitor may be part of a negotiating committee which assists the budget director on issues not related to the budget. For example, the mayor of Wilmington, Delaware appointed a negotiating committee comprised of the city solicitor, the director of finance, and the personnel director. A similar negotiating committee was appointed by New York City's Mayor Wagner in 1958. The budget director and personnel director were given primary responsibility for representing the city in labor negotiations because both individuals had previously represented the mayor in administering the Civil Service Career and Salary Plan and had been responsible for granting and approving wage increases for employees before collective bargaining.

101

Shortcomings of the typical initial model. There are two reasons why the normal response of local government to the emergence of bargaining is to attempt not to disturb the existing management structure: (1) to utilize existing experience or expertise, and (2) to not disturb established authority relationships. Nevertheless, the initial delegation of bargaining authority to the budget director, the personnel director, or other staff officials is usually unstable. One reason is that such staff officials are not professional labor negotiators and often are unable to match the expertise of professional union negotiators who have had considerable experience in negotiating labor contracts. A second reason is that labor relations, especially in large cities, is time consuming and requires the attention of a full-time official. A budget director or personnel director, each of whom has primary responsibilities elsewhere, will not be able to devote sufficient attention or time to the negotiation and administration of labor contracts.

The most serious problem, however, with this delegation of authority is that it leaves unresolved the problem of fragmented authority for labor relations. The budget director or personnel director, or even the chief executive officer if he chooses to negotiate personally, will not be able to transcend existing authority relationships in the city. Semi-independent departments which are not under the budgetary control of the mayor and city council will be untouched; the authority of line managers to negotiate on issues within their discretion will be undefined; and the ability of the legislative body to overrule negotiators on contract provisions will be undiminished. The result is that multiple centers of power will continue to exist, forcing the labor organization to negotiate with numerous city officials on various issues.

At the same time, the lack of clear lines of authority for labor relations permits the unions great flexibility in choosing which representatives of management it will negotiate with on each issue. Generally, the various city officials are anxious to negotiate with the union in the belief that by doing so they will strengthen their own autonomy and authority over their traditional jurisdictions. The city is, however, subject to whipsawing under this arrangement, with favorable terms granted by one part of the city used to justify similar terms for other employees. Even when the unions are not strong enough to force the favorable terms granted by one part of the city on the whole city, the nonstandard terms complicate the city's administrative tasks and invite employee dissatisfaction. Cities which have had even a moderate amount of experience with bargaining through decentralized authority have almost invariably reacted by attempting to reduce the decentralization.

The next section discusses the emerging patterns in the shifts in bargaining structure that are evident in cities with reasonably well developed bargaining relationships.

The Ultimate Impact of Bargaining on Management Structure

Collective bargaining superimposed on the prebargaining management structure is unstable. Stability only emerges as tensions within the management structure are reduced, and this appears to require new organizational forms and often a restructuring of the previous authority relationships. Several trends in the structure of management are clear. These I will discuss in terms of the executive and legislative branches, and the civil service system.

Executive branch. There are three general tendencies concerning the executive branch which will be documented and explained. The executive branch is increasingly gaining effective authority for labor relations, with corresponding losses of influence for the legislative branch and for such independent agencies as civil service commissions and pension boards. Within the executive branch, authority for labor relations is becoming centralized. Also, bargaining authority is being removed from staff officers and transferred to full-time labor relations specialists. These three tendencies are examined in turn.

(1) The executive branch has several clear advantages at the bargaining table. First, management is best able to adopt an integrated position in preparing for negotiations and implementing the resulting agreements. The executive can, for example, coordinate bargaining with the preparation of the budget, which is usually its responsibility, and with its overall legislative program. Similarly, the executive will inevitably be responsible for implementing negotiated agreements, a responsibility which can best be discharged by the officials who negotiate the basic agreement. Second, the executive will usually be more capable of devising appropriate negotiating strategies. The executive is able to formulate a unified policy and confront the union with a single management position.

(2) The most important factor which has led to the centralization of authority within the executive is the need to coordinate management's position on all issues. Another advantage of centralization is that it permits negotiations to be delegated to full-time personnel who can develop expertise in bargaining. Formal collective bargaining requires the attention of full-time negotiators who must negotiate the original contract. In large cities with a multiplicity of bargaining units, this may involve bargaining on a year around basis. The management negotiators must also administer the contract, and are likely to be involved in representational elections and in grievance, fact-finding, and arbitration procedures.

(3) Assuming that the executive branch will become the dominant factor within the management structure, and that authority will be centralized within the executive branch, the next question is: where within the executive should negotiating responsibility be located? Two interrelated trends are evident. Bargaining authority is increasingly being removed from staff officers, such as the budget director or personnel director. The complementary trend is that full-time labor relations specialists are emerging who have responsibility for negotiating and administering labor contracts. In some cities, this second trend has manifested itself in new organizational forms, such as the Office of Labor Relations in New York City.

Legislative branch. Several cities visited in our field work were represented in labor relations by their legislative bodies, at least in early stages of the bargaining relationship. The reliance on the legislature to represent the government in labor relations primarily occurs in counties which do not have chief executive officers and in municipalities which do not have executive budgets.

The main advantage of having the city council or one of its standing committees represent management in collective bargaining is that the councilmen have the ultimate legal authority to make binding commitments, which avoids the delegation of authority problem. Direct control over labor relations enhances a legislature's influence on the outcome of bargaining and insures the legislators that they will share in any political benefit which accrues to the public officials responsible for granting wage increases to a significant part of their constituency.

Usually, however, the participation of elected legislative officials in labor negotiations is short-lived and bargaining responsibility is soon transferred to the executive branch. The main reason is the inability of legislators to be effective negotiators. City councilmen and county commissioners are usually inexperienced in labor negotiations. They do not have detailed knowledge of most items which are subject to negotiations, such as work rules and job security, grievance procedures, union security, and other personnel issues. Furthermore, partially because most local legislators are part-time officials, they do not usually have sufficient time to become experts in these areas or even sufficient time to personally participate in time-consuming negotiations. Especially in larger cities, where there are numerous bargaining units, legislators do not have sufficient time to devote to negotiations.

Exceptions to the rule. Perhaps the extreme case of an exception to the general rule that authority for labor relations is being shifted from the legislative to the executive branch is Milwaukee. The key there, however, quite probably is that the city has a weak mayor form of government, and the city council has never lost control of labor relations. The finance committee of the council also serves as the labor relations committee, which in turn sets policy for the labor negotiator. The city of Milwaukee has strengthened the position of its labor negotiator by requiring a three-fourths vote of the city council to amend any agreement reached by the city negotiator. This institutional requirement has significantly enhanced the ability of the city negotiator to speak effectively on behalf of the city and to make binding commitments in the negotiations. Another part of the explanation for the Milwaukee schema is that the city negotiator is a former councilman who is trusted by the current council members. While Milwaukee does not fit all the normal patterns of cities with emerging bargaining, it is still typical in the sense that the enhancement of the position of labor negotiator has resulted in a centralization of authority for labor relations.

The general rule. The tendency of legislators to abandon rapidly any substantial participation in negotiations is occurring in most cities, and is probably desirable. Legislators, as elected officials, are often subject to political pressures from employee organizations and may be tempted to secure union support through the bargaining process. This "hero syndrome" is most serious in cities where organized labor is particularly strong. Legislators may vie with each other in an effort to be first with concessions to their labor friends; it is difficult to maintain a united front of legislators with diverse political interests. A legislator dependent upon labor support may actively support a union position at the bargaining table or may even divulge management's bargaining strategy to the union. It is unrealistic to expect that management will be able to speak with one voice when numerous independent legislators participate directly in these negotiations.

Delegation of Legislative Authority

In most cities, the executive branch is assuming the primary responsbility for both the negotiation and administration of labor contracts. But institutional or informal arrangements must be developed to insure the effective delegation of authority from the legislative branch, which in precollective bargaining situations generally has legal authority to decide most personnel issues, to the chief negotiator, who is usually in the executive branch. The delegation problem has not yet been solved in many cities, but two mechanisms are worth noting: prior commitment of legislators through consultations, and the Connecticut solution, which eliminates the role of the legislature on some nonwage issues and imposes restrictions on its ratification powers on the balance of the nonwage issues and on budget issues.

The Philadelphia solution. At a minimum, a labor negotiator will attempt to secure the commitment of legislators to a proposed contract by consulting with them in advance, perhaps even to the extent of accepting guidelines established by the legislators. The strategy improves communications between the executive and legislative branches and allows the legislators to participate in the determination of policy. In Philadelphia the management negotiators, all of whom were in the executive branch, conferred with representatives of the city council before each set of negotiations.

The attempt to involve the legislature in the negotiating process was not successful in Philadelphia, and most other cities in our sample have not attempted to institutionalize communication channels between the executive and legislative branches. In no large city in our sample, other than Philadelphia, have councilmen participated in the formulation of bargaining strategy. Chief executives, especially in strong mayor cities, are reluctant to share their negotiating authority with legislators, even if the latter participate only as advisors in policy formulation. Moreover, legislators are unwilling to bind themselves in advance in negotiations which they cannot control and the outcome of which may become a political liability. Therefore, legislators generally have not participated in the negotiating process when the primary responsibility for bargaining has been assigned to the executive branch, but rather have reserved the right to amend or reject agreements when they are submitted for ratification. This insures that the final outcome of negotiations will not be totally repugnant to the legislature, while granting the executive considerable latitude in the actual negotiations.

The Connecticut solution. Connecticut state law vigorously supports executive authority and responsibility for labor relations.[8] The ability of the local legislature to reverse decisions made by the chief executive has been greatly diminished. The 1965 state labor relations law assigns all responsibility for labor negotiations to the chief executive, or his designee, in every unit of local government. Additional provisions of the law enhance the executive authority. For example, negotiated agreements ratified by the legislative body are binding, even if they modify existing rules or regulations of other governmental agencies, such as civil service commissions and police or fire commissions. Also, the legislative body can only review those provisions of a negotiated agreement which require funds for implementation or which conflict with an existing charter, ordinance, or regulation of the municipality or one of its agents or subsidiaries. Purely administrative items, such as union security, grievance procedures, and work rules are not subject to a legislative veto. Furthermore, even if the legislature does reject a provision negotiated by the executive, it may only return the rejected agreement to the executive for further negotiations. The legislative body is prohibited from amending agreements or from participating directly in any negotiations. Management is assured that it will have only one spokesman. Finally, agreements submitted to the legislative body for approval are considered approved if the legislative body fails to approve or reject the agreement within 14 days.

No other state has yet followed the Connecticut precedent. In other areas, legislatures still actively participate in labor negotiations. The local legislatures in Detroit and Boston, for example, have not accepted any limitation on their authority to revise agreements negotiated under the auspices of their mayors. The problem of coordinating the roles of the executive and legislative branches, as the executive assumes primary responsibility for labor relations, has not yet been adequately resolved in most cities we surveyed.

Civil Service

As discussed in the first section, the theory of the civil service merit system is that public employees will be hired, fired, promoted, and paid on the basis of merit, and that this merit principle will be protected by a commission that is independent of the public employer.

Both the existence of the commission and the use of the merit principle are threatened by the emergence of collective bargaining. One reason for the attack on the commissions is that often they are not autonomous agencies, but agents of the employer. In varying degrees, most of the cities in our sample have civil service commissions dominated by management. But truly independent civil service commissions are also under union assault, partially because, as discussed below, they are likely to protect the merit principle and also because their existence as a source of authority over personnel issues complicates the union's role. A theme of this paper has been the diffusion of authority for personnel issues in a typical city, and if the civil service commission can be eliminated as one source of authority, the union's negotiating task is simplified.

Union attacks on the merit principle. The use of the merit principle is also under attack by unions. According to AFSCME:

> *Unions of public employees see the Civil Service agency as a recruiting organ.*
> *... Wages, hours, working conditions, rates of pay, fringe benefits, pensions —*
> *procedures for layoffs where necessary, classifications, reclassifications, appeals*

106

in the discharges or disciplinary actions and on all other work matters—all must be handled as part of the contractual relationship between the employer and the union.[9]

The AFSCME view would limit the merit principle to a narrow scope—the recruitment of new personnel—and for other personnel issues would replace the merit principle with other considerations, such as union membership or seniority. It would also end the adjudicative function of the civil service commission in grievances.

The eventual status of civil service. In most political subdivisions, civil service has been delegated legal responsibility for many personnel issues and has administered a system of industrial jurisprudence which overlaps the potential jurisdiction of collective bargaining. But, as suggested above, the merit principle, administered by an independent civil service commission, is basically incompatible with collective bargaining.[10] The possible consequences for management structure are: (1) collective bargaining will totally replace civil service commissions and the merit principle; (2) civil service commissions will become the bargaining agent for management in negotiations on issues under its control, thus clearly ending the notion that civil service is "neutral" and largely ending the use of the merit principle; or (3) civil service will retain its traditional unilateral authority, but over a limited scope of issues, such as recruiting. Under the third option, civil service and collective bargaining are not totally incompatible.

Summary and Conclusions

This paper undoubtedly overgeneralizes at several points and ignores important exceptions. But at the risk of being compared to the artisans who can write the Lord's Prayer on the head of a pin, let me attempt the ultimate distillation of my views. First, collective bargaining will shift authority for personnel issues to the executive branch at the expense of the legislative branch and the civil service system. Indeed, the civil service system seems doomed. Second, within the executive branch, authority for bargaining will be centralized, and primary responsibility assigned to an individual or office directly responsible to the chief executive.

I have made clear my sympathy with the increasing responsibility of the executive branch, and for the centralization of authority within the executive branch. I find normative judgments about the loss of authority for the civil service merit system more troublesome. Writing a brief for the continued existence of a civil service commission dominated by city management would stretch my competence and conscience. Truly autonomous commissions, though rare, may be worth preserving as an independent check on management, employees, unions, *et al.* But this independence has now been criticized as a hindrance to "sound administrative practices," and for most public jurisdictions the delegation of personnel issues to "a personnel director appointed by, and accountable to, the chief executive" has been recommended by the National Civil Service League, the very organization that helped start the independent civil service commission movement in the nineteenth century.[11]

The case for the merit principle is also debatable. In the private sector, collective bargaining has tempered merit (or ability) with such factors as seniority for many personnel decisions, including promotions and layoffs, and the dilution of the merit principle often has some advantages, such as providing greater job security to workers. Even the use of the merit principle for recruitment purposes is harder to embrace, now that the Supreme Court has discovered that the vehicle for implementing merit recruitment in many firms is unvalidated personnel tests.[12] Perhaps the most severe test of the continued wisdom of the merit principle is provided in the *Model Public Personnel Administration Law* recently released by the National Civil Service League.[13] Section 1 stipulates that all appointments "shall be based on merit and fitness" without regard "to sex, race, religion, or political affiliation." Section 3(9) urges preferential treatment for "members of disadvantaged groups, handicapped persons, and returning veterans." Even a lax constructionist is likely to have problems reconciling those provisions, and yet the underlying sentiments are simultaneously endorsed by many in addition to the League. It is little wonder that the merit principle is plainly on the wane.

APPENDIX A
Population and Form of Government of the 31 Cities Surveyed

Population class	1970 population	Form of government
1,000,000 and over		
New York	7,895,563	Mayor-council
Chicago	3,369,359	Mayor-council
Los Angeles	2,816,061	Mayor-council
Philadelphia	1,950,098	Mayor-council
Detroit	1,512,893	Mayor-council
500,000-1,000,000		
Cleveland	750,879	Mayor-council
Milwaukee	717,372	Mayor-council
San Francisco	715,674	Mayor-council
Boston	641,071	Mayor-council
Memphis	623,530	Mayor-council
St. Louis	622,236	Mayor-council
Seattle	530,831	Mayor-council
Kansas City, Missouri	507,330	City Manager
250,000-500,000		
Atlanta	497,421	Mayor-council
Cincinnati	452,524	City Manager
Portland, Oregon	380,620	Commission
Rochester, New York	296,233	City Manager
100,000-250,000		
Dayton, Ohio	243,601	City Manager
Warren, Michigan	179,260	Mayor-council
Providence, Rhode Island	179,116	Mayor-council
Hartford, Connecticut	158,017	City Manager
New Haven, Connecticut	137,707	Mayor-council
50,000-100,000		
Santa Monica, California	88,289	City Manager
Wilmington, Delaware	80,386	Mayor-council
Binghamton, New York	64,123	Mayor-council
Fairfield, Connecticut	56,487	Mayor-council
LaCrosse, Wisconsin	51,153	Mayor-council
Less than 50,000		
Bloomington, Illinois	39,992	City Manager
Beloit, Wisconsin	35,729	City Manager
Pittsburg, California	20,651	City Manager
Johnson City, New York	18,025	Mayor-council

Footnotes

1. This paper was prepared as part of the *Studies of Unionism in Government* which is being conducted by the Brookings Institution with financial support from the Ford Foundation. The views are the authors' and are not presented as those of the officers, trustees, or staff members of the Brookings Institution or of the Ford Foundation.

   An earlier version of this paper was presented to the "Seminar on the Impact of Collective Agreements on the Administration of Personnel Relations in Public Employment," sponsored by the Institute of Management and Labor Relations, Rutgers-The State University. Useful comments on that draft were received from Paul F. Gerhart and Charles Krider. Considerable assistance in preparing the final draft was provided by Eric Klempner.

2. Extensive interviews in the various local government units were conducted in 1968-1969 by Paul F. Gerhart, Charles Krider, and Arnold Weber. Subsequent developments have been followed in many of these units, although primary attention in this article pertains to the field work period. Because most of the cities had been involved in collective bargaining for several years, the recounting of their experience should be useful to those cities which are just beginning or which have recently begun to bargain with trade unions.

3. While this article concentrates on structural impacts of bargaining in the 31 cities listed in Appendix A, some examples are also provided from ten counties in our sample: Broome (New York), Contra Costa (California), Cuyahoga (Ohio), King (Washington), Los Angeles (California), Milwaukee (Wisconsin), Monroe (New York), Multnomah (Oregon), New Castle (Deleware), and Wayne (Michigan).

4. These forms of government are described by Robert L. Morlan, "Local Government—The Cities," in James W. Fesler, editor, *The 50 States and Their Local Governments* (New York: Knopf, 1967), esp. pp. 469-489.

5. A distinction is often made between strong mayor and weak mayor governments, and the difference has some relevance for collective bargaining developments. See, e.g., David T. Stanley, *Managing Local Government under Union Pressure* (Washington, D.C.: The Brookings Institution, 1972), pp. 7-9, where he distinguishes "strong mayor" and "less strong mayor" governments. However, the distinction between weak and strong mayor forms is not an adequate basis for understanding many local government bargaining developments. For example, Los Angeles has a weak mayor form of government and the council has the primary authority for bargaining on wages and salaries; Chicago also has most of the formal attributes of the weak mayor form—e.g., many of the mayor's appointments must be confirmed by the council—and yet the mayor dominates the bargaining process.

6. O. Glenn Stahl, *Public Personnel Administration*, 6th edition (New York: Harper and Row, 1971), p. 31.

7. An example of the merit principle applied in broad scope is contained in the Intergovernmental Personnel Act of 1967. See *Progress in Intergovernmental Personnel Relations*, Report of the Advisory Committee on Merit System Standards (Washington, D.C.: Government Printing Office, 1969), esp. p. 15.

8. "An Act Establishing a Municipal Employee Relations Act" is reprinted in *Government Employee Relations Report*, Reference File-1; Section 51:1611.

9. *Ibid.*, pp. 52-53.

10. For an extended discussion of the potential collisions between collective bargaining and the merit principle, see Frederick C. Mosher, *Democracy and the Public Service* (New York: Oxford University Press, 1968), Chap. 6, pp. 176-201. Evidence on the actual collisions is included in Stanley, *op. cit.*, esp. Chap. 3.

11. National Civil Service League, *A Model Public Personnel Administration Law* (Washington, D.C.: 1970), p. 5.
12. See *Griggs v. Duke Power Company*, 91 S. Ct. 849 (1971).
13. National Civil Service League, *op. cit.*

THE POTENTIAL FOR EMPLOYER AND UNION ALLIANCES

In examining the structure of public sector bargaining, the focus of the previous section was on internal management and intragovernmental dynamics. In contrast, this section focuses on the potential for intergovernmental and interunion alliances in the public sector—alliances which at present are extremely rare.

In recent years, considerable speculation has emerged concerning the prospects for multiemployer bargaining in government. Such speculation is most commonly focused on teacher-school board labor relations, with some observers and participants foreseeing the development of multiemployer bargaining structures in school districts that are in close geographical proximity to each other, and others envisioning statewide multiemployer arrangements. Despite the speculation, hardly any systematic empirical study of this issue has been reported in the literature.

This deficiency is partially remedied by the first reading selection included in this section, authored by Feuille, Juris, Jones, and Jedel. These authors first review the factors potentially supporting and mitigating the development of multiemployer bargaining in government. Perhaps the key considerations here are the product market monopoly (or near-monopoly) and independent political jurisdiction of each American local government, factors which do not provide strong incentives for intergovernmental cooperation let alone multiemployer bargaining. It is instructive to note that the product market, specifically a highly competitive product market, seems to be the leading variable "explaining" the emergence of multiemployer bargaining in private industry.

Next, Feuille and his associates report the empirical results of their own research conducted in 1975, designed to assess the extent of and climate for multiemployer bargaining in local government. The authors studied 225 governments located in four major metropolitan areas; they focused on teacher, police, firefighter, and public works employees; and they conducted 97 interviews of employers, union representatives, mediators, and fact-finders.

The research uncovered no instances of permanent multiemployer bargaining among these governments and few attempts to establish such bargaining. Instead, the parties seemed to prefer single-employer, single-union bargaining, with the procedural difficulties of coordinating negotiations across diverse jurisdictions and the potential reduction of individual employers' autonomy being the major factors accounting for the lack of formal multiemployer relationships.

110

Then, the authors analyzed the incidence of labor relations information exchanges among these governments. Surprisingly, perhaps, these exchanges were broad, frequent, and widespread. They indicate that some local public employers in major metropolitan areas are well aware of local labor market conditions, the status of negotiations in other governments, and the range of wage and fringe benefit offers made or expected to be bargained over by their counterparts in other jurisdictions. Additionally, a few small governments used the same outside consultants to negotiate their labor agreements. As of yet, however, these information exchanges have not led to alterations of bargaining structure in local government and most certainly not to multi-employer bargaining. Public employers remain strongly wedded to the pro-prietary interest in their own bargaining activity, bargaining data, and decision-making authority. Feuille and his associates conclude, therefore, that while government employers are willing to devote resources to cooperative information sharing, their concern with autonomy translates into very little support for multiemployer negotiations in the public sector irrespective of what some observers presume to be the advantages of this type of bargaining structure.

While many have speculated about the potential for employer alliances in public sector bargaining, few have done so with respect to bargaining alliances among public sector unions. It is known that public sector labor organizations often form alliances to support specific regulatory labor legis-lation, certain broader public policies, and particular candidates for political offices. But the formation of interunion allliances or coalitions to bargain with public employers has rarely been observed and has rarely been proposed. This is no doubt due in part to the aforementioned emphasis on decentralized bargaining in the American system of industrial relations, especially on the integrity and autonomy of the individual bargaining unit. Yet, over the period from the late 1960s to the early 1980s, full-scale coalition bargaining developed in the nation's largest municipal government, New York City, and it is this development which is analyzed in the final paper in this chapter, by Lewin and McCormick.

These authors systematically examine the factors that contributed to the adoption of a coalition bargaining structure. These included the reduction of interunion rivalries, growth of pattern bargaining, and enactment of New York City's Collective Bargaining Law in 1967. The reduction of interunion rivalries was due in large part to the evolution of several large labor organizations with relatively stable leadership, a process that dated to the mid-1950s, when, through mayoral directives, municipal employees were accorded (nonstatutory) unionism and bargaining rights. Pattern bargaining could be said to have developed out of necessity, as the intramunicipal wage comparisons made by the city's 250,000 employees, who at one point were represented by 85 separate unions and were distributed among more than 400 bargaining units, took on the status of wage-setting decision rules. This bargaining phenomenon was reinforced by the decisions of various impasse panels, which were often appointed to resolve negotiating impasses and which viewed pay party relationships as contributing to labor peace. The city's Collective Bargaining Law created a citywide bargaining unit to negotiate certain terms of employment that were required by other statutes to be uniform for career personnel, and it also established a Municipal Labor Committee that was charged with coordinating union participation in the administration of the local bargaining system by the tripartite Office of Collective Bargaining (OCB).

But the main factor that gave impetus to coalition bargaining in New York's municipal government was the fiscal crisis that struck the city in the mid-1970s. Lewin and McCormick show how the crisis spurred the formation of union coalitions and the use of these coalitions to bargain master agreements in 1975, 1976, 1978, and 1980 that covered virtually all municipal workers. In addition to these master agreements, subsidiary agreements covering noneconomic matters were permitted to be negotiated on a unit-by-unit basis, and these helped to preserve the autonomy of individual union leaders which the large coalition otherwise threatened (the authors refer to this as two-tier coalition bargaining). Of particular interest was the city management's support of coalition bargaining (or perhaps more accurately, lack of opposition to it), which aided municipal *and* union officials not only to reach bargaining agreements with each other but to "negotiate" the terms of the city's fiscal rescue with other governing bodies—the state of New York and the federal government—that, in the aftermath of the fiscal crisis, acquired greater control over New York's municipal affairs. Lewin and McCormick thus conclude that coalition bargaining has served both union and management interests in New York City and that this type of bargaining structure is likely to continue in that city as long as fiscal adversity remains on the scene. Whether or not severe fiscal strain will bring about coalition bargaining elsewhere in the public sector is uncertain, but the reader will want to consider carefully the discussion of this possibility in the closing pages of the Lewin-McCormick article.

In evaluating these conclusions and those reached by authors of other papers in this chapter, we remind the reader to consider the empirical bases of the findings, the diversity of public sector labor relations, and especially the relatively short history of collective bargaining in American governments. Changes now underway in the environment of public sector labor relations and those that occur in the future may well cause significant alterations in the structure of collective bargaining. As with other aspects of public sector labor relations, the structure of collective bargaining needs to be periodically reappraised if its dynamic changes are not to go undiscovered.

Multiemployer Negotiations among Local Governments

Peter Feuille, Hervey Juris, Ralph Jones, and Michael Jay Jedel*

Researchers investigating public sector bargaining structure have devoted relatively little attention to multiemployer bargaining relationships. This article partially fills this information gap by presenting and discussing findings from an exploratory study of interemployer negotiating relationships among government employers in four metropolitan areas.

Interemployer Bargaining Relationships

Very few interemployer bargaining relationships have been reported among North American public employers.[1] A large share of this literature has focussed on the key success story of multiemployer bargaining in government: the negotiations between the Minnesota Twin City Metropolitan Area Managers Association and Operating Engineers Local 49, for a succession of contracts covering public works employees in thirty separate jurisdictions. In addition, there have been reports of coordinated and employer association bargaining experiences in British Columbia, multiemployer efforts which apparently have become institutionalized.[2] Various federal agencies of the U.S. government have experimented with a rudimentary form of multiemployer bargaining in which a number of certified bargaining units have been consolidated into larger negotiating units which then negotiate with a higher level of agency management than called for by the original certification.[3] There have been two unsuccessful attempts to establish multiemployer bargaining with firefighter locals, one in California's Alameda County[4] and the other in some Minneapolis-St. Paul suburbs.[5] These reports of selected public sector experiences demonstrate three things: (1) there has been some experimentation with multiemployer negotiating units, but the experiments have involved only a tiny fraction of all negotiations; (2) there are many substantive and procedural obstacles to the success of these efforts, which seem to succeed only when all the parties involved perceive definite benefits resulting from such arrangements; (3) these experiences tell us little about the extent to which multiemployer bargaining is practiced generally.

Further, it is not at all clear on an *a priori* basis that multiemployer bargaining should exist on a widespread scale in public sector labor relations.

*Juris is at the Graduate School of Management, Northwestern University, Jones is an arbitrator and consultant in Washington, D.C., and Jedel is at the School of Business, Georgia State University. The authors gratefully acknowledge the support provided by the Labor-Management Services Administration, U.S. Department of Labor (Contract L-74-207). This paper was presented at the September, 1976 meeting of the Industrial Relations Research Association, Atlantic City, New Jersey, and also appeared in the *Proceedings of the Twenty-Ninth Annual Meeting* (Madison, Wis.: IRRA, 1977), pp. 123-131.

On the one hand, there are some significant incentives for local government employers in a particular metropolitan area to establish such relationships; the employers in each area compete for the bulk of their labor in the same local labor markets; such labor market competition means that individual employers look to other employers in the same area for comparative data to use at the bargaining table and are affected by the terms of bargaining settlements in nearby jurisdictions; the employers in an area frequently may deal with locals of the same union for any particular occupational group; and bargaining consolidation may save each employer substantial time and money. On the other hand, however, the fact that each local government employer enjoys product market monopolies and is an independent political jurisdiction with its own elected and appointed officials dependent for support on separate citizen-voter-taxpayer constituencies, suggests that there are minimal incentives for inter-employer bargaining cooperation.

The private sector bargaining literature[6] similarly presents a bifurcated message. Some employers create and participate in interorganizational bargaining structures because they perceive that they can secure more advantageous terms acting in concert than individually, and these perceptions seem to be associated with several environmental conditions. First, the product market tends to be highly competitive and the employers' products are relatively undifferentiated. Second, the employers tend to compete for labor in the same labor markets. Third, the employers tend to be in close geographical proximity with one another. Fourth, employers tend to deal with the same union or set of unions, and each employer tends to be small relative to the union. To test the validity of these general conditions, consider that employer association bargaining is the norm in the construction, trucking, garment, coal, and many big city local service industries (e.g., hotels, restaurants, laundry delivery); in these industries most of the above conditions exist. However, employers in other industries (e.g., autos, electrical equipment, airlines, oil refining, chemical products) with contrasting conditions have continued to bargain on a single employer basis. Of all these private sector conditions, the only one which does not apply to local government bargaining is the competitive product market dimension. However, the absence of competitive product market pressures may be more important than the presence of all the other conditions that give rise to multiemployer bargaining arrangements in government.[7]

As a separate consideration, it is possible that while the official structure of local government bargaining may adhere to a one employer-one union paradigm, the actual structure may reflect interemployer cooperation through the exchange and use of bargaining information. Employer negotiators may be able to achieve some kind of structural integration across separate bargaining units through formal and informal exchanges of information with their counterparts in other jurisdictions. As a result, we decided to examine the information collection and dissemination practices of selected public employers to see what kinds of interemployer decision connections, if any, emerged from these information exchanges.

Research Design

To assess the extent to which conditions supporting or mitigating multi-employer bargaining might be operating in local government bargaining, we selected for study the interemployer relationships established by local public employers in four geographically diverse metropolitan areas (each with a population in excess of one million): Bay City (in the New England census region), Industrial City (in the Middle Atlantic region), Sun City (South Atlantic), and Lake City (East North Central). The majority of governmental employers in each metropolitan area have been engaged in collective bargaining at least since 1970 (and in one case since 1960), so there was a substantial history of public sector bargaining in each area. Because bargaining structures differ by occupation, and because different types of governmental jurisdictions are involved in teacher and non-teacher bargaining, we selected four occupations for examination: teachers, police officers, fire fighters, and general public works employees. This geographical and occupational diversity should improve the generalizability of our results.

We collected data from a sample of employer and union bargaining representatives for each occupation and from selected neutrals (i.e., mediators and factfinders) in each metropolitan area. The employers in the sample were selected on the basis of size, because larger governmental employers generally have lengthier bargaining histories than smaller ones. Some 97 interviews were conducted during 1975 in the central city, the central city school district, the core county, and several of the larger suburban municipalities and school districts in the four areas. Each interview followed the same format, with the interviewer asking each respondent a set of questions about the interorganizational bargaining and informational exchange relationships in which the respondent participated. Table 1 shows the number of local governments in each metropolitan area for which interemployer cooperation was an option.

Results and Analysis

The interview responses showed two distinct patterns of interorganizational cooperative relationships: the first involves bargaining structure, the second the exchange of bargaining information.

Bargaining structure. Table 1 shows that we found *no* lasting interemployer bargaining alliances in these four areas. The employers in this sample maintain autonomous bargaining relationships, i.e., each of them handles the collective bargaining process on an individual basis and does not engage in association, coordinated, or coalition bargaining with other employers. The few attempts to establish coordinated bargaining serve to emphasize the prevalence of these autonomous relationships.

We discovered two efforts each in the Industrial City and Lake City areas of employers attempting to establish coordinated bargaining. In

TABLE 1

Metropolitan Area (Census Region)	Number of Municipalities	Number of School Districts	Number of Continuing Interemployer Bargaining Relationships	Number of Continuing Interemployer Information Exchange Relationships
Bay City (New England	31	48	0	4
Industrial City (Middle Atlantic)	35	30	0	2
Sun City (South Atlantic)	27	1	0	2
Lake City (East North Central)	21	31	0	3

Industrial City, in 1972, several suburban school district negotiators agreed to coordinate their positions on salaries during bargaining with the respective teacher union locals. This effort consisted of two elements: a common upper limit (apparently five percent) and no salary settlement without group approval. A second Industrial City effort was made in 1973 involving primarily the blue collar or public works employees represented by American Federation of State, County, and Municipal Employees locals of four area employers (the central city, central city school district, sewer authority, and housing authority). All the unions and employers negotiated together at the same bargaining table, and the ostensible goal was to bargain a uniform contract to cover the employees in separate bargaining units. After a few meetings the effort dissolved, apparently because of interpersonal rivalries and a reluctance to make concessions for the sake of uniformity.

In the Lake City area there also were two coordination attempts. In 1973, at the central city's urging, the city, county, city school district, the area vocational education district, the sewage commission, and several of the suburban municipalities coordinated their bargaining efforts with various employee groups, in that they agreed upon common settlement limits and the timing of offers. The key employer negotiator believed that this effort was successful, i.e., the dollar cost of the settlements was smaller than it would have been in the absence of the coordination effort. However, in the next round of negotiations, in 1975, this informal bargaining coalition never really came together as each of the jurisdictions bargained and settled on an individual basis.

A variety of reasons were offered by employer respondents for the prevalence of autonomous bargaining relationships. These may be grouped into two categories: the procedural difficulties of coordinating bargaining across numerous contexts, and a perception that interorganizational relationships would reduce the decision autonomy of individual public employers. Most of the respondents believed that securing and maintaining employer commitment to a united bargaining strategy across multiple employers with varying employment conditions would be a very complex and difficult task, one which would not necessarily result in an improvement in individual employer welfare. In addition, the respondents placed a large positive value on the political autonomy or decision making discretion of their employing organization, and they perceived that an interorganizational bargaining relationship would reduce that autonomy in return for an uncertain outcome.

Consequently, we found very little interemployer bargaining cooperation in general and no continuing coordinative or coalitional relationships in particular. The history of the coordinative failures just described suggest that despite efforts to establish interdependent employer relationships, there are substantial centrifugal pressures on member units to attempt to retain their decision making authority. In turn, the centrifugal pressures seem to be associated with differences in employment conditions across employers, and with a concomitant unwillingness of both employers and unions to make changes for the sake of group uniformity in the absence of any compelling reason to do so. These results suggest that, in spite of their potential benefits, interemployer bargaining interdependencies will not be adopted by local governments until the perceived benefits clearly outweigh the perceived costs.

Information exchange. In contrast to the autonomous nature of the bargaining relationship, the employers surveyed had established a variety of interemployer connections for the purpose of acquiring and exchanging bargaining information. The most visible relationships are the eleven formal organizations (four in the Bay City area, three in the Lake City area, and two each in the Industrial City and Sun City areas) which exist in whole or in large part to facilitate the exchange of bargaining information (e.g. wage and fringe data, contract language, and current negotiation developments) among member employers. While the existence of a few of these organizations antedates the emergence of collective bargaining, and though a few are statewide organizations, all of them devote a major portion of their resources to the exchange of information among employers in the four areas.

These organizations vary considerably in the amount and types of services they provide their members. Some organizations have substantial income (primarily dues and fees from members) and staffs to perform or facilitate information collection and dissemination services. Other organizations have no staff, almost no income, and do little more than hold periodic meetings to facilitate informal, face-to-face information exchanges (primarily "war stories"). For example, in order to prevent whipsawing, the 31 school district employers in the Lake City area school district negotiators association, regularly report to each other via the association on the results of each of their own negotiating sessions. Under the auspices of the county association of school boards, negotiators for the suburban Industrial City area school districts meet regularly to exchange negotiation development and employment condition information. At least five of these organizations regularly conduct wage and fringe benefit surveys and disseminate the results to members. As the foregoing examples indicate, the most structured of these information exchange relationships exist among school district negotiators in three of the four areas surveyed (in the Sun City area there is only one countywide school district).

In addition to these institutionalized information exchanges, the employers in each area engage in substantial *ad hoc* surveys of and discussions, usually via telephone, with other employers as the need arises. In these *ad hoc* exchanges, the surburban employers appear to concentrate primarily on other suburban employers in the same metropolitan area, and, secondarily, on other employers in the state; the central city employers appear to concentrate primarily on other large cities and secondarily on local metropolitan area employers. Also, most of the employers purchase substantial information from publications issued by trade associations, labor relations reporting services, and specialized government agencies. Finally, a special kind of information exchange process exists where consultant negotiators represent employers at the negotiating table. In each of the four areas, we encountered several individuals (typically lawyers) who perform negotiating services on a consulting basis, usually for suburban employers who are too small to support a full time labor relations representative. These consultants establish *de facto* interorganizational information exchanges among the employers they represent.

The large number of continuing information exchange relationships stands in marked contrast to the absence of any continuing coordinated or coalition bargaining activities. These results suggest that the employers in this sample perceive substantial benefits resulting from the exchange of bargaining information. However, these information exchanges have not led to significant interemployer cooperation during the bargaining process, i.e., they have not led to changes in the official or actual structure of bargaining. The employers in this sample, then, are willing to incur substantial costs (in time and money) to collect and exchange information relevant to the discharge of their bargaining responsibilities, but they are unwilling to relinquish their decision making autonomy to an interorganizational system in which group interests may supersede individual interests.

Conclusions

Many worthwhile claims have been made on behalf of multiemployer bargaining in the public sector: it protects against whipsawing, it avoids the costly duplication involved in repeated negotiations for similar contracts among proximate employers, it may result in greater expertise at the bargaining table, and it is a flexible arrangement which can be changed by the participants as they mutually see fit.[9] However, the results of this study suggest that local government employers apparently perceive these potential benefits to be outweighed by the costs associated with a multiemployer arrangement. First, employer respondents anticipated considerable procedural difficulties in coordinating bargaining across several bargaining units with different employment conditions, differential abilities to pay, and different union leaders. These difficulties are compounded by different management structures and decision processes, even in contiguous jurisdictions.[10] Employer respondents were especially dubious of the willingness of the participants to make bargaining concessions for the sake of uniformity in the absence of any compelling reason to do so (e.g., competitive product market pressures). Second, the respondents spoke of employer decision autonomy in strongly positive terms as a behavioral dimension worth preserving (or at least perceived by their respective citizenries as worth preserving).

Finally, our interview responses produced some information that challenges the asserted value of multiemployer bargaining to reduce duplication of negotiations. It was readily apparent from the responses of both union and management representatives that many of them had little or no desire to reduce such duplication because to do so would reduce their organizational stature or even eliminate their current livelihood. For instance, one consultant negotiator in the Industrial City area was strongly opposed to multiemployer bargaining because it would reduce the total number of negotiations and hence the market for his services. The reduction of costly, tax-supported, duplicated services may be a worthy goal, but at the same time such a reduction will negatively affect the self-interest of large numbers of current and future union and management representatives, and this in turn encourages resistance to multiemployer arrangements. In sum, while multiemployer bargaining among local governments has been touted as a very worthwhile phenomenon, our study indicates that it is a phenomenon whose time has not yet come.

Footnotes

1. Cyrus F. Smythe, Jr., "Public-Private Sector Multi-Employer Collective Bargaining—The Role of the Employer Representative," *Labor Law Journal*, 22 (August 1971), pp. 498-508; David L. Norgarrd and Karl Van Asselt, *Cities Join Together for Bargaining: the Experience in Minnesota and British Columbia*, Strengthening Local Government Through Better Labor Relations series no. 10, Labor-Management Relations Service, September, 1971; *California Public Employee Relations*, No. 19 (December 1973), pp. 25-28; Richard Pegnetter, *Multiemployer Bargaining in the Public Sector: Purposes and Experiences*, Public Employee Relations Library series no. 52 (Chicago: International Personnel Management Association, 1975); and Harold W. Davey, "The Structural Dilemma in Public Sector Bargaining at State and Local Levels: A Preliminary Analysis," Industrial Relations Research Association, *Proceedings of the Twenty-Sixth Annual Winter Meeting* (Madison: IRRA, 1974), pp. 67-73.
2. Norgarrd and Van Asselt, *op. cit.*
3. Pegnetter, *op. cit.*, pp. 11-13.
4. California Public Employee Relations, *op. cit.*
5. Pegnetter, *op. cit.*, p. 14.
6. For example, see Arnold R. Weber, ed., *The Structure of Collective Bargaining* (New York: Free Press, 1961); Arnold R. Weber, "Stability and Change in the Structure of Collective Bargaining," in the American Assembly, Lloyd Ulman, ed., *Challenges to Collective Bargaining* (Englewood Cliffs, N.J.: Prentice-Hall, 1967); Jesse T. Carpenter, *Employers' Associations and Collective Bargaining in New York City* (Ithaca, N.Y.: Cornell University Press, 1950); and Edwin F. Beal, Edward D. Wickersham, and Philip Kienast, *The Practice of Collective Bargaining*, 5th ed. (Homewood, Ill.: Irwin, 1976), pp. 111-18, 207-08.
7. For a discussion of the conditions which increase the possibility of multiemployer bargaining units, see Smythe, *op. cit.*, pp. 507-508.
8. Pegnetter, *op. cit.*, pp. 21-26.

9. Pegnetter, *ibid.*

10. For a discussion of this phenomenon in Los Angeles City and County, see David Lewin, "Local Government Labor Relations in Transition: The Case of Los Angeles," *Labor History*, 17 (Spring, 1976), pp. 191-213.

Coalition Bargaining in Municipal Government: The New York City Experience

David Lewin and Mary McCormick*

In both 1978 and 1980, the nation's largest municipal government and its public employee unions used a formal coalition bargaining structure to negotiate basic wage agreements that covered more than a quarter-million workers. These negotiations were preceded by others in the mid 1970s that featured informal coalition bargaining on a smaller scale. The emergence and development of coalition bargaining in New York City, particularly during a period of sustained fiscal crisis, raise several questions about the structure and future direction of public sector bargaining. It is clear that generalizations about coalition bargaining, or, more broadly, bargaining structure in the public sector, cannot rest on the experience of a single government or a group of labor organizations in a single city; yet New York City's experience should not be overlooked, especially since in many respects over the past two decades this city has been a trendsetter in the development of public sector labor relations in the United States.[1]

Why, in view of the aversion to coalition bargaining of most unions and managements in both the public and private sectors, has such a structural arrangement emerged in New York City's municipal government? What historical, environmental, and institutional factors have contributed to this development? Will municipal coalition bargaining stabilize, develop further, or decline in New York City during the 1980s? What are the prospects for coalition bargaining elsewhere in the public sector? These questions will be addressed in this paper.

Bargaining Structure

In recent years, some scholarly attention has been paid to the formation of union and management coalitions for bargaining purposes in the private sector. The basic purpose of such coalitions is to augment the bargaining

*Graduate School of Business, Columbia University. The authors would like to express their appreciation for helpful comments to John C. Anderson, Peter Feuille, Dale L. Hiestand, Raymond D. Horton, James W. Kuhn, members of the Columbia University Labor Seminar, and students in the Public Sector Labor Seminar at Cornell University. Reprinted from *Industrial and Labor Relations Review*, Vol. 34 (January 1981), 175-190.

power of one or the other parties to negotiations.[2] The development of private sector union coalitions has been sparked by the rapid growth of the conglomerate form of corporate organization in the 1960s and 1970s.[3] This is reflected in the efforts of the Industrial Union Department (IUD) of the AFL-CIO to coalesce for bargaining purposes differentially affiliated local unions in companies where single-plant, single-union bargaining has predominated.

But corporate conglomeration is not a necessary precondition to the formation of a union coalition. Recall, for example, General Electric, which was met in the late 1960s by a coalition of thirteen unions countering the company's final-offer-first approach to collective bargaining (known as Boulwarism). Rulings by the National Labor Relations Board and the courts that supported coordinated bargaining at General Electric helped focus attention on this case.[4]

Note that coordinated bargaining occurs when "two or more unions negotiate jointly for *individual* union contracts containing common terms," whereas coalition bargaining refers to situations in which "two or more unions bargain jointly for a *common* 'master agreement' covering all employees they ... represent."[5] Thus, some union coalitions may be engaged in coordinated bargaining while others are engaged in coalition bargaining with a single employer or an employers' association. Furthermore, these two types of bargaining may be distinguished from pattern bargaining, which refers to the negotiation by one union and one employer of terms and conditions of employment that establish targets for other unions and employers.[6]
for other unions and employers.[6]

Considerably more research attention has been devoted to employer than to union coalitions in the private sector, perhaps because as many as 40 percent of all labor agreements in this sector are reached through multiemployer bargaining.[7] Most of the research is addressed to the question of why multiemployer bargaining develops in some industries—construction, garment manufacturing, trucking, coal mining, and local services, for example—but not others.[8] The evidence indicates that the tendency toward multiemployer bargaining in the private sector is strongest where product and labor markets are highly competitive, where employers are in close geographical proximity and negotiate with a common union or set of unions, and where firms are small in size relative to the union.

The structure of bargaining is much less diversified in the public than in the private sector. The dominant pattern in government is bargaining between a single employer and a single union, as both management and labor have opposed coalition structures. Public employers oppose multiemployer bargaining because of (1) procedural difficulties involved in coordinating negotiations across several bargaining units with differences in employment conditions, ability to pay, union leaders, management structures, and decision processes, and (2) the desire to preserve their decision-making autonomy.[9]

Most, if not all, public sector labor organizations also have opposed coalition bargaining, especially on a formal basis. Unions such as the American Federation of State, County and Municipal Employees (AFSCME) and the Service Employees' International Union (SEIU) often have several locals in a particular city or state government. Bargaining involving these locals may proceed (formally or otherwise) on a coordinated basis. But when it comes to the joining of different unions, perhaps with different national affiliations or simply independent local organizations, for the purpose of bargaining a master agreement with a single governmental employer, leaders and members of public employee unions generally have displayed as strong an aversion to coalition bargaining as their management counterparts have shown to multiemployer bargaining.

In addition to employer and union opposition, aversion to coalition bargaining is supported by several other factors: regulatory policy that designates an exclusive bargaining representative for a particular group of employees; decentralized collective bargaining; a labor movement organized on the principles of union autonomy and exclusive jurisdiction; and, in the public sector until just recently, an expansionary fiscal climate.

Despite these and other barriers to coalition bargaining in the public sector, such bargaining is now practiced in the City of New York. The central question is why, given the general aversion to it, did formal coalition bargaining develop in New York City in the late 1970s? In the next three sections, we examine the historical, institutional, economic and political factors that underlie this development.

Developments Prior to the Fiscal Crisis

The City of New York is not only the largest municipal government in the United States, but for a quarter-century it has also been a leader in the development and institutionalization of collective bargaining in the public sector. A review of this labor relations history suggests that interunion relationships, negotiating practices, and regulatory procedures that evolved prior to the fiscal crisis of 1975 contributed in fundamental respects to the development of formal coalition bargaining.[10]

First, by 1975, interunion relationships had matured to the point of relative stability and were marked by a lack of jurisdictional rivalry. This maturity was related to New York City's long tradition of support for the union movement and to the fact that municipal unions had been formally recognized for almost twenty years. A majority of these municipal labor organizations represented single occupational groups, such as teachers, sanitationmen, police, fire and corrections officers, but by 1967, District Council 37 of AFSCME and its several locals had won the right to represent more than two-thirds of the city's non-uniformed, non-pedagogical employees. Thus, by the late 1960s, the municipal unions in New York City generally were secure with respect to their separate constituencies and faced few challenges from rival organizations.[11]

Second, pattern bargaining accompanied the development of collective bargaining in New York's municipal government and contributed to inter- and intra-union stability. In many ways, pattern bargaining was a precursor of the formal coalition bargaining that emerged in the late 1970s. Despite the fact that six major unions dominated the municipal labor relations process during the 1960s and 1970s, the city's 250,000 employees were represented by as many as 85 separate unions and 405 separate bargaining units and were employed in approximately 2,500 different job titles. Some unions had as many as 60 separate locals; in some cases, a single bargaining unit encompassed several local unions. This organizational format resulted in an intricate web of horizontal and vertical parity relationships among unions, bargaining units, and job titles. Pattern bargaining was also reinforced by the rulings of impasse panels, which were often appointed to resolve municipal labor disputes.[12] Although in earlier years no single bargained wage settlement consistently served as the relevant comparison for all others in the city, the 1974 agreement between the Transit Workers Union (TWU) and the Metropolitan Transit Authority (MTA) set the wage pattern for the entire municipal work force.[13]

A third factor that contributed to the emergence of coalition bargaining in New York City was the codification of the municipal labor relations process, which occurred in 1967 when the New York City Collective Bargaining Law took effect. The law institutionalized and extended many of the practices and relationships that developed in the previous decade, several of which fostered coalition-type activity among municipal employees.[14]

One provision of the law mandated, for example, the creation of a citywide bargaining unit to negotiate terms and conditions of employment, such as time and leave benefits and health insurance, that were required to be uniform for approximately 120,000 employees in the city's Career and Salary Plan.[15] Because its members constituted over 60 percent of the total, District Council 37 was designated the exclusive bargaining representative for this unit, but the unit also encompassed employee-members of more than 30 separate municipal labor organizations.

Another provision of the law mandated the creation of the Municipal Labor Committee (MLC), an organization that was to be responsible for coordinating union participation in the tripartite Office of Collective Bargaining (OCB), which was charged with administering the statute. Subsequently, the MLC became the vehicle for developing common bargaining (and political) policies among city labor organizations, both before and during the period of fiscal crisis.

By the early 1970s, then, the municipal labor relations process in New York City was well established. More than 95 percent of all municipal employees were represented in collective bargaining; interunion relationships were relatively stable and peaceful; the turnover of union leadership was infrequent; and, under the auspices of OCB, the number of bargaining units declined from more than 400 in 1968 to approximately 100 in 1975.[16] This reduction of units permitted some municipal labor organizations—District Council 37, for example—to coordinate better their bargaining activity on behalf of constituent locals, and it also facilitated the coordination of management's position in negotiations with municipal unions. Thus, prior to the emergence of the fiscal crisis in 1975, the structure of municipal collective bargaining in New York City had shifted considerably away from strict unit-by-unit and union-by-union negotiations.

The Fiscal Crisis and Bargaining

The fiscal crisis set the stage for further restructuring of the collective bargaining process in New York City's municipal government. The new economic climate provided direct impetus toward a more formal union coalition and also spurred changes in the city's management structure for collective bargaining.[17] The overriding characteristic of municipal labor relations during the 1975-76 period was that the actions the direct participants in the bargaining process—city management and city unions—could take were severely constrained. Underlying all decision making in New York City municipal government during this period, including collective bargaining decisions, was the goal of fiscal solvency.

When the public credit markets closed to the city in the spring of 1975, the municipal government had an operating deficit of $2 billion and faced the task of refinancing $6 billion of outstanding short-term debt. From the perspective of the unions, bankruptcy would have reduced employee benefits, jeopardized pension contributions of member-employees and pension benefits of retirees, further decreased the work force, and significantly diminished the role of municipal union leaders in the labor relations and political processes. For the city's management, bankruptcy implied a dramatic and perhaps permanent curtailment of the power of elected officials. Thus, the threat of bankruptcy and the financing requirements necessary to avoid it made even more salient the interdependent relationship between the city and its organized workers. Furthermore, the willingness of municipal union leaders and the city's officials to bargain on a coalition basis was strengthened by the shifting of responsibility for managing the fiscal crisis from the local to the state and federal governments as well as some private actors and institutions (such as several of the city's largest banks). These were the principal factors underlying centralization of the municipal bargaining structure during the mid-1970s.

Brought about by financing needs required to avoid insolvency, three specific developments served as key precedents for the formal coalition wage bargaining that was to occur in 1978 and 1980. These were the wage-deferral agreement of 1975, the emergence of the municipal unions as the major financiers of the city, and the 1976 contract negotiations.

The 1975 Wage Deferral Agreement

In the spring of 1975, the City of New York's fiscal crisis was initially perceived as a local problem that, it was believed, could be managed at the local level. The mayor laid off municipal employees and reduced nonpayroll expenditures, while leaders of the municipal labor unions indicated their "willingness" to forgo certain negotiated benefits.[18] By June 1975, however, it was apparent that the city was able neither to manage the crisis by itself nor to meet the financing requirements necessary to avoid bankruptcy.

Joint pressures from the city and the state spurred New York's municipal labor organizations to engage in coalition bargaining. On July 1, 1975, a previously negotiated 6 percent wage increase was scheduled to go into effect for almost 200,000 of New York's municipal employees. At that juncture, however, the city was on the verge of default and lacked the funds to pay the approximately $300 million of prospective salary increases. In June, the State had created the Municipal Assistance Corporation (MAC), a public benefit corporation with limited oversight responsibilities that was empowered to help the City of New York restructure its debt, thereby, it was hoped, restoring the city's fiscal credibility. However, the task of financial resuscitation was more difficult that anticipated. To enhance the city's standing with investors, MAC sought proof that the budgetary reductions necessitated by the fiscal emergency were being made. Specifically, MAC called for a wage freeze on the slated 6 percent increase.

At this point, organized municipal employees faced a hostile political climate as well as an unfavorable economic environment. The public generally perceived the municipal unions as major contributors to the city's fiscal problems. Furthermore, as the crisis deepened, it appeared likely that the mayor would be sustained by the courts if he invoked his emergency power to invoke a unilateral wage freeze. Such a ruling would have established a precedent for unilateral managerial actions in the area of labor relations that could well have isolated the municipal labor union leaders from the decision-making process. As the complexity of the situation increased, it also became evident to most municipal union leaders that no one of them alone could count on managing the fiscal crisis to his own or his members' advantage. Thus, responding to these new economic pressures, the major municipal unions (with the exception of the teachers and police), acting in coalition, negotiated a Wage Deferral Agreement with city, state, and MAC officials.[19]

This agreement accomplished several objectives for the labor organizations that made up the coalition: (1) the wage freeze became a wage deferral to be in effect for one year only and was tapered to protect the earnings of low-paid employees;[20] (2) a cost-of-living adjustment (COLA) that had been agreed to in 1974 and that was scheduled to go into effect in fiscal year 1976 was preserved; (3) individual unions within the coalition could negotiate separate agreements provided that these met the conditions of the Wage Deferral Agreement; and (4) a claim was established by employees to receive the deferred wages at a future date. The provision for separate agreements assured each member union of the coalition a measure of autonomy while, more generally, the coalition structure assured each member union that no other labor organization would do better—or worse—concerning the wage deferral provisions.

Municipal Unions as Financiers

Soon after the Wage Deferral Agreement the fiscal crisis forced the municipal unions to assume the even more critical role of financier. By late summer of 1975, it was apparent to political officials that a stronger control mechanism with broader financial and managerial oversight responsibilities than MAC was required for the City of New York to avoid insolvency. In early September, the state legislature passed the Financial Emergency Act and created the Emergency Financial Control Board (EFCB). The board was given the authority to exercise broad powers over municipal affairs, including labor relations. Although the hope was that through EFCB's management of municipal budgetary affairs the city would be able to return to the public credit markets within a few months, its need to finance $5.7 billion of debt between November 1975 and June 1976 overwhelmed the attempts of the state to restore investor confidence in the city.[21]

During this period the city's five major employees' pension systems, with assets of more than $7 billion, emerged as major sources of loans to the city. Controlled by union officials, the pension funds had purchased city and MAC securities in the spring and summer of 1975 on an *ad hoc,* uncoordinated basis. By November, however, the unions became the city's major financiers on a systematic, integrated, long-term basis. Specifically, they agreed to invest $2.5 billion of pension funds in city paper and to "roll over" their earlier $1.2 billion investment as part of a complex $6.6 billion, three-year financing plan that also involved the city's major banks, the state government, and the federal government. As part of this financing arrangement, the federal government guaranteed $2.3 billion in seasonal loans to New York City.

The development of a coordinated policy to manage their pension fund investments in city and MAC securities contributed to the further development of a strong union coalition and formal coalition bargaining. The fact of this major financing role not only expanded the municipal unions' participation in the decision-making processes of the city government, but also placed them in a more collaborative relationship with city officials. This collaborative relationship and the strengthened sense of union solidarity were reinforced by the involvement of a new set of political actors in New York City's municipal government, namely, the federal government, particularly the Department of Treasury and Congress. Thus the fiscal crisis contributed not only to the development of coalition bargaining in New York's municipal government, but to an alliance between the city government and the municipal unions for the purpose of negotiating terms of the city's fiscal rescue with New York State and the federal government.

The 1976 Bargaining Round

The economic and political conditions that prevailed in 1976 further stimulated coalition activity among the municipal unions. A critical factor in the 1976 bargaining round was the role played by the EFCB and the U.S. Secretary of the Treasury. The control board promulgated wage-policy guidelines consistent with the wage freeze that had been mandated by the Financial Emergency Act and to which all participants in the municipal collective bargaining process were bound. Additionally, the board was required to approve all municipal collective bargaining contracts, thereby ensuring conformance with the city's Three-Year Financial Plan.

The wage-policy guidelines were an important limitation on the scope of bargainable issues in the 1976 negotiations. They were intended to serve two purposes: first, to preserve the substance of the city's financial plan; second, to permit some salary adjustments in order to protect employees against inflation, but in a manner that would not increase total labor costs budgeted in the financial plan. A critical condition established by the Department of Treasury was that the municipal labor contracts, scheduled to expire on June 30th, had to be settled before the federal loans, expiring on July 2nd, would be renewed. This stipulation created substantial pressure on the city and the municipal labor organizations to reach a new agreement.

Given the large number of municipal unions and bargaining units, a coalition bargaining structure provided a means of ensuring that the deadline would be met, that all unions would adhere to the wage guidelines, and that no one union would "outdo" any other. Thus, leaders of the municipal unions, again acting in coalition, concluded a two-year agreement with the city on June 30, 1976.[22] This agreement, the Memorandum of Interim Understanding, satisfied federal and state requirements, met the deadline for renewal of federal loans, and incorporated the substance of the EFCB's wage policy guidelines, including a $48 million fringe benefit reduction. As with the 1975 Wage Deferral Agreement, however, the 1976 agreement also provided a two-tier bargaining structure. After labor leaders signed the agreement, the representatives of each bargaining unit (of which there were approximately 100 in 1976) negotiated a separate contract with the city to determine other terms and conditions of employment for members of that unit—which had to be in conformity with the Memorandum of Interim Understanding. Among the major issues dealt with in individual unit bargaining were the manner in which each unit would satisfy the allocated reduction in fringe benefits for its members and the particulars for implementing a productivity program to which the COLA was tied.[23]

In summary, the 1975-76 period of fiscal crisis featured two major instances of coalition bargaining, thereby expanding a bargaining structure that first emerged several years earlier. Throughout this period, the paramount concern of the parties to negotiations was the financial solvency of the city. As the state and federal governments assumed increased responsibility for the city's fiscal and municipal affairs, specific bargaining guidelines and deadlines were set by them. Bargaining through a coalition structure facilitated compliance with these guidelines and deadlines, ensured that all of the municipal labor organizations shared in the costs of retrenchment, and helped to avoid the bankruptcy of the nation's largest local government. Additionally, by ensuring that all municipal labor organizations shared in the costs of retrenchment and by permitting separate nonwage agreements, the two-tier bargaining format addressed some major concerns of municipal unionists, namely, autonomy and interunion competition for resources.

Coalition Bargaining in 1978

Although the City of New York did not face imminent default in 1978, complex state and federal legislation and many delicate financial negotiations were needed in order to secure the municipality's future. Both the state's Financial Emergency Act and the federal seasonal loans were scheduled to expire in mid-1978. The federal government would not consider new legislation to aid the city until the state passed a law containing financial safeguards similar to those provided in the 1975 financial emergency legislation and until municipal labor negotiations were concluded.

These pressures for coalition bargaining were partially offset by local economic and political developments. The city enjoyed greater financial stability in 1978 than at any time during the previous three years; the wage freeze, which was the cornerstone of the 1976 negotiations, did not apply to the 1978 contracts; and a new mayor, Edward I. Koch, assumed office on January 1, 1978. Koch ran for office on a platform that emphasized an adversarial relationship with the municipal unions, in contrast to the cooperative relationship that was advocated during the previous administration of Abraham D. Beame.

Koch initially was reluctant to agree to coalition bargaining, believing that economic and political conditions would favor the city in separate union or unit negotiations. A few municipal union leaders also supported a return to a more conventional bargaining structure. But the difficulties of organizing both a new political administration and a revised (or a return to the traditional) format for labor relations, combined with the need for new federal loan guarantees and perhaps the realization that such guarantees had to be negotiated with other authorities, led the mayor to consent to formal coalition bargaining.

Unlike negotiations over the Wage Deferral Agreement in 1975 and the Memorandum of Interim Understanding in 1976, in which the participants had agreed to basic financial parameters *before* formal bargaining commenced, the 1978 negotiations began without a union-management consensus on the dimensions of the settlement. The only point on which the parties agreed was that in order to ensure that the necessary federal aid would be forthcoming, it would be beneficial if an agreement could be reached simultaneously with the TWU-MTA contract deadline of March 31st.

The scope of bargaining. The two prior negotiations had established a two-tier bargaining structure in city government; the question in 1978 was whether or not both "economic" and "noneconomic" issues should be settled within a single-tier coalition framework. The lack of consensus was especially pronounced within managerial ranks. Some city officials felt that all issues should have been included in coalition bargaining or, alternatively, that bargaining should have proceeded over economic issues only, with unit bargaining suspended and the noneconomic terms of existing contracts carried forward for two more years. These officials believed that a two-tier bargaining format subjected the city to a second round of bargaining in which it could only lose ground. A few union leaders also favored comprehensive (or one-tier) coalition bargaining, believing that they could gain little from separate negotiations.

In contrast, management supporters of two-tier bargaining argued that such bargaining would help achieve the overriding goal of securing new federal aid, even if this arrangement helped one or another union to "do better" than it would have otherwise. If the bargaining experiences of 1975 and 1976 held, the signing of a coalition agreement would satisfy federal authorities. The union leaders who favored a two-tier bargaining structure believed that the coalition arrangement would help reduce interunion rivalries, while unit bargaining would afford each of their organizations some measure of independence and autonomy, if not necessarily a "second bite of the apple."

That the unions were more united than management in their position on this issue was reflected in the 12 demands the union coalition submitted, all of which dealt with wage increases or cost-of-living allowances common to coalition members. By contrast, the city's opening bargaining position reflected the lack of managerial consensus; it included 62 demands or items, ranging from broad wage provisions that affected all employees to very detailed provisions that involved one or another small bargaining unit.

As each self-imposed negotiating deadline approached, the unions and management agreed that there was not sufficient time to bargain to agreement on both economic and noneconomic items. As the various deadlines passed and agreement was not achieved, the scope-of-bargaining issue surfaced again and again, but with less and less force as the ultimate deadline of June 30th drew nearer. No one can say with certainty that, had there been a management consensus one way or another on this issue, the scope of bargaining or the outcomes of the 1978 negotiations would have been different. What is certain is that in 1978, as in 1975 and 1976, the negotiations took place on a two-tier basis, with wages and some additional economic items subjected to coalition bargaining, and other issues, including most "noneconomic" ones, treated in separate unit negotiations. There is no evidence that, in any of these negotiations, some municipal unions did appreciably "better" or "worse" than others in reaching separate unit agreements, a fact that underscores the notion that such two-tier bargaining permits, and is in part motivated by the desire of, union leaders to maintain some measure of autonomy and independence.

Parties to the coalition. The city did not require the unions to declare formally their membership in the coalition. Each union retained the right to autonomy even if it chose not to exercise that right. In fact, only those unions that did not wish to associate themselves with the coalition were explicit regarding their membership status. Nonetheless, all major city employee unions except those representing rank-and-file uniformed personnel (firefighters, police, and corrections officers) eventually participated in the bargaining coalition. The official leadership of the coalition rotated among five labor organizations: United Federation of Teachers, Uniformed Sanitationmen's Association District Council 37, Local 237 of International Brotherhood of Teamsters, and United Fire Officers Association. The presence of the 60,000 member teachers' union in the 1978 coalition was particularly notable, for it formally broadened the basis for the coalition beyond that which had existed previously.

The Negotiations

The union coalition and the city did not reach agreement simultaneously with the contract settlement on March 31st between the TWU and the MTA. Over the next two months, however, the pressures for a settlement were intense, particularly those from the federal government. Finally, on

June 5, 1978, the city and the municipal unions reached a Coalition Economic Agreement (CEA). The cost of this two-year contract was estimated at $1.2 billion; it provided for a total wage increase of 8 percent, payment of the unpaid portion ($567 per employee) of the 1978 productivity-based COLA, and an annual cash bonus payment of $750 per employee in 1979 and 1980 in lieu of productivity COLAs. The provision of a general wage increase, the first in three years, contrasted sharply with the terms of the 1975 and 1976 coalition bargaining agreements.[24] Furthermore, the city abandoned its demand for contractual "givebacks," and $48 million in fringe and pension reductions, which had been required by the Treasury Department and agreed to in the 1976 bargaining round, were cancelled.

By fall 1978, the only major unions that had not signed the CEA—but which nevertheless incorporated its terms and provisions into their separate unit agreements—were the Patrolmen's Benevolent Association and the Uniformed Firefighters Association. In 1978, therefore, coalition bargaining in New York's municipal government directly and indirectly involved virtually all municipal labor organizations and covered most key economic items, while leaving some economic and noneconomic issues to be resolved in individual unit bargaining.

Coalition Bargaining in 1980[25]

Given that New York City was not seeking federal loans in 1980 and that a balanced budget was forecast for fiscal 1981, there seemed to be fewer external pressures for coalition bargaining in 1980 than at any time since the onset of the fiscal crisis. Nevertheless, the 1980 negotiations were conducted in a coalition framework. This may have occurred because, by that time, coalition bargaining had taken firm hold in New York City and was therefore less sensitive to external financial and political pressures. It also may have continued, however, because the parties anticipated serious financial problems resulting from a projected budgetary deficit of approximately $1.2 billion in fiscal 1982.

Many of the issues concerning coalition bargaining that were raised in 1978 surfaced again in the 1980 negotiations but were disposed of with greater dispatch than before. For example, the mayor repeated his reluctance to bargain within a coalition structure, but quickly acceded to this format. Some city officials preferred that economic and noneconomic issues be considered together in single-tier bargaining, but the negotiations were conducted within a two-tier framework.

The major difference between the 1978 and 1980 negotiations was the emergence in 1980 of a second union coalition made up principally of the labor organizations that did not formally join the coalition in 1978—unions of rank-and-file police, firefighters, and corrections officers. These unions formed the nucleus of this 43,000 member Uniformed Coalition. The coalition of 1978 (known as the Municipal Coalition in 1980) continued largely in place, representing about 200,000 city employees in coalition bargaining, including all but one group of uniformed superior officers. The only defections from the Municipal Coalition to the Uniformed Coalition

130

were the Uniformed Fire Officers' Association (UFA) and the Uniformed Sanitationmen's Association (USA).

Negotiations with both coalitions proceeded smoothly, especially by historical standards. The Municipal Coalition reached overall agreement with the city in early June 1980, three weeks prior to the expiration of the master and individual unit agreements. The Uniformed Coalition and the city reached agreement simultaneously with the expiration of the uniformed forces contracts. Members of the Municipal Coalition received annual 8 percent wage increases and adjustments in other benefits for a total two-year settlement of about 17 percent. The uniformed employees received wage increases of 9 percent the first year and 8 percent the second year; the total settlement, including fringe benefit adjustments, was approximately 19 percent. The terms of these new coalition agreements reflected the pattern established by the TWU-MTA agreement, concluded in the spring of 1980, which provided for annual wage increases of 9 percent and adjustments to fringe benefits over the two-year period, 1980-82. Unlike the 1978 negotiations, however, when individual bargaining unit (second-tier) agreements had to be signed before the wage increases were paid, this stipulation was removed in 1980. This meant that wage increases provided under the 1980 master coalition agreements were payable subject only to union ratification of these agreements. Such an arrangement suggests a strengthening in 1980 of the commitment to coalition bargaining in the City of New York, even as a second union coalition appeared on the scene and negotiated a master agreement with city officials. Highlights of the evolution of coalition bargaining in New York City from 1954 through 1980 are shown in the accompanying table.

Summary and Prognosis

New York City has a longer history of municipal collective bargaining than all but a few American cities. During the 1970s, this bargaining took place increasingly on a coalition basis. By 1980, union coalitions encompassed all the city's labor organizations and represented all 243,000 municipal employees covered by collective bargaining. The coalition bargaining agenda included wages, cost-of-living allowances, and some fringe and pension benefits.

Precedents for formal coalition bargaining were established by the reduction of interunion rivalries, the development of widespread pattern bargaining, and the enactment of the city's Collective Bargaining Law in 1967; it was the fiscal crisis of 1975, however, that gave special impetus to coalition bargaining. The goal of fiscal survival served to override the remaining barriers to coalition bargaining. The negotiation within a coalition structure of the 1975 Wage Deferral Agreement and major economic provisions of the 1976 municipal labor contracts provided tangible evidence of union and management responses to the new economic and political climates and were important precursors to broader and more formal coalition bargaining in 1978 and 1980. The coalition structure strengthened the city's ability to carry out fiscal planning within the requirements imposed by other governments and provided the vehicle for municipal labor's "representation" in this critical planning process. Even more fundamentally, this bargaining structure was the mechanism for linking labor *and* management in a *de facto* coalition to negotiate with federal and state authorities over the terms and conditions of the fiscal rescue of the City of New York.

TABLE
Chronology of Key Events in New York City Municipal Labor Relations

Time Period	Events
1954-1965	Mayoral authorization of unionism and bargaining rights for employees; informal negotiation of labor agreements; growth of municipal employee unionism.
1966-1974	Ninety-five percent of municipal employees represented in collective bargaining; development of pattern bargaining and stabilization of interunion relations and union leadership; enactment of Collective Bargaining Law; creation of Citywide Bargaining Unit and Municipal Labor Committee; reduction of bargaining units.
1975-1977	Emergence of fiscal crisis; creation of MAC and EFCB; two-tier coalition bargaining of the Wage Deferral Agreement and Memorandum of Interim Understanding; coordinated investments of employee pension funds in NYC notes and MAC bonds; passage and renewal of federal seasonal loans.
1978-1980	Election of Mayor Koch; long-term extension of EFCB; new federal loan guarantees; two-tier bargaining of the Coalition Economic Agreement; formation of the Uniformed Coalition; two-tier bargaining of the Municipal Coalition and Uniformed Coalition agreements.

Is coalition bargaining likely to persist, expand, or decline in New York City's municipal government? In analyzing private sector labor relations, Weber comments that "bargaining structure will be strongly influenced by the market context within which negotiations take place."[26] The notion of markets is not easily applied to the public sector, but the emergence of severe fiscal constraints on a government, especially to the point of threatening bankruptcy, may be taken as a proxy for market forces. These, in turn, impinge upon bargaining structure. If coalition bargaining in New York City did develop primarily in response to the fiscal crisis and to the related realignment of financial and political relationships among the municipal, state, and federal governments, then the future of coalition bargaining must be linked to the future fiscal condition of the city. Whether economic conditions will worsen or moderate in the near future in New York City is uncertain, but at this point (early 1981) the city projects substantial budgetary deficits and, perhaps more important, probably will not soon regain access to the credit markets. Moreover, the city will remain subject to the powers of the Emergency Financial Control Board, which has been extended by state law (and renamed the Financial Control Board) to the year 2008. All of this implies that coalition bargaining will remain the characteristic form of bargaining structure in New York City, at least for the near future.[27]

Even with severe external economic and political pressures, however, individual unit and union bargaining is unlikely to be entirely eliminated from New York's municipal government. With respect to bargaining structure in the private sector, Weber observes that

> *the formation of a common front inevitably involves a partial relinquishing of individual group goals. Each group will press for, or acquiesce in, the expansion of the worker alliance as long as the rate of substitution between the gains derived from the increment to bargaining power are greater than the perceived losses associated with the denial of autonomy in decision making. At some point, this rate of substitution will become negative, and tensions will develop within . . . the associated bargaining structures for the accommodation of special group interests or the fragmentation of the alliance.[28]*

The mechanism of two-tier bargaining in New York City permits leaders of individual unions to accommodate some of the special interests of their respective members while, at the same time, relinquishing others of their members' interests and some of their own autonomy to a larger coalition. These are difficult tasks for the leaders of otherwise independent and sometimes competing organizations to accomplish successfully.

Thus, if the reduction of interunion rivalries and growth of relatively stable labor organizations were also conducive to the development of coalition bargaining in New York City municipal government during the 1970s, then it is to these characteristics as well as to fiscal conditions that the future of the coalition structure should be linked. On balance, both severe fiscal strain and relatively stable interunion relationships have been instrumental to the development of coalition bargaining in New York's municipal government. As long as these conditions continue, as is anticipated, it is possible to forecast continued adherence to a two-tier coalition bargaining structure that permits common as well as separate union interests to be addressed.

Generalizing from New York City

What are the prospects for coalition bargaining elsewhere in municipal government or in the public sector more broadly? The prospects appear limited. Coalition bargaining has emerged in parts of the public hospital sector, especially in large urban hospitals; in negotiations with publicly employed craft workers at local, state, and federal levels; in some public school districts, such as the City of Chicago; and in some governments that have only recently begun to engage in collective bargaining, such as the City of Los Angeles. However, some of these arrangements represent carryovers of bargaining structures from the private sector; others are limited to unions that enroll only members of similar skills or whose members are employed in but one service or one unit of a government; and still others represent a one-time rather than a sustained bargaining tactic.[29]

These developments point up the need for a more theoretical perspective on bargaining structure in the public sector. Labor relations in the public sector, as in the private, may be conceptualized as diverse rather than uniform.

> *This diversity, which is rooted in historical, legal, functional and political features of government, contains several implications for public sector labor*

133

relations, but, in particular, it suggests that there is no a prior reason to assume that the labor relations process in a (particular) state, county or municipality necessarily will closely resemble the labor relations process elsewhere in government.[30]

Proceeding from this conceptualization, two-tier coalition bargaining of the type that exists in New York's municipal government might be replicated in some other governments. Even if this occurs, however, single-tier coalition bargaining, coalitions limited to unions in single services or agencies, conventional union-by-union bargaining, or various combinations thereof will likely exist in the public sector. The analytical task thus becomes one of identifying the "historical, legal, functional and political features of government" that give rise to a particular form of bargaining structure.[31]

Taking particular account of the economic-political forces that have affected the development of coalition bargaining in New York City, it appears that this form of bargaining structure is not likely to spread throughout the public sector, though it may emerge in some governments. It appears from the New York experience that coalition bargaining is most likely to develop under conditions of intense budgetary and fiscal pressure, which not only heighten the common interests of union organizations but of labor and management vis-à-vis other fiscal and political authorities. Few governments in the United States at present face the degree of fiscal stringency found in New York City; few have had to cede governing powers and managerial control to other public authorities; and few have had to rely· on the federal government to bail them out.

Nonetheless, market forces are dynamic, not static, and the rapid growth of state and local governments in the United States, which marked the third quarter of the twentieth century and stimulated the rapid expansion of public sector unionism and bargaining, has ended. Substantial evidence exists of a fundamental reappraisal by citizens and elected officials of the size, scope, and performance of public institutions. This appraisal implies that the trend toward slower growth, stabilization, and even decline of the revenues made available to governments, which first began to be noticed in the mid-1970s, will continue and perhaps quicken in the 1980s. A more stringent economic climate for government provides less political support for or even outright opposition to public employee unionism and bargaining as well as the reappraisal of management strategies for dealing with labor relations.[32] These developments suggest that, in some instances, the economic and political climates of the public sector may be such as to favor the development of coalition bargaining through which some union leaders and local public officials will seek greater protection of their interests and powers than is afforded them by conventional negotiating structures.

But for reasons identified in the analysis of coalition bargaining in New York City and suggested by bargaining structure and labor relations theory, this prognosis must not be carried too far. Both the labor movement and collective bargaining in the United States are characterized by decentralization and autonomy; public sector labor organizations are particularly heterogeneous. Like the employers with whom they negotiate, public sector union leaders share bargaining information with each other, but, also like public employers, they are chary of structural realignments that threaten their autonomy and livelihood.[33] Thus, to temper union rivalries is not to eliminate them, especially in much of the public sector where (unlike New York City) substantial proportions of employees are unorganized, and to coordinate bargaining is not to engage in coalition bargaining. Furthermore, the fact that a public employer rarely merges with another government means that, unlike their private sector counterparts, leaders of public sector labor organizations do not face the prospect of bargaining with a conglomerate and, consequently, are not pressed to form union coalitions for the purpose of countering that form of employer organization. Indeed, by bargaining as a single labor organization with one employer, individual public employee unions have been found to bring about a reallocation of budgetary resources toward the services in which their members are employed and away from other less well organized services.[34]

In conclusion, the New York City experience suggests more generally that the diminution of interunion rivalries, the spread of pattern bargaining, and the reduction-consolidation of bargaining units are necessary but not sufficient conditions for the development of coalition bargaining in the public sector. It is when fiscal crisis threatens the political viability of a government entity that public sector labor organizations will be motivated to pursue coalition bargaining and that a public employer will be willing to negotiate with a union coalition.[35] In such circumstances, an alliance is struck among the unions and between the unions and a government employer, not only as a way of containing internal rivalries but as a mechanism by which these normally risk-averse parties may negotiate with other political authorities in the hope of achieving a positive "rate of substitution between the gains derived from the increment to bargaining power and the losses associated with the denial of autonomy in decision-making."[36] If and when economic pressures on a particular government ease and local political control and autonomy are less threatened, the perceived rate of substitution may become negative and tensions may develop "for the fragmentation of the alliance"—especially if the public employer judges his interests to be harmed rather than served by continuance of the union coalition.[37] The validity of these observations as generalizations about the public sector awaits cross-sectional research into the determinants of public sector bargaining structures. At present, however, these observations suggest that while coalition bargaining in the City of New York during the 1970s is an important development worthy of close scrutiny, this structural arrangement is unlikely to be widely replicated in municipal government or in the public sector more broadly during the 1980s.

Footnotes

1. Specific examples include the rapid growth of public employee unionism, use of militant union tactics, negotiation of written labor agreements, and legal sanctioning and third-party regulation of public employee bargaining. These developments spread widely throughout the public sector during the late 1960s and the 1970s, but occurred earlier in the City of New York.
2. See William Chernish, *Coalition Bargaining: A Study of Union Tactics and Public Policy* (Philadelphia: University of Pennsylvania Press, 1968), and Arnold

R. Weber, *The Structure of Collective Bargaining* (New York: Free Press, 1961). The formation of union and management coalitions for bargaining purposes may be considered subsets of broader interorganizational relations. See Richard H. Hall, et al., "Patterns of Interorganizational Relationships," *Administrative Science Quarterly,* Vol. 22, No. 3 (September 1977), pp. 457-74.

3. See, for example, Wallace Hendricks, "Conglomerate Mergers and Collective Bargaining," *Industrial Relations,* Vol. 15, No. 1 (February 1976), pp. 75-87, and Kenneth O. Alexander, "Conglomerate Mergers and Collective Bargaining," *Industrial and Labor Relations Review,* Vol. 24, No. 3 (April 1971), pp. 354-74.

4. As reported in *NLRB:* General Electric Company v. NLRB, 69 LRRM 1305, (1968); *Federal Court (Circuit Court):* General Electric Company v. NLRB, 71 LRRM 2418, (1969); and *Federal Court (Circuit Court):* National Labor Relations Board v. General Electric Company, 72 LRRM 2530, (1969). See also James W. Kuhn, "A View of Boulwarism: The Significance of the G.E. Strike," *Labor Law Journal,* Vol. 21, No. 9 (September 1970), pp. 582-90.

5. The quotations are from Phillip J. Schwarz, *Coalition Bargaining.* Key Issues in Industrial Relations Series, No. 5 (Ithaca: New York State School of Industrial and Labor Relations, Cornell University, 1970), p. 3. See also Donald E. Cullen and Louis Feinberg, *The Bargaining Structure in Construction: Problems and Prospects* (Washington, D.C.: U.S. Department of Labor, 1980). The NLRB and court decisions discussed by Cullen and Feinberg as well as those listed in footnote no. 4 above provide legal support for coordinated bargaining but not coalition bargaining in the private sector. The latter can occur where both parties voluntarily agree to merge bargaining units into a single coalition; but if one party objects to negotiating with more than one unit at a time, the other party may not legally force the issue—although it may pursue a coordinated strategy of seeking the same goals in different bargaining units. Consequently, some private sector employees have attempted to characterize the coordinated bargaining activity of unions as coalition bargaining and to make such bargaining the subject of unfair labor practice charges.

6. For a discussion of pattern bargaining in selected manufacturing industries, see Neil W. Chamberlain, Donald E. Cullen, and David Lewin, *The Labor Sector,* 3rd ed. (New York: McGraw-Hill, 1980), pp. 249-53.

7. The Bureau of Labor Statistics reports in *Characteristics of Major Collective Bargaining Agreements, July 1, 1975,* Bulletin 1957 (Washington, D.C.: 1977), that about 43 percent of workers covered under major collective bargaining agreements were in multiemployer units. The proportion of workers so covered in "minor" agreements is presumed to be somewhat smaller. Together these data produce the estimate that 40 percent of all organized workers in the private sector are covered by multiemployer bargaining agreements.

8. Representative works include Weber, *The Structure of Collective Bargaining;* Weber, "Stability and Change in the Structure of Collective Bargaining" in Lloyd Ulman, ed., *Challenges to Collective Bargaining* (Englewood Cliffs, N.J.: Prentice-Hall, 1967), pp. 13-36; and David H. Greenberg, "The Structure of Collective Bargaining and Some of its Determinants," in Industrial Relations Research Association, *Proceedings of the Nineteenth Annual Winter Meeting, December 28-29, 1966, San Francisco* (Madison, Wis.: IRRA, 1967), pp. 343-53.

9. See Peter Feuille, Hervey Juris, Ralph Jones and Michael Jay Jedel, "Multi-employer Negotiations Among Local Governments," in David Lewin, Peter Feuille and Thomas A. Kochan, *Public Sector Labor Relations: Analysis and Readings* (Glen Ridge, N.J.: Horton and Daughters, 1977), pp. 131-38.

10. The history of municipal collective bargaining in New York City prior to the 1970s is well documented. See, for example, Raymond D. Horton, *Municipal*

Labor Relations in New York City: Lessons of the Lindsay-Wagner Years (New York: Praeger, 1973), chapters 2-4.

11. Note also that most municipal union leaders had long tenures in office. As an example, John Delury, who retired in 1978, headed the Uniformed Sanitationmen's Association for more than 40 years and was a key figure in the negotiation of (informal) labor agreements during the three-term administration (1953-1965) of Mayor Robert F. Wagner.

12. See Mary McCormick, "A Functional Analysis of Interest Arbitration in New York City's Municipal Government, 1968-1975," in Industrial Relations Research Association, *Proceedings of the Twenty-Ninth Annual Winter Meeting, September 16-18, 1976, Atlantic City* (Madison, Wis.: IRRA, 1977), pp. 249-57.

13. TWU members are employed by the MTA, a state agency responsible for the subway and commuter rail lines in New York City and its surrounding counties. The city provides an annual operating subsidy to the MTA, but the Mayor has no formal role in negotiations between the TWU and MTA. Municipal union leaders in New York City have sought to institutionalize the pattern-setting role of TWU-MTA agreements because (1) wages for TWU members are tied to the state's rather than the city's fiscal condition; (2) the TWU has greater bargaining leverage than most city labor organizations, given that there are very few substitutes for subway and rail service and that a subway strike in particular can impose substantial economic hardship on the city; and (3) the TWU (unlike most municipal unions) has a tradition of no contract, no work.

14. This law also created some institutional barriers among city labor organizations, though these tended to reflect a traditional division in city government between mayoral and nonmayoral agencies. In particular, employees of mayoral agencies — those under direct budgetary and management control of the mayor—came under the jurisdiction of the city's Collective Bargaining Law and its administrative agency, the Office of Collective Bargaining (OCB), while employees of virtually all nonmayoral agencies came under the aegis of the state's Public Employees' Fair Employment (Taylor) Act and its administrative agency, the Public Employment Relations Board (PERB). The latter group of employees, numbering over 100,000, work principally in the Board of Education, the Board of Higher Education, the Housing Authority, and the Off-Track Betting Corporation.

15. Career and Salary Plan employees are designated as such by a 1954 Civil Service classification. Major exclusions from this category are pedagogical and uniformed employees (police, fire, sanitation and corrections personnel) and prevailing wage workers—certain blue-collar workers whose compensation is set according to the prevailing wage provisions under section 220 of New York State Labor Law.

16. We have neither sufficient information nor space to discuss more fully this remarkable reduction in bargaining units except to underscore the point made immediately below in the text that municipal labor, management, and OCB officials all judged the reduction to serve their particular interests.

17. For other perspectives on the effects of the fiscal crisis on New York's municipal labor relations, see Mary McCormick, *Management of Retrenchment: The City of New York in the 1970s* (Ph.D. dissertation, Columbia University, 1978), and Joan P. Weitzman, "The Effect of Economic Restraints on Public-Sector Collective Bargaining: The Lessons of New York City," *Employee Relations Law Journal,* Vol. 2, No. 3 (Winter 1977), pp. 286-312.

18. According to the city's Office of Management and Budget, New York's municipal work force declined by about 38,000 full-time personnel during calendar year 1975, though it is not possible to distinguish precisely among layoffs, retirements,

and quits. The benefits referred to here included the traditional shorter work week during summer months ("summer hours"), guaranteed overtime (for sanitationmen), and payment (to firefighters) for one day per year for donating blood. These benefits were not actually forgone in 1975, but they were eliminated in subsequent rounds.

19. The teachers were on a different bargaining cycle than other municipal labor groups in 1975 and their contract with the Board of Education was scheduled to expire on September 9th of that year. In addition, intra-union rivalries, which featured major challenges to the leadership of the Patrolmen's Benevolent Association (PBA) in particular, prevented this organization from becoming a party to the 1975 Wage Deferral Agreement.

20. Specifically, the entire 6 percent increase was deferred for municipal employees earning $15,000 or more annually; 4 percent was deferred and 2 percent was granted to employees earning between $10,000 and $15,000 annually; and 2 percent was deferred and 4 percent was granted to employees earning less than $10,000 annually.

21. In November 1975, the state declared a moratorium on the repayment of all outstanding New York City notes, an action that eliminated any short-term restoration of investor confidence in the municipal government.

22. The police were party to this agreement but the teachers were not. Shortly after the agreement was signed, however, the teachers accepted its terms and conditions and incorporated them into their contract. This required a one-year extension of the contract (to 1978) and meant that it would expire in the same year as most other municipal labor agreements. This arrangement facilitated the teacher's union's membership in the 1978 coalition bargaining round, which will be discussed later in this paper.

23. For the 1976-78 contractual period, increases in employee salaries were to be paid as cost-of-living adjustments, referred to as Productivity COLAs. Although it was intended that these payments were to be funded principally through monies raised by productivity improvements, the EFCB wage policy stipulated that COLAs could be funded through "gains in productivity, reduction of fringe benefits or through other savings or revenues." Each bargaining unit was required to develop a program to fund Productivity COLAs. For more on this contractual arrangement, see Mary McCormick, "Productivity Issues," in Raymond D. Horton and Charles Brecher, eds., *Setting Municipal Priorities, 1980* (Montclair, N.J.: Allanheld Osmun, 1979), pp. 171-94.

24. The 1976 agreements, which were in effect for two years, provided for no direct wage increases. The increases scheduled for 1975 (based on 1974 labor agreements) were deferred in the manner described in footnote 20 above. As an incentive for union members to ratify the CEA, the agreement provided for immediate payment of the 1978 COLA ($567) and "timely" payment of the 1979 cash bonus ($750). Municipal employees could not be eligible for wage increases, however, until individual bargaining unit agreements were concluded.

25. It is too early now (early 1981) to provide a detailed analysis of the 1980 municipal labor negotiations, but the leading characteristics of these negotiations are discussed in this section.

26. Weber, "Stability and Change in the Structure of Collective Bargaining," p. 15.

27. As fiscal conditions become less severe, either labor or management may feel freer to move for a departure from coalition bargaining if it believes that such action will serve its particular interests. As noted earlier, a return to unit-by-unit bargaining for the 1980 municipal labor negotiations in New York City was initially advocated by the Koch administration. The fact of some managerial opposition to coalition bargaining serves as a reminder that coalition bargaining

needs to be distinguished from a union coalition. New York's municipal labor organizations may be able to maintain their coalition(s), but coalition bargaining requires the acquiescence of the other party to negotiations. Both parties must judge coalition bargaining to serve their respective interests; if management reaches a different position and sustains that position, then coalition bargaining may recede in New York City even while one or more union coalitions remain on the scene.

28. Weber, "Stability and Change in the Structure of Collective Bargaining," p. 18.
29. Perhaps the clearest example other than New York City of sustained coalition bargaining in the public sector—bargaining that has not been transported from the private sector and that involves several unions whose members represent various skill levels, occupations, and service categories—is in the local government sector of British Columbia. See Shirley B. Goldenberg, "Public-Sector Labor Relations in Canada," in Benjamin Aaron, Joseph R. Grodin, and James L. Stern, eds., *Public-Sector Bargaining* (Washington, D.C.: Bureau of National Affairs, 1979), pp. 254-91, especially pp. 272-74, and David Lewin and Shirley B. Goldenberg, "Public Sector Unionism in the United States and Canada," *Industrial Relations*, Vol. 19, No. 3 (Fall 1980), pp. 239-56.
30. David Lewin, Raymond D. Horton, and James W. Kuhn, *Collective Bargaining and Manpower Utilization in Big City Governments* (Montclair, N.J.: Allanheld Osmun, 1979), p. 9.
31. This task was partially undertaken by Weber, "Stability and Change in the Structure of Collective Bargaiing," pp. 15-22, who identified market forces, the nature of bargaining issues, representation factors, government policies, and power tactics in the bargaining process as determinants of bargaining structure in the private sector, but who did not specify (or test) how the interaction of these variables leads to a particular structural form. See, more recently, D. R. Deaton and P. B. Beaumont, "The Determinants of Bargaining Structure: Some Large Scale Survey Evidence for Britain," *British Journal of Industrial Relations*, Vol. 18, No. 2 (July 1980), pp. 199-216.
32. In San Francisco, for example, where organized labor in the public and private sectors is particularly strong, voters passed several referrenda in the late 1970s revising generous city pay formulas and cutting the salaries of city workers by as much as $4,500 annually. See Harry C. Katz, "Municipal Pay Determination: The Case of San Francisco," *Industrial Relations*, Vol. 18, No. 1 (Winter 1979), pp. 44-58, especially pp. 55-57. Another example is the recent adoption of laws by some state and local governments that permit selected groups of public employees to strike following the exhaustion of one or another impasse procedure. See David Lewin, "Public Sector Collective Bargaining and the Right to Strike," in A. Lawrence Chickering, ed., *Public Employee Unions: A Study of the Crisis in Public Sector Labor Relations* (San Francisco: Institute for Contemporary Studies, 1976), pp. 145-63.
33. On information sharing for bargaining purposes among public employers, see Feuille, et al., "Multiemployer Negotiations Among Local Governments," pp. 131-38. On employer coalitions in the hospital sector, see Peter Feuille, Charles Maxey, Hervey Juris, and Margaret Levi, "Determinants of Multi-Employer Bargaining in Metropolitan Hospitals," *Employee Relations Law Journal*, Vol. 4, No. 1 (Summer 1978), pp. 98-115.
34. See, for example, Stanley Benecki, "Municipal Expenditure Levels and Collective Bargaining," *Industrial Relations*, Vol. 17, No. 2 (May 1978), pp. 216-30, and Harry C. Katz, "The Municipal Budgetary Response to Changing Labor Costs: The Case of San Francisco," *Industrial and Labor Relations Review*, Vol. 32, No. 4 (July 1979), pp. 506-19.

35. That economic adversity in the *private* sector stimulates coalition bargaining is suggested by Alan M. Gustman and Martin Segal, "The Skilled-Unskilled Wage Differential in Construction," *Industrial and Labor Relations Review,* Vol. 27, No. 2 (January 1974), pp. 261-75.
36. Weber, "Stability and Change in the Structure of Collective Bargaining," p. 18. The notion of risk aversion among public employers and public unionists is developed in Henry S. Farber and Harry C. Katz, "Interest Arbitration, Outcomes and the Incentive to Bargain," *Industrial and Labor Relations Review,* Vol. 33, No. 1 (October 1979), pp. 55-63.
37. The quoted phrase is from Weber, "Stability and Change in the Structure of Collective Bargaining," p. 18.

4
Labor-Management Interactions

The text and readings of the first three chapters provide an overview of the economic, political, legal, organizational, and structural contexts in which public sector collective bargaining processes take place. With this background we can now turn to an examination of the interaction process itself. We begin by giving a brief overview of several important concepts that have been used to conceptualize and describe the process of bargaining in the private sector, and then suggest how these concepts need to be modified to fit the public sector context.

THE BARGAINING PROCESS

One of the most widely read theories of collective bargaining has been developed by Walton and McKersie.[1] In describing the bargaining process, they argue that it is important to distinguish between the "distributive" and "integrative" aspects of bargaining. The term distributive bargaining is used to describe interactions between labor and management over which a clear conflict of interest exists. Integrative bargaining, on the other hand, is used to describe interactions where the parties perceive a common interest. In distributive bargaining, the mode of behavior is adversarial and conflict oriented. The parties seek to manipulate information to mount the strongest arguments in favor of their case. Threats, bluffs, and other coercive tactics are considered to be a normal part of the process. In integrative bargaining, the mode of interaction is one of mutual problem solving, that is, openness of communication, joint search for solutions, and examination of alternatives.

The essential argument of the Walton and McKersie model is that all bargaining relationships contain a mix of distributive and potentially integrative issues. The integrative potential arises out of the interdependent nature of the employment relationship—the parties need each other for mutual survival and goal attainment. At the same time, there is an inherent conflict of interest in all employment relationships owing to the different economic interests of employees and employers and the structure of the employment relationship.

We might ask, how would this framework be applied to conceptualizing the bargaining process in the public sector? How does distributive bargaining work in the public sector, given the complexity of the legal, political, and organizational characteristics that have been discussed in the preceding chapters? Is there any potential for integrative bargaining in the public sector, or are the relationships too complex and too immature or unstable to allow joint problem-solving processes to work? The readings in this chapter are included in part to shed some light on these questions.

Since distributive bargaining involves a conflict of interest, the process is very directly affected by the relative bargaining power of the parties. Bargaining power has been described as the basic motivating force that provides the incentive for parties to compromise their positions in order to reach an agreement. Chamberlain and Kuhn provide one of the most widely accepted descriptions of how bargaining power induces parties to reach an agreement.[2] They argue that parties will agree when the "costs of disagreeing" with the proposal of the other party are greater than the "costs of agreeing" to the proposal. In the private sector, the primary costs are the economic ones associated with a strike; therefore, the threat of a strike is viewed as the major motivating force behind the bargaining process.

Thus, at the heart of distributive bargaining is the assumption that two parties are engaged in bilateral negotiations in which they use their willingness and ability to engage in or take a strike to induce their opponent to settle the dispute. In the public sector, this view of distributive bargaining must be modified somewhat because the interests at stake are much more diffuse and, consequently, the bilateral paradigm is less accurate. Instead, bargaining in the public sector has been conceptualized as "multilateral" in nature, that is, involving the interplay of multiple interest groups. In short, the process of distributive bargaining in the public sector must accommodate the interests of these multiple groups or factions before a settlement can be achieved. The process is further complicated by the political nature of the interest groups that share power in public sector bargaining. Therefore, in addition to the economic costs that could be imposed by a strike or a lockout, distributive bargaining in the public sector is affected by the political costs of agreement and disagreement.

The first reading presented in this section on the interaction process reflects the general premises outlined above regarding the nature of public sector bargaining. In it, Kochan develops the notion of multilateralism in the public sector and proposes some conditions under which this type of bargaining process emerges in local governments.[3]

While the literature on multilateral bargaining provides a picture of how distributive bargaining unfolds in the public sector, we have little research or understanding of the extent of integrative bargaining between public employers and public employee organizations. This paucity of research may reflect the reality of practice in government. Though there have been many calls for union-management cooperation in the public sector, especially with regard to the issue of productivity, there seems to be a great deal more talk than action in this area, and few careful and objective studies of the results of labor-management cooperative efforts in the public sector have been conducted.

We are fortunate, therefore, to have an intriguing description of an attempt at productivity bargaining in the public sector, written by Melvin

Osterman, the former Director of Employee Relations for the State of New York. Osterman's paper suggests a number of reasons why productivity bargaining, and perhaps union-management cooperation in general, is not widespread in the public sector. He describes the causes of a failure in productivity bargaining between the state of New York and the Civil Service Employees Association. His interpretation of this effort illustrates the complexity of the problems in successfully structuring an experiment in union-management cooperation in an environment characterized by a broad diffusion of power across multiple interest groups. In a short afterword to the Osterman paper, Robert B. McKersie adds some additional insight into why the New York State experiment failed by comparing the experiment to the two forms of productivity bargaining that have been popularized in previous literature on the subject, namely, the "buy out" and the "gain-sharing" approaches. His comments offer clear guidelines for other practitioners who may venture down this dangerous but essential road in the future.

Indeed, we follow his comments with a brief summary of a productivity bargaining agreement achieved in New York City in late 1980 to illustrate one of McKersie's points, namely, that a "buy out" strategy is more likely to work in large, politically complex jurisdictions in cases involving the introduction of new technology. This case is also instructive for the creative role played by a neutral third party in bringing about the agreement.

We then move to a discussion of some of the thorny legal problems associated with transferring the traditional private sector approach to the scope of issues addressed within the public sector bargaining process. Harry Edwards summarizes the traditional private sector doctrines and gives examples of some of the challenges they pose to public sector bargaining.

The final two papers in this chapter present field studies that show how the bargaining process actually has evolved in two different public sector arenas. McDonnell and Pascal describe how the bargaining process unfolds in a sample of fifteen school districts with diverse political, economic, and legal environments. An important part of their paper illustrates how the negotiations process is integrated into the larger political lobbying efforts of the parties. It also provides ample detail on the "nuts and bolts" of the process, that is, how the parties structure their bargaining teams, prepare for negotiations, and make trade-offs during the negotiation process.

In the final selection included in this chapter, Harry Katz provides an historical overview of the process of pay determination in San Francisco during the post-World War II period. This paper shows that one must view the "bargaining" process very broadly in the public sector if the goal is to understand how unions and public managers influence and set terms and conditions of employment. Despite the absence of a "formal" bargaining process in San Francisco, the mixture of union and other interest group lobbying, municipal ordinances, election politics, shifting public opinion, civil service procedures, public referenda, and strikes all served as important parts of the process by which wages and working conditions were set.

As Katz points out, regardless of the specific process used to make pay decisions, the outcomes were heavily influenced by the relative (and shifting) power of labor, opposing management and business interests, and changing public opinions. Thus this paper shows the power of historical analysis as a tool for analyzing both the dynamics of bargaining and the underlying sources of power at work in the public sector. As such, it points out the close link between our discussion of the process of bargaining contained in this chapter and the outcomes of bargaining discussed in Chapters 6 and 7.

In summary, the case study of San Francisco (and other case studies reported in the literature) illustrates a central theme in all of the papers in this chapter. That is, the nature of the bargaining process in a given public jurisdiction is to a large extent shaped by the broader political relationships among the major power holders in the community. Consequently, collective bargaining processes in the public sector are best viewed as a special subset of the larger political processes in the community.

FOOTNOTES

1. Richard E. Walton and Robert B. McKersie, *A Behavioral Theory of Labor Negotiations* (New York: McGraw-Hill, 1965).
2. Neil W. Chamberlain and James W. Kuhn, *Collective Bargaining*, 2nd ed. (New York: McGraw-Hill, 1965).
3. For an insightful examination of the political strategies employed by public sector unions to affect the interaction process, see Paul F. Gerhart, *Political Activity by Public Employee Organizations at the Local Level: Threat or Promise* (Chicago: International Personnel Management Association, 1974), especially chapters 3 and 4.

A Theory of Multilateral Collective Bargaining in City Governments*

Thomas A. Kochan

Although a vast descriptive and prescriptive literature concerning the nature of the collective bargaining process in the public sector has accumulated in recent years, little progress has been made toward developing theoretical models of these bargaining processes. This paper will address that issue by presenting a behavioral theory of the bargaining process in city governments.[1] In addition, the results of an empirical test of the theory based on data collected from 228 cities that bargain with locals of the International Association of Fire Fighters (IAFF) will also be presented.

The Institutional Context

Collective bargaining in city government can be viewed as a special type of decision-making process that has both inter- and intraorganizational aspects.

*Reprinted from *Industrial and Labor Relations Review*, 27 (July 1974), 525-542.

Traditionally, collective bargaining has been conceptualized as a bilateral process involving the interaction of representatives of employees on one side and management on the other.[2] With the growth of bargaining in the public sector, this traditional view of bargaining has come under serious attack. Since the organizational structures found in city governments have been designed to conform to the principle of separation of powers,[3] a number of semiautonomous management officials often share decision-making power over issues traditionally raised by unions in collective bargaining. Because power is shared by both administrative and elected officials, it has been argued that what often begins as a "variant of private sector bargaining" ends up by becoming an extension of machine politics.[4]

The basic thesis of the model tested in this paper is that these political and organizational characteristics of city government lead to the development of a multilateral bargaining process. Although others have discussed this type of bargaining in the public sector,[5] this paper is believed to be the first to present a formal theory of multilateral bargaining in which the concept is operationally defined and to test empirically several hypotheses concerning the determinants of this form of bargaining.

The Concept of Multilateral Bargaining

Multilateral bargaining is defined as a process of negotiation in which more than two distinct parties are involved in such a way that a clear dichotomy between the employee and management organizations does not exist. In the language of game theory, the concepts of bilateral and multilateral bargaining correspond to two-party and n-party games, respectively. As Caplow has demonstrated, the difference between a two-party and a three-party game reflects a basic qualitative difference between the types of processes that take place within each game.[6] The involvement of any more than three parties, however, is seen as merely an extension of a three-party process.

In this model, it will be the degree of multilateral bargaining experienced in a city that will serve as the dependent variable. The complete model of the bargaining process that was developed and tested in this research project consists of two stages. The first stage addresses the development of internal management conflict. It proposes that internal conflict is a function of the diversity of goals and the dispersion of power within the city management structure. The second stage then relates internal management conflict and a number of other management and union characteristics to the occurrence of multilateral bargaining. It is the second stage of the model that will be discussed in this paper.

A number of researchers have attempted to apply the general concept of multilateral bargaining to the context of local government labor relations and to refine its definition to fit this institutional context. The most basic problem in developing an operational measure of the concept is determining the identity of the parties to the process. McLennan and Moskow have defined a party in this context as any individual or collective body that is capable of imposing a cost on at least one of the other direct parties to the agreement.[7] Those authors were primarily concerned with the impact of interest groups in the community on the bargaining process, however, and thus they did not need to be concerned with identifying the "direct parties" to the process. Juris and Feuille point out that another type of multilateral bargaining is common in city governments—namely, the involvement of what they call "non-labor relations city officials" in the bargaining process.[8] Although these two descriptions suggest that the involvement of both community groups and certain city officials should be included in a definition and therefore a measure of multilateral bargaining, there is still the problem of distinguishing between labor relations and non-labor relations city officials. In order to resolve this problem, characteristics distinguishing bilateral from multilateral bargaining processes must be specified. Unfortunately, this in itself is a problem, since the collective bargaining literature does not provide a clearly defined set of behaviors that are consistent with a bilateral process. Consequently, some assumptions about bilateral bargaining need to be made in order to develop a measure of multilateral bargaining.

It is assumed that a bilateral bargaining process is one in which a formally designated negotiator or negotiating team represents the employer in direct negotiations with a corresponding negotiator or negotiating team representing the employee organization. The purpose of these two individuals or groups is to reach a tentative bargaining agreement. When an agreement is reached, the negotiating representatives take the package back to their respective principals for ratification. An extremely important assumption here is that all interactions between management officials and the employee organization are channeled through the formally designated negotiators. In addition, the negotiators are assumed to serve as the public spokesmen for the parties on bargaining issues.

This is obviously an oversimplification of the way collective bargaining works in any context, but this description is useful as a base line in testing any model that attempts to explain departures from the conventional bilateral pattern of behavior. Thus, the specific types of behavior used in this study to measure the extent of multilateral bargaining in a city are those that clearly violate this assumed pattern of bilateral behavior.[9] Because of the importance of this concept to the model and to bargaining theory in general, the specific types of behavior used to characterize it in this context are described in detail in a later section of the paper.

Determinants of Multilateral Bargaining

Now that the concept of multilateral bargaining has been delineated, its major determinants can be hypothesized. The major proposition in the model is that *the greater the extent of internal conflict among management officials, the more likely that multilateral bargaining will take place.*

To understand why internal management conflict is proposed as the most important cause of multilateral bargaining, it is useful to think of the relationship among city management officials in terms of a coalition. In essence, for bargaining to be bilateral, the management officials who share decision-making authority must coalesce and act as a single unit *vis a vis* the union. If the management coalition does not form or breaks apart at some point during the internal decision-making process so that different officials openly favor different positions on bargaining-related issues, internal conflict occurs. When internal conflict occurs, management officials have two basic options: (1) to resolve their differences internally and then allow the designated management negotiators to represent their mutual interests in bargaining with the union, or (2) to represent their interests separately, by directly intervening in the bargaining process. If they choose the latter option and internal conflicts are carried over into the bargaining arena, either because of tactics of the employee organization or on the initiative of management officials, the necessary condition for multilateral bargaining—the involvement of more than two distinct parties—is fulfilled.[10] Typically, in this type of situation, factions can be identified within management that (1) advocate a position more favorable to the employee organization on an issue, or (2) support a bargaining position that is inconsistent with the positions of either the employee organization or the designated management negotiators.

Although the model proposes that internal conflict is the basic determinant of multilateral bargaining, it also assigns a role of influence to several other variables. For example, it is plausible to assume that the degree of multilateral bargaining would be affected by the extent of management commitment to negotiations. Although most cities that have an established bargaining relationship with their employers have set up formal procedures that specify bilateral negotiations, not all city officials are likely to be equally committed to using these channels as a mechanism for decision making on employment relations matters.[11] Hildebrand suggests that a basic reason for this aversion is that elected officials experience role conflicts when faced with the task of representing the interests of their constituents and acting as a member of a management that is engaged in negotiations with a union.[12] Furthermore, the introduction of collective bargaining into an organization necessarily requires some shifting of the locus of decision making and is bound to be met with resistance from those who feel threatened by such shifts. This is especially true in city governments because of the strong role civil service commissions have traditionally played in making employment relations policy and the interest that those responsible for these functions have in maintaining their autonomy.[13]

Thus, city officials who are not committed to collective bargaining are likely to seek alternative mechanisms for policy making and, by doing so, to reduce the likelihood that bargaining will remain within the formal bilateral channels. It is therefore proposed that *the weaker the commitment of management decision makers to collective bargaining, the more likely that multilateral bargaining will occur.*

Another variable that would influence the level of multilateral bargaining is the conflict resolution policies of management. Some cities have recognized the problems inherent in coordinating the roles of the various management officials in bargaining and have developed policies for achieving the commitment of all relevant decision makers prior to the beginning of negotiations. Hildebrand labeled such policies as mechanisms for obtaining a "family understanding" concerning the procedural and substantive issues related to bargaining. For example, New York and Baltimore and a few other large cities have set up labor policy committees composed of city officials from the various decision-making units within the management structure, and a growing number of cities have established specialized labor relations departments. To the extent that such procedures are successful, a kind of co-opted commitment of the management officials is achieved, and the ability of the parties to influence decisions outside of the formal negotiation process is constrained. Consequently it is suggested that *the greater the number of internal conflict resolution procedures that exist, the less likely that multilateral bargaining will occur.*

Union Political Strength

Up to this point, only city management characteristics that lead to multilateral bargaining have been considered. A number of characteristics of the union involved, however, are also likely to have an important effect on the type of bargaining that occurs. Since multilateral bargaining is basically an outgrowth of the political relationships that exist among city officials, most of the union characteristics that are proposed as determinants of multilateral bargaining reflect some aspect of the union's political strength.

Political pressure tactics by unions, for instance, can produce situations of multilateral bargaining. Chamberlain and Kuhn have suggested that an alert union will be aware of differences among the decision preferences of management officials and will devise tactics to take advantage of these internal differences.[14] In the public sector, the high level of publicity given rivalries among city officials should increase this awareness of employee representatives. As an alternative to engaging in confrontation tactics such as a strike, union leaders might attempt to influence the outcome of bargaining by inducing officials with interests similar to their own to actively represent their position in the management policy-making process. The use of such tactics has been widely discussed in the public sector bargaining literature. Consequently, it is suggested that *the more frequently that employee organizations use political pressure tactics, the more likely that multilateral bargaining will occur.*

For a union to be successful in inducing city officials who are not part of the formal negotiation process to actively support its demands, it must possess sufficient political resources to influence these city officials, or it must feel that the constituency preferences of the officials are similar enough to the union's interests so that the officials will react favorably to the union demands. This type of a relationship has been thoroughly discussed in the political science literature, as the concept of "political access."[15] Thus, it is suggested that *the more political access the union has to city officials, the more likely that multilateral bargaining will occur.*

These three union variables are likely to be highly interrelated. A union is not likely to attempt to apply political pressure during negotiations if it does not have access to city officials, and if it has not been instrumental in putting and maintaining elected officials in office, it is not likely to enjoy access to them. Since these are three distinct sets of union activities or characteristics that help one understand the *process* by which elected officials are motivated to become involved in the bargaining process, however, it will be useful to measure their separate impact on multilateral bargaining before assessing their combined effects.

One final union tactic that needs to be incorporated into the model of multilateral bargaining concerns the effects of pressures applied by a union when an impasse is reached in negotiations. It has already been suggested that if the union chooses to apply political pressure during negotiations, multilateral bargaining is more likely to result. The effects of tactics designed to apply pressures similar to those of a strike—such as a work slowdown, a "sickout," or picketing—are more difficult to predict. For example, city officials may perceive strike pressure to be an external threat and respond to it by resolving their differences. This type of behavior would be consistent with the Walton and McKersie model of intraorganizational bargaining.[17] McLennan and Moskow, however, suggest that exactly the opposite is likely to result.[18] They argue that multilateral bargaining is likely to increase as negotiations move from the initial discussion to the hard bargaining and impasse stages, since the disagreements become more visible to the public during these stages and interest groups become activated.

Throughout this discussion of the nature of the bargaining process in city government, the importance of the "politics" of the relationships both among city officials and with the union has been stressed. Consequently, it is expected in this study that the pressure to assume their roles as political leaders motivates city officials to respond by becoming active participants in bargaining when a visible impasse is reached in negotiations. It is thus proposed that *the greater the number of visible impasse pressure tactics that a union uses in negotiations, the more likely that multilateral bargaining will occur.*

Sample and Methodology

The research design employed in this analysis might best be described as a cross-sectional comparative field study or, in more formal terms, as an *ex post facto* correlation design. Because of the cross-sectional nature of the design, the data are not capable of providing a strict test of the causal propositions presented in the model. This limitation is dealt with by clearly specifying the theory tested and then analyzing the data accordingly. Thus, these data can only provide a test of the plausibility of the relationships posited in the model and can only disconfirm rather than confirm the theory.

Data were collected by means of a series of mailed questionnaires sent to all 380 cities (in forty-two states) that had a formal bargaining relationship with the IAFF in 1971. Questionnaires were sent to the following sets of management officials in each city: (1) management negotiators, (2) city managers or mayors, (3) fire chiefs, (4) a random sample of three city council members, and (5) members of the civil service commission with jurisdiction over the fire department. Data were solicited from all of these city officials in order to increase the reliability of the measures of the variables in the model for each city. The responses from officials in each city were then combined to obtain an overall city score for each variable. In addition, a questionnaire designed to measure union tactics and behavior was sent to a representative of the IAFF local in each city.

Usable questionnaires were returned by 65 percent of the management negotiators, 70 percent of the fire chiefs, 27 percent of the other city officials, and 59 percent of the union representatives. From these responses, enough data were obtained to include 228 cities in the analysis. (The criterion for including a city was responses from two or more management officials.) This provided an overall response rate of approximately 60 percent. A comparison of the characteristics of respondent and nonrespondent cities showed that the cities that responded are slightly smaller and pay slightly higher wages and fringe benefits than those that did not respond. In addition, a comparison of wages and working conditions in 1972 in the 228 cities used in this study and in 667 cities covered by an IAFF wage survey showed that mean wages and fringe benefits were significantly higher in the study sample than in the larger sample.

Measure of Multilateral Bargaining

Table 1 presents the results of applying an index composed of five items that is used as an overall measure of the relative amount of multilateral bargaining that occurs in city governments bargaining with IAFF locals. The city officials who were surveyed in each city were asked to rate on a seven-point scale the extent to which a number of activities had occurred in the past, in the course of bargaining with the Fire Fighters. An overall index was obtained by summing the city responses on the five items.

It has been argued that multilateral bargaining can result from either the involvement of city management officials who are not part of the formal city negotiating team or from the involvement of external community interest groups in bargaining. Only one item is included to assess the extent to which community interest groups become involved in the process, since fire fighter bargaining issues usually have a less visible impact on the community than, for example, the issues discussed in bargaining with teachers or with police. City officials were asked to rate the extent to which "interest groups in the community become involved in bargaining." The mean response to this item was 2.20 on the seven-point scale.

TABLE 1
Means and Standard Deviations of Measures of Multilateral Bargaining and Total Index* (n = 228)

	Mean	Standard Deviation
City officials took actions outside negotiations that affected the bargaining leverage of city negotiators	2.67	1.20
Employee representatives discussed bargaining demands with city officials who are not on the formal bargaining team	3.85	1.29
Interest groups in the community became involved in bargaining	2.20	1.00
City officials overturned or failed to apply agreements reached in negotiations	2.33	0.96
Elected officials intervened in an attempt to mediate an impasse	2.69	1.27
Total multilateral bargaining index	13.73	4.16

*Measures were constructed from ratings by city officials on a seven-point scale.

The other four items used in the construction of the multilateral bargaining index attempt to measure the extent of multilateral bargaining that arises from the actions of some city officials. One of the assumptions underlying the definition of bilateral bargaining is that members of the two parties involved channel all communications to the opposing party through their official representatives and do not engage in actions that are not sanctioned by their spokesmen. One of the most frequent complaints made by city labor negotiators, however, is that the union is constantly making "end runs" around them to other city officials and obtaining concessions not granted in negotiations. For example, in Madison, Wisconsin in 1969, the IAFF local was successful in obtaining a recommendation for a return to parity with police salaries from a Civil Service Board that it was not able to obtain through direct negotiations with the city negotiating team. In Janesville, Wisconsin in 1970, a similar situation occurred in which the city negotiator and the IAFF local had reached an impasse and the union was successful in getting several members of the city council to call the city negotiator to a special meeting with the union in an effort to obtain the essential salary demands that the negotiator had been opposing. Thus, by doing so, the negotiator's bargaining leverage was considerably weakened.[19]

Still a third variant on this same pattern occurs when an elected official (usually the mayor) attempts to intervene when negotiations reach an impasse in an attempt to mediate the dispute. This normally turns the process into a multilateral one, since it involves a member of the management organization attempting to act as a neutral third party rather than as a supporter of the management position. By doing so, the city is no longer able to act as a single entity, since the city negotiator or negotiating team is forced to respond to the mediating party as a new interest. Consequently, both the union and the city negotiators respond to this added party in an attempt to form a coalition against their negotiating opponents.[20]

These activities represent multilateral bargaining through involvement of non-labor relations city officials during the course of negotiations. There are a number of instances, however, in which the city and the union agree to a settlement, but some other city official then overturns or fails to implement the agreement. An example of this occurred in the Madison study: the city agreed to an amnesty clause in a strike-settling agreement with the union, but the Police and Fire Commission later disregarded it by suspending the union president for his leadership role in the strike. In the Janesville study, the city negotiator agreed to a cost-of-living wage increment, but the city council later refused to include enough money in the budget to implement the agreement because of its opposition to this particular clause.[21]

In one of the cities in the current study, a similar situation occurred. The city and the union agreed in negotiations to a change in the job classification of a certain fire department position. When the Civil Service Commission was later asked to implement this change, however, it refused to do so since it felt the change was unwarranted. Most of the examples of this type of multilateral bargaining involve situations in which either civil service commissions or the city department heads are unwilling to abide by what was agreed to and ratified by the city in bargaining. A few cases of this type also involve a rejection by the city council of clauses agreed to by the negotiators or a mayor's veto of agreements ratified by the council.

To measure the extent to which these types of activities occur in the course of bargaining, city officials were asked the extent (on a one- to seven-point scale) to which each of the following had occurred in fire fighter bargaining in the past: "City officials took actions outside of negotiations that affected the bargaining leverage of city negotiators"; "Employee representatives discussed bargaining demands with city officials who are not on the formal bargaining team"; "City officials overturned or failed to apply agreements reached in negotiations"; and "Elected officials intervened in an attempt to mediate an impasse."

The data in Table 1 show that the type of multilateral bargaining that occurs most frequently in fire fighter bargaining in these cities is the end run variety. In addition, the involvement of elected officials at the time of impasse and actions by city officials that affect the bargaining leverage of management negotiators also seem to be relatively frequent phenomena. The failure to implement bargaining agreements and the involvement of community interest groups are less common.

In Table 2, the intercorrelations among the items used to measure multilateral bargaining are presented along with the item-to-total-score correlations. In order to form a reliable index, these items should be positively intercorrelated and highly correlated with the total score. The items clearly meet these criteria. Cronbach's alpha, a measure of index reliability,[22] is .79, clearly indicating that these items combine to form a highly reliable and internally consistent index of multilateral bargaining.

Measurement of Independent Variables

Internal management conflict. Three measures of internal conflict were obtained. City officials were asked to rate on a seven-point scale (a) the

TABLE 2
Intercorrelations Among Multilateral Bargaining Index Items* (n = 228)

Measure	1	2	3	4	5	6
1. Bargaining leverage jeopardized	1.00					
2. End runs occurred	.61	1.00				
3. Interest groups involved	.38	.37	1.00			
4. Contract not implemented	.31	.50	.27	1.00		
5. Elected officials intervened	.49	.36	.33	.41	1.00	
6. Total index	.78	.81	.60	.61	.78	1.00
Total index-item corrected correlation**	.66	.71	.46	.48	.57	

*All correlations in this table are significant at the .01 level. Cronbach's alpha = .79.

**This is the corrected item-to-total-index correlation. It corrects for the bias in the item-to-total-index correlation that occurs because the total score on the index is partially determined by the item. This corrected correlation was computed in the Itempack program for item analysis of the Data and Computations Center, University of Wisconsin.

amount of conflict they experienced with other city officials in general in making bargaining decisions; (b) the amount of conflict they experienced specifically with each set of other management officials (mayors or city managers, city council members, labor negotiators, fire chiefs, and civil service commissioners); and (c) the amount of conflict that they experienced over decision making on five sets of bargaining issues (wages and fringe benefits, departmental work rules, grievance procedures, management rights, and discipline and discharge issues). From the data on conflict among officials and across issues, indices were constructed by summing the aggregated city responses for each of the five items. Cronbach's alpha coefficient is .62 for conflict among officials and .68 for conflict across issues. Each of the three measures of conflict is treated separately in the analysis.

Management commitment to bargaining. City officials were asked to rate on a seven-point scale the extent to which they felt collective bargaining is the most appropriate way to make decisions on the five sets of issues described above (wages, work rules, etc.). A total score for management commitment was obtained by summing the city score for each item. Cronbach's alpha for this index is .68.

Internal management conflict resolution. The chief management negotiator was asked to indicate whether the city had no policy, an informal policy, or a formal written policy for resolving intra-management conflicts on (a) who participates in negotiations, (b) how agreements are ratified by the city, and (c) jurisdictional conflicts between the bargaining process and the civil service commission and conflicts over the substantive bargaining issues. Again, a total score for each city was obtained by summing the ratings assigned to each item. Cronbach's alpha for this index is .64.

Union political pressure tactics. City officials were asked to rate on a seven-point scale the extent to which the Fire Fighters (a) appealed directly to the mayor or city manager, (b) appealed directly to city council members, and (c) attempted to use publicity in the community in order to achieve their bargaining demands. An overall index of political pressure tactics was then obtained by summing the scores on these three items. Cronbach's alpha for this index is .32.

Union election involvement. The union respondent in each city was asked to check whether or not the union engaged in the following activities: (a) endorsing candidates for mayor, (b) endorsing candidates for city council, (c) contributing to the campaigns of city officials, and (d) contributing manpower to city election campaigns. For each item, a score of one was assigned if the union reported that it engaged in the activity; zero was assigned otherwise. An overall election involvement index was obtained by summing the scores on the four items. Cronbach's alpha for this index is .69.

Union impasse pressure tactics. Similarly, the union representatives were asked to indicate which of the following tactics the local had employed: (a) work slowdowns, (b) "sickouts," and (c) picketing. A score of one was assigned for each of these pressure tactics if the union had used it, and zero was assigned otherwise. An overall index was obtained by summing these values. Cronbach's alpha for this index is .50.

Union political access. The city labor negotiator was asked to rate the degree to which the IAFF local possessed political influence with the mayor or city manager, the city council, the fire chief, and the civil service commission. These influence scores were to be summed for each official in order to arrive at an overall access measure. The items, however, did not meet the criterion of internal homogeneity, and thus the overall index was not used in the analysis. Instead, union influence with the city council alone was used as the measure of access.

Zero Order Correlations

Table 3 presents the zero order correlations of each of the independent variables with the multilateral bargaining index, and Table 4 presents the results of a series of multiple regression equations computed to estimate the combined effect of all the hypothesized determinants of multilateral bargaining. Both the correlations and the regression results are presented here in order to provide a complete assessment of both the relative magnitude of the associations of each independent variable and their net effects, holding constant the effects of intercorrelations among the independent variables.

More specifically, Table 3 presents the correlation matrix showing both the intercorrelations among the hypothesized determinants of multilateral bargaining and (in line 8) their correlations with the multilateral bargaining index. The correlations of the three measures of internal management conflict with multilateral bargaining are: .52 for conflict among city officials in general, .44 for conflict across issues, and .34 for conflict with specific groups of city officials. These correlations are all significant well beyond the one percent level and thus provide very strong support for the major proposition in the bargaining model—that internal conflict is the key determinant of multilateral bargaining.

The hypothesis concerning the impact of management commitment is not supported by the data. The .17 ($p<.05$) correlation between management commitment and multilateral bargaining shows that more multilateral bargaining takes places in cities where the management officials are more highly committed to the use of collective bargaining for determining employment relations policies. This suggests that multilateral bargaining is clearly not a transitional phenomenon that disappears once city officials accept collective bargaining and gain some experience with the process. This "lack of experience" argument is often found in the prescriptive discussions of the bargaining process in the public sector.

The existence of procedures for resolving internal management conflicts does not appear to reduce the amount of multilateral bargaining. The correlation is in the hypothesized direction, but is very weak ($-.06$). Thus, the mere existence of procedural devices for coordination does not appear to be sufficient for reducing the general level of multilateral bargaining.

TABLE 3

Intercorrelations Among the Hypothesized Determinants of Multilateral Bargaining and Their Correlations with the Multilateral Bargaining Index (n = 228)

Independent Variable	1a	1b	1c	2	3	4	5	6	7	8
1. Internal management conflict										
1a. Conflict among city officials in general	1.00									
1b. Conflict across issues	.39	1.00								
1c. Conflict with specific groups of city officials	.29	.41	1.00							
2. Management commitment	.12	.17	.12	1.00						
3. Management internal conflict resolution	−.06	.03	.05	−.05	1.00					
4. Union political pressure tactics	.25	.21	.18	.07	.05	1.00				
5. Union election involvement	.17	.03	.19	−.03	−.10	.21	1.00			
6. Union impasse pressure tactics	.21	.11	.02	.08	−.08	.19	.27	1.00		
7. Union political access	.15	.17	.13	.08	−.09	.20	.19	.19	1.00	
8. Multilateral bargaining index	.52	.44	.34	.17	−.06	.34	.21	.32	.19	1.00

$r \geqslant .12$ is significant at the .05 level.
$r \geqslant .18$ is significant at the .01 level.

The strong positive correlations obtained for union political pressure tactics, impasse pressure tactics, and degree of access to the city council support the hypotheses concerning their effects on multilateral bargaining. In no case, however, do these correlations exceed the correlations between internal conflict and multilateral bargaining. They are all significant, however, at the .01 level or above.

The correlations between the use of political pressure in bargaining by the union and the occurrence of multilateral bargaining provide strong support for an underlying argument throughout this research—namely, that there is a strong relationship between the political process in cities and the bargaining process. These data clearly show that one cannot understand the nature of the bargaining process in city governments without first assessing the nature of the political relationships among the parties involved. The high positive correlation between the use of strike pressure tactics (slowdowns, "sickouts," and picketing) and multilateral bargaining provides strong evidence that when city officials are in a position of choosing between their roles as management officials involved in a bargaining situation and their roles as elected politicians responsive to their constituencies, their roles as politicians take precedence.

Regression Analysis

In order to assess the combined efforts of these determinants of multilateral bargaining, three regression equations were computed; each equation included one of the three measures of internal management conflict along with the other management and union variables. Table 4 presents the results of these regressions. The models presented were all linear regression models.

The data in Table 4 confirm the finding in Table 3 that internal management conflict is probably the most important determinant of multilateral bargaining, since the regression coefficients for the internal conflict measures remain highly significant even when all the other management and union characteristics are entered into the equation. Thus, it appears that the strong zero order correlations in Table 3, between internal management conflict and multilateral bargaining, are not a result of an intercorrelation with some other variable in the model.

The addition of the other two management characteristics, commitment to bargaining and internal conflict resolution procedures, increases the

TABLE 4
Standardized Regression Coefficients for the Hypothesized Determinants of Multilateral Bargaining (t-values in parentheses, n = 228)

Independent Variable	Equations		
Conflict among city officials in general	.402		
	(7.03)***		
Conflict with specific groups of city officials		.264	
		(4.43)***	
Conflict across issues			.365
			(6.37)***
Management commitment	.110	.124	.114
	(2.02)**	(2.17)**	(2.07)
Management internal conflict resolution	−.022	.056	−.085
	(0.40)	(−0.97)	(−1.52)
Union political pressure tactics	.189	.232	.208
	(3.28)***	(3.87)***	(3.58)***
Union election involvement	.054	.042	.101
	(0.94)	(0.68)	(1.75)*
Union impasse pressure tactics	.168	.239	.197
	(.293)***	(3.96)***	(3.41)***
Union political access	.039	.040	.001
	(0.70)	(0.68)	(0.20)
R^2	.37	.29	.35

*Significant at the .10 level.
**Significant at the .05 level.
***Significant at the .01 level.

amount of variance explained by only between one and two percent in the three models. By adding the union variables to the model, however, the amount of variance explained increases 13 percent for the model using general management conflict and conflict across issues and 15 percent for the model using conflict with specific groups of officials. Together, the union and management determinants of multilateral bargaining included in this model explained 37 percent of the variance using general conflict, 29 percent of the variance using conflict with specific officials, and 35 percent of the variance using conflict across issues.

Since there are high intercorrelations among the union variables included in the model, it is not surprising that some of the regression coefficients fail to remain significant when all these variables are entered. Those that do remain significant are political pressure and impasse pressure tactics. The results on the impasse pressure variable suggest that city officials are somewhat reluctant to become involved in bargaining—i.e., behavior by city officials that leads to multilateral bargaining seems to be more a *response* to union pressures than an autonomous desire to become actively involved in bargaining. The positive association between visible impasse tactics and multilateral bargaining supports the McLennan and Moskow contention that multilateral bargaining tends to reach a peak after an impasse in negotiations occurs.

Control Variables

In any empirical study that uses a nonexperimental design to test its hypotheses, questions arise over whether some alternative variable can account for the correlations observed between the independent and dependent variables. To resolve this question, a number of control variables were included in this study. Since none of these variables showed a strong relationship with multilateral bargaining, they were not entered in the regression analyses presented in the previous section. The correlations between these control variables and the multilateral bargaining index are presented in Table 5.

TABLE 5
**Correlations Between Control Variables and the Multilateral Bargaining Index
(n = 228)**

Control Variable	Correlation
Comprehensiveness of bargaining law	−.05
Factfinding procedure in the law	−.02
Compulsory arbitration procedure in the law	.06
Age of the bargaining relationship	.13
Years of private sector experience of management negotiator	−.12
Years of public sector experience of management negotiator	.02
Professionalism of management negotiator	.01
City population	.11

$r \geqslant .13$ is significant at the .05 level.
$r \geqslant .18$ is significant at the .01 level.

These control variables were chosen in order to test several aspects of the "conventional wisdom" that is presented in the literature on public sector bargaining. It should be noted that it has seldom, if ever, been explicitly argued that the factors discussed below are causes of multilateral bargaining. Implicit in much of the prescriptive literature, however, is the argument that public sector bargaining is an abnormal deviation from the way collective bargaining "ought to" work and that as soon as the parties gain experience with the process, or public policies formalize and regulate the bargaining process, negotiations will conform more closely to the private sector (presumably bilateral) model.

To test the argument that comprehensive legislation promoting collective bargaining for public employees will encourage negotiations to become more formalized and therefore conform more closely to a bilateral model, an index was developed to measure the comprehensiveness of the law governing bargaining between city governments and fire fighters in each state. Its correlation with multilateral bargaining in these cities is shown to be only −.05.

A few states have attempted to deal more directly with the problem of dispersion of power within management (on the assumption that dispersion of power is the key cause of multilateral bargaining) by spelling out in the state law who management is and further specifying how the bargaining process should operate. Specifically, New York and Connecticut have provisions in their laws identifying the executive as the management representative in bargaining. If these laws are having an effect on the bargaining process, there should be less multilateral bargaining in these states than in the country as a whole, and also the model should overpredict the extent of multilateral bargaining in these states because this provision in their laws is not accounted for in the regression equations. Neither of these results occurred. The average score on the multilateral bargaining index is 14.4 for all cities studied in New York State, 13.2 for all cities in Connecticut, and 13.7 for all 228 cities studied, indicating that neither of these states deviates significantly from the national average. Furthermore, an examination of the residuals of the regression equations showed no tendency to overpredict multilateral bargaining in the cities in these two states.[23]

It might also be argued that the existence of more formalized impasse resolution procedures in the state law should reduce the amount of multilateral bargaining. Again, however, this is not the case—the correlation between multilateral bargaining and the existence of factfinding procedures is −.02, and between multilateral bargaining and the existence of compulsory arbitration procedures, it is .06. Consequently, the extent of multilateral bargaining is affected little by the nature of the laws governing public sector bargaining in each state.

Another argument often found in the literature is that one of the reasons for the lack of bilateralism in the public sector is the lack of "maturity" in the bargaining relationships. Those suggesting this argue that as soon as the parties learn how collective bargaining is "supposed to" work, public sector bargaining will conform to the bilateral pattern that characterizes private sector negotiations. To test this alternative explanation, a correlation was computed between the number of years the city and union have been

158

negotiating labor agreements and the city's score on the multilateral bargaining index. This correlation is .13 ($p<.05$), indicating that the more mature the bargaining relationship between the parties, the *more* multilateral bargaining that occurs. This finding not only rejects the "lack of maturity" hypothesis, it also reinforces the view that multilateralism is not a transitional phenomenon growing out of the parties' lack of expertise and is instead a natural outgrowth of the institutional context of city government decision making.

The same type of reasoning concerning the lack of expertise or understanding of how collective bargaining "ought to" operate led to the examination of the relationship between multilateral bargaining and the extent to which management is represented by professionals with prior experience in labor relations. Again, negative correlations with experience and professionalism variables would be expected if this argument is valid. Yet, Table 5 shows the correlations with the multilateral bargaining index to be .01 for a measure of professionalism (number of professional labor relations associations to which the negotiator belongs), .02 for the number of years of experience the management negotiator has in public sector labor relations, and $-.12$ for the number of years of private sector experience that the management negotiator has. Thus, the only professionalism variable that seems to have any negative relation with multilateral bargaining is the amount of private sector experience the management negotiator brings to city government bargaining, and this effect is slight.

Another control variable that was examined was city size. Since the bargaining process is generally thought to be more formalized in larger cities and since the larger cities have been bargaining longer than smaller cities, it was felt that size of city might be negatively correlated with multilateral bargaining—again based on the "lack of maturity" argument. The correlation between size of city and multilateral bargaining is .11, however, and so again the evidence does not support the alternative explanation.

In summary, none of the control variables show strong enough correlations with multilateral bargaining to provide an alternative explanation for the findings presented in Tables 3 and 4.

Conclusions and Implications

This analysis has demonstrated that variations in the extent of multilateral bargaining within a large sample of cities are systematically related to a number of union and management characteristics. These findings show quite clearly that the nature of the collective bargaining process in city governments is a natural outgrowth of the political context in which it operates. The close relationship hypothesized in the bargaining model between the political conflicts that occur within city governments and the nature of the union-city bargaining process received strong support. The importance of the political relationship among the parties was further reinforced by the correlation found between the political strength of the unions and multilateral bargaining.

Perhaps the model and empirical evidence presented here will put to rest the belief that the type of bargaining often found in city governments is an abnormal deviation from "normal collective bargaining" that will be

159

eliminated as the parties and the laws under which they operate become more sophisticated. Such an argument simply ignores the underlying forces that influence the bargaining process in the public sector. As the evidence presented here suggests, the process responds to the nature of the relationships that exist among the diverse interests that share power over bargaining issues.

Finally, it is hoped that this exercise has shown the applicability of the techniques of theory construction, behavioral measurement strategies, and quantitative analysis to an area of collective bargaining theory. The strategy employed was first to develop an empirically based understanding of the process by means of case study research. This provided the foundation and the general framework for developing the propositions of the model. Then, by formally developing a behavioral model of the process and employing a comparative research design, the model was put to an empirical test.

Hopefully, others will join in similar efforts to expand and improve the model presented here as well as to develop models of the collective bargaining process along other dimensions of interest. By doing so, the overly descriptive and prescriptive orientation of collective bargaining research can be changed to one in which a balance is struck among theoretical, empirical, and prescriptive orientations.

Footnotes

1. The central concepts and propositions in the model were derived from two earlier case studies of collective bargaining in Madison and Janesville, Wisconsin. The present study, therefore, is an effort to expand on, formalize, and test the hypotheses suggested by the results of these case studies. See Thomas A. Kochan, *City Employee Bargaining with a Divided Management* (Madison, Wis.: Industrial Relations Research Institute, 1971).

2. See, for example, F. Y. Edgeworth, *Mathematical Physics* (London: Paul, 1881); Neil W. Chamberlain and James W. Kuhn, *Collective Bargaining*, 2nd ed. (New York: McGraw-Hill, 1965); Richard E. Walton and Robert B. McKersie, *A Behavioral Theory of Labor Negotiations* (New York: McGraw-Hill, 1965); or Myron Joseph, "Collective Bargaining and Industrial Relations Theory," in Gerald G. Somers, ed., *Essays in Industrial Relations Theory* (Ames, Iowa: Iowa State University Press, 1969).

3. Edward C. Banfield and James Q. Wilson, *City Politics* (New York: Vintage Books, 1963).

4. George H. Hildebrand, "The Public Sector," in John T. Dunlop and Neil W. Chamberlain, eds., *Frontiers of Collective Bargaining* (New York: Harper and Row, 1967), pp. 125-154.

5. For one of the earliest theoretical statements on this issue, see Kenneth McLennan and Michael H. Moskow, "Multilateral Bargaining in the Public Sector," *Proceedings of the Twenty-First Annual Winter Meeting* (Madison, Wis.: Industrial Relations Research Association, 1968), pp. 34-41. For a further discussion, see Michael H. Moskow, J. Joseph Loewenberg, and Edward J. Kozaria, *Collective Bargaining in Public Employment* (New York: Random House, 1970).

6. Theodore Caplow, *Two Against One: Coalitions in Triads* (Englewood Cliffs, N.J.: Prentice-Hall, 1968).

7. McLennan and Moskow, "Multilateral Bargaining in the Public Sector," p. 31.

8. Hervey A. Juris and Peter Feuille, *Police Unionism: Power and Impact in Public Sector Bargaining* (Lexington, Mass.: D. C. Heath, 1973).

9. Juris and Feuille used this definition of multilateral bargaining in their study of police bargaining in twenty-two cities. They found that the concept provided a valid description of the union-management interactions in these cities and thus provided further empirical evidence for the construct validity of this characterization of the bargaining process. See Juris and Feuille, *Police Unionism,* pp. 45-51.

10. In other words, the occurrence of internal conflicts within a city management provides the motivation for the various city officials to directly pursue their interests in the interorganizational bargaining process. On the other hand, if little or no disagreement exists among the management officials or if their disagreements are adequately resolved through the internal management decision-making process, there is no incentive for the various officials to intervene directly in the union-city negotiations process. As will be developed more fully below, one reason that this problem is far more prevalent in the public sector than in private industry is that there are multiple points of access to public officials that allow unions to apply pressures that further push the officials toward direct involvement. Also, because decision-making power is so often shared among public officials, they can usually intervene in the bargaining process (if they have the incentive to do so) far more easily and effectively than can management officials in a private company who are not designated negotiators.

11. For an empirical assessment of differences in commitment to the bargaining process by local government officials, see George Fredrickson, "Role Occupancy and Attitudes toward Labor Relations in Government," *Administrative Science Quarterly,* Vol. 14, No. 4 (December 1969), pp. 595-606.

12. Hildebrand, "The Public Sector."

13. See, for example, Murial M. Morse, "Shall We Bargain Away the Merit System," *Public Personnel Review,* Vol. 24, No. 4 (October 1963), pp. 239-243; Chester Newland, "Collective Bargaining Concepts: Applications in Government," *Public Administration Review,* Vol. 28, No. 2 (March/April 1968), pp. 117-126; and Milton Derber, "Who Negotiates for the Public Employer," in Public Employee Relations Library, Special Issue, *Perspectives in Public Employee Negotiations* (Chicago: Public Personnel Association, 1969), pp. 52-58.

14. Chamberlain and Kuhn, *Collective Bargaining,* p. 218.

15. For discussion of the use of these strategies in other political decision-making processes, see Michael Lipsky, "Protest as a Political Resource," *American Political Science Review,* Vol. 62, No. 4 (December 1968), pp. 1144-1158; and Ralph H. Turner, "The Public Perception of Protest," *American Sociological Review,* Vol. 34, No. 6 (December 1969), pp. 815-831.

16. For examples of union election involvement, see James A. Craft, "Fire Fighter Strategy in Wage Negotiation," *Quarterly Review of Economics and Business,* Vol. 11, No. 3 (Autumn 1971), pp. 65-75.

17. Walton and McKersie, *A Behavioral Theory of Labor Negotiations,* pp. 281-351.

18. McLennan and Moskow, "Multilateral Bargaining in the Public Sector," p. 34.

19. See Kochan, *City Employee Bargaining with a Divided Management,* pp. 31-56.

20. *Ibid.,* pp. 39-41.

21. *Ibid.,* pp. 34 and 48.

22. See Jum Nunnally, *Psychometric Theory* (New York: McGraw-Hill, 1967), pp. 210-213. Cronbach's alpha is a measure of the internal consistency of the items combined in an index. Basically, it correlates each item with the total score on the index and serves as a measure of the extent to which the items are similar enough to be combined and interpreted as measures of the same construct.

23. Residuals measure the difference between the predicted and observed values of the dependent variable.

Productivity Bargaining in New York—
What Went Wrong?

Melvin H. Osterman, Jr.
with an afterword by Robert B. McKersie*

I am writing this paper as an advocate of productivity bargaining, with
somewhat tarnished credentials. The subject of the impact of productivity
on labor-management negotiations is a challenging and vital one. It is one
that, particularly in times of an inflationary economy and continuing fiscal
stringency, must be given serious consideration by all who are engaged in
collective bargaining in the public sector. In preparing these remarks,
therefore, I first turned to the excellent material published by the National
Commission on Productivity, the study prepared for the Joint Economic
Committee of the Congress, and to the many scholarly texts that have been
published on this subject. Yet, as I continued preparing material on this
topic, it became clear to me that my remarks might be more valuable if I
were to relate the practical experience that my state—New York—has had
in trying to make productivity bargaining a reality—even though those
efforts have not been successful. There are, I think, valuable lessons that
management, labor, and the public in general may learn from the New York
experience.

On June 20, 1972, I signed a collective agreement with the Civil Service
Employees Association, Inc., a union representing 135,000 employees in the
State of New York. That contract contained a clear commitment to productivity bargaining and looked toward the establishment of mechanisms to
make it a reality.

The State had gone into productivity bargaining with high hopes. In
1972, Dr. T. Norman Hurd, Secretary to Governor Rockefeller, spoke
before the American Statistical Association Convention and commented:

> *In jurisdictions, like New York, which have highly developed collective bargain-
> ing procedures, the desired changes may have to be negotiated and quid pro
> quos offered. We are fortunate that the CSEA, our largest union, seems to
> understand the need for increasing State productivity as evidenced by their
> willingness to take the first step with us.*
>
> *I am sure you know that there are great risks associated with this effort.
> Productivity measurement in the public service, at this time, is more an emerging
> notion than a well-charted program.*

---

*Melvin H. Osterman, Jr., is former Director of the Office of Employee Relations for the State
of New York. He is now in the private practice of law. This article is adapted from a speech
presented in October 1973 to the 10th Annual Conference on Management Analysis in State
and Local Government held at Windsor Locks, Connecticut. Robert McKersie is at the Sloan
School of Management, Massachusetts Institute of Technology. Reprinted with the permission
of the author and the Institute for Public Employment of the School of Industrial and Labor
Relations, Cornell University.

Like all experimentation, however, whatever the initial result we will gain knowledge and insights not available in any other way. And success may well revolutionize the current pattern of public administration in New York and, perhaps, throughout the nation.

The revolution anticipated by Dr. Hurd did not occur.

On June 20, 1973, a year to the day after our first agreement, I signed another agreement with the Civil Service Employees Association (CSEA); this second agreement was wholly silent on the subject of productivity bargaining. In the year that had intervened, both the State and the union had concluded that their respective interests would be better served by avoiding direct reference to productivity.

How we came to our first agreement on productivity bargaining and what went wrong in the intervening year will provide the focus for my remarks in this paper.

New York State, under the Taylor Law, has, since 1967, been committed to meaningful collective negotiations with organizations representing its employees. State employees' salaries, fringe benefits, and all other terms and conditions of employment are determined solely through the processes of collective negotiations. The Office of Employee Relations (OER) is charged under State law with the responsibility for representing the Governor and the Executive Branch in these negotiations. It is assisted in this effort by representatives of the State's Civil Service Commission and the Division of the Budget. Since it will become relevant for later remarks, it is worth noting that, within the Division of the Budget, there is a Management Unit, which has been concerned for many years with assessing the efficiency of State government and devising methods for improving the productivity of State workers and the effectiveness with which State services are delivered.

The largest union with which the State deals, the CSEA, is an independent union with approximately 200,000 members. It represents 135,000 State workers, plus almost all of the noninstructional employees in school districts throughout the State and a majority of the employees in various counties, towns, and villages. CSEA has engaged in an informal bargaining relationship with the State for the past two decades and in a formal negotiating relationship for the past eight years.

Each of CSEA's various collective agreements with the State run to approximately seventy-five pages. They are comprehensive contracts covering wages, health insurance, time and leave matters, and a whole host of working conditions. They all contain the same broad management-rights clause, including, specifically, a provision reserving to the State the right "to direct, deploy and utilize the work force." This clause, as we will see, had a very real impact on our efforts in the area of productivity bargaining.

The State entered negotiations with CSEA in the fall of 1971 with a real problem. It had no money! Managements traditionally commence each round of negotiations with a plea for mercy on the ground that the cupboard is bare. This time, however, our plea was more than a formality. The State was in a period of austerity. Over 10,000 State employees had been laid off the preceding year. We were facing the prospect of a seriously unbalanced budget and the need for even further layoffs in the work force. We were aware of the real need to review State services to assess whether we were doing the best job we could.

Yet, even with these concerns, we were not entirely unrealistic in approaching the negotiations. With all of our problems, we were aware of advances in the cost of living and recognized that CSEA would not lightly accept our pleas of inability to pay as an excuse for deferring a pay increase. We came to the concept of productivity bargaining as a method of bridging our concerns with our budget and efficiency of operation and CSEA's need to protect the interests of its members.

We first broached the subject of productivity in February 1972, several months into the negotiations. We argued that CSEA should seriously consider whether there were methods of enhancing the "productivity" of the State's work force and argued that if there were demonstrable gains in productivity, perhaps they might be the basis for an accommodation of our mutual interests. At that stage of the negotiations, we did not define what we meant by productivity. We simply talked in terms of a trade-off. Indeed, at this stage of the negotiations, we really did not know the parameters of the proposal we were launching. Our exploratory probe fell on deaf ears. CSEA indicated that it was not interested in trade-offs, and the issue was not raised again until the week preceding the expiration of our contract.

By that time, negotiations had proceeded to the point where the State's salary offer had reached 4 percent. The State's negotiators indicated that, to justify an increase in this amount, they would require CSEA to make a variety of "trade-offs," under which the State would receive something back in return for the salary increase.

On the Sunday preceding the expiration date, we advanced a number of specific proposals under the headline "productivity improvements." They included

- the exclusion of temporary employees from leave coverage, at a "savings" of $1.5 million;
- a requirement that employees with less than 100 days of accumulated sick leave charge the first day of sick leave to personal leave credits, at a "savings" of $12 million;
- a requirement that State employees remit fees paid to them for jury duty, at a "savings" of $150,000; and
- the establishment of a uniform forty-hour work week for state employees, at a "savings" of $24 million.

The fact that these items were characterized as productivity improvements perhaps speaks to the naiveté with which we approached the subject of productivity bargaining. It is remarkable, when going through the writings in the area, how rarely the term *productivity* is defined. It is easy to find an explanation of the concept, in which productivity is related to the ratio of inputs to outputs. Perhaps this is the only consistent attempt at a definition that is possible. For when one goes beyond that, one often sinks into an intellectual and verbal morass. Most of what we were talking about at this stage of the negotiations was not real productivity in any technical sense of the term. Certainly requiring employees to remit fees for jury duty or denying holidays and vacation to temporary workers can in no way be characterized as improvements in productivity. On the other hand, they are, in a sense, related to the concept of productivity bargaining—that is, an attempt through the process of collective negotiations to obtain changes in work rules or practices that will permit the employer to reduce the cost or improve the quality or quantity of the services it provides.

We spent the next three days debating the merits of these trade-offs. On Wednesday, with only two days before the expiration of the contract, the union advised us that none of the trade-offs could even be considered acceptable, and discussion moved toward other methods of financing the salary increase.

The other methods of financing did not prove acceptable, and on Friday night, 7,700 union members struck State facilities across New York. Fortunately, the strike occurred on a weekend, and the impact on most State services was minimal. In addition, we received a massive outpouring of volunteer support, which also tended to mitigate the effects of the strike. On the other hand, a strike at a hospital for the mentally retarded or a prison— facilities which are open on the weekend—is never pleasant to contemplate.

During the course of the strike, negotiations continued in Albany. Again, the subject of productivity and trade-offs was introduced. At this point, however, the State itself began to have some second thoughts. During the negotiations, the State's representatives were continuing to refine their perceptions of the concept they were pursuing. They were engaged in a process of considering alternative methods of approaching productivity and attempting to give flesh and blood to that concept. Meanwhile, we were aware that if we intended to pursue productivity bargaining, we should do so on a basis that would be meaningful and would provide real savings to the State. We were not interested in a "public relations" approach, which would merely permit us to claim increases in productivity to justify salary increases to State employees.

It was a keystone of our efforts that we be able to demonstrate actual improvements in service and real savings, a portion of which we would propose to share with employees. We were aware of the difficulties in nailing down a satisactory definition of productivity. We recognized that in government there might be reliable indicators of input, but indicators of output were substantially more ambiguous. For example, how does one measure the productivity of a personnel or budgeting unit? We were also faced with other problems involving evaluation. For example, does one regard a unit that is working at 50 percent of normal efficiency when it brings itself up to 75 percent efficiency? In addition, we were concerned about some special governmental considerations. What would happen to the civil service merit system if employees were paid on the basis of performance as determined by supervisors? These were very real concerns that troubled us deeply. We felt, however, that, if we could start in the direction of solving some of these problems, we could develop a program that would have long-run benefits to both the State and its employees.

Fortunately, several of the union leaders agreed with us. They recognized that there was substantial rank-and-file resistance to the concept of productivity (we ourselves heard employees speak of the spectre of time and motion studies). These union leaders were willing, however, to take some initial steps toward the adoption of this approach, even if only on a limited and tentative basis.

To reinforce this receptiveness among some of the leaders, and to make headway in establishing productivity bargaining, the State offered to increase its salary proposal. On Sunday, thirty-six hours after the strike commenced, we reached agreement with CSEA on a total contract, which included a specific commitment to pursue productivity bargaining. Article 8.1 of that contract provided:

> 8.1. *The State and CSEA agree on the need for cooperative efforts toward increasing productivity in State operations, thereby providing improved efficiencies and service to the public and job enrichment and economic benefits arising from such improvements to employees.*

The agreement called for the establishment of a State-CSEA committee to commence negotiations immediately, with a deadline for reaching agreement of December 1, 1972. The committee's task was specifically delimited. Many of the "trade-offs" that had been debated during the previous week again appeared as subjects of study. The committee was to consider establishment of a standard work week of forty hours, amendment of the system by which the performance of State workers was evaluated, and amendment of time and leave rules so that tardiness would be chargeable against individual leave credits. There were, however, some new items to be considered, which reflected the increasing sophistication of the State's approach. The committee was to study application of a system of flexible hours in which employees would be permitted to select starting and closing times of their work. It was to consider increased flexibility in work assignments, a matter of critical importance to the State, since each of its 3,500 positions has a specific and limiting job description. The committee was to look into applications of the four-day work week and job security in relation to productivity improvement. The agreement provided a guarantee that productivity savings would be shared: 25 percent of any savings would be paid across the board to all employees; 25 percent would be paid to those units and employees who had contributed to the improvement; and the remaining 50 percent would be retained by the State.

In what was perhaps the most important provision, the committee was charged with the development of criteria and procedures for the measurement of productivity and for the allocation of savings resulting from the implementation of proposals in the specific areas assigned to the committee. The State took the position that, in order to be succesful, productivity would have to be launched on a concrete and factually reliable basis. We regarded this commitment to study productivity measurement and methods of allocating savings as the most critical task assigned to the labor-management committee. To help assure the success of the committee's effort, the State promised that if agreements were reached on such criteria and procedures, a bonus of $1\frac{1}{2}$ percent would be paid to all State employees on April 1, 1973.

In retrospect, there were some real problems with our agreement. The mixing of trade-offs and true productivity improvement reflected an initial lack of preparation on both sides to deal with some of the technicalities in this area. A number of the items of study were red flags to particular groups of employees. The inclusion of a specific formula for the allocation of savings was a mistake. The allocation of such savings should have been left flexible so that we would have had greater ability to deal with varying forms of improvements. Finally, our worst miscalculation was our belief that we could motivate a union that was not wholeheartedly and independently committed to productivity bargaining.

Barely a month passed before reservations about the agreement began to surface from all parties concerned. Following the settlement of the strike, the State Legislature appointed a Select Committee to investigate the strike and to evaluate the negotiated agreement. The Legislative Committee recognized that the productivity improvement program as initiated by the agreement might have far-reaching fiscal advantages for the State. It expressed concern, however, that the Legislature was being asked to endorse in advance an agreement that might be used as a justification for the payment of substantial sums to State employees without effective controls. The Committee recommended and the Legislature enacted a specific legislative caveat that would guide the Executive Branch in pursuing the subject of productivity bargaining.

Specifically, the Legislative Committee stated:

> However, we want assurances that proper quality controls are maintained; that bonuses paid are a direct result of increased effort on the part of the employee and not paid where efficiencies are the result of outside factors such as improved equipment or prevailing economic conditions; that work standards be established to insure that bonuses are paid only for extra effort and not for what normally could be expected from an employee.
>
> We applaud the efforts to establish such a program which can benefit the State, the employees and the taxpayers. We are concerned lest inadequate controls work to the State's disadvantage.
>
> For these reasons, we are recommending that this session of the Legislature neither approve nor disapprove the section of the CSEA contracts providing for a productivity improvement program.

Within weeks, further concerns were expressed. A number of the State's managers who had never been enthusiastic supporters of the program, expressed their continuing disagreement with a program that might result in the allocation of funds to State employees without specific and tangible returns. They further expressed concern over the impact of productivity bargaining on the State's own efforts at management improvement, which had been going on without union participation. At meetings of the Budget Director's Management Advisory Council, State managers expressed reservations about the effect of productivity bargaining on what they regarded as their prerogative to seek unilateral changes on a continuing basis. The contractual right to "direct, deploy and utilize the work force" had been won in hard-fought battles in earlier negotiations. State managers were therefore concerned over the possible erosion of this right through concessions made in productivity bargaining.

The summer and early fall of 1972 were busy for the staff of OER. An effort was made to assemble and review a substantial portion of the literature in this field. Field trips were made to a number of firms that had attempted productivity improvements and whose operations were comparable to those of the State government. We met with a variety of consultants who gave us valuable insights into the way we should approach productivity negotiations. We met with the National Commission on Productivity and sought its counsel in determining the appropriate method of launching our program. We developed a strategy for the forthcoming negotiations that was designed to place productivity on a firm basis by developing reliable indicators of output; this would, we hoped, satisfy the concerns expressed by the Legislature and some State administrators.

This period was an equally busy time for the CSEA negotiators. As reports on the implications of the settlement began to flow back from the field, they began to have increasing concerns about the direction they had taken. Many of these concerns were based on misconceptions of either the settlement or what was contemplated under the agreement. Other objections stemmed from actual experiences with productivity improvements. The State, for example, in its period of financial crisis, had established a program of vacancy control. As a result of that program, there were, after two years, approximately 2,000 fewer filled positions in the Department of Mental Hygiene. The employees in that department took the position that since they were doing "the same job" with 2,000 fewer employees, their productivity had increased and they should not be required to participate further in order to share in gains from productivity improvement. Moreover, clerical employees were particularly concerned about the clause in the Committee's charge to study the establishment of a uniform forty-hour work week. These employees regarded their 37½-hour work week with almost religious fervor and were not prepared to participate in any program that even suggested the possibility of its loss. Substantial concern was created by a speech given by one of the legislative leaders at a CSEA conference in which he pointed to the desirability of working people out of title to enrich their jobs and enhance their performance. CSEA had for many years been a firm supporter of the merit system and became concerned that productivity improvement could be used to erode many of the gains it had achieved over the years. The cumulative effect of these pressures and the criticism directed at various of its manifestations dampened whatever enthusiasm many of the CSEA leaders had once had for the program.

When the State-CSEA Committee first met in formal session in October 1972, the chairman of the union's negotiating committee reflected this loss of enthusiasm in a most forceful manner. The first words out of his mouth were, "I don't care about the 1½ pecent for myself. You can take it and stuff it!" His concerns were quickly echoed by the union's first vice president and the chief negotiator for its institutional employees.

With this ominous beginning, the next several negotiating sessions were spent in an effort to reconvince CSEA that the bargain it had struck in April was, in fact, a good bargain and that it would serve our mutual interest to continue pursuing productivity bargaining.

We proposed to CSEA to proceed initially by a deductive process. We recommended that the State and CSEA jointly sponsor a variety of specific projects, testing out various methods of improving productivity. We suggested proposals to test out incentive compensation, flexible work hours, the four-day work week, and a broadening of selected job definitions to permit the employees to take on wider ranges of responsibilities. We solicited the views of State agencies concerning projects they thought might be useful to explore in a collective negotiations context.

Two things quickly emerged. First, CSEA became extremely apprehensive about projects that did not involve all of the employees in the State. Their negotiators argued that if all State employees were to get the benefit of the 1½ percent productivity bonus, all should participate in producing whatever savings might accrue to the State from the program. They also expressed concern that any individual group might receive a benefit that was not shared by the others.

From the State's point of view, we discovered an equally surprising development. Representatives of individual State agencies, however supportive they were of the concept of productivity bargaining, seemed reluctant to put forth specific proposals for discussion with CSEA. In large part, this arose from the fear that if a particular proposal was laid on the table and rejected by CSEA, it would be impossible to put it into effect thereafter. In part, it resulted from an unwillingness to share with other agencies pet projects that individual managers were developing. Finally, and to a more limited extent, it reflected a resistance by certain of the State's managers to admit that a union had any role to play in the determination of the mechanics of productivity improvement.

Negotiations proceeded slowly with CSEA, through the fall of 1972. In an effort to force the union team to grapple with some of the conceptual issues involved in productivity bargaining, we pursued the question of whether a layoff of employees necessarily meant added workload and hence greater productivity for those remaining. We discussed whether improved department performance, which was due to increased supervision, would constitute increased productivity. We discussed whether the substitution of capital for labor, e.g., television cameras to replace prison guards, was a matter in which employees should share, and how capital costs should be set off against estimated savings. We considered methods by which productivity output could be reliably and factually measured. We noted the difficulty of measuring specific jobs and proposed alternate methods of measurement. Finally, we sought to pin down what both the State and CSEA could reasonably expect from productivity bargaining.

While these theoretical discussions were proceeding, however, a series of events occurred, which were to have a profound effect on the negotiations. First, a time and motion study was initiated by the State University in its power plant operation at the SUNY campus at Oswego. This study had been planned for some time and was wholly unrelated to our negotiations. CSEA employees at Oswego argued, however, that this was what "productivity" was all about, and supporting protests were received from throughout the State. At almost the same time, the Department of Mental Hygiene announced the institution of a four-day work week in the food service operation at Pilgrim State Hospital. Again, waves of protest followed. Finally, Mental Hygiene announced the establishment of an overlapping fourth shift at Willowbrook State Hospital in an effort to provide increased coverage at mealtimes to improve the care provided to the institution's mentally retarded children. Although each of the individual employees had been consulted about the need for the change and most in fact had agreed, there were several who were concerned that the new shift would not mesh with local bus service to the institution.

The protests, which came from around the State, soon surfaced at the negotiating table. It soon became quite clear that CSEA was not going to agree to a program that would include specific productivity improvements as one of its elements. The adverse reactions that the various State-initiated projects had invoked had made the union negotiators chary of further exploration.

We were forced, therefore, to move away from individual projects and seek a more conceptual way of moving productivity bargaining forward. We concluded that it was unlikely that we would be able to reach agreement with CSEA at the table on specific standards and criteria. Instead, we proposed a jointly financed study by an outside consultant that would (1) provide research data to the State and CSEA on procedures for measuring output data, (2) develop an inventory of State services and functions to determine which services and functions were measurable, and (3) provide guidance concerning methods of solving problems of job security related to productivity.

Based on the anticipated work of the consultant, we then proposed that we would proceed to develop work measurement data in those areas in which the inventory had indicated measurement was possible. We argued that we should allow the negotiators for each side to evaluate any changes in output-input data and to debate at the negotiating table the reasons for change and whether the employees were entitled to participate in any savings resulting from particular increases in productivity.

We also proposed that an attempt be made to work out some general guidelines for the respective roles of the State and CSEA in further productivity improvements. In this respect, we happened on a bit of good fortune. CSEA had been meeting with Professor Walter Balk of the State University and had sought his counsel regarding how to proceed in the negotiations. He was able to provide many of the technical skills that CSEA had heretofore been unable or unwilling to procure. We were doubly fortunate since Professor Balk's views did not substantially deviate from those of the State. The agreement that we were able to reach is in large part a tribute to the guidance he was able to provide to CSEA.

Our revised proposal, based on principles that we had been developing at the table, was presented to CSEA in December. We debated the language of the proposal throughout the month and on December 26 reached agreement on a method of proceeding.

The preamble to the agreement is perhaps its most important feature. In it, we attempted to analyze the respective roles of the State and CSEA and to lay down guideposts for our future relationship.

170

Let me review some of the important provisions of the preamble. With respect to productivity measurement, we concluded:

> One cannot measure productivity or determine savings without developing some factual data to determine relationships between output and input along with output and service standards. Therefore, knowledge of output is a central and critical factor in productivity measurement. Ease of measurement (or fact-gathering) is often a function of the degree of routineness of tasks. Extremely routine tasks require fewer output indicators and production data is reasonably valid and reliable. Less routine task output indicators must be more numerous and, by their nature, are not as valid and reliable.
>
> State operations differ widely in the amount of routine inherent in their operations. Therefore, predictably, output data "hardness" and the style of interpretation will vary according to the amount and type of task routine in each function. For example, the reliability and interpretation of output data from the Department of Motor Vehicles would be expected to be substantially more firm than that from the Department of Commerce.

With respect to productivity planning, we agreed:

> A major reason why administrators are distinguished from employees is that they are charged with responsibility for and should be trained to innovate and maintain systems to improve productivity. Administrators should have specialized administrative, technical and social knowledge; this leads to better planning, more rational risk-taking and eventually, higher productivity. . . . |T|he preparation of new systems of control depends upon management's initiative and involvement.

Finally, with respect to motivating employees, we stated:

> One safe assumption is that people will be better motivated to do something when they perceive a gratifying personal result. In the case of employees another safe assumption is that often factors relating to pay and job conditions will be more gratifying motivationally than other factors. Experience indicates that it is important to involve employees in the process of implementation so that they understand what is being proposed and how it will affect their jobs and working conditions. In addition, to the extent that there are changes in the terms and conditions of employment, the Taylor Law requires the participation of employee organizations certified or recognized as representatives of employees in the implementation of the proposals.

With these principles as our basis and backed by a commitment of $100,000 from the State and CSEA, we thus engaged a research consultant. We attempted to provide some guidance to the consultant. We directed him first to study State functions in which an improvement would directly benefit the public, ones which were uniform over a period of time and not subject to cyclical or seasonal variations, and ones in which the components contributing to changes in productivity could easily be segregated. On receiving the consultant's report, the State and CSEA agreed to meet further to develop a procedure for the establishment of work-measurement data. We also agreed to consider specific productivity projects primarily in the area of the four-day work week and flex time. We agreed to the establishment of a floating holiday in lieu of Lincoln's Birthday, the net effect of which was to keep State offices open for an additional day.

Our agreement was signed on December 6, 1972 and was ratified by the State Legislature shortly thereafter.

Within two weeks of the signing of the productivity agreement, we went into full-scale negotiations with CSEA for a contract to replace the 1972-73 agreement. We stated as one of the State's initial goals, the continuation of the productivity agreement and, indeed, the expansion of the scope of study.

As the negotiations progressed, however, both the State and CSEA became increasingly concerned about the practical consequences of the course that they had selected. In proceedings under the contractual grievance procedure and before the State's Public Employment Relations Board, CSEA began to argue that the obligation to negotiate over productivity precluded unilateral action by the State to implement any such changes. CSEA acknowledged that the management-rights clause of its contracts had, since 1969, authorized the State to "direct and deploy" the work force. They argued, however, that the new commitment to productivity bargaining prohibited unilateral action by the State to reschedule shifts of individuals, estalish new shifts, or change the starting and closing times of shifts. They resisted, on technical grounds, a proposal to restructure the duties of State Tax Examiners, a proposal which the Division of the Budget estimated might result in savings of $100 million.

CSEA was thus in a difficult position. It was under increasing pressure from employees to resist changes in individual assignments and to utilize the productivity clause as the vehicle to prevent the implementation of myriad changes in terms and conditions of employment. Indeed, virtually every change in State work procedures seemed to be viewed as an application of "productivity bargaining" and to be resisted on that ground alone.

It soon became quite clear to the State negotiators that, having achieved a preliminary agreement and secured the payment of the 1½ percent bonus, CSEA was not interested in a broadscale approach to productivity bargaining. An indication of the degree of CSEA's concern was the fact that it considered and agreed in the closing night of negotiations to trade off a career ladder article under which members of the negotiation units had received $13 million in the preceding two years for a discontinuance of the commitment to productivity improvement. In the State's view, CSEA's resistance to productivity bargaining was so complete that our continued insistence on the concept was becoming counterproductive. Accordingly, in the agreement that was reached in April 1973 and executed in June, the productivity bargaining article was deleted and preparations for the study that had been commissioned in December were discontinued.

The State is now working under a three-year contract that has no commitment to or provision for productivity bargaining. Only vestiges of the commitment remain. These are ongoing studies of out-of-title work and work day/work week. Productivity bargaining itself, however, is not mentioned. Does this mean that productivity bargaining was a failure? Certainly, in the short run our attempts to initiate it on a broad scale failed. I think, however, something was learned from the experience, and, given a continuing commitment on the part of the State to the improvement of service and productivity, it may work in future years.

What lessons can be derived from this experience?

1. Our experience has reinforced the State's belief that productivity bargaining will be profitable only if both parties make meaningful efforts to produce real savings—and not merely use the process as a public relations tactic. It would have been easy, at any stage of the proceedings, to put together numbers that would indicate that the productivity of State workers had increased or that vast savings had been achieved through changes in particular working conditions. Although this might have provided a short-term justification for individual wage increases, it would have served neither the State nor CSEA well. This approach would have exacerbated the very real concerns of those who have apprehensions about the impact of collective bargaining on public service or the expenditure of public funds.

2. The principal lesson we learned is that it is impossible to make productivity bargaining work unless the union is fully committed to the concept and wants to make it work. We thought we could supply incentive with the productivity bonus and that the 1½ percent carrot would move us far enough forward to generate momentum. That just did not work. This is a process that is so delicate and so new that it requires a genuine effort to move forward.

3. It is equally clear that productivity bargaining will not work unless there is a complete commitment to the concept from all levels of management. Those who would resist change or would resist the increasing incursions of collective bargaining must be brought into the process and convinced that they can benefit from trading some of their prerogatives for cooperation from the union. The mere fact that this is a change from the way things have been done in the past generates resistance. There must be a mutual desire to overcome that resistance.

4. There must be technical expertise on both sides of the bargaining table. On management's side, there is often a management-improvement unit that can provide technical advice and counsel. All too often, however, that technical expertise is not shared on the other side of the table. I am reminded of a story that a corporate officer told us as we were preparing for negotiations. A clause in the collective bargaining contract *required* the union to retain a time and motion study expert. At the time I thought the story amusing, particularly when he went on to add that after two years of productivity bargaining, the union fired its own expert because he was agreeing too often with management. In retrospect, perhaps the story isn't funny. If one is going to expect his counterpart across the table to deal with the technical issues of savings and allocation of savings, it may be necessary to require that he obtain the technical support that is essential.

5. Our search for hard data as a precondition to specific improvements probably was the wrong approach. This is an area of collective bargaining that cannot be handled on a theoretical or abstract level. Our experience confirms that there is no way to go about this, other than on a case-by-case basis. Management must search out specific terms and conditions that it wants to change, but cannot change—legally or practically—without the union's concurrence. It then must put those demands on the table. Similarly, unions

cannot expect serious consideration of salary or other demands if these demands are based on amorphous gains in productivity. They too will have to demonstrate specific changes in productivity that are amenable to meaningful evaluation.

6. It was an error to insert in the agreement a specific formula for the allocation of savings. This created an inflexibility and raised expectations among employees, which could not be easily satisfied. Employees who were involved in specific improvements knew that the most they could gain from their improvements was 25 percent of the savings. In larger units in which those savings would have been allocated among many employees, this reward frequently provided no incentive at all. The techniques of productivity bargaining are manifold, and it is necessary to maintain great flexibility to make them succeed. In some cases, management may well be willing to give a greater share to employees in cases in which greater employee incentive is required. In other instances, changes in nonpecuniary terms and conditions of employment may be sufficient to achieve the necessary motivation.

7. Finally, the subject of job security was probably improperly committed as a subject of study to the committee. In this respect, the State is in a dilemma. It is critical for management to realize real savings, and real savings are frequently derived from having fewer people do the same amount of (or more) work. At the same time, it is unreasonable to expect a union to give support to a program that may reduce the size of its membership. Throughout our negotiations, we were concerned over what we were asking CSEA to do to itself. Having come through a period of austerity in which the union had lost substantial numbers of its members, it was perhaps unreasonable to expect it to participate fully in a program which *might* result in even further losses.

Our experience was such that I think it is essential that the contract contain an express guarantee that productivity improvements will not be implemented without a commitment to achieve any reductions in the work force through attrition or to guarantee to retrain those who might be adversely affected by productivity improvements.

As a final note, I might add that, although productivity bargaining was not established in the 1972 contract negotiations with CSEA, there is still hope that it can be initiated in future bargaining situations. To this end, the State should develop its productivity proposals early and formulate them in consultation with the union. I believe that productivity bargaining will work. The task of making it work will be a difficult one, but it will be worth the effort.

AFTERWORD

The paper by Osterman entitled, "Productivity Bargaining in New York State—What Went Wrong?" is a remarkably frank and informative treatment of an attempt by the State of New York to connect productivity improvement with labor-management relations. Although the experiment was not a "success," the experience provided many important lessons, as Osterman carefully documents.

Osterman outlines quite clearly why, despite the compelling circum-

174

stances for productivity bargaining, things went wrong. My comments will not dwell on the State's experience as much as they will compare that experience to productivity bargaining that has been practiced elsewhere, especially in New York City and Nassau County.

One way to explain the failure of productivity bargaining in New York State is that the strategy chosen fell "betwixt and between" the two main modes of productivity bargaining. It was neither pure "buy out" nor pure "gain-sharing." As a result, it experienced the disadvantages of both approaches.

The buy-out approach has been practiced in New York City. Using this strategy, management conducts a thorough analysis of its operations and develops a plan of productivity improvement. Only after it has established its goals and considered the likelihood of their successful implementation does management go to the bargaining table to secure the cooperation of the union in the adoption of the plan.

The gain-sharing approach is open-ended and relies on labor-management cooperation as a means for improving productivity. Rewards are shared after the program of change has been implemented and productivity improvements can be evaluated through a measurement system. This approach has been practiced in Nassau County in negotiations between the County and CSEA and between three towns in the County and CSEA.

The following chart compares the strategies of buy out and gain-sharing with the approach followed in New York State. As the chart indicates, the New York State approach represented a mixture of the two established strategies. For example, money was paid in advance, like the buy-out aproach, but achievement was not specified and was left to the process of labor-management collaboration as in the gain-sharing approach.

COMPARISON OF PRODUCTIVITY AGREEMENTS

	New York State	New York City	Nassau County
Initiative for Program	Management-Labor	Management	Management-Labor
Size of Governmental Unit	Very large	Very large	Large
Time Frame for Program	Presumably during the period of the contract	During the period of the contract	Open-ended
Nature of Rewards	Downpayment with remainder paid 25% to department, 25% uniform and 50% retained by government	Payment in advance and uniform for the union involved	Payment after results and uniform for all employees

If I were to recommend to New York State the strategy to follow, I would strongly recommend the buy-out approach—and for the following reasons:

• The buy-out approach is required when the scope and complexity of operations is large. In a governmental jurisdiction as large as New York City or as large as the State of New York, considerable planning has to be done at

175

the central level, usually by staff specialists. If responsibility for designing productivity improvement is decentralized, usually little will happen in a large organization.

The analysis of the operations and the development of general plans for productivity improvement usually are done much more effectively at the central level. For example, in the case of New York City, the central staff groups delineated the main approaches: technological change (such as the introduction of slippery water for the fire departments), the more rational deployment of the work force (the matching of available manpower to the demand for services in such areas as police and firefighting), better effort utilization (monitoring of start and stop times), and the development of output standards.

• The buy-out approach is required in instances in which labor-management relations tend to be "arm's length" and the union takes a relatively militant approach to collective bargaining. Given the orientation of CSEA at the state level—one of examining every proposal very critically and insisting on quid pro quos—the only approach to productivity bargaining would be the buy out.

What are some of the principles that should be honored if the buy-out approach is to be effective?

• Management must do the preparatory work and develop the rough cut for the productivity improvement program. In some cases, management may need to do some "belt tightening" on its own before bringing the plan to the bargaining table for review and ratification. Since any kind of productivity improvement program puts front-line and middle management on the spot, considerable training and orientation of management itself will be required prior to and during implementation of any productivity agreement.

• Certain key guarantees must be made so that the employees and the union are "set free" to engage in the program. Productivity bargaining, as it has been practiced in the private sector, has usually involved a guarantee from management that no employees will lose their jobs as a result of the program. If fewer employees are required, the excess will be absorbed through attrition. In the case of New York State, where extensive layoffs had occurred in the early 1970s, the atmosphere was negative and productivity bargaining could go forward only if and when management offered employment guarantees.

• The buy out has to be used sparingly. The exchanging of money for productivity improvement is a high-risk process. It may need to be done as a way of removing some barriers, but, if practiced very long, it teaches people the lesson that "looseness is worth money." It also leads to the sort of orientation that developed in New York State—that every time management would make a change in operations, the union would demand that it be considered a part of the productivity improvement program. Such an orientation is clearly counterproductive, and consequently the buy out must be viewed as a particular process that moves in to eliminate specific problems in an organization. The measurement of savings is extremely important in any form of productivity bargaining. Typically, with the buy-out approach, the financial rewards are paid "up front" as a way of inducing acceptance of the desired changes. Management has calculated the expected savings and is willing to share a portion of them through regular wage negotiations in return for assurance from the union that certain changes in work practices will be implemented. The function of measurement is to ascertain whether the savings have been achieved and whether the bargain from management's point of view has been a sound deal.

It is clear that the next several years will see considerable experimentation with productivity bargaining. Productivity in the public sector is "an idea whose time has come." Given the presence of collective bargaining in an increasing number of government jurisdictions, it is likely that management's quest for productivity improvement will intersect, in some fashion, the institution of collective bargaining.

The experience of New York State and the intelligent analysis by Melvin Osterman should serve as an informative source to practitioners as they move into this new field of productivity bargaining.

1981 UPDATE: THE NEW YORK CITY SANITATION AGREEMENT

After (1) numerous start and stop efforts at productivity improvements via labor-management committees, (2) several bargains that made the payment of cost-of-living allowances during the life of the agreement contingent on productivity savings, and (3) at least one major negotiation which promised but failed to deliver significant productivity savings in the transit system, New York City finally appears to have achieved a tangible and real productivity improvement program via a recent "arbitrated" agreement. In December 1980, New York City and its Sanitation Workers' Union announced their acceptance of an arbitration award written by Matthew Kelly that provides the city with the right to introduce larger and more efficient two-man sanitation trucks (replacing three-man trucks) on selected routes. Each worker on a two-person crew in turn will receive an $11 per shift bonus.[1] The city also agreed to put off for two years its plan to experiment with contracting out sanitation services to private firms.

This agreement is important for several reasons. First, it is the most clear-cut and measurable productivity improvement program achieved to date in New York City—a city that has had a long history of trying various strategies to improve productivity in the face of continuous fiscal crises. Second, it demonstrates one of McKersie's main arguments—that is, in large politically complex bargaining units, the buy-out strategy is more likely to work than is an open-ended commitment to develop a gain-sharing plan via a joint labor-management committee. This is especially true when new technology is available and the (potential) cost savings can be carefully estimated before the fact.

Third, it demonstrates the innovative use of a neutral party in bringing about the change. Note that it required an "arbitration award that the parties accepted" to bring about the new agreement. One of the conventional wisdoms regarding arbitration is that it is an inherently conservative procedure—arbitrators tend not to break new ground or innovate, but rather to rely on comparable practice, past practice, or, when interpreting an agreement in grievance arbitration, on the wording and intent of the clause at issue. Thus, this use of arbitration clearly breaks with many of the traditions and conventional practices of the past. It represents a major innovation that was achieved with the help of a dispute resolution process that falls somewhere between the conventional labels we normally use to describe arbitration, fact-finding, and mediation. Clearly, on the one hand, the arbitrator could not have fashioned this type of award unless he sensed the parties were ready and able to accept it. The parties, on the other hand, could not easily agree to this plan on their own and needed the assistance of a knowledgeable and trusted third party.

It may be that this type of heavy-handed yet delicate third party role is needed to confront many of the substantive problems currently found in the public sector. Whether it will be used in other jurisdictions depends on the willingness and ability of the parties to open themselves up to this type of direct attack on their problems and past practices.

FOOTNOTE

1. This case is reported in *Government Employee Relations Report No. 893*, December 22, 1980, pp. 26-27.

The Impact of Private Sector Principles in the Public Sector: The Duty to Bargain

Harry T. Edwards*

The Bargaining Process

In private sector labor relations, the duty to bargain is defined by Section 8(d) of the National Labor Relations Act (NLRA) as:

> the mutual obligation of the employer and the representative of the employees to meet at reasonable times and confer in good faith with respect to wages, hours, and other terms and conditions of employment, . . . but such obligation does not compel either party to agree to a proposal or require the making of a concession. . . .

The obligation to negotiate in good faith has been interpreted by the courts as requiring a duty to participate actively in deliberations with a sincere desire and intention to reach an agreement. Normally, this requirement would encompass give and take on both sides until some agreement is reached, but there is no legal duty to agree. In essence, the requirement of good faith bargaining in the private sector is simply that both parties manifest a type of attitude and conduct conducive to reaching an agreement.

Statutes concerned with public sector bargaining may be divided into

*University of Michigan Law School. This article is excerpted from a larger article titled: "The Impact of Private Sector Principles in the Public Sector: Bargaining Rights for Supervisors and the Duty to Bargain." Reprinted from *Union Power and Public Policy*, David B. Lipsky (ed.) (Ithaca, N.Y.: New York State School of Industrial and Labor Relations, 1975), pp. 51-74.

two categories: those providing for "collective negotiations" and the so-called meet-and-confer statutes. In states such as Michigan and New York that have adopted the collective negotiations approach, the statutory definition of the duty to bargain is often identical or very similar to that found in the NLRA. As a consequence, the process of bargaining in these two states, and in numerous other public sector jurisdictions, closely resembles the practices followed in the private sector. For example, public employers are required to supply relevant information to the employees' bargaining agent, even when the information sought is in the public domain.[1] In addition, although unions and public employers may reserve the right to ratify a negotiated settlement, either by employee vote or legislative action, the negotiating agents for each side must still have sufficient authority to bargain in good faith.[2] In a recent Florida circuit court decision, it was found that the city had failed to negotiate in good faith because

> *the City Manager's function was not to negotiate with the Union on behalf of the Union, but rather to induce the Union to compromise some of its demands in the belief that they were reaching an agreement and then present these compromises to the City Council where further concessions from the Union were to be demanded. The refusal of the City to show any confidence in the preliminary agreement reached by its City Manager (its appointed negotiator) and its attempt to renegotiate the entire agreement and gain further concessions from the Union . . . is not good faith bargaining.*[3]

It has also been held that the parties to the bargaining process retain full discretion to designate their bargaining agents, that unilateral employer action upon a matter that is the subject of collective bargaining constitutes a failure and refusal to bargain in good faith,[4] that it is impermissible for an employer to bypass or denigrate the union by dealing directly with bargaining unit employees,[5] and that employers and unions in the public sector may lawfully participate in private negotiations without violating state "sunshine" or right-to-know laws.[6] All of these policies, which have to do with the bargaining process, have been adapted from the existing private sector case law. Indeed, numerous decisions rendered in New York, Michigan, Wisconsin, and Connecticut have relied specifically on private sector precedent in these areas of concern.

There is one unique aspect to the process of public sector bargaining. Frequently, the employer's bargaining agent in the public sector does not possess absolute authority to make a labor agreement. The Michigan Employment Relations Commission has even suggested that public employers *cannot* delegate the authority to agree to a bargaining agent.[7] Problems of unlawful delegation aside, it is generally true that legislative ratification of proposed settlements is normally required in the public sector. In addition, it has also been held that a legislative body may lawfully reject a proposed settlement or refuse to appropriate the money necessary to implement a settlement reached by bargaining agents.[8] As a consequence, it is not unusual for employee bargaining agents first to bargain with the designated employer agent and then to engage in additional bargaining with the members of a legislative body to ensure ratification of a proposed settlement.[9] In recognition of the problems inherent in such a process, MERC ruled in *City of Saginaw*[10] that "the bargaining representative of a governmental body is under an obligation to keep the governmental body adivsed as to the progress of negotiations." The MERC also ruled that if the governmental body persisted in rejecting a union proposal "on principle," then it could be compelled to appear at the negotiating table "to bargain on the subject." Later in *City of Detroit*,[11] however, the MERC held that

> *It is not required that Municipal Councils, Commissions and Boards bargain directly with the representatives of their employees. This may be done by administrative employees or other agents who are clothed with authority to participate in effective collective bargaining but reserving final approval to the governing body. Such is common practice in the private sector, and it is effective and workable.*

The Wisconsin State Employment Labor Relations Act provides an example of how the legislature may not only legitimize public sector contracts, but also participate more directly in the bargaining process. It requires that agreements, once approved by the unions involved, be approved by a joint legislative committee. The committee then introduces bills in both houses to implement those portions of the agreement, such as wage adjustments and fringe benefits, that require legislative approval. If the committee rejects the agreement or the legislature rejects the resultant bills, the agreement is sent back to the parties for renegotiation. Thus, the parties must remain aware of the attitudes of both the legislative committee and the legislature itself.

Probably the most significant distinction between the public and private sectors is the long-standing and universally followed prohibition against public employee strikes. In most states and in the federal service, there is a common-law or legislated proscription of the right to strike in the public sector. Only Alaska, Hawaii, Montana, Pennsylvania, and Vermont have enacted legislation giving public employees a limited right to strike.

Labor leaders, of course, have argued that the absence of the strike weapon in the public sector reduces collective bargaining to collective begging; yet, the validity of such a conclusion is, at best, speculative. There are enough data to suggest that, in the public sector, there may be a de facto right to strike, despite the legal strike bans in force. The threat or exercise of this de facto right to strike appears to be no less effective than the legal right enjoyed by employees in the private sector. Moreover, it is possible that statutory impasse procedures, such as arbitration, factfinding, and legislative hearings, may be a source of great bargaining leverage for public unions. For example, many municipal employers in Michigan have claimed that the state's compulsory arbitration act for policemen and firemen has produced arbitrated settlements far in excess of what might have been produced by traditional collective bargaining.[12] There obviously is no sure way to test this hypothesis, but the claim at least raises the question of how much, if any, bargaining power unions actually lose by virtue of the strike ban in the public sector.

In short, the process of bargaining is probably essentially the same in many important respects in both the public and private sectors, except in connection with the strike proscription and the process of legislative ratification. Several public sector jurisdictions, however, have apparently attempted to modify the private sector collective negotiations bargaining model by adopting meet-and-confer statutes; therefore, these statutes require some mention.

"Meet-and-confer negotiations" has generally been defined as the

process of negotiating terms and conditions of employment intended to emphasize the differences between public and private employment conditions. Negotiations under "meet and confer" laws usually imply discussions leading to unilateral adoption of policy by legislative body rather than written contract, and take place with multiple employee representatives rather than an exclusive bargaining agent.[13]

This definition fairly describes what was originally intended by the meet-and-confer standard of bargaining. Implicit in the *pure* meet-and-confer approach is the assumption that the private sector bargaining model would be overly permissive if applied without qualification to the public sector. In other words, it is argued that public employers should retain broad managerial discretion in the operation of a governmental agency, subject only to the recall of the electorate. Thus, under the pure meet-and-confer bargaining model, the outcome of any public employer-employee discussions will depend more on management's determinations than on bilateral decisions by "equals" at the bargaining table.

Missouri and California are the best examples of states which have adopted the pure meet-and-confer bargaining model. In *Missey v. City of Cabool,*[14] the Missouri Supreme Court ruled that the state statute does

not purport to give to public employees the right of collective bargaining guaranteed . . . to employees in private industry. . . . The act does not constitute a delegation . . . to the union of the legislative power of the public body, and therefore . . . the prior discretion in the legislative body to adopt, modify or reject outright the results of the discussions is untouched. . . . The act provides only a procedure for communication between the organization selected by public employees and their employer without requiring adoption of any agreement reached.

The Pennsylvania statute adopts an interesting variation on the meet-and-confer model. The Pennsylvania law provides that certain subjects, subsumed under the heading of "wages, hours and other terms and conditions of employment," are mandatory items of "collective negotiations," over which public employees can strike after impasse procedures have been exhausted. The statute also provides that

Public employees shall not be required to bargain over matters of inherent managerial policy, which shall include but shall not be limited to such areas of discretion or policy as the functions and programs of the public employer, standards of service, its overall budget, utilization of technology, the organizational structure and selection and direction of personnel. Public employers, however, shall be required to meet and discuss *on policy matters affecting wages, hours and terms and conditions of employment as well as the impact thereon upon request by public employee representatives [emphasis added].*

Under the Pennsylvania law, the duty to meet and discuss is defined so as to ensure that "decisions or determinations on matters so discussed shall remain with the public employer." In addition, it appears that bargaining disagreements over matters in the meet-and-discuss category may not be appealed pursuant to statutory impasse procedures and, further, that public employees may not strike over such nonmandatory subjects.

At first glance, the Pennsylvania scheme appears to resemble closely and to adopt the private sector model, which distinguishes between "mandatory" and "permissive" subjects of bargaining and forbids bargaining to a point of impasse over permissive subjects. In *State College Education Association v. PLRB*,[15] however, the commonwealth court makes it clear that there are significant differences between the private sector model and the existing law in Pennsylvania. In *State College,* the court made the somewhat astounding finding that "Any item of wages, hours, and other conditions of employment, if affected by a policy determination, is not a bargainable item." The court then went on to rule that a public employer was required to "meet and discuss," but not to "negotiate," over union demands for timely notice of teacher assignments, desks and lockers for each teacher, a cafeteria for teachers, rest periods for teachers, maximum workload for teachers, holidays, maximum class size, and various requests concerning teacher work assignments. The court ruled, in effect, that even though these matters may have concerned wages, hours, and conditions of work, they also affected policy and, therefore, were not negotiable. Many of these same matters would clearly be found to be mandatory subjects of bargaining under the NLRA and, indeed, they have been found to be mandatory subjects for bargaining in numerous other public sector jurisdictions. Thus, the category of "permissive" subjects is substantially greater in Pennsylvania than in the private sector; and, as a result, the employees' right to strike is narrowed accordingly. Public sector unions in Pennsylvania may now seek to avoid the impact of this ruling by camouflaging their real proposals, a difficult undertaking, however, because, if the decision in *State College* is literally enforced, very few, if any, subjects will be found to be mandatory subjects for bargaining.

The Pennsylvania law is plainly an odd statutory creation. Actually, most states have rejected the pure meet-and-confer bargaining model. In practice, most states have adopted either a *modified* meet-and-confer statute, which gives unions more bargaining power than the pure model, or a *modified* collective negotiations statute, which is more restrictive from the union's viewpoint than its private sector counterpart. For this reason alone, it is often difficult to distinguish between the meet-and-confer and collective negotiations concepts in the public sector.

A good example of this problem is seen in Kansas, where the duty to meet and confer encompasses more than a mere exhortation to the public employer to "consider" employee's proposals; it is a joint obligation to "meet and confer in order . . . *to endeavor to reach agreement* on conditions of employment." The supreme court in Kansas recently defined the required duty to bargain under the Kansas teacher bargaining law and clearly put to rest the claim that the statutory reference to meet and confer required something less than collective negotiations. On this point, the Kansas court observed that the "professional negotiation" required by the statute *means not only meeting and conferring but doing so "in a good faith effort by both parties to reach agreement." We think this is where the Board's determination not to be bound runs afoul of the act. If a board were merely required to "meet and confer," there would be no need for the legislative mandates of good faith and a mutual effort to reach agreement. "Agreement," in particular, is hardly necessary if the Board is to be free to ignore what is agreed upon. . . .*

The feature of the act which we think militates most strongly against the rigidity of the Board's position is the statutory provision that agreements when ratified by both parties *are "binding." This is in contrast to the unilateral "implementary action" to make a "memorandum of agreement" effective, as contemplated by the "meet and confer" definitions of the [report by the Advisory Commission on Intergovernmental Relations]. . . . In reaching this conclusion we recognize the differences between collective negotiations by public employees and collective bargaining as it is established in the private sector, in particular by the National Labor Relations Act. . . . We do not, however, believe those differences prevent our reaching the conclusion that a public employer may negotiate and be bound by its agreements relating to terms and conditions of employment.*

The curious mixture of statutory schemes used to define the duty to bargain in the public sector probably just reflects the initial reluctance of state legislatures to adopt the private sector bargaining model in total. Some of this legislative reticence, however, is beginning to mellow. Minnesota and Alaska recently shunned meet-and-confer language in newly adopted statutes, and the word "negotiate" was recently substituted for the word "confer" in the South Dakota statute. The *State College* decision in Pennsylvania is a noteworthy exception to this trend. Even in Pennsylvania, however, it is not clear yet that the *process* of bargaining is actually different with respect to mandatory (collective negotiation) as opposed to permissive (meet-and-discuss) subjects. The *State College* opinion probably reflects an unstated belief by the judiciary that the scope of mandatory bargaining should be narrowed so as to avoid adversary confrontations and strikes over important public policy issues. Unfortunately, the decision is grossly overdrawn in this respect.

The trend in state legislation away from the initial flirtation with meet and confer is not yet complete. Some state legislatures continue to cling to the notion that there ought to be *some* differences between the public and private sectors with respect to the nature of the duty to bargain. It is not clear, however, that legislative attempts to preserve the remnants of a limited bargaining model will have any practical effect on the behavior of the parties at the bargaining table.

The Scope of Bargaining

The issues concerning the *process* of collective bargaining in the public sector raise important and sometimes troublesome questions, especially in connection with questions having to do with the strike proscription, impasse procedures, and processes for legislative ratification. While these issues are not insignificant, more important are the questions related to the range of legally permissible subjects about which the parties may meet and confer or negotiate in the public sector. If, as suggested above, there is no real difference in the technique of bargaining in most meet-and-confer and most collective negotiations states (because the parties negotiate as "equals" only under the latter approach), we are still not told much about the effective scope of bargaining in the states that have opted for the collective negotiations approach. A state statutory requirement that the parties negotiate as "equals" will be insignificant if the statute also narrowly limits the scope of bargaining. To promise the government employee equality at the bargaining table while at the same time excluding most items relating to wages, hours, and working conditions from the mandatory subjects of bargaining would make collective bargaining for the public sector an illusory gain indeed.

In the private sector, the scope of bargaining is derived from the words "wages, hours, and other terms and conditions of employment" found in Section 8(d) of the NLRA. Subjects covered by this phrase are deemed to be mandatory, and the employer must bargain over them. Other matters are either permissive or illegal subjects of bargaining. Bargaining with respect to permissive subjects is discretionary for both parties, and neither is required to bargain in good faith to the point at which agreement or impasse is reached. The parties are not explicitly forbidden from discussing matters that are illegal subjects of bargaining, but a contract provision embodying an illegal subject is, of course, unenforceable.

In the private sector, the line between mandatory and permissive subjects of bargaining is drawn on an ad hoc basis as the NLRB and the courts subject the distinction to constant redefinition and refinement. In the public sector, more is attempted by statute, generally in the form of specific restrictions on the subject matter of bargaining. It is clear that in defining the scope of bargaining, many public sector jurisdictions have attempted to consider the impact of collective bargaining on the allocation of political power. As noted by Wellington and Winter, "the issue is how powerful unions will be in the typical municipal political process if a full transplant of collective bargaining is carried out."[16] This concern is expressly stated in the "declaration of policy" in the Kansas Public Employer-Employee Relations Act, as follows:

> [T]here neither is, nor can be, an analogy of status between public employees and private employees, in fact or law, because of inherent differences in the employment relationship arising out of the unique fact that the public employer was established by and for the benefit of all the people and its authority derives not from contract nor the profit motive inherent in the principle of free enterprise, but from the constitution, statutes, civil service rules, regulations and resolutions; and . . . the difference between public and private employment is further reflected in the constraints that bar any abdication or bargaining away by public employers of their continuing legislative discretion. . . .[17]

Given these expressed concerns, which have been recognized in one form or another in almost every public sector jurisdiction, it is interesting to observe that disparate attempts that have been made to "regulate" the scope of bargaining in the public sector. Indeed, several states appear to attempt to regulate the *scope* of bargaining by limiting the *process* of collective bargaining. For the sake of convenience, some of these various attempts to regulate the scope of bargaining may be listed under the following general headings:

1. *Strike Proscription.* Although the prohibition against public employee strikes does not directly limit the list of bargainable subjects, it does reject the private sector notion that "the use of economic pressure by parties to a labor dispute . . . is part and parcel of the process of collective bargaining."[18] This rejection may be significant if it is assumed that an employer is less likely to capitulate on an important substantive issue if the strike threat is removed.

2. *Legislative Ratification.* As with the strike proscription, the process of legislative ratification may also be an indirect means of limiting the scope of bargaining. For example, New York's Taylor Law requires that each negotiated contract must contain the following notice:[19]

> *It is agreed by and between the parties that any provision of this agreement requiring legislative action to permit its implementation by amendment of law or by providing the additional funds therefor, shall not become effective until the appropriate legislative body has given approval.*

This process of legislative ratification, or budget allocation, obviously may involve judgments on certain substantive items contained in a collective bargaining agreement. The legislative body may be prohibited from attempting to "renegotiate" an entirely new agreement; however, it is not prohibited from refusing to allocate the funds necessary to implement an agreement fully.[20] The net impact of these actions may be the same in some cases and the refusal to appropriate may effectively limit the scope of matters covered by the collective agreement.

3. *Preexisting Legislation and Civil Service Laws.* Some statutory provisions restrict the scope of bargaining by giving precedence to existing state law or municipal ordinance over a collective bargaining agreement. For example, the Pennsylvania law states that

> *The parties to the collective bargaining process shall not effect or implement a provision in a collective bargaining agreement if the implementation of that provision would be in violation of, or inconsistent with, or in conflict with any statute or statutes enacted by the General Assembly of the Commonwealth of Pennsylvania or the provisions of municipal home rule charters.*

4. *Statutory Management-Rights Clauses.* Several states have attempted to limit the scope of bargaining by stating, in general terms, that the public employer shall not be required to bargain with respect to the "mission of the agency" or matters of "inherent managerial policy."

5. *Statutory Exclusions.* Some statutes expressly exclude certain matters from the range of permissible subjects, while other statutes expressly list the matters that may be discussed. For example, the Kansas statute (covering public employees other than teachers) explicitly limits the scope of bargaining to salaries, wages, hours of work, vacations, sick and injury leave, holidays, retirement and insurance benefits, wearing apparel, overtime pay, shift differential and jury duty pay, and grievance procedures.

185

6. *Meet-and-Confer Bargaining.* The pure meet-and-confer bargaining model implicitly limits the scope of bargaining because the employees' bargaining agent can do no more than make suggestions that the public employer is free to ignore. In other words, the scope of "bargaining" is no more or less than what the public employer chooses to make it.

These various methods that have been used to "regulate" the scope of bargaining plainly are not mutually exclusive. Many jurisdictions have adopted two or more of these approaches; this fact alone makes it clear that there has been no uniform adoption of the private sector model in the public sector. Even though these various attempts have been made to "regulate" the scope of bargaining in the public sector, in recognition of the differences between the public and private sectors, it is not clear that the scope of permissible bargaining has been more narrowly defined in the public sector. Indeed, it may be contended that in certain public sector jurisdictions the private sector model has been rejected in favor of a *wider* scope of bargaining.

The experience in Michigan furnishes a good example of this development. The Michigan statute, like the NLRA, defines the duty to bargain as "the mutual obligation [of the parties] to meet at reasonable times and confer in good faith with respect to wages, hours, and other terms and conditions of employment, or the negotiation of an agreement . . . and the execution of a written contract. . . ." In *Westwood Community Schools*[21] MERC construed this language and apparently rejected the mandatory-permissive distinction used in the private sector. Rather, the commission observed that

> *A balancing approach to bargaining may be more suited to the realities of the public sector than the dichotomized scheme — mandatory and non-mandatory — used in the private sector. [The private sector] scheme prohibits the use of economic weapons to compel agreement to discuss non-mandatory subjects of bargaining, but strikes are permissible once the point of impasse concerning mandatory subjects of bargaining is reached. Economic force is illegal in the public sector. . . . In Michigan, in the public sector, economic battle is to be replaced by invocation of the impasse resolution procedures of mediation and fact finding.*
>
> *An expansion of the subjects about which the public employer ought to bargain, unlike the private sector, should not result in a corresponding increase in the use of economic force to resolve impasses. In the absence of legal public sector strikes, our only proper concern in the area of subjects of bargaining is whether the employer's management functions are being unduly restrained. All bargaining has some limiting effect on an employer.*
>
> *Therefore, we will not order bargaining in those cases where the subjects are demonstrably within the core of entrepreneurial control. Although such subjects may affect interests of employees, we do not believe that such interests outweigh the right to manage.*

MERC then went on to find that a school board was required to bargain over the school calendar. On this point, MERC concluded that "the rather substantial interest which the school teachers have in planning their summer activities outweigh any claim of interference with the right to manage the school district."

The Michigan commission's juxtaposition of the duty to bargain and the strike proscription implies that the scope of bargaining ought to be *broader* in the public sector than in the private sector. According to this interpretation, since public employees are ostensibly prevented from using the strike or the threat of a strike to gain leverage at the bargaining table, there is no point in severely restricting the subjects that may be brought up in negotia· tions. The public employer cannot be penalized by work stoppages for taking a hard-line bargaining position and it is not compelled to agree with any position taken by the employees' union on any subject. Therefore, if the strike proscription is in effect *and is enforced,* the agenda at the bargaining table should be open to virtually any subject.

The same rationale was used by the Connecticut Supreme Court in *West Hartford Education Association v. De Courcy*[22] where it was held that class size, teacher work loads, and the length of the school calendar were all mandatory subjects of bargaining. In reaching this result, the Connecticut court ruled that the disputed subjects were not at the "core of entrepreneurial control" (i.e., they were not "fundamental to the existence, direction and operation of the enterprise"); cited private sector precedent to the effect that "while not determinative, it is appropriate to look to industrial practices in appraising the propriety of including a particular subject within the scope of mandatory bargaining"; and suggested that the absence of the strike weapon favored a broad interpretation of the duty to bargain. It may be argued of course that the disputed subjects in *De Courcy* would be found to be mandatory subjects even under the NLRA; however, it is nevertheles noteworthy that the decisions in Michigan and Connecticut, and other jurisdictions as well, indicate that the scope of bargaining in the public sector is *at least* as wide as the duty to bargain in the private sector.

The *Westwood* decision is significant because it suggests that the scope of bargaining may include any subject that "is likely to lead to controversy and industrial conflict." It could be argued that such language may include a number of subjects not within the literal definition of "wages, hours, and terms and conditions of employment," at least as that term has been construed in the private sector. Therefore, the *Westwood* test may in fact foreshadow a movement to free public sector bargaining from the confines of the traditional mandatory-permissive distinction followed in the private sector. The difficulty with the *Westwood* test, however, is that it relies not only on the existence, but also on the effectiveness of the strike proscription. In those states, such as Pennsylvania, where strikes are legal, the *Westwood* test would seem inapplicable. Indeed, it is interesting to note the contrasting opinion on the scope of mandatory bargaining rendered by the Commonwealth Court of Pennsylvania in the *State College* decision. In those states where strikes are illegal but the proscription is not enforced, the application of the *Westwood* test would seem to give public unions an unfair advantage at the negotiating table, perhaps enabling them to coerce agreement on subjects that in the private sector might not be mandatory subjects of bargaining. The recent six-week teacher strike in Detroit highlights this problem.

The Michigan situation is further complicated by the fact that public employers are not relieved from the duty to bargain even when faced with an unlawful work stoppage. In *Saginaw Township Board of Education,*[23] MERC cited the Supreme Court's decision in *NLRB v. Insurance Agents International Union*[24] and ruled that an employer was lawfully bound to continue bargaining with a union even while the employees were engaged in prohibited strike action. The reliance on private sector precedent in *Saginaw* was plainly misplaced. In *Insurance Agents,* the Supreme Court ruled that there was no inconsistency between the application of economic pressure and good faith collective bargaining under the NLRA; consequently, the Court ruled that even when employees are engaged in certain economic action that might be viewed as "unprotected," the employer's duty to bargain was not altered. The same rationale simply is not applicable to the public sector. Most public sector jurisdictions forbid strike action; thus, the strike proscription reflects a policy determination that concerted economic action take by public employees against employers is inconsistent with the duty to bargain as defined in the public sector. Most public sector jurisdictions are not neutral on the strike issue; rather, the economic strike is positively and explicitly forbidden. In this context, it is truly naive to assume that the duty to bargain and the right to strike may be treated as independent problems. Strike action is taken to bring pressure to bear on the bargaining agents who are negotiating at the bargaining table. Such economic pressure is expressly tolerated in the context of private sector bargaining. So long as the strike is banned in the public sector, however, it is not clear why an employer should be required to continue negotiating (and submit to proscribed pressures) in the face of unlawful economic action by the union. The Wisconsin Commission recognized this problem in *City of Milwaukee*[25] when it was held that "We do not believe that labor organizations . . . engaging in a strike, should at the same time be entitled to the benefits of fact finding or other rights granted to them by statute." The commission then went on to hold that it would "decline to process any fact finding petition filed by a labor organization which is engaged in a strike."

The New York approach with respect to the scope of the duty to bargain varies somewhat from that in Michigan. The decisions rendered by the New York PERB clearly reject any expanded interpretation of the scope of bargaining comparable to that suggested in *Westwood.* The New York PERB, however, does appear to adhere closely to private sector precedent in defining the scope of mandatory bargaining. In *City of New Rochelle*[26] PERB upheld the right of a school board to make budget cuts resulting in the termination of the services of teachers. PERB noted that such budget cuts "obviously" affect terms and conditions of employment, but concluded that "the decision to curtail services and eliminate jobs is not a mandatory subject of negotiations, although the employer is obligated to negotiate on the impact of such decision on the terms and conditions of employment of the employees affected." The board was evidently relying on the Supreme Court's decision in *Fibreboard Paper Products Corp. v. NLRB.*[27]

Later, in *West Irondequoit Bd. of Education*[28] PERB ruled that class size was not a mandatory subject of bargaining. In reaching this decision, PERB made it clear that teachers' traditional interest in matters affecting educational policy, was not an adequate justification for expanding the scope of bargaining beyond that in the private sector. In particular, PERB ruled that

> The determination as to the manner and means by which education service be rendered and the extent of such service is the duty and obligation of the public employer. A public employer should not be required to delegate this responsibility.

It is interesting, however, that the same New York PERB, in *City of White Plains*,[29] ruled that a "demand that a minimum number of Fire Fighters be on duty at all times with each engine and each truck constitute[d] a mandatory subject of negotiations." The decision in *West Irondequoit* was distinguished on the ground that "the teachers' interest was limited to workload [whereas] the interests of the Fire Fighters . . . also involved safety."

It is not really surprising to see that states like New York, Michigan, and Connecticut have followed private sector precepts in defining the scope of the duty to bargain. Each of these states has adopted statutory language very similar to that found in the NLRA. Thus, it really may be more interesting to observe the developments in some of the public sector jurisdictions that have enacted statutory provisions at variance with the private sector model.

A good example of such a jurisdiction is Kansas. The Professional Negotiations Act of 1970, which provides for bargaining rights for teachers, defines the scope of the duty to bargain as "meeting, conferring, consulting and discussing in a good faith effort by both parties to reach agreement with respect to the *terms and conditions of professional service*." The Supreme Court of Kansas recently ruled that this language required school boards to bargain about more than just salaries, work load, and fringe benefits.[30] In particular, the court also ruled that the statutory reference to "conditions of professional service" included subjects such as probationary period, transfers, teacher appraisals, disciplinary procedures, and resignations. The Kansas court specifically cited the Connecticut Supreme Court decision in *West Hartford Education Association v. De Courcy*[31] as a useful precedent; however, it declined to follow the Connecticut court's conclusion that class size was a mandatory subject of bargaining.

In defining the scope of bargaining, the Kansas court came close to adopting the impact test frequently followed in the private sector. On this score, the court observed that

> It does little good . . . to speak of negotiability in terms of "policy" versus something which is not "policy". Salaries are a matter of policy, and so are vacation and sick leaves. Yet we cannot doubt the authority of the Board to negotiate and bind itself on these questions. The key, as we see it, is how direct the impact of an issue is on the well-being of the individual teacher as opposed to its effect on the operation of the school system as a whole. . . . The similar phraseology of the N.L.R.A. has had a similar history of judicial definition. See Fibreboard Corp. v. Labor Board, *379 U.S. 203, and especially the concurring opinion of Stewart, J.*

The court then went on to hold that matters such as class size, curriculum and materials, payroll mechanics, certification, use of paraprofessionals, and duties of substitute teachers were not mandatory subjects.

As an aside, it is interesting to note that the scope of the duty to bargain under the Kansas Public Employer-Employee Relations Act is much more narrowly defined and explicitly limited to discussions over salaries, hours of work, vacations, sick leave, holidays, retirement, insurance, wearing apparel, overtime pay, shift premium, jury duty pay, and grievance procedures.[32] Obviously, the Kansas legislature gave favored treatment to teachers in recognition of their traditional interest in matters affecting educational policy.

The Governor's Executive Order in Illinois is another example of a public sector bargaining scheme that rejects the private sector model. Although the order requires negotiations in "good faith with respect to wages, hours and other terms and conditions of employment," it further provides that the state is not required to negotiate on the merit principle, agency policies, programs and statutory functions, budget matters, decision on standards, scope and delivery of service, use of technology, the state retirement system, and anything required or prohibited by law. It might be assumed that this sweeping reservation of management rights might restrict the scope of bargaining; but the Federal Labor Relations Council, which is charged with the enforcement of Executive Order 11491 (regulating bargaining in the federal service), has construed a similar management rights provision very narrowly. In *Department of the Army Corps of Engineers*[33] the council ruled that even though federal agency officials retained the exclusive right to act "to maintain the efficiency of the Government operations," pursuant to the management rights provision in Section 12(b) of Executive Order 11491, the obligation to bargain over "matters affecting working conditions" was not narrowly reduced. The agency had refused to discuss a union proposal designed to curtail the use of swing shifts, contending that swing-shift scheduling minimized overtime and other premium costs to the employer and that, therefore, the union's proposal would impair the agency's ability to maintain efficiency and economy. The FLRC properly recognized that if the management rights provision was construed literally it would effectively nullify the duty to bargain. In rejecting the employer's argument on this point, the FLRC ruled that the Executive Order required:

> Consideration and balancing of all the factors involved, including the well-being of employees, rather than an arbitrary determination based only on the anticipation of increased cost. Other factors such as the potential for improved performance, increased productivity, responsiveness to directions, reduced turnover, fewer grievances, contribution of money-saving ideas, improved health and safety, and the like, are valid considerations. . . . The [management rights section] may not properly be invoked to deny negotiations unless there is a substantial demonstration by the agency that increased costs or reduced effectiveness in operations are inescapable and significant and are not offset by compensating benefits.

A similar ruling was handed down in *United States Merchant Marine Academy*[34] where the FLRC ruled that "an agency may [not] unilaterally limit the scope of its bargaining obligation on otherwise negotiable matters . . . . merely by issuing regulations from higher levels." If these federal precedents are followed in Illinois, then the scope of bargaining will probably

190

be defined as widely as is permitted in the private sector, notwithstanding the management rights provision.

Based on the evidence to date, it is not at all clear that a statutory management rights clause effectively narrows the scope of bargaining. The Nevada Local Government Employee Relations Act[35] sets forth an elaborate management rights provision that seems to remove numerous subjects from the scope of bargaining, but the Nevada Local Government Employee-Management Relations Board in *Washoe County School District*[36] ruled that proposals concerning class size, student discipline, school calendar, and teacher work load were negotiable matters. The board stated in this regard that

> *Although it has been urged upon this Board . . . that the provisions of [the management rights section] limit the areas of negotiability on matters relating to wages, hours, and conditions of employment if said matters also involve any items [listed in the management rights section], the Board rejects this view as untenable. It is presumed the Legislature in enacting [the law] did not enact a nullity. . . . It is the opinion of the Board, therefore, that any matter significantly related to wages, hours, and working conditions is negotiable, whether or not said matters also relate to questions of management prerogative.*

This decision directly conflicts with the decision of the Commonwealth Court of Pennsylvania in the *State College* opinion. Indeed, it appears that the Pennsylvania view concerning the weight to be given statutory management rights clauses is a distinctly minority position. Both the Hawaii Public Employment Relations Board and the Los Angeles County Employee Relations Commission[37] have also defined the scope of bargaining widely, following the same rationale as used in *Washoe County,* notwithstanding the presence of statutory management rights clauses.

Another question that has frequently arisen in the public sector is whether the scope of negotiations should be narrowed pursuant to existing state statutes or municipal ordinances. This subject has been masterfully treated in an article by Hanslowe and Oberer,[38] who framed the question as follows:

> *The general problem . . . is the relationship of the Taylor Law . . . to other laws of the State of New York and to the agencies which administer them, with regard to the determination of the scope of negotiations under the Taylor Law. . . . A question, within the foregoing question is: What impact, if any, does the Taylor Law have on the pre-existing authority of public employers to determine "terms and conditions of employment" of their employees? In other words, is the scope of negotiations under the Taylor Law coterminous with or greater than the scope of the unilateral power held by the particular public employer under pre-existing law. . . . ?*

Several public sector jurisdictions have resolved this issue by giving precedence to existing state law that conflicts with the duty to bargain. For example, the Massachusetts municipal employee bargaining statute provides: "In the event that any part or provision of any such agreement is in conflict with any law, ordinance, or by-law, such law, ordinance, or by-law shall prevail so long as such conflict remains. . . ."[39] Where the matter is not clearly resolved by statute, the duty to bargain has been seen to prevail in at least two important decisions handed down in Michigan and New York. In Michigan, where the public employee bargaining statute makes no mention of precedence, the state supreme court has ruled that those provisions of local civil service laws covering mandatory subjects of bargaining are superseded *pro tanto* by the Michigan Public Employees Relations Act.[40] In 1972 the New York court of appeals, in a landmark decision, *Board of Education v. Associated Teachers of Huntington,*[41] ruled that, in light of the Taylor Act, a school board had authority to enter into a collective bargaining agreement granting benefits to teachers, even though there was no *specific* statutory authorization to do so. In reaching this result, the court stated that

> . . . under the Taylor Law, the obligation to bargain as to all terms and conditions of employment is a broad and unqualified one, and there is no reason why the mandatory provision of that act should be limited, in any way, except in cases where some other applicable statutory provision explicitly and definitely prohibits the public employer from making an agreement as to a particular term or condition of employment.

It is certainly likely that these rulings will influence other states where the statutes do not contain a rule of precedence.

Thus, it may be concluded that, even though the scope of the duty to bargain has been defined differently in many public sector jurisdictions, private sector principles have nevertheless been widely recognized and adopted. It is significant to note that private sector precepts have also had a significant impact on the developing law in connection with the duration and enforcement of the duty to bargain.

Conclusion

It is difficult to generalize from the data at hand, but it probably is fair to conclude that, at least in those states which have adopted a comprehensive statutory scheme to regulate public employee bargaining, the employee (union) interest has thus far fared well in the process of reconciliation in the public sector. It may be that the long history of strong opposition to public sector unionism is now perceived to be unfair and unwarranted by legislators, judges, and other public officials. It also may be that state officials are reacting against the possibility of federal legislation which might control all collective bargaining in the public sector. Whether prompted by a sense of guilt or a practical political problem, however, it would certainly appear that many legislators, judges, and other public officials have been willing to be *relatively* generous in establishing and enforcing bargaining rights for public employees. In any event, it surely may be seen that a number of significant public employee interests have survived well, both because of and without regard to prevailing private sector principles.

Footnotes

1. Saginaw Township Board of Education, 1970 MERC Lab. Op. 127.
2. International Association of Firefighters v. City of Homestead, Case No. 72-9285 (Florida Circuit Court, 1973). See also Board of Trustees of the Ulster County Community College and the Ulster County Legislature, 4 PERB 3749 (1971).
3. International Association of Firefighters v. City of Homestead, Case No. 72-9285 (Florida Circuit Court, 1973).
4. Town of Stratford, Decision No. 1069 (Conn. State Bd. of Labor Relations, 1972).
5. West Hartford Education Association v. DeCourcy, 162 Conn. 566, 295 A.2d 526 (Conn. Sup. Ct. 1972).
6. Bassett v. Braddock, 262 So. 2d 425 (Fla. 1972).
7. City of Saginaw, 1969 MERC Lab. Op. 293.
8. N.Y. Civ. Serv. Law. Sec. 204-a(1) (McKinney 1973); see also City of Detroit, 1971 MERC Lab. Op. 237.
9. See, for example, Board of Trustees of the Ulster County Community College and the Ulster County Legislature, 4 PERB 3749 (1971); City of Saginaw, 1969 MERC Lab. Op. 293.
10. 1969 MERC Lab. Op. 293.
11. 1970 MERC Lab. Op. 953.
12. "Police, Fire Arbitration Opposed by Cities," *LMRS Newsletter* 3, no 11 (November 1972).
13. GERR Reference File 91:02-03 (1970).
14. 441 S. W. 2d 35 (Mo. 1969).
15. GERR no. 510, E-1 (1973).
16. Wellington and Winter, *The Unions and the Cities*, pp. 29-30.
17. Kansas Stat. Ann. Secs. 75-4321 (4) and (5).
18. NLRB v. Insurance Agents, 361 U.S. 477 (1960).
19. N.Y. Civ. Serv. Law Sec. 204-a(1) (McKinney 1973).
20. See City of Detroit, 1971 MERC Lab. Op. 237.
21. 7 MERC Lab. Op. 313 (1972).
22. 162 Conn. 566 (1972).
23. 1970 MERC Lab. Op. 127.
24. 361 U.S. 477 (1969).
25. Dec. no. 6575 B (1963).
26. 4 PERB 3704 (1971).
27. 379 U.S. 203 (1964).
28. 4 PERB 3725 (1971), *aff'd on rehearing*, 4 PERB 3753 (1971).
29. 5 PERB Para. 3008 (1972).
30. National Education Association of Shawnee Mission, Inc. v. Board of Education of Shawnee Mission Unified School District, GERR no. 521, at E-1 (1973).
31. 162 Conn. 566 (1972).
32. Kansas Stat. Ann. Secs. 75-4322 (s).
33. FLRC no. 71A-36 (1972).
34. FLRC no. 71A-15 (1972).
35. Nevada Rev. Stat. Sec. 288.150 (1).
36. Item no. 3 (1971).
37. Hawaii State Teachers Association, GERR no. 480, at E-1 (1972); Los Angeles County Employees Ass'n, Local 600 v. County of Los Angeles, 71 LC Para. 53, 129 (Calif. Ct. of App., 1973).
38. Kurt Hanslowe and Walter Oberer, "Determining the Scope of Negotiations

Under Public Employment Relations Statutes, *Industrial and Labor Relations Review* 24 (1971):432

39. Mass. Ann. Laws chap 149 Sec. 1781 (Supp. 1972).
40. Civil Serv. Commn. v. Wayne County Bd. of Supervisors, 384 Mich. 363, 184 N.W.2d 201 (1971).
41. 30 N.Y.2d 122, 282 N.E. 2d 109, 331 N.Y.S.2d 17 (1972).

Case Study Analysis of Teacher Collective Bargaining

Lorraine McDonnell and Anthony Pascal*

Our primary purpose in conducting this study was not to describe how the collective bargaining process operates, but rather to examine the effects of teacher collective bargaining on school and district operations. However, the negotiations process as well as the contract itself influences how collective bargaining affects local [school] districts. Therefore, our fieldwork analysis needed to include an examination of the collective bargaining process—how the agenda is set, who the major participants are, the effect of the state legal environment, how trade-offs are made, and the role of impasse resolution procedures.

The Collective Bargaining Process

Setting the bargaining agenda. It is clear from our research that the nature of the collective bargaining process greatly influences contractual outcomes. Various aspects, like the stability of the negotiating teams over time and the quality of their relationship with each other, are critical in understanding why collective bargaining has been a very constructive process in some districts and a source of acrimony and divisiveness in others.

The teacher organization agenda. The shaping of bargaining agendas by the teacher organization and the school district comprises the first step in the negotiations process. In formulating its agenda, the teacher organization has two goals. First, because it is a membership organization, it must seek to please the members by negotiating for those items they most prefer. At the same time, the teacher organization has to be realistic and limit its agenda to the items it is most likely to win at the bargaining table. As one teacher organization negotiator notes, "You can't get a good contract if you come in with a Christmas list of stuff."

---

*The Rand Corporation, Santa Monica, California. Reprinted from Lorraine McDonnell and Anthony Pascal, *Organized Teachers and American Schools* (Santa Monica, Ca.: The Rand Corporation, 1979), pp. 35-74.

194

All the teacher organizations in our sample have some formal mechanism for soliciting teacher input. These include surveys conducted by each school-site building representative, a questionnaire in the organization's newspaper, and mass membership meetings held in several locations around the district. Some organizations simply ask their members what they prefer to see in the bargaining package, while others present the members with a number of possible items and ask them to rank-order the possibilities in terms of their preferences. Most organizations form a committee representative of the membership (i.e., elementary, secondary, special education, and school librarians) that refines the results of the surveys into a bargaining agenda. By such methods, the practical day-to-day concerns of teachers guide organizational leadership in their negotiations with school management.

In addition to membership preferences, other factors contribute to an organization's bargaining package. Problems the organization has experienced with the present contract is an example. The leadership knows the source of grievances and concentrates on those areas which have generated a large number. The aim is to get contract language either strengthened or changed altogether. Some teacher organizations rely on a model contract provided by their national or state affiliates. However, we found that except for districts in a few states the use of a model contract is rare and is usually limited to the weakest local organizations with the most immature contracts.

An obvious question is whether solicitation of membership input is anything more than a symbolic action to make the teacher organization appear more open and democratic. Do membership preferences really make a difference once negotiators get to the bargaining table? We found that by and large they do. The leadership of most teacher organizations takes membership concerns seriously even when making trade-offs at the bargaining table. Negotiators try to keep their demands within the general area proposed by teachers. For example, if an organization found it would be unable to obtain dental insurance, it would press for an increase in other medical benefits.

In only two districts in our sample did the teacher organization refuse to negotiate over items proposed by the members. Their refusal was based on a reluctance to anger the school board; it is the policy of these organizations to include in their bargaining package only those proposals they feel will be acceptable to the school board. As expected, these organizations have the weakest contracts of any in our sample. Despite their apparent timidity, only one of these organizations has a friendly, cooperative relationship with the school district, while in the other relations have been extremely troublesome.

Although the majority of organizations were closely guided by members' preferences, some found it necessary to propose additional items that the leadership considered to be important. These fall into three categories: organizational security items such as agency shop, stronger grievance procedures, and items which address problems the leadership anticipates in the future. This latter category includes, for example, more specific reduction-in-force procedures which may result from declining enrollment and district financial problems, and items like involuntary transfer policy which have become more important because of various state and federal mandates. In none of the cases we examined did the membership oppose these items and in most instances, the leadership felt that over time members came to understand their importance.

The school district agenda. While school districts have traditionally formulated very specific economic packages, they have tended to ignore non-compensation items at the proposal stage. Instead, they merely reacted to ones prepared by the teacher organizations. However, we found that over time school districts have begun to formulate their own proposals on non-compensation items. School district respondents felt that such a strategy gives them additional leverage in bargaining over working conditions and professional matters and provides them with something to trade away for teacher concessions. School district negotiators maintained that while they cannot realistically expect to remove items from the contract without concessions to the teacher organization, having a set of definite proposals provides them with a basis for making these trade-offs in a systematic way. In addition, school districts find that, like teacher organizations, they often need to modify problematic contract language.

The effect of federal program mandates on agenda-setting. We expected that external factors like federal program mandates would influence both teacher organizations and school districts. Although school districts seemed relatively unconcerned, teacher organizations did formulate some of their proposals in response to federal programs. The federal government's Education for All Handicapped Children Act (PL 94-142) has important implications for collective bargaining. In the majority of districts we visited school and teacher organization officials reported that the mandates of PL 94-142 would soon become a subject for bargaining, if they had not become so already. Many teacher organizations took cues from national affiliates and demanded that teachers be given release time to prepare Individualized Education Plans, that handicapped students who were mainstreamed into regular classrooms be given extra weight in computing class sizes, and that teachers be provided with adequate in-service education before handicapped children were accepted into their classrooms.

The Emergency School Aid Act (ESAA) has also influenced the course of teacher collective bargaining. This program requires, as a condition of funding, that school faculties be racially balanced (as do many school desegregation decisions). Such a mandate has made the question of involuntary transfer much more important because school districts have had to transfer teachers from one school to another in order to achieve racial balance. In most cases, the teacher organization has attempted to establish explicit criteria (e.g., seniority) for this purpose.

On the other hand, we did not find that state and federal programs like ESEA Title I, which mandate parent advisory councils, and hence affect teacher contact hours with parents, had any effect on bargaining proposals. Most districts and teacher organizations reported that even when there are contractual limits on teacher contact hours, it is usually possible to find enough teacher volunteers to serve on such councils. Therefore, it has not been necessary to propose contract changes to accommodate ESEA's external mandates.

196

Although teacher organizations have found it necessary on occasion to protect contract gains from external pressures, it is important to note that often teacher organizations have worked to accommodate such mandates. For example, one district we visited was beginning to implement a desegregation plan and the teacher organization negotiated, as part of its contract, a lottery system to assign teachers to the new cluster schools. Both district administrators and teachers felt that this negotiated system made the process smoother and more equitable. In other districts, teacher organizations have included provisions in their contracts that exclude some teacher hiring, promotion, and transfer issues from seniority criteria in order to accommodate affirmative action mandates.

The community and the bargaining agenda. The role of the community in setting the bargaining agenda has begun to receive renewed attention. A number of people argue that because the public both consumes and pays for public education, it ought to be included in the teacher collective bargaining process. These community participation advocates believe that mechanisms should be created to obtain public input at the time the bargaining package is formulated and to include public representatives in negotiations as either active participants or observers. They also argue that elected boards of education inadequately represent community interests.

We found that this idea is not only unacceptable to most district and teacher organization negotiators, but also that community groups display little interest in teacher collective bargaining unless there is a strike. Several districts made bargaining proposals public and then reserved time for public comment at board of education meetings. The result was general indifference even in those few cases where community input was actively solicited.

For example, one large Northern district in our sample recently established a community negotiating council (but did not grant it either observer or participant status at the bargaining table). The group was encouraged to obtain consumer input through public meetings. At these meetings, the school district and the teacher organization presented their respective positions and answered questions about the forthcoming negotiations. Although the meetings were not well attended, the council drew up a list of community concerns. This committee is still too new to be able to assess its effect, but its members realize that it can only have a limited influence. Neither the district nor the teacher organization is under any obligation to include items of interest to the community in their bargaining agendas. Still, the committee hopes that over time it can exert more influence on the collective bargaining process and can also educate the community to demand a more active role.

Most school districts and teacher organizations feel that the bargaining process functions better when negotiations are removed from public view. Open negotiations allegedly provoke grandstanding, while privacy facilitates thorough discussion of technical issues. As a result of this agreement between labor and management, the community (however defined) plays no active part at the bargaining table.

In four of the districts we visited, state-mandated sunshine laws allow the general public to observe negotiations. Yet even in these districts, neither the general public nor representatives of groups such as the PTA

197

and the League of Women Voters, nor even the press, attend on a regular basis.

Participants in the collective bargaining process. Not only are parents and the general public uninvolved with teacher collective bargaining, school boards are themselves often divorced from negotiations. Of the fifteen districts we visited, school board members actively participated in collective bargaining in only three. Most boards simply review the packages submitted by the teacher organization and by the school district. In those cases where board members play an active role in formulating the district's package, their interest seems restricted to items having cost implications. Once negotiations begin, the board is kept informed of progress and is advised about probable settlement points. School boards must, of course, ratify any final contract and may contribute to the formulation of the district's final offer. Still, the majority of school boards are one step removed from the negotiations process and play only a consultative role in teacher collective bargaining.

The professionalization of collective bargaining. In an earlier study of collective bargaining, Perry and Wildman noted that over time the role of elected representatives (viz., school boards) becomes limited to the identification of reservation points and the approval of major concessions, while the responsibility for actual negotiations resides with a full-time staff specialist who serves as the board's spokesman.[1] Our study, conducted some ten years after Perry and Wildman's, found that what they identified as a growing trend has become almost universal. There are several reasons for this shift. First, as the incidence of public employee collective bargaining has increased, it has become more complicated: school districts have had to negotiate with a growing number of bargaining units representing not merely teachers, but also bus drivers, clerical and custodial staff, and in some cases principals. Many school boards lack both the time and the technical expertise to participate actively in the process. In addition, many districts have found that the ultimate authority of the board is better protected when it is removed from direct confrontation with teachers at the bargaining table. Such a strategy also gives the board's negotiator a face-saving device. The negotiator can involve the board's authority in a strategic fashion, thus providing a buffer at the negotiations table. A final and very important reason why most school boards are no longer active participants at the bargaining table emerges out of unhappy experience. When board members are present, the negotiations process tends to be more emotional and politicized because they frequently lack the discipline needed to negotiate judiciously and to maintain control over the process. In one of the worst examples of board involvement we encountered, negotiations often deteriorated into shouting matches. The school district attorney saw his primary function at the bargaining table as trying to restrain board members whom he characterized as acting like "wild men." Members were not above name-calling and personal denunciation of teacher organization representatives. Such acrimony had long-term implications when it later spilled over into implementation of the contract. Admittedly this is an extreme example;

however, other districts did report that squabbling was minimized when professional negotiators were responsible for collective bargaining.

In most districts collective bargaining is handled by a director of personnel and/or employee relations who often is also an associate or assistant superintendent, reporting directly to the superintendent. The chief negotiator serves as the primary spokesman for the district, but is usually assisted by other central administrative staff responsible for personnel and district finances as well as by several principals. The school district team typically negotiates with a teacher organization team consisting of the executive director and/or president and a representative group of classroom teachers.

But the use of a professional negotiator does not of itself guarantee the orderliness of the collective bargaining process. The effectiveness of any management negotiator depends on his or her status within the school district and the extent of support by the superintendent and the school board. For example, in one district we visited the chief negotiator is also the director of secondary instruction. He was chosen for the position because, having fewer deadlines than other administrators and retaining fewer financial responsibilities, he can spend sufficient time at the bargaining table. He is dispensable. His position carries low status in the district, just as does collective bargaining. Needless to say, his lack of influence and authority hurts the district's position during negotiations. Ideally, the district's chief negotiator should probably be someone who reports directly to the superintendent, has enough authority to obtain necessary information from district administrators, and has access to the school board at least through the superintendent.

Once a school board decides to use a professional negotiator it is important that the board agree to work through that person and not undercut his or her position. In one district the longtime management negotiator resigned after some members of the school board met independently with teacher organization leadership and leaked strategies and district bargaining positions. Although this was an isolated incident, district negotiators around the state knew of it and reported that it had lowered morale and made them less confident in their own bargaining strategies.

The role of outside assistance. Six of the districts in our sample used outside attorneys on retainer as part of their bargaining teams, while only one teacher organization employed an outside lawyer. We expected that teacher organizations would resent the presence of an outsider on the district's bargaining team. However, we found that most organizations not only did not oppose it, but actually welcomed dealing with such a person. The lawyers usually came from private sector labor relations and thought of collective bargaining as primarily concerned with "bread and butter" compensation items. At the same time, they worked to maintain strong management rights. Yet these professional negotiators also appreciated the advantage of minimizing conflict and regularizing both the collective bargaining process and subsequent labor-management relations under the contract. So, for example, in one district where teachers had not made great strides in bargaining, they welcomed the inclusion of a labor lawyer on the district team. This outsider convinced the district of the importance of a strong grievance procedure, a provision the teachers had previously been unable to obtain. He also devised a precise timetable for bargaining so that teachers would not have to work without a contract, and he obtained release time for the teacher organization negotiators so as to expedite and regularize the bargaining sessions. This pattern also appeared in other districts which employed outside labor lawyers.

Most of the teacher organizations in our sample relied on their own resources for bargaining and did not request special assistance from either their state or national affiliates. In fact, we found that the AFT locals received assistance only at the initiation of the bargaining relationship or in the event of a prolonged strike.

Most NEA affiliates, on the other hand, do receive a form of support from their state and national organizations. In 1970 the NEA established the UniServ Program, which provides one staff person in the field for every 1200 teachers. If a local association does not have 1200 members, it can join with other local associations and share UniServ resources. The NEA pays a portion of each staff member's salary, while the state and local associations contribute the remainder. Staff members are trained in negotiation and grievance procedures, business management, political action, public relations, and the efficient use of state and NEA resources. Aside from this support, however, NEA and state staff do not regularly become involved in local negotiations. Like their AFT counterparts, they only go to the aid of local affiliates in the event of a crisis.

The role of principals in negotiations. School principals are also involved in the collective bargaining process. In most districts, they are represented on the management negotiating team. They advise the district on the potential effect of contract items at the school-site and inform central administrators exactly what principals "can live with." Yet their role is often ambiguous. Are they to be considered a part of the "management team" or is their basic interest on the side of classroom teachers? Traditionally, most principals considered themselves as part of management and have been opposed to inclusion in any type of collective bargaining arrangement. But as teacher collective bargaining spreads, many principals have begun to reevaluate this position. Particularly in large urban districts the individual principal is distant from the top district administrators whose policy decisions the principal must implement at the school level. Many principals also perceive an erosion in their leadership positions as teacher organizations have gained more control over educational decisionmaking.

Some principals have responded by establishing union-like organizations of their own. The case of San Francisco principals who formed an organization affiliated with the Teamsters Union is perhaps the most extreme example of this response. The majority of principals have not chosen such an alternative, however, By early 1975, there were about 1015 public school administrator locals, almost all of which were located in only eight states (Connecticut, New Jersey, Washington, New York, Massachusetts, Michigan, Pennsylvania, and Ohio). But only in Connecticut and New Jersey do unions enroll a majority of school administrators.

The principals we interviewed reflected this ambivalence. They acknowledged that they were managers with responsibility for enforcing the contract in their respective schools. At the same time, many declined to participate on the district's negotiating team because they feared it would adversely affect their day-to-day working relations with teachers. Some districts have attempted to strengthen the principals' allegiance to the administration by promoting a management team concept. An elaborate mechanism is used to solicit principal recommendations and they are sometimes rewarded with benefits (e.g., in-service days, fringe benefits) not granted teachers. Still, the role of principals remains unclear, even though, as we discuss in subsequent sections, they are a critical factor in assessing the effect of collective bargaining on schools and classrooms.

Community attitudes and the bargaining process. While, as we discussed above, direct public participation in collective bargaining is rare, favorable community attitudes toward labor unions in general and teacher organizations in particular seem to be associated with greater collective bargaining gains for teachers. We consistently found that organized teachers do better in areas where private sector organized labor is strong and where there is a tradition of public employee collective bargaining. The narrowest contracts in our sample occurred in places where organized labor is relatively weak. In fact, *local* anti-union attitudes appear to prevail even in states with vigorous labor traditions.

We encountered very narrow contracts in two districts in highly industrialized states. In one district a nonunionized industrial park is the primary source of employment for residents. Most of the community seems firmly opposed to teacher collective bargaining, feeling that teachers have no right to bargain collectively to raise their already high incomes. During the last strike, teachers' property was threatened and many teachers received obscene phone calls. A radio talk-show broadcast during a strike had to be taken off the air in mid-program because callers had become so abusive on the subject of teacher collective bargaining. Although part of this opposition is due to strike action by teachers, most of it stems from strong community disapproval of teacher collective bargaining.

The second district located in a one-industry town where the major employer established its own company union with a sweetheart contract in order to prevent organizing by AFL-CIO affiliates. Negative community attitudes toward organized labor have seriously affected the ability of the teacher organization to attract members and to bargain effectively. (Many teachers, of course, share the ideology of the rest of the community.)

Conversely, we found that in communities where private sector organized labor had secured a stronghold, teachers and other public employees were able to obtain more advantageous contracts. Community ideology obviously has only an indirect influence on teacher collective bargaining prospects. But even given labor-management opposition to and public disinterest in a more active citizen role, community attitudes do seem to affect at least the broad parameters of teacher contracts.

The extent to which the state legal environment actually constrains the bargaining process

Defining the legal scope of bargaining. Defining an appropriate scope of bargaining constitutes one of the knottiest problems in labor negotiations and particularly so for teachers. In the private sector the National Labor Relations Board has limited the topics of mandatory bargaining to "wages, hours, and working conditions." When applied to teacher collective bargaining, this narrow delineation has generated ambiguity and at times, conflict. Central are the practical difficulties in making a clear-cut distinction between "working conditions" and matters of educational policy. For example, is class size a working condition or a policy issue?

Teachers' own notions of professionalism further complicate the definition of scope because they expect to play a larger role in defining their work standards than would nonprofessional employees. Based on this notion of professionalism, teachers have demanded a greater voice in educational programs. Organized teachers argue that as professionals they have superior training in the specifics of the learning process than do most policymakers and can, therefore, more knowledgeably make those decisions which most directly affect the classroom environment. Consequently, the bargaining agendas of local teacher organizations have often included demands for teacher participation in curriculum design, staff evaluation procedures, and student discipline and grading practices.

Obviously, some of these items have cost implications for local school districts. More importantly, many school board members fear that these demands represent a fundamental challenge to managerial authority. In fact, school board members and others who advocate a narrow scope of bargaining argue that elected officials, because of their accountability to the larger community, should be the ones to make educational policy decisions. Proponents of a narrow scope believe that if the scope of bargaining is unduly broadened, narrow economic interests like those of organized teachers will obtain more than their fair share of influence over public policy decisions.

In those states with a statewide agency created by statute to oversee public employee labor relations, legislatures have been reluctant to enumerate the items to be included in the scope of bargaining. Rather, they have allowed the statewide commission to define the actual content of the bargaining process case by case. In those states without a statewide commission, the task of defining the scope of bargaining has often been left to the courts. In many instances, the courts have based their rulings on precedents established in the private sector. For example, in determining the status of class size as either a management prerogative or a working condition, the courts have often based their decisions on principles derived as the result of litigation involving private sector labor relations.

Within the last few years, however, state legislatures have been a major focus of those groups dissatisfied with current statutory provisions. In his summary of recent state experience on the definition of scope, James reports that in 1975 alone, approximately a dozen state legislatures debated proposals to modify the scope provisions of public employee collective bargaining laws. Few states actually enacted new legislation in this area, but those that did defined scope more narrowly and specifically than had been done in the past. For example, new laws in Nevada, Indiana, and Montana list extensive management rights which strengthen the bargaining stance of employers and which put educational policy matters outside the scope of mandatory bargaining.

On the other hand, in states such as Pennsylvania the legal scope of bargaining has broadened over time. There the State Supreme Court ruled that items related to employees' interest in wages, hours, and conditions of employment fell within matters subject to good-faith bargaining even though they might touch upon managerial policy. In practice, this decision has meant that very few items are excluded from the legal scope of bargaining.

In many of the fifteen districts we visited, negotiators bargain with little attention to the state law. Some districts exceed the state law and negotiate over items which are outside the legally permissible scope. For example, one teacher organization was successful in negotiating an assignment and transfer policy which is not permitted under the state statute. Evidence from other sources indicates that even in California, which has one of the most precise scope provisions of any state law, some teacher organizations have been able to obtain contracts which exceed the legal scope of bargaining (just as state teacher organization leadership predicted).

At the other end of the spectrum, some teacher organizations in our sample could not convince school boards to negotiate over items for which bargaining is mandated under state law. For example, one district we visited is located in a state with a broad statute. Yet, this district has one of the narrowest contracts of any in our sample. Community attitudes are strongly against teacher collective bargaining and the school board, which plays a major role in the bargaining process, simply refuses to negotiate on items which are well within the legal scope of mandatory bargaining. The teacher organization, on the other hand, is weak and lacks internal unity. Consequently, it neither presses the board nor files unfair labor practice charges against it. Here, then, the state law as it pertains to scope is irrelevant to this district's negotiations.

However, the fieldwork did reveal that the presence of a state law mandating teacher collective bargaining (rather than its specific scope provisions) makes a difference. Such laws, in effect, provide a floor for teacher organizations where local attitudes or their own organizational weakness would inhibit bargaining gains. Because a state law exists, these organizations are guaranteed recognition and a uniform process.

This is not to say that teacher collective bargaining cannot exist without a state statute, but we did find that districts in states without such laws often had to supplement collective bargaining with alternative strategies in order to maintain the integrity of contracts. For example, one Southern district we visited is one of only a handful in its state with a collective bargaining agreement. Since there is no state law, bargaining is voluntary by the school board and may be withdrawn at its discretion. The teacher organization has had to engage in extensive political action to maintain a pro-teacher majority on the school board. Their political influence, rather than any legal right, guarantees that teachers in this city will continue to work under a contract.

In another district in the Southwest, the school board unilaterally rescinded its negotiated agreement with the teacher organization. A six-day strike (the first for this district) and the mobilization of community support for the teachers convinced the board to consent to reinstate the agreement.

Both these organizations have achieved varied degrees of success without collective bargaining laws. Yet, these districts are unique among those in their respective states; without the minimal guarantees provided by a state law only strong teacher organizations, willing to use strategies supplemental to the negotiations process, are able to maintain collective bargaining relationships. We found that even in strong labor states which lack collective bargaining statutes for public employees, weaker teacher organizations and those in smaller districts are unable to achieve much through negotiations. On the other hand, similar organizations in states with a collective bargaining law are at least guaranteed some minimal success as a result of the protection afforded by the statute.

Trade-offs among items at the bargaining table. We found in all fifteen districts that neither labor nor management have established rules for making trade-offs [in bargaining], but act instead on a case-by-case basis. However, one principle seems to guide deliberations on both sides. While trade-offs occur among economic items and among noneconomic demands, they are rarely made across the two types of demands. One negotiator described the two as the proverbial "apples and oranges."

In other words, trade-offs might be made across provisions which cost money such as salary, fringe benefits, and class size. But these items are seldom traded for others such as evaluation procedures, transfer policy, and instructional policy committees. We found a single exception to this finding among the districts in our fieldwork sample. One district, in severe financial difficulty (its two high schools are in danger of losing accreditation because of out-of-date textbooks and poor library facilities), is so strapped for money that it has been willing to trade salary increases for a number of the teachers' noneconomic demands. For example, it is for the first time willing to negotiate over the school calendar.

The effectiveness of strikes. Strikes, as we noted, constitute one response to impasse. Sixty percent of the districts in our sample experienced at least one strike, ranging in duration from a few days to a month or longer. Yet, the payoff from strikes varied markedly. Some resulted in large gains, while in other districts the teachers actually settled for less than they had been offered prior to the strike. The difference in payoff seems to depend on the strength of the teacher organization and how skillfully it uses strikes as a strategy. For example, one teacher organization in our sample gained its strong contract largely on the picket line. Not only has the leadership been able to maintain rank-and-file commitment during three separate strikes, but it has been willing to endure jail sentences and hundreds of thousands of dollars in fines. In other words, vigorous rank-and-file support (75-90 percent of the teachers walked out of their classrooms each time) and holding out to the bitter end spelled the difference. Other organizations have been less determined in their efforts and have subjected the district, their members, and the community to strike with little or no payoffs. One teacher organization struck four days before the end of the school year, at a point when the district had already received all its annual state aid. Parents were unconcerned about the end-of-the-year loss of class time for their children. Consequently, the teachers looked foolish and gained very little for their efforts. Similar results were obtained in other districts where the teacher organization leadership either misread the willingness of the rank and file to sustain a long strike or where the organization was unwilling to pay the costs imposed by the school district (often through court action).

Respondents uniformly noted that strikes are the result of a high frustration level among teachers which may flow from a hostile relationship between them and the administration. However, it takes skillful organizational leadership to direct and sustain that frustration. Clearly, striking is a high-risk, high-cost strategy which provides no guarantee that benefits will exceed those attainable with less militant tactics. In some cases it may be more accurate to view strikes as the consequence of poor relationships and weak contracts than as devices which will produce strong agreements.

In conclusion, our research on the collective bargaining process indicates that local factors such as public attitudes toward organized labor and the quality of the relationship between labor and management often prevail over more easily measurable financial, organizational, and legal factors. While we did encounter behavior common to most districts—e.g., that negotiating teams are becoming more professional over time and trade-offs are rarely made between economic and noneconomic items—districts vary greatly in their collective bargaining postures, depending on the local political and organizational culture. However, it was quite clear in all the districts we visited that the bargaining process itself affects outcomes. The effect is seen not only in the formal strength or scope of the contract, but also in the extent to which collective bargaining becomes an effective tool for regulating labor-management relations. Where the collective bargaining process works well, the subsequent implementation of the contract and day-to-day relations between teachers and administrators are usually more harmonious and constructive.

In the next section we examine established past practice and political action as alternatives to collective bargaining.

Alternatives to Collective Bargaining

Past district practices and collective bargaining. Some people have suggested that because not all district policies are included in the formal contract, the rights and benefits accorded teachers may be even greater than what is actually included in the contract. In other words, past practice may be an extension of the contract.

Although we did not have the resources to analyze the role of past practice in our entire contract sample, we did examine it for the fieldwork sample. While in the field, we focused on two questions:

- What kinds of items are not incorporated in the written contract by agreement between labor and management?

- Since some past practices may be legally grievable, do these items constitute, in effect, "hidden" contractual provisions?

We found that in the overwhelming majority of our fieldwork districts there were very few past practice items and the number is becoming smaller over time. Although past practices are *legally* subject to grievance procedures in several districts, teacher organization leaders doubted their ability to win such a grievance, particularly at the final, binding arbitration step. Therefore, teacher organizations have generally tried to incorporate as many past practice items as possible in the master contract. In each district there were a few random items which had not yet been included in the contract, but most respondents felt it would only be a matter of time before all were covered.

Past practice items do not seem, then, to constitute a tacit agreement which extends the formal contract. Since past practices are essentially unilaterally extended privileges and depend on the discretion of administrators and school boards, organized teachers seem to have decided that they are better off if as much of their work life as possible is protected by a formal document.

Political action by organized teachers. The two national organizations, along with their state and local affiliates, engage intensively in political action at all three levels of government. They support candidates ranging from school board members to the President of the United States. In conjunction with this electoral activity, teacher organizations lobby to increase federal and state aid to education, to secure more advantageous public employee collective bargaining laws, and to achieve concrete advantages such as reduced class size.

The AFT and the NEA both recognize the real limits on the gains attainable through local collective bargaining. Consequently, these organizations have chosen to commit considerable resources to lobbying and support for political candidates. In 1976, NEA expenditures on behalf of Jimmy Carter exceeded $400,000. This amount was in addition to the over $3 million spent by local and state affiliates. Although the AFT only spent about $400,000 in total on the 1976 campaign, its parent, the AFL-CIO, raised several million dollars for political candidates. Similar efforts were repeated at the state and local levels. For example, the political action arm of the California Teachers Association spent more than $550,000 in the 1974 election. In fact, only the oil industry outspent the AFT and the NEA in that California election.

Local political activity. Organized teachers seem to expect little payoff for their local political activity. Although fourteen of the fifteen teacher organizations studied in depth supported candidates for local school board offices, only two of them seemed to have gained tangibly from having allies on the board. The rest viewed their support of board candidates as defensive action. Because the position of school board members is usually both thankless and unpaid, it is often difficult to encourage competent people to seek the office. Teacher organizations report that they support board candidates to reduce the risks of poor leadership. They hope that if they contribute campaign funds and manpower, they might encourage better candidates to run. But once their candidates win, the teacher organizations seem not to expect the kind of payoff or access that they receive from the state and national candidates they support. Board members who have received such support concurred with the teachers' assessment. Consistently across school districts, members elected with teacher organization support attempted to remain independent even during collective bargaining. Part of the reason for this detachment may be due to the nature of the local political process. School board members, unlike state legislators, make decisions in an arena which is highly visible to their local constituents. If they appear to favor organized teachers too strongly, board members may suffer stronger public disfavor than a state legislator who is making decisions in the distant state capital.

State-level political activity. While this combination of collective bargaining and political action is a relatively new strategy, lobbying by teacher organizations is not. Prior to collective bargaining, lobbying by state teacher organizations accounted for most of the economic and job security benefits teachers obtained. Tenure and continuing-contract laws, statewide joint-contributory retirement plans, and the minimum salary standards established by some states all resulted from legislative action by organized teachers.

However, there is now a difference. A teacher organization can first attempt to obtain a specific benefit at the bargaining table. If it fails at this level, it can bypass the local board of education and lobby at the state level. Here, the teacher organization often finds itself trying to persuade legislators whom it has itself helped elect. The potential for enormous influence is obvious.

In some instances, organized teachers use the political process to facilitate a favorable collective bargaining outcome for themselves. In fact, in a system of shared responsibility among branches and levels of government, public employee unions adopt strategies to exploit the division of authority. Variants on the basic strategy of "bypassing" or "end-run bargaining" abound. Essentially, bypassing is an attempt by the employee organizations to use political pressure on elected officials to undermine the position of the management negotiator.

One form of bypassing exploits the vertical sharing of power among levels of government. A union can use state-level lobbying to gain its ends when local-level negotiations fail. Twice in 1975, for example, the governor of Oregon intervened to avert a threatened strike by teachers. In both instances, he persuaded school boards to increase their offer and break the stalemate.

In many capitals the state affiliates of the two national teacher organizations are among the most powerful lobbies. NEA state affiliates receive the bulk of teacher membership dues and use the funds for professional lobbying as well as for substantial research and public information programs. Typically, teacher organizations pursue three goals at the state level. The first is to obtain greater financial support for public education. In pursuing this objective, the teacher organizations ally themselves with other educational interest groups, including administrator and school board associations. Second, they work for the enactment of public employee collective bargaining laws or toward the improvement of existing laws. Third, organized teachers pursue by means of state statutes the kinds of gains typically associated with local bargaining—minimum salary schedules, class-size maximums, and requirements for the employment of school specialists. Attaining such provisions through state legislation ensures an inflation in the base upon which local bargaining proceeds. Needless to say, these legislatively secured mandates compromise the flexibility of local school management. For example, in one state compliance with 1978-79 statewide salary minimums will require pay raises for two-thirds of all teachers.

State school board associations generally lack the wherewithal to counteract teacher influence at the state level. Often a single large urban district will wield more power in the state capital than the school boards association. In many states the school boards association remains weak and amateurish because it lacks the financial resources and, more importantly, the manpower needed to support political candidates. School board members are few in number and prove no match for large groups of organized teachers when it comes to walking precincts and manning phone banks.

Will state-level political activity by organized teachers increase over time? According to our analysis, there are several reasons to believe it will. First educational policymaking is becoming more centralized. Decisions which were traditionally the sole prerogative of local school boards have escalated to the state and federal levels. For example, recent judicial rulings which direct the equalization of school finance mean less local control over tax and spending policies. Organized teachers have contributed to and responded to this centralization. Its arrival has forced them to recognize that there are real limits on collective bargaining gains at the local level. Consequently, teacher organizations are now concentrating more of their energies on state-level political action.

The recent movement for tax and public expenditure limitations, evidenced by the passage of Proposition 13 in California, also carries profound implications for the collective bargaining process. To the extent that responses elsewhere mirror California's, where the state assumed more of the cost of public education, local collective bargaining could diminish in importance. State control of the purse strings could lead to a two-tier system of bargaining in which most of the negotiating occurs at the state level. Bargaining on items which have no direct cost implications (teacher evaluation, transfer policy, student discipline) could remain at the district level. Such a radical transformation of the collective bargaining system still seems at least several years away. However, it also seems clear that teacher organizations will increasingly look to the state to meet demands formerly made on local school boards.

A second reason for the shift toward state lobbying and political action stems from a growing disenchantment with such militant tactics as strikes. Increasingly, strikes have proven counterproductive. Not only have public attitudes turned against striking teachers, but school boards are now better equipped to deal with teacher strikes. Many school districts have formed mutual aid pacts which allow administrators from nonstriking districts to assist a strike-bound district in keeping its schools open. In addition, the oversupply of teachers usually means readily available substitutes. The following scenario is more and more common: teachers strike; schools remain open; the district receives its per-pupil support from the state; the wage bill, thanks to lower-paid substitutes, actually falls and the district profits from the strike. The only real losers are the striking teachers who often must settle for the district's pre-strike offer or in some cases for even less.

End-run strategies at the local level. Locally, a union may negotiate directly with a professional labor relations expert who represents the school board and at the same time apply political pressure to elected local officials. In public education, particularly, end-run bargaining sometimes consists of pressure on the mayor of a city to intervene in teacher disputes with the local school board.

Nevertheless, the Rand research suggests that political intervention by elected officials has produced very limited results for organized teachers. There were strikes in nine of the fifteen districts in the fieldwork sample. In all but three of them the mayor, city council members, or state legislators attempted to intervene and help resolve the impasses. But in no case did the third-party effort facilitate settlement. Rather, the parties themselves or, on occasion, an outside professional mediator finally succeeded in ending the strike. Interestingly enough, both labor and management in our field sites were critical of intervention by public officials, rarely requested it, and agreed that disputes were best settled by the parties directly involved.

Local teacher organizations with political influence. As we noted earlier in this section, most teacher organizations obtain few benefits from local-level political activity. However, two organizations in our sample do wield real political power and together they are a study in contrasts. Both groups were critical in electing mayoral and school board candidates who were responsive to organized teachers and both had managed to engineer the firing of a recent school superintendent. Here, the similarities end, however. The first organization operates in one of the worst urban school systems in the country. Its problems of poverty, low student achievement, and general deterioration predate the rise of the teacher organization. Yet the organization has failed to use its extraordinary control over school district policy to improve the system. Rather, it has successfully deflected the district's efforts at reform; it uses its veto power over school policy to maintain the status quo in both district and school-site policies.

The second organization, on the other hand, is seen as a progressive political force within the city and school district. Operating in a state without a public employee collective bargaining law and in an environment hostile to organized labor, the organization requires political influence at the local level to survive as a collective bargaining agent. Consequently, it worked to elect a pro-teacher school board. But the organization has used the resulting power constructively and both labor and management feel the relationship is productive. Organized teachers, for example, acted effectively to reduce opposition to school desegregation and to bring about peaceful compliance. Although the organization places it own self-interest first and foremost, it has used its power to improve conditions for students. As an

209

illustration, it negotiated in its current contract a guarantee that all students be given vision and hearing tests.

Since the fieldwork sample was chosen to be representative of a larger, random sample, it is fair to assume that the conslusions reached about local-level political activity are valid for other districts in the country. Most teacher organizations support local candidates, but few receive much payoff for such support, and few expect any. Only a minority of local organizations have attained appreciable political power and a few of these have abused this power. At the same time, others have found a way to pursue their own self-interest and still work to improve the quality of educational services delivered to students.

"Teacher power," then, is generally reflected in the contractual gains made by organized teachers and in their state-level political action. But, as discussed, state-level action has local implications. As teacher organizations target on state and federal political action in the hopes of "leveling-up" control over aspects of collective bargaining and school finance, the responsibilities and autonomy of local school boards are simultaneously weakened.

Footnotes

1. Charles R. Perry and Wesley A. Wildman, *The Impact of Negotiations in Public Education* (Worthington, Ohio: Charles A. Jones Publishing Co., 1970), pp. 124-26.

Municipal Pay Determination: The Case of San Francisco

Harry C. Katz*

The recent expansion of public employee unionization and the fiscal problems confronting many of the nation's central cities have heightened concern over the labor costs faced by municipal governments. In the light of this concern, it is surprising that the public sector labor relations literature provides so few historical studies of the methods by which municipal employees and their unions influence municipal pay determination.[1]

Numerous cross-sectional econometric studies have produced evidence that public employee unions exert little, if any, impact on employee wages. The ability of such studies to assess the impact of unions on pay determination is, however, quite limited. First, because they rely on cross-sectional data, such analyses cannot account for dynamic effects which may be of particular importance given the suddenness with which the public sector became highly unionized. Further, such studies contain scant information regarding the mechanisms by which unions and employees exert their influence on pay

*Sloan School of Management and Department of Economics, Massachusetts Institute of Technology. Reprinted from *Industrial Relations,* Vol. 18 (Winter 1979), pp. 44-58.

determination and also ignore spillover effects that unionization may exert across jurisdictions. Also, cross-sectional studies cannot identify the impact of unions in large cities because the variation in the independent variable (i.e., the degree of unionization) is insufficient owing to the fact that nearly all large cities are highly unionized. Lastly, econometric studies typically use the per cent of workers organized as the measure of union influence. To what extent this measure accurately reflects either union or employee power is left unanswered. These and other deficiences can be remedied—and our knowledge about such issues advanced—through historical analysis.

Wages and Pensions 1945-1976

The municipal workforce in San Francisco is comprised of four distinct groups—craft workers, police and firefighters, transit drivers, and miscellaneous employees—each of whose wages historically have been determined in a different manner.[2] The base wages and the city's pension contribution for each of these four groups from 1945 through 1976 are reported in Table 1.

The wage figures given are only the base wages earned on an annual basis and hence ignore other contributions to total compensation many city employees enjoy such as overtime, holiday, and other pay differentials. These figures must consequently be viewed as only an approximation of total pay received.

A number of factors motivated the choice of the five job titles listed in Table 1. The wage received by the general laborer job title sets the wages of almost half of the city's craft workers. The pay increases received by the clerk typist and assistant engineer job titles are representative of the pay increases received by miscellaneous employees, which comprise almost two-thirds of the city's workforce. Only police are listed in Table 1 because police and firefighter pay and pension benefits have historically been about equal.

As Table 1 indicates, the increase in the wages of craft workers, police, firefighters, and transit drivers was from two to two-and-a-half times greater than the increase in the wages received by miscellaneous employees. The wage increases granted to miscellaneous employees in the early seventies were particularly modest given the high rate of inflation at that time. From 1970 to 1975, the real wages of clerk typists and assistant engineers fell, respectively, by 9.8 and 8.3 per cent. This decrease in real wages was typical of the wages received by almost all miscellaneous employees. In contrast, the real wages paid to police and general laborers increased, respectively, 7.2 and 11.4 per cent over that same five-year period.

By 1970, police and firefighters had become the highest paid city workers largely because of their high pension benefits. Expansion of those benefits continued and even accelerated in the early seventies. By 1976, the city's pension contributions for police and firefighters were, respectively, 73.9 and 67.1 cents per payroll dollar.

What procedures were used to set the wages reported in Table 1 and what role did city employees and their unions play in the design and implementation of those procedures? The following analysis treats these questions

TABLE 1
Base Wage and Pension Costs for a Sample of City Employees 1945-1976[a]

	Transit drivers	Police	(Craft) General laborer	(Miscellaneous employees)	
				Clerk typist	Assistant engineer
1945					
Base wage	2,028	2,700	1,920	2,400	4,500
Pension costs	229	472	217	271	509
Wages plus pension	2,257	3,172	2,137	2,671	5,009
In 1967 dollars	4,366	6,135	4,133	5,166	9,689
1950					
Base wage	3,132	3,780	3,120	3,000	5,640
Pension costs	384	1,015	383	368	691
Wages plus pension	3,516	4,795	3,503	3,368	6,331
In 1967 dollars	5,201	7,093	5,182	4,982	9,365
1955					
Base wage	4,032	5,280	4,380	3,960	6,900
Pension costs	506	1,506	550	497	866
Wages plus pension	4,538	6,786	4,930	4,457	7,766
In 1967 dollars	5,924	8,859	6,436	5,819	10,138
1960					
Base wage	5,412	7,152	6,144	4,980	8,520
Pension costs	563	1,596	640	518	887
Wages plus pension	5,975	8,748	6,784	5,498	9,407
In 1967 dollars	6,805	9,964	7,727	6,262	10,714
1965					
Base wage	6,696	8,820	8,112	5,736	11,292
Pension costs	346	1,393	419	296	583
Wages plus pension	7,042	10,213	8,531	6,032	11,875
In 1967 dollars	7,436	10,785	9,008	6,370	12,540
1970					
Base wage	10,974[b]	12,240	11,208	7,692	14,400
Pension costs	1,044	4,945	1,255	862	1,613
Wages plus pension	12,018	17,185	12,463	8,554	16,013
In 1967 dollars	10,771	15,402	11,170	7,666	14,351
1975					
Base wage	16,473	18,180	17,304	9,612	18,300
Pension costs	2,344	10,472	2,810	1,561	2,972
Wages plus pension	18,817	28,652	20,114	11,173	21,272
In 1967 dollars	11,724	17,852	12,532	6,961	13,254
1976					
Base wage	16,751	18,816	15,720	9,900	19,284
Pension costs	2,859	13,585	2,897	1,824	3,553
Wages plus pension	19,610	32,401	18,617	11,724	22,837
In 1967 dollars	11,529	19,048	10,945	6,892	13,426

[a]The reported base wage for police, clerk typists, and assistant engineers is the maximum amount earned after three years of employment on an annual basis. Pension costs are calculated by multiplying the city's per payroll dollar pension contribution times the annual base wage. San Francisco's retirement system is funded on an actuarial basis, and these pension cost figures can also be interpreted as an approximation of the present value of the pension benefits employees receive upon their retirement. Pension costs (although not benefits) fell from 1960 to 1965 because of the existence of retirement fund surpluses during that period. For details about the pension system, see Harry Katz, *The Impact of Public Employee Unions on City Budgeting and Employee Remuneration—A Case Study of San Francisco,* unpublished Ph.D. dissertation, University of California, Berkeley, 1977, Chapter 5. Wage figures are derived from the annual *Salary Standardization Ordinance,* City and County of San Francisco, various years. The per payroll dollar pension contribution figures are taken from the "Employees Retirement System—Annual Report 1976-77," City and County of San Francisco. Constant dollar figures were derived using a CPI deflator derived from the "C.P.I. For Urban Wage Earners and Clerical Workers," San Francisco-Oakland SMSA, 1947-1977, BLS, All Items—Series A.

[b]From 1968, the transit driver's pay package included a trust fund contribution and as of 1975 also included cost of living increases. These benefits are included in the calculation of base wage.

by examining the specific circumstances pertaining to each of the four components of San Francisco's workforce from 1945 through 1975.

Craft Workers

From 1945 through 1975, city craft workers benefited from a charter pay formula which mandated that craft workers be paid the hourly wage rate set in private sector craft union contracts in San Francisco. Following a suit brought by craft workers in 1962, the courts declared that the dollar equivalent of the holiday, health, welfare, and other fringe benefits received by private sector craft workers must also be paid to city craft workers as part of the formula.

What role did city employees play in the creation of the formula? City craft workers and their union representatives were active supporters of the crafts pay formula in the ballot campaign that surrounded its original adoption as an amendment to the city charter in 1945. City craft workers were then, and still are, represented by craft unions whose membership includes both private and public sector craft workers. In addition to those craft unions, other private sector unions such as the Teamsters and the Longshoremen were active proponents of the pay formula.

It is also interesting to note that campaign supporters of the crafts pay formula included many civic leaders, who saw it as an effective constraint on craft pay scales. Fearful of the effects that unbridled political forces might exert in more flexible pay procedures, many supporters of the formula looked to the private sector as a way to hold down craft wages.

The use of charter formulas to set municipal employee pay is similar to a number of the "reform" procedures which govern the structure and operation of San Francisco's city government. In the wake of a scandalous period of boss rule in the early twentieth century, San Francisco's municipal government had been restructured in accordance with reform (or progressive) notions of good government.[3] As part of that restructuring, power was split among a number of city officials—a mayor, a board of supervisors, a chief administrative officer, and numerous commissions, and a city charter was adopted to provide explicit regulation of municipal affairs. Setting employee wages by charter formula can, in part, be viewed as an extension of this reform tradition.[4]

As illustrated in Table 1, the crafts pay formula yielded rather large wage increases for craft workers over the whole post-World War II period. Those wage increases became particularly large in the late sixties and early seventies when private sector construction wage scales increased dramatically.[5] In the face of these large wage increases, pressure mounted among downtown business groups and other civic leaders to revise the crafts pay formula. Until 1975, however, city craft workers' campaign and lobbying activities successfully defeated all efforts at revision.

Police and Firefighters

Prior to 1951, police and firefighter wage rates were specified by rank in the city charter. Annually, charter amendments appeared on the ballot which specified wage increases for each. Such measures were generally successful, although on a few occasions downtown business opposition led to their defeat. In 1951, frustrated by the tiresome practice of continually going to the electorate for pay increases, police and firefighters, with the support of private sector unions, overruled campaign opposition provided by downtown business groups and passed a charter amendment. That amendment contained a pay formula which provided annual adjustments in police and firefighter's wage schedules equal to the annual increase in the consumer price index for San Francisco.

In 1952, the wage formula for police and firefighters was again revamped. This time the change brought replacement of the rigid CPI wage formula with a flexible pay procedure that transferred wage-setting responsibility to the Board of Supervisors (BOS). The new procedure empowered the BOS to annually set police and firefighter wage rates subject to the constraint that rates of pay not exceed the highest rates paid comparable workers among cities in California with a population greater than 100,000. The charter amendment that provided the new procedure was sponsored by employee unions but had the support of a broad coalition of downtown business groups as well. Business groups were fearful of the high pay increases that might arise from adherence to the CPI formula adopted in 1951, and they looked to the new pay procedure as a way of constraining police and firefighter wage increases.

From 1952 to 1974, the BOS annually chose to match the highest paying city in California.[6] In 1975, the BOS refused to follow that tradition and offered a wage increase below the allowable maximum. A police and firefighter strike ensued with an eventual settlement that fell between the Board's original offer and the maximum allowed by the charter formula. Shortly after the strike, voters passed a charter amendment that once again altered the police and firefighters' pay formula. (The events surrounding this change will be discussed at a later point.)

The charter ordinance that governed police and firefighter wages from 1952 to 1975 obviously allowed substantial discretion to the BOS. The fact that the Board always chose to match the highest allowable rate can, in large part, be attributed to the political pressure exercised by the union representatives of police and firefighters. Over the post-World War II period, a majority of police and firefighters in San Francisco have been members of quite cohesive employee organizations, the Police Officers Association and the International Association of Firefighters. These organizations, which for all practical purposes functioned as unions, successfully combined political lobbying with occasional strike threats to convince the Board to maintain wage rates at the allowable ceiling.

Since World War II, with the single exception of 1963, parity has always been maintained between police and firefighter wage scales. From 1952 to 1963, parity was maintained as a consequence of either the fact that the highest paying city in California (the city the BOS annually chose to match) maintained pay parity between its two safety forces, or the BOS maintained parity as a matter of their own policy. In 1963, in an effort to economize on labor costs, the Board chose to abandon wage parity and set firefighter wage scales 2.5 per cent below police wage rates, saying at the time they felt that

214

the workload attached to firefighter duties did not match that required of police officers. The International Association of Firefighters responded by promoting and successfully passing a charter amendment mandating wage parity between the public safety forces.

Transit Drivers

Union efforts also succeeded in improving transit driver wages by altering municipal wage-setting procedures. In 1946, with the strong backing of both private and public sector unions, a charter amendment passed which required that transit drivers' wages be set equal to the average of the two highest wage schedules for platform employees and bus operators in the state of California. This formula continued in effect until 1954, when downtown business groups succeeded in passing a charter amendment that revised the above formula to require that the Board of Supervisors set transit drivers' wages so as not to exceed the average of the two highest wage schedules in effect in California cities with populations greater than 100,000 and employing more than 100 platform employees. City unions were in vigorous opposition since the new formula, by disallowing consideration of small but high paying cities, produced lower wage increases. Business groups promoted the ordinance as an equitable equivalent to the formula governing police and firefighter wage rates that had been adopted (with employee support) in 1952.

In 1956, a charter amendment revised the ceiling in the transit pay formula to the average of the two highest wage schedules in effect in cities in the United States with populations greater than 500,000 and employing more than 400 platform employees. At the same time, the work week for drivers was reduced from six days (48 hours) to five days (40 hours). This charter amendment had the support of both transit drivers and downtown business groups, who agreed that problems of high vacancy and turnover rates were a product of the inadequate wages provided by the old formula. (This is a rare example wherein labor supply issues were part of a debate over city employee pay rates.)

The next major revision in the transit wage formula came in 1968 with the passage of a charter amendment allowing payment of fringe benefits in excess of the benefits received by miscellaneous employees, by expanding the jurisdiction of the existing pay formula so as to include fringe benefits as well as base wages. The new formula stipulated that the BOS annually *could* make a maximum contribution to a drivers' trust fund equal to the amount by which the retirement, vacation, and health benefits of San Francisco's transit drivers were exceeded by the fringe benefits received by platform employees in the two cities used to compute the drivers' base wage rates. Downtown business groups opposed the ordinance, but did not campaign actively against it.

As was the case for city craft workers, police, and firefighters, transit drivers were represented by a cohesive union, the Transport Workers Union. That union exercised influence by strongly campaigning for the passage of more favorable transit pay formulas and then by lobbying extensively before the Board of Supervisors to affect the way in which they were implemented.

As a result of such efforts, since 1968 transit drivers have succeeded in getting the city to negotiate over the terms of the annual transit pay package. In these negotiations drivers have won both cost-of-living adjustments and annual contributions by the city to their union trust fund. Until 1975, when the city also began to formally meet with miscellaneous employees, these negotiations were the only example of formalized bargaining over wages between the city and any of its employees.

Over the whole post-World War II period, the BOS paid drivers the highest wage allowed by whatever charter pay formula was in effect. The fact that the BOS continually interpreted the wage formulas in favor of the drivers, as they had for police and firefighters, can be attributed to the strength of the employee lobby. However, two other factors should be mentioned. The Board appeared to be anxious to avoid using its discretionary judgment to set employee wages. The avoidance of situations that create political turmoil—what may be called confrontation avoidance—seemed to have been of primary concern. Regularly fixing wages at the maximum allowed in charter formulas enabled the Board to avoid conflict. In addition, once the Board had adopted the pattern of setting wages in that fashion, employees came to expect that sort of interpretation. Deviations from that rule served as a rallying cry for city employees and created just the sort of political turmoil the Board was eagerly trying to avoid.

Miscellaneous Employees

While craft workers, transit drivers, police, and firefighters each have had their wage determination guided by a charter pay formula, miscellaneous employee wages have been set by the BOS in accordance with a "prevailing rate" doctrine. The charter states that miscellaneous employee compensation "shall be set in accord with the general prevailing rate in private employment or in other comparable government organizations in the state."

The determination of pay includes the formation of recommended wage increases for each employee job title by the Civil Service Commission and final determination of wage increases by the BOS. To form their recommendations, the Commission conducts an annual survey of wages in the private sector in San Francisco and the Bay Area and wages in government agencies throughout the state. Although the Board is not bound by the Commission's recommendations, they appear to have weighed heavily in the Board's final decisions.

Historically, employee input into this process has been rather minimal. Input essentially has taken the form of lobbying either behind closed doors with the members of the Civil Service Commission or the Board of Supervisors, or in public hearings before those same bodies. For years miscellaneous employees tried to induce the city to replace the prevailing rate pay procedure with more formalized bargaining. Such efforts have met with only minimal success.

In 1970 and again in 1974, miscellaneous employees engaged in strikes which did produce an increased amount of face-to-face bargaining. The

216

wage settlement in those strikes did not, however, diverge from the pattern of wage increases received in the years before and after those strikes.

In 1973, under employee pressure, the city adopted an Employee Relations Ordinance (ERO) which, among other things, provides impasse resolution and representation election procedures.[7] It was not until 1975, however, that representation elections took place and official union bargaining agents were designated. In 1975 and 1976, in accordance with the ERO, city officials and representatives of miscellaneous employees met and conferred over proposed wage increases. Even in the face of these negotiations, the normal prevailing rate procedures continued in 1975 and 1976 with Civil Service Commission recommendations and final decisions by the BOS. Thus, despite the fact that miscellaneous employees had finally won the right to negotiate the terms of their employment with city officials, such negotiations have not had much effect on wages.

Historically, miscellaneous employees have lacked the kind of cohesive union found among the other employee groups. This can be attributed, in part, to the traditional reluctance office workers (which comprise a large part of the miscellaneous workforce) have shown toward union organization.[8] When pressing their demand for more formalized bargaining, miscellaneous employees also lacked political ties to powerful private sector unions that had increased the leverage of other city employee groups. Miscellaneous employee efforts to bargain over pay also suffered from the absence of statewide legislation requiring local collective bargaining.[9]

As revealed in Table 1, while other city employees reaped the benefits of favorable pay formulas, miscellaneous employees generally received only moderate wage increases which, in the seventies, were particularly modest. A few groups fared much better, however. Lower pay-level employees such as laundry, food service, and clerical workers received large wage increases in the late sixties when the Civil Service Commission recommended them and the BOS approved them. Urban unrest and civil rights protests had become heated political issues throughout the U.S. in the mid-sixties, and the fact that lower level miscellaneous jobs were heavily occupied by members of San Francisco's minority populations became an acute political issue. Large wage increases for those low level jobs were viewed by city officials as a means to answer these political concerns and to present the municipal government as a model nondiscriminating employer.

Some miscellaneous employees received large wage increases by way of their reclassification to craft pay status. Although the charter stated that craft pay status was to be determined as a function of the union status of private sector counterparts, reclassification occasionally appears to have been manipulated for political purposes. For example, in 1972, after a former aide to Mayor Joseph Alioto was appointed as its general manager, the Civil Service Commission reclassified streetsweepers from miscellaneous to craft pay status. The Commission designated that as a consequence of the reclassification, streetsweepers were entitled to the same wages received by city general laborers. As a result, the wages of streetsweepers increased by 17.9 per cent in 1973, and then in later years kept pace with the large wage increases paid to general laborers.

The Board of Supervisors had challenged the reclassification, contending that streetsweepers were not entitled to craft status because there were no laborers covered by private sector union contracts who performed street-sweeping as their primary task. The courts, however, upheld the reclassification, arguing that unless there was a clear showing of fraud or arbitrariness, reclassification was an administrative decision which by charter stipulation was placed in the hands of the Commission.

To understand why the reclassification was proposed in the first place, it is instructive to note that the Laborers' Union, which represented city street-sweepers, had provided active campaign support for Mayor Alioto's election.[10] Throughout the post-World War II period, other miscellaneous employees also benefited from reclassification to craft pay status although the circumstances of their reclassification were typically influenced less directly by political concerns.

Pension-setting Procedures

There are three separate municipal employee pension systems in San Francisco. One system governs the pensions of city craft workers, transit drivers, and miscellaneous employees. Separate pension systems govern police officers and firefighters, although the pension benefits (and costs) of the two public safety forces have remained roughly equal throughout the post-World War II period. Each system is regulated by charter, and each has been periodically upgraded through the years by charter amendments.

Election campaigning in behalf of proposed pension-related charter amendments is an important avenue of municipal employee input into the determination of municipal pay. Formidable opposition to employee interests in those campaigns has been provided by downtown business groups who were led by the city's Chamber of Commerce. In fact, there is no instance when a significant pension improvement amendment passed over the active opposition of the Chamber. Major pension improvements passed in the late sixties and early seventies only when the Chamber either took no position or was distracted from vocal opposition by its concern for other issues.

The drafting of pension-related amendments often involved bargaining between downtown business groups and representatives of both city employees and private sector unions with the mayor sometimes operating as a mediator. As an example, in the mid-sixties, the Chamber of Commerce supported a number of administrative reforms including disability re-examination and the replacement of one of the employee members of the city's Retirement Board with a representative from the community. City employees, on the other hand, were especially anxious to upgrade the pension system owing to their repeated failure (given Chamber opposition) to pass improvement amendments in the preceding years. In 1968, in a compromise effected by Mayor Alioto, the Chamber agreed to support a series of charter amendments with some features that upgraded the pension systems of all city employees but with others that made a number of administrative reforms. City employees thereupon agreed not to oppose a street improvement bond issue favored by the business community. Both the pension amendments and the bond issue passed easily in municipal elections.

218

As Table 1 shows, the pension benefits of city employees (particularly police and firefighters) increased markedly in the late sixties and early seventies. For example, from 1968 to 1976, the city's pension contribution for miscellaneous employees increased from 10.4 to 18.4 cents per payroll dollar. Over the same period, for police and firefighters the city's pension contribution increased, respectively, from 18.1 and 25.6 cents to 73.9 and 67.1 cents per payroll dollar.

How is it that these costly pension improvements occurred in the face of the vigilant stand taken by the downtown business groups? Some of these pension benefit increases followed as a consequence of the amendments the Chamber of Commerce agreed to support in the compromise worked out in 1968. Further improvements resulted from charter amendments which passed in 1973 and 1974, when the Chamber of Commerce's attention was diverted toward promotion of charter amendments that would have revised the crafts pay formula. But the preoccupation of the Chamber with other issues does not provide a complete explanation of the ease by which voters adopted extremely expensive pension improvements in the late sixties and early seventies. The most likely explanation is that the public, as well as the Chamber, were more cost conscious of wage issues whose current costs were clear than they were of pension reforms whose future costs were more difficult to assess.

The Voter Backlash

In the fall of 1975, a backlash against city employees occurred when the voters altered municipal pay procedures in a number of ways to the detriment of city employees. This backlash seems to have been the result of a combination of national and local events. The spring of 1975 had brought news of New York City's default crisis and triggered concern throughout the nation that extravagant public employee pay was in large part to blame for the fiscal plight of the country's central cities. Voters throughout the country responded by reversing many of the gains of public employees.

In the early fall of 1975, the Board of Supervisors responded to the public's mood of fiscal conservatism and moved to break the tradition of providing city police and firefighters with a wage that matched the wages paid public safety forces in the highest paying city in California. The city's move precipitated a joint police-fire strike, an unprecedented event for the city. The public rebelled in anger against the striking workers, anger further inflamed by Mayor Alioto's declaration of a state of emergency and eventual settlement of the strike on terms very close to those demanded by the striking workers. (The strikers won the battle but later lost the war when, as discussed below, the voters accepted a number of revisions to the charter pay formula which left city employees worse off than before.)

Concern over the city's high labor costs had also been fueled by a series of newspaper stories that outlined the benefits received by city craft workers. Attention was repeatedly focused on the excesses of a system that allowed streetsweepers to be paid an annual base salary of $17,300 in 1975.

Shifting public sentiment led to the overwhelming passage in the fall of 1975 of charter amendments removing the crafts pay formula and providing that thereafter craft worker wages be set by the same prevailing rate criterion used to set miscellaneous employee pay. The police and fire-fighters' pay formula was altered to require that these workers receive the average of the wages paid public safety forces in the five largest cities in California. Other charter amendments were adopted which required immediate dismissial of any employee participating in a strike and dictating that future disputes over prevailing pay procedures be decided by public vote.

The following spring, under the new prevailing rate procedure, the Board of Supervisors approved craft wage cuts that averaged $2,000 and went as high as $4,500. With the concurrence of the Civil Service Commission, the Board argued that the new wage scales, though below absolute wages paid in the private sector, nonetheless accurately reflected prevailing rates because city craft workers had a higher expectation of continuous employment than their counterparts in the private sector (i.e., they worked many more hours per year). In protest, city craft workers went on strike with the support of city transit drivers. The craft workers were soundly defeated, however, as they returned to work a month later under the salary terms originally decided by the Board of Supervisors. (It is interesting to note that neither miscellaneous employees nor private sector craft workers were willing to support the strike.)

The voter backlash was not limited to pay restraint, as major revisions were also made in the city's pension plans which eliminated all of the improvements city employees had won in elections in the early seventies. By law, however, the new system could only be applied to new employees.

In 1976, voters further altered the prevailing rate pay procedures used to set miscellaneous employee wage scales (which under the 1975 amendments includes craft pay scales as well). The new pay procedure removed the discretion previously allowed the Civil Service Commission and the BOS by requiring the Commission to first survey a specific list of private and public sector employers and then calculate prevailing rates of pay by computing weighted averages of the wage scales found to exist. The BOS is then required to set miscellaneous wage scales within 10 per cent of those weighted averages.

Summary and Conclusions

The rapid reversal in the fortunes of police, firefighters, transit drivers, and craft workers in San Francisco reveals how heavily these workers have relied on their political influence. When, in 1975, political winds turned against city employees, the power of these employees rapidly dissipated. One simply cannot account for this turnabout if the strength of these employees, as many argue, is founded on the strike threat and/or the in-elasticity of the demand for public services.

It is clear that San Francisco city employees have never relied on the strike (or meaningful strike threats) as a primary method of pressing their demands. No strikes occurred until the seventies, and, when they did, they were either lost altogether or settled for only modest gains. Elsewhere, I report evidence that shows that the city responded to the high pay rates of craft workers, police officers, firefighters, and transit drivers by keeping the number of these employees constant while greatly expanding the number of relatively inexpensive miscellaneous personnel employed by the city.[11] This is further evidence of the fact that city employees did not rely on the essential nature of their services to strengthen their demands.

Municipal craft workers, police, firefighters, and transit drivers did well in San Francisco by using their political muscle to first promote generous pay formulas and, when necessary, to lobby effectively to ensure favorable interpretation of those formulas. Miscellaneous employees, on the other hand, pressed hard for several years to induce the city to engage in formalized collective bargaining, but they lacked the organizational cohesiveness and political leverage necessary to force it to do so. It was not until 1975 that official representatives of miscellaneous employees formally discussed terms of employment with city officials, and, even then, those discussions appeared to have little impact on wage rates. The push for formalized bargaining by this group also suffered from a lack of support from other city employee groups who were doing well with existing pay procedures and simply had no need for collective bargaining.

The presence of multilateralism is often said to be a factor characteristic of public labor relations decision making. My study gives evidence of both forms of multilateralism discussed in the literature—the participation in labor relations of a number of different city officials with different sources of authority (the mayor, Civil Service Commission, and the BOS), and the participation in labor relations decisions by representatives of the community. An example of the latter in San Francisco is the occurrence of negotiations between downtown business groups and public employee representatives regarding the various pension-related charter amendments.

It could be argued that the heavy reliance on political influence by city employees and their representatives is peculiar to San Francisco. Following its reform government tradition, it is perhaps not surprising that San Francisco came to rely heavily on charter regulation and ballot amendments to set employee wages and pensions. This in turn forced city employees and their representatives into the political arena with the result that politically powerful employees and unions fared better than those with less political power.

In cities where public sector labor relations involve more formalized collective bargaining, employee groups may derive their strength from other sources. San Francisco may, however, prove to be more than just an interesting exception. For even in cities that set wages through a system of collective bargaining, what counts most may still be the vote gathering and political lobbying capabilities of employee groups. That relationship may only be more obvious in San Francisco because of that city's tradition of using the ballot box rather than bargaining to provide changes in employee pay. The point is that whether (and to what extent) San Francisco is representative of other cities can only be determined after historical analyses of municipal labor relations in other cities are available.

Footnotes

1. Notable exceptions are Raymond Horton, *Muncipal Labor Relations in New York City—Lessons of the Lindsay Wagner Years* (New York: Praeger, 1972),

and David Lewin, *Wage Determination in Local Government Employment,* unpublished Ph.D. dissertation, University of California at Los Angeles, 1971.

2. The respective 1976-1977 employment of these four groups are: police and firefighters (3,692), craft workers (2,015), transit drivers (1,902), and miscellaneous employees (15,802). Sanitation workers are excluded from consideration because the city contracts with a private employer for refuse collection.

3. A lively account of San Francisco's early political history is provided in Walton Bean, *Boss Reuf's San Francisco* (Berkeley, Calif.: University of California Press, 1952).

4. The author is grateful to Robert Fogelson for clarifying this point.

5. A discussion of the nationwide increase in construction worker wage rates that occurred in the late sixties is provided in Robert Flanagan, "Wage Interdependence in Unionized Labor Markets," *Brookings Papers on Economic Activity,* 3, 1976.

6. The California city paying the highest wage to its public safety forces has traditionally been Los Angeles.

7. It is interesting to note that the impasse resolution procedures outlined in the Employee Relations Ordinance have never been used, even when the city employees went on strike in 1973, 1975, and 1976.

8. A large number of miscellaneous employees traditionally have belonged to a citywide civil service association. This association, however, did not press actively for employee participation in the determination of terms and conditions of employment. Union organization has been somewhat more active among certain miscellaneous employees such as social workers, nurses, and hospital workers.

9. A statute passed in 1968 did require local governments to "meet and confer" with employee groups, but provided no formal mechanism for establishing union representation. See Betty V. H. Schneider, "An Analysis of the Myers-Milias-Brown Act of 1968," *California Public Employee Relations,* February, 1969.

10. Joseph Alioto served as mayor from 1968 through 1975.

11. See Harry Katz, "The Municipal Budgetary Response to Changing Labor Costs: The Case of San Francisco," *Industrial and Labor Relations Review,* 32, July, 1979, pp. 506-19.

5
Dispute Resolution

Dispute or impasse resolution is the most glamorous arena for analysis in public sector labor relations, for it is in the resolution of contract negotiation disputes or impasses that the potential impact upon the parties and the public are greatest and the visibility of union-management relationships most apparent. In large part this impact potential and visibility stem from the strike prohibition and concomitant experimentation with procedural alternatives for reaching settlements. As a result, in this chapter we will pay particular attention to the reasons for and consequences of the reliance on impasse resolution procedures as replacements for the strike, with a special focus on compulsory arbitration.

THE PRIVATE SECTOR BACKGROUND

Since the institutionalization of collective bargaining in the private sector preceded the large-scale emergence of bargaining in government, and since private sector policies, practices, and practitioners had a substantial impact upon the development of governmental bargaining, we begin our analysis with a brief sketch of dispute resolution policies and practices in private industry.

Negotiating disputes in the private sector historically have been resolved by the threat or use of "concerted activities." American unions have relied primarily upon collective bargaining (or private action) rather than government legislation (or public action) to secure direct benefits for their members, and the unions long ago recognized that employers would be unwilling to accede to union demands if the unions could not make such recalcitrance costly. As a result, American unions have developed an imaginative repertoire of concerted activities such as strikes, slowdowns, picketing, and boycotts aimed at interfering with the employers' normal operations and hence increasing their costs of disagreeing with the unions' terms.[1] In most union-management relationships the key source of union power is the strike threat which underlies contract negotiations, followed by the actual strike which will occur if the negotiations do not yield results which satisfy the union's minimum demands.[2]

From a public policy perspective, most strikes existed in something of a no-man's land until 1935. Prior to that time, most American workers had no statutorily protected right to bargain collectively and conduct work stoppages, but neither were they legislatively prohibited from bargaining and striking.[3] The legality of strikes in this legislative vacuum was controlled primary by judges, who until the early 1930s issued antistrike injunctions rather frequently (and who also were willing to apply the Sherman Antitrust Act's penalties to union boycott activities). A long period of judicial hostility toward strikes ended with the passage of the Norris-LaGuardia Act, for with this 1932 statute Congress forbade federal judges from issuing injunctions in labor disputes. In the historic 1935 National Labor Relations (Wagner) Act, Congress took a giant step beyond Norris-LaGuardia by legislatively guaranteeing to most private workers the right to join unions, bargain collectively, and engage in concerted activities. As a result, after 1935 the official labor relations policy of the federal government encouraged the practice of collective bargaining and protected the right to strike.[4]

This right to engage in concerted activities has been steadily abridged since the heady organizing days (for the unions) of the late 1930s, most notably in the 1947 and 1959 amendments to the Wagner Act, and also in the continuing line of National Labor Relations Board and federal court decisions dealing with these activities. Such abridgment does not mean that American workers' strike rights have been emasculated; instead the federal government has established a body of what might be called "means and objectives" rules designed to limit or constrain when, where, how, and why strikes or other activities may occur. The three major thrusts of these rules have been to replace the use of economic muscle with peaceful procedures to resolve particular kinds of disputes (union recognition, jurisdiction over work assignments, etc.), to achieve an approximate balance of power between the contending parties, and to limit the arenas of conflict to the primary combatants and hence protect noninvolved third parties. However, subject to a variety of specific constraints, the general right to strike is still legally protected.[5]

The federal government also has a statutory right to intervene in peacetime labor disputes to assist the parties in reaching agreement, but this authority is rather limited. In the 1947 Labor Management Relations (Taft-Hartley) Act Congress created the Federal Mediation and Conciliation Service, an agency designed to monitor contract negotiations (especially the more important ones) and offer its mediation services in order to help the disputing parties reach agreement.[6] However, the FMCS can only mediate and it has no power to impose a settlement on anyone. In addition, in disputes which could or have become "emergencies," the President has the statutory authority under the Railway Labor Act (covering railroads and airlines) and the Taft-Hartley Act (covering most private industries) to inject the federal government more forcefully into the dispute. Under Taft-Hartley, for instance, the government can secure an injunction which for 80 days will prevent a strike from starting or end a strike that has begun. The primary purposes of these intervention procedures are to protect against strikes which have harmful public or political ramifications and to prod the parties into reaching an agreement. However, it is important to note that the government's statutory intervention authority expires after a fixed term, and then the parties are legally free to resume their concerted activities.[7]

At present there is no general legislative or executive authority for the federal or state government to mandate or impose the terms of settlement upon unions and employers.[8] Congress on three separate occasions has ordered the arbitration of particular railroad industry disputes, but these arbitration authorizations have been applicable only to the specific disputes in question.[9] At the state level, several states in the early post-World War II period statutorily provided for the compulsory arbitration of public utility labor disputes, but a 1951 U.S. Supreme Court decision declaring one of these laws unconstitutional effectively made all of the statutes inoperable.[10] Finally, there has been some experimentation with voluntarily negotiated arbitration procedures (most notably in the basic steel industry), but these experiments involve only a tiny fraction of all private sector negotiations. The lack of arbitral authority over private sector negotiations is the result of a long-standing and deeply held belief on both sides of the negotiating table that the substantive terms of employment relationships are best established through the direct negotiations of unions and managements and should not be imposed by a third party.

We can conclude this oversimplified sweep of private sector dispute resolution policy and practice by noting four highlights:

1. From both a functional and a public policy perspective, the strike is a fundamental—some would say inescapable—part of the American collective bargaining process. The operational implication of this conclusion is that collective bargaining is almost meaningless without the right to strike.
2. Public policy has placed some very definite limits on when, where, why, and how strikes may occur, so this right to strike is not absolute or unqualified.
3. The federal government, in its role as government-as-regulator, has some authority to intervene in labor disputes, but this authority is limited and clearly is secondary to the parties' own efforts to reach agreement.
4. As a corollary of this third point, there is very little use of or apparent desire for compulsory arbitration to settle negotiating disputes.

PUBLIC POLICY IN THE PUBLIC SECTOR

The large-scale emergence of collective bargaining in government has occurred both prior to and in the wake of (primarily) state legislation granting bargaining rights to various groups of public employees. In this section we consider the various kinds of dispute resolution options available to policymakers and some of the arguments for and against their use.

Procedures Instead of Strikes

Our society has long taken for granted that governmental workers do not (and should not) have the right to strike. As Lewin notes, this conventional

225

wisdom is based upon several arguments, the most prominent being governmental sovereignty (i.e., as the sovereign power, government cannot engage in coercive contests with private groups), the essentiality of government services to the public welfare, and the unduly strong power position that government unions presumably would enjoy due to the employer's position as a monopolist.[11] For decades, these (and other) arguments were used to deny public employees the right to strike and also the right to bargain collectively—in part because strikes were seen as an inextricable component of the collective bargaining process.

During the past twenty years this conventional wisdom has been modified considerably by changing events. In 1962 President Kennedy authorized a limited form of collective bargaining for federal employees, and these federal employee bargaining rights were expanded under Presidents Nixon and Carter. Throughout the 1960s and 1970s public employee organizations mounted scores of lobbying campaigns in various state capitols seeking bargaining legislation (the Staudohar article in Chapter 2 provides one example). These lobbying efforts were not uniformly successful, but they did result in the passage of some form of bargaining legislation in more than thirty states, and these laws usually established the right to bargain collectively and prohibited strikes. During these two decades the amount of collective bargaining activity increased substantially, and it is hardly surprising that this increase in bargaining activity has been matched by an increase in strike activity (see Table 1).

There are a variety of policy options available to regulate the strike question. Some states (e.g., Illinois, Colorado) have not passed any bargaining statutes, but strikes in these states usually are illegal as a result of court decisions or attorney generals' opinions. A second option is to statutorily prohibit strikes (either as part of a collective bargaining statute or in a separate piece of legislation). Sometimes these statutory prohibitions are supported by strike penalties (e.g., public employees in New York are fined a day's pay—in addition to the day's pay lost by not working—for each day they are on strike), and a large majority of public sector bargaining statutes contain some kind of strike prohibition.

A third policy option is based on the distinction between the legal right to strike and the operational ability to conduct a strike. As the figures in Table 1 indicate, the number of public employee strikes—most of them illegal—rose dramatically in the late 1960s and continued at a high level in the 1970s. In addition, strikes increased during the latter 1970s, and the preliminary estimate for 1980 suggests that this trend may continue into the current decade. This relatively large number of illegal strikes suggests that operational or *de facto* public policy is not as condemnatory of strikes as the *de jure* policy appears to be on the basis of its statutory strike prohibitions. If it were, policymakers would impose more drastic penalties against strikes than are currently applied. For instance, Ohio's Ferguson Act prescribes some very stiff penalties for strikers, but these penalties are rarely applied.[12] Similarly, some state courts in states with statutory strike prohibitions have ruled that strikes may not be enjoined unless they clearly endanger the public welfare.[13] In other words, it seems fair to conclude that in many jurisdictions there is an unspoken public policy which recognizes that strikes will occur and which tolerates them to an extent that is not readily apparent from statutory prohibitions.[14]

A fourth policy response is to implement procedural substitutes for the strike, and in those states with bargaining legislation this is the route that policymakers have taken most frequently (usually in tandem with strike prohibitions). Operationally, this option involves the legislative implementation of mediation, factfinding, or arbitration, or some combination of these procedures. There have been two key reasons why this option is popular: (1) these procedures strengthen the unions' bargaining position over what it would be with no procedures, and can be justified on the equity grounds that without the strike the unions need some mechanisms to manipulate management's costs of disagreement; (2) these procedures have as their common theme the intervention of a third party to assist the contending parties in reaching a settlement, and thus can be justified as protecting the public's interest in continuously receiving governmental services.

Mediation and factfinding are the more common procedures, and mediation is widely available to most state and local public employee groups.[15] In contrast, compulsory arbitration procedures are less widespread (though there were many more arbitration statutes in 1980 than in 1970) and often are limited to police and firefighter negotiating impasses. Many statutes specify a combination of procedures; for example, negotiating impasses under the Iowa statutory procedure must proceed through mediation and then factfinding before they arrive at the terminal step of arbitration. Finally, there is a great deal of diversity across the states in the shape and operation of their impasse procedures.[16]

Procedures and Strikes

A fifth policy option is the statutory legalization of the right to strike. As noted in Table 2, strike rights have been legislatively granted in several states during the 1970s, and this slow but steady trend represents the most visible evidence of the erosion of the conventional wisdom that governmental sovereignty, service essentiality, and union bargaining power render the strike inappropriate for government employees.[17] This development is consistent with the emergence of a second generation of public sector bargaining, for the many strikes of recent years have resulted in an increasing awareness that such stoppages do not necessarily impugn governmental sovereignty, that many public services are temporarily dispensable, and that union power often is more imagined than real. As a result, policymakers in a few states seem to have concluded that "labor peace"—avoidance of strikes—should not necessarily be the top priority of public sector labor relations policy.

The information in Table 2 suggests that public employee strike rights are considerably more constrained than strike rights in private industry. For example, public employee strike rights can be abridged if such strikes threaten the public health or safety, such rights often become operational only upon completion of dispute resolution procedures (usually mediation and/or factfinding), and sometimes the employer can prevent such strikes altogether by insisting upon arbitration under a "choice of procedures" statute (see the Ponak and Wheeler article later in this chapter).

TABLE 1
Public Employee Work Stoppages by Level of Government, United States, 1942-1980

	Total*			Federal Government			State Government			Local Government		
	Number of Stoppages	Workers Involved (thousands)	Days Idle during Year (thousands)	Number of Stoppages	Workers Involved (thousands)	Days Idle during Year (thousands)	Number of Stoppages	Workers Involved (thousands)	Days Idle during Year (thousands)	Number of Stoppages	Workers Involved (thousands)	Days Idle during Year (thousands)
1942										39	6.0	23.7
1943										51	10.2	48.5
1944							2	0.4	8.0	34	5.3	57.7
1945										32	3.4	20.0
1946							1	†	†	61	9.6	51.0
1947										14	1.1	7.3
1948										25	1.4	8.8
1949										7	2.9	10.3
1950										28	4.0	32.7
1951										36	4.9	28.8
1952										49	8.1	33.4
1953										30	6.3	53.4
1954							1	†	†	9	1.8	9.6
1955							1	0.2	0.5	16	1.3	6.7
1956										27	3.5	11.1
1957										12	0.8	4.4
1958	15	1.7	7.5	—	—	—	1	†	†	14	1.7	7.4
1959	25	2.0	10.5	—	—	—	4	0.4	1.6	21	1.6	57.2
1960	36	28.6	58.4	—	—	—	3	1.0	1.2	33	27.6	67.7
1961	28	6.6	15.3	—	—	—	—	—	—	28	6.6	15.3
1962	28	31.1	79.1	5	4.2	33.8	2	1.7	2.3	21	25.3	43.1
1963	29	4.8	15.4	—	—	—	2	0.3	2.2	27	4.6	67.7
1964	41	22.7	70.8	—	—	—	4	0.3	3.2	37	22.5	57.7

Year	Stoppages (all government)	Workers involved, thousands (all government)	Days idle, thousands (all government)	Stoppages (federal)	Workers involved, thousands (federal)	Days idle, thousands (federal)	Stoppages (state)	Workers involved, thousands (state)	Days idle, thousands (state)	Stoppages (local)	Workers involved, thousands (local)	Days idle, thousands (local)
1965	42	11.9	146.0	—	—	—	—	—	1.3‡	42	11.9	145.0
1966	142	105.0	455.0	—	—	—	9	3.1	6.0	133	102.0	449.0
1967	181	132.0	1250.0	—	—	—	12	4.7	16.3	169	127.0	1203.0
1968	254	201.8	2545.2	3	1.7	9.6	16	9.3	42.8	235	190.9	2492.8
1969	411	160.0	745.7	2	0.6	1.1	37	20.5	152.4	372	139.0	592.2
1970	412	333.5	2023.2	3	155.8	648.3	23	8.8	44.6	386	168.9	1330.5
1971	329	152.6	901.4	2	1.0	8.1	23	14.5	81.8	304	137.1	811.6
1972	375	142.1	1257.3	—	—	—	40	27.4	273.7	335	114.7	983.5
1973	387	196.4	2303.9	1	0.5	4.6	29	12.3	133.0	357	186.7	2166.3
1974	384	160.7	1404.2	2	0.5	1.4	34	24.7	86.4	348	135.4	1316.3
1975	478	318.5	2204.4	1	—	—	32	66.6	300.5	446	252.0	1903.9
1976	378	180.7	1690.7	1	†	†	25	33.8	148.2	352	146.8	1542.6
1977	413	170.2	1765.7	2	0.4	0.5	44	33.7	181.9	367	136.2	1583.3
1978	481	193.7	1706.7	1	4.8	27.8	45	17.9	180.2	435	171.0	1498.8
1979	593	254.1	2982.5	—	—	—	57	48.6	515.5	536	205.5	2467.1
1980**	568	NA	NA	NA	NA	NA	NA	NA	NA	NA	NA	NA

**preliminary

*The Bureau of Labor Statistics has published data on strikes in government in its annual reports since 1942. Before that year, they had been included in a miscellaneous category—other nonmanufacturing industries. From 1942 through 1957, data refer only to strikes in administrative, protective, and sanitary services of government. Stoppages in establishments owned by government were classified in their appropriate industry; for example, public schools and libraries were included in education services, not in government. Beginning in 1958, stoppages in such establishments were included under the government classification. Stoppages in publicly owned utilities, transportation, and schools were reclassified back to 1947 but a complete reclassification was not attempted. After 1957, dashes denote zeros.

†Fewer than 100.

‡Idleness in 1965 resulted from 2 stoppages that began in 1964. NA = Not Available.

NOTE: Because of rounding, sums of individual items may not equal totals.

Sources: U.S. Department of Labor, Bureau of Labor Statistics, Work Stoppages in Government. 1978. Report No. 582 (Washington. D.C.: Government Printing Office, 1980). p. 4: U.S. Department of Labor, Bureau of Labor Statistics, Work Stoppages in Government. 1979. Report No. 629 (Washington. D.C.: G.P.O., March 1981). p. 4; and U.S. Department of Labor, Office of Information, News Release USDL 81-74, Work Stoppages, 1980 (Washington. D.C.: November 28, 1980), pp. 4 and 10.

TABLE 2
Summary of State Bargaining Laws That Permit Public Employee Strikes

State	Strike Policy
Alaska	Strike prohibited for essential employees; permitted for semi-essential employees (utilities, snow removal, sanitation) but may be enjoined if there is threat to public health, safety, or welfare; strike permitted for nonessential employees if approved by majority of unit in secret ballot election; no direct provision governing teachers.
Hawaii	Pertains to state and local government employees, police, firefighters, and teachers; strike prohibited for 60 days after factfinding report; 10-day notice required; strike not permitted where public health or safety is endangered; can be enjoined by circuit court.
Minnesota	Nonessential employees may legally strike if (1) an agreement has expired or, if there is no agreement, an impasse has occurred, (2) the employer and union have participated in mediation sessions for at least 45 days and (3) written notification of intent to strike has been served. Also, if a request for binding arbitration has been rejected or an employer fails to comply with a valid arbitration award, the strike right is available. The strike right is also available for teachers under the same conditions except that they must have participated in mediation for at least 60 days, 30 days of which have occurred after the expiration date of the collective bargaining agreement. State nonessential employees may strike if the legislature fails to ratify a negotiated agreement or arbitration award, or if the legislative commission on employee relations does not approve a negotiated agreement or arbitration award within 30 days during a legislative interim.
Montana	Pertains to state and local government employees, transit workers, police and firefighters; strike permitted; also pertains to nurses, but stoppage prohibited if simultaneous strike occurs within 150 miles; labor organization must give written notice and specify strike date.
Oregon	Pertains to state and local government employees, and teachers; limited right to strike for employees included in appropriate bargaining unit certified by PERB for which final and binding arbitration is not provided; mediation and factfinding and other statutory procedures must have been exhausted; injunctive relief can be granted if the strike is a threat to public health, safety and welfare; strike is prohibited for police and firefighters, but the dispute must be submitted to binding arbitration if unresolved after mediation and factfinding.
Pennsylvania	Pertains to state and local government employees, teachers (police, fire, and court employees excluded); limited right to strike after exhaustion of impasse procedures unless strike creates clear and present danger to public health, safety and welfare; injunction may not be issued prior to strike.
Vermont	Pertains to local government employees, police, firefighters and teachers; limited right to strike; stoppage is prohibited and enjoinable if it occurs 30 days after a factfinder's report, after parties have submitted dispute to arbitration, or if it is shown that the strike will endanger public health and safety; for teachers, a strike may be disallowed if it is ruled a clear and present danger to a sound program of education by a court of competent jurisdiction.

230

TABLE 2 (continued)

Strike	Strike Policy
Wisconsin	Pertains to local government employees and teachers (but excluding police and firefighters); mandates mediation and final offer arbitration, except that if both parties withdraw their final offers prior to arbitration the labor organization may strike after giving 10 days written advance notice.

Sources: David Lewin. "Collective Bargaining and the Right to Strike." in A. Lawrence Chickering. ed.. *Public Employee Unions* (Lexington. Mass.: D.C. Heath. 1976), pp. 155-56: Bureau of National Affairs. *Government Employee Relations Report Reference File:* and Commerce Clearing House *Public Employee Bargaining.* Vol. 2.

Consequently, we must conclude that the trend toward legal public employee strikes is a slow and cautious one of rather modest proportions. However, this trend does indicate a much wider acceptance of public employee strikes than existed fifteen years ago.

THE PRACTICE OF DISPUTE RESOLUTION

It is relatively easy to describe how various dispute procedures are designed to operate; it is much more difficult to assess their impacts upon bargaining processes and outcomes. Much of the difficulty can be traced to two methodological problems: the problem of obtaining the relevant operational data, and the problem of controlling the multitude of other variables which influence bargaining processes and outcomes. As a result, it is fashionable for writers in this area to proclaim how little is known about these subjects and consequently how necessary further research is. Although we do not disagree with these proclamations, in this chapter we emphasize the dispute resolution information that is available in order to reach some conclusions— however tentative—about how settlements are achieved in governmental bargaining.

Strikes

The vast majority of negotiations produce agreements without strikes, but a large number of these agreements are created as a result of strike threats, and each year several hundred of these threats become reality. The experiences with public employee strikes suggest several conclusions.

First, the Table 1 and Table 3 data show that these strikes occur primarily between local government employers and employees, principally over money issues. In almost any given year 90 percent or so of all government strikes occur among the municipalities, counties, school districts, and special districts which compose local government. Teachers are the most strike prone occupation and several states account for a disproportionate share of strikes. This array of strike facts is hardly surprising when one considers that local governments employ more than half of all public

TABLE 3
Work Stoppages by Major Issue, Occupation, and State, 1978

Major Issue		California	23
All issues	481	Colorado	2
		Connecticut	6
General wage change	330	Delaware	2
Supplementary benefits	9	District of Columbia	3
Wage adjustments	12	Florida	3
Hours of work	1	Georgia	2
Other contractual matters	20	Hawaii	—
Union organization and security	26	Idaho	1
Job security	20	Illinois	38
Plant administration	52	Indiana	23
Other working conditions	9	Iowa	—
Interunion or intraunion matters	2	Kansas	2
		Kentucky	3
Occupation		Louisiana	7
		Maine	4
All occupations	481	Maryland	1
Teachers	125	Massachusetts	9
Teachers and other professional		Michigan	74
and technical	16	Minnesota	6
Nurses	9	Mississippi	3
Professional and technical	11	Missouri	8
Clerical	10	Montana	7
Sanitation workers	9	Nebraska	1
Craft workers	3	Nevada	—
Blue-collar and manual	134	New Hampshire	1
Police	21	New Jersey	25
Fire fighters	15	New Mexico	—
Police and fire fighters	4	New York	16
Other protective	5	North Carolina	6
Professional, technical and		North Dakota	—
clerical	16	Ohio	67
Clerical and blue-collar	25	Oklahoma	1
Professional, technical and blue-		Oregon	4
collar	31	Pennsylvania	69
Sales and blue-collar	2	Rhode Island	5
Protective and blue-collar	12	South Carolina	—
Professional, clerical, and blue-		South Dakota	—
collar	33	Tennessee	10
		Texas	3
State		Utah	—
		Vermont	3
All states	481	Virginia	1
Alabama	14	Washington	16
Alaska	2	West Virginia	4
Arizona	2	Wisconsin	4
Arkansas	3	Wyoming	—

Source: U.S. Department of Labor, Bureau of Labor Statistics, *Work Stoppages in Government 1978,* BLS Report 582 (Washington, D.C.: G.P.O., 1980), pp. 9, 19, and 21.

employees, that these workers are more solidly organized and usually more militant than state and federal employees, that local governments tend to be faced with greater financial scarcities than state and federal governments, and that there is a lot more bargaining in some states than in others.

Second, the data in Table 4 show that public employee strikes have somewhat different characteristics than work stoppages in private industry. Public employee strikes are much shorter than strikes in public industry, and as a result the days of idleness per striker is much lower in government. The number of workers involved in the average public or private strike is not dramatically different, but because there are proportionately fewer government strikes a smaller fraction of public employees than private employees are involved in strikes in any year (though the fractions for both groups are quite small). In addition, the comparatively small number and short duration of government strikes means that the proportion of all work time lost due to strikes is much lower in the public sector than in private industry (though, again, proportions for both groups are very small).

Third, there is some recent research which shows that strike penalties may reduce the number of strikes. In a study of the "propensity to strike" among teachers, police, firefighters, and other municipal employees in several states during the middle 1970s, Olson and his colleagues found that strong and consistently enforced strike penalties reduce strikes compared to situations where strikes are legal or where strikes are illegal but strikers and their unions are not penalized. For example, after controlling for several other factors which influence strikes, they found that the highest to lowest rank order probability of teachers strikes occurs in Pennsylvania, Illinois, Ohio, Indiana, and New York (it is important to note that teacher strike propensities in these five states are compared only with each other and not with strike propensities in other states). Teacher strikes are legal in Pennsylvania, are illegal but usually not penalized in Illinois and Ohio, are moderately

TABLE 4
Selected Work Stoppage Measures, All Industries and Government, 1978

Measure	All Stoppages	Government Stoppages		
		Total	State	Local
Days of idleness as a percent of working time	0.17	0.04	0.02	0.06
Workers involved as a percent of total employment	1.9	1.3	.5	1.8
Average number of workers involved per stoppage	384	403	398	393
Average days of idleness per worker	22.7	8.8	10.1	8.8

Source: U.S. Department of Labor, Bureau of Labor Statistics, *Work Stoppages in Government,* 1978, BLS Report 582 (Washington, D.C.: G.P.O., 1980), p. 5.

penalized in Indiana (i.e., school teachers cannot be paid for strike days that are rescheduled later in the school year and unions of striking teachers lose their dues check-off privileges for a year), and are more strongly penalized in New York (i.e., strikers lose two days pay for each day on strike and unions of striking employees lose their dues check-off privileges for a period of time). Similarly, there were lower strike probabilities for police, firefighters, and other municipal employees in those states where strike penalties existed and were consistently enforced.[18] These results are at odds with previous research[19] which found no consistent and significant relationship between strikes and strike prohibitions and penalties. However, the Olson *et al.* research is far more intensive than previous public sector strike research.

The Olson *et al.* findings do not necessarily lead to the straightforward policy conclusion that strong and consistently applied strike penalties are the best way to prevent public employees from striking. For one thing, their research may not have been able to account for some factors which influence strikes. For another thing, they found that compulsory arbitration also was a very effective method for reducing the probability of a strike. Third, the implementation and use of strong strike penalties against public employees and their unions raises numerous equity considerations which cannot be answered in a multiple regression analysis. However, their findings do suggest that when policymakers have decided that public employee strikes and compulsory arbitration are inappropriate, strong and consistently enforced strike penalties seem to prevent many strikes which otherwise might occur.

Fourth, there is little systematic data on the relationship between strikes and bargaining outcomes. Logical reasoning suggests that strike-induced settlements may be more favorable to the employees than nonstrike settlements on the grounds that the struck employers are willing to pay a premium to have the withheld services restored. This in fact may happen, but it has not happened to such an extent that it is readily apparent. For instance, Gerhart correlated an index of favorable union bargaining outcomes with a state strike activity index and found a positive but weak association.[20] Kochan and Wheeler correlated firefighter strikes with favorable union outcomes and found no discernible relationship, but they did find favorable outcomes correlated with union pressure tactics such as picketing and slowdowns.[21] Anderson's study in this chapter shows that over the long run Canadian federal employees have not been able to use strikes or strike threats to obtain more wages or contractual benefits than their peers who bargained under a compulsory arbitration system, but in particular years actually going on strike seemed to yield large payoffs. Further, since about 1975 public management has shown an increasing willingness to "hang tough" in strike situations, and many strikes have ended on less than victorious terms for the unions involved (including, in a few cases, the permanent discharges of striking employees).[22] As a result of this mixed bag of information, we are unwilling to offer any generalized conclusion about the impact of strikes upon bargaining outcomes.

Fifth, the relationship between government strikes and the maintenance of the public welfare is similarly ambiguous. As a general conclusion, we believe that the danger most public employee strikes pose to the citizenry's

234

health, safety, or welfare is more rhetorical than real, for the public appears to survive the vast majority of these strikes with a minimum of apprehension and inconvenience. To take one prominent example, the citizens of Chicago survived a twenty-three-day strike by most of the Windy City's firefighters in early 1980 with about the same amount of fire-related death and destruction that occurred in comparable periods in previous years.[23] More generally, Feuille argues in his selection in this chapter that it is very difficult to demonstrate systematically that the public needs to be protected from strikes of its own employees. However, we recognize that our assessment needs to be qualified with three important considerations: (a) there are widely varying degrees of essentiality to the public welfare across the range of government services, so a police strike is more troublesome than a parks and recreation strike; (b) the essentiality of the same services (say, fire protection) can vary across jurisdictions along such dimensions as size, density, population composition, income level, and so on, with large central cities appearing more vulnerable than small suburbs; and (c) various citizens' proximity to and need for the deprived services may vary greatly.

Finally, the high level of strikes that has prevailed since 1969 indicates that these activities are occurring more and more as "normal" events which increasingly are built into the parties' expectations. This admittedly subjective assessment is supported by the increasing legalization of strikes and by the apparent increasing willingness of management to take strikes in order to implement "less" relative to union demands for "more." Just as this society has learned to cope with private sector strikes, so we perceive the same process occurring in the public sector.

Mediation

Mediation probably is the most used and least studied dispute resolution procedure. The usage rate and the relative lack of systematic investigation are not surprising, however, considering that: (1) mediation is the least visible of all the various procedures, with the mediator working privately and informally to assist the parties in reaching agreement; (2) its behind-the-scene nature makes it very difficult for researchers to obtain pertinent information; and (3) mediators seem to be convinced that their unstructured craft is more "art" than "science" and hence not very amenable to systematic inquiry and resultant generalization. One of the few studies which has probed into the dynamics of mediation is the Kressel selection, which we believe presents an interesting and at times fascinating account of how a sample of mediators work to bring contending parties together.[24]

The most accessible mediation data consist of the number and proportion of impasses referred to and settled at this impasse step, and these data show that a large proportion of all impasses are settled via mediators' efforts. For instance, in New York during 1968-74, about 30 percent of all negotiations went to impasse, and slightly less than half of these impasses were settled in mediation.[25] In Iowa, Gallagher's analysis in this chapter shows that about 80 percent of all impasses are settled at the mediation step of that state's three-step statutory impasse procedure (though the declaration of "impasses" in

Iowa is artificially inflated by a statutory filing requirement). In addition, in many states a large number of disputes are mediated into agreement at the factfinding or arbitration steps. There is a conventional wisdom in dispute resolution circles which says that mediation is the most preferred (or least undesirable) form of third-party intervention because it is much less coercive than factfinding or arbitration; hence any mediated settlements primarily reflect the desires of the parties. The large proportion of all impasses settled via mediation tends to support this conventional wisdom.

The increasing availability of factfinding and arbitration has posed an important question for the continued effectiveness of mediation: how does the availability of these more structured and coercive procedures affect mediation's usefulness? There are no conclusive answers to this question, in part because of a scarcity of information. For instance, one study reported that a sample of mediators perceived that mediation is more effective in reaching agreement when followed by arbitration rather than factfinding, and that mediation is more effective under final offer than conventional arbitration.[26] However, these perceptions were not supported by any statistical evidence. A careful investigation of this question has been made by Kochan and his associates in their study of New York police and firefighter impasse resolution before and after the introduction of conventional arbitration. They found that mediation appeared to be equally effective—as measured by the proportion of mediated agreements and by the perceptions of union and management negotiators—when factfinding was the final impasse step as when conventional arbitration was the final step.[27]

The nature of the negotiating impasse probably has more impact upon mediation's usefulness than post-mediation procedures. It has been hypothesized that mediation works well in those disputes where the parties are inexperienced in bargaining and hence unsure of themselves, lack knowledge of contract language, and are especially susceptible to personality conflicts. In these situations mediators can play a useful role as they help the parties develop an improved appreciation of the negotiating process. Mediation may work less well in situations where there are strong constituent pressures, scarce resources, and sophisticated negotiators who know how to manipulate dispute procedures to their advantage. In cases where these factors are present and where mediation is followed by factfinding or arbitration, the proportion of impasses settled via mediation is likely to be relatively small.

Another important factor influencing mediator success is the style or philosophy of the mediator or mediation agency, usually expressed on an aggressive-passive or degree-of-intensity continuum. For instance, Kochan and Jick found that aggressive mediators were more successful in obtaining mediated settlements than were passive mediators.[28] Going a step further, Gerhart and Drotning found that "high intensity" mediators were more effective than "low intensity" mediators in facilitating settlements in "tough" bargaining cases.[29] These differences in mediator styles are not only a function of the preferences and personalities of individual mediators, they also may reflect different mediation philosophies across mediation agencies. Kolb compared mediator activities in a regional office of the Federal Mediation and Conciliation Service and in a state mediation agency and found that the state mediators (the "dealmakers") were uniformly aggressive in trying to achieve settlements while the federal mediators (the "orchestrators") were comparatively much more passive.[30] We still need a great deal more research to discover which specific mediator activities are best suited to various bargaining circumstances, but it is readily apparent that "mediation" encompasses a very wide variety of dispute resolution behaviors.

As the preceding discussion suggests, mediation and the other impasse procedures should not be regarded as procedures which are utilized only after the parties have thoroughly explored every settlement possibility in direct negotiations and have bargained to exhaustion. Although some impasses accurately are described in such a manner, it is more likely that negotiators manipulate impasse procedures to gain tactical negotiating advantages, and the first step in such manipulation usually is to move to mediation (see the Kressel selection for an elaboration of this phenomenon). Further, the unions are more likely than management to be the party initiating these impasse steps. Bargaining purists may decry this procedural manipulation, but the fact that the parties have incorporated such manipulation into their negotiating strategies should not be surprising given (a) the absence of the right to strike in most states and (b) the requirement in some states that these procedures be utilized prior to conducting a legal strike.

Factfinding

Factfinding is a misnamed process—rarely does it produce "facts" not already found—which combines elements of mediation and arbitration. It has much of the structure and ritual of arbitration, including a hearing, testimony from each side, and a written report, but as in mediation the third party's settlement recommendations are not binding upon the parties. Further, the ostensible purpose of the procedure is to use a third party to create a settlement range which the two contending parties will find acceptable, and in that sense the factfinder's function is conceptually similar to that of a mediator. In addition, mediation and factfinding often overlap, and in some disputes it is difficult to tell where one stops and the other begins. In part, this blurred distinction results from the mediation efforts of many factfinders[31] and from the mediation efforts which sometimes occur after a factfinding report has been issued.[32]

During the 1970s factfinding acquired an increasingly poor (though largely undeserved) reputation, and its bad name resulted primarily from a deadly mixture of high expectations and low performance. Expectations are high because the procedure appears quasi-adjudicative, but performance often is low because either party can—and often does—reject the factfinder's report. The strongest condemnations of factfinding have occurred in states where factfinding was (or still is) the terminal step in the official impasse procedure. The evidence from these jurisdictions suggests that factfinding's lack of finality limits its usefulness as a substitute for strikes, that some parties may incorporate factfinding into their negotiating strategies and may not begin to bargain seriously until after receipt of the factfinder's report, and that public pressure upon the parties to accept the factfinder's recommendations—one of the key reasons for factfinding's existence—almost never occurs (usually because the public doesn't know or doesn't care that the process is being used).[33] In addition, factfinding may be ineffective in bringing the parties together when it is followed by conventional arbitration, as occurred in New York police and fire impasses during 1974-77.[34] Finally, factfinding may be least useful in situations involving financial scarcity, for there often is a wide gap between the employers' and employees' expectations that cannot be bridged simply with the well-meaning suggestions of a third party.

During the 1970s compulsory arbitration and the right to strike became more common as the terminal step in statutory dispute procedures, in part because of employee and union dissatisfaction with factfinding. This dissatisfaction indicates that certain forms of factfinding, for example, when it is the terminal step in a dispute procedure, may be doomed to a fairly short effective life once the parties have become experienced at manipulating the impasse process to their own advantage. However, factfinding can play a very useful role in helping unions and managements resolve their differences, as Gallagher indicates in his selection on factfinding and arbitration in Iowa. The key to factfinding's success in Iowa—more than half of the factfinding cases are settled at factfinding and do not go on to arbitration; arbitrators tend to confirm factfinder recommendations in those cases where an arbitration award is necessary—is the possibility that an arbitrator will impose the factfinder's judgment upon the parties. Knowing this, the parties can—and do—use this information to fashion their own settlements. In addition, the Iowa impasse process has not had to operate in the same environment of financial scarcity as has occurred in some other states.

The Gallagher selection suggests that factfinding may be effective in those states which have not been hard hit by fiscal scarcity and/or where factfinding has a direct impact on arbitration. In addition, the substantial number of mediated and negotiated settlements at the factfinding step in several states indicates that many parties are willing to use the factfinder's help in resolving their disputes.[35] Finally, the lack of a binding award may be factfinding's greatest virtue, for the procedure's open end leaves room for the parties to fashion their own agreement—which is the purpose of collective bargaining.

Compulsory Arbitration

During the past few years arbitration seems to have captured the lion's share of the attention that has focused on governmental impasse resolution procedures. For instance, there are at least twenty states that have implemented compulsory statutes; in 1965 there was only one.[36] The desire for arbitration seems to be based on four factors: (1) its binding award creates a final resolution of a dispute; (2) it reduces strikes; (3) it tends to equalize the power of the parties in negotiations; and (4) it provides a face-saving tool which union and management representatives may find useful. After examining these points in more detail, we will analyze the impact of arbitration upon bargaining processes and outcomes and upon the political process in a democratic society.

The most important publicly stated rationale supporting the existence of arbitration statutes is that arbitration reduces strikes. Most of these statutes apply to police and firefighters—who arguably provide government's most essential services—and thus they insure that the citizenry will continuously receive vital public safety protection. The available evidence does show that in those jurisdictions where arbitration exists there have been very few strikes, especially over arbitrable issues.[37] Critics respond by pointing to the 1969 Montreal police strike, the 1974 New York City fire strike, and several police strikes in Michigan and Pennsylvania in the 1970s, all of which took place while arbitration procedures were in effect in those jurisdictions. These isolated incidents do not destroy the validity of the strike prevention rationale; instead they demonstrate that in a democratic society there is no feasible way to insure a total and complete absence of such stoppages.

Arbitration reduces strikes because its binding award eliminates almost any opportunity for one side to provoke or conduct a work stoppage for terms more favorable than those provided by the arbitrator. However, we believe it is incorrect to view arbitration as the *quid pro quo* for the right to strike, for the employee groups are not giving up any right they previously enjoyed.[38] A more accurate interpretation of arbitration statutes is that they represent political and functional *quid pro quos*. Politically, the arbitration advocates—mostly police and fire unions—have been able to convince state legislators of the desirability of such statutes, and the politicians presumably collect political IOUs in return. Functionally, such statutes represent a procedural compromise with the police and fire unions in return for the latter giving up their ability to conduct (illegal) strikes.

The fact that such statutes have come into existence primarily because of vigorous union lobbying—frequently over the opposition of municipal management—illustrates our third point: arbitration is perceived by the unions as a low-cost power equalizer which increases their strength at the bargaining table. Under an arbitration procedure, management cannot realistically adopt a "take it or leave it" bargaining posture, for such a tactic may be rendered useless by the arbitrator's binding award. Similarly, management cannot bargain to impasse and unilaterally implement its desired changes. Further, arbitration is a much lower-cost route for seeking benefits than strikes, for strikes are risky and many engender negative public and managerial responses. In contrast, arbitrators usually award the employees more than the employer has offered, and hence the downside risk of an antagonistic arbitration award is minimal.

Although most municipal managers appear unenthusiastic about and even hostile toward arbitration, the process is not devoid of benefits for them (benefits in addition to the absence of strikes). Arbitration provides both union leaders and managerial officials with the ability to save face when coping with constituent pressures. The binding nature of the arbitrator's award enables union and management representatives to use the arbitrator as a scapegoat if there is constituent backlash toward the outcome. This face-saving feature assumes the greatest importance in those large and financially constrained central cities where union member militancy tends to be high and municipal ability to pay rather low.[39]

In sum, what sets arbitration apart from mediation and factfinding is its binding award, for this is what creates the results just discussed. In those impasses where the parties are unable or unwilling to reach a mutually satisfactory agreement without a work stoppage, this quality of finality offers a useful guarantee of the continued availability of essential public services.

The binding nature of arbitration, though, has raised three important questions about the process: (1) does the existence of arbitration reduce the parties' incentives to engage in the hard bargaining necessary to reach agreement? (2) does arbitration provide for more expensive settlements than would result from direct negotiations? (3) is arbitration, with its delegation of governmental authority to a private party, constitutionally and politically compatible with our democratic system of representative government?

Conventional compulsory arbitration is alleged to have a "chilling effect" on the parites' incentives to reach their own agreement. The reasoning behind this allegation is that if either one of the parties perceives—for whatever reasons—that it may get a better deal from an arbitrator than from a negotiated agreement, it will have an incentive to cling to excessive demands in the hope of tilting the arbitration award in its favor. If one side acts this way, the other side has no realistic choice but to respond in like manner, and the result is surface bargaining on top of a wide gap between the parties' positions. This lack of hard bargaining will occur because of the very small costs attached to remaining in disagreement: there will be no strike by the union, no unilateral changes by the employer, and the compromise nature of the typical award will give the employees less than the union has asked for but more than the employer has offered. This compromise award is made possible by the discretion the arbitrator possesses to fashion the award he deems appropriate on the disputed issues.

This reasoning applies to the bargaining process under conventional arbitration, which is the more common kind. However, policymakers in several jurisdictions—including Wisconsin, Iowa, Massachusetts, Michigan, and Eugene, Oregon—have implemented final-offer arbitration, a process which attempts to preserve the strike prevention and impasse finality features of conventional arbitration while simultaneously increasing the parties' incentives to reach their own agreement. This kind of arbitration attempts to increase the parties' costs of not reaching agreement by eliminating arbitral discretion and thus forcing the arbitrator to select one or the other party's final offer—with no room for compromise. The final offer theory predicts that each side will develop ever more reasonable negotiating positions in the hope of winning the award, and these convergent movements will result because of the fear that the arbitrator will select the other side's offer. Consequently, final-offer arbitration should not have a chilling effect upon the parties' incentives to negotiate because its potentially severe costs of disagreement should push the parties together in a "strikelike" manner—in a way that conventional arbitration does not.

There is evidence which confirms the existence of a chilling effect under conventional arbitration, and some of this evidence is presented in the selections by Anderson, Kochan and Baderschneider, and Ponak and Wheeler in this chapter. In negotiations under the strike and arbitration options for Canadian federal government employees, Anderson found that the unions relied more heavily on arbitration awards than on strikes (or strike threats) to resolve their negotiating disputes. Similarly, in police and firefighter bargaining in New York, Kochan and Baderschneider found that the factfinding and conventional arbitration processes developed a clientele of frequent and repeated users. Ponak and Wheeler examined strike and arbitration decisions in four jurisdictions (Canadian federal government, British Columbia, Minnesota, and Wisconsin) where the parties can choose either to strike or arbitrate, and they found that managements and especially the unions preferred to arbitrate their negotiating disputes rather than strike over them. However, the data in these and other studies should not hide the fact that, in almost all jurisdictions where arbitration exists, the majority of negotiations are settled through negotiated or mediated agreements. In other words, arbitration has not destroyed good faith collective bargaining.

A second line of criticism directed at compulsory arbitration—conventional and final offer—is that it may result in excessively generous awards, especially on economic issues. Although there is no precise definition of "excessive," presumably it refers to a comparison between the cost of arbitration awards and negotiated agreements. The available evidence suggests that arbitration is associated with favorable union outcomes, but the magnitude of this effect is not large. For instance, Kochan and Wheeler report a significant positive correlation between the presence of arbitration and the favorableness to the union of firefighters' contracts—on both dollar and nondollar items.[40] Olson examined the influence of arbitration on firefighter wages, and found that over a five-year period (1972-77) the presence of an arbitration statute produced wages about 3 to 6 percent higher than would have been the case without arbitration.[41] It is not surprising that favorable union outcomes are associated with arbitration given that arbitration is designed in part to increase the union's bargaining power vis-a-vis management. However, the magnitude of this favorable union impact strikes us as something less than "excessive."

The third category of criticism is aimed at arbitration's alleged constitutional and political incompatibility with our democratic system of representative government. In this system the citizens elect government officials who are responsible for the allocation of scarce public resources—both dollar and nondollar. If a majority of the citizenry is dissatisfied with these allocation decisions the relevant officials may be voted out of office. In addition, the government's financial resources are coerced from the citizenry in the form of taxes, and government officials should be accountable for the use of these funds. Arbitration critics point out that under the typical arbitration procedure the arbitrator often is appointed by an outside agency, enters an impasse on an *ad hoc* basis, issues an award and leaves the scene. He is not elected to his position and he is not accountable to those groups—employees, employer, citizens—who must live with and bear the impact of his award. Further, the arbitration process itself rarely, if ever, provides an opportunity for the direct involvement of citizen interest groups. Consequently, arbitration is said to be an unwarranted delegation of governmental authority to a private party and is inconsistent with our system of government.

If the above argument were compelling we would expect to find the courts striking down compulsory interest arbitration as unconstitutional.

However, the legal record to date tends to support arbitration, as the highest state courts in Maine, Massachusetts, Michigan, Minnesota, Nebraska, New York, Pennsylvania, Rhode Island, Washington, and Wyoming have upheld the constitutionality of arbitration in those states, while the high courts in California, Colorado, South Dakota, and Utah have struck down arbitration statutes (Utah, South Dakota) or municipal ordinances (Colorado, California) as unconstitutional.[42] To date, then, the constitutional batting average clearly favors the vaility of arbitration.

Part of the governmental incompatibility criticism focuses on the political wisdom of using arbitration as a mechanism for allocating government resources for altering public sector bargaining power and for regulating interest group conflict, and these are the subjects of the Feuille selection on various costs and benefits of compulsory arbitration. The author's three main points are that (1) arbitration statutes are implemented and renewed to serve selfish interests rather than the "public interest," (2) arbitration does a lot more than prevent strikes, and as a result, (3) arbitration rhetoric often diverges from arbitration reality.

Finally, the arbitration experiences in many American and Canadian jurisdictions strongly suggest that in order to fully understand how these various procedures influence union and management attempts to reach agreement, we must pay careful attention to the procedural fine points and complexities of the various impasse processes. The selections by Gallagher, Ponak and Wheeler, and especially Anderson indicate that arbitration procedures can differ dramatically in their operation. These operational differences, in turn, can have a strong influence on the outcomes and the acceptibility of these outcomes to the affected unions and managements. Expressed another way, once you have seen one arbitration procedure you have *not* seen them all!

Third-Party Dependency

As long as public sector labor relations policy prohibits strikes, impasse resolution procedures will be implemented and used. Much of our analysis has focused on how often governmental unions and managements rely on third parties to help them reach agreement (via mediation or factfinding) or to impose a settlement (via arbitration). One of our concerns is that unions and managements will rely too much on third parties to the detriment of the effective functioning of the collective bargaining process, and we have seen that in selected jurisdictions the availability of various procedures—especially conventional arbitration—has substantially reduced the parties' efforts to negotiate their own agreements. Further, this third-party dependency seems to be greater in those states with lengthier public sector bargaining histories, which tentatively suggests that, over time, unions and managements learn how to incorporate the manipulation of these procedures into their negotiating strategies.

However, we should qualify our perceptions by repeating an earlier point: there is no formula to determine how much third-party intervention is "too much." For example, some observers will conclude that a 25 percent arbitration award rate is evidence of too much dependency, while others will emphasize that three-fourths of the negotiations ended in agreement. In addition, if policymakers place greatest weight on protecting the public from strikes, then the extent of third-party intervention is of secondary importance. Further, any settlement achieved via mediation or factfinding can occur only with the combined approval of the two contending parties, so there is an inherent limit to the role played by third parties in nonbinding procedures. In sum, it seems fair to say that public sector experiences with third-party impasse resolution procedures have demonstrated that most of the time collective bargaining can function effectively without the right to strike.

CONCLUDING COMMENTS

We close this introductory portion of Chapter 5 by reemphasizing our earlier point about the tremendous diversity that exists in the impasse procedures and practices across the federal government, fifty states, and countless local governments. This diversity is well illustrated by the numerous dimensions along which these procedures can and do vary (in addition to those already mentioned): the employee groups covered, who initiates the process, who provides the impasse services, the procedural timetable, the requirements for moving from mediation to factfinding to arbitration (if available), the criteria to be used by the third parties in reaching their decisions, who pays the costs, and so on. Adding to this diversity is the changing nature of the impasse resolution scene over time, especially the growth of arbitration statutes, and the increasing aggressiveness of management. We believe this diversity is healthy, for it means that there is more impasse experimentation than would be the case otherwise. In turn, this experimentation means that the public sector can offer some valuable impasse resolution suggestions to the private sector.

Earlier in this chapter we briefly examined private sector dispute practices, emphasizing the reliance on the strike—subject to the government's rules regulating its use—and the relative unimportance of third-party intervention. We have discussed two public sector trends, one of which converges with private sector practice and another which diverges from it. We believe that the growth of the right to strike and management's apparent increasing tolerance of strikes indicate that, on the one hand, public sector practices may be moving—however slowly—toward private sector norms, and this assessment is strengthened when one considers the relative absence of legal and illegal governmental strikes prior to 1966. On the other hand, the public sector continues to increase its reliance on third-party procedures— witness the growth of arbitration statutes—and this phenomenon contrasts with private industry. On balance, then, we believe the public and private sectors will be distinguished for some time to come by their respective reliance on procedures and strikes to resolve negotiating disputes, but that in the long run this difference will narrow.

FOOTNOTES

1. See Neil W. Chamberlain and James W. Kuhn, *Collective Bargaining*, 2d ed. (New York: McGraw-Hill, 1965), chap. 7, for a perceptive analysis of bargaining power as the manipulation of the adversary's costs of agreement and disagreement.
2. See Albert Rees, *The Economics of Trade Unions* (Chicago: University of Chicago Press, 1962), chap. 2, for an insightful treatment of the sources of union power.
3. The basic source for most of this paragraph is Charles O. Gregory, *Labor and the Law*, 2d rev. ed. with 1961 supplement (New York: W.W. Norton, 1961).
4. For an analysis of why these fundamental changes in American labor relations law emerged, see Sanford Cohen, "An Analytical Framework for Labor Relations Law," *Industrial and Labor Relations Review*, 14 (April 1961), 350-362.
5. Section 13 of the amended National Labor Relations Act reads in its entirety: "Nothing in this Act, except as specifically provided for herein, shall be construed so as either to interfere with or impede or diminish in any way the right to strike, or to affect the limitations or qualifications on that right."
6. Many states have their own mediation agencies which provide the same kind of dispute settlement services.
7. For a very readable and insightful analysis of emergency strikes, see Donald E. Cullen, *National Emergency Strikes*, ILR Paperback no. 7 (Ithaca, N.Y.: New York State School of Industrial and Labor Relations, Cornell University, 1968).
8. The 1971-74 wage and price controls were an exception to this statement, but these controls established financial ceilings which settlements could not exceed and they did not attempt to write contract language.
9. See Benjamin J. Taylor and Fred Witney, *Labor Relations Law*, 2d ed. (Englewood Cliffs, N.J.: Prentice-Hall, 1976), pp. 488-491.
10. Maurice S. Trotta, *Arbitration of Labor-Management Disputes* (New York: ANACOM, 1974), chap. 11.
11. David Lewin, "Collective Bargaining and the Right to Strike," in A. Lawrence Chickering, ed., *Public Employee Unions* (Lexington, Mass.: D.C. Heath, 1976), pp. 145-163.
12. Paul D. Staudohar, "Prison Guard Labor Relations in Ohio," *Industrial Relations*, 15 (May 1976), 179.
13. Two such states are Michigan and Rhode Island; see U.S. Department of Labor, Labor-Management Services Administration, Division of Public Employee Labor Relations, *Summary of State Policy Regulations for Public Sector Labor Relations* (Washington, D.C.: U.S. Government Printing Office, 1975).
14. We are not suggesting that public employees inevitably go unpenalized when they strike. We are suggesting that the usual strike penalties are light enough that each year many thousands of public employees decide they are worth risking.
15. B.V.H. Schneider, "Public-Sector Labor Legislation: An Evolutionary Analysis," in Benjamin Aaron, Joseph R. Grodin, and James L. Stern, eds., *Public-Sector Bargaining* (Madison, Wis.: Industrial Relations Research Association, 1979), pp. 191-223.
16. Thomas A. Kochan, "Dynamics of Dispute Resolution," in Benjamin Aaron, Joseph R. Grodin, and James L. Stern, eds., *Public-Sector Bargaining* (Madison, Wis.: Industrial Relations Research Association, 1979), pp. 150-190.
17. This erosion has not yet reached police and firefighters, for these groups almost always are specifically excluded from any strike rights.
18. Craig A. Olson, James L. Stern, Joyce Najita, and June Weisberger, "Public Sector Strikes and Strike Penalties," unpublished report to the U.S. Department of Labor, Labor-Management Services Administration, 1981.

244

19. John F. Burton and Charles E. Krider, "The Incidence of Strikes in Public Employment," in Daniel S. Hamermesh, ed., *Labor in the Public and Nonprofit Sectors* (Princeton, N.J.: Princeton University Press, 1975), pp. 135-177; Robert C. Rodgers, "A Replication of the Burton-Krider Model of Public Employee Strike Activity," Industrial Relations Research Association, *Proceedings of the Thirty-third Annual Meeting* (Madison, Wis.: IRRA, 1981); and James L. Perry, "Public Policy and Public Employee Strikes," *Industrial Relations,* 16 (October 1977), 273-282.

20. Paul F. Gerhart, "Determinants of Bargaining Outcomes in Local Government Labor Negotiations," *Industrial and Labor Relations Review,* 29 (April 1976), 347-349.

21. Thomas A. Kochan and Hoyt N. Wheeler, "Municipal Collective Bargaining: A Model and Analysis of Bargaining Outcomes," *Industrial and Labor Relations Review,* 29 (October 1975), 55-56.

22. Thomas A. Kochan, "Dynamics of Dispute Resolution," in Aaron, Grodin, Stern, *op. cit.,* pp. 167-169.

23. Bureau of National Affairs, *Government Employee Relations Report,* No. 853 (March 17, 1980), 27-28.

24. The interested reader might also examine William E. Simkin, *Mediation and the Dynamics of Collective Bargaining* (Washington, D.C.: Bureau of National Affairs, 1971), and Carl M. Stevens, "Mediation and the Role of the Neutral," in *Frontiers of Collective Bargaining,* John T. Dunlop and Neil W. Chamberlain, eds. (New York: Harper and Row, 1967).

25. New York State Public Employment Relations Board, *PERB News,* 8, 3 (March 1975), 1.

26. James L. Stern, Charles M. Rehmus, J. Joseph Loewenberg, Hirschel Kasper and Barbara D. Dennis, *Final-Offer Arbitration* (Lexington, Mass.: D.C. Heath, 1975), pp. 126, 175.

27. Thomas A. Kochan, Mordechai Mironi, Ronald G. Ehrenberg, Jean Baderschneider, and Todd Jick, *Dispute Resolution under Factfinding and Arbitration: An Empirical Evaluation* (New York: American Arbitration Association, 1979), chap. 5.

28. Thomas A. Kochan and Todd Jick, "The Public Sector Mediation Process: A Theory and Empirical Evaluation," *Journal of Conflict Resolution,* 22 (June 1978), 209-238.

29. Paul F. Gerhart and John E. Drotning, "Dispute Settlement and the Intensity of Mediation," *Industrial Relations,* 19 (Fall 1980), 352-359.

30. Deborah M. Kolb, "Roles Mediators Play," *Industrial Relations,* 20 (Winter 1981), 1-17.

31. Jack Steiber and Benjamin W. Wolkinson, "Fact-Finding Viewed by Fact-Finders: The Michigan Experience," *Labor Law Journal,* 28 (February 1977), 89-101.

32. Thomas A. Kochan, "Dynamics of Dispute Resolution," in Aaron, Grodin, Stern, *op. cit.,* pp. 177-182.

33. For instance, see William R. Word, "Factfinding in Public Employee Negotiations," *Monthly Labor Review,* 95 (February 1972), 60-64; William R. Word, "Implications for Factfinding: The New Jersey Experience," *Journal of Collective Negotiations in the Public Sector,* 3 (Fall 1974), 339-343; and Lucian G. Gatewood, "Factfinding in Teacher Disputes: The Wisconsin Experience," *Monthly Labor Review,* 97 (October 1974), 47-51.

34. Thomas A. Kochan, *et al., Dispute Resolution under Fact-Finding and Arbitration, op. cit.,* chap. 7.

35. Thomas A. Kochan, "Dynamics of Dispute Resolution," in Aaron, Grodin, Stern, *op. cit.*

36. These states include Alaska, Connecticut, Hawaii, Iowa, Maine, Massachusetts, Michigan, Minnesota, Montana, Nebraska, Nevada, New Jersey, New York, Oregon, Pennsylvania, Rhode Island, Vermont, Washington, Wisconsin, and Wyoming (which passed its firefighter arbitration statute in 1965).
37. Thomas A. Kochan, "Dynamics of Dispute Resolution," in Aaron, Grodin, Stern, *op. cit.;* Craig A. Olson, *et al., Public Sector Strikes and Strike Penalties, op. cit.*
38. This *quid pro quo* reasoning does apply, for instance, to private sector grievance arbitration, for most unions have surrendered their right to strike over contract interpretation disputes in return for the employer's promise to arbitrate such disputes.
39. For a more elaborate discussion of arbitration's face-saving characteristic, see Mollie H. Bowers, "Legislated Arbitration: Legality, Enforceability, and Face-Saving," *Public Personnel Management,* 3 (July-August 1974), 270-278.
40. Thomas A. Kochan and Hoyt N. Wheeler, "Municipal Collective Bargaining: A Model and Analysis of Bargaining Outcomes," *op. cit.*
41. Craig A. Olson, "The Impact of Arbitration on the Wages of Firefighters," *Industrial Relations,* 19 (Fall 1980), 325-339.
42. Joseph R. Grodin, "Judicial Response to Public-Sector Arbitration," in Aaron, Grodin, Stern, *op. cit.,* pp. 224-253; and Bernard C. Diemer, "Final Offer Arbitration and Collective Bargaining," unpublished M.A. thesis, Institute of Labor and Industrial Relations, University of Illinois, 1980, chap. 4.

Labor Mediation: An Exploratory Survey

Kenneth Kressel*

The Study and Its Setting

Labor mediation, one of the most highly institutionalized methods of resolving social conflict, has infrequently been the subject of systematic inquiry. . . . The present investigation was undertaken as an exploratory study of the attitudes of labor mediators towards various aspects of their craft. . . .

The interview. The interview schedule was designed to obtain information on a wide range of topics. Because of the exploratory nature of the inquiry, respondents were given considerable latitude in framing their answers, and prepared questions were modified or abandoned when it seemed desirable to pursue topics which had not been anticipated originally.

Interviews lasted, on the average, about an hour and a quarter. They were conducted at each respondent's office, and tape-recorded for later transcription. All respondents were assured of anonymity.

The respondents. Thirteen labor mediators served as respondents. By any standards they constituted an elite group. Four held top administrative posts

*Teachers College, Columbia University. Reprinted from Kenneth Kressel, *Labor Mediation: An Exploratory Survey.* Association of Labor Mediation Agencies, 1972.

in public mediation agencies and two others had previously held such positions. Respondents included seven with law degrees and three Ph.D.s. Three were university professors, one was a university dean, and two had private labor arbitration practices. Eight of the group had written one or more articles for professional journals, and, during the 3-month course of the study, at least four of the respondents were involved, either as mediators or as members of impasse panels, in disputes of sufficient importance to be prominently reported in the public press. The average age of the group was 53.

The plan of the report. The report is divided into two parts. In the first section, respondents' views on the *process of mediation* are discussed. The material in this section deals with the respondents' accounts of their behavior as mediators and their reasons for behaving as they do.

In the second section, the respondents' perceptions of *mediation as a profession* are documented. The primary threme is that of mediation as "art" rather than "science," and aspects of the professional life of the mediator which appear related to this view are examined. . . .

Given the small number of respondents and the unique character of the sample, several caveats seem in order. First, it is clear that the views documented cannot by interpreted as representing the attitudes of the profession at large. Second, when an attempt is made to "explain" certain expressed attitudes on the basis of other information provided by the respondents, the admittedly speculative nature of the effort should be borne in mind. Finally, it should be noted that while explicit disagreement among those interviewed is often pointed out, for certain purposes it seemed desirable to develop a composite account of how the mediator conceives of his work. This composite should not be taken as indicating consensus among the respondents in every respect.

The Process of Labor Mediation

The framework. It may be helpful to begin with a brief sketch of the institutional context in which mediated collective bargaining occurs.

There are two broad types of mediation to be distinguished: That which is conducted under the auspices of some public mediation agency and that which is arranged for privately by the parties. By far the larger volume of labor mediation is conducted by public agencies, and can, in turn, be divided into mediation in private enterprise (the "private sector") and that involving government employees on either federal, state, or local levels (the "public sector").

Among the mediation agencies, the Federal Mediation and Conciliation Service has jurisdiction in disputes in the private sector as well as in those involving federal employees. Nearly every state has its own state board of mediation which operates in private industry within the state. In those states which have granted public employees the right to bargain collectively, a separate state agency may exist to handle public sector disputes. Mediators may be full-time employees of an agency, or they may be affiliated with it on a *per diem* basis, being called upon only when the existence of a dispute requires their services.

Among the present group, four respondents were full-time members of public sector agencies, and eight were, or had been, full-time members of state mediation boards, operating in the private sector. Most of those interviewed had had some experience in both sectors at some point in their careers. Unfortunately, it was not possible to interview members of the Federal Mediation and Conciliation Service.

Entering a dispute. Three major issues related to entering a dispute may be identified from the respondent's remarks: (a) The *acceptability* of the mediator; (b) the strategic implications of a request for mediation; (c) the "timing" of entry.

The acceptability of the mediator. On the matter of acceptibility respondents were in universal agreement. Since a mediator's success depends in large measure on the willingness of both parties to confide in him and accept his suggestions, the more eager both are to have him mediate their dispute the easier his job will be.

> *It's the individual and his acceptability that is more important than anything else. Jones, they will take him. "We like him. We trust him." Smith, who has the same credentials may be totally unacceptable. And, I might say, possibly for irrational reasons. I know some mediators—very fine mediators—who are unacceptable to one side or the other for reasons that don't make any sense. You say, "Why don't you, why can't you, use so and so?"*
>
> *Well it's hard for us to explain," they say. "But we don't feel comfortable with him." That's all you have to hear. You don't really probe much deeper. One side or the other says to you, "We just don't feel comfortable with that fellow," that's enough to rule him out. Unless, of course, there's nobody else and he's the least objectionable.*

However desirable mutual acceptability of the mediator may be in theory, in practice—as the last sentence hints—it may be compromised in a variety of ways. In particular, the method by which the mediator makes contact with the dispute, and the public statutes which govern his intervention, may place constraints on the enthusiasm with which the parties receive him.

The respondents discussed three principal ways that a mediator may make contact with a dispute: (a) Both parties may make a joint request for mediation to the agency with jurisdiction; (b) One of the parties may request mediation; (c) The agency itself may take the initative in contacting the parties.

From the point of view of the acceptability, a joint request is clearly preferable. It is even better if, in making their request, the parties indicate a desire for a particular mediator.

Unfortunately, joint requests for mediation are in the minority. (In a recent year one of the agencies represented handled approximately 200 joint requests for mediation as opposed to 400 unilateral requests). Moreover, when joint requests are made they do not always include a request for a specific mediator. In that case, agencies handle the matter somewhat differently. One provides the parties with a list of potential mediators from which the parties then choose. The process of choosing argues for a degree of investment in the individual selected. This same agency also requires that both parties share the cost of paying for the mediator's services on the grounds that this too increases their commitment to him. (This is in distinction to the traditional practice of providing mediation gratis.)

Another agency prefers to assign the parties a mediator of its own choosing. Since its clients are primarily inexperienced public sector disputants, this method had the advantage of permitting the Director of Mediation to select a man who may be particularly qualified for the dispute in question. Whatever their merits, however, both methods involve the probability of a somewhat lower level of commitment to the mediator than is theoretically desirable.

Acceptability can also be compromised by the inability of the disputants legally to refuse mediation. This, at least, can be inferred from the respondent's descriptions of impasse procedures in the public sector. Historically, mediation has been a voluntary process, and this is entirely consistent with the notion that to be effective the mediator must be more or less welcomed into the dispute. In recent years, however, what may be termed "compulsory mediation" has developed in public sector bargaining. The parties are required by law to accept mediation as the first step in an impasse procedure. Only after they have "exhausted" mediation may the parties proceed to the next stage, which may be some form of arbitration or fact-finding, and, if necessary, a legislative hearing. Since the parties have no choice, and since they are also aware that mediation is only the first stage in what may be a long and complex process, it seems entirely possible that, in such a context, the mediator's efforts may be met with only pro-forma compliance.

Acceptability was often linked with another concept, that of impartiality. The majority of those interviewed felt that a prerequisite for the mediator's acceptability was the belief of both sides that he was genuinely neutral. Any behavior which could be taken as evidence that the mediator was more favorably disposed to one side or the other was to be scrupulously avoided. As one may put it, "A mediator, like Ceasar's wife, must be beyond reproach."

A minority of the respondents expressed a different opinion about the relationship between acceptability and impartiality. In their view, the major component of acceptability was the belief of both sides that the mediator can *effectively* represent their best interests. The belief that the mediator is also impartial is of decidedly secondary importance. Indeed, "impartiality"— in the sense of equal personal distance from each side—is likely to be a handicap, since, according to these respondents, in the collective bargaining situation it is the union, not the employer, who experiences the greatest control over the outcome; that being the case, it is to the mediator's advantage—and ultimately to that of the employer—for the mediator to establish a close relationship with the union leaders. To do this it may be necessary to transcend the bounds of what, in legalistic terms, would be regarded as "scrupulous neutrality." Thus, for several of the respondents it is apparently common practice to socialize with union leaders, speak at union affairs, and in other ways familiarize themselves with the attitudes and feelings of union members. Having established their "credentials" with the union, they are then in a position to oppose firmly some of the more injudicious union demands in the interests of a settlement that will be mutually acceptable.

The ambiguous relationship between acceptability and impartiality was perhaps best illustrated by a respondent, himself an advocate of "strict" neutrality, who cited the remark of a well-known union leader during a major strike. The leader, after listening patiently to all the distinguished individuals who were available to mediate the dispute—a list of which, however, omitted the name of a mediator particularly dear to his own heart—demanded to know why Mr. X had not been mentioned. Where, he wanted to know was *his* "impartial"?

The strategic implications of a request for mediation. Respondents had no illusions that a call for mediation was divorced from the strategy of bargaining. Since they conceived of a request for mediation as a tacit admission of a willingness to compromise, if only one of the parties feels the need for mediation, (and several respondents noted that such a feeling might be a sign of a sophisticated understanding of the uses of mediation rather than a difficult bargaining position), the problem of introducing the mediator can be a delicate one: how to do so without seeming "weak"?

Respondents also noted that requests for mediation are not always made out of an honest desire to resolve a dispute. It has already been noted that in some states disputants in the public sector are required to accept a mediator. Responents also observed that mediators were sometimes called in when one or both disputants merely wish the facade of mediation without its substance. It may be politically inexpedient, for example, for either side to refuse mediation and be publicly branded recalcitrant, even though neither has any real intention of bargaining in good faith, and both may be convinced of the need for a strike (to prove their mettle, to encourage group solidarity, etc.). In some instances collusion may be involved. The leadership on both sides, having worked out an agreement between themselves, may wish to create the impression in the minds of the public, the rank and file, or a regulatory agency, that the dispute has been honestly fought. The presence of the mediator may seem to provide such evidence. Blatant abuses of the latter kind were characterized as chronic but relatively infrequent, and all who discussed the problem were agreed that a mediator who becomes aware that he is being used in such a fashion has an obligation to withdraw immediately.

The timing of entry. There were two views on the most favorable time to enter a dispute. A sizeable majority of those interviewed favored coming in "late."

250

The majority preference for "late" entry was founded on the belief that mediation is most effective when the parties' motivation to bargain is at its highest. Motivation is highest when the pressure to settle is highest, i.e., when there is a clear and impending deadline.

Aside from the level of the parties' motivation to bargain, there were several other factors cited as justifying late entry. One interviewee felt that the major contribution of the mediator is his ability to suggest novel solutions, to be a "new voice," as he put it.

Perhaps the most important concept of their role which respondents held was the notion that they should be instrumental in bringing about a settlement which the parties could "live with." In a later section the matter of "livability" will be explored at greater length. It is sufficient to note here that the ability of the parties to "live with" a settlement is enhanced if they feel that it is largely of their own devising. Consequently, an additional argument for late entry is that it gives the parties maximum opportunity to resolve by themselves all but a few of the most intractable issues.

The goals of the mediator. Once a mediator enters a dispute his behavior is likely to be varied and complex. As a context for viewing this behavior it will be useful to examine first some of the concepts of mediation and collective bargaining which respondents bring with them to a dispute.

Respondents were asked about their over-all objectives in entering a dispute. The most frequent response was to disavow any goal other than settlement, and it was stressed that this settlement was to be an expression of the parties' needs and desires, not those of the mediator. Respondents included in their disclaimers a concern for equity and, in particular, the "public interest."

> I do not take the view, I've never taken the view, that the mediator is the third party at the bargaining table to protect the public. I think its an erroneous view that the mediator is a public official in there to reach a general accord within the guidelines, or within the prescribed goals, or within the economic requirements of the community. . . . I think the management official, in the case of the public employer, is there to protect the taxpayer; that's his role and if he doesn't protect them properly he ought to be thrown out of office. In private industry the company negotiator is there to report to the board of directors and if he doesn't properly protect them he ought to be thrown out. The marketplace should seek its own level.

In addition to this laissez-faire interpretation of collective bargaining, two additional reasons were given for declining the role of public protector. The difficulty of defining the public interest was one. Perhaps more fundamental, was the explanation that a mediator who attempts to protect the "public interest" runs the considerable risk of alienating the disputants and, hence, of losing his usefulness altogether.

There is some evidence, however, that the recent emergence of the public sector as a critical bargaining area has raised the salience of the public interest in the minds of many of the respondents, even if they end up by disavowing such responsibility—and not all of them do. Three interviewees accepted some explicit responsibility for protecting the public welfare. Interestingly, all of them worked primarily in the public sector—where pressures to protect the public interest might be expected to be greater—and all appeared somewhat conflicted about their admission.

Although the majority of respondents were most comfortable with the view that their obligation was to get a settlement and not to defend some abstract notion of public well-being or equity, nearly all of them were willing to sketch a variety of criteria by which to distinguish "good" settlements from the less good and the downright poor.

By far the most common response to a request to define a good settlement was the phrase, "something the parties can *live with*." A settlement that can be "lived with" may refer to:

1. A settlement that the negotiators feel is their own, and not one into which they have been manipulated or finessed by the mediator—whether or not the mediator's role has, in fact, been a large one.
2. A settlement which the parties like.
3. A settlement which is ratified by the respective constituencies. (Several respondents did observe that since, (a) the vast majority of agreements are ratified anyway, and (b) there are times when the constituents are going to reject an agreement no matter what its terms, ratification per se is a poor criterion by which to judge the quality of an agreement.
4. A settlement in which neither side feels that it has been forced to accept terms imposed by the other. While there was little willingness to endorse overt efforts to prevent such settlements from being reached, there appear to be things that mediators can do to try to avoid creating a feeling of "victory" for one side and "defeat" for the other. Several respondents expressed an enthusiasm for "complex" settlements for this reason.
5. A settlement that does not have adverse political consequences for the leadership—particularly the union leadership. This criterion is related to the previous one, in the sense that "defeat" is not the sturdiest platform from which to hold elected office.
6. A settlement in which the terms of agreement are unambiguous, all major issues are resolved, and little, if anything, is left for later determination. In essence, this is the idea that a good settlement is one which produces stability in the relationship.

Apart from the umbrella term of "livability," several other criteria of a good mediated settlement were mentioned. These included:

7. Settlements which succeed in averting physical violence.
8. Settlements which give the parties an understanding of "what the collective bargaining process is all about, what mediation is all about, the art of compromise." Public sector bargaining was singled out as an area in which such an achievement was especially desirable.
9. Settlements which violate no law.

252

10. Settlements in which the parties have bargained in good faith, as opposed to those in which the mediator has been called in to give the appearance of honest bargaining.
11. Settlements which fall within the range established in comparable plants or industries.

When the respondents' criteria for good settlements have been enumerated, however, the question of whether they attempt to promote such settlements receives no clear answer. As in the case of protecting the public interest, there appear to be honest differences of opinion, as well as some genuine, albeit implicit, conflict.

To the observer, the surest source of such conflict is the exceedingly large and impressive list of activities which the respondents deemed appropriate for the mediator. The range of these activities will soon become clear. It is sufficient to note that a modest, retiring conception of the mediator's role was by no means a popular one.

Even those who indicated that a more passive demeanor was sometimes desirable—particularly when the parties were resolving issues on their own—stressed that mediation is an active process, whatever the outward appearance may be. "I think the mediator has to recognize when he is supposed to be passive, and that is an active determination in and of itself."

But if the mediator's role is to be an active one, what is it that guides his activity? Since the needs and desires of the parties are not unalterable, nor clearly visible at the outset, and since, in fact, by many of their actions mediators may be instrumental in forming and modifying those needs and desires, it appears somewhat ingenuous to say the mediator has no goal other than settlement; that he does not propound his own views; and that everything which is decided is decided voluntarily.

The Strategies and Tactics of Mediation

At first glance, the respondents' remarks about their behavior as mediators appear so varied and so dependent on the particular dispute being discussed, that any attempt at a general summary seems apt to prove an unfruitful exercise. This, in fact, was the explicit opinion of several of those interviewed. Nonetheless, it is possible to discern three broad types of strategies and some of the tactics which cluster around them. I shall refer to *reflexive, non-directive,* and *directive* strategies of mediation.

By *reflexive* strategies is meant those behaviors by which the mediator attempts to orient himself to the dispute and to establish the groundwork upon which his later activities will be built. As the term implies, reflexive strategies are designed primarily to affect the mediator, rather than the parties: to make the mediator the most effective instrument for the resolution of conflict possible under the circumstances. *Non-directive* and *directive* strategies, on the other hand, are aimed specifically at the conflict and the parties to it. In a concrete sense they are what the mediator "does" to resolve a dispute.

Non-directive interventions refer to attempts at increasing the probability that the parties themselves, with a minimum of manipulation or suggestion from the mediator, will hit upon a mutually acceptable solution to the dispute. If one thinks of the mediator as an instrument for assisting at the "birth" of a settlement, then one might describe non-directive strategies as a "mid-wifery" kind of mediation.

In contrast, directive interventions refer to those strategies by which the mediator actively promotes a specific solution or attempts to pressure or manipulate the parties directly into ending the dispute. Pursuing the obstetric analogy, one might think of directive interventions as the "caesarian" approach to mediation.

Reflexive strategies

Gaining the trust and confidence of the parties. The respondents were in general agreement that this was the first and most important task of the mediator.

Tactics designed to achieve the necessary rapport include:

1. Explicitly stating the mediator's role. The mediator's introductory remarks to the parties will generally include a statement to the effect that under no conditions will he reveal a confidence unless given permission to do so, and that he is the servant of the parties and of nobody else. This, of course, is nothing more than a statement of purpose; by itself it will not elicit confidence or trust. Nonetheless, it puts the mediator's conception of his role on record. With naive parties such a preamble may avoid uncessary confusions, i.e., the suspicion that the mediator is an agent of the governor's office with instructions to get a settlement in the "public interest"; that he is the personal choice of the union, there to do its bidding, etc.

2. Explicitly stating concern with the dispute. This is another tactic that does not, by itself, inspire confidence. It is, however, additional evidence to the parties, that they are no longer alone in their difficulties.

> *I open with a general discussion which means nothing; that I'm very concerned that a high public interest is involved; ten, twelve thousand employees are out of work, and a large business is not operating, and money is being lost, and the public is being hurt. Now this is not to tell them how to settle, but just as a general statement which they know beforehand, but they listen; I'm saying something.*

3. Speaking the "language" of the parties. Respondents observed that it is important to convey to the disputants that the mediator is the type of person who is capable of understanding their problems. Respondents warned, for example, about the dangers of appearing patronizing. Several interviewees also referred to the fact that mediation unlike arbitration, tends to be an informal process. A highly judicial hearing and an insistence on protocol are not generally desirable. It is the mediator's task to set the tone of informality in his own manner and speech (unless, of course, the parties clearly expect a more formal proceeding).

Once past the initial joint meeting the mediator's ability to inspire confidence depends on a wide range of skills.

254

4. Demonstrating competence. It is important for the mediator to be able to handle substantive matters expertly.

Part of the ability of the mediator's acquiring confidence has to do with his ability to have some mathematical soundness; to sit there while the parties are talking, while somebody throws out a number, to say: "Well, that's 1.2% and that would represent 18 million, or if you did it this way, it would be 13 and let me show you how." And after you do this a few times, the parties get to the point where they wil trust anything you say.

The mediator must also demonstrate that he understands the bargaining process and the occasional necessity for the parties to strike poses.
5. Using humor effectively.

I think a lot of it is the ability to have a good story, to have a repertoire of good jokes. I can go into a union committe of 30 guys who look at you like a stone-age man. You know, they're glaring at you; they each got a hammer. And you tell a joke and they laugh. And then you tell another joke and you leave them there. And when you go out they invariably say to each other, "Jesus, that was a great story he told." And then when you go down the hall, the guy will say, "Hey, that was a great story." Now he's talking to you.

6. Demonstrating an empathic understanding of each side's position. It is essential for the mediator to convey to both sides that he understands their respective positions fully, and does so without passing judgement.

Discovering the real issues

It will hardly do to walk into a dispute at the first meeting and say to an employer: "You really ought to give them another 25 cents an hour to satisfy their demands." That's the best way I know to become an ex-mediator very quickly. There must be a reason why the situation is polarized; there are reasons why it can be unpolarized. The difference in the two situations lies in the needs and feelings of the people and you've got to find out what they are.

As a newcomer to a dispute one of the mediator's first tasks is to educate himself to the important issues in the conflict. This task is made more complicated by the fact, noted earlier, that the genuine issues may not have been clearly formulated by the time of his arrival.

"Just listening" was frequently cited as a tactic for uncovering the salient issues. The mediator must be alert not only to what is being said, but to what is *not* being said. If, for example, wages are being completely omitted from the discussion, the mediator might wonder if this is an issue touching such deep-seated feelings that neither side is willing to discuss it openly for fear that the entire negotiations may be jeopardized. On the other hand, does it seem likely that matters receiving all the initial attention are going to be of ultimate importance? Here the mediator must use whatever knowledge he has of the industry and the disputants, as well as healthy amounts of common sense.

While listening with the "third ear" remains characteristic of the mediator's behavior throughout the dispute, in the effort to uncover the central issues, it gradually gives way to a more active probing of each side's position. Probing usually occurs when the mediator has separated the parties. (Although most of the respondents felt that separate meetings were the most effective means for clarifying issues, one interviewee preferred to continue joint sessions for as long as possible. He felt that the mediator can all too easily lose his perspective when confronted with the arguments of but one side, whereas direct and even heated exchanges, permit him to keep contantly in view all the forces and interests at play.)

On one point all respondents agreed: the worst possible tactic for eliciting the parties' genuine feelings about the issues, is to ask for them directly. Since for reasons of strategy, honest answers to direct questions will generally not be given, such questions can put a premature end to any useful dialogue between mediator and negotiators.

> *I, at all times, avoid asking the parties what their final position is. That's a dirty question, because you are seeking to penetrate the bargaining facade the parties have put up; you imply by that, that you don't believe what they're saying whereas it's important to give the impression that you believe a bargaining position is a sincere position. It's also a futile question because it's not going to be answered and, therefore, you're encouraging a form of dishonesty with someone with whom you are trying to establish an open relationship.*

Identifying the real leaders. Just as the real issues may be masked at the outset of the mediator's entry into the dispute, so too for the real leaders, i.e. the persons with the power to "make or break" a proposed settlement. The mediator's problem here appears to be on two levels.

First, there is the problem of identifying those few individuals, *physically present* at the bargaining table, who are most able to determine the direction which their side will take in the bargaining. The second problem of identification facing the mediator is establishing the *effective,* as opposed to the theoretical, constituencies of both sides; that is, the parties (individuals or groups) who are most able to make the negotiator's experience produce consequences—either favorable or unfavorable. Unfortunately, effective constituencies are sometimes difficult to locate. It is a well-known fact that not every membership effectively holds their leaders to account. In public sector disputes it is particularly difficult to separate the theoretical from the effective constituency. The "public" is always the constituency of record for the public employer. Effectively, however, it is more likely to be a mayor, a city council, or a school board that is in a position to strike down a proposed settlement, or, at the least, make the negotiator wish that he had gotten into another line of business. The lines of responsibility may be difficult to trace.

Understanding the relationship between the disputants. Several respondents noted that negotiations frequently have a past and that this past can effect the present in a very decided fashion. Parties can become accustomed to having agreements written down and meticulously spelled out. In other disputes, expectations about the physical form a contract ought to take may be considerably more flexible. In other instances, the parties may expect formal reports to the membership at a specific time during the talks, or it

256

may be understood that the company attorneys are to report back periodically to the employer for further instructions. It may even be the case that, as a matter of tradition, the parties have gotten used to doing without mediators altogether. One respondent cited an entire industry where just such a tradition had developed. The more familiar the mediator is with these historical matters, the easier it will be for him to avoid pitfalls and understand resistance to his interventions.

More contemporaneous aspects of the parties' relationship was stressed by many respondents. Interviewees referred repeatedly to the need for the mediator to understand the "nature of the power relationship" between the parties, or the importance of "getting an assessment of the people and their relationships with one another," or of getting to know the "problems" that exist in a particular relationship. The mediator becomes aware of the present state of the parties' negotiating relationship in the same way that he identifies the real issues: by keen observation of the parties' interactions in joint meetings and by observing the responses to his questions when he meets with the parties separately.

Non-directive strategies. Non-directive strategies may be sub-divided into two categories: (a) those designed to make *the context* in which bargaining occurs more favorable to settlement, and (b) those designed to help *the parties* become more adept bargainers.

Of the strategies designed to affect the context of bargaining, the following may be noted:

Producing a favorable climate for negotiations. The first tactic under this heading has already been encountered: patient listening. The psychological benefits of such attention can be considerable. Another, more active, technique for improving the bargaining atmosphere consists of creating positive expectations by obtaining agreement on small, relatively easy to resolve issues early in the negotiations. Later, when the going gets rougher and the negotiators begin getting discouraged, the mediator may point to these earlier achievements as evidence that agreements are possible.

The mediator also has a role to play in controlling the expression of hostility, or what one writer has referred to as "ludic" outbursts, in general. Several respondents noted that the open expression of anger was sometimes to be encouraged. The cathartic effects of an occasional mediator-arranged confrontation was noted by one man, who remarked:

> There are some times when I know some steam will be blown off and the best way to do it is to call a joint session. For example, if I hear one side say something particularly vindictive about the position of the other and I can see the anger and hostility is just at the breaking point, I'll say: "I'm not going to tell that to the other side. Nah, you feel that way about it, you're going to tell them yourself. Now, you tell them yourself what you think of them when they ask for that."
>
> "All right, we'll tell 'em," and off he goes. And there's a wild explosion and that's done with. You have to be careful about it because you can't bring them together to the point where the explosion is so extreme as to break off talks.

There are two things to note in these comments. In the first instance, it is the mediator's responsibility to *control* the expression of anger. How exactly he does this is not entirely clear. The simplest answer is that he "knows" when things are going too far (by using his "antennae" or "intuition") and will then intervene and suggest separate meetings.

Second, and perhaps implied in the notion of "intuition," the mediator permits the expression of hostiliy which is *issue* oriented—not personally oriented. To be sure, attacking the bargaining stance of the opponent may involve disturbing reflections on his personal character or antecedents. Nonetheless, it is the mediator's job to distinguish in a relative fashion between the two types of anger. (The respondent spoke, for example, of hearing one side "say something indicative about the bargaining *position* of the other side.")

Handling "administrative" details. It is clear from the remarks of several respondents that the "administrative" role of the mediator, while at first glance constituting the most mundane of his activities, has important implications for the atmosphere under which negotiations will be conducted. Perhaps the simplest of these administrative activities is alerting the parties to logistical problems involved in collective bargaining—housing, meeting space, transportation to and from meetings, etc.—and advising them on the objectives to be served in solving such problems.

Perhaps the central administrative function of the mediator is establishing an agenda for the bargainers: What issues will be considered first? Can issues be broken down and farmed out to sub-committees for more efficient use of time and personnel? The technique of "bulking" issues—identifying those problems which can be handled more or less as a unit, i.e., all those matters related to fringe benefits, all the "economic" issues, etc.—was mentioned by three respondents as being of special importance.

Bulking issues is useful for three reasons. First, disputes with a great number of issues have a tendency to overwhelm the parties: there appears to be so much disagreement on so many separate questions that a strike seems all but inevitable. By grouping the issues the mediator brings a sense of order and manageability to the proceedings. There really aren't 50 separate issues, but only 3 or 4 major areas of disagreement.

Second, by classifying issues under larger headings the mediator makes it easier for the parties to see where "trade-offs" and "swaps" may be arranged. Previously it may have seemed that all 50 issues were on more or less the same footing.

Pacing the negotiations. It is the mediator's job to insure that movement towards settlement proceeds at an orderly pace; too slow, as well as too rapid movement is to be avoided.

Too slow movement is bad because it produces discouragement, fatigue, and frustration. Personal attacks are likely to become more frequent and the goal of settlement lost sight of. One respondent noted that too slow a pace may also provide a little too much time for reflection.

> When I have a sense of momentum, when I feel a sense of momentum is there, I don't want to break for supper, I don't want to break for sleep, I don't want to

break for anything. You have to exploit that, because once there is time for reflection and then for figuring out the political consequences and trying to find everything that's wrong with a settlement, you can tear any settlement apart — so you don't leave that time for reflection available.

Too rapid achievement of a settlement may be inadvisable for another reason: the political nature of the bargaining process requires that the negotiators give evidence to their constituents that the battle has been hard fought.

The committees that represent both the employer and the union will have to go back; and since they settled at 3 o'clock in the afternoon when people know that people settle difficult situations at 3 in the morning; somebody is going to get up in the back of the room and say, "What was your big rush? If you would have held out another two hours we would have gotten another 7 cents." And politically, you see, the committees know this, and they're not there to settle quickly unless they have *to.*

Unfortunately, it is very difficult to capture precisely what "pacing" involves. How does the mediator *know* when the pace is too fast or too slow? As in so many other areas of mediator behavior the only answer is to be found in such words as "intuition" or "instinct."

Maintaining the privacy of the negotiations. Respondents generally agreed that a "goldfish bowl" atmosphere is inimical to dispute settlement. The dangers of "public" mediation, as the respondents saw them, were two-fold. First, public statements tend to fix bargaining positions prematurely. A negotiator who, in the heat of the moment, has declared before the radio microphones or T.V. cameras that he will *never* agree to a 30 cent an hour wage increase, will find the inevitability of such a settlement much more difficult to face than one who has kept his opinions restricted to the bargaining table. (Of course, it is precisely for such reasons that the parties may find opportunities to unburden themselves publicly so alluring. It is the mediator's job to prevent this kind of maneuver by pledging the parties to a ban on public statements.)

Second, public statements about the substance of bargaining can lead to the growth of internal resentments which can eventually force a negotiator to rescind an offer, or to the failure of the constituency to ratify the settlement.

The second category of non-directive strategies are those aimed, not at affecting the context in which bargaining occurs, but rather at helping the parties become more adept bargainers. The most frequently discussed strategies of this kind included:

Helping the parties establish which issues are significant to them. Just as the mediator is concerned with educating himself to the "real" issues, he may also wish to give each side a clearer understanding of where its own true interests appear to lie. As a non-directive strategy the emphasis is not on attempts to convince one side or the other that a specific proposal should be accepted or rejected, but rather on getting each to see the broad requirements of a satisfactory settlement.

The mediator, in focusing discussions in this manner, may also make some effort to give each party a certain amount of insight into the reasons behind the stand taken by the opposition. The purpose is to defuse feelings of anger and resentment by pointing out that the other side is attempting to satisfy pressing practical needs of its own (i.e., to run for re-election, to compete successfully in the marketplace, etc.).

Educating the parties to the nature of the bargaining process. This function is particularly important with naive parties. In addition to an explicit statement that he is the confidante of both sides and is acting exclusively in their interests, the mediator may also use the initial joint meeting to make explicit some other aspects of mediated collective bargaining. He may stress to the parties that they must be willing to compromise, and that his job is to mediate, not to do their bargaining for them. The educating process will continue by example, of course, as the negotiations proceed. (Respondents who dealt with public sector disputes were more prone to stress this educative function than mediators in the private sector where the parties are usually sophisticated).

Directive strategies

Discovering areas of compromise. This function of the mediator is closely related to reflexive attempts to discover the underlying issues in a dispute. It is included under directive strategies primarily because it was most often mentioned as an important preliminary to the formulation, in the mediator's mind, of the type of settlement that will ultimately be acceptable to both sides, and consequently, as the first clear step on the road to the mediator's direct efforts to bring about an agreement.

Most of the mediator's attempts at discovering areas of compromise occur in private caucuses. By careful probing the mediator begins to get a notion of just how far apart the disputants are, and what compromises it will take from each side to get a settlement. One respondent referred to this process as discovering the "ambit of expectancy" of the parties. The mediator is aided in these efforts by the trust he has established with each side. Respondents were aware, however, that no amount of high regard for the mediator will suffice to get feuding parties to instantly abandon strategically adopted positions.

Making the parties face "reality." The mediator may force the parties to confront facts that, swept up in the conflict, they are unable or unwilling to face. In other cases, "reality testing" may be required for quite the opposite reason: one of the parties is unmotivated to bargain out of the mistaken belief that their position is so invulnerable that there is nothing to lose by *not* bargaining. It may be the mediator's job to correct such impressions. Some of the "realities" which the mediator may discuss with the parties include:

1. The financial costs of a strike. Several respondents alluded to the occasional necessity of making one or both parties face squarely the potential costs involved in not coming to terms until after a strike has occurred.

260

2. The range of settlements in similar industries or situations. One of the important guidelines in helping the parties develop an overlapping "ambit of expectancy" is a knowledge of what others in similar situations have agreed to. Part of the mediator's expertise consists of having a broad acquaintance with patterns of settlement.

3. The needs of the constituencies. Earlier it was observed that the mediator may aid each party in clarifying its own objectives by getting it to review the needs of its total membership. This tactic may also be used to blunt a demand which threatens to stall negotiations. The mediator wants the demand retracted or modified without antagonizing the party making it.

4. The high priority issues. The mediator may not only help the parties discover which issues are salient for them, he may also assist each party to see where each issue fits into the total scheme of settlement.

5. The position of the opponent. Earlier this tactic was described as functioning to reduce anger by making the opponent's position more understandable. It may also facilitate the intelligent formulation of compromise proposals which have some realistic chance of being accepted.

As a directive strategy it may involve more than a logical explanation of the other side's point of view. Rather, the mediator becomes a forceful advocate of each side's position. Of course, the mediator runs a risk in becoming an advocate for the opposition and, indeed, in all his efforts at pressing home unpleasant facts of life: He may so alienate and antagonize the parties that his usefulness is all but over. Something of the art of dealing with "resistances" is conveyed in the following remarks.

> Now you say, "Well, why don't they throw you out of the room?" Maybe sometimes they do. They never have to me. I've gone as far as I can sometimes without antagonizing people all the way. I've had committees say to me, "Look, we don't have to take this from you." And I say to them, "We're just talking. We're friends. I have a record: I have a track record; I have an experienced record. Check with anybody. Most of you guys know me. I'm not taking you over the coals, but I'm just telling you my view. Now don't get offended by it. You don't have to accept it, but at least let me tell it to you. I think you're crazy." And you say it long enough, you'll find that out of a committee of 20 guys, two or three of them say, "He's right, we are crazy." You tell them, "Look, maybe you'll get a $1,000 a week raise if you're out on strike for five years, you know, I mean, you want to take a five year strike or you want to start talking sense?"

In this small illustration it is possible to identify at least five different tactics aimed at bringing disputants bluntly but not disruptively into touch with reality: (a) reassurance of the mediator's fundamental empathy ("We're just friends"; "most of you guys know me"); (b) reiteration of the mediator's competence ("I have a track record"); (c) emphasis on the voluntary nature of the relationship with the mediator ("You don't have to accept it."); (d) disarming use of colloquial language ("You're crazy"); (e) the entire presentation leavened with a touch of humor, which, not incidentally, also introduces a needed perspective ("Look, maybe you'll get a $1,000 a week raise if you're out on strike for 5 years"). It is performances such as these that mediators have in mind when they pronounce mediation an "art" rather than a "science."

Making suggestions for settlement. This aspect of the mediator's role may range from tentative speculations aloud ("fishing expeditions") through the formal issuance of public recommendations. At its most imperceptible it may not involve suggestions at all, but rather re-discussions of the issues in a fashion calculated to stimulate the parties to novel reformulations of their own.

From the respondents' remarks three types of suggestions for settlement may be identified.

1. Suggestions for modifying proposals already made by the parties. This is the art of restructuring or rephrasing, and one of its major objectives is to make things more palatable. It is also the most active type of proposal making with which the respondents, as a group, felt comfortable. The making of such proposals follows familiar guidelines: they must be tactfully put ("Does it make any sense to . . .?" and well-timed (when confidence and trust have been established and the "crisis" point close enough to make acceptance probable).

2. Formal mediator recommendations for settlement (made to the parties only). This was a tactic mentioned by only a few respondents, and then with distaste. The problem with explicit, detailed, and formal recommendations for settlement, is that, having been made, the mediator must thenceforth operate under one, and possibly two disadvantages. First, he can no longer make a claim to the status of true neutral. He now has a "position" like the parties themselves, and the presumption is that he will attempt to promote this position. Second, and perhaps more damaging, if one or both sides have been displeased by his recommendations—as they almost certainly are if the proposal has not ended the dispute—any further discourse becomes compromised by an atmosphere of hostility and suspicions of betrayal.

3. Public recommendations. This is the extreme form of mediator proposal making and, in general, respondents expressed aversion to it. It belongs conceptually with "pressure" tactics discussed below.

Applying pressure for settlement. This was not a function for which the respondents expressed a great deal of enthusiasm. However, they did feel, as has already been seen, that crises—usually in the form of a strike threat—are a necessary motivating force in collective bargaining. In some cases, particularly in the public sector where strikes are generally illegal, it may be necessary for the mediator to "create" a crisis. The most commonly cited tactic was to inform the parties that after a certain date the mediator would no longer be available because of personal or professional commitments that could not be deferred. Other pressure tactics mentioned were the controlled and strategic expression of anger and dissatisfaction with the way the parties are negotiating; the use of the press, either to express hope that negotiations will soon reach a successful conclusion, or more bluntly, to brand one side or the other as intransigent; the making of public recommendations. . . .

"Selling" the proposed settlement to the bargaining committees. Much of the actual work of collective bargaining is carried out either by small subcommittees or by two or three key people on each side. The proposal which is arrived at in this manner must be ratified by the entire union bargaining committee before it can be submitted to the union membership for a final vote. One respondent indicated that his function included motivating the principal negotiators to "sell" the proposal to the rest of the bargaining committee. In the event that they have difficulty in this regard, he is available to help them argue their case.

By way of summarizing the respondents' views on strategies and tactics of mediation, it can be observed that reflexive, non-directive, and directive strategies appear to correspond in a rough way to three distinct stages of the bargaining process.

In the *early* stage, issues are of subsidiary importance. There is, instead, a staking out of bargaining positions for later compromise, accompanied, perhaps, by ritual displays of anger and indignation. The parties are feeling out each other as well as the mediator. This early stage is dominated, from the mediator's point of view, by *reflexive* strategies. What are the most pressing issues? How can he establish his credentials and get the disputants to rely on his judgement and abilities?

In the *middle* stage of negotiations, more active but still tentative bargaining has begun. The parties may now be meeting in separate caucuses at the mediator's request, and through him are beginning to exchange offers and counteroffers. Small sub-committees may have been formed to work out particularly difficult issues. Here the mediator's role may be primarily *non-directive*. If possible he would like the parties to hit on a settlement with minimal intrusiveness on his part. He may confine himself primarily to working on the "atmosphere" surrounding the negotiations: establishing a workable agenda; dealing with disruptive, angry outbursts or permitting hostility to be vented when this appears fruitful; educating naive parties to the nature of the bargaining process. He may also be probing gently to discover areas of potential compromise that he will exploit later on, when the parties seem to have reached an impasse.

The *final* stage may be characterized by feverish exchanges of proposals or by an apparent total lack of movement. In retrospect, however, it will be clear that the parties were very close to a solution. In this last stage, *directive* strategies predominate. The mediator may attempt to "bridge the gap" with more frequent suggestions at compromise. He may put these forward with less of his earlier hesitancy, and sometimes, with veiled or not so veiled attempts at pressuring the parties to accept.

The Profession of Labor Mediation

Mediation: "art" versus "science." Perhaps the best place to begin an examination of the professional situation of the mediator as it is reflected in these interviews, is with a more thorough investigation of the respondents' distrust of generalizations about their work. They preferred to view mediation as "art" rather than "science." In nearly every case warnings were given to the interviewer that nothing being said about the mediator's behavior should be taken as having very wide applicability. The most common explanation for this presumed state of affairs was the idiosyncratic and ever-changing nature of the work. Respondents also took a dim view of the desirability of establishing professional schools to train mediators. Some, in fact, did not accept the premise upon which the idea was based; namely, that mediation is a professional discipline. Interviewees did consider a knowledge of industrial relations, economics, labor law, and the process of collective bargaining, important adjuncts to the mediator's personal skills. These subjects, however, are already incorporated into various professional and graduate curricula, and respondents saw no reason to tailor a program specifically to the needs of mediators.

To the relative unimportance of formal academic preparation, respondents contrasted the salience of personal qualifications:

> It is more a field of men than it is law. There's no law on mediation; there's no statute that tells you how to mediate—what the parties have to do and what the mediator should do.

> The key to the whole thing is: Do the parties trust you? Do they have confidence not only in your integrity but in your ability? Have you demonstrated to them that you are sensitive to their needs? That you will work hard on the part of both of them in the interest of a common solution? That you maintain confidences and never breach them? That they feel comfortable with you? So it's the individual and his acceptability that is more important than anything else.

When asked for personal traits desirable in a mediator, respondents mentioned intelligence, tenacity, physical stamina, a sense of humor, the ability to persuade, subtlety, the ability to empathize with and understand positions not one's own, self-effacement, and ingenuity in proposing novel solutions. However desirable such qualities may be, they are not the stuff of which professional curricula are made. As one man put it: "How do you teach a course in 'I'll think of something?'"

Aspects of Professional Development. The view that mediation depends primarily on idiosyncratic combinations of elusive personal qualities, rather than on general principles capable of being inculcated by formal training, undoubtedly reflects a fundamental truth: Labor mediation, like any intervention which attempts to affect complex human relationships, must, in some fundamental sense, remain a mystery, even to its most successful practitioners. Nonetheless, the insistence with which this view was reiterated appears related to aspects of the mediator's professional life which extend beyond the complex, demanding nature of the work. Four such aspects can

264

be identified: (a) the absence of clear criteria for success; (b) professional isolation; (c) unstructured methods of recruitment and training; (d) the changing social environment for mediation with the advent of public sector bargaining.

The absence of clear criteria for success. The respondents balked at the notion that straightforward criteria of success are available to the mediator. Settlement, the most obvious criteria of success, was rejected as unsatisfactory on at least two grounds: first, the great majority of all contracts are settled without mediators and work successfully; second, since the parties are mutually dependent on one another they will settle regardless of what the mediator does, and, indeed, whether or not he makes an appearance at all.

It is conceivable, of course, that criteria of success could be developed. It would appear, however, that for the same reason that they are reluctant to admit attempting to produce "good" settlements, so the respondents are unwilling to promulgate notions of "successful" mediation: viz. the process is a voluntary one which rests largely on the disputants' belief that the mediator's goals are parallel to their own. A mediator whose explicit idea of "success" in any fashion gave cause for doubt on this score might soon find himself *persona non grata.*

Whatever the explanation, the lack of criteria of success poses a dilemma for professionalization: without criteria of success, techniques which lead to success cannot be identified; without identifying techniques which lead to success, training must remain confined mainly to the hope that, by whatever lights are given him, each new recruit will become a skilled "artist" in his own right.

Professional isolation. The theme of professional isolation was a strong one. The commonest explanation for this condition was the fact that mediation requires privacy and confidentiality. It is not hard to see how such professional autonomy and isolation could produce, in an almost Darwinian fashion, a diversity of approaches genuine enough to establish the notion that mediation is an irreducibly "artistic" enterprise. Moreover, a high level of pluralistic ignorance could further magnify the differences which exist: each man imagining that, like him, everybody has struggled through to their own unique solutions to the problems which mediation presents.

The informal process of recruitment and training. The multiplicity of styles that is often taken as evidence that mediation is art rather than science may reflect the recruitment of candidates with a wide range of prior experience and the absence of concerted efforts to establish uniform criteria of selection, as much as the ethereal demands of the job. The best description of how an individual becomes a mediator was given by one respondent who characterized the process thusly:

> *I don't know anybody who starts out with the determination that he is going to school and become a mediator who becomes a mediator. I don't think anybody anticipated becoming a mediator. He slides into it laterally somewhere along the*

line, unintentionally, by force of circumstances, by opportunities that arise, but not because he does it intentionally.

The growth of the mediation services seems to have produced more formalization than is reflected in the above two acounts. There are now civil service examinations which must be passed before a candidate is eligible for training. Even so, requirements tend to be broad, usually specifying only general experience in industrial relations and some knowledge of collective bargaining, economics, and labor law. Oral examinations, where they exist, are, according to one respondent more or less improvised on the spot by the examiners. Criteria of evaluating candidates' responses appear equally spontaneous.

Once a man is deemed an acceptable candidate, there is far less chance in mediation, as compared to many other professions, that major differences in orientation between him and his more experienced colleagues will be eliminated in the course of training.

Overall, however, there was little indication that respondents were much concerned about improving training in any systematic fashion. Most appeared satisfied that the best way to learn to mediate is to start mediating.

Choice of Procedures in Canada and the United States

Allen Ponak and Hoyt N. Wheeler*

A recent and intriguing addition to dispute settlement mechanisms for public sector workers is choice of procedures, a system which explicitly permits one or both negotiating parties to select either arbitration or a possible work stoppage as the next step in effecting an agreement if previous negotiations and various mediation steps have failed to do so.[1] Choice of procedures provides a distinctive alternative to traditional single dispute resolution systems, which are based either in arbitration or work stoppages and have been criticized on a variety of grounds (see Kochan, 1980; Feuille, 1979). Choice of procedures was first introduced in the 1967 Canadian Public Service Staff Relations Act (PSSRA) and has since been adopted for public sector groups in British Columbia (1973), Minnesota (1973), and Wisconsin (1978). Although the manner in which the impasse machinery operates varies among these jursidictions, the concept of an explicit strike/ arbitration choice is present in all four systems.

Our first objective in this article is to describe each of the four systems and their development and analyze the institutional contexts in which they are imbedded.[2] While the PSSRA has already received attention in the literature (Anderson and Kochan, 1977), choice-of-procedures systems in

*Faculty of Management, McGill University, and Industrial Relations Center, University of Minnesota, respectively. Reprinted from *Industrial Relations*, Vol. 19, No. 3 (Fall 1980).

British Columbia, Minnesota, and Wisconsin have yet to be systematically explored. Second, we suggest a theoretical framework for explaining bargaining processes under choice of procedures and then develop a set of propositions deriving from the theory. These propositions are examined in terms of (1) the overall performance of the four systems in terms of the degree to which negotiated settlements have been reached (overall settlement rates); (2) the behavior of labor and management in making procedural choices (choice behavior); and (3) the ability of the negotiating parties to reach agreement under each procedural alternative (strike or arbitration) after the alternative has been selected (post-choice settlement rate). Lastly, because the incidence of strikes is an important public policy issue, we examine strike experience under each of these systems.

Our findings suggest that the choice-of-procedures systems are capable of fostering negotiated settlements and reducing the incidence of strikes. The data also show that, contrary to conventional wisdom, both labor and management in the public sector prefer arbitration to strike procedures.

Institutional Context

Each jurisdiction considered in this study has adopted one of three basic choice-of-procedure structural alternatives. The Canadian federal service and British Columbia give the union the choice; Minnesota gives the employer the choice; and Wisconsin gives both parties the choice, jointly.

The Canadian federal civil service. Collective bargaining for Canadian federal civil servants began in 1967 with the passage of the Public Service Staff Relations Act (PSSRA).[3] Today, more than 250,000 employees in 100 bargaining units bargain under the PSSRA's provisions. Bargaining units are drawn along occupational lines, with each distinguishable occupational group entitled to its own unit. Seventeen unions currently hold bargaining rights for at least one unit, although the Public Service Alliance of Canada represents 38 units, covering three-quarters of the unionized employees. On the employer side, the Treasury Board bargains on behalf of the government for more than 90 per cent of the employees. The remainder, in 25 bargaining units, work for special agencies of the government (e.g., National Film Board), with which they bargain.

The PSSRA's choice-of-procedures impasse resolution system arose largely as a compromise to satisfy divergent employee concerns within the civil service. When the bill that led to the PSSRA was introduced in 1965, it banned strikes and provided for binding arbitration. While the bill was under debate, postal workers engaged in an illegal work stoppage. This action, combined with pressure from a number of labor organizations opposed to arbitration, convinced policymakers that denying all employees the right to strike might seriously jeopardize their new bargaining scheme. At the same time, it was clear that many employees in the federal government preferred arbitration to a strike-based system.

The choice-of-procedures system reflects the decision to accommodate both employee factions. Under the Act, the union representing employees in a bargaining unit specifies, prior to the start of each bargaining round, whether disputes will be resolved through a work stoppage or arbitration. Once the choice of procedures is made, it cannot be altered until the next round of bargaining. The union's choice is binding on the employer. Both the arbitration and strike options require that certain intermediate conciliation steps be completed before either an arbitration hearing or a work stoppage may occur.

The right of employees to strike is not unfettered. If the strike option is chosen, and an impasse is imminent, certain employees in the bargaining unit may be designated as essential by the Public Service Staff Relations Board. Should a strike occur, these "designated employees" are obligated to continue working.[4]

British Columbia. Police and firefighters in British Columbia have bargained since the Second World War.[5] Twenty-five hundred firefighters in 35 municipalities currently are organized and represented by the International Association of Fire Fighters. Although most municipalities in British Columbia are served by the Royal Canadian Mounted Police, 12 cities maintain their own police forces. The 1,500 police officers in these municipalities belong to locals of the independent British Columbia Federation of Police Officers.

Pattern-following and employer centralization trends characterize police and firefighter bargaining in the province. While each local is responsible for its own negotiations, the outcome of bargaining in Vancouver, British Columbia's largest city, establishes patterns for the rest of the province. In several municipalities, labor and management sign memoranda agreeing in advance to be bound by the Vancouver settlement. Even where pattern-following is less explicit, negotiations rarely are completed elsewhere until agreement has been reached in Vancouver. In addition, in several areas some municipal employers have formed bargaining associations with which the police and firefighter locals negotiate.

Choice of procedures was introduced in 1973 with the enactment of a completely revised Labour Code by the newly elected labor-oriented government. Prior to 1973, police and firefighter interest disputes were submitted to binding arbitration. As with the PSSRA, choice of procedures arose as a compromise. When the Labour Code first was introduced in the British Columbia legislature, police and firefighters were given a simple right to strike. Subsequent criticism, however, resulted in changes making it possible for a union to voluntarily choose to relinquish its strike right and send a dispute to arbitration.

There is no fixed point in negotiations at which the arbitration/strike choice must be made. In fact, the union may serve the 72-hour notice of an impending strike—as required by the Labour Code—and still retain its right to arbitrate. (As under the PSSRA, in the event a strike does occur, certain employees may be designated as essential by the British Columbia Labour Relations Board and required to continue working.)

Wisconsin. Wisconsin has a relatively long history of collective bargaining in the public sector, having enacted a comprehensive law in 1959. Approximately 65 per cent of the state's 150,000 municiapl employees and teachers are unionized (Wisconsin Bluebook, 1979). They are divided into about

268

1,200 bargaining units. As in many states, the collective bargaining structure is highly fragmented, with a large number of unions representing diverse types of employees. The principal unions are the Wisconsin Education Association; the Wisconsin Federation of Teachers; American Federation of State, County, and Municipal Employees; Milwaukee Teachers' Education Association; Wisconsin Professional Policemen's Association; International Association of Fire Fighters; Milwaukee Professional Police Association; and the International Brotherhood of Teamsters.

Choice of procedures was enacted in Wisconsin in 1978, following an increase in illegal work stoppages and general public employee dissatisfaction with the existing impasse machinery which banned strikes and provided factfinding as the terminal dispute resolution step. Choice of procedures was selected partly because, compared to arbitration, strike, or factfinding, it was the system least objectionable to all major interest groups, the governor, and the state legislators (Ponak, 1976).

In Wisconsin, choice of procedures involves both parties in the selection process. At or after the inception of negotiations, either party may petition for mediation-arbitration. If the mediator-arbitrator fails to achieve a settlement through mediation, then he notifies the parties of his intention to arbitrate the dispute by final-offer arbitration on a total package basis. At this point, either party may signify its preference for a test of strength by withdrawing its final offer before arbitration begins. Only if both sides withdraw, however, may the union strike (after ten-days notice). Otherwise, arbitration proceeds as if neither offer had been withdrawn. This provides a *mutual* choice of procedures.

Minnesota. Compulsory arbitration laws covering employees in county, municipal, and private hospitals have existed in Minnesota since 1947. However, it was not until 1971 that the state introduced a general public employee collective bargaining law, the Public Employment Labor Relations Act (PELRA). In 1973, the present choice-of-procedures provisions were inserted into the law.

Minnesota's state and local government employees number about 200,000 and are highly unionized. As in Wisconsin, the bargaining structure is fragmented. The Minnesota Education Association; Minnesota Federation of Teachers; International Association of Fire Fighters; International Brotherhood of Teamsters; and International Union of Operating Engineers are the principal employee representatives.

The choice-of-procedures provisions in Minnesota vest the choice in the public employer, partly because the legislature believed that extending strike rights to public employees should be done cautiously. It was also argued that the existence of a strike system should be a matter of local option. That is, elected officials in a particular community should be able to make the decision regarding whether a public employee strike would be allowed in that community.[6]

In the Minnesota choice-of-procedures system, mediation is actively pursued until the Director of the Bureau of Mediation Services determines that an impasse has been reached. Typically, his declaration of an impasse comes only after an extended period of voluntary settlement efforts. Once an impasse is declared, either the union or the employer may request arbitration. If the employer requests arbitration, this will be the procedure utilized. If the union requests arbitration, it will occur unless the employer rejects it. Should the employer reject arbitration, the union has the right to strike. The union may also strike in the event that arbitration occurs and the employer refuses to abide by the arbitrator's award. During the period covered by this study, arbitration for all nonessential employees was of the conventional variety, without final-offer selection. Effective July 1, 1979, however, state employees and essential employees were made subject to an item-by-item final-offer system.

Theory

At the core of the debate over dispute settlement lies the alleged inability of procedures culminating in arbitration to produce a high rate of negotiated (as opposed to arbitrated) settlements (Stevens, 1966). By contrast, work stoppage systems are said to produce a high rate of settlement prior to strike because the costs of disagreement generally will outweigh the costs of agreement for one or both of the parties (Anderson and Kochan, 1977). The costs of not settling, and using arbitration, are substantially less in most cases than the costs associated with a work stoppage. Thus, under an arbitration system there is a greater chance (compared to a strike system) that the costs of disagreement will *not* outweigh the costs of agreement. Furthermore, arbitration systems may introduce a disincentive to compromise because concessions offered by a party during negotiations may be used against it if introduced as evidence before an arbitrator. Anything which discourages compromise during negotiations reduces the likelihood of settlement. For these reasons, arbitration systems are expected to produce a lower settlement rate than systems under which work stoppages are permitted.

Data for private sector work stoppage systems in the U.S. and Canada indicate settlement rates in the 85-90 per cent range.[7] Under public sector work stoppage systems, which may provide a more meaningful basis for comparison, settlement rates have been higher.[8] For Alaska, Pennsylvania, Oregon, and Montana, Dunham (1976) reported that settlement rates in 1974 averaged 95 per cent and ranged from 86 to 99.5 per cent. Anderson (1980) found a settlement rate of 92.5 per cent for Canadian local governments in 1976-1977. For Hawaiian public employees over a six-year time period, Klauser (1977) reported a settlement rate of 86 per cent. Finally, Wolkinson and Stieber (1976) found that in Michigan, where limited enforcement of strike prohibitions created a de facto strike-based system, settlement rates were in excess of 95 per cent for the period 1971-1974.[9]

Among jurisdictions using arbitration, settlement rates appear generally lower than in systems permitting work stoppages. Studies by Kochan *et al.* (1979) and Anderson (1978), and reviews by Feuille (1975), Dunham (1976), and Downey (1979), together covering more than 15 arbitration systems, indicate that: (1) settlement rates ranged from 68 to 95 per cent, with a median rate of 80 per cent; (2) in only three instances were settlement rates greater than 90 per cent, while in seven cases they were less than 75 per cent; and (3) higher settlement rates seemed to be achieved in relatively new systems, since the data show that settlement rates decline over time within a given arbitration system. Despite some data limitations and methodological shortcomings,[10] the evidence indicates that systems anchored in work stoppages are characterized by higher settlement rates than systems which rely on arbitration to resolve impasses.

Choice of procedures. The critical element explaining settlement rates under all impasse resolution systems is the potential costs of disagreement that failure to achieve a negotiated settlement will impose on labor, management, or both. In a choice-of-procedures system, the choosing party is in a unique position to manipulate the costs of disagreement through its control of the selection of the dispute procedure. To determine whether the choosing party will select the procedure likely to impose the highest costs of disagreement on the other (nonchoosing) party, the reasons underlying labor and management decisions in collective bargaining must be examined.

For the public sector, the literature suggests that the parties make decisions on the basis of three types of considerations: strategic, political, and ideological.[11] *Strategic* decisions are aimed at obtaining the best possible collective agreement for the constituents on whose behalf negotiations are being conducted. *Political* decisions are primarily motivated by the desire of management and union officials to protect their own incumbencies. For union representatives, this means acting in a way that will insure re-election and deter rival unions; public sector employers attempt to gain the favor, or at least avoid the wrath, of the voting public. *Ideological* decisions reflect labor and management's philosophical convictions regarding certain bargaining tactics or behavior.

The decision to choose the strike or arbitration option under choice-of-procedures will reflect the strategic, political, and ideological motivations of the parties involved. For example, union leaders facing re-election may choose the strike option in response to pressures from a militant group of rank-and-file members, even though the leaders believe that choosing arbitration would ultimately produce a better collective agreement. In such a case, the choice of strike can be said to reflect primarily political factors. An illustration of a largely ideological decision is the position taken by the Province of Quebec against arbitration in the early seventies. In the course of several rounds of highly conflict-prone negotiations with a coalition of public employees, the Quebec government rejected arbitration on the grounds that such a move would constitute an abdication of governmental responsibilities. It held to this decision in the face of dubious strategic gains and disastrous political consequences culminating in an election rout (see Boivin, 1975; Goldenberg, 1975).

Although we acknowledge the potential importance of political and ideological motivations on the part of labor and/or management, our expectations about differential settlement rates (discussed below) are based on the assumption that a party's selection of the strike or arbitration option is generally governed by strategic factors. To the extent that political or ideological considerations prove to be important, our general predictions about choice-of-procedures settlement rates will have to be revised.

271

Propositions

In the propositions below, we assume that settlement rates will be upwardly influenced only if the choosing party can gain a substantial advantage by choosing one procedure over the other. That is, we would expect high settlement rates in situations where the choosing party gains a substantial advantage in terms of potential costs of disagreement through its selection of either the strike or arbitration. Conversely, if neither procedure will provide the choosing party with a substantial power advantage, lower settlement rates would be anticipated.

> *Proposition 1:* Management will choose the strike procedure in a greater percentage of cases than will the union.

Sanford Cohen (1979) has convincingly argued that the financial constraints under which many governments now operate and the decreasing likelihood of public panic in the face of service interruptions have strengthened the bargaining position of the public employers, compared to just a few years ago. Add to this the recent taxpayer revolt, the fact that a public employer may realize substantial financial savings during a work stoppage, and the public's tremendous concern over possible inflationary wage increases, and it becomes clear that many public employers may enjoy a substantial power advantage if the strike option is selected. Strategic considerations, then, should lead mangement to choose the strike procedure more frequently than would the union.

> *Proposition 2:* Overall settlement rate will be higher where management has the right to choose the impasse resolution procedure than where the union has this right.

We assume that management occupies a substantially more powerful position when it is the choosing party. Giving management a monopoly on the strike threat is likely to place enough pressure on the union to result in settlement. However, giving the union the same monopoly is not expected to have as powerful an effect on management. We assume that unions, when given the choice, will select arbitration—where settlement rates are generally relatively low—with greater frequency than would management. The recurring line-up of union support for arbitration legislation and managerial opposition to it reflects the differing preferences of labor and management (Feuille, 1979).

> *Proposition 3:* Overall settlement rate under management choice of procedures should be equal to, or perhaps slightly greater than, overall settlement rate under a simple strike system.

Giving management the choice of procedures creates a large power imbalance to management's advantage. The impetus toward settlement in this situation is expected to be strong. It is also strong under a simple strike system.

> *Proposition 4:* Overall settlement rate under union choice of procedures will be approximately equal to this rate under a simple arbitration system.

272

As stated above, unions are expected to have strategic preference for arbitration. However, unions that have a strong strike capability will probably choose the strike procedure, as will those with a strong ideological commitment to the strike.

Proposition 5: Overall settlement rate under union choice of procedures will be lower than under a simple strike system.

Because union choice of procedures is generally similar to simple arbitration, it is expected to give the parties less impetus toward settlement than a simple strike system.

Proposition 6: Post-choice settlement rates will be higher when the strike procedure is chosen than when arbitration is chosen.

This expectation reflects our view that the prospect of a strike strongly impells the parties toward settlement, and that arbitration may not.

Results and Discussion

In order to examine the propositions stated above, and to generally view the experience under choice of procedures, we gathered the following data from all four jurisdictions: (1) number of negotiations; (2) number of choice opportunities; (3) number of times arbitration was the procedure chosen; (4) number of times strike was the procedure chosen; (5) number of arbitration awards; and (6) number of strikes. This information is presented in Appendix A and cross-tabulated in Tables 1 and 2.

It should be emphasized that our data interpretations are subject to significant limitations. The jurisdictions studied differ politically, economically, and culturally. The choice-of-procedures systems vary with respect to the timing of the strike/arbitration choice and form of arbitration (final-offer versus conventional). The use of mediation differs across jurisdictions, and in Wisconsin, mediation-arbitration is used. The type of employee (e.g., firefighter, teacher, etc.) covered in each jurisdiction also varies. Differences in impasse resolution experience might well arise from these or other (unknown) variables. Because we are unable to control for this potentially wide range of variation, we can only inquire whether the data are consistent with or support our propositions, not whether these propositions are confirmed.

Finally, references to experiences under the Wisconsin system are necessarily limited by two factors. First, because adoption of the strike option requires a joint decision, it may never occur. It is questionable whether, as a practical matter, the Wisconsin system is really any different from a simple arbitration system. Second, we have data for only the first year of experience in Wisconsin. This is really too short a period of time to provide a basis for judgments about how the system is functioning.

Proposition 1. Procedural choice was primarily in the direction of arbitration in all jurisdictions (see Table 1). However, in line with expectations, the strike option was favored more often by management. The strike option was chosen more frequently in Minnesota, where the employer makes the

TABLE 1
Choice Behavior and Settlement Rates

Jurisdiction	Choosing Party	Type of Employee	Choices	Selected Strike (per cent)	Number of Negotiations	Overall Settlement Rate (per cent)
Canadian federal	Union	Professional/administrative	351	10	351	71
		Clerical/technical	80	18	80	93
		Technical/operational	251	35	251	83
		All above	682	20	682	78
British Columbia	Union	Police	8	13	53	91
		Firefighters	23	4	158	87
		All above	31	6	211	88
Wisconsin	Both	Municipal/teacher	90	0	726	91
Minnesota	Employer	State	15	0	81	85
		Teachers	148	20	1,311	94
		Municipal/metro agency	54	44	n.a.	n.a.
		County	51	63	n.a.	n.a.
		All above	268	32	1,392	94

Source: See Appendix A.

selection, than in the Canadian federal sector or in British Columbia, where the procedural choice is vested in the union. These findings are consistent with our suggestion that choice behavior is primarily strategic and that it is the employer that usually enjoys the power advantage in a situation where a strike can occur.

The major exception to this pattern of choice behavior, technical and operational personnel in the Canadian federal service, offers an example of an exception that proves the rule. Technical and operational employees' rate of strike choice approached the employer average in Minnesota. This is understandable in view of the fact that these employees are among those most capable of conducting an effective strike. The services they provide are sufficiently important (e.g., air traffic control, postal service) that their disruption places substantial pressure on the public employer. A more detailed breakdown of the data than we make in our tables shows that it was the largest of the technical/operational bargaining units, i.e., those most capable of imposing high costs of disagreement on the employer, which most often chose the strike option.

That this proposition is supported by the data is also interesting in light of the conventional wisdom that it is labor that eschews arbitration and management which opposes the strike. The few attitudinal surveys available offer conflicting evidence (see, e.g., Ponak, 1976; Wheeler and Owen, 1976). Our present findings suggest that where there is an actual choice to be made, public managers favor a strike-based situation and public employee unions prefer arbitration.

Proposition 2. Overall settlement rates are shown in Table 1. They are roughly the same across all jurisdictions, lending only a small degree of support to the proposition that overall settlement rates would be higher in a system where management had the right to choose the dispute procedure than in a system where the union was the choosing party. As expected, settlement rates were substantially higher in Minnesota than in the Canadian federal sector. Contrary to expectations, however, the Minnesota rates were only marginally higher than those in British Columbia, where the union chooses. It may be that the tradition of pattern bargaining in British Columbia contributes to high overall settlement rates. Once settlements have been achieved in Vancouver, contracts are negotiated elsewhere without much difficulty. The British Columbia system also gives unions a great deal of flexibility in timing the strike/arbitration choice. The fact that the union retains the right to strike throughout negotiations, even if this right is rarely exercised, may induce the employer to make concessions.

Proposition 3. It appears that management choice of procedures may provide at least as powerful an impetus toward settlement as does the more traditional system which is modeled on the private sector. The data generally support our third proposition. The overall settlement rate in Minnesota, which has management choice of procedures, is 94 per cent. Simple strike systems have settlement rates in the same general range, i.e., over 90 per cent.

Proposition 4. The data give only mixed support to our expectation that the overall settlement rate under union choice of procedures would approximate that found in a simple arbitration system. The settlement rate in the Canadian federal system, 78 per cent, is consistent with the level of settlement which other studies have found in simple arbitration systems. The 88 per cent rate in British Columbia, however, is higher than we expected. (We have speculated above on the reasons for this high rate.)

Proposition 5. The data only weakly support the proposition that the overall settlement rate should be lower under union choice of procedures than under a simple strike system. Again, while the 78 per cent settlement rate in the Canadian federal system is lower than rates reported under simple strike systems, British Columbia's settlement rate is in the same general range as that experienced in simple strike systems. This may be due, in part, to the flexibility in timing available to the union in the B.C. system.

Proposition 6. The data in Table 2 show that post-choice settlement rates are higher where the strike route is chosen. This is true for all jurisdictions, although the number of strike choices in British Columbia is very small. Only for technical and operational employees in the Canadian federal service was the settlement rate the same under both options. This gives a clear indication, we believe, of the contrast between the impetus toward settlement provided by the prospect of a strike and that provided by the prospect of arbitration.

Strikes and choice-of-procedures systems. One of the more important findings of this study is that the jurisdictions which have choice of procedures have a low incidence of strikes. There were no strikes in Wisconsin. British Columbia police and firefighters struck only once in more than 200 negotiations. In the Canadian federal sector, only 2 per cent of all negotiations resulted in a work stoppage. For Minnesota, the strike rate cannot be completely calculated because of lack of data on number of negotiations for county, municipal, and metro agency employees. The rate can, however, be calculated for Minnesota state employees and teachers, who struck in less than 1 per cent of their negotiations.

There is some evidence to suggest that strike rates may increase in Minnesota, particularly in rural areas. There is already a relatively strong preference for the strike procedures by Minnesota county government employers. If this preference is combined with exceptionally tough employer bargaining, unions might find themselves in a position where concessions are not possible, and be forced to strike, even under very unfavorable circumstances. In some rural Minnesota counties, it appears to have been politically fruitful for county officials to force foredoomed strikes by county employees. The political benefits appear to stem at least in part from the fact that many of these county workers are social workers serving welfare clients. Their salaries represent rather unpopular expenditures of funds in some areas.

TABLE 2
Post-Choice Settlement Rates

Jurisdiction	Choosing Party	Type of Employee	Number of Arbitration Choices	Settlement Rate after Arbitration Chosen (%)	Number of Strike Choices	Settlement Rate after Strike Chosen (%)
Canadian federal	Union	Professionals/administrative	316	68	35	97
		Clerical/technical	66	91	14	100
		Technical/operational	163	83	88	83
		All above	545	64	137	88
British Columbia	Union	Police	7	29	1	100
		Firefighters	22	9	1	0
		All above	29	14	2	50
Wisconsin	Both	Municipal/teachers	90	29	0	n.a.
Minnesota	Employer	State	15	20	0	n.a.
		Teachers	119	41	29	72
		Municipal/metro agency	30	70	24	83
		County	19	47	32	66
		All above	183	45	85	73

Source: Appendix A.

Conclusions

The question of whether public sector collective bargaining impasses should be settled by arbitration or by a work stoppage is extremely controversial in both Canada and the United States. Impasse procedures which culminate in arbitration seem to preordain an excessive usage of arbitration. This is said to violate the norms of voluntarism in collective bargaining, ultimately damaging the relationship between the parties. Impasse procedures anchored in work stoppages, although more likely to produce agreements negotiated by the parties themselves, risk service disruptions that are unacceptable to many policymakers.

Our findings suggest that choice of procedures may be capable of resolving this apparent dilemma. The ability of labor and mangement to reach negotiated agreements was higher in three of the four jurisdictions examined than would normally be expected under a simple arbitration system. At the same time, the incidence of work stoppages was substantially lower than the strike rates reported for simple strike systems. Choice-of-procedures systems thus seem to have fulfilled multiple policy objectives: (1) fostering negotiated agreements; (2) avoiding work stoppages; and (3) providing unions with the right to strike (albeit circumscribed in Minnesota and Wisconsin), a right of considerable philosophical importance to many unions.

Our data also show that, with the exception of county employers in Minnesota, labor and management in the public sector preferred an arbitration procedure to a strike procedure in the majority of cases. Unions were much more inclined to choose arbitration than were employers. These results suggest that conventional wisdom regarding labor and management dispute procedure preferences needs re-examination. In particular, unions may not be nearly as strongly wedded to dispute resolution via work stoppages as is commonly believed. It may well be that certain types of employees, especially professionals and white-collar workers, would be much more comfortable operating under an arbitration system than under a strike system. Perhaps private sector white-collar workers would find unionism more appealing if the potential for a strike did not necessarily accompany a union card.

We proposed here a theoretical framework within which settlement rates under choice of procedures could be analyzed, and derived a series of propositions based on the framework. Neither the theory nor the propositions could be tested adequately because of our inability to control for variables in addition to the dispute mechanisms which might influence settlement rates. Future investigations of choice procedures should explicitly consider the effects on settlement rates of social, economic, and political factors, type of employee, and details of the dispute settlement mechanisms.

In addition, our assumption that choices were made mainly on strategic grounds demands further examination. A richer understanding of impasse experience under choice of procedures is contingent upon knowledge of when decisions are politically and ideologically motivated. More broadly, choice behavior provides a unique opportunity to examine employer and union decision making in collective bargaining. In any set of negotiations decisions are made regarding tactics, issues, and other matters. A researcher is rarely able to examine what decisions each party makes, what the alternatives are, and what factors influenced the decisions. In a choice-of-procedures system the selection of strike or arbitration is explicit. It is a behavioral measure rather than a hypothetical statement of what a negotiator would or should have done in a given situation. Systematically examining union and management choices is a potential source of insight into collective bargaining decision making.

Lastly, in examining choice behavior, the incidence of strikes, and settlement rates, our research focused almost exclusively on the *process* side of collective bargaining. It is crucial that attention be directed as well to the bargaining *outputs* of choice-of-procedures systems, such as the quality of collective agreements under choice of procedures; who succeeds and who fails to achieve their bargaining objectives; and the impact of choice of procedures on working relations among the various actors in the system. In part, we are concerned that placing the choice of procedures in the hands of management, as does Minnesota, may create a power imbalance which overwhelms the employee, and public, interest in an acceptable level of wages and conditions of work for public employees. A consideration of the outputs of the system is necessary before a complete evaluation of choice of procedures can be made.

Footnotes

1. Note that choice of procedures is distinct from a traditional right to strike system where the parties may mutually forego a work stoppage in favor of an arbitrated settlement.
2. This research was supported by the Canada Department of Labour-University Research Committee. The authors would like to thank Sharon Angel, Greg Hundley, and Kathy Timmons for their research assistance.
3. Our description of the situation in the Canadian federal civil service is based largely on Anderson and Kochan (1977) and Connell (1973).
4. The proportion of employees so designated has varied considerably from unit to unit. Over 85 per cent of the firefighters have been deemed essential and prohibited from striking, while virtually no postal workers have been so designated.
5. The following discussion is based on interviews with police, firefighter, and municipal government representatives, Fisher and Starek (1976), and Matkin (1975).
6. Minnesota law may still be in a state of flux. On February 21, 1980, a bill was introduced in the Minnesota legislature which would make sweeping changes in PELRA. This proposed legislation arises from a legislative commission on employment relations which was created by the 1979 legislature. This bill would give "nonessential" employees the right to strike. Arbitration would take place only if both parties so agreed. Telephone conversation, February 21, 1980, with Peter Obermeyer, Director, Minnesota Bureau of Mediation Services.

    (Editor's note: At press time, the author informed *Industrial Relations* that the Minnesota legislature has amended PELRA by abolishing the choice-of-procedures system and granting to nonessential employees the right to strike [ch. 617 Acts of Minnesota Legislature, 1980].)
7. Very few private sector studies exist which report strike data in terms of settle-

ment rates. A study of 1,400 settlements involving units of 250 or more employees in Ontario, covering the years 1970-1973, showed a settlement rate of 89 per cent (Kelly, 1974). For U.S. manufacturing bargaining units over 1,000 employees, a settlement rate of 87 per cent was found for the years 1954-1975. However, the settlement rate was only 81 per cent in the more recent 1970-1975 period (see Kaufman, 1978).

8. Differences in the dynamics of bargaining between the private and public sectors, particularly the costs of agreement and disagreement on the employer side, dictate that comparisons between the two sectors with respect to impasse experience be made very cautiously.

9. The data bases (and limitations) vary among these studies. Dunham presents number of strikes as proportion of bargaining units, which exaggerates settlement rates to the degree each unit did not negotiate a collective agreement in the year examined. Bargaining units per jurisdiction are as follows: Alaska—7; Pennsylvania—800; Oregon—519; and Montana—60. Anderson's data are based on 53 sets of negotiations involving 28 municipalities, almost all of which had populations in excess of 100,000. Klauser's analysis was based on 51 negotiations; in 12 per cent of the cases the parties voluntarily relinquished their ability to engage in a stoppage, agreeing instead to accept binding arbitration. Wolkinson and Streiber's figures are estimates, based on more than 1,000 negotiations per year.

10. Some caution should be exercised with respect to the data cited above. First, with the exception of Anderson's study of the experience at the Canadian local government level, environmental and institutional variables have not been controlled across jurisdictions. Such variables may be important in determining settlement rates. Second, private sector settlement rates may not be good benchmarks. Third, data on public sector work stoppage based systems tend to be based on very narrow time periods with little information provided on the representativeness of the period under scrutiny. Nevertheless, the thrust of the data seems sufficiently clear, especially in light of the number of jurisdictions surveyed, to warrant the conclusion reached.

11. These categories reflect our synthesis of the case and analytical literature. See, for example, Schick and Coutourier (1977) and Perry (1979).

References

Anderson, John. "Determinants of Collective Bargaining Impasses: The Effect of Dispute Resolution Procedures," paper presented at the conference, "Industrial Relations and Conflict Management: Different Ways of Managing Conflict," Nijenrode, The Netherlands, July, 1980.

———. "Evaluating the Impact of Compulsory Arbitration: A Methodological Assessment," paper presented to the 39th Annual Meeting of the Academy of Management, Atlanta, Georgia, August, 1978.

——— and Thomas Kochan. "Impasse Procedures in the Canadian Federal Service: Effects on the Bargaining Process," *Industrial and Labor Relations Review,* XXX (April, 1977), 283-301.

Boivin, Jean. *The Evolution of Bargaining Power in the Province of Quebec Public Sector.* Quebec: Department of Industrial Relations, Laval University, 1975.

Cohen, Sanford. "Does Public Employee Unionism Diminish Democracy," *Industrial and Labor Relations Review,* XXXII (January, 1979), 189-196.

Connell, J. P. "Collective Bargaining in the Federal Service of Canada." In J. F. O'Sullivan, ed., *Collective Bargaining in the Public Service.* Toronto: Institute of Public Administration of Canada, 1973, pp. 45-56.

Downie, Bryan. *The Behavioral, Economic, and Institutional Effects of Substituting Compulsory Arbitration for the Right to Strike,* paper prepared for the Economic Council of Canada, August, 1979.

Dunham, Robert. "Interest Arbitration in Non-Federal Public Employment," *The Arbitration Journal,* XXXI (March, 1976), 45-57.

Feuille, Peter. "Selected Benefits and Costs of Compulsory Arbitration," *Industrial and Labor Relations Review,* XXXIII (October, 1979), 64-76.

————. "Final Offer Arbitration and the Chilling Effect," *Industrial Relations,* XIV (October, 1975), 302-310.

Fisher, E. G. and Henry Starek. "Mediation-Arbitration and Vancouver Police Negotiations: 1945-1975." Working paper, Institute of Industrial Relations, University of British Columbia, 1976.

Goldenberg, Shirley. *Industrial Relations in Quebec Past and Present.* Industrial Relations Centre Reprint Series, No. 28, Kingston, Ontario, 1975.

Klauser, Jack. "Public Sector Impasse Resolution in Hawaii," *Industrial Relations,* XVI (October, 1977), 283-287.

Kochan, Thomas. "Dynamics of Dispute Resolution in the Public Sector." In Benjamin Aaron, Joseph Grodin, and James Stern, eds., *Public Sector Bargaining.* Madison, Wisc.: Industrial Relations Research Association, 1980, pp. 150-190.

————, Mordehai Mironi, Ronald Ehrenberg, Jean Baderschneider, and Todd Jick. *Dispute Resolution Under Fact Finding and Arbitration.* New York: American Arbitration Association, 1979.

Matkin, James. "Government Intervention in Labour Disputes in British Columbia." In Morley Gunderson, ed., *Collective Bargaining in the Essential and Public Service Sector.* Toronto: University of Toronto Press, 1975, pp. 79-100.

Ponak, Allen. "Public Sector Dispute Resolution: An American Twist to a Canadian Approach," *Relations Industrielles,* XXXI (1976), 437-551.

Stevens, Carl. "Is Compulsory Arbitration Compatible with Bargaining," *Industrial Relations,* V (February, 1966), 38-52.

Wheeler, Hoyt N. and Frank Owen. "Impasse Resolution Preferences of Fire Fighters and Municipal Negotiators," *Journal of Collective Negotiations in the Public Sector,* V (1976), 215-224.

Wisconsin Bluebook 1979-80. Madison, Wisc.: State of Wisconsin, 1979.

Wolkinson, Benjamin and Jack Stieber, "Michigan Fact Finding Experience in Public Sector Disputes," *The Arbitration Journal,* XXXI (September, 1976), 228-247.

APPENDIX A
Choices and Settlements in Choice-of-Procedures Jurisdictions

Jurisdiction	Choosing Party	Years	Type of Employee	Number of Negotiations	Choice Opportunities*	Arbitration Procedure Chosen	Strike Procedure Chosen	Arbitration Awards	Strikes
Canadian federal	Union	1967-1979	Professionals/administrative	351	351	316	35	101	1
			Clerical	80	80	66	14	6	0
			Technical/operational	251	251	163	88	28	15
British Columbia	Union	1974-1979	Police	53	8	7	1†	5	0
			Firefighters	158	23	22	1‡	20	1
Wisconsin	Both	1978	Municipal/teachers	726†	90	90	0	64	0
Minnesota	Employer	1973-1978	State	81†	15	15	0	12	0
			Teachers	1311†	148	119	29	70	8
			Municipal/metro agency	n.a.	54	30	24	9	4
			County	n.a.	51	19	32	10	11

*For the Canadian federal data, a choice opportunity was judged to exist in every negotiation; in *British Columbia*, when strike notice was given or arbitration applied for; in *Wisconsin*, when an arbitrator was selected; and in *Minnesota*, when an impasse was certified.

†These data are estimates based on the best information available.

‡There were three cases in which a police or firefighter local in B.C. served strike notice, but then decided to go to arbitration. These cases are treated as if the union chose arbitration.

Source: Canadian federal—Records of the Pay Research Bureau, Ottawa: *British Columbia*—(1) Questionnaires sent to all police and firefighter locals, (2) Bureau of Arbitration and Special Services, B.C. Ministry of Labour, (3) information provided by Greater Victoria Labour Relations Association and the Okanagan Mainline Employers Association; *Wisconsin—Biennial Report*, State of Wisconsin Employment Relations Commission, July 1, 1977 to June 30, 1979 (Madison, Wisc.: State of Wisconsin, 1979), Letter from General Counsel, Wisconsin Employment Relations Commission (December 19, 1979); *Minnesota*—Minnesota State Labor Negotiator, Minnesota Bureau of Mediation Services, Minnesota Federation of Teachers, Minnesota Education Association.

Dependence on Impasse Procedures: Police and Firefighters in New York State

Thomas A. Kochan and Jean Baderschneider*

One of the central criteria for evaluating the effectiveness of the collective bargaining process is the extent to which unions and employers are able to resolve their differences without dependence on third parties. George W. Taylor noted the importance of this concern shortly after World War II:

> One conclusion invariably emerges whenever and wherever "the labor problem" is subjected to impartial analysis. It is: collective bargaining must be preserved and strengthened as the bulwark of industrial relations in a democracy. This is just another way of saying that organized labor and management should settle their own differences by understanding, compromise, and agreement and without government interference.[1]

The concern for promoting "free collective bargaining" is especially important in public sector jurisdictions that have established impasse procedures as alternatives to the right to strike. For example, the Final Report of the Taylor Committee (the committee chaired by George Taylor that recommended the collective bargaining law for public employees in New York) cautioned:

> The design of dispute settlement procedures must consistently avoid at least two pitfalls. The first is that impasse procedures often tend to be overused; they may become too accessible and as a consequence, the responsibility and problem-solving virtues of constructive negotiations are lost. Dispute settlement procedures can become habit-forming and negotiations become only a ritual.[2]

Similarly, Willard Wirtz feared that the existence of impasse procedures may create a "narcotic effect" whereby once the parties start using the procedures they become increasingly reliant on them in subsequent rounds of negotiations.[3] Since a variety of alternative dispute resolution procedures exist, it is important to compare the relative effectiveness of each in achieving settlements without resort to third parties. Thus, one component of any

*Baderschneider is at the School of Business, University of Kansas. This research was supported by the National Science Foundation (grants no. APR75-15217 and APR77-17120) and carried out with the cooperation of the New York State Public Employment Relations Board. The views expressed herein, however, are solely those of the authors and do not reflect the official policies of either of these organizations. Reprinted from *Industrial and Labor Relations Review*, Vol. 31, No. 4 (July 1978).

evaluation of an impasse procedure (although certainly not the sole focus) should be an assessment of the rate of settlement without use of the procedure.

Because of the conflicting goals unions and employers bring into negotiations, impasses are an expected and natural part of any collective bargaining system. They are likely to be more frequent in systems where the right to strike is constrained since the costs of a failure to agree are less severe than when an impasse is synonymous with the beginning of a strike. We must be careful, therefore, not to view the occurrence of any single impasse as an indication of a breakdown in the bargaining system. Only when the reliance on the impasse procedures reaches an unacceptable level or becomes a routine part of bargaining should we become concerned. It is thus important for policy purposes to identify trends in the rate of dependence on the procedures, to compare rates of dependence across alternative systems of dispute resolution, and to identify the basic causes of impasses. Ultimately, the line between an acceptable and unacceptable rate of impasse is a subjective judgment, and must be balanced against the other policy goals that must be considered in evaluating the effectiveness of a bargaining and dispute resolution system.[4]

Since impasses can be caused by a wide array of factors in addition to the nature of the impasse procedure, these other causes must be controlled before the effects of the procedures can be estimated. A theory that identifies these other causal forces must therefore be developed, and since the effects of a procedure may change over time, any specific estimates of the effects of a procedure must be placed in their historical context. This paper will present a theory of impasses in public employee bargaining and use it to estimate the effects of a change in impasse procedures for police and firefighters in the State of New York.

In 1974 the procedure governing police and firefighters was changed from one providing factfinding with recommendations followed by a legislative hearing to one providing factfinding but terminating in conventional compulsory arbitration.[5] Both procedures provided for mediation as the initial step following impasse, which is defined as the point at which one or both parties submit a request to the Public Employment Relations Board (PERB) for a mediator. Although the data are drawn from a study of the New York experience, the theory and methodology used here should be applicable to studies of impasse procedures and collective bargaining in other contexts as well.

Determinants of Impasses

All theories of collective bargaining begin with an underlying assumption that a structurally based conflict of interest exists between the job-related goals of employees and the organizational efficiency and effectiveness goals of their employer.[6] The collective bargaining process is one means of periodically confronting and resolving these conflicts. While the underlying conflict of interests between employees and employers stems from their different economic roles in industrial relations, collective bargaining is also a political, organizational, and interpersonal process. Impasses may arise because of pressures from any of these aspects of the bargaining relationship. Consequently, any comprehensive theory of why impasses occur in negotiations must attempt to incorporate variables that reflect the interplay of these diverse forces in negotiations. The propositions presented below attempt to identify the critical variables within each of these aspects of a bargaining relationship that are expected to affect the probability of an impasse occurring.

Environmental Sources of Impasse

The economic environment. It is exceedingly difficult to specify a priori propositions concerning the impact of the economic environment on the probability of an impasse since the economic factors that contribute to management resistance in negotiations may have offsetting effects by lowering union resistance.[7] We might expect, for example, that factors creating an inability to pay would increase management resistance and therefore increase the likelihood of an impasse; yet, these same conditions might lead unions to reduce their expectations concerning their ability to present a strong case in factfinding or arbitration and thereby lower their resistance in negotiations. Similarly, unions might be expected to resist to the point of an impasse most persistently in cities where wage levels or increases have been or are low relative to some community or occupational norm; yet, in such situations management might be less resistant to union arguments. These offsetting factors may in fact explain the inability of previous studies to predict impasse experience in the public sector with economic variables.[8] Consequently, although we will examine the predictive power of tax and income characteristics of communities in our sample, our expectations for them are not very great.

Economic theory and private sector bargaining theory would lead us to predict a negative effect on the probability of impasses developing when unemployment is high in a community.[9] It has been argued that high unemployment should lead unions to moderate their bargaining demands, but it has also been argued that the wage inelasticity of the demand for police and firefighters should limit the impact of outside market forces.[10] Given the threats of manpower cuts that have occurred in recent years in cities in New York, however, the wage inelasticity argument may be losing its applicability and outside market forces may be beginning to play a more important role. Consequently, we would expect that the higher the rate of unemployment, the lower the probability of an impasse.

The political environment. Similar offsetting effects are likely to be found in measures of the political environment of the relationship. Clearly a favorable environment for public sector unions exists in a community in which a high proportion of the labor force is unionized, the elected officials are liberal, the population has a liberal voting record, and blue-collar workers predominate in the private sector labor force. Since there is some empirical evidence to suggest that impasses are more likely in relationships where the unions are stronger and more militant,[11] and we would expect unions to be more militant when the environment is favorable to their interests, we would predict a positive relationship between each of these measures of the political environment and the probability of an impasse. We would especially expect to find this result in bargaining under the factfinding procedure since the impact of adverse publicity of the factfinding report to management in a city with a union-oriented constituency is likely to be higher than in a conservative community. Under arbitration, however, the reverse may be true. Since the arbitrator's decision is final, the unions in the more conservative communities should have more to gain from going to arbitration and the management representatives might find the arbitrator to be a useful scapegoat for the adverse public reaction that is likely to result from higher cost settlements. Indeed, Stern et al. found some support for this latter argument in their interview data: arbitration seemed to be used relatively frequently in conservative suburbs surrounding the city of Milwaukee, even though these suburbs had been oblivious to the union political and public relations pressure tactics under factfinding.[12] Thus, while a positive relationship between liberalism of the environment and probability of impasse is expected, offsetting considerations may moderate the strength of this relationship.

The legal environment. The major variable to be considered in the legal environment is the change in the law from factfinding to compulsory arbitration in 1974. Our prediction here is that the move to arbitration will act as a source of power to the unions and that they will tend to be more resistant to concessions in bargaining, thereby increasing the probability of going to the impasse procedure. In an earlier study, Wheeler found that in prior negotiations under arbitration firefighter unions tended to move or compromise right up to the point at which they expected to settle, but under factfinding they showed a greater tendency to move beyond that resistance point.[13] Thus, the available evidence suggests that a higher proportion of negotiations will reach an impasse under arbitration than under factfinding.

Size of city. Stern et al. and Lipsky and Drotning found positive relationships between size of city and dependency on third parties in negotiations.[14] These results have been interpreted as suggesting that size is a proxy for a complex array of characteristics that differentiate bargaining relationships in small and large cities, such as: (1) fewer overlapping social, religious, family, and business relationships between union and management representatives; (2) greater professionalization of the management function; (3) less paternalism in the management style; (4) greater politicalization of city management; and (5) more formalization of the labor-management relationship. Whatever theoretical and behavioral factors city size actually represents, the finding that impasses are more probable in larger cities is consistent with previous studies of the impact of city size on industrial relations. Consequently, we expect a positive relationship between size of city and the probability of an impasse.

Structural-Organizational Sources of Impasse

The inability to predict the impasse experience in the public sector on the basis of environmental characteristics has led several research teams to

286

suggest that future research should concentrate on identifying the organizational and interpersonal factors that affect the course of bargaining.[15] Several key structural and organizational factors are included in our model.

Police-fire pattern bargaining. Since wages of police and firefighters in a city often tend to be set at some specified relationship to each other—parity in many cases—bargaining with one of the services is often dependent on the outcomes of bargaining with the other. It is therefore necessary to control for the influence of these alternative pattern arrangements in our analysis. We would expect that the probability of going to impasse in any given bargaining relationship would be higher if the bargain is a pattern setter, or if the bargain is a pattern follower *and* the pattern setter has also gone to impasse.

Intraorganizational conflict. It is normally assumed that collective bargaining involves both bargaining between officially designated representatives of the parties at the negotiating table and intraorganizational bargaining or decision making in which each party assigns priorities to the various issues that may be taken up in negotiations.[16] To the extent that this intraorganizational bargaining over priorities is not successfully resolved and internal conflicts, power struggles, or political factions still exist when the negotiations take place, this friction will be felt at the negotiations table.[17] In this situation most negotiators will hold back on making concessions since they are uncertain about the internal organizational consequences of compromising. One way of handling internal pressure is to call an impasse in negotiations and allow a neutral third party either to put pressure on one's constituents or take the responsibility for an unpopular settlement; thus, the existence of internal political-organizational conflicts within one or both of the parties is likely to increase the probability of an impasse. We propose, consequently, that the greater the intraorganizational conflicts or political power struggles within the union or the management, the higher the probability of an impasse.

Management negotiator authority. Another organizational problem that has received much attention in the public sector concerns the allocation of decision-making power among the various officials in the executive and legislative branches. The introduction of collective bargaining has created a conflict with the traditional distribution of powers among those decision makers. The pressure for effective negotiations has led to demands by both public sector unions and management negotiators for the delegation of decision-making power to a management negotiator who sits at the formal bargaining table. Because of their concern for the loss of their own power, however, some public officials have been reluctant to redistribute power in this fashion. Although this issue involves an important underlying conflict between the values of designing an effective negotiations process and keeping control of policy making in the hands of elected representatives of the public, the lack of sufficient decision-making power or discretion at the bargaining table can be expected to increase the probability of an impasse.

Consequently, we propose that the less power is delegated to the management negotiator, the higher the probability of an impasse.

Previous research has shown, however, that cities delegate more power to their management negotiators in situations in which the unions are strong.[18] Consequently, the impact of the lack of management power may only be observable when the other sources of union power are controlled. The only empirical study of impasses that examined this variable experienced a problem identifying the net effects of the power of the management negotiator and consequently found inconclusive results for this variable.[19]

Union pressure tactics. Previous studies of firefighter negotiations have identified a number of political, public relations, and negotiations pressure tactics that are used to induce movement or compromising by city officials.[20] These tactics serve much the same function as does a strike: to communicate the strength of the union's resolve to achieve its demands and to seek to impose higher costs of disagreement on the management officials. One might expect that these pressure-inducing tactics would induce concessions by management and therefore help to avoid an impasse. On the other hand, these tactics are an indicator of how militant the local union is and may thus be positively related to the likelihood of an impasse. This second interpretation is strengthened by a previous study that found that the use of political and negotiations pressure tactics was part of a more generalized local union strategy of pushing a dispute to an impasse in order to activate the political access that union representatives enjoy to local elected officials.[21] Thus, the use of pressure tactics by the union appears to be part of a larger set of organizational strategies designed to pursue the union's demands aggressively in negotiations. We therefore expect a positive relationship between the use of these tactics and the probability of an impasse in negotiations. It should be noted, however, that although we hypothesize that pressure tactics lead to impasses, one could also argue that unions feel compelled to engage in pressure tactics in situations where an impasse has already occurred.

Other Sources of Impasse

Personal characteristics of the negotiators. One element of the conventional wisdom concerning public sector bargaining is that the parties at the bargaining table often are inexperienced and lack adequate skills to make collective bargaining work effectively. It is undoubtedly true that many public sector negotiators are inexperienced, but there is almost no empirical evidence concerning the impact of experience and bargaining skill on the ability of the parties to reach an agreement short of an impasse. An examination of the independent effects of these characteristics is difficult, however, since experienced and skillful negotiators are most likely to be found in situations that otherwise have a higher probability of going to impasse. It is clear, though, that some impasses may be caused by a lack of skill and expertise, and, consequently, it is proposed that the less experience and skill the union and management negotiators possess, the greater the probability of an impasse.

Interpersonal characteristics of the relationship. The attitudes of the parties in collective bargaining toward each other have been the subject of a good deal of theoretical analysis but very little empirical research.[22] Clearly, however, low trust or a high degree of hostility in the bargaining relationship can be expected to make the parties more resistant to compromise and lead to a greater reliance on third parties to facilitate the communication process. Consequently, we propose that the more hostile the attitudes of the parties toward each other, the greater the probability of an impasse.

Bargaining history. To the extent that a narcotic effect has developed, the probability of an impasse in any given round of negotiations is partly a function of whether or not an impasse occurred in previous negotiations. It is not yet clear, however, whether a narcotic effect exerts an autonomous impact on the probability of impasse that is independent of the factors discussed above or whether the narcotic effect occurs *because* of the repeated existence of these other sources of impasse. We will test for these alternative views of the narcotic effect by holding constant the other factors described and measuring the effect of the percentage of times the parties went to impasse in their previous negotiations.

This completes our specification of the model of impasses to be tested in this study. Although the measures chosen to verify this model are somewhat specific to the sample, we believe the general framework and the propositions developed here have validity for bargaining in other contexts as well.

Data and Methodology

The sample for this study consists of all municipalities in the state of New York that bargain with units of both firefighters and police (excluding New York City, which is covered by its own impasse procedure).[23] These cities range in size from 4,000 to 363,000. The average size of the cities in the police sample is 42,300 and the average size in the firefighter sample is 39,700.

Data were collected between 1974 and 1976 in semistructured personal interviews with the union and management negotiators in these units. Originally 74 municipalities were included in the sample but several were dropped because (1) they did not negotiate with both police and firefighters, (2) their representatives who negotiated contracts in the last round under factfinding were no longer in the area, or (3) they had not finished the first round under arbitration. The test of the model and the estimate of the effects of the change in the procedure are based on 133 negotiations that took place during the last round of bargaining under the factfinding procedure and 118 negotiations that took place under the first, and, in a few cases the second, round of bargaining under the experimental arbitration statute. The negotiations under factfinding took place between January 1972 and June 1974, those under arbitration between July 1974 and June 1976.

The analysis proceeds by first tracing the aggregate or statewide impasse histories between 1968 (the first year of bargaining under the Taylor Law) and 1976. To estimate the effects of the change in the law, a set of correlations and regression equations are generated to test the propositions outlined above using the data from bargaining under the factfinding procedure in effect between January 1972 and June 1974. A reduced set of variables are then included in an equation to predict whether or not an impasse would have been expected in the July 1974-June 1976 period if the law had not been changed. The actual experience under the new arbitration procedure between July 1974 and June 1976 is compared to the expected outcomes to generate an estimate of the effects of the change in the law. A more conventional pooled regression equation that includes a dummy variable for the nature of the procedure in effect is also computed to check on the stability of our estimate from the prediction technique.

Impasse History 1968-1976

To test for the existence of a narcotic effect, the impasse histories of the police and firefighter units were analyzed in two ways. First, the rate of impasses for each bargaining unit across its complete bargaining history since 1968 was calculated. Second, the conditional probability of going to impasse in the later rounds of bargaining, given that the parties went to impasse in earlier rounds, was calculated.[24] The first set of data provides a descriptive overview of the variation in the reliance on procedures while the second provides a more formal test of the narcotic hypothesis.

As indicated in Table 1, between 1968 and 1975, 8.5 percent of the cities and police units in the sample never went to impasse while 18.3 percent of these groups went to impasse each time they bargained. Of the remainder, 35.2 percent went to impasse at least once but in fewer than 50 percent of their negotiations, and 38 percent went to impasse in at least 50 percent but fewer than 100 percent of their negotiations. The distribution of experiences is quite similar for the firefighters. Thus, while wide variations exist in the extent to which the parties relied on the procedures, a majority of bargaining relationships depended on the procedures to reach a settlement in more than 50 percent of these negotiations. Furthermore, across these first five rounds of bargaining, the percentage of disputes going to an impasse steadily increased. These percentages for police and fire units combined are: 41 percent in round one, 47 percent in round two, 59 percent in round three, 61 percent in round four, and 65 percent in round five. There was, therefore, a definite trend toward higher rates of reliance on the impasse procedures in each successive round of bargaining since the passage of the Taylor Act.

The narcotic hypothesis can be formally tested by determining whether going to impasse in one period increases the probability of going to impasse in subsequent rounds and whether this increase is significantly different from the probability of going to impasse for units that settled on their own in previous periods. These "conditional probabilities" are shown in Table 2.

The results shown in Table 2 indicate that the probability of going to impasse increased in subsequent rounds of bargaining for those units that had previously gone to impasse. Only in the second and third rounds of negotiations, however, was the difference in the probability of going to impasse significantly greater for those units that went to impasse in prior rounds. Specifically, 63 percent of those units that went to impasse the first time they bargained also went to impasse the second time. Similarly, 77

290

TABLE 1
Reliance on Impasse Procedures in all Police and Firefighter Negotiations between 1968 and 1975
(in percentages of all units)

Measure	Police	Fire
Units that never went to impasse	8.5	15.0
Units that went to impasse at least once but in fewer than 50% of negotiations	35.2	27.0
Units that went to impasse in at least 50% but fewer than 100% of negotiations	38.0	44.0
Units that went to impasse in every negotiation	18.3	14.0

percent of those units that went to impasse in their second round (and 80 percent of those that went to impasse in both round one and round two) went to impasse in round three. By the fourth and fifth rounds, the increasing usage of the procedures was more a general phenomenon than a function of the specific bargaining unit's past impasse experience.

Tests were also performed to assess the effect of going beyond mediation to factfinding in a given round on the probability of going to factfinding in subsequent rounds. Although the results of these tests are not shown here because of space limitations, they indicate that going to factfinding in the previous round increased the probability of going to factfinding in the second and third round by over 20 percent. In later rounds, however, there was again such an increase in the probability of all units going to factfinding that prior impasse experience failed to have a significant effect.

The data also indicate that the proportion of *impasses* that went to factfinding increased during the period in addition to the increase in general usage of procedures. For police this proportion increased from 38 percent to 45 percent between the second and fifth contract rounds, for firefighters, from 47 percent to 59 percent. These increases did not occur at an even rate over the period, however.

In summary, the probability of going to impasse in rounds two and three increased if the parties went to impasse in rounds one and two respectively, and similarly parties were more likely to go to factfinding in rounds two and three if they had gone to factfinding in rounds one and two respectively. Also, this pattern was not statistically significant in the fourth and fifth rounds only because those that had settled on their own in prior rounds were themselves using the impasse resolution process at an increasing rate.[25]

Test of the Model

The propositions developed earlier in this paper were all stated in terms of their impact on the probability of an impasse. Their relevance for explaining the tendency to go to later stages of the settlement process, however, will

TABLE 2
Probability of Going to Impasse in Round 2 and Round 3

		Police		Fire		Combined	
		No Impasse	Impasse	No Impasse	Impasse	No Impasse	Impasse
Round 1				Round 2			
No Impasse		.62	.38	.62	.38	.60	.40
Impasse		.47*	.53	.31*	.69*	.37*	.63*
Round 1	**Round 2**			Round 3			
No Impasse	No Impasse	.56	.44	.77	.35	.60	.40
Impasse	No Impasse	.38**	.62	.72**	.28	.53**	.47
No Impasse	Impasse	.31**	.69	.12**	.88**	.23**	.77**
Impasse	Impasse	.23**	.77	.19**	.81**	.20**	.80**

*Difference from figure in row above is statistically significant.
**Difference from figure in top row for round 3 is statistically significant.

also be examined, through the use of three measures of "stage of the settlement":

(1) *An index of the specific point of settlement.* The point-of-settlement index takes on the following values: 1 if settled without an impasse, 2 if settled in mediation, 3 if settled in factfinding without a report, 4 if settled in factfinding with a report, 5 if settled after factfinding but with further intervention (hereinafter called superconciliation), and 6 if settled by a legislative hearing prior to July 1974 or by arbitration after July 1974. This measure allows the identification of factors that cause the dispute to go further into an impasse procedure in a given round of negotiations.

(2) *A measure of declaration of impasse.* The measure takes on the value of 2 if an impasse was declared and 1 if the dispute was settled without an impasse. This measures the probability of going to impasse but does not pick up any effects of going to the later stages of the procedure.

(3) *A factfinding measure.* The measure takes the value 2 if the dispute went to factfinding or beyond and 1 if it was settled prior to the factfinding stage. This is designed to identify the factors that lead the parties to go all the way to the final step of the procedure.

Correlations and preliminary regressions. The first step in the analysis was to compute the correlations between each of the independent variables and each of the three measures of the settlement process for the 1972-74 cases negotiated under the factfinding procedure. Several sets of preliminary regressions were then computed to (1) compare the relative predictive power of the environmental, structural-organizational, and interpersonal-personal characteristics, and (2) to choose the most significant variables within each of these categories for inclusion in the final prediction model. (The data sources and measurement procedures for these variables are presented in Appendix I and the correlations in Appendix II.)

The most striking result obtained in these correlations and preliminary regressions was that the environmental characteristics showed less consistent and weaker relationships with the measures of the stage of settlement than did the structural-organizational or the interpersonal-personal characteristics. In addition, the correlations and regression coefficients in all three categories were generally stronger for police negotiations than for firefighter negotiations.

Very few of the correlations between measures of the economic environment and stage of settlement were significant. The two that had the strongest relationships for police were previous salary and the unemployment rate in the community. The lower the previous salary and the higher the unemployment rate, the less likely the parties were to go to impasse or to factfinding and the earlier in the impasse procedure they tended to settle. While the correlations were in the same direction for the firefighters, none of them were significant. The correlations between the measures of the financial status of the cities—closeness to the constitutional tax limit, change in total revenue, and the tax rate—and the stage of settlement were all insignificant. The one measure of the economic pressure on the *employees* for higher wages—the change in the cost of living in the last 12 months of the previous contract—was significant for both the police and firefighter negotiations. The direction of the correlation, however, was negative, contrary to our hypothesis.

Overall, the economic conditions in the cities in our sample did not distinguish those cities that settled on their own from those that relied on impasse procedures. Cities with severe financial problems in the state relied heavily on the procedures, but so did enough cities of all sizes without serious financial problems so that measures of financial condition did not discriminate between cities that settled without third parties and those that relied on procedures. Thus, although economic problems obviously are important causes of some impasses, improving the economic positions of the cities would not appear to guarantee better bargaining.

The one measure of the political environment included in our analysis, the percentage voting Democratic in the 1972 presidential election, was positively correlated with the dependent variables in the police cases but showed no consistent relationship in the firefighter cases.

A strong positive correlation was found between size of city and reliance on impasse procedures. This finding is not only consistent with previous studies of public sector bargaining but was also supplemented with other data collected in this research. The largest cities in the state have a record of heavy dependence on impasse procedures throughout the first decade of bargaining under the Taylor Law. The five largest upstate cities (Buffalo, Yonkers, Rochester, Syracuse, and Albany), for example, have gone to impasse in approximately 90 percent of their negotiations with police and firefighters and to factfinding and beyond in over 70 percent of all their negotiations.

Buffalo, the largest city with the most severe financial problems and the most politicized bargaining environment, has gone to factfinding or beyond (or arbitration after the change in the law in 1974) with its police and firefighters *every* time it has negotiated. Sick outs, threatened slowdowns, court challenges of arbitration awards, improper practice charges, and other delays in resolving contract disputes have all been common. In fact, since mediation at the initial impasse stage in previous years has proved futile and since the intensity of the disputes has been so strong, the parties have recently bypassed the initial mediation step and gone directly to factfinding. While bargaining in the other large cities appears to be somewhat less intense, the interplay of the political process and the bargaining process is clearly also present.

The experience of these large cities highlights the dismal record of bargaining in highly complex, highly politicized environments. Our qualitative notes reinforced the statistical evidence that the change in impasse procedures from factfinding to arbitration had minimal effects on the dependence of the parties on impasse procedures or on their incentive to bargain. The pattern of heavy dependence started almost immediately with the cities' first experiences under the Taylor Law and has continued up to the present time.

Appendix II also shows that strong negative correlations were found between the amount of authority delegated to the management negotiator and each of the three measures of the stage of settlement for both police and firefighters. On the other hand, strong positive relationships were found between the dependent variables for both employee groups and the use of political and negotiations pressure tactics by the union and the amount of internal pressure on union officials going into negotiations.

The correlations of pattern follower and stage of settlement were positive and significant for police but negative and insignificant for firefighters. In conducting our interviews it became clear that a strategy of pattern setting and following was affecting police and firefighter negotiations in many cities. However, the direction of the effect and the link between the bargaining process and the use of the impasse procedures was unclear. Our general impression was that the police tended to be pattern setters more frequently than the firefighters, but in a number of cities the firefighters' local was highly aggressive and did act as pattern setters.

One interpretation of these correlations is that where the firefighters are militant and therefore tend to go to impasse, the police (if they are pattern followers) are likely to go to impasse too, in order to await the settlement of the fire contract. A number of examples were clearly documented in interviews showing that parties in one unit were obviously holding back to allow the pattern to be set by the other unit. In other cases, one of the unions would hold back to await the other's settlement and then go to the next step of the impasse procedure insisting that the pattern settlement must be surpassed. (These efforts failed in most, but not all, cases.) Thus, it is clear that the pattern setting and following process between police and firefighters in most of the cities in our sample is quite strong and has an important impact on the negotiations process. The complexity of this setter-follower relationship, however, is too great to capture effectively by our measures. Furthermore, being a pattern follower is more strongly correlated with the probability of going to the terminal step of the procedures. This is further evidence that followers often bide their time until the pattern has been set.

The correlations between the interpersonal and personal characteristics and the measures of stage of settlement were also quite consistent and strong. The level of hostility between the parties had the strongest correlations with the measures of stage of settlement in this set (and one of the strongest of all the correlations examined). These correlations were negative (indicating a positive relationship between hostility and use of procedure) and significant for both the police and fire groups. The fact that hostility was more strongly correlated with the probability of an impasse than with the probability of going to factfinding suggests that hostility is one source of impasse that is amenable to resolution in mediation.

Although the effects of a high level of hostility in bargaining were uniform—the probability of going to impasse was increased—our interviews indicated that the causes of hostility were quite varied. Often relations simply reflected personality conflicts between the chief negotiators. In other relationships hostility had built up over a number of years because of unkept promises made in previous negotiations, or it was largely a function of severe economic pressures on the parties. Finally, in a number of the smaller, more conservative communities, which have not experienced some of the economic hardships of the larger cities, hostility had developed because of the general lack of acceptance of collective bargaining by the community's political leaders. In a few of the relationships it was clear that the hostility between the parties was so great as to preclude any effective bargaining or problem solving, regardless of the type of impasse procedure available. Hostility also often carried over from one negotiation to the next. In view of these observations, it is not surprising that the degree of hostility showed such strong correlations with the probability of impasse.

Several of the personal characteristics of the negotiators were also related to stage of settlement. The strength of these correlations, however—and in some cases even their direction—varied across the police and firefighter groups. Perhaps the most interesting results were found for the use of an outside professional negotiator by the union: for police there was a strong negative correlation between using an in-house union official as the chief negotiator and the stage of settlement. This implies that those police locals that used an outside consultant or attorney were more likely to go to impasse and go further into the impasse procedure than their counterparts. The correlations for the firefighter were in the same direction, but not as strong as for the police. The correlations between the years of negotiating experience of the management representative and stage of settlement were consistently positive, contrary to our expectations. The correlations between the stage of settlement and the use of in-house negotiators for management were all negative, but the magnitudes varied considerably. Similarly, the measures of the parties' ratings of the skills and abilities of their counterparts' negotiators were significantly negative (as expected) for the firefighter negotiations; however, there was no consistent pattern to the police correlations.

The finding that the use of outside professional negotiators increased the probability of impasse reinforces the impressions obtained in our interviews with the parties and the neutrals involved in these cases. A lawyer who represented a large number of police locals in one section of the state, for example, views everything that goes on prior to the factfinding stage of the impasse procedure as a futile waste of time. His basic strategy has been to proceed to factfinding without making any compromises in an effort to obtain one favorable factfinding recommendation to use in "whipsawing" the other municipalities in the region into comparable settlements. While this is the strongest and most obvious effect of the impact of outside professional negotiators, all of our interviewers recorded similar experiences in other jurisdictions. The finding that the more experienced the management negotiator the higher the probability of an impasse is also consistent with the outside-negotiator effect on the union side. Apparently the more experienced professionals are able and willing to press the demands and counterdemands of their side harder and farther into the impasse procedures. Thus, instead of the bargaining process becoming more effective and the impasse procedures more successful over time as the parties become more professionalized, the opposite effects seem to have occurred. This relationship is somewhat contrary to the conventional wisdom on public sector bargaining.

We should be extremely wary of relying too heavily on the simple correlations between these interpersonal and personal variables and the stage of settlement, however, since they are likely to be rather highly intercorrelated with other measures in our framework and may not exert an independent effect on the bargaining process once these other variables are controlled. While this caveat applies to our entire discussion of these correlations, it is most serious with this set of variables. Consequently, we will await the results of the final regression model before assessing the net effects of these personal and interpersonal characteristics of the bargaining relationship.

Final equation under factfinding. On the basis of the correlations and preliminary regressions discussed above, the follwing variables were included in the final model used to estimate the effects of the change in the impasse procedure:[26] (1) four measures of the environment—closeness to the tax limit, cost-of-living change, city size, and previous starting salary; (2) three structural-organizational characteristics—whether or not the unit is a pattern follower, authority of the management negotiator, and union pressure tactics; and (3) four interpersonal and personal characteristics—degree of hostility, whether or not the union negotiator is an outside consultant or attorney, the skill of the union negotiators, and the experience of the management negotiator. The results of running regression equations with these variables on the factfinding sample are reported in Table 3.[27]

The variables that are significant in these equations are clustered largely in the categories measuring interpersonal-personal and structural-organizational characteristics. The previous starting salary, closeness to the tax limit, and cost of living are each significant in one of the equations.

Estimates of the Change in Procedure

Two tests were conducted using the model developed under factfinding to determine whether the change in the impasse procedure from factfinding to arbitration increased or decreased the probability of going to impasse or affected the stage of settlement. First, the regression coefficients derived in the models for police and for firefighters (presented in Table 3) were used to predict the probability of impasse and the probability of going to arbitration during the first round of negotiations under arbitration. Second, the data for the last round of bargaining under factfinding and the first round of bargaining under arbitration were pooled (combined) and a regression equation was estimated using the same variables as were included in the final equation under factfinding with the addition of a "dummy" variable that estimated the impact of the nature of the impasse procedure in effect (factfinding or arbitration). Descriptions of these two tests and their results are provided below.

The prediction test. Multiplying the unstandardized regression coefficients estimated in the last round of negotiations under factfinding times the observed (or measured) values of the independent variables obtained during

TABLE 3
Regressions of Probability of an Impasse Under Factfinding

Variables	Police (n=64)		Firefighters (n=69)	
	Unstandardized Coefficients	Standardized Coefficients	Unstandardized Coefficients	Standardized Coefficients
Closeness to tax limit	0.01	.02	0.40	.12
Cost-of-living increase	0.00	.00	-0.00	-.02
Union pressure tactics	-0.12	-.05	-0.43	-.16
Management negotiator authority	-0.01	-.02	-0.04	-.08
Pattern follower	-0.02	-.05	-0.02	.03
Hostility[a]	-0.36	-.56**	-0.16	-.24**
Union in-house negotiator	-0.25	-.22**	-0.14	-.11
Union negotiator skill	-0.04	-.07	-0.16	-.28**
Management experience	0.01	.35**	0.00	.00
City population	-0.01	-.23**	0.00	.13
Previous starting salary	-0.00	-.05	-0.00	-.05
Constant	3.43		3.43	
F Value	5.47**		2.88*	
R^2	.54		.35	
$\overline{R}^2$	.44		.23	

[a]The sign on this variable is reversed; therefore, a negative coefficient indicates a positive effect and vice versa.
* = Significant beyond .05 level.
** = Significant beyond .01 level.

the first (or in a few cases the second) round of negotiations under arbitration gave us a prediction test. By summing across these products and adding the constant from the factfinding equation we obtained an estimate of the probability of impasse for each negotiation conducted under the arbitration procedure. This estimated probability of impasse was then compared to the actual value of the dependent variable under arbitration. By comparing the estimated and the actual values on the dependent variable we could determine which of the observations were correctly classified by the model. If the model systematically predicted that certain cases should have gone to impasse (based on the pattern of characteristics found in the bargaining relationship under arbitration and the estimated effects of this pattern of characteristics under factfinding), and we found that these cases were actually settled without an impasse, for example, we would conclude that the arbitration procedure had reduced the probability of going to impasse. On the other hand, if the model systematically predicted certain cases should have settled and we found that in fact they went to an impasse, we would conclude that arbitration had increased the probability of going to impasse.[28]

The results for the prediction equations are summarized in Table 4. For the police, the model predicted that nine of the cases in the arbitration sample that actually went to impasse would be settled short of impasse. Thus, the model underestimated the number of impasses under arbitration and implied that the effect of the change in the statute would be to increase the number of police impasses. This effect can be expressed in percentage terms by dividing the number of unpredicted impasses that occurred by the total number of negotiations. Using this calculation, our model estimated an increase in impasses of 15.78 percent (9/57). A very similar estimate was obtained for the firefighters, although here we found that we both under- and over-predicted settlements in some cases. Specifically, the model predicted that 15 cases should have been settled that actually went to impasse and 5 cases that should have gone to impasse in fact were settled. Thus, on balance the model estimated that 10 more cases from our sample of 61 firefighters negotiations under arbitration went to impasse than would have been the case under factfinding. Expressed in percentage terms, the model provided an estimate of a 16.39 percent (10/61) increase in firefighter impasses under arbitration. Thus, taking the police and firefighter estimates together, this technique suggests that about a 16 percent increase in impasses during the first round of negotiations under arbitration was caused by the change in the statute. Thus, even though the firefighter equation is somewhat suspect because of the problem noted in footnote 28, the estimate of the net effects of the change in the law for firefighters is almost identical to that for the police.

Comparison with the pooled regression estimates. A further check on the stability of these estimates was made by comparing them with estimates of the effects of the change in legislation obtained when the data were pooled and a regression equation computed in which the effects of the law were estimated by including a dummy variable that takes the value of 1 under arbitration and 0 under factfinding. These regression equations are shown in

TABLE 4
Comparison of Predicted with Actual Impasses Under Arbitration

Predicted Experience	Actual Experience Under Arbitration			
	Police (n=57)		Firefighters (n=61)	
	No Impasse	Impasse	No Impasse	Impasse
No Impasse	14	9	21	15
Impasse	0	34	5	20

Table 5. There, in addition to the probability of an impasse as the dependent variable, equations are also presented in which the dependent variables are the stage of settlement and the probability of going to the terminal step of the procedure (legislative hearing under the old statute and arbitration under the new). The unstandardized regression coefficients in the probability-of-impasse equation in Table 5 corresponding to the dummy variable measuring the type of procedure are .140 for the police and .113 for the firefighters.[29] This procedure, therefore, provides an estimate of an 11.3 percent increase in firefighter impasses due to arbitration and a 14.0 percent increase in police impasses due to arbitration. These estimates are very close to those obtained with the prediction model.

Equations were also computed in which the variable measuring the percentage of times the unit had gone to impasse previously was included. The addition of this variable increased the estimates of the effects of the change in the law by between 2 and 3 percent, indicating that those units that were more likely to go to impasse under arbitration than under factfinding were units with few impasses in the past.

The equations for the probability of going to the terminal step of the procedure and for the stage of settlement provide similar results. The unstandardized coefficients indicate that the probability of going to the final step in the procedure increased approximately 17.8 percent under arbitration for the police and approximately 13.8 percent for the firefighters. Here again a combined estimate for the two groups lies in the range of a 15-16 percent increase due to arbitration.

The coefficients for the arbitration procedure are consistently larger and somewhat more significant for the police than for the firefighters. This is also consistent with the prediction results since for the police there were no cases in which the effect of the law was to increase the probability of settlement without an impasse whereas for the firefighters five cases fell into this group. Thus, the effects of the law for the firefighters were more varied, and the standard errors on the regression coefficients larger, than for the police, reducing the statistical significance of these coefficients. The regression coefficients were somewhat smaller for the firefighters as well. In any event, however, the differences between the police and firefighter coefficients are small and should probably not be taken very seriously.

It should be noted, however, that there are several variables in the pooled regression equations that exert an effect as strong as or sometimes even stronger than the arbitration statute. For police, the impact of the level of hostility is significantly stronger than or equal to that of the arbitration statute in all three equations, and management experience and previous starting salary have such an impact in two of the equations. For firefighters, management negotiator authority, level of hostility, and city population exert a significantly greater impact than the arbitration statute in two of the equations. Other variables exert a significantly greater impact than the arbitration statute in at least one of the equations for both police and firefighters. Thus, the change in legislation ranks at best equal to, and in some cases below, all of these characteristics in importance as a determinant of the probability of settlement without an impasse or in the early stages of

TABLE 5
Standardized Regression Coefficients from Pooled Regressions of Stage of Settlement

Independent Variables	Police (n=121)			Firefighters (n=130)		
	Point of Settlement Index	Probability of Impasse	Final Step	Point of Settlement Index	Probability of Impasse	Final Step
Closeness to tax limit	-.01	-.06	.02	.07	.08	.03
Cost of living	-.07	.02	-.10	.02	-.01	.02
Union pressure tactics[a]	-.15**	-.08	-.12	-.22***	-.10	-.12
Management negotiator authority	-.03	-.00	.01	-.17***	-.04	-.20***
Pattern follower	-.03	-.08	.06	-.06	-.07	.03
Hostility[a]	-.33***	-.50***	.22***	-.25***	-.32***	-.11
Union in-house negotiator	-.16***	-.20***	-.05	-.09	-.17***	-.01
Union negotiator skill	-.12**	-.03	-.10	-.14***	-.16	-.14**
Management experience	.21***	.25***	.16**	.08	.13*	.12
City population	-.02	-.12*	.09	.28***	.17	.31***
Previous starting salary	.20***	-.03	.22***	-.10	-.10	-.11
Arbitration statute	.19***	.14*	.22***	.14**	.11	.17***
F value	11.3***	9.71***	6.07***	7.38***	4.68***	4.54***
R^2	.56	.52	.40	.43	.32	.32
$\bar{R}^2$	.51	.46	.34	.37	.26	.25

[a]The sign on this variable is reversed; therefore a negative coefficient indicates a positive effect and vice versa.

* = Significant beyond .10.
** = Significant beyond .05.
*** = Significant beyond .01.

impasse. This result should be kept in mind in order to place the role of the legislative change in perspective.

The impact of the legislation can be further understood by examining which specific bargaining relationships were misclassified under the arbitration procedure. An examination of the jurisdictions that we predicted should have settled but actually went to impasse indicated that these cities were almost universally confined to small and medium-sized (ranging from 5,000 to 50,000 population) upstate cities, excluding those in the New York City area. This was true for both the police and firefighter samples; in fact, many of the same cities were misclassified for both. This finding suggests that the effects of the change in the statute were largely confined to those cities.

Summary and Implications

When taken together, the results presented in this rather complex aggregate and micro analysis lead to the following conclusions. Since 1968, the probability of going to impasse increased in each successive round of negotiations, and it increased at a faster rate for those that went to impasse in early years. The switch to arbitration in 1975 increased the probability of going to impasse and to the final step of the procedure by about 16 percent;[30] the effects of this change, however, were limited mainly to small to medium sized up-state cities. In addition, the change in the law was less important than a number of underlying organizational and attitudinal characteristics of the bargaining relationships and the characteristics of the individual negotiators. Also, the larger cities were generally not affected by the change to arbitration because they had already fallen into a pattern of heavy reliance on the procedures under factfinding. Thus, while the change in the statute did increase the number of impasses experienced in the state, the effects of the change were limited to a specific subsample of cities and the presence of arbitration was not nearly as important a determinant of the stage of bargaining or the impasse procedure that the parties settled at as were several more basic and, unfortunately, recurring problems found in these bargaining relationships.

Perhaps the most important theoretical contribution of this study is that by going beyond the analysis of environmental determinants of impasses—through the addition of critical organizational, interpersonal, and personal variables to a prediction equation—it has been more successful than previous efforts at explaining the probability of an impasse occurring in a given round of negotiations. This confirms a view, previously advanced, that the effects of economic and political environmental characteristics tend to be offsetting and therefore do not discriminate well between units that are likely to settle on their own and those that are likely to go to impasse.[31]

This is the second study of impasse resolution to use the technique of examining rounds of bargaining rather than annual averages. In contrast to the more optimistic findings of several other public sector studies that have utilized annual averages in examining use of impasse procedures, both these studies have revealed a definite pattern of reusage (a narcotic effect).[32]

303

Future studies, therefore, should be sensitive to the differences in results that may occur with these different techniques. We believe that analyzing rounds of bargaining provides a better method of tracing the experience of the same units through time and therefore provides a better assessment of the performance of the bargaining system on the absolute level and trends in use of impasse procedures.

When the correlation and regression results are considered together with the impasse history data, a picture of this system emerges that suggests that since 1968 the parties have experienced a relatively high and consistently increasing rate of dependence on third parties. A narcotic effect is especially observable in the largest cities in the state. The problems that cause impasses in the bargaining relationships appear to get carried over from one round to the next and to have spread to a larger number of relationships in each successive round of bargaining. This trend continued under the first round of bargaining under arbitration.

In an earlier paper it was suggested that observers of public sector bargaining and impasse procedures could be divided into three groups: the optimists, pessimists, and fence sitters.[33] Clearly, the record of dependence on third parties in these jurisdictions over the first decade of the Taylor Law provides little support for the optimists. The performance of the system on the criterion of dependence on third parties deteriorated as the parties became more experienced and the role of professionals increased. Within the confines of this time period, the pessimists (those who expect the narcotic effect to be a permanent and increasingly dominant characteristic of the bargaining system) can find strong support for their views. The fence sitters (those who would expect the dependence on the procedures to rise and fall as the environment changes) could argue, however, that the declining rate experienced since 1968 reflects the general overall economic decline and subsequent increase in political hostility toward public employees that occurred in New York State as its fiscal crisis worsened. Therefore, it may still be too early to argue that the experience of the first decade indicates that heavy reliance on third parties is an inevitable characteristic of bargaining under impasse procedures without the right to strike. It is clear, however, that some shifts in the pattern of bargaining and dispute resolution in these jurisdictions will be necessary if the parties are to reverse the trend established in the first decade.

Footnotes

1. George W. Taylor, *Government Regulation of Industrial Relations* (Englewood Cliffs, N.J.: Prentice-Hall, 1948), p. 1.
2. *Final Report of the Governor's Committee on Public Employee Relations* (Albany: State of New York, 1966), p. 33.
3. Address by Willary Wirtz before the National Academy of Arbitrators, Chicago, February 1, 1963. Reprinted in *Daily Labor Report* (Washington, D.C.: Bureau of National Affairs, February 1, 1963), pp. F1-F4.
4. See, for example, the comment by Peter Feuille and the reply by Mark Thompson and James Cairnie in *Industrial and Labor Relations Review,* Vol. 28, No. 3 (April 1975), pp. 432-38.
5. The amendments were passed on a three-year experimental basis. In 1977, a two-year extension of the amendments was passed by the legislature and signed

by the governor. The new 1977 amendment modified the procedure by eliminating factfinding, imposing the costs of arbitration on the parties, and changing the content and application of the criteria for arbitration awards. This paper is drawn from chapter 3 of a larger evaluation of the impasse procedures before and after the 1974 amendments: Thomas A. Kochan, Ronald G. Ehrenberg, Jean Baderschneider, Todd Jick, and Mordehai Mironi, *An Evaluation of Impasse Procedures for Police and Firefighters in the State of New York* (Final Report Submitted to the National Science Foundation, 1977). We will refer to this as the *Final Report* in future footnotes. A condensed version of this report will be published in 1978 by the American Arbitration Association.

6. Jack Barbash, "The Elements of Industrial Relations," *British Journal of Industrial Relations,* Vol. 2, No. 10 (October 1964), pp. 66-78.

7. For a discussion of this problem see John C. Anderson and Thomas A. Kochan, "Dispute Resolution in the Federal Public Service of Canada: Impacts on the Bargaining Process," *Industrial and Labor Relations Review,* Vol. 30, No. 3 (April 1977), pp. 283-301. For theoretical discussions of union and management resistance in the bargaining process see Carl M. Stevens, *Strategy and Collective Bargaining Negotiations* (New York: McGraw-Hill, 1963), and Richard E. Walton and Robert B. McKersie, *A Behavioral Theory of Labor Negotiations* (New York: McGraw-Hill, 1965).

8. See, for example, John F. Burton, Jr. and Charles E. Krider, "The Incidence of Strikes in Public Employment," in Daniel S. Hamermesh, ed., *Labor in the Public and Non-Profit Sectors* (Princeton: Princeton University Press, 1975), pp. 135-78; David A. Huettner and Thomas L. Watkins, "Public Sector Bargaining: An Investigation of Possible Environmental Influences," in Gerald G. Somers, ed., *Proceedings of the Twenty-Sixth Annual Winter Meetings of the Industrial Relations Research Association* (Madison, Wisc.: IRRA, 1974), pp. 178-87; Norman Solomon, "Environmental Factors Facilitating Industrial Peace in the Police Sector," (Master's thesis, Industrial Relations Research Institute, University of Wisconsin, Madison, 1974).

9. Orley Ashenfelter and George Johnson, "Bargaining Theory, Trade Unions and Industrial Strike Activity," *American Economic Review,* Vol. 59, No. 1 (March 1969), pp. 35-49.

10. See, for example, Orley Ashenfelter and Ronald G. Ehrenberg, "The Demand for Labor in the Public Sector," in Hamermesh, *Labor in the Public and Non-Profit Sectors,* pp. 49-78.

11. Burton and Krider, "The Incidence of Strikes," and Huettner and Watkins, "Public Sector Bargaining."

12. James L. Stern, Charles M. Rehmus, J. Joseph Loewenberg, Hirschel Kasper, and Barbara D. Dennis, *Final-Offer Arbitration* (Lexington, Mass.: D. C. Heath, 1975), p. 32.

13. Hoyt N. Wheeler, "The Impact of Compulsory Arbitration on Movement in Public Sector Bargaining," *Industrial Relations* (forthcoming).

14. Stern et al., *Final-Offer Arbitration,* and John E. Drotning and David B. Lipsky, "The Relation Between Teacher Salaries and the Use of Impasse Procedures Under New York's Taylor Law: 1968-1972," *Journal of Collective Negotiations in the Public Sector,* Vol. 6 (1977), pp. 229-44.

15. Huettner and Watkins, "Public Sector Bargaining"; Solomon, "Environmental Factors Facilitating Industrial Peace"; and Anderson and Kochan, "Dispute Resolution."

16. Walton and McKersie, *A Behavioral Theory;* John T. Dunlop, "The Social Utility of Collective Bargaining," in Lloyd Ulman, ed., *Challenges to Collective Bargaining* (Englewood Cliffs, N.J.: Prentice-Hall, 1967), pp. 168-75; Thomas A. Kochan, George P. Huber, and L. L. Cummings, "Determinants of Intraorganiza-

tional Conflict in Collective Bargaining in the Public Sector," *Administrative Science Quarterly*, Vol. 20, No. 2 (June 1975), pp. 10-23.

17. Thomas A. Kochan, "City Government Bargaining: The Path Analysis," *Industrial Relations*, Vol. 14, No. 1 (February 1975), pp. 90-101.
18. Thomas A. Kochan, "Determinants of the Power of Boundary Units in Inter-organizational Bargaining Relations," *Administrative Science Quarterly*, Vol. 20, No. 3 (September 1975), pp. 434-52.
19. Solomon, "Environmental Factors Facilitating Industrial Peace."
20. Thomas A. Kochan and Hoyt N. Wheeler, "Municipal Collective Bargaining: A Model and Analysis of Bargaining Outcomes," *Industrial and Labor Relations Review*, Vol. 29, No. 1 (October 1975), pp. 46-66; James A. Craft, "Fire Fighter Strategy in Wage Negotiations," *Quarterly Review of Economics and Business*, Vol. 11, No. 3 (Autumn 1971), pp. 65-75.
21. Thomas A. Kochan, "A Theory of Multilateral Bargaining in City Governments," *Industrial and Labor Relations Review*, Vol. 27, No. 4 (July 1974), pp. 538-39.
22. See, for example, Walton and McKersie, *A Behavioral Theory*, pp. 185-270; or Ross Stagner and H. Rosen, *Psychology of Union-Management Relations* (Monterey, Calif.: Brooks-Cole, 1975).
23. A more complete description of the design and methodology of the larger study can be found in chapter 2 of the *Final Report*.
24. For a complete description of the techniques used to compute these probabilities see chapter 3 of the *Final Report*.
25. For an analysis of how the experience of the police and firefighters compares with teachers in New York State and with police and firefighters in several other states, see pp. 40-54 of the *Final Report*.
26. Ordinary least squares regression equations are used throughout this paper since they provide a simple way of applying the prediction technique used. The procedure is basically analogous to a discriminant function when used with a dichotomous dependent variable. For a description of how regression analysis can be used with these types of dependent variables, see Fred N. Kerlinger and Elazar J. Pedhazur, *Multiple Regression in Behavioral Research* (New York: Holt, Rinehart and Winston, 1973), pp. 336-39. Although a dichotomous dependent variable raises problems of heteroskedasticity, it has been shown that the results of using ordinary least squares regressions do not differ significantly in this type of problem from results obtained using the more complex and less straight-forward logit or probit techniques. See Morely Gunderson, "Retention of Trainees: A Study with Dichotomous Dependent Variables," *Journal of Econometrics*, Vol. 2, No. 1 (May 1974), pp. 79-94.
27. No serious problems of multicollinearity were found among the independent variables included in the final prediction equation. Most of the coefficient correlations were well below .40, with the degree of hostility and use of union pressure tactics the only exceptions (.58 for police and .60 for firefighters). We decided to keep both of these in the equations, however, since our interview notes suggested that while hostility normally was high when unions used pressure tactics, the obverse was not necessarily true. Thus, although there is some overlap between these two variables, they still appear to be reflecting different aspects of the negotiations. A complete table of the intercorrelations is available from the authors.
28. Use of the prediction model assumes that (1) nothing *not* measured in the two equations affects the dependent variables under one procedure but not the other, and (2) the independent variables not in the model exert roughly equivalent effects on the settlement process under the two procedures. Tests of these assumptions were made by comparing the percentage of variance explained by

the equation presented in Table 3 using the arbitration data. The first assumption was tested by comparing the R²s in these equations. The second was tested by computing a Chow test to determine whether the structure of coefficients in the equations differed significantly. There was almost no change in the explanatory power of the equations for the police or the firefighters under the two procedures, suggesting that the overall model works equally well under both procedures for both groups. The Chow tests found no significant differences in the structure of coefficients for the police (F=0.67) but a significant difference (F=2.18, p<.05) for the firefighters. We should therefore be cautious in interpreting the results of applying the prediction model to the firefighters since we might expect more random prediction errors with these data than with the police data.

29. The unstandardized coefficients (which are not shown in Table 5) give an approximate estimate of the probability of an impasse due to the independent variable. Because of the limitations of ordinary least squares regressions with a dichotomous dependent variable, these estimates only approximate the true effects of the independent variables. We prefer to use the standardized regression coefficients in reporting the rest of the regression results since they allow direct comparisons of the relative importance of the independent variables in the equations. They cannot be interpreted as probability estimates, however.

30. There is still the possibility that some of this 16 percent may represent a continuation of the longer term upward trend in the impasse rate that would have continued in the absence of any change in the procedure. To the extent the control variables in the model adequately capture the reasons causing this trend, our estimates should be accurate. To the extent that the model does not completely capture these trends, however, we may overstate the effects of the procedure somewhat. Thus, if there is any systematic bias in our estimates, the bias would be in the direction of overstating the effects of the change in the law.

31. Anderson and Kochan, "Impasse Procedures."

32. Ibid., pp. 285-86.

33. Ibid., pp. 291-92.

APPENDIX I
Variable Description and Data Sources

Tax Limit
Total Revenue
Equalized Tax Rates
City Population
Source: All municipal finance data are from *Report of the State Comptroller on Municipal Affairs* (Albany, New York: Office of the State Comptroller, Bureau of Audit and Control) 1972, 1973, and 1974 editions, Tables 3, 4, and 5.

Cost-of-Living Increase
Source: U.S. Department of Labor, Bureau of Labor Statistics, Consumer Price Index News Releases and Reports, various issues 1972-76.

Percent Voting Democratic in 1972 Presidential Election
Source: *County and City Data Book* (Washington, D.C.: Bureau of the Census, 1973)

Unemployment Rate
Source: *Employment Review* (Albany: New York State Department of Labor) various issues.

Data for all the following variables were obtained in interviews:

Previous Starting Salary (starting salary existing at the time of negotiations).

Previous Impasse Experience (percent of previous negotiations going to impasse).

Management Negotiator Authority (average scores of management and union response to questions concerning the amount of discretion the management negotiator had in determining bargaining positions [based on a 1-5 scale with 1=none and 5=a very great deal]).

Internal Management Conflict (average score on eight items concerning the amount of disagreement among various city officials and city negotiators concerning bargaining positions).

Union Pressure Tactics (sum of the various activities engaged in by the union during negotiations, such as slowdowns, "sick outs," and door-to-door campaigns).

Pressure on Union Leaders (average score on three items concerned with the pressure on the negotiations team to get more in this round of bargaining—based on 1-5 scale).

Pattern Follower and Pattern Setter (whether the negotiation was viewed as a pattern follower or pattern setter for other jurisdiction—1 if pattern follower, 0 otherwise; 1 if pattern setter, 0 otherwise).

Hostility (average score of management and union on five items dealing with the nature of the relationship between the city and union during negotiations).

Union Negotiator Skill (average score of management responses to three questions concerning the bargaining skill of the union negotiator).

Management Negotiator Skill (average score of union responses to three questions concerning the bargaining skill of the management negotiator).

Union Negotiator Experience and Management Negotiator Experience (number of previous collective bargaining agreements negotiated by respective representative).

Union In-House Negotiator and Management In-House Negotiator (whether the negotiator was an outside consultant or a union or paid city official—0 if in-house consultant, 1 if outside consultant).

Characteristics	Point of Settlement		Impasse-No Impasse		Going to Factfinding or Beyond	
	Police	Fire	Police	Fire	Police	Fire
Environmental						
Closeness to tax limit	-.09	.02	-.11	.02	-.04	.10
Changes in total revenue	-.05	.13	-.09	.00	.00	.17
Equalized tax rate	-.04	.06	.03	.08	-.13	-.01
City population	.36***	.25**	.20*	.13	.30**	.17
Cost-of-living increase	-.17	-.20*	-.07	-.20*	-.22*	-.18
Percent voting Democratic in 1972	.28**	.02	.30**	.09	.19	-.07
Unemployment rate in 1973	-.25**	-.09	-.20*	.02	-.21*	-.10
Previous starting salary	.44***	.13	.26**	.11	.46***	.06
Previous impasse experience	.32***	.37***	.35***	.37***	.23*	.23*
Structural/Organizational						
Management negotiator authority	-.20*	-.36***	-.29**	-.27**	-.18	-.34***
Internal management conflict	.15	.17	-.05	.27**	-.15	.16
Union pressure tactics [b]	-.61***	-.65***	-.47***	-.46***	-.49***	-.64***
Pressure on union leaders	.23*	.16	.25**	.18	.21*	.15
Pattern follower	.29**	-.11	.42***	-.10	.13	-.14
Pattern setter	.00	.02	-.10	-.03	.06	.02
Interpersonal and Personal						
Hostility [b]	-.54***	-.45***	-.61***	-.47***	-.35***	-.39***
Union negotiator skill	-.11	-.34***	-.16	-.39***	.05	-.28**
Management negotiator skill	.03	-.36***	-.17	-.32***	.16	-.36***
Union negotiator experience	.34***	-.13	.21*	-.10	.48***	-.11
Management negotiator experience	.35***	.18	.36***	.21*	.36***	.05
Union in-house negotiator	-.38***	-.09	-.34***	-.15	-.37***	-.14
Management in-house negotiator	-.01	-.15	-.15	-.27**	.06	-.04

[a]Police correlations are based on 64 observations, firefighter on 69. Five joint police and firefighter negotiations are included in the firefighter sample. Pearson product moment correlations are used for all variables in this study.

[b]The sign on this variable is reversed; therefore a negative correlation indicates a positive effect and vice versa.

*Significant beyond the .10 level.
**Significant beyond the .05 level.
***Significant beyond the .01 level.

Selected Benefits and Costs of Compulsory Arbitration

Peter Feuille*

In 1965 Wyoming became the first state to adopt compulsory arbitration[1] to resolve public employee bargaining disputes; by 1979 twenty states had implemented arbitration statutes covering various public employee groups.[2] Our understanding of the potential impact of such arbitration, however, may

*The author wishes to thank John Anderson, Milton Derber, Raymond Horton, Michele Hoyman, Thomas Kochan, Margaret Levi, David Lewin, Gary Long, Myron Roomkin, George Sulzner, and Hoyt Wheeler for their helpful and generous comments. Reprinted from *Industrial and Labor Relations Review*, Vol. 33, No. 1 (October 1979).

not have kept pace with this rapid growth in coverage. Labor relations scholars, for instance, who have done the lion's share of the writing on the subject, have focused on the labor relations functions and effects of arbitration, while generally ignoring its political functions. Similarly, the analyses of these various functions have been shaped by some easily identifiable normative premises, but these premises have received little explicit attention. Furthermore, arbitration is most often viewed as an independent variable that affects such outcome variables as wages, strikes, or bargaining incentives; rarely is it seen as a dependent variable that might indicate the degree of interest group conflict or the distribution of political influence in a jurisdiction.

Accordingly, the following analysis considers three sets of benefits arbitration may provide and two sets of costs the process may impose. It does so by examining the normative premise and operational mechanisms associated with each of these five attributes and by discussing some tests (and accompanying research) that can be used to measure how well or poorly arbitration performs the various functions ascribed to it.

Part of this analysis focuses upon arbitration as a negotiating dispute-settlement process, and thus it deals primarily with the role of *government as employer* representing managerial interests in a unionized workplace. Another part of the analysis focuses upon arbitration as a political process, and thus it deals primarily with the role of *government as regulator* of the entire polity. The first role is based on the relatively narrow efficiency and budgetary interests historically associated with management in employer-employee relations; the second is based on the broader regulatory and service-providing functions of government: managing conflict in matters of public importance and providing the services that policy makers have decided should not be provided through private markets.[3] Although the employer and regulator roles are analytically different, they overlap considerably at the operational level. Therefore, it should be profitable to examine how public dispute-resolution policies directed toward government as employer might also affect government as regulator.[4]

Guardian of the Public Interest

Arbitration's most visible attribute is the ability of its binding award to guarantee (almost) the absence of strikes among covered employees and hence to prevent the interruption of covered public services. Arbitration proponents have used this strike prevention function more than any other to explain why arbitration is desirable, arguing that the prevention of such strikes protects the public's interest in continuously receiving such services. After all, few political slogans are as attractive (and vague) as "the public interest."[5] Because strike prohibitions and arbitration tend to coexist, arbitration may at first seem superfluous as a device to prevent interruptions of public services. Yet policy makers have long recognized that prohibiting strikes merely makes illegal the strikes that do occur. Arbitration serves, therefore, as a no-strike insurance policy. This strike-prevention function ostensibly explains why public safety services—presumably the most "essential" of local government services—are most likely to be covered by arbitration statutes. Of the twenty arbitration states, twelve require arbitration only for public safety personnel,[6] and the remaining eight cover public safety as well as other groups.

The usual test for whether arbitration has protected the public is comparing strike occurrences in jurisdictions with and without arbitration. The available evidence shows that far fewer strikes occur where arbitration is mandated.[7] Although arbitration substantially reduces the probability of strikes compared to other impasse-resolution procedures, it is not a perfect form of no-strike insurance. It does not protect against wildcats or against stoppages over issues outside the scope of bargaining and, as the Montreal police demonstrated in 1969, it may not always prevent an unusually militant union from striking in defiance of an unsatisfactory award (in other words, there may be strikes authorized by the union leadership over issues within the scope of bargaining).

The connections among the public's interests, strikes, and arbitration are more complex, however, than the extent to which strikes and arbitration are negatively correlated. Arbitration's public interest protection function assumes, first, that some or all public employee strikes are inappropriate and, second, that the public's overriding interest in governmental labor relations is "labor peace." In turn, the strength of this first assumption rests upon the reasons why some or all public employees should not have the right to strike, and the second assumption requires a demonstration of a clear public preference for labor peace over all other labor relations alternatives. These two assumptions need to be carefully examined, for if they wilt under critical scrutiny so does much of the support for the public interest protection function of arbitration.

The justification for denying public employees the right to strike is generally argued on the following bases: government is sovereign, elected and selected to reflect the collective desires of the citizenry, and hence it should not be subject to adversarial pressure tactics on behalf of the few at the expense of the many; because most governmental services are offered on a monopolistic basis, unions enjoy tremendous (and unfair) bargaining power when they threaten to strike; and some or all public employee strikes actually harm the public (or will after a certain duration).[8]

In response to the first argument, an appeal to popular sovereignty is an article of faith, not capable of being empirically tested; however, such an appeal ignores the pluralist and selfish nature of the group interests and pressures that pervade the U.S. political system and that form the basis for many (perhaps most) governmental actions.[9] Second, if the unfair bargaining power argument had merit, we should see public employee unions negotiating very favorable contracts. Yet, while there is a substantial body of evidence that public unions have a positive impact on wages,[10] the magnitude of this impact is not large. In fact, it appears to be smaller than in the private sector[11]—where the unions presumably do not enjoy such monopolistic protection. Furthermore, Kochan and Wheeler found that the presence of compulsory arbitration laws contributed much more to firefighter unions' ability to bargain favorable contracts than did the unions' use of militant tactics, such as slowdowns, sickouts, and picketing.[12] In addition, there is no evidence that the public unions in the seven right-to-strike states[13] have fared noticeably better at the bargaining table than their more constrained counterparts in other states. Thus, there is no systematic support for the belief that arbitration should or will serve as a check upon public union monopoly power, nor is there any systematic evidence that supports the proposition that the unions possess such tremendous bargaining power in the first place.

In considering the third argument—that public employee strikes harm the public or will cause such harm after a certain duration—the observer wonders why this assertion never has been systematically documented. There certainly have been enough public employee strikes upon which to perform strike-impact research.[14] Even police and fire strike impacts, which are supposed to be horrendous, have received rather cursory attention. In fact, the industrial relations research community so far has seemed content to rely primarily upon the commercial news media for "data" about the service-deprivation effects of government strikes. Furthermore, it is possible to interpret the public employee strike experience in this country as demonstrating that this strikes-will-cause-harm assertion contains more rhetoric than substance. The hundreds of public employee strikes since 1965 (including 338 protective service strikes during 1965-75[15]), the relatively minor (or even nonexistent) strike penalties, and the slow growth of the legal right to strike strongly suggest that such strikes, including those by police officers and firefighters, are rather minor threats to the public interest (in other words, the public can tolerate such strikes better than conventional wisdom suggests).[16] This *de facto* tolerance of strikes may have occurred because government services are less "essential" to the short-run public welfare than is commonly believed and because government managers are better at providing short-run substitutes for struck services than the conventional wisdom has suggested.[17]

The second assumption inherent in the notion of arbitration as the guardian of the public interest is that the public's only interest, or at least its primary interest, in public labor relations is "labor peace," and that any other interests are relatively unimportant.[18] Expressed another way, this assumption ignores the possibility that the "public" may actually consist of numerous "publics" with multiple interests in public labor relations processes and outcomes that go beyond a desire not to be inconvenienced by strikes.[19] To take an obvious example, parents of school-age children and nonparents alike may prefer no teacher strikes; but the nonparents may be much more willing than the parents to have school district managements use strikes as a tool to support managerial demands for "less" relative to union demands for "more." Furthermore, there are public opinion poll data that suggest that the public may be more accepting of strike rights for some public employee groups than is commonly believed.[20] In addition, the conventional wisdom suggests that public management represents the interests of the public at the bargaining table and in the hearing room. If this suggestion has any merit, recent managerial behavior may also indicate changing public attitudes toward the strike (and certainly changing managerial attitudes). It still may be politically risky for candidates for public office to advocate public employee strike rights, but increasing numbers of public administrators

312

seem to be more accepting of the right to strike, at least when the alternative is compulsory arbitration.[21] Instead of assuming a unitary public with an overriding interest in "labor peace," research might profitably focus on the extent to which different groups hold convergent or divergent views about the costs and benefits of various labor relations impasse arrangements.

The apparent normative premise underlying the public interest protection function of arbitration is that the public is a monolithic entity that is rather helpless in the face of a collective withdrawal of important public services and hence needs and wants to be protected from such withdrawals. The assertions that flow from this premise are either normative expressions of faith or empirically undocumented, and thus it is difficult to demonstrate systematically that the public needs to be protected from such strikes—even those involving "essential" services. Arbitration may substantially reduce the probability of public employee strikes, but the case supporting the need for such a strike prevention device rests on empirically shaky ground.

Guardian of Employee Interests

Arbitration advocates argue that public employee strike prohibitions may make collective bargaining a one-sided process because employees have no readily available mechanism to manipulate management's costs of disagreeing with employee demands. Management can continue the status quo, ignore mediator or factfinder recommendations, or implement unilateral changes (at least after impasse), but the employees have no countervailing weapons; thus there is a serious imbalance of negotiating power in management's favor. Arbitration should correct this imbalance, for it eliminates management's ability to prolong the status quo indefinitely, ignore third party recommendations, or impose its own terms (it also eliminates union abilities to do these same things, but it is rare that the unions want or are able to do them). Arbitration, then, should increase the employees' negotiating strength until it is approximately equal with management's.

Some relevant tests of arbitration's effectiveness in fulfilling this function are the extent to which it promotes good-faith negotiations and the extent to which arbitrated and negotiated outcomes are distributed in a manner that balances union and management interests. There are reports from some jurisdictions that the introduction of arbitration promotes more genuine negotiating behavior by management,[22] but there is also evidence that in many instances arbitration inhibits the parties' ability or willingness to negotiate their own agreements.[23]

The distribution of outcomes could be measured by comparing the parties' bargaining goals with actual outcomes, by comparing bargained agreements with arbitrated awards, by comparing award winners and losers under final-offer arbitration, or by examining the parties' satisfaction (or lack of it) with the distributional nature of negotiation-arbitration processes. Some labor relations observers have concluded that arbitration outcomes are distributed in a balanced manner,[24] but many municipal managers object to arbitration, in large part because they perceive the process as more supportive of employee than employer interests.[25] Furthermore, the recurring line-up in state legislatures of union support for arbitration and managerial opposition to it[26] means that the unions perceive that arbitration is to their advantage in bargaining and managements perceive it is to their disadvantage. Some evidence suggests that these perceptions are accurate,[27] and so parties seem to be acting rationally. This line-up of support and opposition plus more rigorous research evidence suggest strongly that arbitration has worked effectively to enhance public employee negotiating interests.

Arbitration also may protect employee interests by acting as a labor market leveling mechanism. To the extent that Ross's "orbits of coercive comparisons" paradigm accurately specifies the process by which employee wage demands are formulated,[28] and to the extent that arbitration decisions are made primarily on labor market comparability criteria,[29] arbitration becomes "the visible hand" by which members of similar bargaining units seek to be treated similarly (at least within the same state). There is some evidence that on wages such an impact does occur, especially on behalf of covered employees in small bargaining units at the low end of the wage distribution.[30] This levelling or "regression to the mean" impact may cause some observers to conclude that arbitration is an efficient and effective method for ensuring equity and hence protecting employee interests, while others may question the need for such a mechanism in the absence of any persuasive reason why the covered employees should have such a protective device and other employees should not.

The normative premise upon which this arbitration function is based is that public employees with no right to strike should be protected against managerial domination of the bargaining process. The logical implication of this premise is that arbitration should be most prevalent in those situations in which the employees are on the short end of the largest power imbalances. As discussed earlier, however, arbitration laws apply disproportionately to those groups with the greatest withholding power and who typically have acquired considerable political influence—police officers and firefighters.[31] Thus, the two occupational groups who would be expected to negotiate most effectively without arbitration are the two groups with the highest incidence of arbitration coverage. This fact suggests that there are distinct limits to the policy makers' acceptance of the employee interest-protection function as a rationale for why arbitration statutes should be enacted: such a rationale applies only to those employees represented by unions who happen to have the ability to manipulate skillfully the legislative process to their own advantage. In short, the incidence of arbitration coverage seems to reflect less concern among policy makers for the general welfare and more concern for accommodating the requests of influential interest groups.

Regulator of Interest-Group Conflict

From a broad political perspective (in contrast to the narrower labor relations perspectives just examined), arbitration may perform a useful conflict regulation function. The unionization of public employees brought out into the open a set of group interests (those of the various employees and their representatives) that represent claims upon public resources that were potentially rather costly. Although such unionization did not create these claims, it certainly made them more visible, and it helped make overt the potential conflicts between public employees and the public. The widespread use of collective bargaining, with its militant posturing and strident rhetoric, and the increasingly frequent use of the strike became the visible manifestations of these interest-group conflicts.[32] One policy response to this situation has been to provide third party impasse resolution procedures to regulate and contain the interorganizational and intraorganizational pressures that contribute to such overt conflict.[33]

These impasse procedures, including arbitration, regulate public–public-employee conflict by institutionalizing trilateral decision mechanisms for the formation of public employment conditions and by absorbing the advocates' demands for particular outcomes. Arbitration performs this regulatory function primarily through the finality, impartiality, compromising, and face-saving features of the process. Supposedly, all the parties affected by an award will accept it because of legal requirements to do so and because of its issuance by a neutral third party who has attempted to balance employee and employer interests. Furthermore, managerial and union leaders can protect themselves from intraorganizational retaliation from their constituents by blaming the arbitrator for any unfavorable outcomes. As a result of these attributes, arbitration is said to absorb the interest group pressures that might cause strikes or other disruptions and, by absorbing them, to contribute to political and social stability. The normative premise underlying this arbitration function is that society needs such conflict-absorption mechanisms to contribute to societal stability.

Arbitration's effectiveness in performing this regulatory function can be measured by examining the legality of the process and the extent to which affected unions and managements comply with or accept the process and awards, strikes are prevented, arbitration reduces bargaining hostility, and the affected parties believe their legitimate interests have been adequately considered in the process. A review of relevant court decisions suggests that most of the time arbitration is constitutionally acceptable and hence its awards are legally enforceable.[34] The evidence also suggests that union and management compliance with the process is widespread, if not always enthusiastic, at least in those states with substantial bargaining and arbitration histories.[35] In addition, as noted previously, arbitration is associated with a general absence of strikes.

There is little systematic evidence about the extent to which arbitration has reduced bargaining hostility or fostered impasse-resolution legitimacy perceptions among the parties. To the extent that arbitration prevents strikes and strike threats it may reduce bargaining hostility, but these nonevents are very difficult to measure. There is a substantial body of evidence that union representatives believe arbitration legitimately considers employee interests, but this is not so for management representatives. And there simply are insufficient data to determine if citizens' views about arbitration are supportive, hostile, or apathetic.

The available evidence suggests, then, that arbitration effectively absorbs selected employer and employee pressures that might emerge as overt conflict and, in so doing, contributes to the institutionalized resolution of workplace conflict already begun by collective bargaining. However, the sharp divergence in enthusiasm for arbitration displayed by union and management representatives suggests that there are very different perceptions about the costs and benefits attached to arbitration's conflict-regulation function, and it appears unlikely that these perceptions will be reconciled. Furthermore, because empirical testing of this arbitration function may be difficult given its process (rather than outcome) focus, this function will win support primarily through a value judgment by those who place great importance on political pluralism and political stability.

Inhibitor of Representative Government

The conclusion that arbitration performs a useful political function is contrary to the conclusion that arbitration is a decision process inimical to the tenets and operation of our system of representative democratic government. This latter conclusion is based on the normative premise that our political system should be structured to reflect the will of the governed, as expressed through a pluralistic diffusion of interests, by allowing for active and legitimate groups to make themselves heard during public decision processes.[36] However, compulsory arbitration contains two related elements that detract from this desired governmental system: a lack of accountability for public decisions and an intensification of the bureaucratic forces that insulate public decision processes from public influence.

Arbitration allows for authoritative public allocation decisions to be made in a relatively private manner by a nonelected third party who is not directly accountable for his or her decisions.[37] Regardless of whether this delegation of authority is constitutionally permissible, it is deemed politically undesirable because it reduces management's accountability for these allocations of scarce public resources and allows public officials (and union leaders) to evade their responsibilities for these allocations by using arbitrators as mechanisms to absorb any constituent dissatisfactions with these decisions. In other words, arbitration is a classic example of the delegation of public authority to private actors that has pervaded our post-New Deal political system.[38]

Similarly, arbitration represents an undesirable intensification of the bureaucratic-professional control over governmental employer-employee relations begun by civil service and carried forward by collective bargaining.[39] As civil service and collective bargaining have come to be administered by professionals in numerous state and local bureaucracies, so arbitration is administered in a similar manner by labor relations professionals. One of the procedural costs of such professionalization, however, may be to increase the proportion of allocative decisions that are made by labor relations professionals whose primary allegiances are to the arbitration process itself and to their immediate union and management clients and who are much less concerned with the interests of the larger groups (such as taxpayers and other employees) affected by arbitration awards.[40] A second cost may be the development of arbitration constituencies among these professionals that act to ensure the continuation of arbitration legislation because of the tangible benefits (such as budget appropriations, income, and prestige) that arbitration provides to them.[41]

The major weakness of this critical view is that it tends to overlook the extent to which arbitration procedures can be "structured and limited in such a way as to preserve both the appearance and reality of the democratic process. . . ."[42] For instance, legislative bodies may restrict the scope of arbitrable subjects, limit the coverage of the arbitration legislation, specify exceedingly tight decision criteria, require that decisions be made by tripartite panels instead of single arbitrators, and mandate final-offer selection rather than conventional decision making. These and other procedural attempts to limit arbitral discretion may help make arbitration and the "democratic process" more compatible, though it is likely that arbitration critics would argue that the search for these procedural characteristics is an explicit admission that arbitration is inimical to democratic government.

This critical view of arbitration is difficult to test empirically, for it is not addressed to substantive differences between arbitrated and negotiated outcomes but to the processes used to produce those outcomes. Similarly, it is difficult to demonstrate empirically that arbitration is or may be inimical to democratic government without first formulating an explicit and normative definition of democracy. Furthermore, even with such a formulation, it may not be possible to give operational and hence measurable meaning to such key phrases as "accountability" and "professionalization." Instead, it is likely that this arbitration function will attract adherents and critics on the basis of its appeal to personal preference.[43]

Inhibitor of Genuine Bargaining

The belief that arbitration has a costly impact on bargaining incentives is often used to criticize the arbitral process. This conclusion is based upon the normative premise that collective bargaining is a valuable and desirable decision-making process that should be protected from inimical forces. Arbitration is cast as a villain because it does not have the voluntary and joint decision-making properties of bargaining and because it may lure unions and managements away from the bargaining process.

More precisely, arbitration may be a too-easily-used escape route from the difficult trade-off choices that must usually be made in order to negotiate an agreement. Arbitration will be invoked because one or both sides believe that an arbitration award may be more favorable than a negotiated agreement *and* because one or both believe the costs of using arbitration are comparatively low (none of the trauma and costs of a work stoppage and none of the uncertainty of using other forms of political influence). As a result of this cost-benefit calculus, the availability of arbitration may have a "chilling effect" upon the parties' efforts to negotiate an agreement, and over time there may be a "narcotic effect" as the parties become arbitration addicts who habitually rely upon arbitrators to write their labor contracts. The logical conclusion of this reasoning is that arbitration will destroy and replace collective bargaining.

Researchers and practitioners have searched diligently for techniques to make arbitration and bargaining compatible, and this search has produced such proposals as final-offer arbitration (in all its permutations), closed-offer arbitration, and labor-management arbitration screening committees. In addition, there has been considerable research to measure this compatibility (or lack of it). The most widely used method seems to be the cross-sectional or longitudinal comparison of arbitration awards, as a proportion of all settlements, with other settlement techniques within or across one or more jurisdictions.[44] A second method measures the number of issues taken to arbitration under different procedures.[45] A third method tracks the amount of movement, usually on wages, exhibited during negotiations under arbitration, compared with no arbitration, to see if the availability of a binding award affects compromising activity.[46] While most of this research gathers data from actual negotiations, recently some researchers have used laboratory simulations to test more carefully arbitration's impacts on negotiating behaviors.[47] Another method examines negotiator and arbitrator attitudes about various arbitral features.[48] In short, we probably have a larger body of research results on arbitration's impact on bargaining than on any other aspect of the process.

Generalizations are hazardous, but this research seems to support the following conclusions. First, the availability of arbitration has not destroyed bargaining, for in practically all arbitration jurisdictions a majority of agreements are negotiated. Second, in many cases the parties use the arbitration process as a forum for additional negotiations (or perhaps as a forum for their truly serious bargaining). Third, however, there are many union-management pairs who seem to have become quite dependent upon arbitration, with such dependency influenced by employer size, degree of fiscal scarcity, prior use of impasse procedures, bargaining hostility, and so forth. Fourth, the shape of the impasse-arbitration procedure may affect the parties' use of such procedures, for negotiating behaviors seem to vary with the nature and extent of arbitral discretion (the presence of a final-offer selection requirement or the availability of factfinding recommendations, for example). In short, collective bargaining generally functions as a viable process in the presence of arbitration, but there is no doubt that arbitration has also increased union and management dependency upon third parties to resolve their disputes and in so doing has frequently sapped the vitality of the bargaining process.

Perhaps most important, there are no precise formulas with which to evaluate the research results. This means that a given body of data can be used to support differing and even opposing conclusions[49] and that personal preferences can play a strong role in the conclusions reached. Given that both collective bargaining and compulsory arbitration represent strongly held labor relations value judgments, the influence of personal preferences on these conclusions should not surprise anyone.

318

Discussion

The major components of each of these arbitration functions are summarized in the following table. The components include the impact that the procedure has (or is designed to have), the normative premise upon which each function is based, the operational mechanisms by which each impact occurs, and some of the measures that might be used to evaluate how well or poorly arbitration performs these various functions. As the table suggests, arbitration advocates can point to three major benefits that arbitration might provide, while the skeptics can emphasize two sets of costs that these procedures may impose. The connecting thread among all these positive and negative functions is the set of premises upon which they are constructed, for each

TABLE
Selected Components of Arbitration Functions

Arbitration's Purpose or Impact	Normative Premise	Operational Mechanisms	Measurement Tests
Protector of the public interest	The public needs and wants to be protected from strikes.	A binding award prevents strikes.	Absence of strikes.
Protector of employee interests	Employees should bargain from position of equal strength with management.	Union can invoke arbitration over employer's objection and employer must accept award.	Comparison of awards with negotiated outcomes where arbitration is not available.
Regulator of interest-group conflict	There is a need for social and political stability.	Third party decision making absorbs and accommodates conflicting group presures.	Comparison of the degree of overt labor relations conflict and hostility with and without arbitration.
Inhibitor of representative government	Public decision processes should be accesible and accountable.	Public authority is delegated to nonaccountable third parties.	Comparison of accessibility and accountability of labor relations decision processes with and without arbitration.
Inhibitor of genuine collective bargaining	Bargaining incentives should be protected and strengthened.	There exists a high probability of satisfactory award and low usage costs.	Comparison of bargaining behaviors with and without arbitration.

premise assumes that there is some group, process, or political condition that needs to be protected or enhanced. Much of the debate among students of arbitration seems to result from the different normative premises they hold; and since there is no formula for determining the relative importance of these premises, there is no reason to expect that there will emerge a single arbitration paradigm upon which everybody can, will, or should agree. These same students, however, should agree that since arbitration has multiple impacts, it should be evaluated along several dimensions rather than simply looking at how well it prevents strikes.

This diversity of impact leads to a second point—that although arbitration is directed at government acting in its role as (unionized) employer, arbitration's more important long-run effects may be upon government as regulator of the polity. For instance, artibration's most valuable long-run function may be the manner in which it quietly absorbs and accommodates conflicting interest group claims over scarce public resources. The price for this accomodation, however, may be the insulation of these allocative decisions from the direct influence of many individuals or groups with strong interests in these decisions. In addition, such insulation may be particularly unwelcome because it occurs primarily at the local level, which is the level of government supposedly most responsive to citizen influence.

Whatever arbitration's political impacts may be, they need to be discussed in tentative terms, for there seems to be a sort of Gresham's Law of Arbitration Research in which researchers' attention is drawn toward arbitration's labor relations impacts.[50] With all its labor relations labels, though, public sector interest arbitration is established through the political rule-making process (primarily at the state level) and then operates as a surrogate for the political resource-allocation process (primarily at the local level).[51] Even though these political roles and impacts may be somewhat "messy" to study, they deserve more research attention than they have received to date. In particular, there needs to be a careful examination of the balance struck between the public-interest and private-interest impacts of arbitration.

As noted earlier, the most visible rationale for arbitration has been the perceived need to protect the public from the withdrawal of supposedly vital public services (though such perceptions seem to be based on little or no empirical foundation). However, the public interest appears to refer only to this strike-prevention objective, for once an arbitration system is implemented and working there seems to be little or no room for formal public participation in the arbitration proceedings. Furthermore, arbitration's availability reduces outcome uncertainty by eliminating the need for unions (or managements) to assume the risks of work stoppages or other forms of political-influence manipulation to press their demands.[52] Even if arbitration is not used, its availability tends to ensure that over time the level of negotiated benefits in a jurisdiction will not diverge substantially from the level of benefits obtainable via arbitration.[53] In short, the passage of arbitration legislation is consistent with Downs's theory that producers will influence government action more than consumers "because most men earn their incomes in one area but spend them in many. . . ."[54]

The adoption of the view that arbitration is primarily a response to interest group pressures should have a salutary effect on public labor relations research and policy making. Such a view seems far more consistent with how arbitration legislation actually is passed and renewed than the suggestion that such legislation results from the policy makers' concern for the general welfare. Similarly, this view might provide a useful framework for investigating and explaining why different jurisdictions have adopted so many different arbitration procedures. Further, this view would explicitly allow for the use of arbitration as a dependent variable that measures the distribution of political influence necessary to shape public labor relations systems in a desired direction. In addition, the interest group concept should focus more attention than has occurred to date on the political roles and effects of arbitration. Finally, thinking of arbitration as a response to interest-group pressures suggests the replacement of the unverified assumption that public employee strikes are inappropriate with empirical investigations of the comparative costs and benefits of strikes and arbitration. These investigations should produce much more informed debate about the desired shape of public dispute-resolution arrangements than has occurred so far.

Footnotes

1. In pursuit of brevity and clarity "arbitration" shall henceforth be used in this analysis to refer only to compulsory and binding interest arbitration, except when specifically noted otherwise.
2. Alaska, Connecticut, Hawaii, Iowa, Maine, Massachusetts, Michigan, Minnesota, Montana, Nebraska, Nevada, New Jersey, New York, Oregon, Pennsylvania, Rhode Island, Vermont, Washington, Wisconsin, and Wyoming. (In addition, the supreme courts in South Dakota and Utah declared unconstitutional compulsory arbitration statutes in those two states.) These statutes vary considerably in age, coverage, scope, and procedural requirements, but they all mandate the binding resolution of bargaining impasses between covered employees and employers.
3. Edward C. Banfield and James Q. Wilson, *City Politics* (New York: Vintage Books, 1963), p. 18.
4. Some caveats: no claim is made that the arbitration functions examined here exhaust the total possible list; relatively little attention is given to arbitration's procedural variations; and this analysis deals with bargaining and arbitration primarily among local governments in the United States.
5. For a complex definition of "the public interest" (in the context of public sector labor relations), see Richard P. Schick and Jean J. Couturier, *The Public Interest in Government Labor Relations* (Cambridge, Mass.: Ballinger, 1977), ch. 1. For a much shorter definition (in the same context), see Raymond D. Horton, "Arbitration, Arbitrators, and the Public Interest," *Industrial and Labor Relations Review,* Vol. 28, No. 4 (July 1975), p. 503. For an insightful general discussion of the use of the phrase, see Murray Edelman, *The Symbolic Uses of Politics* (Urbana: University of Illinois Press, 1967), pp. 134-38.
6. Hawaii, Massachusetts, Michigan, Minnesota, Montana, Nevada, New Jersey, New York, Oregon, Pennsylvania, Washington, Wyoming.
7. Hoyt N. Wheeler, "An Analysis of Fire Fighter Strikes," *Labor Law Journal,* Vol. 26, No. 1 (January 1975), pp. 17-20; J. Joseph Loewenberg, Walter J. Gershenfeld,

H.J. Glasbeek, B.A. Hepple, and Kenneth F. Walker, *Compulsory Arbitration* (Lexington, Mass.: D.C. Heath, 1976), p. 165; James L. Stern, Charles M. Rehmus, J. Joseph Loewenberg, Hirschel Kasper, Barbara D. Dennis, *Final-Offer Arbitration* (Lexington, Mass.: D.C. Heath, 1975), p. 189; and Peter Feuille, *Final Offer Arbitration,* Public Employee Relations Library Series No. 50 (Chicago: International Personnel Management Association, 1975), pp. 10-11.

8. This list borrows heavily from David Lewin, "Collective Bargaining and the Right to Strike," in A. Lawrence Chickering, ed., *Public Employee Unions* (San Francisco: Institute for Contemporary Studies, 1976), pp. 145-63.

9. For instance, see David B. Truman, *The Governmental Process* (New York: Knopf, 1951); Edward C. Banfield, *Political Influence* (New York: Free Press, 1961); Banfield and Wilson, *City Politics.*

10. For a review of these studies through 1976, see David Lewin, "Public Sector Labor Relations: A Review Essay," *Labor History,* Vol. 18, No. 1 (Winter 1977), pp. 133-44.

11. Sharon P. Smith, *Equal Pay in the Public Sector: Fact or Fantasy* (Princeton: Industrial Relations Section, Princeton University, 1977), pp. 120-29.

12. Thomas A. Kochan and Hoyt N. Wheeler, "Municipal Collective Bargaining: A Model and Analysis of Bargaining Outcomes," *Industrial and Labor Relations Review,* Vol. 29, No. 1 (October 1975), pp. 46-66. Gerhart found a positive relationship between favorable union contract provisions and a strike-activity index among local government employees, but this relationship was not statistically significant in the presence of other explanatory variables. See Paul F. Gerhart, "Determinants of Bargaining Outcomes in Local Government Labor Negotiations," *Industrial and Labor Relations Review,* Vol. 29, No. 3 (April 1976), pp. 331-51.

13. Alaska, Hawaii, Oregon, Montana, Minnesota, Pennsylvania, and Vermont. In 1978 Wisconsin started allowing municipal employees to strike if both the union and the employer refused to use final-offer arbitration to resolve their dispute.

14. Contrast the apparent scarcity of current public sector strike impact research with the fairly substantial amount of research on "emergency" strike impacts in the private sector performed mostly in the 1950s, which is nicely reviewed in Donald E. Cullen, *National Emergency Strikes,* ILR Paperback No. 7 (Ithaca: Cornell University, New York State School of Labor and Industrial Relations, 1968), ch. 2.

15. This number is the sum of figures extracted from a variety of U.S. Bureau of Labor Statistics publications on government work stoppages: *Work Stoppages in Government, 1958-68,* Report 348 (1970); *Government Work Stoppages, 1960, 1969, and 1970,* summary report (November 1971); *Work Stoppages in Government, 1972, 1973, 1974, 1975,* Reports 434 (1974), 437 (1975), 453 (1976), and 483 (1976), respectively. The 1965-70 strikes are for employees providing "administration and protection services"; the 1971-75 figures are for employees in "protective occupations." Thus, the two categories are not strictly comparable, and they include more than just police and fire strikes.

16. There is no doubt that many public employee strikes can and do cause considerable apprehension, annoyance, and inconvenience, but they rarely seem actually to hurt the public health and safety. Such assessments, however, inevitably reflect the assessor's definitions (which usually are implicit rather than explicit) of such terms as "inconvenience," "hurt," and "health and safety." See John C. Meyer, Jr., "Discontinuity in the Delivery of Public Service: Analyzing the Police Strike," *Human Relations,* Vol. 29, No. 6 (June 1976), pp. 545-57. In addition, it is quite likely that the views espoused here will differ sharply from those of public managers (and union leaders) who have worked

eighteen-hour days struggling with the many apprehensions, annoyances, and inconveniences created by such strikes.

17. The belief that public employee strikes will harm the public is based in large part on a very negative view of the ability of public managers to cope with such strikes. While there is little or no systematic research addressed specifically to this topic, several case studies suggest that public managers have learned to cope rather effectively with strike situations. For reports on a variety of police strikes, see Hervey A. Juris and Peter Feuille, *Police Unionism* (Lexington, Mass.: D.C. Heath, 1973), pp. 85-89; Richard M. Ayres, "Case Studies of Police Strikes in Two Cities — Albuquerque and Oklahoma City," and William J. Bopp, Paul Chignell, and Charles Maddox, "The San Francisco Police Strike of 1975; A Case Study," *Journal of Police Science and Administration,* Vol. 5, No. 1 (1977), pp. 19-31 and 32-42, respectively.

18. See Lewin, "Collective Bargaining and the Right to Strike," pp. 152-57.

19. The assertion that the public's paramount labor relations objective is to avoid or minimize the inconvenience of strikes (which is said to be a prime source of union power) has never been specifically tested, but it has received considerable publicity. See Harry H. Wellington and Ralph K. Winter, Jr., *The Unions and 'he Cities* (Washington, D.C.: The Brookings Institution, 1971), ch. 1. Similarly untested is the corollary of this assertion, that the public, when inconvenienced, will always pressure management to settle the strike and terminate the inconvenience. For a well-publicized example of contrary behavior, see "Strike of San Francisco City Craft Unions Fails to Win the Support of Public or Labor," *Wall Street Journal,* April 15, 1976, p. 30.

20. See Schick and Couturier, *The Public Interest in Government Labor Relations,* pp. 244-45; and Victor E. Flango and Robert Dudley, "Who Supports Public Employee Strikes?" *Journal of Collective Negotiations in the Public Sector,* Vol. 7, No. 1 (1978), pp. 1-10.

21. For example, the Missouri Municipal League recently approved a campaign to lobby for right-to-strike legislation in that state — for the express purpose of preventing compulsory arbitration legislation. See Bureau of National Affairs, *Government Employee Relations Report,* No. 779 (October 2, 1978), p. 17. For reports of statements by various managerial representatives or commentators that managements prefer strikes to compulsory arbitration, see Bureau of National Affairs, *Government Employee Relations Report,* No. 696 (February 21, 1977), pp. 15-17; No. 702 (April 4, 1977), pp. 12-13; No. 725 (September 12, 1977), pp. 21-22; and No. 754 (April 10, 1978), p. 19.

22. See the reports on arbitration in Michigan, Pennsylvania, and Wisconsin in Stern, et al., *Final-Offer Arbitration.*

23. See Hoyt N. Wheeler, "How Compulsory Arbitration Affects Compromise Activity," *Industrial Relations,* Vol. 17, No. 1 (February 1978), pp. 80-84; John C. Anderson and Thomas A. Kochan, "Impasse Procedures in the Canadian Federal Service," *Industrial and Labor Relations Review,* Vol. 30, No. 3 (April 1977), pp. 283-301; and Peter Feuille, "Final Offer Arbitration and the Chilling Effect," *Industrial Relations,* Vol. 14, No. 3 (October 1975), pp. 302-10. As would be expected, this (and other) research also suggests that negotiating incentives may vary with the shape of arbitration procedures and the nature of dispute-resolution alternatives available.

24. Stern, et al., *Final-Offer Arbitration.*

25. Thomas A. Kochan, Ronald G. Ehrenberg, Jean Baderschneider, Todd Jick, and Mordehai Mironi, *An Evaluation of Impasse Procedures for Police and Fire-fighters in New York State* (Ithaca: Cornell University, New York State School of Industrial and Labor Relations, 1977), ch. 10; and Hoyt N. Wheeler and Frank

Owen, "Impasse Resolution Preferences of Fire Fighters and Municipal Negotiators," *Journal of Collective Negotiations in the Public Sector,* Vol. 5, No. 3 (1978), pp. 215-24.

26. Stern, et al., *Final-Offer Arbitration;* Thomas A. Kochan, "The Politics of Interest Arbitration," *The Arbitration Journal,* Vol. 33, No. 1 (March 1978), pp. 5-9; Bureau of National Affairs, *Government Employee Relations Report,* No. 717 (July 11, 1977), pp. 13-14.

27. Kochan and Wheeler, "Municipal Collective Bargaining"; Stern, et al., *Final-Offer Arbitration,* ch. 6; Kochan, et al., *An Evaluation of Impasse Procedures,* ch. 6; Paul C. Somers, "An Evaluation of Final-Offer Arbitration in Massachusetts," *Journal of Collective Negotiations in the Public Sector,* Vol. 6, No. 3 (1977), pp. 193-228.

28. Arthur M. Ross, *Trade Union Wage Policy* (Berkeley: University of California Press, 1948).

29. Charles J. Morris, "The Role of Interest Arbitration in a Collective Bargaining System," *Industrial Relations Law Journal,* Vol. 1, No. 3 (Fall 1976), pp. 470 and 477; Irving Bernstein, *The Arbitration of Wages* (Berkeley: University of California Press, 1954), pp. 26-33; and David B. Ross, "The Arbitration of Public Employee Wage Disputes," *Industrial and Labor Relations Review,* Vol. 23, No. 1 (October 1969), pp. 3-14.

30. Stern, et al., *Final-Offer Arbitration,* pp. 144-45; Kochan, et al., *An Evaluation . . . ,* pp. 216-17.

31. Political influence is difficult to measure, but there are some sources that attest to the reputation for political expertise police and fire unions have acquired: Juris and Feuille, *Police Unionism;* Don Berney, "Law and Order Politics: A History and Role Analysis of Police Officer Organizations," Ph.D. dissertation, University of Washington, 1971; Philip Kienast, "Police and Fire Fighter Organizations," Ph.D. dissertation, Michigan State University, 1972; Jack Steiber, *Public Employee Unionism* (Washington, D.C.: The Brookings Institution, 1973), pp. 204-07.

32. For two contrasting paradigms about the role of collective bargaining in the conflict between public employees and the public, compare Wellington and Winter, *The Unions and the Cities,* ch. 1 and Clyde W. Summers, "Public Employee Bargaining: A Political Perspective," *Yale Law Journal,* Vol. 83, No. 6 (May 1974), pp. 1156-1200.

33. Perhaps the best exposition of this regulatory function is in George T. Sulzner, "The Political Functions of Impasse Procedures," *Industrial Relations,* Vol. 16, No. 3 (October 1977), pp. 290-97. Much of the material in this section is based on Sulzner's analysis.

34. For such a review, see Morris, "The Role of Interest Arbitration in a Collective Bargaining System," pp. 487-91. As Morris notes, a few state supreme courts have struck down arbitration statutes as unconstitutional, usually on the grounds that such statutes unlawfully delegate legislative authority. For reports on two such state supreme court decisions (in Colorado and Utah), see Bureau of National Affairs, *Government Employee Relations Report,* no. 708 (May 16, 1977), pp. 10-11, and No. 726 (September 19, 1977), pp. 12-13.

35. Stern, et al., *Final-Offer Arbitration.*

36. This premise is contained in Wellington and Winter, *The Unions and the Cities,* ch. 1, and appears to be based on Robert A. Dahl, *A Preface to Democratic Theory* (Chicago: University of Chicago Press, 1956).

37. For a more complete statement of this characterization of arbitration, see Raymond D. Horton, "Arbitration, Arbitrators, and the Public Interest," *Industrial and Labor Relations Review,* Vol. 28, No. 4 (July 1975), pp. 497-507.

38. Lowi refers to this phenomenon as "interest-group liberalism"; see Theodore J. Lowi, *The End of Liberalism* (New York: Norton, 1969), ch. 3.
39. For a brief discussion of the professionalization of governmental collective bargaining, see Thomas M. Love and George T. Sulzner, "Political Implications of Public Employee Bargaining," *Industrial Relations,* Vol. 11, No. 1 (February 1972), pp. 23-25.
40. For instance, there is some evidence that advocate representatives, mediators, and factfinders pay little if any attention to the "public interest" during contract negotiations or impasse resolution. See Thomas A. Kochan, George P. Huber, and L.L. Cummings, "Determinants of Intraorganizational Conflict in Collective Bargaining in the Public Sector," *Administrative Science Quarterly,* Vol. 20, No. 1 (March 1975), pp. 10-23, esp. Table 1; Kenneth Kressel, *Labor Mediation: An Exploratory Survey* (Albany: Association of Labor Mediation Agencies, 1972); and Jack Steiber and Benjamin W. Wolkinson, "Fact-Finding Viewed by Fact-Finders: The Michigan Experience," *Labor Law Journal,* Vol. 28, No. 2 (February 1977), pp. 89-101.
41. An interesting research effort would be to examine the actions or positions of state arbitration administrative agencies and arbitrators in those situations in which the renewal of an arbitration statute is being considered by the legislature. For a report on the position of the New York State Public Employment Relations Board during the 1977 arbitration renewal debate in that state, see Thomas A. Kochan, "The Politics of Interest Arbitration," *The Arbitration Journal,* Vol. 33, No. 1 (March 1978), pp. 5-9.
42. Joseph Grodin, "Political Aspects of Public Sector Interest Arbitration," *Industrial Relations Law Journal,* Vol. 1, No. 1 (Spring 1976), p. 24. In this article Grodin explores how arbitration procedures can be made more compatible with the democratic process.
43. For an example, see Horton, "Arbitration, Arbitrators, and the Public Interest," and then see Joseph Krislov's "Comment" and Horton's "Reply" in *Industrial and Labor Relations Review,* Vol. 31, No. 1 (October 1977), pp. 71-77.
44. In addition to the sources cited in footnote 23, see Stern, et al., *Final-Offer Arbitration;* Peter Feuille, "Final-Offer Arbitration and Negotiating Incentives," *The Arbitration Journal,* Vol. 32, No. 3 (September 1977), pp. 203-20; Thomas A. Kochan and Jean Baderschneider, "Dependence Upon Impasse Procedures: Police and Firefighters in New York State," *Industrial and Labor Relations Review,* Vol. 31, No. 4 (July 1978), pp. 431-49; Hoyt N. Wheeler, "Compulsory Arbitration: A 'Narcotic Effect'?" *Industrial Relations,* Vol. 14, No. 1 (February 1975), pp. 117-20; Daniel G. Gallagher, "Interest Arbitration Under the Iowa Public Employment Relations Act," *The Arbitration Journal,* Vol. 33, No. 3 (September 1978), pp. 30-36; and David B. Lipsky and Thomas A. Barocci, "Final-Offer Arbitration and Public-Safety Employees: The Massachusetts Experience," Industrial Relations Research Association, *Proceedings of the Thirtieth Annual Winter Meeting* (Madison: IRRA, 1978), pp. 65-76.
45. Mollie H. Bowers, "A Study of Legislated Interest Arbitration and Collective Bargaining in the Public Safety Services in Michigan and Pennsylvania," Ph.D. dissertation, Cornell University, 1974; and Stern, et al., *Final-Offer Arbitration.*
46. Wheeler, "How Compulsory Arbitration Affects Compromise Activity"; Kochan, et al., *An Evaluation of Impasse Procedures.*
47. William W. Notz and Frederick A. Starke, "Final Offer versus Conventional Arbitration as Means of Conflict Management," *Administrative Science Quarterly,* Vol. 23, No. 2 (June 1978), pp. 189-203; A.V. Subbarao, "The Impact of Binding Interest Arbitration on Negotiation and Process Outcome: An Experimental Study," *The Journal of Conflict Resolution,* Vol. 22, No. 1 (March 1978), pp. 79-104.

48. Stern, et al., *Final-Offer Arbitration;* Kochan, et al., *An Evaluation of Impasse Procedures.*

49. For instance, see Mark Thompson and James Cairnie, "Compulsory Arbitration: The Case of British Columbia Teachers," *Industrial and Labor Relations Review,* Vol. 27, No. 1 (October 1973), pp. 3-17; Peter Feuille, "Analyzing Compulsory Arbitration Experiences: The Role of Personal Preferences—Comment," and Thompson and Cairnie, "Reply," *Industrial and Labor Relations Review,* Vol. 28, No. 3 (April 1975), pp. 432-38.

50. A recent review of political science and industrial relations journals revealed that almost all the scholarly writing on arbitration, including the few examinations of its political role and impacts, has appeared in industrial relations outlets. Quite naturally, most of this writing focuses on how well or poorly arbitration and collective bargaining fit together. Given the labor relations training and interests of these authors, and the availability of relatively precise (or quantifiable) data about the labor relations impacts of arbitration, this concentration of research efforts is not surprising.

51. A particularly useful research topic is whether arbitration alters the proportionate shares of government resources allocated to covered and uncovered employee groups.

52. Arbitration may be particularly important to the unions as a risk-avoidance mechanism when they are faced with hostile environmental forces, such as "taxpayer revolts." During such periods, arbitration may be less important to the unions as a mechanism to get "more" and more important as a mechanism to protect against "less."

53. One recent analysis demonstrated that within a single jurisdiction negotiated and arbitrated outcomes are quite interdependent. Henry S. Farber and Harry C. Katz, "Interest Arbitration, Outcomes, and the Incentive to Bargain: The Role of Risk Preference," *Industrial and Labor Relations Review,* Vol. 33, No. 1 (October 1979), pp. 55-63. See Stern, et al., *Final-Offer Arbitration,* and Kochan, et al., *An Evaluation of Impasse Procedures,* for empirical results showing that the differences between negotiated and arbitrated wage increases are rather modest.

54. Anthony Downs, *An Economic Theory of Democracy* (New York: Harper and Row, 1957), p. 254.

Arbitration in the Canadian Federal Public Service

John C. Anderson*

With the inception of collective bargaining in the public sector in Canada and the United States came a continuing debate over the right of public employees to strike. The encroachment on governmental sovereignty, the essential nature of many government services, and the availability of political rather than economic power have each been cited as reasons for the removal of the

---

*Graduate School of Business, Columbia University. This paper was written especially for this volume.

right to strike.[1] As a consequence, the adoption and use of some variety of compulsory arbitration has become increasingly widespread. Currently all eleven Canadian jurisdictions and 20 U.S. states have implemented some form of arbitration for select public employees groups.[2] The federal government of Canada was the first jurisdiction to provide choice of dispute resolution mechanisms, either strike or arbitration, to the parties.[3] The purpose of this paper is to evaluate the arbitration procedure under this system. In doing so, I will (1) describe the law and impasse procedure provided for federal government employees, (2) outline and discuss a number of criteria for assessing the effectiveness of an impasse procedure, (3) present the results of an examination of the experience of bargaining units under the procedure over eight rounds of negotiation between 1967 and 1979, and (4) discuss the implications of the analysis for the future of arbitration in the federal public service.

The Public Service Staff Relations Act

Public service employees of the Government of Canada were granted the right to organize, to be represented by unions of their own choosing, and to bargain collectively in 1967. In drafting the Public Service Staff Relations Act (PSSRA), the preparatory committee had been charged with developing a collective bargaining process with an arbitration mechanism to resolve disputes.[4] However, demands by staff associations and an illegal strike by postal employees convinced the committee that a collective bargaining statute which did not provide for the right to strike would not be acceptable to the employee representatives. At the same time, it was believed to be necessary to provide smaller and professional groups with an alternative to the strike. For that reason, the PSSRA allows the bargaining unit to have the option of selecting the arbitration route or the conciliation board and strike route for settling disputes. The method chosen, however, must be specified prior to giving notification to bargain and cannot be altered until a subsequent round of negotiations.

Regardless of the route chosen, if negotiations break down either party may request a conciliator to be appointed to assist them in reaching a settlement. Within fourteen days (or a longer period agreed upon by the parties) the conciliator must report the probability of success or failure to reach an agreement to the chairman of the Public Service Staff Relations Board (PSSRB). Beyond the conciliator stage, the alternatives for dispute resolution available to the parties vary depending on the route specified.

When a bargaining unit has decided that arbitration will be the final stage in the impasse procedure, either party may submit the issues in contention to an arbitration tribunal, along with a list of provisions already included in the collective agreement. The other party to the dispute is then allowed to add other issues with which the arbitrator must deal. The PSSRA limits the scope of arbitration, however, to issues involving rates of pay, hours of work, leave entitlements, standards of discipline, and other terms and conditions of employment directly related thereto. Moreover, no award may require additional legislation other than for the appropriation of funds or include references to subjects of the merit system covered by the Public Service

Employment Act. The parties may also limit the scope of arbitration, of course, since the arbitration tribunal can only render an award on the issues submitted by the parties.

The PSSRA provides for the establishment of a permanent arbitration tribunal, the Public Service Arbitration Tribunal (PSAT). The tribunal has a permanent chairman, a pool of alternate chairmen, and a pool of "partisan" members to represent the interests of each of the parties. When arbitration is requested, the chairman of the PSAT is charged with forming an arbitration board comprised of himself (or an alternate chairman) and one member of the panel to represent each of the parties. In issuing their award, an arbitration tribunal is constrained to base its award on the following five criteria established in section 68 of the act:

(a) the needs of the Public Service for qualified employees;
(b) the conditions of employment in similar occupations outside the Public Service including such geographic, industrial, or other variations as the Arbitration Tribunal may consider relevant;
(c) the need to maintain appropriate relationships in the conditions of employment as between different grade levels within an occupation and as between occupations in the Public Service;
(d) the need to establish terms and conditions of employment that are fair and reasonable in relation to the qualifications required, the work performed, the responsibility assumed, and the nature of services rendered; and
(e) any other factor that appears to be relevant to the dispute.

Any arbitral award is binding and must be implemented within ninety days.

Under the conciliation board-strike method of dispute resolution, when a conciliator is unsuccessful and when either party requests factfinding, or the chairman of the PSSRB deems it beneficial, an ad hoc conciliation (factfinding) board may be established. The board is comprised of three members: one nominee from each party to the dispute and a mutually agreed-upon chairman. It is then the responsibility of this body to convene, review the statements of the parties, and, within fourteen days (or a longer period mutually agreed upon), make a report covering the issues of concern. As with arbitration awards, no factfinding report may recommend legislation other than for the appropriation of funds or changes in matters under the jurisdiction of the Public Service Commission. Unlike the arbitration route, however, the conciliation board may deal with all issues presented before it (except the aforementioned) and also may add or delete issues at its discretion. Moreover, no restrictions exist on the factors that may be considered in making the determination. Furthermore, the parties may mutually agree prior to the proceedings to make the recommendations of the conciliation board binding.

If the dispute is not settled within seven days after the issuance of the conciliation board report, the bargaining unit attains the legal right to strike. This right is limited only by the designation of certain employees as essential to the safety and security of the public; those employees so designated are not allowed to participate in any strike. It is important to note, however, that in reality the designation process has often resulted in a vast majority of the bargaining unit members (up to 95 percent) being designated as essential. As a consequence, the right to strike is frequently severely restricted.

Criteria for Evaluating Arbitration Procedures

The increased adoption of arbitration procedures in the public sector has led to substantial discussion among researchers, policy makers and practitioners regarding the long run impact of arbitration on the bargaining process. Three main dysfunctional consequences have been identified. First, given that arbitrators are presumed to split the differences between the final positions of the parties, representatives of union and management are likely to hold back concessions during bargaining in anticipation of arbitration or to return to extreme positions prior to submitting the dispute to an arbitrator. This has been referred to as the chilling effect of arbitration.[5] Second, it is argued that once the parties use a procedure, they are likely to become addicted to continued reliance on it in future rounds of negotiations. In other words, arbitration is also proposed to exhibit a narcotic effect.[6] Third, Anderson and Kochan, in an earlier study of the Canadian federal system, identified a half-life effect.[7] Over time, impasse procedures may lose their effectiveness as the parties, through experience, become aware of the shortcomings of the process. As a result, their disenchantment may lead to the search for ways to circumvent the whole dispute resolution system. Finally, more recent research has suggested that the existence of arbitration as the final stage of an impasse procedure may change the importance attached to various factors which cause the negotiators to reach impasse in the first place.[8]

While most of the controversy over arbitration has focused on the effects on the process of collective bargaining, Feuille indicates that we may have been too narrow in our views of the costs and benefits of arbitration.[9] Arbitration is also designed to protect the public interest and employees' interests, and to regulate interest group conflict. As such, it is important to assess the outcomes of collective bargaining in situations with and without arbitration. Outcomes, in this case, would include not only wages and benefits but also strike activity and the degree of overt hostility and conflict between the parties. Arbitration should reduce strike activity and hostility in the relationship, and by reducing unilateral action by management, equalize wages and benefits across strike and arbitration systems.

Beyond evaluating the impact of arbitration on the process and outcomes of collective bargaining, for an arbitration procedure to survive it must be acceptable to the parties. As Mitchell points out, interest arbitration does not simply apply rules of law but relies on the judgment of the arbitrator to fashion an award which will gain acceptance and be implemented by the parties.[10] While the notion of acceptability of an arbitration procedure has not received substantial attention by researchers, several areas of acceptability may be identified.[11] The nature of the tribunal, the scope of arbitral decision making process and criteria, innovation and time delays in the procedure as well as the nature of judicial review and enforcement are all important to the parties in evaluating how well a particular procedure is functioning.

Thus, in order to assess the effectiveness of arbitration it is imperative that the evaluation not only examine its impact on the process and outcomes of collective bargaining but also that attention be directed toward the acceptability of the procedure. An attempt is made in this paper to evaluate arbitration in the federal public service of Canada according to each of the above criteria. The analysis is based on the experiences of all those bargaining units negotiating with the Treasury Board (the employer) between 1967 and 1979.

Results

Impact of arbitration on the bargaining process[12]

The chilling effect. This argument states that arbitration is likely to reduce the extent of good faith bargaining prior to the terminal step in the impasse procedure. Table 1 presents an indirect test of this effect by showing the stage of settlement under the arbitration and the conciliation board-strike routes over eight rounds of bargaining covering the period 1968-1979.

The data related to settlement under the arbitration route show a relatively clear trend away from settling without going to impasse. Specifically, the percentage of units settling without going to impasse were: 83, 47, 56, 46, 64, 32, 41, and 40. It is interesting to note that the one exception to the trend is in round five, which was during 1976 and 1977, the initial years under the Anti-Inflation Board. It appears that many of the units believed that it was unlikely that an arbitration award would have been more favorable than a negotiated settlement under the circumstances. While a trend is evident, it appears, however, that a substantial proportion of the units are still likely to settle on their own even when arbitration is the final step in the procedure. In fact, in the first five rounds, a higher proportion of units settled on their own under the arbitration route than under the conciliation board-strike alternative. That trend is reversed, however, in the last three rounds.

The probability of settling in the intermediate stages of mediation and conciliation also seems to vary systematically by impasse procedures. The percentage of mediated settlements are higher under the conciliation board-strike route. Under the arbitration route, for example, from the first to the eighth round of bargaining 1, 20, 10, 12, 4, 5, 14 and 0 percent of the units settled in the intermediate stages while under the strike route the comparable figures were 38, 67, 70, 40, 30, 40, 18, and 25 percent. The range of settlements in the intermediate stages under the arbitration procedure was 0 to 20 percent while it was 18 to 70 percent under the conciliation board-strike route. Thus, once a dispute went to impasse under the arbitration route, there was a much higher probability that it would go all the way to arbitration rather than getting settled through conciliation and mediation. The costs of disagreement associated with a strike appear to provide much higher pressure or motivation for the parties to settle in mediation or conciliation than the associated costs of going to arbitration.

There was also a general trend under the arbitration route for disputes to go all the way to the terminal step in the procedure. For example, across

TABLE 1
Stage of Settlement by Impasse Resolution Route Chosen and Round of Bargaining: 1968-1979

Stage of Settlement	Round One			Round Two			Round Three			Round Four		
	A*	C-S*	Total†	A	C-S	Total	A	C-S	Total	A	C-S	Total
Negotiations	82.9	50.0	77.5	47.5	22.2	49.2	56.4	00.0	44.9	46.2	36.3	41.7
Conciliation officer	12.2	25.0	14.3	7.5	22.2	10.2	5.1	30.0	10.2	3.8	9.1	6.3
Conciliation board	—	12.5	2.0	—	22.2	4.1	—	10.0	2.0	—	22.7	10.4
Mediation	—	—	—	10.0	—	8.2	2.6	10.0	4.1	7.7	9.1	8.3
Post-conciliation bargaining	—	—	—	2.5	22.2	6.1	2.6	20.0	6.1	—	4.5	2.1
Arbitration	4.9	—	4.1	32.5	—	26.5	33.3	—	26.5	38.5	—	10.8
Work stoppage	—	12.5	2.0	—	11.1	2.0	—	30.0	6.1	—	18.2	8.4
Total percent	83.6	16.4	100.0	81.6	18.4	100.0	79.6	20.4	100.0	54.2	47.8	100.0
Total n	41	8	49	40	9	49	39	10	49	26	22	48

Stage of Settlement	Round Five			Round Six			Round Seven			Round Eight		
	A	C-S	Total	A	C-S	Total	A	C-S	Total	A	C-S	Total
Negotiations	64.0	56.5	60.4	32.0	45.0	37.8	40.9	63.6	48.5	40.0	75.0	50.0
Conciliation officer	4.0	8.7	6.4	—	10.0	4.9	—	—	—	—	—	—
Conciliation board	—	17.4	8.3	—	10.0	4.9	—	—	—	—	—	—
Mediation	—	—	—	8.0	5.0	6.7	13.6	9.1	12.1	—	25.0	7.1
Post-conciliation bargaining	—	4.3	2.1	—	15.0	6.7	—	9.1	3.0	—	—	—
Arbitration	32.0	—	16.6	60.0	—	33.3	45.5	—	30.3	60.0	—	42.9
Work stoppage	—	13.0	6.2	—	15.0	6.7	—	18.2	6.1	—	—	—
Total percent	52.1	47.9	100.0	55.5	44.5	100.0	66.7	33.3	100.0	71.4	28.6	100.0
Total n	25	23	48	25	20	45	22	11	33	10	4	14

*A indicates arbitration route; C-S indicates conciliation-board-strike route;
†Total refers to all negotiations regardless of route chosen. All figures except "Total n" are percentages.
Source: Canada Department of Labour, *Collective Bargaining Review*, various issues from 1968-1979 and *Annual Report of the Public Service Staff Relations Board*, various years.

331

the eight rounds of bargaining, the percentage going to arbitration was as follows: 5, 32, 33, 39, 32, 60, 46, and 60. However, as discussed in the subsequent section on the half life effect, this trend may in part be due to the strong units switching away from the arbitration alternative. The proportion of units which ended in a strike under the conciliation board-strike route tended to be more stable over time: 13, 11, 30, 18, 13, 15, 18, and 0. Thus, there were two major differences in the percentage of cases going to the terminal stage of the procedures under the two routes: (1) a higher percentage went to the terminal step under arbitration; and (2) the percentage increased consistently over time under the arbitration procedure while under the conciliation board-strike route the percentage was much more consistent across rounds.

Therefore, the overall pattern of results supports the existence of a chilling effect. Over time, the proportion of units settling on their own, with no third party assistance, decreased. Furthermore, the chilling effect appeared to be greater under the arbitration route.

The narcotic effect. The data presented above which suggest an increased use of impasse procedures over time may be viewed as indirect evidence of a narcotic effect. A more specific test of this hypothesis, however, is to examine the impasse history of individual bargaining units to determine whether a unit is more likely to go to impasse if it has utilized the assistance of third parties in the past.

A detailed examination of the experience of those units with 500 or more employees reveals that there is not overwhelming evidence that once a bargaining unit goes to arbitration that it will always return to arbitration. However, once a bargaining unit has received an arbitral award, in over two thirds of its subsequent negotiations for which arbitration is the final stage, the unit will go all of the way to this terminal step. This is preliminary evidence of a narcotic effect. However, once again it may overstate the strength of this effect given that those units which were dissatisfied with arbitration are more likely to switch to the strike route.

A more general (as it only looks at the probability of impasse and not specifically arbitration) but also more rigorous test is provided in Table 2. The results show that in all rounds the probability of going to an impasse was greater if the unit had gone to an impasse in the immediately preceding round. The probability of using third party intervention in the seven rounds of bargaining for those that had not gone to impasse in the preceding round were 0.50, 0.48, 0.27, 0.15, 0.59, 0.40, and 0.86 versus 0.64, 0.63, 0.80, 0.50, 0.78, 1.00, and 1.00 for those units that had gone to impasse in the preceding round. It also appears that overall the probability of going to impasse has increased no matter what the previous experience of the bargaining unit has been. Thus, the data suggest that a history of experience with the impasse procedure increases the probability of relying on third parties in the subsequent round of bargaining.

The half-life effect. The Canadian system provides a unique opportunity to examine whether or not an impasse procedure has a natural half-life—that is, whether after a period of time the procedure loses its acceptability and

TABLE 2
Probabilities of Impasse Given Prior Impasse Experience: The Narcotic Effect*

Round 1	Round Two		Round Three		Round Four		Round Five	
	No Impasse	Impasse	No Impasse	Impasse	No Impasse	Impasse	No Impasse	Impasse
No impasse	.50	.50	.52	.48	.73	.27	.85	.15
Impasse	.36	.64	.37	.63	.20	.80	.50	.80

Round 1	Round Six		Round Seven		Round Eight	
	No Impasse	Impasse	No Impasse	Impasse	No Impasse	Impasse
No impasse	.41	.59	.60	.40	.14	.86
Impasse	.22	.78	0.0	1.00	0.0	1.00

*The test for the narcotic effect is whether the probability of going to impasse in a given round of negotiations is higher for those units that went to an impasse in the prior round of bargaining. For example, 64 percent of those units that went to an impasse in round one also went to an impasse in round two while only 50 percent of those units that settled on their own in round one went to an impasse in round two.

thereby leads one or both of the parties to turn to an alternative for resolving their differences. Evidence of switching from the arbitration to the conciliation board-strike route in a nonrandom manner would support the existence of this effect.

In the first round of bargaining, 83.6 percent of the bargaining units selected the arbitration route (see Table 1). From that point, there was increasing movement away from the arbitration route in favor of the conciliation board-strike route. The largest shift occurred between the third and fourth rounds of bargaining, dropping from 80 to 54 percent choosing arbitration. An examination of the units that switched from arbitration to the strike route shows that the decision to switch occurred most often (67 percent of the cases) following the receipt of an arbitration award in the immediately previous round of negotiations. Another 11 percent of those units which switched did so after settling in the previous round after requesting arbitration, but prior to receiving an award. Thus, in 78 percent of the cases the switching party had some experience with arbitration in the past set of negotiations. Overall, these results suggest that most units that switched to the strike route had become dissatisfied with arbitration for some reason, perhaps recognizing that future innovations or breakthroughs would come only through the use of more aggressive (strike threatening) strategies.

The nature of the bargaining process. The nature of the bargaining process may be different where the terminal stage of the impasse procedure is the right to strike or compulsory arbitration. Specifically, negotiations ending with the right to strike are likely to be shaped primarily by the bargaining power of the parties. On the other hand, the arbitration process is likely to shift the negotiators' approach to attempting to second guess the arbitrator with respect to the types of data and arguments which best support the parties' positions. Furthermore, the parties are more likely to allow the arbitrator to resolve problems in the union-management relationship or political problems with their constituencies or the public than would be the case in the strike system. Thus, the arbitrator can be used as a scapegoat for unacceptable relationships or settlements.

There is some evidence that both of these situations arise in the Canadian federal public service. First, an examination of hearing briefs reveals that there was a much heavier reliance on reporting statistics, like those prepared by the Pay Research Bureau,[13] than appears to be the case in negotiations under the strike alternative. Whether or not these statistics actually make any difference is difficult to discern given that arbitrators do not provide reasoning for their awards. Second, the use of arbitration to resolve political problems for one or the other of the parties was evidenced in awards made in 1973 (2), 1974, 1976, and 1977. In all of these cases, union and management agreed upon a new collective agreement which the union's membership subsequently refused to ratify. As a result, the parties requested arbitration. The bargaining agents involved submitted a full set of demands to the arbitrator, in most cases retreating to preagreement positions. The employer, on the other hand, submitted the terms and conditions of the tentative agreement to the arbitrator. In each instance, the arbitration board accepted the position of management on each issue under each jurisdiction, and in doing so ratified the negotiated settlement which had been rejected by the membership.

The data presented so far provide partial support for the dysfunctional consequences that arbitration procedures may have on the bargaining process. Although it could be argued that only 25 percent of the total sample (on average over eight rounds of bargaining), or 38 percent of the units under the arbitration route, used arbitration, the percentage of cases increased steadily over time. Moreover, other data were presented to support all of the four effects—narcotic, chilling, half-life, and nature of the bargaining process—in addition to the actual use of arbitration.

These results raise a question of whether or not all effects on the bargaining process can occur simultaneously. While it seems plausible that the nature of the bargaining process could be altered and the chilling and narcotic effects can coexist, a half-life effect in cross sectional data would suggest the opposite of the chilling and narcotic effects. That is, a reduction in the use of impasse resolution machinery would be expected. The data indicate a sequential process whereby the unit relies on the impasse procedure (narcotic and chilling effects) until some point at which dissatisfaction with the whole procedure causes the unit to switch to the conciliation board-strike route (half-life effect). In systems without a legal procedural alternative, the switching may take such forms as political action or illegal strikes.

Impact of arbitration on bargaining outcomes. An arbitration procedure is hypothesized not only to have negative impacts on the bargaining process by inhibiting genuine negotiations but also to have a positive impact by protecting employee interests. Feuille argues that in the absence of arbitration (and the right to strike) there may be "no readily available mechanism to manipulate management's costs of disagreeing with employee demands. Management can continue the status quo, ignore mediator or factfinder recommendations, or implement unilateral changes (at least after impasse), but employees have no countervailing weapons; thus there is a serious imbalance of negotiating power in management's favor."[14] Thus, if an arbitration procedure is working correctly there should be no difference between the wages and benefits negotiated by the employees' representatives under a strike or arbitration procedure.

Effect on wages. A recent study by Subbarao reveals substantial differences in wages for three occupational categories between the strike and arbitration routes in the 1974-1975 period.[15] These results would suggest that arbitration has not, in fact, protected employee interests. However, his results should be interpreted with caution. In another study which examined changes in wages of units over 500 employees negotiating with the Treasury Board, Anderson discovered that after other determinants of wages were controlled, the choice of impasse procedure had no effect.[16] Further, a comparison of arbitration awards with negotiated settlements under both the arbitration and conciliation board-strike routes reveals that arbitral awards tended to be within a much narrower range (less variance in settlements) than negotiated settlements. For example, in round one, 100 percent of the arbitral awards granted a seven or eight percent increase while negotiated settlements ranged from three to nine percent; in round two, 80 percent were between six and eight percent under arbitration versus a range of three to eleven percent increases for negotiated settlements; 75 percent of the arbitrated settlements were between six and nine percent in round three in comparison with a range of five to fourteen percent in negotiations; and in round four, 85 percent of the arbitral awards were for eight to eleven percent versus a range of seven to twenty-one percent for non-arbitrated settlements. Thus, while on average the wage outcomes under conciliation board-strike and arbitration alternatives may not be significantly different, there is a distinct tendency for restricted variance to exist in the wage increases granted by arbitration tribunals.

Effect on nonwage bargaining outcomes. In order to determine whether or not choosing the arbitration or conciliation board-strike route had any impact on the nonwage terms and conditions of employment in the federal public service, collective agreements were coded in terms of their favorableness to the union. In total, 92 provisions in the collective agreements were analyzed over four rounds of bargaining. These provisions were then broken down into five general areas: contract administration, leave, vacations, fringe benefits, and pay supplements. The mean contract index score for each of these areas by impasse resolution route is presented in Table 3.

An examination of the results reveals that the scores on each of the five areas of the collective agreement do not differ significantly across dispute resolution procedures. This fact is further confirmed when the determinants of nonwage outcomes and changes in nonwage outcomes over the four rounds of bargaining are investigated. When other factors are controlled, the choice of impasse resolution procedure does not significantly effect nonwage outcomes.[17] Thus, it appears that, at least, in the federal government of Canada, arbitration does not provide the employees with any particular long-run advantage or disadvantage in terms of negotiated outcomes. In contrast, however, the results of this same study do indicate that in the third and fourth rounds of bargaining, actually going on strike did provide a significant increase in wage and nonwage outcomes. Therefore, a slight disadvantage to bargaining units under the arbitration route may exist because of the forfeiture of the ultimate impasse weapon.

Acceptability of the arbitration procedure. It can be hypothesized that one of the major reasons that arbitration procedures become less effective is a decline in their acceptability to the parties. Acceptability may have many dimensions: the administrative structure of the tribunal; the scope of the issues which may be arbitrated; the manner in which decisions are made as well as the actual decisions; the innovations or lack of them resulting from arbitration; time delays in the arbitral process; and the enforcement and review of arbitral decisions. To investigate these areas of acceptability of arbitration, all of the arbitration awards rendered in negotiations between employee representatives and Treasury Board during the 1969 to 1979 period were analyzed.

TABLE 3
Non Wage Outcomes Under Arbitration and Conciliation Board—Strike Routes over Four Rounds of Bargaining: 1968-1975

Contract Provisions	Possible Values	Round One		Round Two		Round Three		Round Four	
		A*	C-S†	A	C-S	A	C-S	A	C-S
Contract administration	0-20	11.4	10.8	11.7	11.8	11.7	11.6	12.0	11.9
Leave provisions	0-36	19.5	16.5	19.4	16.4	19.2	19.3	19.2	19.8
Vacation provisions	0-16	10.8	10.8	11.7	11.2	11.9	11.3	11.9	11.6
Fringe benefits	0-34	8.0	7.1	8.5	8.6	9.0	8.2	10.1	8.7
Pay supplements	0-59	19.1	21.5	21.5	24.9	22.3	22.8	25.6	24.4

*A indicates arbitration route; C-S indicates conciliation-board strike route.

†Collective agreements for units of over 500 employees negotiating with Treasury Board between 1968 and 1975

337

Nature of the arbitration tribunal. In reviewing the literature on the acceptability of arbitration procedures, Kochan, Mironi, Ehrenberg, Baderschneider and Jick indicate that the tripartite arbitration panels (neutral, employee and employer representatives) tend to be more effective because of the psychological effects of participation and control over the process and subsequent commitment to the award.[18] Tripartitism is also expected to increase the quality of the award. This occurs as a consequence of the partsisans' ability to provide additional input, to sensitize the chairperson to the political realities faced by the parties as well as to convey their expectations concerning the award. Therefore, the award should be better balanced within the zone of acceptability.

The use of a tripartite panel rather than a single arbitrator, may also have some dysfunctional outcomes, however. A three or five person tribunal often creates time delays and administrative inefficiency. Moreover, a neutral may be forced to side with an extreme position of one of the partisan members of the board to get a majority, which in turn may make it more difficult to follow statutory criteria established to guide the writing of arbitral awards. Tripartitism, therefore, appears to have costs and benefits associated with it.

The PSSRA differs from many jurisdictions with respect to the nature of the arbitration tribunal. While the panel appointed in any given dispute is comprised of a chairman and a representative of both labor and management, the parties have no influence over the selection of the individuals. All members of the board are selected from a permanent rather than an ad hoc slate of individuals. Moreover, it is the chairman of the PSAT who assigns employer and employee representatives (on a rotating basis) to arbitration cases as they arise, without any input from the parties. This creates several problems for the true operationalization of the tripartite philosophy in the federal public service.

Because the vast majority of arbitration hearings do not last longer than a single day, employer and employee representatives to the tribunal have little opportunity to communicate with the individuals preparing the arbitration submission. While contact prior to the hearing is not prohibited, it is certainly not encouraged. Thus, board representatives are limited in their information to the formal briefs and presentations made by the parties. As a consequence, several of the underlying reasons for having partisan representatives in the arbitration process are restricted. This presents an even more serious problem when the parties' representatives to the tribunal do not tend to have extensive experience in the federal public service. Moreover, an examination of the background and experience of the members of the panels reveals that the majority of the employer representatives are either management officials or lawyers, while employee representatives are academics, lawyers, or in a few cases, union representatives. Because many of these individuals are also practicing arbitrators, it is unclear that they would be likely to act as strong advocates for employee or employer positions. Furthermore, few employee representatives have had any union experience. Thus, the permanent panel may not increase the acceptability of the process to the extent that an ad hoc panel does.

In marked contrast to the nature of the arbitration tribunal is the

338

composition of the conciliation board under the strike route, for each conciliation board is formed on an ad hoc basis. Each of the parties within seven days is asked to nominate a representative to the board. The employer and employee representatives when appointed are expected within five days to nominate a chairman of the board. In the event that they are unable to do so, the chairman of the PSSRB is required to appoint the conciliation board chairperson. Thus, the procedure and composition of the conciliation board is similar to arbitration boards in many other jurisdictions and as such has most of the benefits of a tripartite procedure.

Scope of issues. One of the greatest differences between the arbitration and conciliation board procedures is in the scope of issues which can be considered by the respective tribunals. In arbitration, only rates of pay, hours of work, leave entitlements, standards of discipline and other terms and conditions of employment directly related thereto can be considered. In addition, items requiring legislative implementation, issues covered by the merit system, and items not submitted to the board may not be dealt with by an arbitral award. Conversely, a conciliation board is only restricted from including issues requiring legislative implementation and items in the merit system. As such, the scope of arbitration is comparatively narrow.

The Act provides that other terms and conditions of employment directly related to the above four areas are also arbitrable. However, arbitration tribunals have consistently interpreted this provision strictly and have denied jurisdiction over most issues. In total, over the 1969-1979 period, 39 issues have been rejected as not arbitrable. Between five and thirty percent of the issues submitted have been considered outside the jurisdiction of the tribunals in each year. Many of these are issues which have been dealt with by conciliation boards. Thus, the reluctance of arbitrators to expand their jurisdiction has further limited the scope of the procedure.

Decision criteria used by arbitrators. The PSSRA stipulates that the arbitration tribunal *must* consider the five factors specified earlier when making any award. Unfortunately, although criteria are specified, the arbitrators are not required to provide reasons or a rationale for their decisions and therefore, it is virtually impossible to assess the extent to which these criteria are actually used.

Another aspect of arbitrator decision making which is of interest is the extent to which the procedure results in a compromise between the final positions of the parties. In order to analyze the decision making process, all arbitration awards were examined and for each issue the award was coded as accepting the exact position of union or management or some compromise between them. Any change in wording or substance by the arbitration tribunal was coded as a compromise. The results of this investigation are presented in Table 4.

An examination of the results reveals that few issues are withdrawn from arbitration after the hearing and prior to the award. In four of the eleven years, no issues were resolved by the parties. The percentage of issues where the union, management, or a compromise position is selected provides some interesting information about the arbitration process in the Canadian federal

TABLE 4
Decision Making in the Arbitration Process

Decision Made (percentages)	1969	1970	1971	1972	1973	1974	1975	1976	1977	1978	1979
					Year of Arbitration Award						
Parties agreed during arbitration	13.5	2.1	0.0	3.1	3.4	0.0	0.0	2.0	0.0	6.6	5.0
Union position selected	30.2	5.3	20.0	1.5	3.4	2.6	8.7	15.3	5.7	8.8	7.5
Management position selected	27.5	37.2	40.0	58.9	69.5	67.9	45.7	33.7	37.7	29.9	26.2
Compromise position selected	9.6	23.4	29.2	27.6	18.6	25.0	39.1	43.9	39.3	38.2	53.8
Jurisdiction denied by board	19.2	32.0	10.8	9.2	5.1	4.5	6.5	5.1	14.8	16.5	7.5
Status quo position selected	21.2	38.3	27.6	44.6	16.9	17.9	23.9	26.5	26.2	27.9	25.0
Average number of issues	17.3	8.5	9.3	8.1	7.4	8.6	9.2	6.5	6.4	7.5	4.7

public service. First, it appears that in the first year of the procedure the process worked much like a final offer selection by issue procedure. Either union or management's position was selected on most of the issues. Subsequently, however, the percentage of issues on which a compromise award is rendered increases steadily from 9.6 percent in 1969 to 53.8 percent in 1979. The union seems to fare least well under this arbitration procedure with less than ten percent of their demands being directly granted by the arbitration tribunal in most years. On the other hand, the procedure would seem to strongly favor management's position, with arbitrators adopting from 26 to 70 percent of their demands, depending on the year. Without any other data, these results would suggest a strong management bias within the system. In fact, those years in which close to 70 percent of the issues were awarded in favor of management's position precede the end of the third round of bargaining and the substantial switch of bargaining units from arbitration to the conciliation board-strike route. Thus, one plausible explanation for the half-life effect of this arbitration procedure is its bias towards management.

It is important, however, not to accept this conclusion too quickly. Several other explanations must be explored. First, it is possible that the employee organizations have a tendency to submit a number of superfluous demands to the arbitration tribunal as give-aways for the more important issues. While this explanation is plausible, the relatively narrow scope of bargaining coupled with the low number of issues which are submitted on average to arbitration suggests that it cannot be accepted as a major factor. A second explanation is that management only made demands it knew would be accepted by the arbitrators, either through past experience with the process or for some other reason. Some evidence is available which supports this contention. In the three years in which the employer was most successful (1972-74), they requested arbitration in 50, 25, and 46 percent of the negotiations, respectively. This is in sharp contrast to the situation in other years where Treasury Board only requested arbitration for one case in 1976 and in 1978. Thus, this is certainly a partial explanation for management's success. Finally, arbitration, in this jurisdiction, appears to be inherently conservative and in many cases the employer position selected was no change in the existing provision. These two factors help to explain both the apparent bias in the system as well as the switching behavior from arbitration to conciliation board-strike route.

Innovation in the arbitration process. One of the major complaints about the acceptability of the arbitration process is the inability to make breakthroughs in terms and conditions of employment. This problem is readily apparent, as indicated by several pieces of information. First, Table 4 presents the percentage of demands for which the response of the arbitration tribunal was to award no change in the provision, or in other words, where the decision was to uphold the status quo. In most years, in excess of 25 percent of the demands resulted in no change; in one year it went as high as 45 percent of the issues. In addition, the PSAT has refused to accept jurisdiction over a large number of issues, and thus the overall result is an extremely conservative process. The one significant innovation over the eleven year period, the granting of a COLA clause to the Information Services

Group in 1974, was not repeated in subsequent awards and the tribunal chairman who granted this provision was not allocated any more cases. Third, a few chairmen dominate the arbitration tribunals. A careful reading of their awards reveals that there is a strong tendency for an arbitrator to establish and follow his own pattern. Finally, arbitration appears to act primarily as a catchup process for the weaker and smaller bargaining units. As more and more units opted for the conciliation board-strike route, increasingly the units remaining were ones which would be unable to wield the necessary bargaining power to demand changes in their collective agreements.

Time delays in the arbitration procedure. Arbitration systems have also been considered unacceptable if there are substantial delays between the request for arbitration and the actual handing down of the award. Under the PSSRA, where one party requests that issues in dispute go to arbitration, the Secretary of the PSSRB must notify the other party, who within seven days must provide written notice of any additional matters in dispute. At the time of notice, the Chairman of the PSAT is also expected to form an arbitration tribunal within 14 days. Once formed, it is to proceed immediately to consideration of the matter.

In actuality, the average time between the parties' request for arbitration and the establishment of an arbitration tribunal is closer to three weeks than two as established by statute. Moreover, in most cases it takes over a month from the establishment of the board to a formal hearing with the parties. Thus, rather than the two weeks contemplated by the law, it takes an average of six or more weeks to have the dispute heard. While this is at variance with the law, it is similar to the experience of police and firefighters under New York State's Taylor Law.[19] On average, after the hearing it has taken anywhere from 21 to 120 days for the award to be completed depending on the year. However, the majority of awards are made in less than three months. Unfortunately, a four or five month process may well be unacceptable to the membership and leadership of the bargaining unit. It appears that during the last two years the average times have dropped drastically, which may be attributable to the increased number of arbitration tribunal chairmen who are being appointed.

Review of arbitral awards. The PSSRA also provides that the parties may resubmit the arbitral award to the tribunal for reconsideration under two circumstances: (1) if the tribunal failed to address any issue submitted by the parties; or (2) there is a need for further clarification of an issue which was addressed in an award. The increased need to resubmit awards for review is likely to take its toll in the degree of acceptability of the process as it will substantially increase the actual time to obtain a binding, implementable award. A substantial proportion of the awards have been reconsidered by the arbitration tribunals. The figures for 1969 to 1979 show that 0, 36, 0, 63, 50, 62, 40, 53, 26, 17, and 24 percent of the awards, respectively, were sent back for review. Again, it is interesting to note that the proportions are greatest during the years just prior to the substantial switch away from arbitration.

Thus, once again it is possible that the need to frequently send awards back to the arbitrator results in a substantial reduction in the credibility and acceptability of the arbitration procedure, which in turn reduces the effective half-life of the procedure.

Conclusions and Implications

The purpose of this chapter was to evaluate the arbitration procedure adopted for public employees in the Canadian federal government. To do so, a number of criteria were established which focused on the impacts of arbitration on the collective bargaining process and outcomes and on the acceptability of the procedure itself. The results provide partial support for the arguments that arbitration, as the terminal step in the impasse procedure as compared to the right to strike, may have a chilling effect on good faith bargaining as well as inducing reliance on the procedure over time. Most interesting, however, is the clear half-life effect. That is, as the parties learn about the shortcomings of the procedure and become disenchanted with it, they are likely to attempt to find alternate methods to resolve their disputes. In this case, the parties have a readily available option of switching to the dispute resolution method culminating in a conciliation board and the right to strike.

An analysis of the acceptability of the procedure helped to pinpoint some of the reasons why the bargaining units may have been switching routes. First, the decision making process appears to favor both management and the status quo. Second, time delays in the procedure lengthen the negotiating period greatly. Third, the extent to which awards once granted must be resubmitted to the arbitration tribunal reduces the procedure's credibility substantially. Finally, the composition of the panel itself limits the extent to which a tripartite representation system can function.

Overall, these results have one major implication for theory and policy with respect to compulsory arbitration systems. The vast majority of the research which has evaluated the effectiveness of these systems has paid little or no attention to the administrative procedures which are established to govern the implementation and operation of the laws.[20] This study suggests that it is the acceptability of these characteristics which may determine the overall effectiveness of the system.

Footnotes

1. For a review of the literature on the right to strike in public employment see A. Aboud and G. Aboud, *The Right to Strike in Public Employment,* Key Issues Series No. 15 (Ithaca, N.Y.: NYSSILR, Cornell University, 1974).
2. All Canadian provinces and the federal government have compulsory arbitration procedures available to select groups. In the United States the following states have adopted arbitration: Alaska, Connecticut, Hawaii, Iowa, Maine, Massachusetts, Michigan, Minnesota, Montana, Nebraska, Nevada, New Jersey, New York, Oregon, Pennsylvania, Rhode Island, Vermont, Washington, Wisconsin, and Wyoming.

3. Since that time New Brunswick, British Columbia, Wisconsin and Minnesota have adopted choice of procedures. See A. Ponak and H. Wheeler, "Choice of Procedures in Canada and the United States," *Industrial Relations*, Vol. 20, No. 3 (Fall 1980), pp. 292-308.

4. Canada, *Report of the Preparatory Committee on Collective Bargaining in the Public Service* (Ottawa: Information Canada, 1965).

5. For the first direct test of the chilling hypothesis, see Hoyt Wheeler, "How Compulsory Arbitration Affects Compromise Activity," *Industrial Relations*, Vol. 17, No. 1 (February 1978), pp. 80-84.

6. For a discussion of the narcotic effect see, "Willard Wirtz, Address Before National Academy of Arbitrators in Chicago, February 1, 1963 (see Daily Labor Report, No. 23, February 1, 1973 F1-F4). Also see Robert J. Hines, "Mandatory Contract Arbitration—Is It a Viable Process?" *Industrial and Labor Relations Review*, Vol. 25, No. 4 (July 1972), pp. 533-44; Jacob J. Kaufman, "Procedures Versus Collective Bargaining in Railroad Labour Disputes," *Industrial and Labor Relations Review*, Vol. 25, No. 1 (October 1971), pp. 53-70; and Herbert R. Northrup, *Compulsory Arbitration and Government Intervention in Labor Disputes* (Washington, D.C.: Labor Policy Association, 1966).

7. John C. Anderson and Thomas A. Kochan, "Impasse Procedures in the Canadian Federal Service: Effects on the Bargaining Process," *Industrial and Labor Relations Review*, Vol. 30, No. 3 (April 1977), pp. 283-301.

8. John C. Anderson, "Determinants of Collective Bargaining Impasses: The Role of Dispute Resolution Procedures," paper presented at the conference, Industrial Relations and Conflict Management; Different Ways of Managing Conflict at the Netherlands School of Business, Nijenrode, Breukelen, June 29-July 3, 1980.

9. Peter Feuille, "The Selected Costs and Benefits of Compulsory Arbitration," *Industrial and Labor Relations Review*, Vol. 33, No. 1 (October 1979), pp. 64-76.

10. Leon Mitchell, "Interest Arbitration in the Federal Public Service," unpublished paper, PSSRB, Ottawa, 1979.

11. Thomas A. Kochan, Mordehai Mironi, Ronald Ehrenberg, Jean Baderschneider, and Todd Jick, *Dispute Resolution Under Fact-Finding and Arbitration: An Empirical Analysis* (New York: American Arbitration Association, 1979).

12. The majority of this section is an update of Anderson and Kochan, *op. cit.*, pp. 283-301.

13. For a description of the Pay Research Bureau see, Felix Quinet, "The Role of Research in Centralized Bargaining: The Pay Research Bureau," *Relations Industrielles*, Vol. 26, No. 1 (1971), pp. 202-212.

14. Feuille, "Selected Costs and Benefits," *op. cit.*, p. 68.

15. A. V. Subbarao, "Impasse Choice and Wages in the Canadian Federal Service," *Industrial Relations*, Vol. 18, No. 2 (Spring 1979), pp. 233-236.

16. John Anderson, "Determinants of Bargaining Outcomes in the Federal Government of Canada," *Industrial and Labor Relations Review*, Vol. 32, No. 2 (January 1979), pp. 224-241.

17. Anderson, "Bargaining Outcomes," pp. 231-234.

18. For a review see, Kochan et al., *op. cit.*, chapter 8.

19. Kochan, et al., *op. cit.*

20. John Anderson, "Evaluating the Impact of Compulsory Arbitration: A Methodological Assessment," *Industrial Relations*, Vol. 21, No. 2 (Spring 1981), 129-148.

Factfinding and Final Offer Arbitration in Iowa

Daniel G. Gallagher*

Accompanying the tremendous growth of collective bargaining activity in the public sector has been a considerable amount of researcher and practitioner comment on the design and implementation of impasse procedures for resolving disputes that may occur during the bargaining process. This emphasis is based on a general belief that public sector employment relationships are distinct from those in the private sector and that resort to strike activity as a means of impasse resolution should be prohibited or severely constrained.

A cursory review of public sector bargaining statutes reveals that the use of mediation as an initial step in bargaining impasse resolution is almost universal. However, considerable diversity exists among statutory impasse resolution procedures in the number and types of forums utilized subsequent to mediation. Procedural steps after mediation often include one or more of the following: factfinding; interest arbitration; and, to a limited extent, the right to strike. Further variation is created by legislation that establishes, if applicable whether or not arbitration is voluntary or mandatory, whether arbitration is conventional or final offer (FOA) and if FOA, whether on an issue by issue or total package basis and the maximum possible number of final offers. This diversity is magnified by the differences that may exist within a particular jurisdiction depending upon the occupational group to which the statutory procedure applies.

One of the more novel approaches to impasse resolution in the public sector is the statutory procedure established under the Iowa Public Employment Relations Act (IPERA).[1] In 1974, the Iowa law extended collective bargaining rights to all categories of public employees. The Iowa law is atypical not only in the scope of employee coverage but also in the inclusion of a statutory three step dispute resolution mechanism consisting of mediation, factfinding and issue by issue FOA. Another distinguishing aspect is the unique relationship between the factfinding and FOA steps of the impasse procedure. If a bargaining dispute advances beyond factfinding to issue by issue FOA, the arbitrator is presented the factfinder's recommendation for each impasse item as an alternative third offer from which to select a binding award.

Following is a description and analysis of the Iowa statutory impasse mechanism for public sector disputes. This discussion focuses primarily on the impact which factfinding prior to FOA has had upon the impasse resolution and bargaining processes.

---

*Department of Industrial Relations and Human Resources, University of Iowa. This paper was written especially for this volume.

Structure of the Iowa Statutory Impasse Procedure

Under the provisions of the IPERA, the procedure for resolving potential bargaining impasses is determined by the parties to the bargaining relationship. The IPERA requires that the parties in their duty to bargain "shall endeavor to agree upon" their own methods for resolving deadlocks.[2] The parties are thus encouraged to establish by mutual agreement an "independent" procedure. However, independent procedures may not include the right to strike as an alternative action. In the absence of an independent impasse procedure, the statutorily prescribed procedure outlined in Sections 20-22 of the IPERA prevail. To date, approximately 80 percent of the public sector bargaining relationships have used the statutory impasse procedure.

The Iowa statutory impasse process is a carefully structured, three-tiered dispute adjustment procedure consisting of mediation, factfinding, and FOA.

If parties adopting the statutory impasse procedure fail to reach an agreement 120 days prior to the required budget certification date and an impasse exists, either party may request a mediator. The Iowa Public Employment Relations Board (IPERB), which is responsible for appointing a neutral, relies upon three major sources for mediation services—the Federal Mediation and Conciliation Service (FMCS), the PERB staff, and a cadre of ad hoc mediators—and assumes the costs associated with the mediation process. Mediation is restricted to a period of 10 days following the neutral's initial meeting with the parties. Should medition prove unsuccessful in resolving all the issues, the dispute automatically advances to factfinding.

The responsibility for appointing a factfinder resides once again with the IPERB but the costs associated with the factfinding process are shared equally by both parties. Under the provisions of Section 21 of the Act, the factfinder conducts a hearing, secures evidence and makes written recommendations for the resolution of the impasse no later than 15 days from the date of appointment.[3] The IPERA does not specify standards or criteria which the factfinder must consider in formulating the recommendations nor does the Act prohibit the factfinder from engaging in further mediation efforts. Once the factfinding report is issued, the parties have ten days in which to accept or reject it or engage in further negotiations before the report is made public by the IPERB.

The parties may continue to negotiate after the public issuance of the factfinding report or either party may request that the unresolved items be submitted to FOA. As specified under the Act, the parties may submit the impasse items to a three member panel to which each party independently appoints a single arbitrator and by mutual agreement selects a chair. In the majority of cases, the parties have exercised an option under the Act that permits them by mutual agreement to use a single arbitrator insted of a panel.[4] In the absence of agreement on the selection of either the panel chair or single arbitrator, the arbitrator is chosen by elimination from a list provided by the IPERB. Similar to factfinding, the fees and associated costs are shared equally by the parties.

The procedure requires that each party submit to the IPERB within four days after the request for arbitration its final offer for each impasse issue.

Arbitration is limited to those issues presented at factfinding and remaining unresolved. In order to prevent arbitration from operating as an extension of the bargaining process, the parties are prohibited from revising their final offers after submitting them to the IPERB and the arbitrators are prohibited from engaging in mediation efforts.[5]

The most novel aspect of the Iowa statutory procedure is that in addition to the final offers submitted by the employer and employee representatives for each impasse issue, the arbitrator receives the factfinder's recommendations. In formulating the award for each impasse item, the arbitrator must choose one of three alternatives: the final offer of the employer, the employee representative's final offer, or the factfinder's recommendation. In effect, the factfinder's advisory recommendation reappears as a third final offer from which the arbitrator may select a final and binding award in an issue by issue FOA procedure.

The singularity of the Iowa statutory impasse procedure lies primarily in the function of factfinding, first as an advisory mechanism between mediation and mandatory FOA on an issue by issue basis, and second in the inclusion of the factfinder's recommendations as final offer alternatives that the arbitrator may select. Although the inclusion of factfinding and arbitration in the same impasse procedure is not particularly unusual, the use of both forums tends to be restricted to statutes applying to protective service employees and not to all categories of employees as provided under the Iowa statute.[6] Inclusion of the factfinder's recommendations in FOA has been the mandated impasse technique in only one other state. Only Massachusetts, since 1974, has utilized a three step procedure of mediation, factfinding and FOA that also includes the factfinder's recommendation as a final offer alternative.[7] However, the Massachusetts tri-offer scheme applies only to protective service employees and, secondly, the FOA procedure is on a total package basis rather than an issue by issue approach, as utilized in Iowa.

The New Jersey Fire and Police Arbitration Act of 1977 has some limited similarities with the Iowa and Massachusetts arbitration procedures. The New Jersey Act affords the parties a choice of five terminal impasse procedures as an alternative to the compulsory procedure specified in the law.[8] Two of these alternatives are tri-offer FOA on either an issue by issue or total package basis. However, a recent study of the New Jersey experience indicates no utilization of the tri-offer FOA format by public safety employees.[9] In summary, the Iowa statutory impasse procedure is unique in its provision for FOA at the request of either party and tri-offer issue by issue procedure for all categories of public employees.

The inclusion of factfinding as an intermediary step and mandatory FOA as the terminal step was adopted by the Iowa legislature to accomplish two objectives. First, factfinding prior to FOA was seen as an opportunity for the parties to submit unresolved bargaining issues to a neutral for review and receive recommendations that could guide the parties in reaching a voluntary settlement. Factfinding could have a "sobering effect" by requiring the parties to realistically reappraise their own positions in light of the neutral factfinder's recommendations.[10] Second, including mandatory FOA as the final step was adopted by the Iowa legislature to establish "finality" in the resolution procedure, given the absence of the right to strike. Adopting FOA was based primarily on the expectation that the parties would be more likely to converge in their impasse positions, and thus reach a voluntary agreement, than if conventional arbitration were adopted.[11] However, the efficacy of FOA was criticized by some proponents of the IPERA. FOA could produce situations in which both parties' final offers were untenable, thereby legally forcing the arbitrator to select one of two unworkable or inequitable alternatives. In the spirit of compromise and conservatism, the FOA procedure was modified to include the factfinder's recommendation as a third alternative submitted to the arbitrator.[12] Theoretically, including an experienced neutral's recommendation as a third final offer for each impasse issue would minimize the possibility of an untenable award. This explicit connection between the factfinding and FOA procedures also could benefit the former, for the parties should give considerably more weight to the factfinder's report since, if a voluntary settlement is not reached, the factfinder's recommendations may be selected by a subsequent arbitrator.[13]

Despite the potential benefits of including factfinding as an intermediary step between mediation and FOA, the availability of factfinding and the use of the factfinder's recommendations as final offer alternatives are subject to some concern. The use of factfinding after mediation but prior to arbitration may have a chilling effect on the bargaining process.[14] In particular, the mediator's ability to facilitate an agreement may be reduced as the mediation step is further removed from the arbitration step of the impasse procedure.[15] The effectiveness of mediation may be diminished if the parties view factfinding primarily as an additional, subsequent opportunity for mediation efforts.[16] Most problematic is the situation in which the parties withhold their concessions until after the issuance of the factfinder's recommendations in an attempt to maximize their bargaining positions and options.

Concern has also been expressed over the possiblity that factfinding prior to arbitration will essentially reduce the arbitration step to a "show cause" hearing.[17] Of primary concern is the belief that arbitrators may rely too heavily upon the factfinder's recommendations when formulating a binding award. Should arbitrators prove consistently to award the factfinders' recommendations, factfinding would, in practice, operate as de facto arbitration.

Usage of Procedures

A number of measures can be applied to judge the effectiveness of the Iowa impasse procedure. One of the most commonly utilized indicators of the "success" or "failure" of a procedure is the degree to which the parties rely upon adjudicative steps, in particular arbitration, rather than voluntary settlement to reach a contract. Concentrating on those bargaining relationships that utilized the statutory impasse procedure, Table 1 shows the step at which the parties reached an agreement during each of the first five years of negotiations.

During the first five years of bargaining under the statutory procedure, 1316 contract negotiations utilized mediation (about 55 percent of all negotiations). Of this total, 1045 or 79.4 percent settled with the assistance of

TABLE 1
Steps Utilized Under the Statutory Procedure

	Year 1 1976-76	Year 2 1976-77	Year 3 1977-78	Year 4 1978-79	Year 5 1979-80	Total
Total negotiations to impasse	155	207	265	314	375	1316
Mediation only	113 (72.9)*	149 (72.0)	226 (85.3)	237 (75.5)	320 (85.3)	1045 (79.4)
Mediation and factfinding	32 (20.7)	37 (17.9)	24 (9.1)	57 (18.1)	36 (9.6)	186 (14.1)
Mediation, factfinding and FOA	10 (6.4)	21 (10.1)	15 (5.7)	20 (6.4)	19 (5.1)	85 (6.5)

*Percentage of impasse cases by stage of settlement.

mediation either during the mediation sessions or prior to the commencement of the factfinding step. Two hundred and seventy-one contract disputes proceeded beyond mediation to factfinding. Of these 271 disputes, 186 or 69.0 percent reached a voluntary settlement after the issuance of the factfinder's report without using FOA.[18] For the first five years, only 6.5 percent of all contract negotiations advanced to FOA. Considering contract negotiations that utilized the statutory impasse resolution procedure and those that reached an agreement without any neutral assistance, only about 3.5 percent of all negotiations required an arbitrated settlement. A year by year analysis of bargaining relationships that relied on the impasse procedure reveals no specific trend in the increased or decreased use of factfinding or arbitration.

Despite some annual fluctuations, the Iowa experience under the statutory impasse procedure compares well with impasse resolution rates reported in other public sector jurisdictions. A review of other jurisdictions' experiences reveals that the percentage of bargaining impasses advancing beyond mediation to arbitration was much lower in Iowa than in New York State, Massachusetts, Michigan, Pennsylvania, Wisconsin, Minnesota, the Canadian federal government, and British Columbia.[19] Such comparison, however, must be carefully interpreted due to the existing variations in statutory procedures and the categories of employees that are included under various statutes. A further caveat in interpreting the Iowa impasse usage summary is that bargaining relationships primarily occur in small rural communities. As a result, the environment may differ substantially from that of more urban states which typically have more experience with the collective bargaining process.[20]

As presented in Table 1, the use of factfinding prior to arbitration shows a strong "filtering effect" or reduction in the number of cases advancing beyond factfinding to arbitration.[21] More specifically, 186 of 271 cases (69.0%) submitted to factfinding were resolved without arbitration. But another basis on which to evaluate the effectiveness of factfinding is the extent to which it reduces the number of items at impasse should the dispute advance to FOA. Based on all available factfinding and arbitration reports during the first four years of bargaining under the Iowa statute, an average of 6.5 issues per case were submitted to factfinding. Where a complete settlement was reached prior to arbitration, an average of 6.2 issues per case were resolved after the issuance of the factfinder's report. (See Table 2.) For those cases advancing to arbitration, the number of issues at impasse per case was reduced from 6.9 at factfinding to 4.0 at arbitration. Thus, an additional benefit of the factfinding procedure is the extent to which it assists the parties in reducing the number of issues at impasse even though complete agreement is not reached on all isssues. Factfinding's impact on issue reduction is seen by comparing the number of issues submitted to arbitration in those disputes using factfinding prior to FOA (statutory procedure) with those disputes proceeding directly from mediation to FOA (independent procedure). As presented in Table 2, those parties using fact-finding prior to arbitration referred an average of 4.0 issues to arbitration compared to an average of 6.2 issues by those parties using independent procedures.

Besides evaluating the efficacy of factfinding as an intermediary step between mediation and tri-offer FOA on the bases of usage rates and filtering effects, two additional dimensions can be used. The impact of the factfinding process can be judged on the extent to which the factfinder's recommendations serve as the foundation for voluntary settlements or encourage position modification should the dispute advance to FOA. And, secondly, for disputes advancing to tri-offer FOA, the factfinding process can be evaluated on the extent to which arbitrators tend to reaffirm or reject the factfinders' recommendations.

Methodology

To determine the impact of factfinders' recommendations on both voluntary and arbitrated settlements, available factfinding and arbitration reports were reviewed for impasse cases involving teachers and municipal employees using the statutory procedure. Available factfinding reports provided the following for each case: the number and type of issues at impasse; the union and employer representatives' impasse positions; and the factfinders' recommendations. Secondly, for those impasse cases that totally or partially resolved the bargaining dispute voluntarily after the issuance of the fact-finding report, the resulting collective bargaining agreement was studied. The parties' impasse positions at factfinding and the factfinder's recommendation were compared with the contract to reveal the extent to which the voluntary agreement reflected terms similar or divergent from the fact-finder's recommendation. For those bargaining disputes advancing to tri-offer FOA, each party's final offers were identified to determine the amount of position convergence that occurred between the issuance of the fact-finder's recommendation and the submission of final offers. Finally, arbitra-tion awards were studied to show whether factfinders' recommendations were typically reaffirmed in the final offers of either party to the dispute.

The sample studied consisted of 147 factfinding cases of which 57 cases advanced to FOA. There were 859 issues submitted to factfinding of which

TABLE 2
Issue Reduction: Number of Issues Presented at Factfinding and Arbitration

Settlement Stage	Year 1 1975-76	Year 2 1976-77	Year 3 1977-78	Year 4 1978-79	Total
	Mean Number of Issues per Case				
Complete settlement after factfinding	6.8 (29)*	4.8 (29)	6.6 (19)	6.6 (43)	6.2 (120)
Factfinding to arbitration					
at factfinding	10.4	5.2	7.8	6.9	6.9
at arbitration	5.4 (8)	3.2 (21)	6.0 (15)	2.8 (18)	4.0 (63)
Arbitration without factfinding	5.4 (14)	6.9 (15)	7.3 (10)	3.5 (4)	6.2 (43)

*Number of cases examined.

624 issues or 72.6 percent were voluntarily resolved after the issuance of the factfinding report. The remaining 235 issues advanced to FOA.

Factfinding Recommendations

Table 3 shows that for about 73.0 percent of the issues the factfinder's endorsed one party's position. However, the factfinders' recommendations disproportionately favored the employer representatives' impasse position

TABLE 3
Location of Factfinding Recommendations by Issue: 1975/76-1978/79

Factfinding Recommendation	Number Issues	Percentage of Recommendations	Number of Issues Advancing to FOA	Percentage of Recommendations Advancing to FOA
Adopt union position	217	25.2%	56	25.8%
Adopt employer position	410	47.6%	100	24.4%
Compromise terms	211	24.5%	75	35.5%
Adopt existing	21	2.4%	4	19.0%
Total	859	100.0%	235	27.3%

(47.6 percent) while the union position was endorsed for 25.2 percent of the issues. Surprisingly, a mid-range or compromise position was recommended for only 24.5 percent of the impasse items, suggesting that the factfinders' propensity to split the difference between the parties' positions is not extensive. And, for 21 of the 859 issues (2.4 percent) examined, the factfinder recommended maintaining the status quo where both parties sought a change in the existing contract.

A review of the type of issues for which the factfinder supported either party's position or recommended a compromise position revealed some interesting results. The factfinder typically endorsed the union position on issues relating to contract duration and grievance procedures, while employers disproportionately received the factfinders' endorsement on items relating to supplemental salary allowances, work hours, and fringe benefits. Compromise recommendations were most often made for issues of base salary and wage rate changes. A year by year analysis revealed no major variation in the distribution of the factfinders' recommendations.

As shown in Table 3, about one in four of the issues presented at factfinding advanced to arbitration. Impasse issues for which a compromise solution was recommended were more likely to advance to arbitration than those issues for which either party's position was endorsed. However, most of the issues receiving compromise recommendations involved base salary and wage rate change disputes which are typically the most critical issues in most impasse cases. Thus, the failure to resolve salary and wage rate disputes is often the compelling reason to submit the dispute to arbitration.

Voluntary Settlements

Of those impasse cases utilizing factfinding, the parties voluntarily settled 624 or 72 percent of all items after receiving the factfinders' reports. In 90 of the 147 cases examined, the dispute was completely resolved after the issuance of the factfinding recommendations, while in 34 of the 57 cases that advanced to FOA, the number of issues at impasse was voluntarily reduced. Table 4 summarizes the extent to which the parties adopted or modified the factfinder's recommendation to reach a voluntary settlement.

The results tend to confirm the general expectation that voluntary agreements reached after factfinding will be on terms identical to the factfinder's recommendations. In 84.9 percent of all voluntary settlements, the factfinder's recommendations were incorporated into the contracts. On only 94 or 15.1 percent of the issues settled voluntarily after the issuance of the factfinding report did the parties deviate from the recommended terms. For 62 or 10.0 percent of all issues settled voluntarily after factfinding, the party receiving the factfinder's endorsement modified its position. This suggests that to some extent a party receiving the factfinder's endorsement will modify its own position to reach a voluntary settlement rather than use the factfinder's support to justify its impasse position and advance the dispute to FOA.

Cases and Issues Advancing to FOA

The 57 cases, reflecting 235 impasse items, advancing to tri-offer FOA were examined to identify first, the occurrence of position modification between

TABLE 4
Voluntary Settlements by Factfinding Recommendation and Contract Terms
(column percentages in parentheses)

| Contract Terms | Factfinding Recommendations | | | | |
	Union Position	Employer Position	Compromise	Existing	Total
Factfinding recommendation	129 (80.1)	280 (90.3)	106 (77.9)	15 (88.2)	530 (84.9)
Union's factfinding position	—* —	13 (4.2)	4 (2.9)	1 (5.9)	18 (2.9)
Employer's factfinding position	19 (11.8)	— —	9 (6.6)	1 (5.9)	29 (4.6)
Favors union	0 (0)	16 (5.2)	11 (8.1)	0 (0)	27 (4.3)
Favors employer	11 (6.8)	1 (.3)	5 (3.7)	0 (0)	17 (2.7)
Existing	2 (1.2)	0 (0)	1 (.7)	— —	3 (.5)
Total issues	161	310	136	17	624

*Same as contract equals factfinding terms.

factfinding and arbitration, and second the propensity by arbitrators to award the factfinders' recommendations.

Table 5 summarizes impasse position modification between factfinding and arbitration. The data report the change in impasse positions by the parties for all 235 issues submitted to FOA during the first four years of bargaining activity relative to the factfinder's recommendation.

Theoretically, the Iowa impasse procedure and tri-offer FOA scheme suggest that post-factfinding modification will be less likely to occur if the factfinder endorses the party's position and more likely to occur if the party fails to receive such endorsement. The results partially support this expectation. In the 56 items advancing to FOA for which the factfinders recommended the unions' positions, the unions submitted their factfinding impasse position as the final offer for 54 or 96.0 percent of these issues. Employers received the factfinder's endorsement on 100 issues that advanced to arbitration and, similarly, submitted the same position as their final offer for all 100 issues. But surprisingly, very limited post-factfinding position modification occurred by the nonendorsed party. For example, of the 56 union positions endorsed by factfinders, the employers converged toward the factfinders' recommendations only 12.5 percent of the time. Similarly, the unions modified their impasse positions on only 16 of the 100 issues where the factfinders supported the employers' positions. Typically, the nonendorsed party modified its position when the disputed issue involved wage level changes rather than non-wage issues.

In contrast to this very limited change where one party's position was endorsed, post-factfinding modification occurred most often if mid-range or compromise solutions were recommended. For the 75 issues receiving compromise solutions, the unions modified their factfinding positions for 52.0 percent of the issues while the employer representatives altered their positions for about 31.0 percent of all issues. The higher propensity to modify impasse positions in compromise situations may be more a function of the types of issues in dispute than the position of the factfinder's recommendation. As previously indicated, factfinders recommended compromises for impasse items involving base salary and wage rate changes. Where this occurred, the unions modified their impasse positions in 73.0 percent of such cases and the employers modified their positions in 67.0 percent of the cases. However, in four years of impasse activity, both unions and employers in general showed limited position modification between factfinding and FOA.

Arbitration

As previously indicated, the FOA step of the Iowa statutory impasse procedure limits the arbitrators to selecting one of three final offers for each impasse item: the final offer of the employer or employee representative, or the factfinding recommendation. However, the probability that the arbitrator will receive three separate final offers for each issue is reduced if the factfinder endorses one party's position. As a result, the arbitrator receives only two distinct final offers: the final offer of the party endorsed by the factfinder and the other, nonendorsed party's final offer. The number of final offers may also be reduced if the factfinder recommends a compromise solution and one party adopts it. Because of the factfinders' propensity to endorse one party's position and the occasional post-factfinding position modification by a party to a final offer recommended by the factfinder, arbitrators received three distinct final offers for only 20.0 percent of the 235 issues submitted to FOA during the first four years.

During the entire four year period, factfinders' recommendations, either as a third distinct alternative or as an endorsement of one party's final offer, were awarded by the arbitrators for about 72.0 percent of the issues. For 186 impasse issues for which only two distinct offers were available, the party's position that was equivalent to the factfinder's recommendation was awarded for 76.0 percent of the issues. In the limited situations where the arbitrators received three distinct offers, the factfinders' recommendations were selected for approximately 56.0 percent of the awards. Furthermore, an annual analysis of arbitration awards revealed that over the four year period the selection of the factfinders' recommendations as the binding award increased substantially.

Reviewing the relationship between post-factfinding position modification and arbitration awards indicates that the party receiving the factfinder's endorsement and maintaining that position at arbitration had a high probability of receiving a favorable arbitration award. Conversely, failing to engage in post-factfinding position modification if the other party's position was endorsed usually meant rejection by the arbitrator. If the factfinder

TABLE 5
Post Factfinding Position Changes

| Factfinding Recommendation | Modification | | | |
| | Union | | Employer | |
	Change	No Change	Change	No Change
Adopt union position (N = 56)	2* (3.6)†	54 (96.4)	7 (12.5)	49 (87.5)
Adopt employer position (N = 100)	16 (16.0)	84 (84.0)	0 (0)	100 (100)
Compromise terms (N = 75)	39 (52.0)	36 (48.0)	23 (30.7)	52 (69.3)
Adopt existing terms (N = 4)	1 (25.0)	3 (75.0)	2 (50.0)	2 (50.0)
Total (N = 235)	58 (24.7)	177 (75.3)	32 (13.6)	203 (86.4)

*Number of issues.
†Percentage of modifications based on factfinding recommendation.

recommended a compromise solution, the party modifying its final offer equivalent to the factfinder's recommendation greatly enhanced the probability of its position being selected by the arbitrator. However, only partial modification of the final offer to incorporate some of the factfinder's recommendation yielded no recognizable advantage, particularly if the other party adopted the factfinder's recommendation as its final offer. In summary, the results suggest that arbitrators have been inclined to select the position of the party receiving the factfinder's endorsement or modifying its impasse position equivalent to the terms recommended by the factfinder.

Conclusions

The bargaining and impasse resolution experiences under the IPERA clearly suggest that the focus of the parties in bargaining relationships has been on voluntary settlement. Data pertaining to negotiations under the statutory impasse procedure indicate that third party intervention is requested in slightly more than one-half of all bargaining relationships, and that when the three step impasse procedure is utilized, approximately four-fifths of such impasses are resolved without neutral assistance beyond mediation. Although the number of voluntary settlements in public sector bargaining in Iowa appears to exceed voluntary settlement rates reported in other jurisdictions, the extent to which such favorable findings are a function of the structure of the impasse procedure is still unclear. More specifically, the absence of adjudicated settlements to resolve bargaining disputes within Iowa could be more a function of various characteristics of the bargaining units rather than the structure of the impasse procedure itself.

355

Factfinding appears to have functioned very effectively as an intermediary step between mediation and FOA. The principal benefit of factfinding is the opportunity for relatively inexperienced negotiators to have their impasse positions evaluated by a neutral party and receive recommendations or directions from the neutral for resolving the dispute. Typically, the factfinder's nonbinding recommendations have been adopted by the parties as the terms on which to resolve their bargaining impasses.

The parties' willingness to reach an agreement on the terms recommended by the factfinders could be the result of two principal factors: the wisdom demonstrated by the factfinders, or the expectation that advancing the dispute to FOA will likely result in the factfinder's recommendation being reaffirmed by the arbitrator as the final and binding award. Thus, the extent to which arbitrators have reaffirmed the factfinder's recommendations when issuing a binding award suggests that the factfinding procedure operates as *de facto* arbitration. In essence, the Iowa experience indicates that what the factfinder recommends is what the arbitrator is likely to award.

A potentially negative effect associated with the operation of factfinding as *de facto* arbitration is the possible chilling effect on the negotiation process. Since the factfinder is not constrained to selecting final offers when formulating recommendations, the parties may approach negotiations prior to factfinding in a manner similar to negotiations prior to conventional arbitration, that is, the parties may withhold concessions prior to the adjudicative step expecting that a compromise award (or recommendation) will be forthcoming. But the extent to which such behavior has occurred prior to factfinding under the Iowa procedure is not entirely certain. The importance of the factfinders' recommendations in the impasse resolution procedure does suggest that the parties may be encouraged to limit their concessions prior to completing factfinding. However, since factfinders have tended to endorse on an issue by issue basis one party's impasse position, it does not appear that the parties adhere to extreme positions prior to factfinding. In addition, about 88 percent of all negotiations are settled prior to factfinding.

Even though the factfinders' recommendations often assume the force of an arbitration award, the principal benefit of retaining factfinding prior to FOA is the opportunity for the parties to mutually adjust through further negotiations the factfinder's advisory award into a voluntary settlement. In essence, the parties receive a strong indication of the terms of a final and binding award but are able to mutually adjust them to reach a voluntary agreement. Finally, although the Iowa experience indicates that arbitrators are likely to reaffirm the factfinders' recommendations, sufficient departure from the factfinders' recommendations has occurred to encourage some parties to an impasse to pursue the dispute to arbitration. In these cases, the use of FOA under the Iowa procedure has assumed the quality of a "court of appeals," where one or both parties seek to overturn an unacceptable factfinder's report.

Footnotes

1. Chapter 20, Code of Iowa, 1977.
2. Chapter 20.19, Code of Iowa, 1977.
3. Chapter 20.21, Code of Iowa, 1977.
4. Chapter 20.22(2) Code of Iowa, 1977.
5. Chapter 20.22(7), Code of Iowa, 1977.
6. T.A. Kochan *et al., An Evaluation of Impasse Procedures for Police and Firefighters in New York State* (Ithaca, N.Y.: New York State School of Industrial and Labor Relations, Cornell University, 1977). p. 94.
7. L. Holden, "Final-Offer Arbitration in Massachusetts," *The Arbitration Journal,* Vol. 31, No. 1 (March, 1976), pp. 26-35.
8. D.E. Bloom, "Customized 'Final-Offer': New Jersey's Arbitration Law," *Monthly Labor Review,* Vol. 103, No. 9, (September, 1980), p. 31.
9. *Ibid.,* p. 32.
10. D.G. Gallagher and R. Pegnetter, "Impasse Resolution Under the Iowa Multi-step Procedure," *Industrial and Labor Relations Review,* Vol. 32, No. 3, (April, 1979), P. 333.
11. P. Feuille, "Final Offer Arbitration and the Chilling Effect," *Industrial Relations,* Vol. 14, No. 3 (October, 1975), pp. 302-310.
12. E. Bittle, "The Fact-Finding Process In Iowa," paper presented at the Sixth Annual Conference of Society of Professionals in Dispute Resolution, Detroit, Michigan, October 31, 1978.
13. Gallagher and Pegnetter, *op. cit,.* p. 333.
14. A. Zack, "Final Offer Selection—Panacea or Pandora's Box?", *New York Law Forum,* Vol. 19 (1974); T. Kochan, "Dynamics of Dispute Resolution in the Public Sector," in B. Aaron, et al., editors, *Public-Sector Bargaining* (Washington, D.C.: BNA, 1979), pp. 176-185.
15. Kochan, *ibid.,* p. 180.
16. A. Zack, "Improving Mediation and Fact-Finding in the Public Sector," *Labor Law Journal,* Vol. 21, No. 5, (May, 1970), p. 270.
17. J.T. McKelvey, "Fact Finding in Public Employment Disputes: Promise or Illusion?", *Industrial and Labor Relations Review,* Vol. 22, No. 4, (July, 1969), p. 542; L. Holden, *op. cit.,* p. 29.
18. In 20 of the 186 cases presented at factfinding, the factfinder engaged in mediation efforts which resulted in a settlement without the issuance of a written report.
19. For a summary of impasse usage rates in other jurisdictions see: Gallagher and Pegnetter, *op. cit.,* p. 331; F. Champlin, *et. al.,* "A General Theory Of Interest Arbitration In Bargaining Behavior," Working Paper 79-03 (Industrial Re-lations Center, University of Minnesota, 1979), pp. 29-31; A. Ponak and H. Wheeler, "Choice of Procedures In Canada And The United States," *Industrial Relations,* Vol. 19, No. 3 (Fall, 1980), pp. 303-308; and T. Kochan, *op. cit.,* pp. 171-177.
20. McKelvey, *op. cit.,* p. 539.
21. Gallagher and Pegnetter, *op. cit.,* p. 330.

PART III

COLLECTIVE BARGAINING IMPACTS

6
Wage Impacts of Unionism

In previous chapters, we examined the public sector collective bargaining process as a dependent variable shaped by external economic, political, and legal contexts as well as by the characteristics of union and management organizations. In this chapter and the one to follow, bargaining is conceptualized as an independent variable, and the focus is on the outcomes or impacts of the collective negotiations process. The wage impacts of public employee unionism are explored in Chapter 6, nonwage impacts in Chapter 7.

For several reasons, it would be difficult to understate the importance of such impact research. First, despite the voluminous literature on public sector labor relations, relatively little systematic study of collective bargaining impacts actually has been undertaken. Second, much of what is perceived to be known about the impacts of unionism on and the consequences of bargaining in government is based on conventional wisdom, assertion, unsupported generalization or limited case study. Third, the conceptual frameworks, research methodologies, and analytical techniques employed to study public sector bargaining impacts vary widely, often are partially or whollly unarticulated, and, on balance, have substantial limitations. Finally, public policies regarding unionism and collective bargaining in government continue to be made largely in the absence of data obtained from systematic impact research.

Measurement Problems

Essentially, impact research on public sector labor relations is concerned with the question, "What substantive difference does the existence of unionism and collective bargaining make?" Though simple to pose, the question is a difficult one to answer. By substantive difference, one may mean the depth or extent of bargaining's impact on a specific employment characteristic, such as the hourly wage rate, amount of overtime worked, pension benefits, or disciplinary practice. Alternatively, one may regard the range or breadth of issues negotiated as a measure of bargaining impact.

Moreover, the latter focus may extend beyond formal bargaining over, say, wages, working conditions, and management policy issues to the impacts of public employee unionism on government structure and informal politics. Ideally, both depth and breadth criteria would be considered in any attempts to measure public sector bargaining impacts, but the practical limitations that confront researchers in this field generally mitigate such comprehensive assessments. Nevertheless, this discussion points up one of the key problems of impact research on public sector collective bargaining, namely isolating the union's impact on a specific issue from its impact on all other issues.

A second and in some ways more vexing problem confronting students of this subject is that of isolating the impacts of unionism from those of other factors that affect the subject matter of bargaining. To gain perspective on this problem, recall the conceptual framework used to organize this book, as illustrated in Figure 1 of the introductory chapter. There, bargaining was conceived as an intervening variable between environmental contexts and organizational characteristics on the one hand, and outcomes or impacts on the other. What may at first glance appear to be outcomes of bargaining in the public sector may, in fact, be due to other, more fundamental forces. In other words, bargaining is a conduit for environmental and organizational variables that impact wages, working conditions, and other issues that are negotiated at the bargaining table. These forces, in addition to unionism itself, are determinants of bargaining outcomes in government, and the researcher must attempt to separate them out in order to obtain accurate measures and identify the impacts of unionism.

This problem is a familiar one within the field of industrial relations and is further complicated by the tendency of bargaining participants and observers to attribute the terms of a contract settlement solely to the formal negotiations process. Thus, upon the conclusion of a labor agreement in the private sector, a manager typically will assign to the union responsibility for wage and other labor cost increases, and may then use this "explanation" to rationalize subsequent price increases for the firm's products. Similarly, a union leader will take credit for the totality of wage, benefit, and working condition improvements he has negotiated. Union members generally accept this claim, and, when they do not, usually turn to new leadership that promises to extract even more from management in subsequent negotiations. The public readily seems to believe the contentions of labor and management about the terms and conditions they have negotiated, even if sometimes holding them in opprobrium for having done so.

Quite the same phenomenon, perhaps to an even greater degree, has emerged in the public sector. Consequently, popular opinion tends to overestimate the impacts of unionism and to be insufficiently appreciative of other variables—economic, political, legal, organizatonal—that affect the terms and conditions of public employment and the costs of government services. In such a context, it is incumbent upon researchers carefully to design their studies of public sector collective bargaining so as to isolate the union impact from all other sources of impact. When unable to do so completely, they should be cautious in interpreting their findings and drawing conclusions about collective bargaining outcomes. Readers may judge for themselves the extent to which these caveats are heeded by the authors of articles presented in this chapter.

We turn now to another problem encountered in public sector collective bargaining research, one which for lack of better terminology might be labeled an aggregation problem. It becomes salient as one inquires into the data base upon which generalizations about public sector bargaining impacts rest. For example, available evidence indicates that the relative wage impact of public employee unions in the United States is, on average, between five and fifteen percent. Yet the empirical basis for this conclusion consists primarily of studies of teacher and protective service worker bargaining in local government. Most other groups of public employees—sanitationmen, clerical employees, hospital attendants, social workers, nurses—have received little or no attention in wage impact research. Therefore, the generalization about the wage outcomes of public sector bargaining noted above must be regarded as a narrow one and its limitations recognized.

That the impacts—wage and non-wage—of government employee unions may vary across occupational groups seems especially plausible in light of the diversity thesis of public sector collective bargaining recently forwarded in the literature and underscored in this book.[2] This diversity may manifest itself among public jurisdictions and within each of them. Thus, in a recent article,[3] Lewin noted the multiple patterns of labor relations that exist among the large local governments of Los Angeles, California, and the four major types of public employee labor organizations in that city. In another article, Kleingartner highlighted the different job-related concerns and hence potential bargaining impacts of publicly-employed professional and nonprofessional workers.[4] Similarly, Derber has detailed the heterogenity of organizational arrangements that public sector managers have adopted to deal with unionism and collective bargaining.[5] Such diversity limits the generalizability of conclusions about public sector bargaining impacts that are based on disaggregated single-union, single-occupation or single-work group studies, including those that encompass more (even many more) than one public employer.

The case approach to public sector bargaining impact research has somewhat different limitations. While it permits the investigator to explore in depth and usually over time multi-faceted dimensions of public sector labor relations, including those that may best be examined qualitatively (as reflected in the Staudohar reading in Chapter 2 and the Lewin-McCormick reading in Chapter 3), it simply does not permit generalization to other governments at the same level. Put differently, the more disaggregated the approach to public sector bargaining research (and the case study is the ultimate in disaggregation), the more limited is the potential for linking the findings to a larger setting and for building broad-based generalizations about the impacts of public employee unionism.

This limitation is partially overcome by the cross-sectional methodology that has been used by several researchers to study one or another aspect of public sector labor relations. For example, Anderson recently employed such an approach to study various outcomes of local government bargaining (see his reading selection in Chapter 7). In the narrower area of wage

impact research, Bartel and Lewin similarly used the cross-sectional methodology, as reported later in this chapter. The conclusions of these researchers
provide a broader and more systematic basis for generalizing about the
outcomes of public sector bargaining than was available heretofore.

These types of cross-sectional research also permit the application of
quantitative techniques to public sector collective bargaining processes and
outcomes, yielding a thoroughness of testing and a level of validity usually
not obtainable through other methodologies. Because of their exclusive
focus on municipal government, however, these studies do not provide the
basis for generalizing about all local government or, of course, the public
sector more broadly. Indeed, labor relations in the federal and state
governments, especially the area of bargaining impacts, remain relatively
unexplored by researchers.[6]

The cross-sectional methodology has one other limitation (perhaps
inherent less in the technique than in its application), namely the difficulty
of measuring changes over time in public sector bargaining impacts. The
bulk of both the wage and non-wage impact studies reported in this and the
next chapter, most of which employ some type of cross-sectional research
design, yield findings at a particular point in time—typically the late 1960s or
early 1970s. As such, they provide a static or snapshot view which may not
endure over time. This is an especially significant limitation in light of the
recent changes that have occurred in the economy of the American public
sector, changes that have brought about a more constrained environment
for the second generation of public sector bargaining.

To illustrate this point further, consider the data presented in the table
below. For the five-year period ending in 1977 (the last year for which
complete data are available), the minimum pay scales of publicly employed
police, firefighters and refuse collectors increased by between 5.9 and 6.5
percent annually, on average, while maximum pay scales for these groups
rose by between 6.5 and 7.1 percent. These rates of increase were well below
the average annual growth rate of privately employed production and
nonsupervisory workers' pay scales over the same period, 7.5 percent. In the
white-collar category, the salaries of urban public school teachers rose at an
average annual rate of 6.9 percent between 1972 and 1977, which was below
the rates of pay increase for clerical and beginning technicians and experienced professionals in industry, though it exceeded the rates of increase for
privately employed entry level professionals and advanced technicians.
(Note that inclusion of rural public schools teachers in these data would very
likely result in lower overall rates of teachers' salary increases). Federal
employees under the General Schedule, of whom there are about 1.4
million, experienced average annual salary growth of 5.1 percent over the
1972-1977 period, or well below the rates of increase for blue-collar
and white collar personnel employed in industry. Additionally, though the
federal government has just recently begun to obtain information on pay
settlements in public sector collective bargaining agreements, the single
year's worth of data that are available, for 1979, show that in that year the
average first-year wage rate adjustment in major agreements in state and
local governments was 6.8 percent, compared with 7.4 percent in major
private sector agreements.[7] When changes in wages *and* fringe benefits were
considered, the average first-year adjustment in state and local contract

362

TABLE 1
Percentage Increases in Average Pay and Salary Scales for Selected Groups of
Public and Private Employees and in the Consumer Price Index over the Five-Year
Period Ending in 1977

Occupational Group	Average Annual Rate of Increase
Public Sector:	
Police	
minimum salary scales	5.9
maximum salary scales	6.8
Firefighters	
minimum salary scales	6.3
maximum salary scales	6.8
Refuse collectors	
minimum salary scales	6.1
maximum salary scales	6.5
Urban public classroom teachers	6.9
Federal employees under the general schedule	5.1
Private Sector:	
Production and nonsupervisory workers in the private, nonfarm economy	7.5
Professional administrative, technical and clerical employees:	
Clerical and beginning technicians	7.1
Entry level professionals and advanced technicians	7.0
Experienced professionals	7.0
Consumer Price Index	7.3

Source: U.S. Bureau of Labor Statistics, *Government Employee Salary Trends,* reprinted from *Current Wage Developments,* February and March, 1978 (Washington, D.C.: G.P.O., n.d.).

settlements was 7.0 percent in 1979, or well below the 9.0 percent average first-year settlement in private sector settlements.[8]

Though they are in no sense conclusive, these data clearly indicate that in the cyclical, generally restrictive economic climate of the mid-to late 1970s, public employee pay increases were below—in some cases well below—the pay increases received by privately employed workers. As the table also shows, public sector pay increases between 1972 and 1977 were below the average annual increase in consumer prices over this period. All this suggests that the pay advantage over comparable privately employed workers that some public employees, both unionized and nonunion, enjoyed in earlier years has since eroded.[9] Although better data would help to establish firmer conclusions in this respect, it does appear (as was noted in the introductory chapter of this book) that the era of "catchup" wage increases for public employees has ended. In a nutshell, the second generation of public sector bargaining in the United States features environmental characteristics that are less favorable for public employees than those that existed during the first generation of bargaining, and this seems to be reflected in the declining relative and real wage position of the public work force. Because we expect these restrictive environmental conditions to continue (and perhaps worsen) in the near future, we anticipate considerable conflict and tension in the public sector bargaining arena over the next several years.

363

From an empirical standpoint, researchers will want to examine and compare the impacts of public employee unionism at various stages in the "business" cycle, rather than simply (and in disaggregated fashion) in the expansionary state. To do so will require the application of longitudinal methodologies to the study of public sector bargaining impacts.[10] This type of analysis hopefully will permit the establishment of broader-based generalizations about bargaining impacts in the American public sector than are presently available.

Some Normative Concerns

We concluded the introductory chapter of this book by discussing explicitly the personal preferences of public sector labor relations researchers and the ways in which those preferences may influence the choice of research topics and interpretation of findings. Before presenting the major readings on wage and nonwage impacts of public employee unions, we want to share with the reader some of our views of and concerns about such impact research.

First, it is our considered judgment that wage impact research is overemphasized and nonwage impact research is underemphasized, not only in the study of public sector labor relations but in the field of industrial relations generally. This is not to denigrate the value of wage impact research—indeed, at the present time, we believe it to be, on balance, of higher quality than nonwage impact research—but, rather, to underscore its limitations, especially if we wish to answer the questions posed earlier in this chapter about the substantive consequences that derive from the existence of unionism and collective bargaining in government.

The strong emphasis placed on union wage impacts in industrial relations research is understandable. Because a major rationale for the existence of labor organizations is to take wages out of competition, it is natural to inquire into and perhaps focus centrally on union wage impacts. In such research in the private sector and, with some modifications, in the public sector as well, investigators make use of neoclassical price theory and its underlying analytic framework to examine systematically the wages of unionized workers compared to those of their nonunion counterparts. No other area of impact research has at its disposal a comparably well-developed theory or analytical framework and, consequently, such research must proceed in relatively "looser" fashion. Furthermore, wage impact research deals in the finiteness and tangibility of numbers, and permits the application of quantitative techniques which are particularly appealing to social science researchers generally and economists in particular.

Yet to draw conclusions about the consequences of unionism and to evaluate the institution of collective bargaining solely on the basis of wage impact research is shortsighted, comparable perhaps to judging the whole by one of its parts. Consider, for example, the comments of Albert Rees concerning private sector union wage impact research:

> My own best guess is that the average effects of all American unions on the wages of their members in recent years would lie somewhere between 15 and 20 per cent. . . . Unions, insofar as they have the power to raise relative wages, reduce employment in the union sector and increase it in the non-union sector. This is a worse allocation of labor than would exist without unions. . . .[11]

He goes on to add, however:

> *The view that unions make for a worse allocation of labor does not necessarily imply an unfavorable judgment of the total effect of unions. There are many other aspects of union activity yet to be considered, and an economy has other and perhaps even more important goals than the most efficient allocation of resources.*[12]

Thus does Rees cogently state the case for avoiding judgments about the impacts of unionism based on partial (even if soundly derived) evidence. The caveat applies as well to public as to private sector unionism and collective bargaining.

Second, important aspects of the public sector employment relationship have escaped the scrutiny of collective bargaining researchers. Most students of public sector union wage impacts, for example, have as yet failed to deal adequately with fringe benefits, most notably employee pensions, in their analysis (although see the Bartel-Lewin reading in this chapter). Broadening the focus of such studies beyond wages to total compensation would provide a broader, more complete basis for judging the monetary impacts of public employee unionism.

Similarly, such nonwage issues as productivity and job security in the public sector have been subjected to little systematic research. The former is commonly alleged to be low, the latter high, in relation to the private sector, but virtually no comparative studies across the sectors or even just among governments have been undertaken, particularly in terms of how these aspects of public employment are impacted by collective bargaining. This probably bespeaks less of the orientation of researchers than of the limited availability of data concerning productivity and job security in government, and also perhaps of the apparent disinterestedness of labor and management in these issues during the first generation of public sector collective bargaining. As bargaining continues in a second generation featuring more restrictive economic and political climates, however, public management may move aggressively to tie wage and benefit increases to productivity improvements (rather than simply dealing in the cosmetics of productivity bargaining), and public employees may make stronger claims on broadened job security or, more generally, property rights in work. Collective bargaining researchers may then have access to a more substantial data base in attempting to assess the nonwage impacts of public employee unionism.

Finally, the methodologies employed to study public sector labor relations, specifically the nonwage impacts of unionism, will have to be refined and improved. It is unlikely that such studies can match the methodological sophistication of the wage impact research reported later in this chapter. Nevertheless, Anderson's analysis of bargaining outcomes in municipal government and the analytical frameworks and methods used by the authors of other readings contained in Chapter 7 of this book provide tangible evidence of the potential for methodological improvement in studying the nonwage impacts of public employee unionism. We should add, however, that the lack of advanced analytical frameworks and methodologies to examine such bargaining impacts is due partly to the complexity of these nonwage issues. It would be unfortunate, in our view, if the absence of precise measures of nonwage bargaining impacts should lead readers—and researchers—to ignore the available evidence about these impacts (some of this evidence is also presented in Chapter 7) or especially to base their judgments about the consequences of collective bargaining solely on the wage impacts of public employee unions. In essence, we prefer a broad over a narrow assessment of public employee unionism, even if this means accepting the methodological and measurement limitations of existing research.

GOVERNMENTAL WAGE-SETTING AND BUDGET-MAKING PROCESSES

Prior to considering empirical evidence concerning the wage impacts of public employee unions, it is necessary to understand some of the characteristics of wage setting and, more generally, cost determination in government. Referring, once again, to the model presented in Chapter 1, these processes may be regarded as organizational characteristics—independent variables— with which collective bargaining, where it develops, subsequently interacts. If the impacts of public employee unions are to be properly gauged, then the outcomes of bargaining must be compared to outcomes that occur in governments without formal collective negotiations or to outcomes that resulted in the pre-union period within a specific public jurisdiction. Bargaining outcomes should not be compared with an ideal model of wage or cost determination in the public sector.[13]

In the first article in this section, Fogel and Lewin identify and analyze some of the consequences of governmental wage-setting processes. Underlying these processes in many governments is the prevailing wage principle which, as the authors note, seemingly makes good sense on both economic and political—i.e., efficiency and equity—grounds. Yet in applying this principle, one that is pervasive in the American public sector and which presumably commits governments to base their wages on prevailing community and especially private industry rates, public employers systematically overpay their blue-collar and lower level white-collar workers, while underpaying their professional and managerial personnel, relative to the private sector. These equalitarian wage structures may perhaps satisfy some equity objective or presage a restructuring of wage relationships in the broader society, but they have negative efficiency consequences and, in any case, are made without the explicit judgment of the voting—and taxpaying—public.

The Fogel-Lewin article not only demonstrates that public employers depart from their own expressed ideals in the determination of wages, it supports the view that bargaining wage impacts should be measured against empirical reality. By distinguishing the narrower wage-related concerns of government employees from the broader issues of interest to the general (voting) public and by identifying the ways in which the former can influence the political processes that govern wage determination, this article implies that government workers can affect their wages prior to or in the absence of unionism and formal collective bargaining. To the extent that such effects occur, they are extremely difficult if not impossible to detect, even by the sophisticated analytical methods employed in the wage impact studies reviewed later in this chapter. Consequently, those studies may misstate the impacts of collective bargaining on public sector wages.

366

The second article in this section, by Derber and Wagner, focuses on the integration—or lack thereof—between formal collective bargaining and the public budgeting process. Studying labor negotiations during the late 1970s in 27 public units in Illinois (a state without a public employee bargaining law, incidentally), the authors found a close relationship between the bargaining and budget-making processes in those units where a "tight" economic situation prevailed, but a much looser connection between the two processes in units where a favorable economic environment existed. In the former government units, bargaining over new agreements typically was completed before or at about the same time as the submission of the budget to a legislative body for approval, whereas in the latter units bargaining proceeded beyond budget completion deadlines. Furthermore, retroactivity of terms and conditions of employment characterized most of the negotiations that took place in a favorable economic climate, but only one of the negotiations that occurred in a tight fiscal environment. Where bargaining and budget-making in public institutions is not closely integrated, public officials who are charged with budget-making responsibilities do not know at the beginning of the relevant fiscal period the true costs of providing government services. Hence, they often must pursue revenue-generating measures, notably tax increases, to meet actual expenditures during the fiscal year—including where putatively formal prohibitions on such actions exist.

The Derber-Wagner study is also of interest because it replicates research conducted by these authors in the early 1970s in the same governmental units.[14] At that time, most of the units faced reasonably favorable economic environments, and the researchers found at best a very loose relationship between the bargaining and budget-making processes. Following the recession of 1974-75 and the more general slowdown in the growth of public sector (including in Illinois) during the 1970s, a more restrictive economic climate existed, particularly in some governmental units. As Derber and Wagner demonstrate, this generated pressures for a much closer link between bargaining and budget making in these Illinois governments. It is likely that, as the second generation of public sector bargaining continues, even stronger pressures will emerge on union officials and managers to integrate the bargaining and budget-making processes. Such integration may permit the more realistic appraisal, and perhaps even containment, of the costs of government services, and may also enable the citizenry to hold elected officials more closely accountable for their managerial performance.[15] To determine whether or not such consequences actually materialize as a result of tightening economic conditions will require longitudinal research, including of the type undertaken by Derber and Wagner in their examination of the relationship between bargaining and budget making in selected Illinois governments.

Finally, Derber and Wagner report a bimodal distribution of union responses to public employer claims (for bargaining purposes) of fiscal stringency. Roughly half of the union negotiators accepted these claims and adjusted their negotiating behavior accordingly. The other half either rejected such employer claims or contended that it was management's responsibility to obtain the funds necessary to finance the pay increases sought by the union negotiators. Derber and Wagner conclude, therefore, that the level of trust between the parties is an important determinant of the degree of integration between bargaining and budget making during periods of fiscal strain. The reader should consider this conclusion in light of the discussion in Chapter 4 of integrative and distributive bargaining.

Taken together, these two articles provide the reader with specific analyses of some important, if unappreciated, characteristics of the governmental sector, especially in terms of how these characteristics affect the costs of government services. As such, they provide a useful backdrop against which to appraise studies of the wage impacts of public employee unions.

FOOTNOTES

1. By relative wages we mean the wages of organized public workers compared to the wages of their unorganized counterparts.
2. Raymond D. Horton, David Lewin, and James Kuhn, "Some Impacts of Collective Bargaining in Local Government: A Diversity Thesis," *Administration and Society,* 7 (February 1976), 497-516, and David Lewin, Raymond D. Horton, and James W. Kuhn, *Collective Bargaining and Manpower Utilization in Big City Governments* (Montclair, N.J.: Allanheld Osmun, 1979), especially chaps. 1 and 6.
3. David Lewin, "Local Government Labor Relations in Transition: The Case of Los Angeles," *Labor History,* 17 (Spring 1976), 191-213.
4. Archie Kleingartner, "Collective Bargaining Between Salaried Professionals and Public Sector Management," *Public Administration Review,* 33 (March-April 1973), 165-172.
5. Milton Derber, "Management Organization for Collective Bargaining in the Public Sector," in Benjamin Aaron, Joseph R. Grodin, and James L. Stern, eds., *Public-Sector Bargaining* (Washington, D.C.: Bureau of National Affairs, 1979), pp. 80-117.
6. But see Anne H. Hopkins, George E. Rawson, and Russell L. Smith, "Public Employee Unionization in the States: A Comparative Analysis," *Administration and Society,* 8 (November 1976), 319-341, and James E. Martin, "Application of a Model from the Private Sector to Federal Sector Labor Relations," *Quarterly Review of Economics and Business,* 16 (Winter 1976), 69-78.
7. See U.S. Department of Labor, Office of Information, "BLS Introduces Data on the Size of Collective Bargaining Settlements Covering State and Local Government Employees," *News* (Washington, D.C.: U.S. Department of Labor, August 18, 1980), p. 5; and U.S. Department of Labor, Bureau of Labor Statistics, "Major Collective Bargaining Settlements, First 9 Months, 1980," *News* (Washington, D.C.: U.S. Department of Labor, October 27, 1980), p. 17.
8. Note that the wage data for state and local governments include contract settlements covering 5,000 or more workers, while the wage data for the private sector include settlements covering 1,000 or more workers. Because wage increases tend to be greater in large than in small bargaining units, it is likely that the average wage settlements in state and local government contracts covering 1,000 or more workers would be below the figure reported above for the larger settlements—and hence the gap between public and private sector contract settlements in 1979 would be even larger than is reported here. It is true that the average annual change in wages over the life of the contracts in the 1979 state and local governments' settlements was 6.3 percent, or greater than the 6.0 percent in private sector settlements. However, for wages and benefits combined, the average change over the life of the contracts in state and local government settlements reached during 1979 was 6.3 percent compared to 6.6

368

percent in private sector settlements. See the sources cited in footnote 7 for further details.

9. An analysis of public sector-private sector pay differentials can be found in the reading by Fogel and Lewin included in this chapter and in Sharon P. Smith, *Equal Pay in the Public Sector: Fact or Fantasy?* (Princeton, N.J.: Princeton University Press, 1977).

10. One such application is reported in Lewin, Horton, and Kuhn, *op. cit.,* chap. 4.

11. Albert Rees, *The Economics of Trade Unions,* rev. ed. (Chicago: University of Chicago Press, 1977), pp. 74 and 87-88.

12. *Ibid.,* pp. 88-89.

13. This is comparable to the caveat issued by Rees, *op. cit.,* p. 65: "In judging the consequences of union wage effects, we shall seek to compare the operation of organized labor markets with the operation of unorganized labor markets as they exist in the United States, for it would be unfair to compare the organized market with some theoretical model of a perfect market that never existed."

14. Milton Derber, Ken Jennings, Ian McAndrew, and Martin Wagner, "Bargaining and Budget Making In Illinois Public Institutions," *Industrial and Labor Relations Review,* 27 (October 1973), 49-62. Three of the 30 governmental units studied in the early 1970s were not included in the follow-up study for reasons explained in the article by Derber and Wagner.

15. This theme is developed in Raymond D. Horton, *Reforming the Labor Relations Process in New York City* (New York: State Charter Revision Commission, January, 1975). See also Lewin, Horton, and Kuhn, chap. 6.

Wage Determination in the Public Sector

Walter Fogel* and David Lewin

There is a growing body of evidence that government employment is attractive in terms of both wages and job security. A recent U.S. Bureau of Labor Statistics survey found that clerical, data processing, and manual workers employed by municipalities in eleven large urban areas were substantially better paid than their counterparts in private industry.[1] In most cases, federal employees in the same cities also were paid more than comparable private sector workers. Fringe benefits in the public sector are also as good or better than those in the private sector, according to a national survey of U.S. municipalities.[2] Furthermore, job hiring and tenure practices provide considerable security to public workers: in 1971, 57 percent of nonfarm private employees worked a full year, whereas in the public sector the proportion was 77 percent.[3] Attractive wages and salaries, steady demand for public services, and tenure practices all combine to produce low rates of employee turnover—19 percent in state and local government and 22 percent in the federal service in 1970, compared to 58 percent in private manufacturing.[4]

*Graduate School of Management, University of California, Los Angeles. Reprinted from *Industrial and Labor Relations Review,* 27 (April 1974), 410-31.

Because these rather surprising findings conflict with popular notions about government pay, it is appropriate to examine the process of wage determination in the public sector and the outcomes of this process for different occupational groups in government employment. Governmental wages and salaries affect the respective government budget and, therefore, the citizens' tax burden; they influence the relative attractiveness of employment in the public and private sectors; and they are an important factor in the continuing debate over the size and role of government in American society.

The Prevailing Wage Principle

Almost all levels and agencies of government in this country, at the city level or higher, are required to pay wages comparable to those received by private employees performing similar work. This rule is commonly called the "prevailing wage" principle. For example, the Federal Salary Reform Act of 1962 requires that "federal pay rates be comparable with private enterprise pay rates for the same levels of work." The city of Los Angeles, one of the largest local government employers in the United States, is required by its charter to "provide a salary or wage at least equal to the prevailing salary or wage for the same quality of service rendered to private employers."[5]

These prevailing wage requirements are sensible in terms of both equity and efficiency. The output of government does not pass through the marketplace where its relative worth can be assessed by customers. In the absence of a product market discipline imposed on pay practices (a discipline which, incidentally, is not present in all parts of the private sector), what could be more fair than to pay government employees what their private industry counterparts are getting? Furthermore, to attract employees of at least average quality to the government, the pay offered must be comparable to that available in the private sector. For the government to pay more than the private sector, however, would be unneccesary and would waste government revenues. Therefore, the prevailing wage rule is efficient as well as equitable.

On the surface, the procedure seems quite simple and "fair" for all concerned. As one examines the application of this rule closely, however, things appear less simple and certainly not "fair" for everyone. Aside from the administrative problem of applying the prevailing wage rule to an occupational structure that may include hundreds or even thousands of job classifications, this rule is dependent on the existence of smoothly functioning private labor markets. If these markets all operated like the textbook model of perfect competition, the prevailing wage rule would always provide efficient and equitable wages — and, in fact, such laws would probably not be needed at all. Private markets, however, are influenced by noncompetitive forces and also contain jobs that differ widely with respect to their nonwage attractiveness. The latter phenomenon produces a range of wage rates, rather than a single rate; the noncompetitive forces often produce a wage (or range of wages) above or below that which would prevail in a truly competitive market.

370

The existence of a range of wages for most occupations presents difficult administrative problems for government wage-fixing authorities. What rules should be applied to the range in order to come up with a prevailing wage? Should the average of the entire range be used, or the first quartile, or the mean, or the median? The decision could be made simpler by precisely defining the labor markets in which the government employer must compete for a work force. Rarely is this done, however. Instead, it will be shown that the more common practice is to seek wage information over the geographical area included within the governmental jurisdiction and then only from medium- and large-sized employers. Although this practice holds down the cost of wage surveys—surveying small firms or firms outside of the local market is costly relative to the information obtained—it also imparts an upward bias to prevailing wage determinations, since only the "core" economy is surveyed. The "periphery" economy, which pays low wages, is excluded.[6]

Other Problems

The existence of a private sector market that pays wages that are either above or below the competitive wage presents a more difficult policy problem for governmental wage setters. Suppose that a private sector wage is depressed because the market is monopsonistic or, more likely, because discrimination or other factors that impede mobility confine some workers to a small part of the total labor market. In such cases, is it appropriate for government to pay a wage that has resulted from the market power of the employer or from employee inability to compete? We will show that many government wage-setting authorities apparently think not, and in these cases they often establish rates above those prevailing in such private markets.

In contrast, suppose that a union, professional association, or licensing agency has achieved a wage above that which would otherwise prevail. For example, Lewis has estimated that, on average, American unions have a 7 to 15 percent impact on the wages of those for whom they bargain,[7] and, because of their ability to influence labor supply, some unions, especially craft unions, have an even larger impact on wages. Should governments match wage rates that have been achieved through the exercise of private market power and, in effect, support and expand such power? For reasons to be stated later, we assume that, in their wage-setting actions, governments will indeed tend to match private market rates that have been raised through market power, even in instances in which lower rates would clearly attract an adequate supply of labor.

Another potential bias in government wage-setting practices occurs because of the narrow view of employment compensation contained in most prevailing wage statutes. Any reasonably sophisticated view of the labor market recognizes that the wage is merely the most variable part of employment compensation, the part that firms most easily adjust to offset other aspects of compensation (fringe benefits, working conditons, location, etc.) that are discernibly advantageous or disadvantageous. A private firm can experiment with its wage rates, relative to those of other firms, in order to discover the rates that, along with other characteristics of the firm, will attract an adequate work force. In contrast, government employers required to pay prevailing wages almost always interpret that requirement as precluding any attempt to take into account the attractiveness of nonwage aspects of government employment. As previously noted, one such nonwage aspect—job security—appears to be very attractive in government compared to the private sector. Failure to consider this difference in job security on the part of government wage setters would seem, *a priori,* to produce public wage rates that are higher than necessary to attract a work force.

Finally, for some public sector jobs (e.g., policemen, firemen, social worker), there is either no private market or, because of government's dominant employment position in these occupations, wage rates in the private market that does exist are pegged to the public sector rather than the reverse. Government employers probably overestimate the number of occupations of this type, but some do exist. How should the pay for such jobs be established?

To summarize, four aspects of labor markets create serious policy problems whenever public employers attempt to translate prevailing wage statutes into wage rates for their employees: the wide range of wages paid for most private sector jobs; the existence of wage rates established through the exercise of market power; the multifaceted nature of employment compensation; and the absence of a private market for some government occupations.[8] Because of these factors, much discretion must be exercised by public authorities in implementing prevailing wage statutes and fixing public sector wages. It will be argued here that this discretion in decision making, plus the political processes involved in wage setting, produce upwardly biased wage rates for most government jobs.

The Politics of Wage Setting

Recently, several researchers have summarized the shortcomings of traditional wage theory in explaining public sector wage determination.[9] Major weaknesses include the absence of a motive for profit maximization in government and the related lack of a conventional demand curve for labor. Public employers' demand curves are inferred indirectly through "voter expressed demands for government services and directly through political bargaining between governments and employee groups," rather than through a marginal revenue product curve.[10] Thus, construction of a relevant public sector wage model apparently requires more explicit consideration of the motivations of public managers and public workers, as well as the political processes through which these motivations are filtered.

In his seminal work on democratic theory, Anthony Downs notes that "the main goal of every party (defined as a team of individuals) is the winning of elections. . . . Thus, all its actions are aimed at maximizing votes."[11] In pursuit of that goal, parties view the electorate as a number of interest groups, and they seek to determine and respond to the relative importance of such groups.

Thus, in their wage-setting decisions, political bodies are sensitive to two constituencies. First, there are the government employees directly affected by public wage decisions. In general, the larger the group whose wages will be affected by a legislative decision, the more responsive elected decision makers will be to the preferences of this group. The second constituency is the general public. The public is, of course, interested in keeping down its tax burden, but beyond this general constraint, it is usually uninformed and not especially interested in the specifics of government wage setting.

> *In order to influence government policy-making in any area of decision, a citizen must be continuously well-informed about events therein. . . . The expense of such awareness is so great that no citizen can afford to bear it in every policy area. . . . If he is going to exercise any influence at all, he must limit his awareness to areas where intervention pays off most and costs least.*[12]

Consequently,

> *many voters do not bother do discover their true views before voting, and most citizens are not well enough informed to influence directly the formulation of those policies that affect them.*[13]

These considerations suggest that lawmakers are relatively more responsive to the first group—those directly affected by wage decisions—than to the second. Government employees will watch lawmakers' reactions to their proposed wage increases, and these reactions, especially negative reactions, can be the major determinants of employee voting behavior in subsequent elections. The general public, however, will probably not recall the lawmakers' votes on government wage questions, and furthermore, will be concerned with a variety of other issues in its voting decisions. In general, then, the combination of the direct interest of government employees in their wages and the diffusion of issues (including public sector pay issues) among the general constituency create the potential for an upward bias in public sector wage rates. Obviously, the potential bias increases with the size of the government sector in question.

An organization of public employees will attempt to exploit this political condition. First, it will try to bring about solidarity among employees who are to be directly affected by wage decisions. Second, it will attempt to convey the force of this solidarity to the appropriate political body. Finally, it may attempt to gain broad support for its wage objectives by appealing directly to the public. At least part of the relative increase in public sector wage rates over the last ten to fifteen years is due to the effectiveness with which some public employee organizations have carried out these activities.[14]

In summary, because of the nature of the political process involved, there is a tendency for lawmakers and other elected officials to support the wage preferences of government employees. Indeed, "the position of public employees as voters and opinion-makers who partially determine whether or not the employer retains his job" has been cited as the major factor underlying motivational differences between public employers and private, profit-maximizing employers.[15] The tendency toward "high" public wages varies with the size of the group in question, its public "image," and its cohesiveness. Finally, this tendency has been increasing as government services have expanded and as employee organizations continue to develop in the public sector.

Major Patterns

In the balance of this paper, we shall present evidence showing that wage determination in the public sector tends to be characterized by the following practices:

1. Government employers deal with the range of private sector wages for any given occupation, in part, by excluding small firms from their wage surveys. This has the effect of giving an upward bias to the results of such surveys.
2. The public sector pays rates that are higher than existing private rates for jobs for which the private sector wage is relatively low because of monopsony or highly elastic supplies of unskilled laborers who are relatively immobile.
3. The public sector pays wages that are at least equal to those that exist in private markets where wage levels have been increased by supply-side institutional power.
4. Public agencies do not take into account favorable nonwage aspects of public sector employment or unfavorable aspects of private sector employment that have affected the private market wage.
5. Administrative procedures used to fix wages for "unique" public sector jobs bias the results upward.

These practices result from the effect of the political process underlying public sector wage setting on the discretionary areas inherent in the prevailing wage concept as it is applied to imperfect labor markets. The general result of these practices is that public sector wages tend to exceed those of the private sector for all occupations except high level managers and professionals. These relationships flow directly from the politicization of public sector wage determination. There are many more votes in the low-skill and middle-skill occupations than in managerial-professional jobs. Furthermore, public employees in the latter jobs tend to be more visible to a public that is skeptical, at best, of the contributions of "highly paid" government employees.

The Evidence

Government employers deal with the range of private sector wages for any given occupation, in part, by excluding small firms from their wage surveys. The Bureau of Labor Statistics (BLS) annually conducts wage surveys of (a) office clerical, (b) professional and technical, (c) maintenance and power plant, and (d) custodial and material movement occupations in more than ninety major metropolitan areas of the United States. In reporting the results of these surveys, BLS states explicitly that "establishments having fewer than a prescribed number of workers are omitted because they tend to furnish insufficient employment in the occupations to warrant inclusion."[16] Therefore, to be included in the survey in most areas, an establishment must employ at least fifty workers in manufacturing; transportation, communication, and other public utilities; wholesale trade; retail trade; finance, insurance, and real estate; or services. In twelve of the largest areas, the minimum establishment size is one hundred workers in manufacturing;

374

transportation, communication and other public utilities; and retail trade.[17] Because wages vary directly with firm size,[18] these procedures have the effect of biasing survey results upward. Public wages set on the basis of survey rates will be similarly biased.

Since 1959, the BLS has also conducted the *National Survey of Professional, Administrative, Technical and Clerical Pay* (PATC), the results of which are used in the determination of wages for white-collar (i.e., "general schedule") civil service workers as well as employees in the postal field service and those covered by a few other statutory pay systems. Minimum establishment size requirements in this survey range from 100 employees in most industry divisions to 250 employees in manufacturing and retail trade. As in the area wage surveys, exclusion of relatively small, low-wage establishments results in upwardly biased wages in the PATC survey.

State and local government employers, especially those with large labor forces, sometimes undertake their own wage surveys. For example, in Los Angeles, four local public jurisdictions jointly conduct an annual survey of wages and salaries in Los Angeles County. To be included in this survey, an establishment regardless of its industry classification must employ more than 250 persons. Industry coverage parallels that of the BLS survey.

The exclusion of small establishments from public wage surveys produces both a direct and indirect upward bias in the survey results. The direct bias occurs, of course, because of the positive relationship that exists between size of firm and wage levels. The indirect bias occurs from the overrepresentation of high-wage industries and underrepresentation of low-wage industries produced by the exclusion of small establishments. For example, wholesale and retail trade accounted for only 9 percent of surveyed employment in Los Angeles County in 1970, when actually 26 percent of all workers in that county were employed in those industries. On the other hand, employment in the manufacturing and utilities-transportation sectors is overrepresented in this survey.[19]

The magnitude of the bias produced by the exclusion of small firms from wage surveys is probably large. Approximately 60 percent of all nonfarm private sector employees work in establishments employing fewer than 250 employees.[20] Such workers are likely to be paid 15 to 20 percent less than employees of establishments with 1,000 or more employees.[21]

Low-Wage Jobs

The public sector pays more than existing private rates for jobs for which the private sector wage is relatively low because of the monopsony or highly elastic supplies of unskilled laborers who are relatively immobile. Rather than ferret out the existence of monopsony and labor supply characteristics of private labor markets, we will present evidence on the simpler proposition that, *for most low-wage occupations, government pays more than the private sector.*

Table 1 shows that there is proportionately more low-wage employment in the private sector of the American economy than in the governmental sector. For example, among full-time, year-round, privately employed workers, about 12 percent earned less than $4,000 and 42 percent earned less than $7,000 in 1971, when the comparable proportions in the public sector were only 6 and 30 percent. Note that the proportion of low-wage employment is particularly small in the federal government, in which the median annual salary was $11,809 in 1971.[22] The relative advantage of the public sector would be increased by inclusion of private self-employed workers in the comparisons and, of course, by inclusion of part-time and part-year workers.

These public-private differences in earnings distributions could reflect differences in occupational composition rather than rates of compensation. Table 2, therefore, presents salary comparisons for low-wage occupations common to municipal, federal, and private employment in eleven large cities, including five of the six U.S. cities with populations over one million. In nine of these cities, municipal governments consistently paid higher salaries than private employers in 1970. Only in New Orleans and Kansas City did private sector pay exceed municipal pay for the occupations listed. The size of the municipal-private differential is often substantial. Of the fifty-six observations in Table 2, twenty-seven show a municipal wage of at least 20 percent.[23] It should be remembered, as well, that the private sector wages that are used to make the comparisons in Table 2 contain some upward bias, since they do not encompass the rates paid by small establishments.

The superiority of municipal over private pay in major American cities is further accentuated when hours of work are considered. In Los Angeles, Houston, Kansas City, and Atlanta, municipal white-collar employees worked

TABLE 1
Earnings Distribution for Full-Time, Year-Round Wage and Salary Workers in the U.S., by Sex and Employment Sector for 1971 (in percentages)

Employment Sector and Sex	Earning Below				
	$3000	$4000	$5000	$6000	$7000
Private sector					
Male	3.4	6.5	11.3	18.2	26.3
Female	11.4	25.7	45.0	64.3	77.9
Average	5.8	12.3	21.5	32.1	41.8
Public sector					
State and local government					
Male	1.5	4.6	7.2	12.5	19.8
Female	4.4	10.8	20.3	32.3	45.8
Average	2.6	6.4	12.4	20.3	30.1
Federal government (both sexes)	0	1.6	2.7	6.6	16.2

Source: U.S. Bureau of the Census, "Money Income in 1971 of Families and Persons in the U.S.," *Current Population Reports,* Series P-60, No. 85 (Washington, D.C.: G.P.O., 1972), Tables 52 and 58, pp. 135-38; and U.S. Civil Service Commission, *Pay Structure of the Federal Civil Service* (Washington, D.C.: G.P.O., June 30, 1971), Tables 11-14, pp. 29-32.

TABLE 2
A Comparison of Monthly Salaries in Municipal Government and Private Industry in Seven Low-Wage Occupations and Eleven Cities for 1970

(Private Industry Salary = 100)

Occupation	Equivalent Federal Salary (GS) Grade	New York	Chicago	Los Angeles	Phila-delphia	Houston	Newark	Boston	New Orleans	Kansas City	Atlanta	Buf-falo
Messenger	1	114	98	107	136	123	125	107	86	–	–	–
Keypunch op.–B	2	102	101	120	114	111	120	103	91	95	104	115
Switchboard op.–B	2	105	112	134	–	142	107	–	105	–	119	135
Typist–B	2	102	105	123	142	–	107	102	89	101	102	122
Tab. mach. op.–C	2	109	107	–	140	–	–	–	–	–	–	–
Tab. mach. op.–B	3	–	103	–	131	–	–	114	83	–	112	–
Janitors, porters, and cleaners	–	98	137	122	131	124	109	127	88	95	100	111

Source: Stephen H. Perloff, "Comparing Municipal Salaries with Industry and Federal Pay," *Monthly Labor Review,* Vol. 94, No. 10 (October 1971), Tables 1-3, pp. 47-50.

377

a "standard" 40 hour week in 1970, but in Philadelphia, the work week for these employees was 37.5 hours; in Chicago, Boston, New Orleans, and Buffalo, 35 hours; in Newark, 30 hours; and in New York City, municipal employees worked a 35 hour week for nine months and a 30 hour week during the remainder of the year.[24] Although these differences in work schedules partially reflect differences in area practices generally, the municipal work week is typically shorter than the work week in private employment. For example, in New York City in 1970, "96 percent of the white-collar workers in local government worked 35 hours or less per week as compared with 58 percent of private office workers."[35] Thus, pay differentials between municipal and private employment are even greater when considered on an hourly rather than monthly basis.

The pattern of relatively high governmental pay for low-skill occupations may be even more pronounced in suburban areas than in central cities. This very tentative conclusion emerges from analysis of recently published data, presented in Table 3, on the salaries of local government workers in the New York City area. For the individual occupations shown in that table, average salaries in the two types of suburban governments ranged from 18 percent above to 6 percent below those in New York City. In only two cases, however, did suburban pay fall below central city pay in the New York area.

TABLE 3
Average Weekly Earnings for Janitors and Office Clerical Occupations in New York Area Local Government[a] for April 1970

Occupation	New York City Municipal Government Earnings (dollars)	New York Area Earnings as a Percentage of New York City	
		Counties	Suburban Cities and Towns
Typist–B	102.40	102	100
Messenger	103.00	102	112
Keypunch operator–B	106.00	108	116
General stenographer	107.50	102	107
Accounting clerk–B	108.00	116	113
Transcribing machine operator–B	111.00	101	94
Janitors, porters, cleaners	111.20	112	113
Bookkeeping machine operator–B	113.50	118	100
Switchboard operator–B	114.00	97	106
Senior stenographer	125.00	113	111

[a] Includes New York City municipal government and the governments of five counties and fifty-three cities and towns located in the New York standard metropolitan statistical area.

Source: U.S. Department of Labor, Bureau of Labor Statistics, *Wages and Benefits of Local Government Workers in the New York Area,* Regional Reports, Number 26, December 1971 (Washington, D.C.: G.P.O., 1972), Tables 2, 4, and 6; and pp. 16, 21, and 25.

Pay differentials between New York counties and the City exceeded 10 percent in four occupations; differentials between suburban municipalities and New York City exceeded 10 percent in five occupations. It is possible, of course, that this differential is "neutralized" by similar differentials in private industry salaries between the suburbs and the central city.

Relatively high minimum wages in government employment are sometimes explicitly mandated by legislative statute. In 1970, for example, the salary ordinance governing the largest local government employer in Southern California, the County of Los Angeles, required that, "notwithstanding any other provisions of this ordinance, the minimum salary for all positions . . . shall be $417 per month . . . or $2.40 per hour, as the case may be."[26] Similarly, the city of Los Angeles required that

> the salary rate of any person . . . employed in any class, the salary schedule of which is fixed at Schedule 23 or lower, and who is receiving salary at a lower rate than the third step of the schedule for such class . . . shall be increased to the third step of the schedule prescribed for his class of position.[27]

The city's statute resulted in a minimum wage of $2.54 per hour in 1969. Minimum wages in the county and city of Los Angeles were thus 50 and 59 percent higher respectively than the minimum hourly wage of $1.60 then mandated for private employment under the Fair Labor Standards Act. These ordinances account for at least some of the public-private differentials that exist in the Los Angeles area, as shown in Table 2 and also, using different sources and data, in Table 4.

Craft Wages

The public sector pays wages at least equal to those that exist in private markets where wage levels have been increased by supply-side institutional power. Among American unions, market power is perhaps most strongly exercised by construction unions. Moreover, governmental pay policies have broadened the wage impact of construction unions in the private sector and have extended it to public employment.

For example, at the federal level, the Davis-Bacon Act requires private contractors engaged in construction work valued at two thousand dollars or more and paid for by federal funds to compensate employees on the basis of prevailing wages. Secretaries of Labor have generally considered the union rate to be the prevailing rate even in nonunion areas. Consequently, "unions need only secure a wage increase in a few locations where their control of the labor supply is firm . . . and under the law the government extends the wage gain far and wide."[28] It is little wonder that this act has been labeled a "superminimum wage law."[29]

At the state and local level, especially in very large cities, this approach has been carried one step further: through explicit policy or administrative practice, government craft employees are often paid construction industry rates and frequently only the union rates within construction. In these cases, public employers ignore the lower wages paid by nonconstruction employers for the same jobs. This practice undoubtedly accounts, at least in part, for the relatively high salaries for public craft workers in five of the eleven

TABLE 4
Monthly Salaries in Low-Skill Occupations and the Private and Public Sectors for the County and City of Los Angeles, Fiscal Year 1969-70

Occupation	Private Sector	Public Sector County Government	Public Sector City Government	Differences Between Public and Private Sectors (percentage) County	Differences Between Public and Private Sectors (percentage) City
Laundry worker	287	428	–	49.1	–
Institutional food service worker	358	447	–	24.9	–
Hospital attendant	385	453	–	17.7	–
Clerk	385	428	464	11.1	20.5
Clerk typist	418	447	489	6.9	17.0
Custodian	447	489	491	9.4	9.8
Gardener	495	–	591	–	19.4
Transcriber typist	480	518	–	7.9	–
Bookkeeping machine operator	475	489	516	2.9	8.6
Telephone operator	474	489	505	3.1	6.5
Vocational nurse	494	577	–	16.8	–

Sources: Derived from City of Los Angeles *et al.*, *Wage and Salary Survey in Los Angeles County*, March 1, 1969 (Los Angeles: City of Los Angeles, Printing Division, 1969); County of Los Angeles, *Salary Ordinance of Los Angeles County,* Ordinance Number 6222, as amended to July 1, 1969; and City of Los Angeles, City Administrative Officer, *Salary Recommendations* (processed, April 1969).

major cities for which data are presented in Table 5.

Public employers are not unaware of the substantial public-private differentials for craft workers. In Los Angeles, for example, local government employers annually obtain data on craft wages in all sectors of the private market. Yet, when setting wages for municipal craft workers, these employers discard all market rates obtained through their survey and adopt, instead, construction industry-negotiated wage levels. This occurs despite important differences (to be discussed later) in the characteristics of craft employment between the public and private sectors. Consequently, an analysis of the 1969 local agency survey (not the BLS data reported in Table 5) showed that Los Angeles government agencies paid craft workers salaries that were between 10 and 46 percent higher than those paid by private employers, and the differences would have been even larger if small (low-wage) employers had been included in the government's wage survey.[30]

Nonwage Factors

Public agencies do not take into account favorable nonwage aspects of public sector employment or unfavorable aspects of private sector employment that have affected the private market wage. As previously noted,

380

TABLE 5
Municipal Salaries as a Proportion of Private Industry Pay in Selected Crafts, 1970*

(Private Industry Salary = 100)

Occupation	New York	Chicago	Los Angeles	Phila- delphia	Houston	Boston	New Orleans	Kansas City	Atlanta	Buf- falo	Newark
Carpenter, maintenance	162	125	118	106	91	91	76	80	98	88	141
Electrician, maintenance	162	148	121	107	113	–	87	87	91	82	141
Helper, maintenance trades	–	–	–	113	–	99	–	–	–	83	171
Painters, maintenance	136	108	107	114	95	101	75	81	100	93	139
Plumbers, maintenance	160	111	121	113	–	–	–	–	–	–	144

*Comparisons are of monthly salaries.

Source: Stephen H. Perloff, "Comparing Municipal Salaries with Industry and Federal Pay," *Monthly Labor Review*, Vol. 94, No. 10 (October 1971), p. 49.

government employment generally offers more favorable fringe benefits, employment stability, and job security than private employment. Yet government employers fail to take this into account when establishing their own wage rates.

In addition to the evidence previously cited of the favorable nonwage aspects of much government employment,[31] it is useful to examine comparative turnover data in more detail. Among thirty-three federal agencies reporting separation data, only three—Interior, Agriculture, and the Tennessee Valley Authority—experienced rates higher than those incurred by manufacturing industries in 1972, and the layoff rate alone was 75 percent lower in the federal service than in manufacturing.[32] Although state governments experienced about the same separation rate as the federal sector (22 percent) in 1970, county and city governments experienced rates only three quarters and two thirds as large respectively as the federal government's.[33] These rates are especially significant in light of the fact that local governments employ more than two and one-half times as many workers as state governments in the United States.

The failure of public employers to consider the nonwage aspects of employment is most generally shown by the methods commonly used to implement the prevailing wage rule. When they are undertaken, governmental wage surveys generally solicit only wage and salary information. Recently, the Department of Labor expanded some (but not all) of its area wage surveys to include selected fringe benefits, such as work scheduling, paid vacations and holidays, and health and welfare plans.[34] Most state and local public employers, however, have not similarly intensified their survey efforts, and the government has not yet sought unemployment or turnover data from private employers as part of its wage-setting process. Thus, public employers focus too narrowly on wages to the exclusion of other factors determining comparative net advantage in the labor market.

Inconsistent treatment of nonwage differences in employment is shown by pay determination procedures for public craft occupations. On the one hand, the higher public fringe benefits are often recognized by setting public wages for these jobs at the level of unionized industry rates minus some percentage reduction for the superior fringe benefits paid by the public jurisdiction. On the other hand, use of the negotiated construction rates ignores the fact that most public sector craft employees are more fully employed and apparently perform much more nonconstruction work (for which private sector wages are lower) than private sector construction workers. These procedures help to bring about heavy civil service filing and waiting lists for most craft occupations in many cities.[35]

Unique Jobs

Administrative procedures used to fix wages for "unique" public sector jobs bias the results upward. Various methods are used to set pay for jobs unique to the public sector.[36] Although these procedures do not uniformly result in upwardly biased wage rates, on balance, they have probably escalated rates beyond efficient levels.[37]

Because private market wage data are unavailable for jobs exclusive to government, public administrators often set pay for these positions on the basis of interagency or intergovernmental comparisons. For example, in Los Angeles, the Department of Water and Power, a city agency with independent salary setting authority, has historically been a high-wage employer, compensating some uniquely public occupations at rates more than 20 percent above those of other departments. Because of this, city agencies in similar positions face continual upward pressures on wages, even in cases in which substantial civil service eligibility and waiting lists are maintained.

The County of Los Angeles determines pay for social work, probation, property appraisal, sanitation, and inspection positions by comparing its rates with those of the ten other largest counties in California and then making any pay adjustments required to maintain at least a third-place ranking among these governments.[38] Because the county is the principal employer of public service personnel in Southern California, its wage decisions set the pattern for other governmental bodies in the area. To the extent that the other large California counties (and local governments) make similar pay comparisons, this practice creates the potential for circular wage escalation in positions exclusive to the public sector.

A procedure that establishes wage rates for many "unique" public employees is the "parity" arrangement. Wage parity between policemen and firemen is especially widespread; this arrangement was adhered to by more than 60 percent of all American municipalities in 1969. Because of dissimilarities between the labor markets for policemen and firemen, the parity rule probably results in the underpayment of policemen and certainly the overpayment of firemen, judged by market criteria.[39]

In some cities, sanitation workers are treated as a component (with police and firemen) of the uniformed services. Where this occurs, there exists pressure for a more expanded form of wage parity—tripartite parity. Although sanitationmen have not yet achieved outright parity with police, and are generally paid about one-quarter less than police, the differential in 1970 was only about 15 percent in the largest cities (those with populations of more than one million) and about 13 percent in Northeastern cities.[40] In New York, sanitationmen now earn 90 percent of police base pay, up from 60 percent in 1940, and the differential is even smaller when interdepartmental variation in overtime scheduling is considered. Because of this wage level, New York City experiences substantial queuing for positions in the sanitation service.

It has been suggested that pay for uniquely public jobs should be based on private sector wages for "occupations . . . to which individuals of comparable training and interests might be attracted."[41] Thus, in some cities, police and fire salaries are based on rates paid to skilled trades occupations in the local labor market, on the assumption that the two occupational groups attract persons of similar characteristics.[42] Aside from its dependence on a market sector that is strongly influenced by union power, this is not an unreasonable procedure, provided that its results are periodically checked against job turnover and vacancy experience.

A widely practiced procedure for dealing with exclusively public jobs is to establish their wage *levels* at a point in time by some system of internal job evaluation or salary comparisons and to base subsequent wage *increases* on the average rate of wage change occurring in the local private market. This is a generally commendable technique and is practically the only means of setting wages for some public jobs. All job evaluation systems, however, incorporate a large element of subjectivity and, consequently, are subject to the politicization process described earlier.

The Total Wage Structure

Public sector wages tend to exceed those of the private sector for all occupations except high-level managers and professionals. Evidence demonstrating a tendency for public wages to exceed private levels for low-skilled and craft occupations has already been presented. There is ample information showing the reverse relationship for high-level occupations.

The National Manpower Council noted in 1964 that

> *government employers have been handicapped by the salaries they offer . . . scientific, professional and managerial and executive personnel. . . . The discrepancy between public and private compensation for these categories of personnel . . . are larger on the upper rungs of the salary ladder.*[43]

Table 6 presents federal government—private industry salary comparisons for the ten lowest and ten highest ranking positions included in the most recent *National Survey of Professional, Administrative, Technical and Clerical Pay*. These data show that in 1972, for jobs with GS 1 through GS 3 classifications, the federal government paid between 1 percent and 13 percent more than private industry, whereas for jobs with GS 13 through GS 15 grades, federal salaries ranged between 1 percent above and 19 percent below private salaries. In the same year, the highest pay schedule in government, that for the federal executive branch, contained salaries ranging from $36,000 to $60,000—well below the $144,000 median salary then paid to the chief executive officers of America's 774 highest paying corporations.[44] Although progress has been made, the conclusion reached ten years ago by the Advisory Panel on Federal Salary Systems still holds: "Federal agencies . . . lag far behind private employers in the monetary rewards they can offer executive and managerial . . . personnel even though they have duties and responsibilities equal to or greater than any to be found in private enterprise."[45]

Similar relationships between public and private occupational pay exist in state and local government. An analysis of wage data for one hundred governmental job classifications in Los Angeles produced public-private wage ratios ranging between 153.3 for the lowest ranked position (Laundry Worker) to 76.5 for top-ranking executive jobs (Health Officer, M.D., and County Counsel).

Moreover, eight of the twelve lowest ranked positions in these governments had ratios exceeding 100 percent, whereas all sixteen highest ranked occupations had ratios below 90 percent.[46] The low salaries of city managers and chief executive officers in major cities, as displayed in Table 7, provide additional support, when compared to the average salary of $144,000 for top

TABLE 6
Relationship of Federal Salaries to Private Industry Salaries for Selected Occupations, 1972

Occupation and Job Grade	Average Annual Salary for Private Industry (dollars)	Annual Federal Salaries as a Percentage of Private Industry Salaries
File clerk I (GS 1)	4,602	109
File clerk II (GS 2)	5,027	113
Messenger (GS 1)	5,087	99
Typist I (GS 2)	5,229	109
Keypunch operator I (GS 2)	5,756	99
Accounting clerk I (GS 3)	5,870	109
Typist II (GS 3)	6,093	105
General stenographer (GS 3)	6,181	104
File clerk III (GS 3)	6,214	103
Draftsmen – Tracer (GS 3)	6,288	102
Engineer VI (GS 13)	21,402	96
Attorney IV (GS 13)	23,443	88
Engineer VII (GS 14)	24,367	99
Director of personnel IV (GS 14)	24,738	98
Chemist VII (GS 14)	25,888	93
Chief accountant IV (GS 14)	26,521	91
Attorney V (GS 14)	27,528	88
Engineer VIII (GS 15)	27,885	101
Chemist VIII (GS 15)	30,827	91
Attorney VI (GS 15)	34,828	81

Source: Derived from U.S. Department of Labor, Bureau of Labor Statistics, *National Survey of Professional, Administrative, Technical and Clerical Pay, March, 1972,* Bulletin 1764 (Washington, D.C.: G.P.O., 1973), Appendix D, pp. 68-69.

executives in industry, of the fact that the occupational pay structure is more compressed in the public sector than in private industry.

Conclusion

The available data indicate that public-private pay relationships in the United States can be explained, at least in part, by a combination of two factors: the discretion that public employers must exercise in implementing the prevailing wage rule adopted by most cities and larger government units and the nature of the political forces that affect governmental wage decisions. The result is an occupational pay structure that is more "equalitarian" in the public sector than that in private industry, in the sense that public employers tend to pay more than private employers for low-skill and craft jobs and to pay less for top executive jobs.[47]

It is not appropriate for us to render a judgment about the equity of the public sector wage structure. The collective judgment of the American

TABLE 7
Average Salaries for Chief Administrative Officers or City Managers of Selected Major U.S. Cities, 1971 (in dollars)

City	Mean Salary
Atlanta	29,068
Boston	27,500
Chicago	31,000
Dallas	40,452
Los Angeles	42,888
New York	45,000
Philadelphia	34,000
Phoenix	37,500
Seattle	25,188
Washington, D.C.	36,000

Source: International City Management Association, *The Municipal Yearbook – 1971* (Washington, D.C., 1972), p. 244.

people may be that government wage structures should be more egalitarian than those existing in private industry. This is doubtful, however, since the relevant political pressures work toward producing that kind of public wage structure without benefit of any implicit or explicit public judgment about the equity question.

We can, however, draw a conclusion about the market efficiency of the public sector wage structure, and that conclusion is negative. Government employers frequently pay more than necessary to attract a work force at the low- and middle-skill ranges and generally pay less than necessary to attract employees of average quality at the upper managerial and professional levels. It is doubtful that high worker productivity offsets the high public wages, although research on this question is needed.[48]

Given the great increase in the number of college graduates expected during this decade, the public wage structure may well be a precursor of a general restructuring of wage relationships in society as the wages of highly educated workers suffer a relative decline. Such restructuring, however, is far from certain,[49] and until it occurs, there is need for a dialogue on whether the equity benefits of the public sector wage structure are worth their costs in efficiency.

Finally, Ehrenberg has recently presented evidence confirming a widely held view that employment elasticities in state and local government are very low. Thus, "market forces do not appear to be sufficiently strong to limit the size of real wage increases which state and local government employees may seek in the future."[50] Consequently, he suggests, and we agree, that careful attention should be given to the evolving structure of collective bargaining in the public sector.

Footnotes

1. Stephen H. Perloff, "Comparing Municipal Salaries with Industry and Federal Pay," *Monthly Labor Review*, Vol. 94, No. 10 (October 1971), pp. 46-50.

2. Edward H. Friend, *First National Survey of Employee Benefits for Full-Time Peronnel of U.S. Municipalities* (Washington, D.C.: Labor Management Relations Service, October 1972). As an example, municipal workers in New York City receive four weeks' paid vacation after just one year of service. In New York's private industries, less than one fourth of plant and one third of office workers are eligible for four weeks' vacation, *even after 15 years' service.* See U.S. Department of Labor, Bureau of Labor Statistics, *Wages and Benefits of Local Government Workers in the New York Area,* Regional Reports, No. 26 (Washington, D.C.: G.P.O., 1971), pp. 40-42.

3. U.S. President, *Manpower Report of the President—March, 1973* (Washington, D.C.: G.P.O., 1972), Table B-16, p. 185. Also see Bennett Harrison, "Public Employment and the Theory of the Dual Economy," in Harold L. Sheppard, Bennett Harrison, and William J. Spring, eds., *The Political Economy of Public Service Employment* (Lexington, Mass.: D.C. Heath and Co., 1972), pp. 66-67.

4. Jacob J. Rutstein, "Survey of Current Personnel Systems in State and Local Governments," *Good Government,* Vol. 87 (Spring 1971), p. 6; and U.S. Civil Service Commission, Bureau of Manpower Information Systems, *Federal Civilian Manpower Statistics* (Washington, D.C.: May 1971), Table 6, p. 14. See also, Robert E. Hall, "Turnover in the Labor Force," *Brookings Papers on Economic Activity,* No. 3 (Washington, D.C.: The Brookings Institution, 1971), p. 715. The data cited in the text are separation rates.

5. Charter of the City of Los Angeles, Section 425. Also see *Pay Policies for Public Personnel: A Report of the Municipal and County Government Section of Town Hall* (Los Angeles, 1961), p. 15.

6. These concepts underlie developing theories of labor market behavior. See Harrison, "Public Employment and the Theory of the Dual Economy," especially pp. 45-55; and Barry Bluestone, "The Tripartite Economy: Labor Markets and the Working Poor," *Poverty and Human Resources,* Vol. 6 (July-August 1970), pp. 15-35.

7. H. Gregg Lewis, *Unionism and Relative Wages in the United States* (Chicago: University of Chicago Press, 1963), p. 193.

8. We have purposely avoided some additional, largely administrative problems of governmental wage determination, e.g., deciding which public jobs should be directly compared with their private sector counterparts. These problems are reviewed in David Lewin, "The Prevailing Wage Principle and Public Wage Decisions," *Public Personnel Management,* Vol. 3 (November-December, 1974), 473-85.

9. Robert J. Carlsson and James W. Robinson, "Toward a Public Employment Wage Theory," *Industrial and Labor Relations Review,* Vol. 22, No. 2 (January 1969), pp. 243-48; Donald Gerwin, "Compensation Decisions in Public Organizations," *Industrial Relations,* Vol. 9, No. 2 (February 1969), pp. 174-184; Robert J. Carlson and James W. Robinson, "Criticism and Comment: Compensation Decisions in Public Organizations," *Industrial Relations,* Vol. 9, No. 1 (October 1969), pp. 111-113; and James A. Craft, "Toward a Public Employee Wage Theory: Comment," *Industrial and Labor Relations Review,* Vol 23, No. 1 (October 1969), pp. 89-95.

10. Mark V. Pauley, "Discussion Comments: Manpower Shortages in Local Government Employment," *American Economic Review,* Vol. 59, No. 2 (May 1969), p. 565.

11. Anthony Downs, *An Economic Theory of Democracy* (New York: Harper and Row, 1957), p. 35.

12. Downs, *An Economic Theory of Democracy,* p. 258.

13. *Ibid.,* p. 259.

14. The other major influence over this period has been the growth in the number of

public employees, as this number (votes) has been brought to bear on the wage-setting process. Some authors casually assign a large wage impact to public employee unions. Cf. Harry H. Wellington and Ralph K. Winter, Jr., *The Unions and the Cities* (Washington, D.C.: The Brookings Institution, 1971), especially pp. 7-32. Yet, as Lewin suggests, the extent to which governmental wage increases are due to unionization as distinct from the increasing politicization of public wage-setting processes is not clear. See David Lewin, "Public Employment Relations: Confronting the Issues," *Industrial Relations*, Vol. 12, No. 3 (October 1973), pp. 309-321.

15. Bernard Lentz, "A Democratic Theory of Economics: Wage and Salary Determination in Municipal Employment" (Ph.D. dissertation, Yale University, in progress). Stanley notes further that "employees in the public sector exert influence not only as employees, as do private workers, but also as pressure groups and voting citizens." See David Stanley, *Managing Local Government Under Union Pressure* (Washington, D.C.: The Brookings Institution, 1972), p. 20.

16. See, for example, U.S. Department of Labor, Bureau of Labor Statistics, *Area Wage Survey, The Los Angeles-Long Beach and Anaheim-Santa Ana-Garden Grove, California, Metropolitan Area, March 1972,* Bulletin No. 1725-76 (Washington, D.C.: G.P.O., 1972), p. 1.

17. U.S. Department of Labor, Bureau of Labor Statistics, *Wage Differences Among Metropolitan Areas, 1970-71* (Washington, D.C., July 1972), p. 1. Major exclusions from BLS wage surveys are construction, the extractive industries, and government.

18. See Richard A. Lester, "Pay Differentials by Size of Establishment," *Industrial Relations,* Vol. 7, No. 1 (October 1967), pp. 57-67.

19. David Lewin, "Wage Determination in Local Government Employment" (Ph.D. dissertation, University of California, Los Angeles, 1971), pp. 77-110. The Los Angeles Survey does not weight its sample results to reflect the actual industry composition of the county.

20. U.S. Bureau of the Census, *County Business Patterns: 1970* (Washington, D.C.: G.P.O., 1971), p. 29.

21. Lester, "Pay Differentials by Size of Establishment," p. 59.

22. U.S. Civil Service Commission, Bureau of Manpower Information Systems, *Pay Structure of the Federal Civil Service, June 30, 1971* (Washington, D.C., 1971), Table 2, p. 18. The data are for domestically employed general schedule employees.

23. As a proportion of private pay, municipal salaries for the entire group of 16 office clerical positions surveyed by the BLS were as follows: New York—101; Chicago—108; Los Angeles—118; Philadelphia—133; Boston—109; New Orleans —93; Kansas City—97; Atlanta—108; Buffalo—122; and Newark—106. Perloff, "Comparing Municipal Salaries with Industry and Federal Pay," Table 2, p. 49.

24. *Ibid.,* Table 1, pp. 47-48.

25. U.S. Department of Labor, Bureau of Labor Statistics, Middle Atlantic Regional Office, *Wages and Benefits of Local Government Workers in the New York Area,* Regional Report No. 26 (Washington, D.C.: G.P.O., December 1971), p. 53.

26. County of Los Angeles, *Salary Ordinance of Los Angeles County,* Ordinance No. 6222, as amended to July 1, 1969, p. 30.

27. City of Los Angeles, *Salary Standardization Ordinance,* Ordinance No. 89, 100, revised to September 20, 1966, amended to July 1, 1969, p. 25.

28. James W. Kuhn, "The Riddle of Inflation: A New Answer," *The Public Interest,* Vol. 27 (Spring 1972), p. 73.

29. Gordon F. Bloom and Herbert R. Northrup, *Economics of Labor Relations,* 7th ed. (Homewood, Ill.: Richard D. Irwin, Inc., 1973). p. 493.
30. Derived from Lewin, "Wage Determination in Local Government," pp. 187-190. Because construction unions have recently shown increased willingness to exercise market power, the differences between public and private sector craft wages are probably even larger than suggested here. By 1972, the hourly earnings of construction workers were about 60 percent more than those of manufacturing workers; in 1947, the differential was little more than 25 percent. See U.S. President, *Manpower Report of the President—March, 1973* (Washington, D.C., 1972). Table C-3 pp. 190-191.
31. See the first paragraph of this article and the sources cited in footnotes 2, 3, and 4.
32. Derived from U.S. Civil Service Commission, Bureau of Manpower Information Systems, *Federal Civilian Manpower Statistics* (Washington, D.C., March 1973), Tables 7 and 8, pp. 17-18.
33. Rutstein, "Survey of Current Personnel Systems in State and Local Governments," p. 6. In this survey, counties reported a separation rate of 16.6 percent, cities 14.5 percent.
34. See U.S. Department of Labor, Bureau of Labor Statistics, Area Wage Survey, *The Newark and Jersey City, New Jersey, Metropolitan Areas, January 1972,* Bulletin 1925-52 (Washington, D.C., 1972), pp. 28-35.
35. Lewin, "Wage Determination in Local Government," pp. 165 and 196-198; and Eugene J. Devine, *Analysis of Manpower Shortages in Local Government* (New York: Praeger, 1970), Tables 5 and 6, pp. 42-43.
36. Some jobs commonly regarded as unique to government, such as teaching and protective service positions, are also found in private markets. In this section, we discuss occupations for which government is an exclusive or dominant employer.
37. "The method of salary setting for . . . classes peculiar to the public service . . . may have raised the cost of government without a demonstrated need to increase these salaries as high as they have gone." See Louis J. Kroeger *et al., Pricing Jobs Unique to Government* (Chicago: Public Personnel Association, n.d.), p. 5.
38. Lewin, "Wage Determination in Local Government Employment," pp. 260-275.
39. For further analysis of this issue, see David Lewin, "Wage Parity and the Supply of Police and Firemen," *Industrial Relations,* Vol. 12, No. 1 (February 1973), pp. 77-85; and David Lewin and John H. Keith, Jr., "Managerial Responses to Perceived Labor Shortages: The Case of Police," *Criminology,* 14 (May, 1976), 66-92.
40. See Urban Data Service, Stanley M. Wolfson, *Salary Trends for Police Patrolmen, Firefighters and Refuse Collectors* (Washington, D.C.: International City Management Association), Vol. 4, No. 10 (October 1972), pp. 5-6. These data are for cities with populations in excess of 100,000.
41. Kroeger *et al. Pricing Jobs Unique to Government,* p. 4.
42. See the Jacobs Company, *Report on Police and Fire Classification and Pay Studies,* City of Los Angeles (Chicago: The Jacobs Company, 1970), p. 31.
43. National Manpower Council, *Government and Manpower* (New York: Columbia University Press, 1964), pp. 34-35.
44. Derived from "Who Gets the Most Pay," *Forbes,* May 15, 1972, pp. 205-236. The cited federal salaries exclude those of the President and Vice-President.
45. National Manpower Council, *Government and Manpower,* pp. 159-161.
46. David Lewin, "Aspects of Wage Determination in Local Government Employment," *Public Administration Review,* Vol. 34 (March-April 1974), 149-55.

47. Obviously, we do not purport to explain all elements of public wage structures. For example, we suspect that in some regions and in relatively non-urban areas, public sector wages are comparatively low. If, indeed, this is correct, our hunch would be that the political forces described in this article, particularly public worker organization, have not developed very far in these areas.
48. A strong believer in the efficiency of markets might argue that high government wages attract highly qualified workers but that productivity is unaffected because government agencies are unable or unwilling to identify and hire these workers or are unable to use them efficiently when they are employed.
49. See Lester Thurow, "Education and Economic Equality," *The Public Interest,* Vol. 28 (Summer 1972), pp. 66-81.
50. Ronald G. Ehrenberg, "The Demand for State and Local Government Employees," *American Economic Review,* Vol. 53, No. 3 (June 1973), p. 378.

Public Sector Bargaining and Budget Making under Fiscal Adversity

Milton Derber and Martin Wagner*

In 1971-72 we conducted a field study of relations between collective bargaining and the budget-making process in a sample of thirty public units in Illinois. Our central findings were that the two decision-making processes have their separate dynamics, influence each other only in a rather loose and general way, and are highly flexible processes that can be readily adjusted if they do not initially mesh.[1] Most governmental units at that time were in reasonably favorable economic conditions. A few years later, however, the national recession hit Illinois and most governmental units found themselves under considerable economic stress. Both the popular media and the professional literature began to focus attention on the relations between bargaining and public finance, including budgeting. A restudy of our sample seemed a potential aid to an understanding of the interactions. Fortunately for the state but rather unfortunately for our research plans, the economic situation had improved noticeably by mid-1977 when our follow-up study got under way. Nonetheless, as we soon discovered, a tight fiscal situation continued to confront about half our sample, thus enabling us to do some unanticipated cross-sectional comparisons. This article presents the results.

A few introductory methodological remarks are in order. Our 1971-72 sample of governmental units was broken down into five categories—higher education (two universities and four community colleges), public schools, cities, counties, and special districts. The sample was not random; it was purposely selected to assure a wide distribution of bargaining units on the basis of geography and size. By 1977 three units had to be dropped, two because they no longer engaged in collective bargaining and the third be-

*Institute of Labor and Industrial Relations, University of Illinois. Reprinted from *Industrial and Labor Relations Review,* 33 (October 1979), 18-23.

cause it was shifted from a county to the state's jurisdiction, the bargaining process being drastically altered by the change. We decided not to make substitutions for these three cases, thereby reducing our county category to four and our special districts category to five.

In developing our interview schedule, we planned to enlarge our data supply by asking the respondents about two bargaining periods, the most recent (of which 2 occurred in early 1978, 20 in 1977, 4 in 1976, and 1 in 1975) and the immediately preceding negotiations (of which 1 occurred in 1977, 11 in 1976, 9 in 1975, 5 in 1974, and 1 in 1972).[2] It was expected that the earlier period would reflect more of the recession experience. The data on the earlier negotiations were disappointing, mainly because the respondents often had only a fuzzy recollection of the period, but partly because there was a high turnover in the people who had participated in the negotiations. We therefore have been obliged to discard most of the data on the earlier negotiations.

The chief hypothesis guiding the study was that collective bargaining would be tied much more closely to the budget-making process under conditions of fiscal adversity than under favorable economic conditions. To elicit the information necessary for testing this hypothesis, we included questions on the following topics in the interview schedule.

1. The names and positions of the members of the bargaining teams, to determine which of them, if any, were associated with budget making.
2. The dates when bargaining and budget making began, when a bargaining agreement was reached, when the budget was submitted to a legislative body, and when the budget was adopted. A question on retroactivity was also included.
3. Assumptions made by the management and union negotiators about the budget in formulation of bargaining positions.
4. The extent to which management negotiators consulted with the budget makers and the extent to which union negotiators requested and obtained budget information from management.
5. Ability to pay as an issue in negotiations.
6. Work stoppages and their issues.
7. The substance of the agreements reached.
8. How the agreed upon increases were financed.
9. Whether the negotiations had any impact on the labor-management relationship.
10. Assessments by the parties of the bargaining-budget making nexus overall.

As in the earlier study, we interviewed at least one and usually two representatives for both management and the union who had been involved in the bargaining process. A total of 102 interviews were conducted, excluding those in the three discarded cases. In addition to the interviews, we collected copies of available collective bargaining agreements, budget reports, and relevant miscellaneous materials.

Subdivision by Economic Situation

The sample was subdivided into three categories: 11 cases in which both parties described the economic situation as "tight" (hereafter referred to as *T*), 10 in which both described the situation as "favorable" (hereafter referred to as *F*), and 6 in which the parties differed in their perceptions of the economic situation (hereafter referred to as *M*). Category *T* included 5 of the 6 public schools and 1 or 2 of each of the other four groups. Category *F* included only one case from higher education and none from the schools, but it encompassed 4 of the 6 cities, 2 of the 4 counties, and 3 of the 5 special districts. Category *M* had 3 of the 6 higher education cases, and 1 from each of the remaining groups, except for the special districts.

The reports on the economic situation were consistent with the responses to the question of whether "ability to pay" was an issue in the negotiations. The answer in 8 of the 11 *T* cases was yes and in 2 others the parties gave a mixed reply. In contrast, in 5 of the 10 *F* cases the answer was no and in only 2 cases was there a clear yes response. In the 6 *M* cases there were 3 no, 2 yes, and 1 mixed responses.

Bargaining Teams and Budget Makers

There was no significant difference among the three categories. Seven of the 11 *T* teams included a budget man and in 4 of these cases the chief negotiator was a key budget person. In 4 cases the budget makers were not represented on the bargaining team: in 2 the negotiators were given general limits on how large a pay increase they could agree to but otherwise the negotiators did not consult with the budget makers and in the other 2 cases there was continuous consultation throughout the negotiations.

Nine of the 10 *F* teams included a budget maker and in the tenth case, the chief negotiator consulted often with the chief executive who reported to the governing board.

Three of the 6 *M* bargaining teams included a budget maker: in one case a budget man served as "resource" to the negotiators, in one case the budget maker and negotiator were in close and constant touch, and in the last case the budget maker consulted with the chief negotiator before negotiations started and set limits on cost concessions.

The assumptions of the negotiating parties about the budget, on the other hand, differed rather significantly among the three categories. In the 11 *T* cases the management negotiators assumed that little if any money was available for pay increases in the budget. Among the comments reported were these:

- no money available for pay increases—need to increase workload
- had to be a freeze on salaries
- any pay increase would cause a deficit
- would need to borrow to meet salary increases
- although funds were not available, a small increase (5 percent) would be necessary
- very little change from the past level

- were "broke" and needed to get by as cheaply as possible
- will not negotiate wage issues until budget is finalized
- question of priorities once available funds were so limited

The union responses, however, varied with the trust level. In five cases the union negotiators accepted the management's report on the tightness of the budget and restrained their money demands. In 5 cases they either disbelieved the reports ("We never believe anything they tell us about the budget.") or they adopted the position that it was up to management to get the funds or to change their priorities. In the eleventh case they noted that the budget was determined by the governor and the legislature and bargaining involved only the distribution of a fixed amount.

In the 10 F cases management generally operated on the basis that money was available in the budget for a "fair" increase. Their criteria of "fair" were "parity with other groups" (3 cases), the cost of living (1 case), or "living within means," thus avoiding a deficit (1 case). In the other 5 cases the budget makers gave the negotiators a fixed amount, percentage, or range to guide their bargaining, derived either from past experience or a variety of other considerations. The union negotiators, on the other hand, uniformly assumed that there was plenty of money available ("plenty of money for a good increase," "city had surplus," "budget was full of fat") and concentrated on such wage criteria as prevailing rate, the cost of living, parity, and as much as they could get.

In the 6 M cases, the management assumptions about the budget for negotiating purposes were quite varied whereas the union negotiators were virtually unanimous in believing funds for a "reasonable" increase were available. In one case the management negotiator stated that management would defer an agreement until the budget was finalized; in a second case management felt secure about the availability of funds for a reasonable settlement; in a third case, a small (5 percent) increase figure was tentatively put into the budget; in a fourth case, management arbitrarily assumed that salaries would not exceed 80 percent of the total budget; and in the remaining two cases limits were set by the budget makers on a variety of revenue assumptions. The union positions were all of the order: "plenty of money," "the legislature would provide additional funds," "a sizeable fund was available following passage of a referendum," or "management will find money."

Timing of bargaining and budgeting. Did the economic situation of the sample unit influence the time nexus between bargaining and budgeting? The start of budget making preceded the start of bargaining in 8 of the 11 T cases, in 9 of the 10 F cases, and in 5 of the 6 M cases. In all but one of the other cases, budgeting and bargaining started about the same time. On the other hand, bargaining was completed prior to or about the same time as the formal submission of the budget to a legislative body in 8 of the T cases, in only 3 of the F cases and in none of the M cases. Furthermore, retroactivity was a factor in only 1 T case, but in 8 F cases and in 3 M cases.

These data suggest that the tight economic situation limited the duration of the bargaining period and led to a much closer relationship between the budgeting and bargaining processes. In contrast the favorable economic environment appeared to encourage more latitude in the budgeting-bargaining nexus since bargaining settlements typically occurred after the completion of the budget. This latter conclusion, it should be noted, was similar to the finding in the 1971-72 survey at which time economic conditions for state and local governments were generally on the favorable side.

How the settlements went. The natural expectation that the settlements in the *T* cases would be smaller than in *F* or *M* is generally borne out by the data, with a few interesting exceptions. Despite the stringency of their budgets, only 2 of the 11 *T* units actually froze pay. Five other cases, however, settled for 5 percent increases or less (below the rise in living costs), and the remainder were around 6 or 7 percent. Equally significant were the very limited adjustments in fringe benefits. No changes occurred in paid holidays and vacations; only 4 units increased sickness and medical benefits and 1 reduced the employer portion of a contributary health insurance plan.

The 10 *F* cases generally reported much more generous pay and fringe settlements. In 4 of these units there were varying wage increases in addition to the cost-of-living adjustments provided in the agreements; in 3 others the increases were in the 6 to 7 percent range; the remaining 3 appeared to fall below the rise in living costs during the contract periods. Moreover, in 6 cases holidays or vacation benefits were increased and in 8 cases sickness and medical benefits were improved. One unit cut back on the number of paid holidays (from 12 to 10) but increased the vacation period for those with ten years' service or more.

The 6 *M* cases were much closer to the *F* cases than to the *T* group. They ranged from 6 to 9 percent in the first year of pay settlements and from 5 to 7 percent in the second or third years. Four of them also reported some increase in sickness or medical benefits. On the other hand, with one very minor exception, none improved either paid holidays or vacations.

How the settlements were financed. As might be expected, the financing of the settlements posed much more complex problems for the *T* group than for the *F* or *M* groups.

Of the 11 *T* cases only 5 indicated that the settlements were financed within existing resources, and 4 of these 5 qualified their answers. Three units relied upon special (i.e., not regularly recurring) federal grants, 4 borrowed money, 3 raised taxes or fees, 3 froze hiring and reduced employment through attrition, and 2 each transferred money from nonpersonnel funds, laid off employees, or reduced or eliminated services. These numbers exceed the number of cases because 5 units used two or more of these revenue-raising or cost-cutting devices.

In contrast, in 8 of the 10 *F* cases, and in 5 of the 6 *M* cases, the parties reported that existing revenue sources were sufficient. Only 1 *F* unit and 2 *M* units[3] raised taxes or fees and only 2 *F* units and 1 *M* uinit transferred money from nonpersonnel to personnel funds, but a scattering of other financing steps were reported by individual units. In addition, two *F* units were aided by extra grants from other levels of government.

Explaining the Relationship

We attempted through several questions in our interviews to gain insight into the controlling forces at work in these bargaining relationships. First, of those who had reported that they negotiated in a tight economic climate, we asked: *Was bargaining tied more closely to budget making as a result of the tight economic climate?* Seven of these 11 units said "yes," 2 said the tie was always close, and 2 alleged that it did not make much difference.

When asked a related question, however—*Did the tight economic situation affect the bargaining process?*—all but 1 of the units responded affirmatively. It is noteworthy that in 7 of the 11 T cases, the responses were conflict-oriented and in 4 cases they were cooperation-oriented. By far the most common response among the former was that the negotiations were longer and more difficult than in prior bargaining, when economic conditions were more favorable.[4] Similar reflections included the following: "It strengthened management's resistance," "It led to management demands for givebacks," "People got madder," and "It reduced management flexibility." The cooperation-oriented responses included: "The union settled more quickly," "Management provided more information to the union," "The union restricted demands," and "The union understood the situation."

Another question we asked was: *Did the tight economic situation affect the impasse resolution process or the attitudes of the parties to strike or to take a strike* (as compared to those that prevailed in more favorable economic conditions)? In 4 cases no changes were noted; in 2 management appeared to be more willing to take a strike; in 1 management was unwilling to accept binding arbitration; in 1 the union was more willing to strike while in another the union was less willing to strike; and in 3 there was greater reliance on mediation expressed.[5] Only one strike actually occurred during the 11 T negotiations. In contrast, in the 6 M units there were 2 strikes and in a third the union members refused to cross the picket line of another union. Among the 10 F units, 2 strike votes were taken but strikes were enjoined by court orders.

We pursued our inquiry from another angle by asking the following question: *Did negotiations* [regardless of economic impact] *have any impact on the labor-management relationship?* Many changes were reported, including replacement of management and union negotiators,[6] reorganization of management and union bargaining procedures, a decline or increase in employee grievances, and a shift in the duration of the bargaining agreement. None of these yielded significant results, however, when distributed on the basis of the three economic climate categories. Four of the 11 T cases, 4 of the 10 F cases, and 2 of the 6 M cases, for example, reported a replacement of management negotiators. A change in union negotiators was reported in 4 of 11 T cases, 6 of 10 F cases, and 4 of 6 M cases. The other distributions appeared equally random.

Our survey instrument concluded with a general open-ended question inviting any comments that the respondent might care to make. These results had no statistical significance, but a number of comments were made that may shed some additional, or at least heuristic, light on the subject. Five management respondents felt that the main bargaining-budgeting problem was the uncertainty about revenue (including state and federal aid), and some suggested more careful planning for negotiations and research into the cost implications of the terms of the agreements. Another noted that higher levels of government were requiring local units to perform more functions that they were not adequately funded to perform. There also were expressions of concern that collective bargaining was reducing management's flexibility in handling fiscal problems and of discontent with the union's reluctance to be concerned with the costs of settlement.

The union responses seemed to be bimodal. One set emphasized good working relations with management and recognized management difficulties in getting state aid or a tax increase. The other charged management with bad faith and deception in fiscal matters, saw little or no connection between the budget and the bargaining process, wanted to avoid "being bludgeoned" by the budget, or lamented the lack of union bargaining power and the increased toughness of management. A few expressed the need for a state bargaining law and mandatory arbitration.

In Conclusion

The findings of this modest study are correspondingly modest. They clearly support the hypothesis that led to the conduct of the study: under conditions of fiscal adversity, collective bargaining is tied more closely to the budget-making process than under favorable economic conditions. This is shown in at least six ways.

First, the ability to pay was an important issue in virtually all negotiations under tight (T) fiscal conditions but in only a few of the negotiations under generally favorable (F) fiscal conditions.

Second, in T conditions the management team entered negotiations with the assumption that little if any money was available for pay increases, whereas the F case negotiators generally operated on the assumption that money was available for a "fair increase."

Third, under T conditions bargaining was generally completed prior to or about the same time that the budget was submitted to the legislative body responsible for final approval, whereas in a majority of the F cases bargaining continued beyond the formal budget deadline and retroactivity was resorted to. This finding suggests, fourth, that tight economic conditions restricted or dampened the bargaining process as compared with more favorable economic conditions. In two-thirds of the T cases the attitudes of the negotiators became more conflictive and the negotiations were described as more difficult and prolonged, even though only one experienced a strike. In the remaining third of the T cases the negotiations were more cooperative with both sides recognizing the seriousness of the situation.

Fifth, the money settlements in the T cases were more modest than in the F cases, particularly with respect to fringe benefits, in which virtually no improvements were made. Finally, whereas most of the F settlements required additional action, which ranged from grants by other levels of government and raising taxes or fees to freezing employment, layoffs, and the reduction or elimination of services.

One of the most interesting findings of the study was the bimodal character of union responses. About half the union negotiators accepted management's claims of budget constraints and accommodated their bargaining to the situation. The other half disbelieved management or asserted that, regardless, it was up to management to get the necessary funds for acceptable pay increases. In short, the level of trust between the parties was a significant element in how bargaining and budget making were related during periods of economic adversity. Given a condition of mutual trust and freeflowing communications and information, one might expect a reasonable accommodation of the two processes.

Footnotes

1. Milton Derber, Ken Jennings, Ian McAndrew, and Martin Wagner, "Bargaining and Budget-Making in Illinois Public Institutions," *Industrial and Labor Relations Review*, Vol. 27, No. 1 (October 1973), p. 61.
2. Of the most recent contracts, 6 were for 1 year, 18 for 2 years, and 3 for 3 years. Fifteen of these contracts had the same duration as their preceding contracts, 8 had shifted from 1 to 2 years, 2 from 1 to 3 years, 1 from 3 to 2 years, and 1 from 2 to 1 year.
3. In one of these units the management representatives were divided on whether existing revenue sources were sufficient or the settlement depended on the increase in fees.
4. The reports of "longer" negotiations seem to contradict the data on the timing of the conclusion of negotiations in relation to budget making. . . . The apparent discrepancy might be explained by an analysis of actual time devoted to negotiations as distinguished from the duration of the negotiating period, but such information was not obtained.
5. In one case, two different responses were offered.
6. The nature of these replacements is of interest. Some reflected the turnover among individuals holding the negotiator positions due to such normal factors as job mobility and competition in elections; others, particularly on the management side, reflected a policy decision either to use outside professionals instead of internal staff as chief negotiators or (in a few instances) to replace such outside professionals by internal staff.
7. Although this study clearly indicates that economic adversity will bring about a closer tie between the budget-making and bargaining processes than more favorable economic conditions, it does not preclude the possibility that in the normal development of public sector bargaining over time, there will be a tendency for the two processes to interact more closely.

THE IMPACT OF UNIONS ON PUBLIC SECTOR WAGES

The paper by Bartel and Lewin in this section and others that are summarized below generally follow the approach developed by H. Gregg Lewis for estimating the impact of unions on wages in the private sector.[1] The measure of the effect of unions used in that study is the extent to which a union raises the wage of its members above the wages of comparable unorganized workers. Usually this is presented as a ratio of the union to nonunion wage, expressed in percentage terms. Numerous studies of this type have been carried out on samples of private sector employees; they have provided a wide range of estimates of the average effect of unions on wages. In general, it has been shown that the relative impact of unions tends to be strongest during recessionary periods, since unions make it difficult for employers to reduce the wage or drastically moderate the rate of wage increase. Both union and nonunion employers have incentives to increase wages during periods of relatively full employment irrespective of their workers' union status.

Overall, as Rees notes, the relative wage impact of unions has varied over time and across occupational groups.[2] He concludes that unions had their peak wage impact during the Great Depression of the 1930s. At that time, according to his analysis of the evidence, the relative union effect was 25 percent or more. By the end of the decade, however, as inflation occurred and employment expanded, the union impact decreased to between 10 and 20 percent. The decline continued through World War II and beyond, so that by 1947 the relative union wage impact was only between 0 and 5 percent. Since the late 1940s, Rees estimates the union impact to be between 15 and 20 percent, but cautions that some of the stronger unions, such as those in the construction trades, may have had considerably larger relative wage impacts.

A more recent summary of the evidence by Johnson essentially reinforces Rees' findings. However, Johnson adds further estimates of the union impact on an individual worker's wage; these range up to a maximum of 33 percent in some cases. Furthermore, the impact of unionism on an individual's wage varies across age, education, and racial groups. In summary, Johnson concludes that unions in the private sector have had their strongest effects on the wages of blacks, very young and very old workers, and those with lower levels of education.[3]

There are essentially three ways to apply this type of analysis to the wage impacts of public sector unions. The first is to examine wages of union and nonunion employees at a single point in time, that is, cross-sectionally. The second way, only rarely applied to public workers, is a longitudinal or time series analysis comparing the wages of employees during the period prior to unionization (and collective bargaining) with the wages established through collective bargaining after employees have unionized. The third, also only rarely applied to public workers, is to compare the wages of individual unionized and nonunion workers over time—a methodology that may become more widely used now that longitudinal data on samples of workers are more readily available.[4] In all three types of analysis, the researcher must develop a model which effectively controls for the impacts of economic, political, and institutional factors other than unionization and bargaining on wage levels or wage changes. Thus the accuracy of any estimate of union wage impacts depends partly, indeed largely, on the ability of the researcher to specify adequately other causal variables affecting the dependent variable.

Most of the studies produced so far have done a relatively good job of isolating economic forces other than unionism that affect public employee wages. Some progress is also being made in capturing political and institutional characteristics affecting bargained wage outcomes. For example, the impacts of government structure and the political climate of the community on public employee wages have been examined in several studies.[5] Some researchers have attempted to include in their analyses variables measuring the nature of the law governing bargaining in the public sector, the nature of impasse procedures and the rate of strike activity among public employees.[6] These all represent steps in the proper direction, in our judgment. Further progress is needed, however, before most practitioners would be confident that the critical institutional factors affecting wage and fringe benefit settlements in the public sector have been adequately captured within existing analytical frameworks. The reader need only recall the characteristics of public sector wage determination and budget-making that were discussed earlier to appreciate this point.

A further problem that confronts those attempting to assess the average effects of unions on wages within the models and methodologies outlined above concerns the "spillover" effects of union wage settlements. This problem arises because nonunion employers sometimes look at settlements negotiated by unionized workers and then adjust their own wage structures accordingly. They do so either in order to continue to attract workers of equal quality or to avoid creating an incentive for their own employees to unionize. To the extent that this type of spillover occurs, the ratio of union to nonunion wages declines and, therefore, estimates of the impact of unions on public sector wages are biased downward. Although this problem has long plagued industrial relations researchers, recent public sector studies have made important progress in attempting to resolve it. Several investigators have sought to measure the geographic and occupational spillovers of union wage settlements utilizing a variety of ingenious adjustments.[7] As expected, to the extent that they have been able to account for the effects of these spillovers, the researchers' estimates of public sector union wage impacts are increased.

Two other problems are encountered in seeking to isolate the impact of unions on public sector wages, and both of them are treated in the single reading included in this section, by Bartel and Lewin. The first of these concerns fringe benefits. It is well recognized that fringe benefits are an important and growing portion of compensation in both the public and private sectors, and also that unions negotiate with employers over such benefits. Consequently, studies that are limited to the pay outcomes of public sector bargaining may be missing a key area of union impact. The absence of suitable data has prevented most researchers from investigating this issue, but Bartel and Lewin were able to analyze fringe benefit data from municipal police departments and they report that the impact of police unions on such fringes exceeded the impact on direct pay.[8] (The reader should pay particular attention to the limitations of this portion of the Bartel-Lewin paper, limitations which the authors themselves point out.)

The second problem is more complex, concerning as it does the determinants of wages *and* unionism in the public sector. Consider that while many factors, including unionism, may determine the level of wages (or wage changes) for a certain type or group of employees, many factors, *including perhaps the level of wages,* may determine whether or not workers are organized. Virtually all studies of union wage impacts, whether in the private or public sector, have examined only the determinants of wages and, thus, have treated unionism as an independent or exogenous variable. But if the level of wages is one of the factors (variables) determining unionism, then it may be erroneous to treat unionism as exogenous; instead, it should be treated as endogenous. This is what Bartel and Lewin in fact do, as they formulate separate wage and union equations in a simultaneous determination model.

Testing this model with wage and unionism data from 215 municipal police departments, Bartel and Lewin report two key results: (1) the measured impact of unionism on police wages (in 1973) doubled to around 14 percent when the simultaneous determination of wages and unionism (rather than only the determination of wages) was considered; and (2) the demand for unionization among police—the probability of a police union existing in a municipal police department—was greater in low wage cities. Thus, American police apparently are most likely to unionize for the purpose of raising their relatively low salaries and seem to have been reasonably effective in raising those salaries. The reader is advised to consider carefully the quantitative techniques, the distinction between unionism and collective bargaining (i.e., the CONTRACT variable), and the treatment of public sector bargaining laws in the Bartel-Lewin paper. Those who are especially interested in this subject may care to pursue some recent studies of private sector union wage impacts—studies that also employ simultaneous equation models but that reach conclusions somewhat different from those offered by Bartel and Lewin.[9]

Furthermore, the Bartel-Lewin study is only one among many that deal with public sector union wage impacts. To place this study in perspective, we provide in Table 2 a summary of all such studies reported in the literature through 1980.[10] It can readily be observed from this study that the wage impacts of teacher and hospital employee unions are smaller than the impacts of unions of protective service workers, particularly firefighters. Also note that the studies that employ data for samples of individual workers (instead of occupations, departments or services) report comparatively large union wage effects. On balance, we interpret these findings to provide support for the thesis that public sector bargaining outcomes are diverse rather than singular, varied rather than monolithic.

It is unfortunate, however, that there are very few longitudinal studies of the wage impacts of government employee bargaining. Note, in particular, that none of the studies summarized in Table 2 employ data more recent than 1975, yet it has been since that time the economy of the public sector has undergone its sharpest contractions. Furthermore, as unionism expands in the public sector, the utility of cross-sectional analysis of the type presented in the Bartel-Lewin paper and most of the studies listed in Table 2 become more limited. This is because both the size and comparability of the non-union group will decline, making them subject to potentially larger wage spillovers emanating from the unionized sector. Consequently, future studies of public employee union wage impacts will require either a purely longitudinal research design or a pooled (combination) cross-sectional and longitudinal approach. From such research, we feel, will emerge a better understanding of how public sector bargaining affects the wages of government employees.

Moreover, such longitudinal studies hopefully will identify more concretely some of the impacts of bargaining on fringe benefits in the public

TABLE 2
A Summary of Public Sector Union Wage Impact Studies

Author†	Employee Group and Year	Principal Finding(s)
Kasper	Teachers, 1967-68*	Insignificant; adds 0% to 4% to average salary
Ashenfelter	Firefighters, 1961-66	Significant; adds 6% to 16% to hourly wage
Thornton	Teachers, 1969-70*	Significant; adds 23% to highest step, 1% to 4% to all other steps
Baird and Landon	Teachers, 1966-67*	Significant; adds 4.9% to beginning salary
Hall and Carroll	Teachers, 1968-69*	Significant; addes 1.8% to average salary
Schmenner	Teachers, police-fire, other municipal employees	Mixed results, some significant, some not. Adds 0% to 15% to beginning salaries and/or average earnings
Ehrenberg	Firefighters, 1969	Significant; adds 2% to 18% to hourly wage
Ehrenberg and Goldstein	Ten categories of noneducational municipal employees, 1967	Significant; adds 2% to 16% to average monthly earnings
Lipsky and Drotning	Teachers, 1967-68*	Insignificant over entire sample; significant in subsample, adding 0% to 15% to salary change
Freund	Municipal employees, 1965-71	Insignificant; adds about 1% to changes in average earnings
Frey	Teachers, 1964-70	Insignificant; adds 0% to 1½% to beginning and maximum salaries
Hamermesh	Bus drivers, craftsmen, other	Significant for bus drivers; adds 9% to 12% to wage changes. Insignificant for all others; adds −4% to 4% wage changes and/or earnings
Ichniowski	Firefighters, 1966 and 1976	Generally significant; adds from −1.6% to +3.4% to hourly wage and from 7.2% to 18.0% to fringe benefits

401

TABLE 2 (continued)

Author	Employee Group and Year	Principal Finding(s)
Lewin, Horton, and Kuhn	Seven blue- and white-collar occupations in four municipal governments, 1951-1976	Generally significant; adds from 1% to 8% to annual salaries
Lewin and Keith	Police, 1971-72	Insignificant; adds −1% to 6% to beginning and maximum salaries
Fottler	Hospital employees	Significant; adds +4.0% to 5.5% to weekly wages
Hall and Vanderporten	Police, 1973	Significant; in independent (monopsonistic) cities, insignificant elsewhere; adds $250 to $1000 to beginning and maximum salaries
Shapiro	Blue- and white-collar government workers at federal, state, and local levels, using 1971 National Longitudinal Survey (NLS) data	Significant; adds −20% for white-collar workers and +22% for blue-collar workers
Victor	Police and firefighters, 1972	Significant; adds 6% to 12% to beginning and maximum salaries or average hourly earnings
Smith	Individual federal, state, and local government employees, 1975	Significant; adds 0 to 17% to annual salaries of individuals employed by governments
Bartel and Lewin	Police, 1973	Significant; adds 9% to 19% to beginning and average salaries or to average hourly earnings

*School year.
†See full citation in references on pp. 404-405.

sector. The available cross-sectional research has hardly dealt with this problem. Yet, there is accumulating evidence from other sources that not only are fringe benefits, especially pension benefits, substantial in the public sector, but that in some respects the benefit levels surpass those of private industry.[11] Thus, it is important for researchers to deal empirically with this issue, and thereby broaden their estimates of the monetary impacts of public sector bargaining beyond the wage area.

In summary, we may conclude that during the first generation of public sector collective bargaining in the United States, there was an initial effect, a shock effect, on governmental wage structures that produced gains for unionized workers relative to those employees who neither organized nor engaged in formal collective bargaining. Whether these wage gains are accelerating, moderating or remaining unchanged during the second generation of bargaining in the public sector is a major research issue. It is particularly important that studies of the wage impacts of public employee unions continue to be made during periods of economic upheaval and contraction in the public sector in order that we may judge whether, like their private sector counterparts, organized public workers are better able than the unorganized to protect themselves from wage erosion.[12]

FOOTNOTES

1. H. Gregg Lewis, *Unionism and Relative Wages in the United States*, (Chicago: University of Chicago Press, 1963).
2. Albert Rees, *The Economics of Trade Unions*, Revised Edition (Chicago: University of Chicago Press, 1977), pp. 70-75.
3. George E. Johnson, "Economic Analysis of Trade Unionism," *American Economic Review*, 65 (May 1975), 23-28. Two other studies that employed data on individual workers to study the wage impacts of public employee unions are Sharon P. Smith, *Equal Pay in the Public Sector: Fact or Fantasy?* (Princeton, N.J.: Princeton University Press, 1977), and David Shapiro, "Relative Wage Effects of Unions in the Public and Private Sectors," *Industrial and Labor Relations Review*, 31 (January 1978), 193-204.
4. See, for example, the sources of data used by Smith, *op. cit.*, and Shapiro, *op. cit.*
5. A case in point is Ronald G. Ehrenberg, "Municipal Government Structure, Unionization and the Wages of Firefighters," *Industrial and Labor Relations Review*, 27 (October 1973), 36-48.
6. Note that we do not discuss here the impact of other institutional forces in public sector wage determination, such as impasse procedures. Refer back to Chapter 5 for discussion of this issue. A recent study that examines the effects of one type of impasse procedure on public sector pay is Craig Olson, "The Impact of Arbitration on the Wages of Firefighters," *Industrial Relations*, 19 (Fall 1980), 325-339.
7. See David B. Lipsky and John E. Drotning, "The Influence of Collective Bargaining on Teachers' Salaries in New York State," *Industrial and Labor Relations Review*, 27 (October 1973), 18-35, and Ronald G. Ehrenberg and Gerald S. Goldstein, "A Model of Public Sector Wage Determination," *Journal of Urban Economics*, 2 (July 1975), 223-245.
8. A similar finding for firefighters is reported in Casey Ichniowski, "Economic Effects of the Firefighters' Union," *Industrial and Labor Relations Review*, 33 (January 1980), 198-211.
9. Orley Ashenfelter and George E. Johnson, "Unionism, Relative Wages and Labor Quality in U.S. Manufacturing Industries, *International Economic Review*, 13 (October 1972), 488-508, and Peter Schmidt and Robert Strauss, "The Effect of Unions on Earnings and Earnings on Unions: A Mixed Logit Approach," *International Economic Review*, 17 (February 1976), 204-212.
10. This summary is an updated version of those contained in David Lewin, "Public Sector Labor Relations: A Review Essay," *Labor History*, 18 (Winter 1977), 133-

144, and David Lewin, Raymond D. Horton, and James W. Kuhn, *Collective Bargaining and Manpower Utilization in Big City Governments* (Montclair, N.J.: Allanheld Osmun, 1979), pp. 84-86.

11. See, for example, *Report of the Permanent Commission on Public Employee Pension and Retirement Systems, Recommendation for a New Pension Plan for Public Employers: The 1976 Coordinated Escalator Retirement Plan* (State of New York, Executive Department, March, 1976), popularly known as the "Kinzel Report"; *The Fiscal Impact of Fringe Benefits and Leave Benefits,* Some Proposals for Reform, Seventh Interim Report to the Mayor (of New York City) by the Temporary Commission on City Finances, (New York, June, 1976); and Robert Tilove, *Public Employee Pension Funds* (New York: Columbia University Press, 1976); and Edward H. Freind and Albert Pike, III, *Third National Survey of Employee Rights for Full-Time Personnel of U.S. Municipalities* (Washington, D.C.: Labor-Management Relations Service of the United States Conference of Mayors, 1977).

12. Private sector studies generally show the wage impacts of unionism to be greatest during the early years of a collective bargaining relationship. On this point, see Rees, *op. cit.,* pp. 82-89.

REFERENCES

Ashenfelter, Orley. "The Effect of Unionization on Wages in the Public Sector; The Case of Firefighters." *Industrial and Labor Relations Review,* 24 (January 1971), pp. 191-202.

Baird, Robert N., and Landon, John H. "The Effects of Collective Bargaining on Public School Teachers' Salaries Comment." *Industrial and Labor Relations Review,* 25 (April 1972), pp. 410-17.

Bartel, Ann P., and David Lewin. "Wages and Unionism in the Public Sector: The Case of Police." *Review of Economics and Statistics,* 63, (February 1981).

Ehrenberg, Ronald G. "Municipal Government Structure, Unionization and the Wages of Firefighters." *Industrial and Labor Relations Review,* 27 (October 1973), pp. 36-48.

Determination," *Journal of Urban Economics,* 2 (July 1975), pp. 223-45.

Fottler, Myron, D. "The Union Impact on Hospital Wages," *Industrial and Labor Relations Review,* 30 (April 1977), pp. 342-55.

Freund, James L. "Market and Union Influences on Municipal Employee Wages." *Industrial and Labor Relations Review,* 27 (April 1974), pp. 391-404.

Frey, Donald E. "Wage Determination in Public Schools and the Effects of Unionization," in Daniel S. Hamermesh, ed. *Labor in the Public and Nonprofit Sectors* (Princeton, N.J.: Princeton University Press, 1975, pp. 183-219.

Hall, W. Clayton, and Carroll, Norman E. "The Effects of Teachers' Organizations on Salaries and Class Size." *Industrial and Labor Relations Review,* 26 (January 1973), pp. 834-41.

Hall, W. Clayton, and Vanderporten, John. "Unionization, Monopsony Power, and Police Salaries." *Industrial Relations,* 16 (February 1977), pp. 94-100.

Hamermesh, Daniel S. "The Effect of Government Ownership on Union Wages," in Hamermesh, ed. *Labor in the Public and Nonprofit Sectors* (Princeton, N.J.: Princeton University Press, 1975) pp. 227-55.

Ichniowski, Casey. "Economic Effects of the Firefighters' Union." *Industrial and Labor Relations Review,* 33 (January 1980), pp. 198-211.

Kasper, Hirschel. "The Effects of Collective Bargaining on Public School Teachers' Salaries." *Industrial and Labor Relations Review,* 24 (October 1970), pp. 57-72.

Lewin, David, Horton, Raymond D., and Kuhn, James W. *Collective Bargaining and Manpower Utilization in Big City Governments.* Montclair, N.J.: Allanheld Osmun, 1979, chapter 4.

Lewin, David, and Keith, John H., Jr. "Managerial Responses to Perceived Labor Shortages: The Case of Police." *Criminology,* 14 (May 1976), pp. 65-92.

Lipsky, David B., and Drotning, John E. "The Influence of Collective Bargaining on Teachers' Salaries in New York State." *Industrial and Labor Relations Review,* 27 (October 1973), pp. 18-35.

Schmenner, Robert W. "The Determination of Municipal Employee Wages." *Review of Economics and Statistics,* 55 (February 1973), pp. 83-90.

Shapiro, David. "Relative Wage Effects of Unions in the Public and Private Sectors." *Industrial and Labor Relations Review,* 31 (January 1978), pp. 193-204.

Smith, Sharon P. *Equal Pay in the Public Sector: Fact or Fantasy:* Princeton, N.J.: Industrial Relations Section, Princeton University, 1977.

Thornton, Robert J. "The Effects of Collective Negotiations on Teachers' Salaries." *The Quarterly Review of Economics and Business,* II (Winter 1971), pp. 37-46.

Victor, Richard B. *The Effects of Unionism on the Wage and Employment Levels of Police and Firefighters.* Santa Monica, Ca. The Rand Corporation, 1977.

Wages and Unionism in the Public Sector: The Case of Police

Ann Bartel* and David Lewin

I. Introduction

One of the most important developments in government during the last two decades has been the growth of public employee unions. Because personnel expenditures comprise a substantial portion of the cost of providing public services, there has been considerable concern that unionization has severely exacerbated budgetary problems of governments, especially local governments. Consequently, a large literature on the wage effects of public employee unionism has developed in recent years.[1] In general, these studies have found rather modest union wage impacts in the public sector, with unions raising the wages of municipal employees by about 5%, on average.

There are several reasons, however, why these estimates may be misleading. First, much public sector union wage impact research has focused on teachers and the demand for teacher services is considerably more elastic than the demand for other public services such as police protection, fire protection and medical care. Second, previous studies have treated public employee unionism as an exogenous variable, and studies of

---

*Graduate School of Business, Columbia University. Reprinted from *The Review of Economics and Statistics,* Vol. 63 (February, 1981), 53-59.

We received helpful comments on this paper from participants in seminars held at The Urban Institute, Princeton University, the University of California at Berkeley and Columbia University. Lewin's research was supported in part by the Faculty Research Fund of the Columbia University Graduate School of Business.

405

private sector unionization have shown that the estimated wage impacts of unions change substantially when unionism is treated as an endogenous variable.[2] Finally, the earlier studies have not considered how public employee unionism has affected fringe benefits, which represent a substantial and growing component of governmental compensation.

This paper attempts to deal with each of these problems. First, we focus on the effects of unionism on the wages of municipal police officers.[3] Because police services are commonly thought to be among the most essential of all public services, organized police should be in an especially powerful position when bargaining with local governments. Second, we estimate a system of equations in which wages and unionism are simultaneously determined and compare these results to the estimated wage impacts from a single equation model. Finally, some estimates of the effects of unionism on police fringe benefits are presented.

II. A Conceptual Framework

A. A model of police wages when unionism is exogenous. To model the determinants of police wages, we rely on previous research on the determinants of public sector wages in general,[4] and police wages in particular.[5] In the absence of police unionism, police wages are assumed to be a function of a community's ability to pay and its "tastes" for police services, the form of municipal government, and the opportunity wage for potential applicants for police jobs. Ability to pay is proxied by median family income *(INC)* while a community's tastes for police services can be captured by such variables as city size *(POP)*, population density *(DEN)*, the median value of housing in the community *(HOUSE)*, and a vector of geographic region dummies *(REGION)*.[6] The form of government is generally considered to be an important determinant of the demand for police services, given that city-managers have professional training and consequently may be relatively more efficient in "producing" police services.[7] This hypothesis can be tested by using two dichotomous variables in the wage equation: *MAYOR,* which equals one if the form of government is mayor-council, zero otherwise, and *COMM,* which equals one if the form of government is commission, zero otherwise. The opportunity wage can be proxied by the average hourly earnings of manufacturing production workers in the municipality *(OPPW)*.

Now suppose that in some municipalities police officers are unionized. Police unions may be expected to raise the wage above the market clearing wage, thereby creating an excess supply of labor.[8] In attempting to measure this union effect, previous studies have employed such variables as the existence of a police labor organization, the percentage of police organized, or the type and affiliation of the police labor organization.[9] However, we prefer a different measure, namely, the presence of collective bargaining among police. This is because the behavioral importance of a workers' organization is not simply its existence, but rather the joint decision making that it engages in with management through collective bargaining. Thus, a dummy variable *(CONTRACT)*, which equals one if the city has a written labor agreeement covering wages, hours and conditions of employment for police personnel, zero if it does not, is used here to measure the impact of collective bargaining on police wages.[10] The superiority of this variable over a dummy measuring the existence of a police labor organiztion is shown in part III.

Given the assumption that unionism is exogenous, we can estimate the following equation for police wages:

$$\ln W = \beta_0 + \beta_1 INC + \beta_2 POP + \beta_3 DEN + \beta_4 HOUSE + \beta_5 REGION$$
$$+ \beta_6 MAYOR + \beta_7 COMM + \beta_8 \ln OPPW + \beta_9 CONTRACT$$
$$+ u_1 \tag{1}$$

where β_1, β_2, β_3, β_4, β_6, β_7, β_8 and β_9 are hypothesized to be positive and u_1 is the residual.

B. A simultaneous model of police wages and unionism. Equation (1) assumes that police unionism (and collective bargaining) in a municipality is exogenously determined. However, if the level of police wages in a municipality partially determines whether or not police are organized and engage in collective bargaining, then CONTRACT will be correlated with u_1 and the estimated coefficient on CONTRACT in equation (1) will be biased. The following section suggests how the complete simultaneous model may be specified.

As discussed by Stigler (1971), the "economic theory" of regulation treats regulation or legislation as the result of the interplay of demand and supply forces such that individuals who presumably would benefit from the legislation determine demand, and individuals who stand to lose from the legislation determine supply.[11] Within the context of this theory, the level of police wages that prevails in the absence of a union could positively or negatively affect the probability that police will unionize. First, the lower the wage, the greater will be the increase in taxes necessary to finance the increased labor costs resulting from collective bargaining and, thus, the greater should be a community's opposition to unionism and collective bargaining by police. Another way of interpreting such a positive relationship is that legislation sanctioning unionism and collective bargaining by police may merely codify existing behavior. In other words, it is in those municipalities where police are already paid relatively high wages that there will be less opposition to unionization.[12] An alternative argument is that the lower the wage, the greater will be the benefits to the police from unionizing and hence the greater the demand for unionization.[13] While we cannot predict a priori the sign of the wage variable in the police unionization equation, we can at least conclude that it is an important determinant of the costs and/or the benefits of police unionism.

Other variables can also be suggested as empirical measures of the costs and benefits of police unionism. For example, in their organizing efforts police presumably would be aided by other organized workers, or at least would encounter less opposition to their goals in areas that are heavily unionized; in other words, the supply of public sector unionism would be greater in these areas. In the absence of data on local work force unionization, we use the percentage of private sector workers organized in the state (*PSU*) to measure this variable. Second, the form of government can also influence the ease with which police gain collective bargaining rights. The relatively greater direct personal control that city managers have over municipal services as well as their professional training should make it easier for them to prevent police officers from gaining enough political support to organize and to engage in collective bargaining; therefore, *MAYOR* and *COMM* should have positive signs in the police unionization equation. Third, it can be argued that the higher the median family income in a municipality (*INC*), the less reluctant will be the city's population to finance the increased wage costs which may result from police collective bargaining. In addition, holding *INC* constant, police may find it more difficult to bargain collectively in municipalities with a relatively highly educated population to the extent that a more educated citizenry has greater awareness of the costs that police collective bargaining may impose on them. Median education in the municipality (*EDUC*) should therefore have a negative effect in the unionism equation. Finally, a vector of geographic region dummies (*REGION*) can be added to the equation to capture unmeasured "tastes" for police unionism.

In summary, the following equation (with u_2 as the error term) is used to explain variations across cities in police collective bargaining activity:[14]

$$CONTRACT = a_0 + a_1 \ln W^* + a_2 PSU + a_3 MAYOR + a_4 COMM$$
$$+ a_5 INC + a_6 EDUC + a_7 REGION + u_2 \qquad (2)$$

Note that the wage that is included in this equation is W^*, i.e., the wage that prevails in the municipality in the absence of police unionism, or, from equation (1), $\ln W^* = \ln W - \beta_9 CONTRACT$. By estimating the simultaneous system represented in equations (1) and (2), we obtain unbiased estimates of the parameters in both equations.[15] The specifications insure that both equations are identified.[16]

III. Empirical Analysis

A. Data. Equations (1) and (2) are estimated for a sample of cities that responded to the 1973 Survey of Personnel Policies in Municipal Police Departments conducted by the International City Management Association. These cities had populations of at least 25,000. The survey elicited information on size of the police force, the structure of police salaries, total police labor costs, whether or not the city had a written labor contract with police officers, the form of government in the municipality, the city's total budget, and training, retirement and pension provisions for police. From the 1972 County and City Data Book, we obtained information on the economic and demographic characteristics of the municipalities. Information on private sector unionization in the state was obtained from the U.S. Bureau of Labor Statistics (1975). Deletion of the cities that did not report the information necessary to estimate equations (1) and (2) resulted in a sample of 215 municipalities.[17]

B. The impact of unionism on police wages. Table 1 presents the coefficients on *CONTRACT* from wage equations that were estimated alternatively by ordinary least squares (OLS) and two stage least squares (TSLS) techniques.

To conserve space, the coefficients on the other variables in the wage equation are not presented. With the exception of form of government, the coefficients on all of these variables had the hypothesized signs and were significant at the 5% level. Several different measures of the police wage were used in the equation: the minimum (entry) salary for police privates (*MINSAL*), the "hourly" minimum wage for police privates (*MINHW*), calculated by dividing *MINSAL* by the average weekly hours for police privates times 52,[18] the maximum (base) salary for police privates (*MAXSAL*), and the average salary for all police officers (*AVGSAL*), calculated by dividing the city's annual cost for salaries for full-time uniformed police by the number of full-time uniformed police.[19]

The results in Table 1 show that when the wage equation was estimated under the assumption that unionism is exogenous, *CONTRACT* was positive and significant in three of the four equations. Annual minimum and maximum salaries were found to be about 6% higher in cities with contracts; controlling for the labor supply of police privates in column (2) raised the union effect slightly, indicating that policemen work fewer hours, on average, in cities with a contract.[20] In addition, the average salary of all uniformed policemen was 3.9% higher in municipalities with a written labor contract, but this effect was not statistically significant. Before turning to the results of the simultaneous model, it should be noted that we examined the suitability of an alternative measure of unionism, the existence of a police labor organization, by creating two dummy variables to replace *CONTRACT*: (1) *ORGC* = 1 if the municipality has a police labor organization *and* a written labor contract, and (2) *ORGNC* = 1 if the municipality has an organization but no contract. The superiority of the *CONTRACT* variable is shown by the fact that in the case of the dependent variable MINSAL, the coefficient on

TABLE 1
Coefficients on CONTRACT from Police Wage Equations*
(t-values are given in parentheses)

Dependent Variable†	(1) MINSAL	(2) MINHW	(3) MAXSAL	(4) AVGSAL
A. OLS Results‡	0.0590	0.0640	0.0639	0.0393
	(3.90)	(3.72)	(3.86)	(1.34)
B. TSLS Results				
1. Collective bargaining law excluded from *CONTRACT* equation	0.1505	0.2070	0.0998	0.0917
	(3.71)	(4.02)	(2.43)	(1.32)
2. Collective bargaining law included in CONTRACT equation	0.1336	0.1722	0.1190	0.1190
	(4.57)	(4.81)	(3.80)	(2.24)

*All of the other variables shown in equation (1) in the text are included in the wage equation.
†See text for definitions.
‡In columns 1, 2, and 3, the R^2 is approximately 0.65. In column 4, it is 0.47.

409

ORGC is 0.0769 and is significant, while the coefficient on *ORGNC* is 0.0316 and is not significant. Further, the difference in these coefficients is statistically significant.

If we relax the assumption that unionism is exogenous and assume that police wages and police unionism are simultaneously determined, the estimated union wage impact increases considerably.[21] As can be seen in Table 1, we now estimate that municipalities with a *CONTRACT* have annual minimum salaries that are about 14% higher than annual minimum salaries in cities without a *CONTRACT*. This effect is more than twice the size of the union impact estimated from the single-equation model. Hourly starting wages are now estimated to be between 17% and 21% higher in contract than in non-contract cities, while annual maximum (base) salaries and average annual salaries are about 10% higher. These results support the hypothesis that the demand for unionization is greater in low wage municipalities; therefore, single-equation estimates understate the impact of police unionism on police wages.

C. The impact of wages on police unionism. To demonstrate further the need for a simultaneous model of police wages and unionism, we present in Table 2 the coefficients on the police wage from unionism equations (equation (2) in part II above) that were estimated alternatively by OLS and TSLS. Again, in order to conserve space, we do not report the coefficients on the other variables in the equation but discuss them briefly here. The predictions about private sector unionization and a state's collective bargaining law were borne out; in addition, the coefficients on median family income and median education had the predicted signs but were not significant.[22] The only unexpected result in the unionism equation was the finding that police collective bargaining was more likely to occur in municipalities with a city-manager form of government. Perhaps city managers are more willing to accept unions because they are better able to obtain productivity gains to offset relatively higher police salaries.[23]

The wage coefficients in Table 2 demonstrate the need for a simultaneous model of wages and unionism in order to understand the determinants of municipal variations in police unionism. When the wage is treated as exogenous, the wage coefficient is either zero or positive. Allowing for the endogeneity of wages results in a negative wage coefficient which is significant in some of the specifications. Thus the simultaneity bias present in the single-equation estimate of the determinants of police unionism would have prevented us from reaching the important conclusion that a *CONTRACT* is more likely to be present in a low wage than in a high wage city. This finding supports the hypothesis that the demand for police unionization is greater the lower the police wage.

D. The impact of police unionism on fringe benefits. Our analysis has focused on the impact of unionism on police salaries via the collective bargaining process. It is well known, however, that fringe benefits account for a large proportion of total compensation for public employees generally and for police in particular. In this section we consider the role of unionism through collective bargaining in the determination of police fringe benefits.

410

TABLE 2
Coefficients on 1n (WAGE) from CONTRACT Equation*
(t-values are given in parentheses)

	Wage Measure†			
Independent Variable(s)	(1) MINSAL	(2) MINHW	(3) MAXSAL	(4) AVGSAL
A. OLS Results‡				
1. Collective bargaining law	0.3975	0.3289	0.4814	0.0512
excluded from equation	(1.50)	(1.31)	(2.02)	(0.31)
2. Collective bargaining law	0.0492	−0.0026	0.1695	−0.1162
included in equation	(0.19)	(−0.01)	(0.73)	(−0.73)
B. TSLS Results				
1. Collective bargaining law	−0.8248	−0.8079	−0.6474	−0.6491
excluded from equation	(−1.40)	(−1.33)	(−1.27)	(−1.31)
2. Collective bargaining law	−1.443	−1.619	−1.091	−1.130
included in equation	(−2.35)	(−2.38)	(−2.08)	(−2.13)

*All of the other variables shown in equation (2) are included in the *CONTRACT* equation. In some cases, as indicated, the presence of a state collective bargaining law variable is added to the equation.
†See text for definition.
‡The R^2 in each of these equations is approximately 0.30 when the collective bargaining law is excluded and increases to 0.38 when this variable is included.

Since the data set we are using contains rather limited information on fringes, the results in this section should be interpreted cautiously.

In panel A of Table 3 we attempt to gauge the impact of collective bargaining on total fringe benefits. This is done by defining two variables: *LGACOST,* which equals the logarithm of the municipality's annual expenditures for personnel costs for full-time uniformed police divided by the number of full-time police; and *LGASAL,* which is the logarithm of the municipality's annual expenditures for salaries for full-time uniformed police divided by the number of full-time police.[24] We believe that the first variable includes salary expenditures plus expenditures for all fringe benefits. If this assumption is correct, then we can compare the impacts of unionism on salaries and fringe benefits by estimating equation (1) for each of the two variables we have defined.[25] Since the dependent variables are in logarithmic form, we can compare the estimated *CONTRACT* coefficients and thereby determine whether unionism has a larger impact on salaries or on fringes.[26] The results in panel A of Table 3 show that *CONTRACT* has a larger coefficient in the *LGACOST* equation than in the *LGASAL* equation. This indicates that collective bargaining has had a greater impact on the fringe benefits than on the salaries received by police.

In panel B of Table 3 we focus on police retirement benefits and use five variables to measure these benefits: *AGE* = the minimum regular retirement age, *YEARS* = the minimum number of years of service needed to receive a pension for regular retirement, *EXPEND* = the annual employer expenditure for retirement benefits as a percentage of payroll, *ECONT* =

411

TABLE 3
Effects of CONTRACT on Police Fringe Benefits* (t-values in parentheses)

Dependent Variable†	OLS	TSLS	Sample Size
A. All Fringe Benefits			
LGACOST	0.0891	0.1723	121
	(1.77)	(1.83)	
LGASAL	0.0575	0.1241	121
	(1.43)	(1.65)	
B. Retirement Benefits			
AGE	−1.750		180
	(−1.69)		
YEARS	−1.234		198
	(−1.30)		
EXPEND	3.457		161
	(1.89)		
ECONT	0.9892		161
	(0.82)		
PCSAL	0.8423		164
	(0.43)		

**HOUSE. POP. INC. DEN. OPPW. MAYOR. COMM* and *REGION* are included as independent
variables in these regressions.
†See text for definitions.

the employee contribution to the retirement system as a percentage of
annual salary, and PCSAL = the percentage of salary received for minimum
regular retirement. The results show that unionism has significantly reduced
the age at which policemen retire and has significantly increased employer
expenditures for retirement benefits as a percentage of payroll.

Admittedly, much better data are required in order to sort out the role
of collective bargaining in the determination of police fringe benefits. But it
appears that, even with these fragmentary data, we have documented a
significant impact of unionism on the nonwage benefits received by police.

IV. Summary

This study has examined the determinants of police wages and police
unionism in American cities, with unionism measured by the presence of a
collective bargaining *CONTRACT* rather than simply by the existence of a
police labor organization. Ordinary least squares estimates of union impacts
on police wages range between 3.9% and 6.4%, which are consistent with the
findings of other investigators.[27] However, the impact more than doubles to
around 14% (in the case of minimum salaries) when police unionism is
treated as an endogenous variable. Our results also show that the demand
for unionization is greater in low wage cities and that, consequently, an
analysis that ignores the simultaneous determination of wages and unionism
seriously underestimates the effect of police unionism on police wages.

When the analysis was extended to incorporate fringe benefits, we
calculated that unionism has had a greater impact on fringes than on

salaries. Further, unionism appears to have significantly improved the retirement benefits attained by police. However, better data are needed before we can draw firm conclusions about the nonwage impacts of police unionism.

In conclusion, it appears that the wage impacts of police unionism are larger than previously thought and large compared to the wage increases achieved by other organized public employees; so too may be the nonwage impacts of police unionism. But in order to gauge the true impact of police unionism on municipalities, we must know how police productivity is affected by police unionism and bargaining activity. Brown and Medoff (1978) have shown that unionization has had a substantial positive effect on output per worker in U.S. manufacturing industries. Perhaps police unionism analogously serves to improve the productivity of police so as to fully offset (or even exceed) the increased costs that result from unionism and collective bargaining. Testing this hypothesis is beyond the scope of the present paper, but provides an important topic for further research.

Footnotes

1. This literature is summarized in Lewin (1977).
2. See Ashenfelter and Johnson (1972) and Schmidt and Strauss (1976).
3. Schmenner (1973), Ehrenberg and Goldstein (1975), Lewin and Keith (1976) and Hall and Vanderporten (1977) have examined the impact of unionism on police wages. None of these studies considered the simultaneity problem or the fringe benefit issue that we discuss here.
4. See Lewin (1977).
5. See the sources cited in footnote 3.
6. Since variations across municipalities in *INC, POP, DEN* and *HOUSE* will capture much of the variation in the crime rate, it is not necessary to include a variable for the crime rate.
7. See, for example, Ehrenberg and Goldstein (1975).
8. For a discussion of the excess supply of police labor, see Wolitz (1974).
9. See the review in Lewin (1977).
10. By doing this we are implicitly assuming that the percentage wage increase is the same in all unionized cities and that nonunionzed cities are unaffected by the existence of these unions.
11. Edwards (1978) used this theory to specify a simultaneous model of school enrollment rates and compulsory schooling laws.
12. In their private sector interindustry analysis, Ashenfelter and Johnson (1972) predicted a positive relationship between wages and unionism on the grounds that unionism is a normal good and that, holding constant the cost of union membership, higher wages will increase the worker's desire to join a union. Their empirical results supported the hypothesized relationship, as did the later findings of Schmidt and Strauss (1976).
13. This is consistent with the work of Moore (1978) who found a negative relationship between teacher income and teacher unionism in a model that treated income as exogenous.
14. It can be argued that the existence of a state collective bargaining law (*CBL*) also belongs in equation (2). However, this variable could be construed as endogenous. In our empirical work, we estimate equation (2) with and without this variable.

15. Note that this simultaneous model implicitly assumes that variations in the variables over time within a city are small relative to variations across cities at a point in time. We would therefore expect wages to be highly correlated over time within a city. In fact, the simple correlation of 1963 police salaries (when few cities had contracts) and 1973 salaries (when 50% of the cities had contracts) is 0.85. This result testifies to the consistent role of the demand-supply variables in the wage determination process. Given this framework, our model enables us to estimate the effect of W^* (not W) on $CONTRACT$ in a simultaneous system. It must be stressed that ordinary least squares estimation of equation (2) could not provide us with this parameter. Heckman (1978) discusses the statistical properties of this type of model given in equations (1) and (2).

16. As our empirical results show, the wage equation is identified simply because of the strong role of PSU in the $CONTRACT$ equation. We believe it is reasonable to argue that PSU belongs only in the union equation. While private sector unionists could be expected to favor the expansion of unionism in the public sector, it is not at all obvious that their activities would increase the demand for police services, holding the other demand variables constant. In some of our work we did include PSU in both equations, using the state collective bargaining law to identify the wage equation; the results showed that PSU had a significant effect only in the contract equation.

17. It was not possible to perform this analysis for years after 1973 because, unlike police salary and fringe benefit data, police unionism and bargaining data have not been published since then. Obviously, this also prevents us from conducting a time-series analysis of police wages and police unionism.

18. This is the only information on labor supply that was available to us. The assumption of zero unemployment implicit in this calculation is perhaps unrealistic, but far less so than it would be in the case of private sector employees.

19. Note that the salary variables as well as all the other variables that are measured in money terms were deflated by a city cost-of-living index. Data on the cost of living were available for one-third of the municipalities. Using these data, we estimated an equation in which the cost of living was a function of the region of the country and the size of the municipality. A cost of living index was then predicted for the remaining municipalities. The results using the deflated variables were very similar to those that used the undeflated variables. The undeflated results are available from the authors.

20. Although $CONTRACT$ has a significant effect on average weekly hours, the actual reduction in hours is only about 1%.

21. Equations (1) and (2) were estimated using a standard two stage least squares technique. Heckman (1978) shows that this approach gives consistent estimates even though one of the endogenous variables is dichotomous. Note, however, that the estimates of the variances of the coefficients in the $CONTRACT$ equation will be biased unless this equation is estimated by $PROBIT$ or $LOGIT$. Since we are primarily concerned with the way in which the estimated union wage impact changes when a simultaneous model is specified and less concerned about the significance levels of coefficients in the $CONTRACT$ equation, we chose not to incur the high costs of estimating a simultaneous model using $PROBIT$.

22. The fact that the "political" variables are significant while the "economic" ones are not may indicate that the taxpayer's political identification with a unionized police force is the motivating factor behind a community's willingness to let its police bargain collectively.

23. Since the available data do not contain productivity measures we are unable to test this hypothesis directly.

24. Note that only 121 cities provided the information necessary to construct both of these variables.
25. Professor Martin Segal of Dartmouth University and an anonymous referee pointed out that the fringe benefit data used in this analysis are unlikely to include the employers' unfunded pension liabilities, thereby making our fringe benefit estimates imperfect measures of the true value.
26. This is because the union elasticity in the *LGACOST* equation will be a weighted average of the union elasticities on salaries and fringes, with the weights being the shares of salaries and fringes in total personnel costs.
27. For example, Ehrenberg and Goldstein (1975) and Victor (1977).

References

Ashenfelter, Orley, and George E. Johnson, "Unionism, Relative Wages and Labor Quality in U.S. Manufacturing Industries," *International Economic Review* 13 (Oct. 1972), 488-508.

Brown, Charles, and James Medoff, "Trade Unions in the Production Process," *Journal of Political Economy* 86 (June 1978), 355-378.

Edwards, Linda N., "An Empirical Analysis of Compulsory Schooling Legislation, 1940-1960," *Journal of Law and Economics* 21 (Apr. 1978), 203-222.

Ehrenberg, Ronald G., and Gerald S. Goldstein, "A Model of Public Sector Wage Determination," *Journal of Urban Economics* 2 (July 1975), 223-245.

Hall, W. Clayton, and Bruce Vanderporten, "Unionization, Monopsony Power and Police Salaries," *Industrial Relations* 16 (Feb. 1977), 94-100.

Heckman, James J., "Dummy Endogenous Variables in a Simultaneous Equation System," *Econometrica* 46 (July 1978), 931-959.

Lewin, David, "Public Sector Labor Relations: A Review Essay," *Labor History* 18 (Winter 1977), 133-144.

Lewin, David, and John H. Keith, Jr., "Managerial Responses to Perceived Labor Shortages: The Case of Police," *Criminology* 14 (May 1976), 65-92.

Moore, William J., "An Analysis of Teacher Union Growth," *Industrial Relations* 17 (May 1978), 204-215.

Schmenner, Roger W., "The Determination of Municipal Employee Wages," *Review of Economics and Statistics* 55 (Feb. 1973), 83-90.

Schmidt, Peter, and Robert Strauss, "The Effect of Unions on Earnings and Earnings on Unions: A Mixed Logit Approach," *International Economic Review* 17 (Feb. 1976), 204-212.

Stigler, George J., "The Theory of Economic Regulation," *Bell Journal of Economics and Management Science* 2 (Spring 1971), 3-21.

U.S. Bureau of the Census, *County and City Data Book,* 1972, 1977.

U.S. Department of Labor, Bureau of Labor Statistics, *Directory of National Unions and Employee Associations,* Washington, D.C., 1975.

Victor, Richard B., "The Effects of Unionism on the Wage and Employment Levels of Police and Firefighters," Rand Corporation Report, August 1977.

Wolitz, Louise B., "An Analysis of the Labor Market for Policemen," unpublished doctoral dissertation, University of California at Berkeley, 1974.

7
Nonwage Impacts of Unionism

DETERMINANTS OF BARGAINING OUTCOMES

We begin this chapter with a paper that presents both a conceptual framework for analyzing public sector bargaining outcomes and an empirical test
of the underlying model. The study of the determinants of bargaining
outcomes in Canadian municipalities by John C. Anderson adapts a model
that was developed and first applied to the analysis of bargaining outcomes
in local governments in the U.S.[1] This framework and its application are
instructive for several reasons. First, it illustrates that a wide range of issues
in addition to wages are covered in bargaining agreements and are systematically related to characteristics of the environment, structure, and process
of bargaining and the organizational characteristics of the union and the
employer. This points out the importance of considering the nonwage
aspects of the bargaining agreement in assessing the effects of unions in the
public sector and the relative power of the parties. Second, when the results
of the Canadian study presented here are compared with the earlier U.S.
research, one sees how the sources of power that drive the bargaining
process and influence its outcomes can vary across political settings and
over time. Bargaining outcomes in American cities during the initial generation of bargaining appear to have been heavily influenced by differences in
the legal environments (collective bargaining laws and impasse procedures)
across states and by the political effectiveness of local unions. The Canadian
data, drawn from older bargaining relationships and across jurisdictions with
less marked differences in law, appear to be most heavily influenced by the
economic and political environments and the managerial responses to
collective bargaining. Thus, to the extent that the responses of U.S. public
sector managers are being modified as a result of the economic and political
changes now taking place, we may see changes in the relative importance of
different sources of power and ultimately a different configuration of bargaining outcomes. In short, there is no reason to believe that the sources of
power that were dominant during the first generation of public sector
bargaining in the U.S. will continue to be so in the future.

Indeed, the second article by Charles R. Perry, using a longitudinal and
more qualitative methodology, clearly demonstrates how the sources of
power and perhaps even the relative power of the parties have changed over

417

time in a sample of school districts. This paper provides empirical support for a number of the perceptions of the current state of affairs in the public sector that we offered in our introductory chapter. By comparing the outcomes and related experiences in his sample districts circa 1978 with the results of his research in these districts a decade earlier, Perry reached the following conclusions: (1) management resistance to union demands had stiffened; (2) the strike had become less effective as a source of union power; (3) unions had achieved some wage gains through direct increases and changes in salary structures, however the gains tapered off in recent years and the magnitude of the union impact over the time period does not support those who fear excessive union power from collective bargaining; and (4) unions have made incremental gains in contract language which reduce managerial discretion, but they have not yet exercised their new rights in ways that seriously constrain managerial policy development.

Taken together, the Anderson and Perry articles illustrate the benefit gained by examining both quantitative and qualitative data before forming conclusions about the effects of collective bargaining. Anderson's paper and its forerunners provide estimates of the impact of alternative sources of power on the range of issues in bargaining. Perry's paper provides a more intensive description and interpretation of how these sources of power vary in impact over time.

PERSONNEL AND HUMAN RESOURCE MANAGEMENT POLICIES

The next set of papers turn to the analysis of union impacts on more specific aspects of the personnel and human resource management function. Papers of this type all owe an intellectual debt to the classic private sector study of these issues by Slichter, Healy, and Livernash.[2] That study, published by the Brookings Institution in 1960, concluded that the arrival of a union produces a "shock effect" on management. Unions force management to formalize their personnel policies, restructure, specialize, and professionalize their personnel and labor relations functions, and in general, search for managerial improvements to recoup the potential efficiency losses associated with union induced wage gains. The methodology employed in their study, as in the ones presented here, is generally qualitative and judgmental in nature as it is based on intensive fieldwork in specific organizations.

A number of these types of studies have been conducted to date in the public sector and appear to reach remarkably similar conclusions. An early example was conducted in nineteen cities and counties in the late 1960s and early 1970s by David Stanley.[3] He found very little evidence of union impacts on the traditional civil service standards dealing with employee selection, promotion, and training. This finding would probably still hold, with the major exception of the growth of stronger seniority provisions in contracts covering layoff, transfer, and in some cases, promotions. In contrast, grievance procedures had generally taken hold in the local governments studied by Stanley and were based on established private sector standards, principles, and practices of due process, progressive discipline, and most importantly, binding arbitration. Stanley also concluded, that with a few notable exceptions, such as New York City, unions had not imposed major restrictions on management in the areas of subcontracting, manning, and workload policies.

Two selections that are presented here from a study of twenty-two police departments conducted in the early 1970s by Juris and Feuille provide more detailed but similar conclusions regarding the impact of police unions on police management. The authors discuss specific instances in which police unions have influenced overtime pay, work scheduling, shift differentials, manning provisions and broader areas of management policy. Furthermore, they show how these union impacts vary across cities and argue that many of the gains were achieved in the early years of bargaining by unions' taking advantage of the political power and access that they enjoyed to different political bodies and officials at the local and state levels. Hence this analysis supports the contention noted throughout this book regarding the importance of political power and internal management structure and conflict as important determinants of bargaining outcomes.

Substantially similar conclusions to the Stanley and Juris and Feuille studies of the late 1960s and early 1970s have been reached in two more recent studies of union impacts—one in the federal sector by George Sulzner and the other in school districts by McDonnell and Pascal.[4] Both of these more recent studies found support for the shock effect hypothesis. Both also found instances where unions have achieved contractual provisions which limit management's ability to innovate but, on average, found little support for the notion that public sector unions have hamstrung public managers, as some had feared. Thus, a consistent story seems to be emerging from the qualitative studies in the Slichter, et al. tradition, namely, that unions have major effects on the *procedures* for making and administering personnel policies, have some effects on the *substance* of these policies, but, on average, have not placed restraints on management's ability to manage. All these studies caution, however, that the union impact on management varies considerably—examples of unions that have substantially raised labor costs and imposed restrictive practices can be found in some cities, while contrasting examples of minimal union impacts can be found in other cities.[5]

This final point on the diversity of union impacts leaves us with a very uneasy feeling with regard to the state of research in this area. We noted earlier the intellectual debt that research in this area owes to Slichter, et al. The other side of that statement is that we really have not advanced the state of analysis in this area very far since 1960! We have yet to find systematic studies that go beyond analysis of the contract provisions and subjective assessments of the impacts of these provisions on actual behavior at the workplace. To assess adequately the ultimate impacts of collective bargaining on the bottom line of goals of employers, the key job related goals of workers, and the public service goals of communities, we need to go well beyond these studies to compare actual labor costs, safety and health experiences, employment levels, layoff experiences, and other indicators of the quality of working life across bargaining settings in the public sector. These issues lie on the frontier of research in public sector bargaining.

INTRODUCING CHANGE IN
BARGAINING RELATIONSHIPS

The final issue we wish to take up in this chapter involves the increasingly key question of how labor and management in the public sector adjust to external shocks on the bargaining system. Change does not come easily in collective bargaining, particularly when it involves threats to job security or to other vital economic and organizational interests of the parties. Yet all of the financial and demographic trends introduced in Chapter 2 suggest that employment cutbacks have been and will continue to be important features of the public sector landscape for some time to come. Other pressures for change are likely, as external actors begin to probe the collective bargaining relationship for ways to assert or reassert their interests. Thus, the final two papers in this chapter summarize two fundamentally different strategies for managing change—a joint labor-management-neutral committee and a court ordered and supervised procedure. The labor-management committee example is drawn from the work of Robert B. McKersie, Leonard Greenhalgh, and Todd Jick on the Continuity of Employment Committee in New York State. This committee perhaps deserves the label as the best example of integrative bargaining in the public sector to date. The authors' story of how the Committee helped search for effective ways of managing major workforce reductions speaks for itself.

Throughout this book we have stressed the increasing pressures that are impinging on public sector bargaining relationships from the external environment. Indeed, we have argued that the growing importance and impact of external community and governmental forces has been one of the major distinguishing characteristics of public sector bargaining in recent years. Thus it is fitting that our final selection by Harry Katz docuuments a specific type of external influence on bargaining, namely, the effects of a major desegregation plan in a large urban school district. In this case the key external agent is the Federal Court, however the larger lesson to be drawn from the example is that public sector bargaining is indeed a permeable institution and cannot be isolated from the larger economic, social and political pressures that can force adjustments in public institutions. If our hunch is correct, then the growing assertiveness of the public, combined with continued fiscal austerity, will, in the years ahead, produce many more examples of externally induced changes in public sector bargaining practices and relationships.

FOOTNOTES

1. See Thomas A. Kochan and Hoyt N. Wheeler, "Municipal Collective Bargaining: A Model and Analysis of Bargaining Outcomes," *Industrial and Labor Relations Review,* 29 (October 1975), 46-66; Paul F. Gerhart, "Determinants of Bargaining Outcomes in Local Government Negotiations," *Industrial and Labor Relations Review,* 29 (April 1976), 331-351.
2. Sumner Slichter, James J. Healy, and E. Robert Livernash, *The Impact of Collective Bargaining on Management* (Washington, D.C.: The Brookings Institution, 1960).

3. David T. Stanley, *Managing Local Government under Union Pressure* (Washington, D.C.: The Brookings Institution, 1972).
4. George T. Sulzner, *The Impact of Labor Management Relations upon Selected Federal Personnel Policy and Practices,* U.S. Office of Personnel Management, January 1979 (OPM Document 124-76-1), and Lorraine McDonnell and Anthony Pascal, *Organized Teachers in American Schools* (Santa Monica, Ca.: The Rand Corporation, 1979). A portion of the latter work is reprinted in Chapter 4 of the present volume.
5. Such diversity is further analyzed and theoretically elaborated in David Lewin, Raymond D. Horton, and James W. Kuhn, *Collective Bargaining and Manpower Utilization in Big City Governments* (Montclair, N.J.: Allanheld Osmun, 1979).

Bargaining Outcomes:
An IR System Approach

John C. Anderson*

Substantial debate still exists about the relevance of the private sector collective bargaining model to the public sector. For example, it has been argued that the inelasticity of demand for public services, the predominance of political rather than economic power, the diffuse nature of management, resulting in intraorganizational conflict, and the existence of multilateral and not bilateral negotiations combine to produce a set of influences on the wage and benefit determination process unique to the public sector. Nevertheless, most wage determination research has not yet gone beyond economic models of bargaining power to explain the outcomes of the bargaining process. Typically, conditions of the labor market (e.g., unemployment, monopsony, demand for labor), inflation, and private sector wage comparisons are used as the primary predictors of public sector wages. Those studies going beyond these environmental context variables are typically limited to dummy variable measures of the impasse procedures available, the existence of a union contract, or the form of government. Thus, while public sector bargaining *theory* identifies a number of critical characteristics of the non-economic context, the management and union organizations, and the bargaining process which may impact wage and benefit levels, *research* has remained generally limited to economic explanations.

Recent studies, however, evince a new interest in developing empirically testable models of the bargaining process which identify a wide range of potential sources of bargaining power that may affect the outcomes of collective bargaining in the public sector.[1] Moreover, these studies have gone beyond wages to examine the determinants of the contents of collective agreements. The present study extends this nascent trend first by using an industrial relations system conceptual framework to identify the character

*Graduate School of Business, Columbia University. Reprinted from *Industrial Relations,* Vol. 18 (Spring 1979), pp. 127-143.

istics of the environment, management and union organizations, and bargaining process which may act as sources of union bargaining power affecting bargaining outcomes. Second, both wage and nonwage bargaining outcomes are examined separately as dependent variables. Finally, propositions relating the components of the industrial relations system to bargaining outcomes are developed and tested with a cross-sectional analysis of the outcomes of bargaining between Canadian municipal governments and 95 local unions. The results generally confirm findings in recent research and imply the need for several new directions in future research

The Conceptual Framework

To develop a more comprehensive approach to the determinants of bargaining outcomes in the public sector, it is first necessary to select a conceptual framework to aid in the choice of independent variables. Perhaps the most well-known theoretical perspective is Dunlop's industrial relations system, which he defined as "an analytic subsystem of an industrial society on the same logical plane as an economic system."[2] The system is comprised of three actors—government, employers and their associations, and workers and their associations—bound together by an ideology, with an output of a "web of rules" of the workplace and the work community. The technical, power, and market contexts of the system are viewed as determinants of the web of rules, with each context having a selective impact on the subset of rules (e.g., market context affects compensation).

The present study uses four conceptual categories from the industrial relations system framework: (1) the environment or context; (2) the actors; (3) the mechanisms for converting inputs into outputs or the procedures for establishing rules; and (4) the outcomes of the industrial relations system. Each of the first three sets of factors may act as a source of bargaining power for union and management, shaping the outcomes of the system. That is, the characteristics of the economic, political, legal, and social environments, the organizational characteristics and expertise of union and management, and the nature of the bargaining process all are likely to influence the costs of agreement or disagreement between negotiating parties and hence affect the outcomes of collective bargaining. Consequently, in the present research, all of these factors are identified and measured as sources of union bargaining power. The hypothesized relationships between these sets of characteristics and wage and nonwage bargaining outcomes are presented with the results.

Research Design

Sample. The sample population consists of police officers, fire fighters, clerical employees, and manual workers in 26 major Canadian municipalities. All cities over 100,000 people were included and then supplemented so that at least the two largest cities in each of the ten provinces are represented. Personal interviews were conducted with representatives of each of the 95 local unions selected and with the negotiator acting for each of the municipalities. In the majority of cases, separate bargaining units are certified for each of the four occupational groups examined. Manual and clerical employees, and in several provinces police and firefighters, are under the jurisdiction of private sector labor legislation.

Dependent variables. Both wages and an index of nonwage collective bargaining outcomes are included as dependent variables. Similar to the approaches of Kochan and Wheeler, Gerhart, and Perry and Levine, provisions in collective agreements are identified and assigned values according to their favorability to the union.[3] Categories representing the degree of favorability of the provisions are developed from a comprehensive list of contract provisions. The least favorable provision is assigned the lowest value and the most favorable one, the highest value. For example, union security provisions have the following values: no reference (0), maintenance of membership (1), agency shop (2), modified union shop (3), and union shop (4). A total score is calculated for each contract by adding the scores on each of the 45 provisions included in the particular contract. The base wage rate for each occupational group (local union) is used as the wage dependent variable. Because it is the base wage that is altered directly through negotiations (the higher steps in the wage scale being adjusted accordingly) and because of its comparability across bargaining units, the base wage rate is preferable to the average or maximum rate.

As both wages and the nature of issues demanded in collective bargaining vary systematically by occupational group, two forms of each dependent variable are examined: the raw score and the normalized score. Wages and bargaining outcomes scores are normalized within a particular occupation (i.e., police, fire fighters, clerical, manual) to a mean value of zero and a standard deviation of one. This enables direct comparisons on bargaining outcome measures across occupations.

Independent variables. The independent variables are characteristics which the industrial relations system framework and previous public sector collective bargaining research suggest might enhance the union's ability to attain favorable outcomes. Measures of the characteristics of the environment, union, management, and bargaining process are taken from published data sources and interviews with union and management representatives. Most measures are specifically developed or adapted for this study and have acceptable estimates of reliability. The definitions of the independent variables and the data sources are presented in Table 1.

Hypotheses and Zero-order Correlation Results

Environmental sources of union power. Environmental characteristics may be classified into economic, political, legal, social, and task categories. As previous research on the public sector wage and benefit determination process has emphasized, the objective conditions of the environment have a substantial impact on the costs of agreement or disagreement both for the union and management. Specifically, it has been hypothesized that the greater the employers' ability to pay for wage and benefit increases; the greater the demand for city services; the greater the municipality's demand

TABLE 1
Correlations of Sources of Bargaining Power with Bargaining Outcomes

Independent Variables	Hypothesis	Wages	Bargaining Outcomes
Economic environment			
Inflation rate[a]	+	.27***	.05
Unemployment rate[b]	−	−.44***	−.08
City's ability to pay[c]	+	−.08	−.22***
Demand for city services[d]	+	.37***	.20**
Private sector wage rate[e]	+	.33***	.19**
Political environment			
Per cent voting NDP[f]	+	.31***	.34***
Municipal election year[g]	+	.23***	−.17**
Legal environment			
Comprehensiveness of the law[h]	+	−.27***	−.23**
Social environment			
Per cent of labor force unionized[i]	+	.22***	.04
Rate of strikes in the city[j]	+	.24***	−.22**
Per cent of labor force in manufacturing[d]	+	.16*	.51***
Task environment			
Support from task environment[g]	+	−.32***	.13*
Management structure			
Negotiator authority to bargain[g]	−	.17**	.17**
Internal management conflict[k]	+	−.19**	−.15*
Elected official on bargaining team[k]	+	.12	.14*
Form of city government (manager)[m]	−	−.33***	.12
Departmental representatives on bargaining team[k]	−	.02	−.15*
Management preparation for collective bargaining			
Negotiator skill and experience[g]	−	.12	.05
Professional negotiator training[k]	−	−.19**	−.22***
Management commitment to industrial relations[k]	−	.10	−.39***
Union structure[l]			
Specialization of labor	+	.04	.22***
Standardization of activities	+	.09	.01
Formalization of activities	+	.21**	.23***
Centralization of decision making	+	.07	.13**
Vertical differentiation	+	.15*	−.02
Professional staff/members	+	.10	−.02
Internal union processes			
Leadership competence[k]	+	.07	.15*
Union democracy[g]	+	.09	−.01
Union tactics[g]			
Militant tactics	+	.07	−.09
Public relations tactics	+	−.05	−.17**
Political pressure tactics	+	−.07	−.13*
Overall index	+	−.03	−.17**

TABLE 1 (continued)

Independent Variables	Hypothesis	Wages	Bargaining Outcomes
Bargaining process			
Multilateral collective bargaining[g]	+	.10	.10
Joint collective bargaining[k]	+	.05	−.04
Stage of impasse resolution[k]	+	.01	−.02
Control Variables			
Age of bargaining relationship[k]	+	.28***	−.06
Union-management hostility[g,k]	−	.11	.14*
Union size[k]	+	.21**	−.00

Note: *p $< .10$; **p $< .05$; ***p $< .01$

Sources:

[a]Statistics Canada, *Prices and Price Index* (Ottawa, Canada: Information Canada, 1975, 1976).

[b]Statistics Canada, *The Labor Force*, monthly (Ottawa, Canada: Information Canada, 1974-1976).

[c]Statistics Canada, *Municipal Revenue and Expenditures* (Ottawa, Canada: Information Canada, 1973).

[d]Statistics Canada, *1971 Canada Census* (Ottawa, Canada: Information Canada, 1973).

[e]Labour Canada, *Wage Rates, Salaries and Hours of Labour, Volume I—Community Rates* (Ottawa, Canada: Information Canada, 1973).

[f]Election Canada, *Twenty-ninth General Election, 1972—Report of the Chief Electoral Officer* (Ottawa, Canada: Information Canada, 1974).

[g]These data were obtained in union interviews.

[h]This index was developed by classifying provincial bargaining laws into 12 categories and assigning a value to each category according to the degree to which it provides for a more formalized bargaining relationship. For a description of the coding scheme see Thomas A. Kochan, "Correlates of State Public Employee Bargaining Laws," *Industrial Relations*, XII (October, 1973), 322-337.

[i]Labour Canada, *Corporations and Labor Unions Returns Act* (Ottawa, Canada: Information Canada, 1975).

[j]Labour Canada, *Strikes and Lockouts in Canada* (Ottawa, Canada: Information Canada, 1970, 1971, 1972).

[k]Management interviews.

[l]The approach to organizational structure of unions used in this research is based on the Aston studies and adapted for local unions. See Lex Donaldson and Malcolm Warner, "Structure of Organizations in Occupational Interest Associations," *Human Relations*, XXVII (August, 1974), 721-738.

[m]ICMA, *Municipal Year Book* (Washington, D.C.: ICMA, 1974).

for labor; the greater the level of comparable private sector wages; the greater the erosion of wages by inflation; and the lower the level of unemployment, the higher the ratio of costs of disagreement to costs of agreement for the employers, and, thus, the greater the bargaining power of the union. The results presented in Table 1 generally support these hypothesized relationships, especially with respect to the wage dependent variable. Only the measure of the city's ability to pay does not appear to be significant. On the other hand, only demand for city services and high private sector wages increased the favorability of nonwage bargaining outcomes to the union. Interestingly, the greater the city's ability to pay, as measured by per capita revenues, the lower the level of nonwage bargaining outcomes.

A favorable political environment may also increase union bargaining power. Political support in the form of a greater level of citizen vote for Canada's labor party (the New Democratic party) is associated with increased levels of both wages and nonwage bargaining outcomes. However, bargaining in a municipal election year has opposite effects on wages and bargaining outcomes. This result possibly indicates the existence of trade-offs, such that during an election year the union may be willing to push for increased wages at the expense of fringe benefits.

The favorableness of labor and other related legislation to the position of unions also may be a significant source of power for the union. The comprehensiveness of the law would be expected to reduce employer resistance, increasing union bargaining outcomes. Kochan and Wheeler found measures of the legal environment to have the strongest impact on bargaining outcomes. The most surprising result of this research is the consistent negative impact of a comprehensive labor relations statute on the dependent variables. This may be due to the relatively standardized nature of labor legislation across Canadian provinces and to the fact that some of the most comprehensive statutes are in less industrialized provinces (e.g., Saskatchewan) which also have lower wages.

The more favorable the characteristics of the community and community sentiment toward industrial relations and unions, the more power the union would be expected to have in the bargaining process. Thus, it could be hypothesized that bargaining outcomes would be generally more favorable to public sector unions where a greater proportion of the labor force is unionized and concentrated in highly unionized industries, and where the labor force is generally militant. Each of these conditions raises the probability of support for public sector unions and, thus, increases the potential costs to the employer of disagreement.

As Table 1 indicates, unionization, militancy, and a more industrial base in the city are all positively related to wage levels. The relationships are not as clear for nonwage outcomes. For example, the city strike rate has a negative effect on nonwage outcomes. Thus, once again it is possible that the results are suggesting the existence of a trade-off between wages and benefits. The per cent of the city's labor force in manufacturing is strongly correlated with the nonwage variable. Industrial communities are more likely to have comprehensive collective agreements governing the workforce; therefore, this independent variable may represent a private sector comparability measure for nonwage outcomes.

The union's environment is comprised not only of the economic, political, legal, and social setting but also of a network of other organizations with which the union interacts. Support from these outside organizations may significantly impact the employers' perception of unions' ability to impose costs, and hence, where support exists, the outcomes are likely to be more favorable to the union. This contention receives some support in nonwage outcomes, but the results suggest that unions with lower wages are more likely to seek help from other organizations.

Management characteristics as sources of power. The manner in which management is organized and the extent to which it is prepared for collective bargaining may be reflected in the ability to impose costs on the union. Several authors have identified the problems of dispersion of authority among management officials in the public sector as a source of internal conflict. The existence of conflict within management increases the probability of union success through multilateral bargaining. Thus, the union's ability to impose costs on management should be increased when: authority is not delegated to the negotiator; internal conflict is present; an elected official is on the bargaining team; the city does not have a city manager form of government; and only a few city departments are represented in collective bargaining.

The relationships appear to be weaker for this set of characteristics than for the environmental variables (see Table 1). Moreover, several of the associations are not in the expected direction. Contrary to the hypothesis, the delegation of authority to the management negotiator increases the favorability of the settlement to the union. Kochan and Wheeler discovered the same relationship and suggested that delegation of power may be a result rather than a cause of union success. Alternatively, experienced negotiators may be more willing to negotiate a broad range of issues since they accept the value of a comprehensive contract. The results of the present study also strongly refute the hypothesis that internal management conflict aids the union because it allows the use of a divide and conquer strategy. However, a qualitative analysis of the situations where internal conflict occurred reveals that, in most cases, the conflict involved an individual powerful enough both to resist union demands and to have those demands rejected at the political level.

The remaining variables assessing management structure are consistent with the hypotheses, although only for one of the two dependent variables. Furthermore, they support multilateral bargaining theory. That is, having an elected official and only a few departmental representatives on the bargaining teams are positively related to nonwage bargaining outcomes; and having a mayor-council form of government positively affects wage outcomes.

Management's preparation for collective bargaining is also important. Where the city's negotiator is trained, skillful, and has greater expertise in collective bargaining, and where management is committed to the industrial relations function, it might be expected that management would be better able to manipulate the costs of agreement and disagreement as perceived by the union representatives. The data presented here indicate that having a professionally trained negotiator on the management team limits the ability of the union to obtain greater bargaining outcomes. A management committed to the importance of industrial relations functions is also likely to be able to halt union demands. The skill and expertise of the negotiator are not related to bargaining outcomes.

Union characteristics as sources of power. Previous research on the determinants of bargaining outcomes has been more concerned with the existence of a union or contract than with the actual characteristics of the union organization. However, it could be hypothesized that the manner in which the union is organized would have an impact on its ability to achieve its goals through the collective bargaining process. For instance, Bok and Dunlop view the lack of coordination, supervision, and specialization; the failure to develop goals and strategies; the failure to ensure that leaders are administratively competent through planned selection and promotion procedures; and the reliance on part-time officers as causes of ineffective union performance.[4] Similarly, Barbash argues that rationalization, "making of union decisions through rules, organization and expertness rather than through trial by struggle, ideology, and hit-or-miss,"[5] is a requirement for the continued effectiveness of unions. The use of staff experts has also been identified as a criterion of effectiveness.[6] These arguments suggest that the development of an administrative bureaucracy is not only inevitable in unions, but also needed to enhance their effectiveness. Thus, it is possible to hypothesize that increased specialization of functions, formalization and standardization of activities, centralization of decision making, and differentiation of structure will enhance union effectiveness in collective bargaining. The results of testing this hypothesis are generally disappointing (see Table 1). Only five associations are significant, and only a single variable is correlated with both wage and nonwage outcomes. It appears that specialization, formalization, and centralization are positively associated with nonwage outcomes. This implies that the development of an administrative structure may increase the ability of the union to prepare demands and rationales for nonwage components of the collective agreement. Only formalization of activities and a taller union hierarchy are correlated with better wages.

Internal union processes such as leadership and democracy have received a substantial amount of attention in the literature. A competent, well trained leader can manipulate the employer's perceptions of the costs of agreement and disagreement in such a way as to increase the level of bargaining outcomes. The extent of union democracy, while a popular topic of debate, has rarely been included in discussions of the outcomes of collective bargaining. Possibly, this is because predictions have ranged from negative, through no effect, to positive. The present results indicate that leadership competence is only related to increased nonwage bargaining outcomes: union democracy is not significantly correlated with either dependent variable.

The third set of union characteristics examined is the extent to which the union used militant, public relations, and political pressure tactics to place extra pressure on management to accede to union demands. None of the union tactics is significantly correlated with wages, but both public relations and political pressure tactics reduced the level of nonwage outcomes. It appears that bargaining tactics are not necessarily relevant within the Canadian system, and that, in fact, the use of political means to obtain benefits may be harmful to the union's position.

Characteristics of the bargaining process as a source of power. Because unions are able to strategically select the government official or body with which they will deal, the existence of multilateral collective bargaining is likely to raise bargaining outcomes. Furthermore, when two or more municipal unions jointly negotiate with an employer, they are likely to be able to inflict a greater cost, and therefore should be able to negotiate more favorable outcomes. Lastly, pushing the dispute further into the impasse procedure will increase the costs of agreement for unions, and, therefore, they are unlikely to settle without substantial increases in bargaining outcomes.

Testing these propositions results in none of the relationships being significantly different from zero. Because of the theoretical importance of the multilateral bargaining concept to public sector research, the index was broken down into its five component items and the correlations with bargaining outcomes were examined. Three of the five items are significantly correlated with both wage and nonwage outcomes: (1) bargaining leverage of management is jeopardized by actions of other management officials (wages, r = .13, outcomes, r = .18); (2) union representatives discuss their demands with city officials who are not on the formal negotiating team (wages, r = .18, outcomes, r = .18); and (3) elected officials intervene when an impasse occurs to mediate the dispute (wages, r = .18, outcomes, r = .15). The associations are only significant at the 10 per cent level, however.

Control variables. Theory and research indicate that bargaining outcomes more favorable to the union are more likely to exist under certain conditions which are not directly related to the power of the parties. The older the collective bargaining relationship, the less hostility in the union-management relationship, and the larger the union, the more likely the union is to have favorable bargaining outcomes. These variables are therefore included as controls. The age of the bargaining relationship is correlated positively with the level of wages but not nonwage outcomes. The degree of union-management hostility is only slightly related to nonwage outcomes (negative). Finally, larger unions tend to have higher wage levels.

Regression Results

In order to examine the relative importance and combined effect of the independent variables and sets of characteristics as sources of union power on bargaining outcomes, a series of regression equations were estimated. The first equation for each dependent variable in Table 2 uses the unstandardized form of the variable and dummy variables to estimate union effects. The second and third equations use the normalized form of the dependent variables, with the results in equation three representing a reduced model of the second. All variables which attained a significant correlation at the 10 per cent level were entered into equation two. Overall, these variables explain approximately two-thirds of the variance in both wage and nonwage outcomes. Past research has typically explained less than 50 per cent, which suggests that there is some efficacy to the model presented.

The results of the regression analyses are generally consistent with the correlational findings. For both wage and nonwage outcomes, only the environmental and management characteristics make unique contributions

TABLE 2
Regression of Bargaining Outcomes on Characteristics of the Environment, Management and Union Organizations, and Bargaining Process

Independent Variables	Wages			Nonwage Outcomes		
	1	2	3	1	2	3
Environment						
Inflation rate	.06	.02	—	—	—	—
Unemployment rate	−.22***	−.48***	−.48***	−.42***	−.43***	−.44***
City's ability to pay	.13	—	.17*	.32**	.36***	.37***
Demand for city services	.04	.14	—	.04	.04	—
Private sector wage rate	−.03	−.11	—	−.01	.03	—
Per cent voting NDP	.10***	.04	.15**	−.001	−.03	—
Municipal election year	−.10	.16*	—	.10	.02	—
Comprehensiveness of the law	.003	−.08	—	.57***	.47***	.52***
Per cent of labor force in manufacturing	.11	.07	—	—	—	—
Per cent of labor force unionized	.20***	.07	.31***	−.07	−.18*	−.17**
Rate of strikes in the city	−.13**	.33***	−.26***	.31***	.30***	.32***
Support from task environment	—	−.24***	—	—	—	—
Management:						
Management commitment to IR	—	—	—	−.31***	−.42***	−.43***
Form of city government (manager)	−.17***	−.27***	−.25***	−.03	−.21*	−.23**
Professional negotiator training	−.07	−.21**	−.21***	−.02	.04	—
Negotiator authority to bargain	−.03	.01	—	−.08	−.04	—
Internal management conflict	−.08	−.15	−.18**	−.002	.03	—
Elected official on bargaining team	—	—	—	−.02	−.01	—
Departmental representatives on bargaining team	—	—	—	—	—	—
Union:						
Specialization of labor	—	—	—	.02	.02	—
Formalization of activities	−.001	−.15	−.13	.02	.07	−.06

Centralization of decision making	—	-.05	-.02	—	—	—
Vertical differentiation	-.05	—	—	—	-.02	-.06
Leadership competence	—	-.001	-.01	—	—	—
Union tactics	—	-.05	-.02	—	—	—
Process:						
Union discusses with elected officials (multilateral collective bargaining)	.15	.20*	.31**	—	—	-.01
Control:						
Age of bargaining relationship	—	—	—	.17**	.15	.07
Union size	—	—	—	-.13	-.14	-.12*
Union-management hostility	—	.12	-.02	—	—	—
Manual workers	—	—	.001	—	—	.28***
Fire fighters	—	—	-.48***	—	—	.64***
Police officers	—	—	-.27*	—	—	.78***
$R^2(R^2)$	.63(.58)	.64(.51)	.75(.62)	.64(.59)	.66(.55)	.92(.88)
Overall F-value	12.25***	4.88***	5.73***	11.67***	6.38***	23.59***
Unique contribution:						
R^2—Environment (R^2)	.26***(.21)	—	—	.18***(.11)	—	—
R^2—Management (R^2)	.50*(.44)	—	—	.50**(.44)	—	—
R^2—Union (R^2)	.63(.58)	—	—	.60(.56)	—	—
R^2—Process (R^2)	.62(.57)	—	—	—	—	—
R^2—Control (R^2)	.62(.57)	—	—	—	—	—

Note: Equation 1 uses the unstandardized dependent variable: Equation 2 uses the standardized dependent variable: Equation 3 is a reduced model. — indicates that the variable was not entered into the equation

*p < .10; **p < .05; ***p < .01.

431

to the variance explained. Union characteristics and characteristics of the bargaining process are not significant in either of the regression equations. Age of the bargaining relationship alone exhibited a significant beta coefficient in the control variables. That is, as the relationship matures, management may become more generous with its wage concessions.

Unions appear to be more effective in obtaining higher wages when: unemployment is low; the demand for city services is high; it is a municipal election year; the city has greater per capita mandays lost due to strikes; the local union is autonomous of task environment support; a mayor-council form of government exists; a professionally trained negotiator does not exist; internal conflict is low; and the parties have been bargaining for some time. Nonwage bargaining outcomes are higher, on the other hand, when: ability to pay is low; demand for city services is high; the base of the city is manufacturing; strike activity is low; there is support from the task environment; commitment to the industrial relations function is low; and a professionally trained negotiator is not present. Thus, there is only minimal overlap between the determinants of wage and nonwage outcomes. In fact, in several cases the signs on the variables change direction across outcomes.

While Kochan and Wheeler discovered the comprehensiveness of the law to be the strongest predictor of bargaining outcomes, it is insignificant in this analysis. Two explanations are possible. First, unlike the United States, the characteristics of public sector bargaining laws in Canada are relatively standard across jurisdictions. Thus, a lack of variance may explain the results. Alternatively, it seems possible that the law is an important source of union power in the initial stages of collective bargaining, when the parameters of the union-management relationship are not well defined. Subsequently, however, when the units have been negotiating for 30 years, as is the case in Canada, neither the comprehensiveness of the law nor the type of impasse procedures may be particularly important.

An examination of the relationship between union dummy variables and bargaining outcomes (equation 1) demonstrates the relative impact of the four occupational groups represented by municipal unions. In the wage level equation, as a result of the distribution of wages among occupations, the dummy variables increase the variance explained to over 90 per cent. The results indicate that clerical workers have the lowest wages, followed by manual employees, fire fighters, and, finally, police officers. Although the differences are not as dramatic with nonwage outcomes, the same pattern is apparent. Police and fire fighters have significantly less comprehensive collective agreements than clerical or manual workers. These results point out that the nature of the work may result in different types of union demands. The findings also support the use of dependent variables normalized by occupation.

Conclusions

The results presented here are generally consistent with previous research. The findings also include several implications for future research on public sector labor relations. First, it is clear from investigating wages and benefits as separate dependent variables that different factors influence the wage level than affect the nonwage package. While the pattern of results does not instantly reveal any underlying dimensions to these differences, it is apparent that we need better theorizing about the determinants of each. In several cases, the relationship of a given independent variable was positive for one of the dependent variables and negative for the other. Despite the fact that the two dependent variables were uncorrelated ($r = -.02$), the results suggest that we need to consider the possibility of trade-offs between wages and benefits. While industrial relations theorists have emphasized the give-and-take of the collective bargaining process, research has not formally pursued this issue. Furthermore, these results reiterate the need for longitudinal rather than cross-sectional research designs which are better able to capture the dynamic nature of the bargaining process.

The findings also raise concerns about the ability of the union to affect the outcomes of collective bargaining, as environmental and management characteristics were of prime importance. It may be that the measures of union structure, process, and tactics were not designed with a specific enough reference to collective bargaining, weakening the results. On the other hand, the unions interviewed relied heavily on changes in environmental conditions as a basis for demands, and, hence, the results may to some extent reflect the ability of the union to use that information in the bargaining process. Although we have relatively good economic models of bargaining outcomes, our conceptualization and empirical measures of other characteristics continue to be sorely lacking.

Public sector collective bargaining theory is based in large measure on a rather limited set of experiences in the United States. Most states have only enacted public sector labor legislation during the past decade. Prior to that, political processes rather than collective bargaining were the norm. Thus, in a relatively new, experimental, and unstable context, the role of the law, political pressure, and other union tactics are stressed. Conversely, in Canada, municipal employees have enjoyed the full right to collective bargaining since the forties, and many have had formal negotiations prior to that time. This suggests that stability in the system and the maturity of the relationship between the parties may change the nature of the process. Over time, bargaining may tend to move from a reliance on hard core tactics and political pressure to an emphasis on more rationalized and professional negotiations. If this is true (qualitative findings do provide some support), it would help to explain several of the present findings which conflict with previous research: (1) the unimportance of the comprehensiveness of the law; (2) the negative impact of union pressure tactics; (3) the negative sign on internal management conflict; (4) the insignificance of the multilateral bargaining index; and (5) the relative importance of the age of the bargaining relationship as an independent predictor.

An emphasis on the difference between public and private sector labor relations may be misguided if we are only experiencing a reflection of the maturity of the system and the relationships between the parties within the system. Moreover, it is possible that the application of different standards of evaluation to public sector policies could lead to inappropriate policy decisions. Therefore, in addition to improved specification of the characteristics of unions, management, and the bargaining process, future research should also consider the maturity of the industrial relations system.

Footnotes

1. For the most complete study of the determinants of bargaining outcomes to date, see Thomas A. Kochan and Hoyt N. Wheeler, "Municipal Collective Bargaining: A Model and Analysis of Bargaining Outcomes," *Industrial and Labor Relations Review*, XXIX (October, 1975), 46-66.
2. John T. Dunlop, *The Industrial Relations System* (New York: Holt, 1958), p. 5.
3. See Kochan and Wheeler, *op. cit.*, Appendix I; Paul F. Gerhart, "Determinants of Bargaining Outcomes in Local Government Negotiations," *Industrial and Labor Relations Review*, XXIX (April, 1976), Appendix I; and James L. Perry and Charles Levine, "An Interorganizational Analysis of Power, Conflict, and Settlements in Public Sector Collective Bargaining," *American Political Science Review*, LXX (December, 1976), 1185-1201.
4. Derek Bok and John Dunlop, *Labor in the American Community* (New York: Simon and Schuster, 1970), pp. 138-188.
5. Jack Barbash, "Relationalization in the American Union," in Somers, ed., *op. cit.*, p. 147.
6. For example, see Arie Shirom, "Union Use of Staff Experts: The Case of the Histadrut," *Industrial and Labor Relations Review*, XXIX (October, 1975), 107-120. Unfortunately, the author did not provide an empirical assessment of the validity of the assumption that the use of experts is related to effectiveness.

Teacher Bargaining:
The Experience in Nine Systems

Charles R. Perry*

The past decade has produced a staggering abundance of scholarly literature on the process and results of collective bargaining in the public sector. That literature is as diverse as it is abundant, encompassing "theoretical" works on the basic nature of bargaining relationships,[1] empirical studies of the character of bargaining outcomes,[2] and efforts to relate the two through analyses of determinants of bargaining outcomes.[3] Relatively little attention, however, has been given to the way in which bargaining relationships develop over time or to the institutional and economic forces that shape the evolution of those relationships.[4] This study endeavors to fill that gap through a longitudinal analysis of bargaining processes and results in nine public school systems of widely varying size and circumstance. All of these systems were engaged in hard bargaining with teacher unions by 1965, when they were the subject of an earlier study of bargaining in public schools,[5] and all have continued to engage in bargaining with teachers since then.

An intensive analysis of bargaining process and results can only be undertaken in a limited sample of relationships. The virtue of such a sample rests in the detailed information that can be obtained. The obvious weakness

*The Wharton School, University of Pennsylvania. Reprinted from *Industrial and Labor Relations Review*, Vol. 33 (October, 1979), pp. 3-17.

in this approach rests in the problem of generalizing any findings, particularly if there is substantial diversity in experience within the sample. At this point in the development of the literature on collective bargaining in the public sector and in public education, there is a need for institutional detail to test more global theories and generalizations. To meet this need nine systems were chosen from among the larger set of twenty-four studied in 1965, which had then been selected on the basis of size of the system, character of the community, and evidence of teacher militancy at an early stage in the evolution of bargaining.

The sample of nine systems used in this study encompasses a diverse cross-section of school districts. Two of the systems are large urban districts, two are much smaller urban districts, two are suburban systems of varying size, and three are essentially rural systems, again, of varying size. The systems are also diverse with respect to their operating structure and fiscal condition. (These characteristics are summarized in Table 1.)

In each of the nine systems, school or union officials or both were interviewed at length and asked to describe the character and course of their bargaining relationships since the conclusion of their 1965 negotiations. In addition, interviewees were asked a series of specific questions regarding such matters as: (1) the relationship of bargaining to the budget cycle; (2) the role played by the press and the public in the bargaining process; (3) the issues that have been the most significant source of conflict in bargaining; (4) the incidence of full-scale impasses in negotiations (those resulting in a strike, strike threat, or recourse to some procedure other than mediation); and (5) the response of the public in general, and of public officials, in impasse situations. Finally, interviewees were asked to evaluate the impact of bargaining in three general areas: (1) teacher compensation; (2) teacher work loads; and (3) administrative procedure and educational policy.

The descriptive information gained through interviews was augmented by contractual and budgetary data for each of the systems. In all cases, interviewees were asked to provide copies of each contract covering the classroom bargaining unit beginning with the 1967-68 school year. In some situations copies of all contracts could not be provided, but it was possible in all to secure at least copies of the 1967-68 and 1977-78 contracts, plus copies of the salary schedules for all the intervening years. In addition, copies of the system budget or audit report were obtained to provide data on expenditures, enrollment, and employment over the 1967-77 period.

Bargaining Relationships

It is difficult, if not dangerous, to draw conclusions from a study of only nine bargaining relationships in public education, but two conclusions appear to be justified by the experience of the systems studied. First, collective bargaining relationships in public education, as in the private sector, have become incredibly diverse in almost every respect. Second, collective bargaining relationships in public education, as in the private sector, have matured quite rapidly, judged by the acceptance of the legitimacy of bilateral decision making.

TABLE 1
Characteristics of the Systems Studied

System	Type	Population	Fiscal Control	Pupil/Teacher Ratio in 1977	Expenditure/Pupil 1977	Percentage Change from 1967-1977		
						Teachers	Pupils	Budget
1	Urban	2,000,000	Dependent	17.4	2400	−13	−10	+190
2	Urban	1,500,000	Independent	23.8	1460	−9	−14	+90
3	Suburban	200,000	Independent	21.2	1370	+22	+30	+180
4	Suburban	50,000	Dependent	19.8	1700	+5	−7	+108
5	Urban	80,000	Dependent	16.5	1400	+24	−5	+165
6	Urban	70,000	Independent	16.8	1890	0	−10	+138
7	Rural	50,000	Dependent	21.7	1540	+10	+20	+200
8	Rural	40,000	Dependent	18.0	1850	+20	+3	+250
9	Rural	25,000	Independent	20.3	1310	+48	+44	+270

Source: Data supplied by the school systems.

436

The most striking characteristic of this set of bargaining relationships was its diversity in terms of procedure and process. In most systems, management was represented in negotiations by the administration; in two of the systems, however, board members continued to play a leading, or at least active, role in negotiations. Most systems operated with relatively compressed timetables to conclude an agreement, but two scheduled regular weekly negotiation sessions throughout the school year as the basis for bargaining. Most used closed negotiation sessions, but some opened bargaining sessions formally or informally to the press; and one system conducted negotiations entirely through bargaining sessions open to both the press and the general public.

The tone of individual relationships varied almost as much as their procedures. In all of the relationships, however, "institutional" issues of principle and control had given way to more pragmatic questions of power and money as those relationships matured. Notably absent were serious vestiges of the basic institutional conflict over "lay vs. professional" control that had characterized these same relationships in the early 1960s. Also absent were the questions of personal and institutional integrity that had been associated with early impasses in many of these systems.

Basic questions of money and power have not been easily resolved in any of the nine systems. Many reported repeated recourse to mediation in their negotiations over the period. All acknowledged that they had close to the point of a formal impasse in one or more of their negotiations between 1967 and 1977, but only five of the nine systems had actually reached that point. (See Table 2.) The overall conflict record of these nine systems suggests two interesting patterns: (1) overt conflict has been concentrated in larger, urban systems and (2) overt conflict intensified in the early 1970s. The explanation for these cross-sectional and longitudinal conflict patterns must be sought in the basic constraints on the parties to these public sector bargaining relationships. Those constraints can be placed in three overlapping categories—political, economic, and institutional.

Political constraints. The existence of political constraints on bargaining relationships is difficult to deny, but the character, strength, and mode of operation of such constraints are equally difficult to pinpoint. The clearest manifestation of such constraints would be the emergence of true "multilateral" bargaining in which community groups seek and receive full and independent participation rights in the bargaining process.[6] The existence and operation of such constraints can also be inferred from efforts by either or both protagonists to appeal directly to the public for its support on substantive conflict issues.

The experience in the nine systems over the past decade provides little concrete evidence of an emerging system of explicit political or public constraints on the bargaining process, particularly short of a strike. In most cases, both parties expressed the view that the community was not actively interested in what went on in negotiations either procedurally or substantively. Few of the protagonists reported any serious efforts to enlist the

TABLE 2
The Bargaining Record of the Nine Systems

System	First Impasse	1967	1968	1969	1970	1971	1972	1973	1974	1975	1976	1977
1	—	—	Strike Threat	—	Strike Threat	—	Strike	—	—	—	X	—
2	—	Strike	—	X	—	X	—	Strike	X	X	—	X
3	1965	X	—	—	Strike	Strike	—	Strike	—	X	X	—
4	1965	X	X	X	X	X	X	—	X	—	X	—
5	1965	X	X	Strike Threat	X	X	X	Strike	—	Strike	X	—
6	1965	X	Strike Threat	X	Strike	X	—	X	X	—	X	—
7	1965	X	X	X	X	X	X	X	X	Near Impasse	—	X
8	1964	X	X	X	X	Near Impasse	X	X	X	X	X	X
9	1965	X	X	X	X	X	X	X	—	X	—	Near Impasse

X = Agreement reached without recourse to a strike, strike threat, or some dispute-resolution procedure other than mediation.
— = No negotiation held that year (multiyear contract).

support of community groups in the negotiation context on a regular basis. As a result, collective bargaining in most systems was a remarkably private and apolitical process.

The most significant exceptions to this apolitical rule were the two large urban systems, in which bargaining did become highly politicized in the early 1970s. In both cases, there was evidence of conscious efforts by both sides to frame and publicize conflict issues in such a way as to enlist the support of specific interest groups, both in anticipation of and in reaction to an impasse and a strike. In both cases, management took the initiative in such action, an initiative that has since been repeated in one of the systems with the same result—a strike. The success of all three of these management initiatives is open to serious question.

The only evidence of community pressure for multilateral bargaining appeared in these two urban systems and then only in the context of a strike. In both cases, more militant and radical community groups attempted to gain hearings in the bargaining process; in both cases, they failed. In one case, a "radical" group in the form of a "parents' union," which emerged as a result of a strike, sued to overturn the resulting contract and, in the subsequent set of negotiations, published a formal position paper on substantive issues. The suit was dismissed and the paper largely ignored by all concerned, including the press. Interestingly, in this same system, "reponsible" community groups, such as the PTA or established civic groups with a special interest in education, had been invited to sit in on negotiations at one point, but had quickly lost interest in light of the time required. In the second system, a similar group attempted to gain a formal role in negotiations on two separate occasions, but was rebuffed by the union. The union did, however, agree to meet outside negotiations with the group in the first instance but not the second.

Outside the major urban systems, there was almost no management or union activity intended to involve the community in bargaining, except through a strike. A few of the systems did maintain active community-public relations programs, but in all cases those programs were directed toward building or sustaining favorable attitudes toward the system generally, not merely in the bargaining context. There were a few isolated cases of community relations efforts by teacher organizations, but those, too, were not designed or used to seek strategic advantage in bargaining. Even in strike situations, public relations efforts were remarkably limited. Only one Board of Education went so far as to hold a series of public board meetings at various schools across the community during one of its strikes.

Outside of the major urban systems the level of community interest in participation in or understanding of decisions reached through bargaining appeared to be surprisingly limited, even in the smaller rural communities. In one such system in which the press was welcome at all negotiation sessions, the only sessions that were attended regularly were those at which money issues were to be discussed, and even those sessions were not reported in any detail. Similar reports of the extent of press interest were made by interviewees in most of these systems. The system with totally open negotiations reported that public attendance and participation were extremely limited, to the point of making "off-the-record" meetings unnecessary. However, it was clear that neither party encouraged public attendance and that both parties were capable of being deliberately "oblique" in any discussions of issue on which they perceived that the public was and should be kept "vague."

The absence of evidence of the emergence of growing community interest or participation in decision making through bargaining does not mean that political constraints do not exist or are not significant. It does suggest, however, that such constraints operate primarily through normal political channels. Thus, bargaining in public education, as in the private sector, is a bilateral process of decision making. The primary difference between the two sectors is the potential diffuseness of constituent expectations and control on the management side, which can create both opportunities and problems for unions in the bargaining process. Thus far, unions in most of these nine systems have not actively sought to exploit their opportunities, except at the point of impasse, nor have managements sought consciously to negate those opportunities. It may well be that both sides gain from the flexibility accorded them by an "uncommited" community that leaves open the possibility of a non-zero—sum bargain for a management and union that share a common interest in the "educational system."

Fiscal constraints. The budgetary resources available to a public school system in the short run constitute the most significant potential constraint on the decisions reached in collecting bargaining, particularly since education is a highly labor-intensive industry. The existence of such fiscal constraint, in theory, is difficult to dispute. The practical clarity and stringency of such constraint, however, has been seriously debated. At the core of this debate is the question of whether available resources determine bargaining outcomes or bargaining outcomes determine available resources.

The budgetary cycle, itself, imposes a form of potential discipline on the bargaining process. That discipline played a prominent role in the early stages of bargaining in virtually all of the nine systems in two ways: (1) management often was reluctant to move on basic economic issues until it had a clear picture of what its revenues were likely to be and (2) management often was forced to hold the line once it had such a picture of its resources. The same is true today, but to a far less significant extent. The integration of bargaining and budgetary cycles has become far more a matter of convenience than principle with management, although a number of smaller systems have resisted multiyear contracts that involve a clear break in the bargain-budget link. Smaller systems generally maintained stronger budget-bargain links over the period—in terms of timing of settlements, one year contracts, and avoidance of a cost-of-living allowance (COLA)—that did their larger counterparts in the sample.

Decisions in bargaining necessarily continue to be made with far less than perfect knowledge of the resources available to finance the costs of even a one-year agreement, due to uncertainty over such matters as state-aid formulas, appropriations from local fiscal authorities (in the case of dependent districts), and the outcome of millage (taxing-authority) referenda (in independent districts). Despite such uncertainty, it was clear that management generally approached negotiations with some concept of the total package it could afford to accept, based on estimates of probable revenues and expenditures in the coming year or years. The fact that such estimates could only be highly tentative at the outset of negotiations provided the basis for some flexibility. Problems tended to arise when this flexibility disappeared as budget deadlines approached and passed, making it increasingly clear that further deadlines approached and passed, making it increasingly clear that further compromise might require either deficit of resources.

The original study revealed that many school managements were willing to accept one or both of these alternatives to resolve an impasse at the time of their first impasse in the mid 1960s, despite the economic or educational risks involved. For the most part, those risks turned out to be minimal at the early stage, given the ability of most systems to pass on the costs of settlements to the community or to local or state government in the short run. Subsequent experience in these nine systems suggests little change in this basic predisposition of management until or unless an actual or imminent budget crisis makes risk-avoidance imperative. Thus, much of the intensified overt conflict in the nine systems in the early 1970s was the product of short-run budget crises rather than emerging managerial concern over the long-run fiscal stability of the system.

None of the nine systems faced particularly stringent fiscal constraints during the latter part of the 1960s. All experienced growing enrollments and employment and were the beneficiaries of growing real revenues. In this context, overt conflict was limited and relatively easily resolved in all the systems. Four of the nine did, however, experience impasses in this period; but none of these impasses resulted in long or serious strikes. In all cases, the disputes were perceived by the parties, and particularly by the unions involved, as having been necessary to pave the way politically to "free-up" some available resources for the school system or the salary bargain. In all cases, the impasse appeared to have served this purpose very effectively.

The three rural systems have continued to operate without serious fiscal constraints since 1970 and have continued to be successful in concluding agreements without overt conflict. The roots of this success rest in both the ability of school management to neutralize community pressure for fiscal restraint and its willingness to share the fruits of its efforts with teachers. Managements in these systems have been able to offset pressure for fiscal restraint by building strong political support for the public schools through extensive community relations and services programs, close cooperative relationships with the local fiscal authority, and, where necessary, active bargaining with the community through real or threatened curtailments in services—most notably athletics and extracurricular activities. Managements in these systems generally have not sought to impose more stringent limits in negotiations than they themselves are subject to in dealing with the community. In two of these systems, however, management recently has attempted to impose such limits in negotiations—in one case on the issue of resistance to the introduction of COLA and in one case on the issue of fringe benefit cost containment. In both cases, the result was a near impasse and substantial managerial withdrawal from its initiative.

The six remaining systems did not fare as well after 1970 as the three rural systems. Two of the three rural fiscally independent systems experienced an absolute drop in local tax support as a result of failures of millage issues in the early 1970s and the third experienced a relative decline in the real rate of growth of such support as its tax base ceased to grow. The three fiscally dependent systems experienced similarly adverse circumstances in the form of budget cuts or limits imposed by local fiscal authorities. As a result, management in all six systems felt compelled to impose stringent limits in negotiations, which led to strikes in five of the six cases. These strikes were generally both prolonged and bitter, which is not surprising in that they marked a transition from what was described as the "easy affluence" of the 1960s to the "hard reality" of the 1970s. This transition was not easy and may not yet have been completed in all of the systems, for the following reason. The credibility or legitimacy of fiscal constraints is still open to question in the minds of teachers in at least three of the systems—those in which such constraints stem from seemingly arbitrary limits on the growth rate of local tax support imposed by the allocational decisions of either city or system management in the budgetary process. Thus far, teachers have been reasonably successful in challenging such "arbitrary" allocational decisions where they are internally imposed by managerial reluctance to reallocate resources or to seek additional resources, but not where they are externally imposed by a city government or similar outside agency.

Insitutional constraints. The basic strategies of the parties, and particularly teacher organizations, in these nine systems in dealing with impasses in negotiations have changed markedly. At the early stage, considerable emphasis and faith were placed on factfinding, a process that worked reasonably well in a number of cases. Over time, however, the emphasis on, faith in, and effectiveness of factfinding have waned rapidly and dramatically, and the parties have turned to the strike and related activities as the basis for impasse resolution.[7] This phenomenon was evident even in "non-impasse" systems (those four systems in which no full-scale open impasse occurred). In those systems, as well as in "impasse" systems, those unions confronting a possible impasse have considered such activities as picketing of schools and board offices in nonschool hours, distribution of literature, and one-day protest strikes or sick-outs rather than factfinding or arbitration.

The growing emphasis on the strike model does not mean that impasse procedures have not proved helpful in isolated cases. Mediation was relied on heavily in a few systems. In two systems ad hoc interest arbitration was used to resolve issues of implementation that threatened to renew or prolong a strike. In a third system, the parties faced with the possibility of their second prolonged strike in two years were able to accept factfinding and to agree to abide by the recommendations of the factfinder before the fact.

The reaction of the local community to strikes generally took the form of demands that solution be found so that schools could be opened. The sources of these demands were varied, including organized and unorganized groups of parents, ad hoc groups of civic or religious leaders, and the local press. The primary focus of such demands tended to be on management.

442

There was little evidence, particularly in the eyes of management, that community reaction extended beyond the question of simply ending the strike to a concern about the substance of the issues in the dispute.

Information from the five systems that experienced formal impasses over the period suggests a growing willingness on the part of school management to "stand the political heat" of a confrontation with teachers. In only one of these five districts did the Board of Education attempt to open school during their first strike experience. Three of the five, however, threatened or actually attempted to open schools in subsequent impasse situations. Similarly, in the first strikes management in none of these five systems sought legal sanctions against the union, but in subsequent impasses, management in three of the systems sought and secured injunctions against strikes, which in two cases resulted in the jailing of union leaders.

The effectiveness of these managerial actions is open to serious question, particularly in large systems and urban areas. The two systems that did not attempt to open schools simply perceived no prospect of success in such a more; the three systems that did attempt to open schools fared little better. One system tried and failed, whereupon groups of parents responded by opening schools in their homes, but with little real effect on the strike situation. A second system tried twice to open schools one fall, finally succeeding by hiring substitute teachers and running double shifts. The third system was able to operate schools with administrative personnel and some non-striking teachers, but not effectively enough to preclude one parent group from seeking a court order to provide "adequate education." Attempts to open schools generated considerable teacher bitterness and handed unions in the large cities a potent basis for appealing to the larger labor movement for support—the charge of "union busting." This action may ultimately have increased the price of a settlement in some systems.

The changing posture of school mangement in responding to strikes has been paralleled by changes in the response of other public officials to strikes. The potential for political credit constitues a powerful incentive for intervention by elected officials at the local level, particularly in fiscally dependent districts, and at the state level, particularly in the case of large urban systems. Several instances of such intervention noted in the original study resulted in tripartite or multilevel bargaining, based on the ability of the intervening party to provide or promise added resources.[8] Over time, both the frequency and form of such intervention has changed. After 1970, there was a marked drop in the apparent propensity of local and especially state officials to intervene in disputes and, where such intervention occurred, it was increasingly confined to mediation in search of agreement within the limits of available resources rather than negotiations in search of added resources.

The changing fiscal environment and attitudes of management and other officials seem to have resulted in longer strikes and less generous settlements. For example, one fiscally dependent district experienced a one-week strike in the early years, which led to intervention by the Mayor and a settlement involving a deficit for that year, which would become the Mayor's problem in the following year. In a later three-week strike in the same system, the same Mayor declined to intervene and a settlement was reached that did not involve additional resources. Similarly, the first strike in a fiscally independent district ended after four weeks when the district accepted a settlement that involved deficit financing, but the same district later took a twelve-week strike to avoid such a settlement. Finally, another system in which a strike threat and later a short strike had produced intervention and augmentation of resources in the 1967-70 period, finally took a twelve-week strike without either intervention or augmentation.

Bargaining Results

The accomodations made and agreements concluded in nine diverse bargaining relationships cannot provide a basis for definitely assessing the impact of bargaining in public education. The experience in those relationships, however, can provide valuable insight into the direction in which collective bargaining and collective action are moving public school systems, the extent to which such movement has been substantial, and the potential implications of that movement for the educational process.

The first problem that confronts any effort to assess bargaining outcomes in the public sector is that of defining the effective scope of bargaining. The original study found that the formal scope of teacher bargaining (all the terms and conditions of employment dealt with in contracts) was actually far broader than the effective scope of bargaining (the terms and conditions that teachers try to change). Teacher contracts, that is, were found to contain many provisions that simply called for the continuation of "past practices" that had been established by the employer and that teacher unions made no effort to change. Subsequent research has added another dimension to this problem—recognition that effective bargaining can and does occur over issues not covered in the contract.[9]

The formal scope of bargaining in the nine systems covered in the present study became both broader and more uniform across districts than had been the case in the mid-1960s. The effective scope of bargaining within the contractually defined range also was broader and more uniform than had been the case earlier, although to some extent this effective bargaining range varied directly with size of the school system. Finally, the "true" effective scope of bargaining in all districts was significantly expanded by formal and informal commitments to discuss or to confer or consult on various matters independent of the normal process of contract negotiation or administration. the scope of this "informal" bargaining varied greatly among the systems.

The original study identified three central thrusts of unions in the collective bargaining arena—compensation, work loads, and participation rights in "policy" decisions. Clearly, all three remain relevant today to the interests both of teachers and the public in the outcome of bargaining. It seems worthwhile, therefore, to ask the question, "As a consequence of bargaining, have teachers gained more pay for less work while achieving more control?"

Wage bargains. It is difficult to measure the wage gains of teachers over time, much less to assess the contribution of collective bargaining to any such gains. Teachers usually receive, at one time or another, three kinds of wage increases: across-the-board increases, increments for service (up to some maximum), and differentials for added academic credit (at established credit-hour intervals). Unions can enhance teachers' wage gains by expanding the magnitude of those three types of increase, of course, and also by increasing the frequency or number of increments and differentials that produce added compensation. Consequently, the wage gains of individual teachers, groups of teachers, or teacher organizations will not be reflected accurately in average teacher salary in either growing or snrinking systems.

The original study concluded that collective bargaining did produce larger salary increase packages for teachers than would have been forthcoming in the absence of bargaining, with much of the gains of bargaining coming in the form of increased service increments or educational differentials.[10] The marginal impact of these gains on the earnings of individual teachers, the level of incremental resources required by the systems, or the way in which such incremental resources were allocated was significant in several cases; the overall impact on average teacher salary, budget size, and budget structure, however, was not equally substantial.[11]

The experience of the nine systems over the 1967—77 period offers little evidence to contradict the conclusions of the earlier study. Collective bargaining in these systems has continued to add varying amounts to the total cost of salary settlements, but the cumulative effect of these increases on average teacher salary, overall budget size, and percent of budget devoted to teacher salaries has not yet been substantial in aggregate terms. Collective bargaining has also continued to result in an increase in the size and frequency of both service and educational increments—with obvious implications for the earnings potential of individual teachers, but far more limited implications for district salary costs until or unless turnover drops sharply (which it is beginning to do in many of the urban systems).

The pattern of salary increases over time and across the systems suggests that collective bargaining in public education has not produced dramatically different results than it has in the private sector. Overall, negotiated increases in the nine systems slightly exceeded increases in the cost of living in the late 1960s when the labor market for teachers was tight, and increases fell slightly short of cost-of-living increases in the 1970s when the labor market for teachers was loose,[12] suggesting only the same limited degree of isolation of wage determination from market conditions as that found in the private sector. At the same time, overall percentage salary increases over the period were larger in the small than in the large system, suggesting the possible existence of a pattern effect in which large and small districts tended to receive the same dollar increases during this period. This tendency is probably consistent with an explanation based on differences in ability-to-pay, but not, however, with differences in need to pay as reflected in rates of turnover. Finally, there can be little doubt that collective bargaining has served to enhance the salaries of long-service teachers who lack mobility alternatives in either a tight or loose labor market, which suggests the operation of an egalitarian wage policy not unlike that encountered in unions elsewhere.

Effort bargains. A second set of bargaining issues that were the subject of considerable attention, if not action, in the early stages of collective bargaining in public school systems encompassed hours of work, work loads, and work responsibilities. Specifically, the original study suggested that collective bargaining could or would have an impact on one or more of the following: (1) length of the school year and school day; (2) student contact time during the school day; (3) nonteaching responsibilities; and (4) class size.

The original study found that collective bargaining had resulted in a shortening of the effective school year or day in a few systems. This thrust of bargaining appears to have continued and expanded, although systems in which a dramatic impact seemed evident remained limited in number. The school calendar was discussed in bargaining in all of the systems except one, which placed the responsibility for recommendations on the calendar on a committee of parents, teachers, and administrators; the school day was a subject of bargaining in all the systems. The length of the school year or school day, however, was specified in the contract in only five systems. In these five systems, which included the three largest, there was evidence that collective bargaining had contributed to a discernible reduction in hours. All five of these systems experienced a trend toward the minimum school year required by state law. In three of the five systems, collective bargaining was credited with producing a reduction in the length of the school day of between thirty and fifty-five minutes. In a fourth district, collective bargaining was instrumental in preventing a lengthening of the school day until it became evident that the system was failing to meet state standards on instruction time.

The issue of preparation periods was not a prominent one in 1965, but had become one at some point since then in all of the nine systems. The question of preparation time during the school day for secondary school teachers was resolved in their favor by 1970. Elementary school teachers, however, did not receive preparation periods in most of the systems until the early 1970s and, in at least three systems, still do not enjoy as much preparation time as their counterparts at the secondary level. Once preparation periods were established, a second issue arose over the permissible uses of such time. That issue also has now been universally resolved in favor of teachers in the nine systems through contract provisions that place control over such time in the hands of the teacher or severely limit any administrative infringement on such "free time."

The issue of relief from nonteaching duties received a limited amount of attention in bargaining in the early 1960s and has received continuing attention since then. In all of these nine systems, teachers had achieved a duty-free lunch period and some measure of relief from administrative duties by 1967. Since then, this thrust has carried into nonteaching activities such as faculty meetings, parent conferences, preparation of report cards, supervision of sporting events, and leadership of student activities. The goal of teachers in this area has been to make such activities voluntary or compensable. Teachers across the nine systems have been quite successful in this quest as a direct result of collective bargaining. Most systems now provide for faculty meetings, parent conferences, and report-card prepara-

446

tion on school time and require little or no teacher participation in after-school activities. Most systems now also provide far larger and more pervasive pay premiums for teacher participation in student extracurricular activities, and some systems are beginning to face demands that teachers can be assigned to such activities only with their consent.

The class-size issue was the most contentious work-load issue in the mid-1960s, primarily because it was debated as a "policy" issue. That debate has now effectively been resolved and class size accepted as a working condition in the bargaining context in all nine of the systems. Despite that fact, unions in these systems have made relatively little concrete progress in achieving definite, enforceable limits on class size or in reducing those limits where they exist. Contracts in eight of the nine systems continued provisions governing class size in 1977, but only four of these eight established specified class size maxima by grade level. The remaining four contracts stated only goals or ranges for class size, although in two cases target average class sizes were stated and in one an amount of money to be expended each year to achieve the target was also stipulated. Contractual provisions for enforcement of class-size limits, targets, or goals were equally diverse. Three contracts were silent on the subject of enforcement, presumably leaving that matter to arbitration. Two other contracts required only that the superinten-overage. One contract provided only that "prompt action" will be taken to eliminate class-size overages and another provided for a review of overage eliminate class-size overages and another provided for a review of overage situations by a special union-management review board. Finally, one contract did call for extra pay for teachers with class-size overages.

The relative weakness of provisions governing class size in the nine systems reflects, at least in part, the substantial economic costs of reducing or even standardizing class size in any school system. These costs apparently have forced unions to accept the inevitability of a trade-off between wages and class size, particularly in the face of increasing fiscal stringency in the early 1970s. Class size does not appear to have fared well in this context. The union initiative on this issue across the nine districts reached its peak well before 1970, after which the issue was by-and-large dropped or increases tacitly accepted.

The experience in the nine districts clearly suggests that collective bargaining has had a discernible effect on teacher work loads, primarily in the areas of contact time and extracurricular responsibilities. The cost of these gains to the school systems has been subtle, but substantial—a fact that some are only now beginning to appreciate in the face of declining enrollments and increasing fiscal stringency. Such an appreciation has already led one of the systems in the sample to propose (unsuccessfully) a cut back in preparation periods and class-size limits. Most managements in the sample, however, would prefer to pursue a strategy of absorbing declining enrollments through smaller class sizes, as several have already begun to do in a quiet fashion. This strategy should not prove repugnant to teachers or their unions unless it requires unacceptable trade-offs between wages and job security, which it will most certainly do if communities perceive that declining enrollment should mean declining tax support as opposed to increasing quality as measured by class size or professional morale.

Rights bargains. We found that the basic dimensions of the contractual system of teacher rights across the nine systems were fairly well set by 1967. The central elements in this system were provisions governing teacher personnel files, teacher evaluation procedures, and teacher assignments and transfers. The major additions to these systems since 1967 have been provisions regarding promotion and layoff. The net effect of these new provisions has been to expand significantly the importance of seniority in an "industry" in which both employees and employers have long stressed the importance of professional qualifications and ability.

Contractual provisions limiting management discretion in promotions were rare and weak in the early 1960s. By 1977, however, relatively strong provisions governing promotions existed in six of the nine systems, including one in which "peer ratings" were to be considered in decisions on promotions out of the bargaining unit into administration. The provisions on promotion within the bargaining unit were evenly divided on the relative weight to be given to seniority—half stipulated that promotions were to be made on the basis of seniority only when ability was equal and half specified that promotions were to be made on the basis of seniority unless one candidate was "substantially superior."

Contractual provisions regarding layoffs, which had been virtually non-existent at the time of the original study, were found in eight of the nine systems by 1977. In six systems, layoff was to be strictly on the basis of seniority within area of past or present teaching certification and in one system the contract specified only that the procedures to be used to effectuate a reduction in staff would be worked out jointly should that contingency occur. In the remaining system, layoff was to be based on a point system under which teachers could earn fifteen points for seniority, twelve for advanced education, five for [evaluated] teaching performance, and one for participation in extracurricular activities. This system had just been tested at the time of this study and was not expected to survive without serious challenge from the union in the next set of negotiations.

The contractual rights of teachers in many of the nine systems have been extended well beyond the specific substantive terms of the agreement to encompass the broad universe of past policy and practice that constitute the *status quo*. The first step in this process of institutionalizing the *status quo* was taken relatively early in a number of the systems in the negotiation of definitions of a "grievance" that went well beyond allegations of a violation of the contract to encompass, for example, "a complaint involving the work situation; that there is a lack of policy; that a policy or practice is improper or unfair; or that there has been a deviation from . . . a policy or practice." A next step taken in some of the systems was the negotiation of "maintenance of standards" clauses along the following lines: "all conditions of employment shall be maintained at not less than the minimum standards in effect at the time this agreement is signed. . . ." A third step recently taken in a few of the nine systems has been the extension of "just cause" clauses to protect teachers against the effects, among other things, of the type of "technological change" dealt with in the following clause:

> *A teacher shall not be laid off because of curricular change unless such change would render him non-qualified under the State Certification Code, and he has*

refused other assignment opportunity or turned down training provided by the employer (at the employer's expense) to certify him for existing vacancies.

There is a discernible pattern in the incidence of these restrictive provisions. The contracts of the three largest systems contain some form of each. The contracts of the three next largest systems contain or have contained both broad definitions of a grievance and some form of maintenance of standards, although management in one of these systems has been successful in "ridding itself" of a maintenance-of-standards clause. The three smallest systems thus far have escaped all three types of clauses, although one has had to resist strong union demands for maintenance of standards and all have had to deal with repeated union proposals to expand the concept of a grievance in the contract.

There has been considerable speculation that collective bargaining can and will lead to the extension of teacher rights to the control of some or all matters of educational policy. The original study found little evidence of such an impact, despite the existence of contract clauses covering such policy issues as class size, teacher transfers, school integration, student discipline, and pupil grading and promotion. The more recent experience in in the nine systems does not provide evidence to contradict this conclusion, despite the addition in some contracts of clauses dealing with academic freedom, "quality integrated education,"[13] and teacher accountability[14] to the historic list of what was and remains a sparse population of substantive "policy" provisions.

The fact that policy issues generally have not become part of the formal scope of bargaining does not mean that bargaining has not resulted in greater informal teacher participation in policy decisions. The original study pointed out significant potential for such participation through the basic bargaining process and the generalized consultative arrangements at all levels that have come to be part of that process in education. These avenues for participation have been used in all the systems; policy issues have often been raised and discussed in negotiations and consultation between administration and union representatives at both central and school levels.

Above and beyond this very basic avenue for participation and influence, the original study also suggested that bargaining might lead to expanded teacher participation through institutionalization and extension of the prebargaining "joint committees" approach to the "study of issues." The experience in the nine systems clearly suggests that this has been the case. The basic system of generalized consultation rights—regular meetings between union and administration at the central and school level to discuss matters of mutual concern—was fairly well in place in most of the systems by 1967 and has not changed significantly since then. What has changed is the number and variety of joint committees—both ad hoc and standing—that are recognized in contracts particularly, but not exclusively, in the larger systems. This large and constantly changing universe of special committees was assigned tasks ranging from reviewing the schedule of increments for extracurricular activities to evaluating a teacher-aid program and developing a teacher evaluation program. The more stable and less diverse universe of standing committees typically dealt with such matters as sabbatical leaves, materials and supplies, textbook selection, and curriculum development.

449

The operational significance of this complex web of teacher rights is difficult to measure or assess. Spokesmen for teacher organizations have often pointed to the results of rights bargains as important evidence of the gains achieved through collective bargaining. Spokesmen for management, however, have equally often indicated that the expanding network of teacher rights has created only procedural as opposed to substantive barriers in the development or implementation of policy. The fact that in two of the systems studied management has felt compelled to seek a "rollback" of the concessions it made in rights bargainings raises questions about the validity of this view but does not undermine it as a general statement of impact. At the same time, however, it was clear in many of the systems that the procedural or due-process requirements embodied in contracts had posed a serious if not insurmountable barrier for management in implementing some policy decisions and administrative actions.

There was a surprising consensus among union and management spokesmen that rights and policy issues were likely to receive far more intensive attention in the future than they have to date. The basis for this consensus is a shared perception that increasing fiscal stringency coupled with increasing barriers to mobility will turn teacher attention inward and to noneconomic issues. Only one system in the sample as yet appears to have reached this point. Its experience can only be regarded as idiosyncratic, but it is interesting, nonetheless. Management in that system has been forced to live within clear and stringent fiscal constraints. In order to secure the cooperation of the union in living within those constraints, it has given effective control over internal budget allocation decisions to the union, with clear implications for the control of "educational policy." The fact that the budget, per se, is within the "effective" scope of bargaining in this system clearly has not been reflected fully in the contractual definition of the "formal" scope of bargaining, which recognizes only that:

> The Union Fiscal Committee shall work directly with the Fiscal Department of the District in preparing budgets. All budgetary income and expenditures shall be discussed by the Fiscal Department with the Fiscal Committee and with the Superintendent before [being] submitted to the Board for approval.

Summary and Conclusions

The most fundamental conclusion that can be drawn from the long-term negotiation experiences of the nine systems is that collective bargaining in public education is not radically different in process and results from collective bargaining in the private sector. Bargaining relationships in both sectors have become highly diverse and have adapted to changing circumstances. Both the nature and magnitude of bargaining results also have been remarkably similar in the two sectors.

The fact that there appears to be little that is revolutionary about collective bargaining in the experience of these school systems does not mean that there is no basis for concern over the implications of bargaining for the distribution (or redistribution) of control over decisions and resources in the public sector, in general, or public education, in particular. The experience in this small sample of school systems suggests that political constraints on bargaining are and tend to remain relatively weak and diffuse.[15] Similarly, the experience in the nine systems indicates that institutional constraints on bargaining, such as formal community involvement in negotiations and fundamental managerial concern over long-run rights and fiscal responsibilities, are weak or difficult to implement, or both, particularly from the managerial standpoint. Thus, the primary burden of discipline in the bargaining context must fall on fiscal constraints, which appear to come into play only at or near a point of imminent crisis and then only with respect to issues with obvious short-run implications for the size of the system budget rather than the structure of that budget or of the educational effort it can sustain.

This lack of effective short-run constraints on the process and results of bargaining, absent an immediate and dramatic crisis, is not unique to public education or the public sector, nor are the bargaining outcomes that have flowed from this undisciplined system. Teachers have achieved real incremental, if not yet fundamental, gains in earnings through collective bargaining by forcing a redefinition of short-run ability to pay up to the limits of long-run willingness to support public education. They have not yet been successful, however, in producing a basic change in such willingness to pay. Teachers have also been able to achieve gains in the effort area through collective bargaining, as have unions in the private sector, but those apparently noneconomic gains are also beginning to encounter fiscal constraints, particularly since declining enrollments and employment must ultimately force both management and unions to choose between higher salaries and higher pupil/staff ratios in the allocation of available resources.

The most interesting and controversial aspect of teacher bargaining remains that involving employee and management rights. The past ten years have produced a substantial expansion in the contractual job rights of teachers in terms of both protection against arbitrary treatment and participation in decision making. Their protective rights are hardly revolutionary when contrasted to the rights of workers in the private sector; their participatory rights, however, appear to be far more substantial. The procedural implications of these participatory rights are clear; their substantive impact is not. Thus far, such impact appears to have been limited more by lack of teacher interest or consensus than by political or managerial constraints. Mounting economic constraints, however, may force teachers and teacher organizations to devote more attention and energy to their participatory rights and, if so, it will be interesting to see whether or when countervailing public or managerial interest emerges.

Footnotes

1. Much of this literature is heir to the "disproportionate power" theory put forth by Wellington and Winter; see Harry H. Wellington and Ralph K. Winter, Jr., *The Unions and the Cities* (Washington, D.C.: The Brookings Institution, 1971), chap. 1. Some more recent thoughts on this subject by Wellington and Winter and others can be found in A. Lawrence Chickering, ed., *Public Employee Unions: A Study of the Crisis in Public Sector Labor Relations* (San Francisco:

Institute for Contemporary Studies, 1976).

2. For example, see James L. Freund, "Market and Union Influences on Municipal Employee Wages," *Industrial and Labor Relations Review,* Vol. 27, No. 3 (April 1974), pp. 391-404; and David B. Lipsky and John E. Drotning, "The Influence of Collective Bargaining on Teachers' Salaries in New York State," *Industrial and Labor Relations Review,* Vol. 27, No. 1 (October 1973), pp. 18-35.

3. For example, see Thomas A. Kochan and Hoyt N. Wheeler, "Municipal Collective Bargaining: A Model and Analysis of Bargaining Outcomes," *Industrial and Labor Relations Review,* Vol. 29, No. 1 (October 1975), pp. 46-66; and Paul F. Gerhart, "Determinants of Bargaining Outcomes in Local Government Labor Negotiations," *Industrial and Labor Relations Review,* Vol. 29, No. 3 (April 1976), pp. 331-51.

4. Some attention has been given to the developmental aspects of bargaining relationships in the context of the New York City fiscal crisis. For example, see Raymond D. Horton, "Economics, Politics and Collective Bargaining: The Case of New York City," and David Lewin, "Collective Bargaining and the Right to Strike," both in Chickering, *Public Employee Unions.*

5. Charles R. Perry and Wesley A. Wildman, *The Impact of Negotiations in Public Education: The Evidence from the Schools* (Worthington, Ohio: Charles A. Jones Publishing Co., 1970).

6. Kenneth McLennan and Michael H. Moskow, "Multilateral Bargaining in the Public Sector," *Proceedings of the Twenty-First Annual Winter Meeting, Industrial Relations Research Association* (Madison, Wisc.: IRRA, 1968), pp. 31-40.

7. This same phenomenon was noted in Lucian B. Gatewood, "Fact-Finding in Teacher Disputes: The Wisconsin Experience," *Monthly Labor Review,* Vol. 97, No. 10 (October 1974), pp. 47-51.

8. The potential advantages of such intervention to unions in the public sector may be significant. See Kochan and Wheeler, "Municipal Collective Bargaining," p. 59.

9. Charles R. Perry, *The Labor Relations Climate and Management Rights in Urban School Systems* (Philadelphia: Industrial Research Unit, Wharton School, University of Pennsylvania, 1974), pp. 21-27. For a more general treatment of these distinctions between real and formal scope of bargaining, see Paul F. Gerhart, "The Scope of Bargaining in Local Government Labor Negotiations," *Labor Law Journal,* Vol. 20, No. 8 (August 1969), pp. 545-52.

10. These findings subsequently have received support from empirical studies of broader samples of school systems. See, for example, Lipsky and Drotning, "The Influence of Collective Bargaining," pp. 33-35.

11. This finding is consistent with the results of other studies of the impact of bargaining on wage levels in the public sector.

12. In part, the weaker salary gains of teachers over this period may reflect the dramatic growth in fringe benefit costs experienced by most systems over this period, which amounted to almost $1200 per year per teacher.

13. This clause covers matters such as "Textbook and Curriculum Improvement," "Staff Integration," "Achievement and Intelligence Test Revision," and "Pupil Integration." The clause originally was proposed by the union with the encouragement of management.

14. This clause refers to a union statement of "Goals of Accountability," which is "not to be regarded as a compilation of conditions of employment or work standards but rather as goals of excellence which both the Board and the Union endorse." The clause and the statement it refers to were adopted in response to a management initiative linking pay to accountability in negotiations.

15. This conclusion appears to be at odds with that reached by Sanford Cohen in his article, "Does Public Employee Unionism Diminish Democracy?" *Industrial and Labor Relations Review,* Vol. 32, No. 2 (January 1979), p. 195. I do not dispute Professor Cohen's conclusion directly; indeed, my findings on substantive impact are consistent with his. I do, however, question whether those results are a product of "political" constraints independent of the "economic" constraints imposed by fiscal considerations. Thus far, this distinction has not been highly significant, primarily because unions have focused their attention on economic issues. If in the future the growing stringency of economic constraints should force unions to alter this focus of attention, political constraints per se may have to bear increasing responsibility for disciplining the bargaining process. There is little evidence yet in these nine systems that one can be optimistic that such constraints are or will quickly become operative.

Police Union Impact on the Chief's Ability to Manage

Hervey Juris and Peter Feuille*

The Scope of Bargaining: Hours of Work

In this section we consider the questions of instituting a fourth shift, shift changes, the shorter workweek, paid lunch, overtime, night-shift differential pay, court time, call-in, call-back, standby, out-of-turn work, and roll-call pay. The first three topics are covered under the heading "Direct Impact on Scheduling" and the remainder under the subhead "Indirect Impact."

Direct impact on scheduling

The fourth shift. One of the recommendations made most often by writers in the police management field and by consultants who evaluate police departments is that the patrol force be deployed on some rational basis related to crime patterns and other needs. Communities traditionally have deployed men in three shifts of approximately eight hours each. Most research has shown that the greatest number of calls for service probably come between the hours of 6 P.M. to 2 A.M. In most cities this period lies within two shifts—the 4-12/12-8 or 3-11/11-7, both of which are equally staffed, meaning an excess of men before 6 P.M. and after 2 A.M. and too few from 6 P.M. to 2 A.M. Thus the recommendation of consultants has been to establish a fourth shift to begin around 6 P.M. and run until the end of the peak crime period.

*Hervey Juris is at the Graduate School of Management, Northwestern University. Reprinted from Hervey Juris and Peter Feuille, *Police Unionism* (Lexington, Mass.: D.C. Heath and Co., 1973), pp. 125-150. These findings are based on the authors' field research and analysis of union-management employment relationships in 22 medium to large size municipal police departments [editors].

The question of establishing a fourth shift in the face of union pressure was explicit in only four cities in our sample. In Cleveland, the proposal came from the CPPA in response to a management proposal for a four-day week with ten hour days. In New Haven, management wanted a volunteer tactical squad to work the fourth shift with $500 per year extra pay. The union refused, saying it would agree to doubling up on the 4-12. The city refused the counterproposal and the police used their off-duty time to picket in civilian clothes.[1] When both sides returned to the bargaining table they agreed to a compromise in which the idea for a fixed fourth shift was dropped in return for which the chief got the right to use new men during their first two years of service anywhere he wanted.[2] In Boston, the union wanted an eight-hour day rather than the ten hours then in effect on day shifts.[3] The union went to the state legislature where they were able to obtain a permissive local option bill allowing the eight-hour day if adopted by the city council. The union then lobbied in the city council where they lined up sufficient support to go to the city and through bargaining work out an agreement providing eight-hour shifts, a night-shift differential and, for the city, the right to establish a fourth shift from 6 P.M. to 2 A.M.

In the New York State Legislature during the 1960s, New York City tried many times to change a 1911 state law mandating three eight-hour shifts of equal strength. The PBA took the position that there were not enough men to man three shifts let alone four and that it should be a bargainable issue. The city took the position that this was a management prerogative. In 1969 a bill was passed which gave New York City the right to establish a fourth shift. A fourth shift then was established but it was manned with volunteers as a compromise to avoid a full-scale confrontation. In the most recent contract the parties have agreed to the assignment of a significantly larger number of men to the 4-12 shift, meeting management's manpower needs while still meeting the union's objections to a mandatory fourth shift.

Shift changes. Changing the hours of shifts was an issue in four cities (although in New York City the issue was still on the table and there was no indication of what might happen). In one of the three cities the chief already had a 6 P.M. to 2 A.M./2 A.M. to 8 A.M./8 A.M. to 6 P.M. arrangement. The 2 A.M. to 8 A.M. shift was a skeletal force. What he sought was the ability to move men freely from one shift to another so that he could beef up the 6 P.M. to 2 A.M. shift. While he had not yet made any changes, he did indicate that he would neither consult the union nor warn them ahead of time even though a bargaining relationship exists in the city.

In a second city the International Association of Chiefs of Police (IACP) had recommended that a new shift structure be instituted ostensibly to break up a graft operation which had existed in the 8 P.M. to 4 A.M. shift. The rank and file threatened a strike if the shifts were changed but the union leaders were able to talk them out of it. A few months later the new shifts were implemented without trouble. The union then sent two men on a fact-finding trip in 1969 to gather information with which to discredit the IACP. A publicity campaign was launched charging the IACP was unqualified; that it had caused havoc elsewhere; that the shift changes were upsetting the personal lives of the men, and that there was a lack of adequate coverage from midnight to 2 A.M. However, the department held tight until early 1971 when in a unilateral decision they went to a schedule only one hour different from the original schedule.

Shorter workweek. In one eastern city, the police had been working a forty-hour week. They wanted shorter hours and the city agreed to a 5-2, 4-2 plan which made weekly hours average out to 38.7. In return the city won the right to fill many jobs with civilians, thus freeing sworn men for street duty to make up for the man hours of sworn service lost in the change. In a New England city, management negotiated a 4-2 plan which left the department six men short. The city, however, refused to provide the extra men so the chief is forced to call back people at time and one-half whenever someone is sick. In another New England city, the police were asking for a thirty-two hour week in the 1971 negotiations as part of their continuing parity drama with the city and the firefighters.

Indirect impact on scheduling

Paid lunch and roll-call pay. These two union demands are difficult to separate. The work day for a police officer involves a roll call prior to the shift which may run as long as one-half hour; this is not part of the shift. To compensate, many departments allow lunch to be taken on company time during the eight-hour shift. The catch is that the lunch time is not really the officer's: he is on call and cannot get a haircut, go shopping, or run some other errand.

In Los Angeles, the work day was eight hours to be worked in eight hours and forty-five minutes. Officers report forty-five minutes before the shift and then take a forty-five minute break during their eight-hour tour. However, in some sectors the men were unable to get away for lunch. The union suggested overtime pay for those men who could not get lunch. The chief refused and the union filed suit. The judge awarded the suit to the union subject to appeal and ordered the city to set up an escrow account for back pay. The chief responded by cutting the roll call to 23 minutes and lunch to 23 minutes. The Oakland union also won paid lunch time by court action.

In an eastern city the police get one hour for lunch but they are on call throughout the hour. One district commander was receiving grievances from men who were missing the whole lunch period every day of the week. Faced with a shortage of manpower he finally agreed with the union that he would overlook a relaxed atmosphere in low crime periods if the men would continue to respond during lunch hours. This settlement was possible because shifts rotate weekly in their department giving each man only one week in three when he is on a high pressure tour that requires missing the midshift meal.

Cincinnati, Dayton, Buffalo, and New York City have all sought some form of roll-call pay. Cincinnati dropped the demand during bargaining; the Dayton FOP has filed suit seeking this benefit; in New York the issue was on the table. In Buffalo the union has been successful in getting fifteen minutes pay on both ends of the shift for turnout and end of shift time.

Roll call and paid lunch are important issues because many departments use this time for in-service training, announcements, or even closed circuit TV communication with the chief or commissioner. By putting a straight time or overtime price on these minutes, the union may cut them to a fraction of their previous importance. On the other hand, few other occupations require people to report early and stay late with little or no added compensation.

Overtime. Overtime is, of course, an accepted feature in the private sector. The Fair Labor Standards Act has guaranteed most workers time and one-half after forty hours in a week for more than thirty years. In the police service, however, paid overtime has been only of recent origin. Officers traditionally have been compensated for overtime with straight time compensatory time off or more recently with compensatory time off at a time and one-half rate. We present here some interesting police overtime situations. In three cities it was the department itself which brought on the pressure for premium pay for overtime. In Rochester, officers as late as 1970 were getting straight time compensatory (comp) time off for overtime work. In May of that year 150 men were called in one evening because of rumors of possible civil strife in the minority community. The men rebelled at being called in for straight-time pay and refused to go out on the street. They took a strike vote but the city refused to negotiate under a strike threat so the next day the men went out for six to eight hours. An amnesty agreement brought them back and ultimately a fact-finding panel awarded them the time and one-half among other benefits.

In 1966 the Boston city council passed a time-and-one-half overtime ordinance which was vetoed by the mayor. While the council overrode the veto, the mayor refused to appropriate the funds. In 1967 just before the election to determine a bargaining agent for the city's police, the patrolmen's union filed a $300,000 suit against the city for thousands of hours of overtime worked during 1967 summer civil disturbances (and no doubt also for votes in the election). The first contract did give the union time and one-half for overtime.

In one western city the department had a practice of reassigning days off in order to avoid paying overtime to men. The union and the city were able to work out a procedure where reassignment of days off would be for emergency reasons only. In Omaha, in 1968, the police and firemen both got overtime at time and one-half by going the referendum route. Cleveland had a plan which awarded straight time comp time for overtime. What an officer didn't take during his career could be converted to *cash* at retirement. The austerity program forced the city to reconsider this policy and now while all previous rights are grandfathered, any new comp time must be taken every thirty days or lost.

In summary, the overtime issue is one where the unions are moving toward the standard time and one-half after eight hours in a day and forty hours in one week. This aspect of overtime, however, will probably not have as great an effect on scheduling and deployment as will penalties imposed on call-back, call-in, and standby, which we consider next.

Call-in, call-back, and standby. Call-back is the situation in which a man has left the station house and is called back for duty before eight hours has elapsed. Call-in is a call to work on an off day. Standby is a requirement that a man be available on his off day or off time. His physical presence may or may not be required but at least he may not be far away from a telephone, imbibe alcoholic drinks or in general make independent use of his time. This last category became a real issue during the civil disturbances of the late 1960s in the United States.

In 1968 Boston negotiated a four-hour minimum for call-in. Cincinnati has time and one-half comp time or straight time cash (officer's choice until the money runs out) but no minimum for call-back and call-in. Seattle, however, in its 1970 contract provided for time and one-half for call-ins with a four-hour minimum and 50 percent straight-time pay for standby. Rochester provides a four-hour minimum for call-backs and a two-hour minimum for holdovers on a shift, both at time and one-half with the officer's choice of pay or comp time. Dayton has a two-hour recall guarantee. In one city the call-in clause got into the contract because the men used to work parades and other events on their off days for no extra compensation.

In Boston men were often moved from one shift to another with little or no advance warning. The department claimed that this was necessary but the union negotiated a clause requiring that all out-of-turn work be compensated at time and one-half unless a man is placed on the shift for more than fourteen days. It is clear from talking to management personnel that this kind of clause has indeed infringed on the traditional prerogatives of the chief as have call-back and call-in. However, no one in this or any other department complained to us that they had been hamstrung. Rather the feeling we got was one of being "inconvenienced." A couple of departments who found their overtime budgets pressed by the demands of the contract were able to get supplementary funds as the occasion demanded.

In the case of standby we found that most abuses were covered by the call-back and call-in procedures. The chief had ceased requiring excessive standby at home and the amount of excessive call-ins for parades, riots, and special events had also been decreased; as management found money to be a scarcer resource, they began to husband it more carefully. In one department there was a cash penalty for standby and a group of detectives were able to collect a sizable back-pay settlement because an overzealous detective sargeant had ordered them to standby for over three months after the order prohibiting standby was issued.

Court-time adjustments. In the past police officers were scheduled to go to court on off days at straight time pay or no pay at all. The unions have moved rapidly on this front in many cities. Most of the cities now provide some kind of premium pay, although the form may vary. Rochester has a four-hour minimum at straight time; Boston has time and one-half with a three-hour minimum; Cincinnati has straight time with a two-hour minimum (three hours for grand jury or common pleas court); this is an improvement from the previous situation in which an officer got a two-hour slip regardless of hours actually worked. One western city provides a three-hour guarantee at time and one-half. Department records indicate that most men actually come out ahead. Pittsburgh pays a $5.00 witness fee for each appearance as does Baltimore.

The question of court appearances has raised a managerial response in three of the cities in our sample. In Buffalo where an officer gets a four-hour minimum guarantee at straight-time rates, a city court judge warned that he would not permit the repeated appearances of officers due to continuances because it cost the city too much. In addition, the city judges voted to have police fill out a sworn statement when making misdemeanor arrests which could be forwarded with the prisoner, thus obviating the need for the officer's appearance.[4] In a city where the city pays time and one-half for actual time, the chief has worked out an agreement with the juvenile court in the county seat whereby arresting officers will not have to appear. He is also exploring with the union other ways to cut court-time costs. In a New England city the chief has two problems. The first is money, since the contract provides for a four-hour guarantee even in the case of continuances. The second is a provision that a man who spends *over* four hours in court in a given day cannot be called to work a second or third shift that day. In an attempt to deal with both problems, the chief plans to station a man with a two-way radio in court to call detectives as their cases are called.

In other cities the police have made efforts to talk with the presiding judge about schedule coordination but they have been rebuffed.[5] Court time has always been an abuse to police officers. Now that they are able to put a cost on the practice, the burden shifts to management. If experience follows the private-sector model, what started as penalty overtime should in due course come to be considered as a right, further complicating the management problem.

Night-shift differential. A second and/or third-shift pay differential (usually seven to fifteen cents per hour) is fairly common in the private sector. In the police service, however, it is a relatively new benefit. The experience in Boston is instructive. The department had worked under a three-shift schedule with shifts of 10, 6 3/4, and 7 1/4 hours respectively. When the union sought to negotiate three eight-hour shifts, they also requested a $15.00 per week night-shift differential to compensate the second and third-shift men for the loss in shorter hours. The city, in return, got the right to establish a fourth shift.[6] In a New England city the union was offered an increase of $5.00 per month in the uniform allowance but asked for and received a $1.00 per week night-shift differential. The union had hoped this would open the door to future increases once the principle was established. So far, however, this has not happened. In San Francisco, the night-shift differential was included in the charter amendment which also asked for an end to firefighter parity. As indicated, the amendment lost 3 to 1.

While there have not yet been any changes in manpower allocation as a result of these differentials, we include the night-shift differential in this section to call attention to the potential impact of this benefit.

The Scope of Bargaining: Conditions of Work[7]

These are the nondollar conditions of work over which there has been conflict in several of the jurisdictions visited. Each subject clearly has an impact on the chief's ability to manage. However, in each case there are two sides to the story. Our format in this section is to discuss the issue briefly and cite some examples of behavior from the field.

Manning

The use of civilians. Management would like to introduce civilians into jobs previously performed by sworn personnel in part because the sworn personnel are not really trained to handle these administrative and clerical tasks and in part because the patrolmen's new salaries have priced them out of the market for these jobs. Most unions in our sample opposed civilianization, although few were successful. Union reasons for opposition primarily focus on some variant of the need for security and confidentiality, the need for the arrest power (available only to sworn personnel) in order to gain respect, or the need for experience in the field to properly perform the function (as in handling the dispatcher's job). The most novel reason given by one major union president was that civilians don't always obey orders while sworn officers always do; and civilians always leave for lunch at noon whereas sworn officers stay until the work is done. The economics of the situation is such that civilianization will probably become more important in the future.

A hopeful sign—in the sense of promoting the development of professionalism in the leadership of police agencies—is the number of departments in our sample in which management brought in civilians in top line and staff jobs without significant union opposition—New York City, New Haven, Hartford, Baltimore, and Dayton. This is consistent with our prior observation that the potential for professionalization is probably greatest at the management level.

One-man versus two-man squad cars. The number of men in a squad car is one of the most emotional issues we encountered. Management wants the freedom to assign one-man cars and two-man cars on the basis of its perception of the data on crime by areas and shifts; the unions want to maximize patrolman safety under street conditions they perceive as tantamount to wartime. In our sample we saw both aspects of the issue: cities where the union was attempting to pressure a move from one-man to two-man cars and cities where management was attempting to move from two-man cars to one-man cars.

In three of our cities there was an increase in two-man cars. Recently one New England city made fourteen of the thirty-four cars on the 6 P.M. to 2 A.M. shift two-man cars. These are the fourteen cars in the high-crime area and the move was probably the result of perceived need and union pressure; however, it was a unilateral management decision. Similarly, in a California city, where in 1970 the city went to all two-man cars on the swing shift where the union had been calling for two-man cars, there was a demonstrated need but the decision was made by management. In Boston where patrol cars had been 70 percent two-man, Mayor White gave the union 100 percent two-man cars prior to the gubernatorial primary in which the union subsequently endorsed him.

In three other cities, the movement was away from two-man cars toward single patrol. In one western city, even though a couple of officers had been injured in one-man cars over the eighteen months preceding our visit, and even though the union was pressuring for two-man cars, management unilaterally changed the ratio of one-man/two-man from 30/70 to 50/50. When the union objected, management indicated it was not the union's decision to make. In a midwestern city, the union has pressured for no more one-man cars and presented a general grievance to the chief. The result is a freeze on the *status quo;* one-man cars stay but there is no increase. In an eastern city an elaborate walkie-talkie communications system has staved off union pressure for two-man cars. The union has basically accepted manpower deployment as a management function.

Moonlighting and paid details. Moonlighting, or the holding of a second job by sworn officers was not an issue in all the jurisdictions we visited, but it does illustrate a situation where collective bargaining can lead to a creative solution to a mutual need. Many departments are faced with demands for service they cannot meet because of resource scarcities. The men, on the other hand, often feel that the salary from the regular job is not sufficient to provide the style of life to which they would prefer to grow accustomed. One bridge between these two concerns is for off-duty police officers to perform police-type duty in their off hours at a comparable hourly wage. Police agencies frequently receive calls for uniformed officers to chaperone parties, to direct traffic at shopping centers, sports events, or construction sites, or to serve as private supplemental police for particular neighborhoods in the community. In New York City, police officers moonlight as cab drivers. In San Francisco a few police officers moonlight as bank tellers. The reported effect of this added presence has been to reduce robberies in both categories in the respective cities.

There are a number of problems connected with the department providing uniformed officers on a moonlighting basis. Some involve the city's liability in case of accident or death or civil suit against the officer . from an incident which occurs during moonlighting. Other problems concern the nature of jobs and the number of hours of moonlighting permitted. Usually jobs are prohibited which would increase the probability of contact with undesirable elements in the community such as those persons engaged in vice or gambling. For this reason bartending is almost always excluded. The hours question is one of how many hours a man can work a second job without infringing on his ability to perform in his primary job.

Some unions (Providence, Cranston, Boston, New Haven) have negotiated a paid detail contract clause. Whereas previously moonlighting opportunities had been assigned on a favoritism basis, the clauses provide for sign-up lists, allocation of opportunities by seniority, minimum pay rates, and other conditions. As we indicated above, this is an emerging area and one where the liability problem may cause spottiness in the diffusion of the pattern. But it does represent an example of how the bargaining process has provided an integrative solution to a mutual problem.

Name tags. One of the issues achieving prominence during the civil disturbances of the late 1960s was the question of name tags on uniforms. Protesters claimed that when police officers violated their civil rights they had no way of identifying the perpetrator because the badges and other identifying insignia had been removed. The officers countered that the badges had been removed to prevent their being used against the police as weapons. The men resisted sewn on name tags because they said this would open the door to harassment of their families by protestors who read the names off the tags during demonstrations. In Seattle the city painted badge numbers on the riot helmets and sewed them on overalls. While the men objected, the union took no action. In Detroit the union opposed the order to wear name tags on the grounds that they had not been consulted and that this was a violation of the maintenance of conditions clause in the contract. The issue went to arbitration with the city claiming the issue was not arbitrable. The arbitrator ruled it was arbitrable, ordered the department to confer with the union but said that the department did have the right to require name tags be worn. As a result, the tags are now worn.

At a 1969 disturbance at Harvard University, the Boston police removed their badges claiming that the stick pins could be used to jab them. Mayor White proposed sewing on name tags and the commissioner agreed. The union objected, claiming that this would lead to harassment of their families. The commissioner ordered the tags sewed on and arranged for union tailors to come to headquarters to sew them on. The police threw up a picket line and the union tailors refused to cross. The police-union attorney filed a greivance and the department agreed to hold off until the grievance was resolved.[8] The union lost the grievance and took it to arbitration. Simultaneously the union attorney introduced a local option permissive bill in the legislature which would, if adopted by a city, ban the wearing of name tags if identifying numbers were worn. The union got the bill through but the governor sent it back for redrafting. Finally, the governor signed it and the union got the bill passed in the city council. The arbitrator finally came down with his award supporting the city but by this time the issue was moot and the men do not wear name tags.

Sick leave. Sick leave is not so much an issue over the generosity of the benefit as it is over the lengths to which a police agency will go to control abuses of the sick-leave privilege. In general, management is concerned that there are abuses of sick leave while the men object to the fact that management sends supervisors to their homes to verify illnesses. In three cities in our sample, however, management crackdowns led to quite significant decreases in sick-leave days taken. In one city, management made its move when it found that an excessive number of sick days were being taken on Friday and Saturday evenings. There is, of course, a potentially expensive interrelatedness between residency requirements and policing sick leave; for example, in New York City many of the men reside in the suburbs, and the sargeants who check on those claiming to be sick must travel long distances. The significant factor in this discussion, however, is that while the unions do object strenuously, they have taken no actions that would infringe on management's prerogatives in this area.

Reorganization and management studies. In several cities in our sample major changes in procedure or complete reorganization were attempted. In some cases it was with the union's cooperation and in other situations over their opposition. In a third subset, the unions were opposed but the opposition was ineffective. We cite two examples of positive departmental-union cooperation. In one New England city, the new mayor in conjunction with the police union, but over the opposition of police management, brought in the Public Administration Service for a management survey; with the cooperation of the union and despite the opposition of some departmental leaders, the changes recommended by PAS were implemented. In a California city, the new chief introduced a large number of changes, including a new workweek of four ten-hour days but only after extensive consultation with the union and with his command staff. Almost all of these changes were implemented smoothly.

In three other cities, the unions have been neither supportive nor effectively deterrent. In Baltimore the IACP management survey led to the appointment of a new commissioner with broad sweeping powers to institute change. The two unions have not been pleased with all the changes instituted, but neither have they been effective in keeping change from occurring. The same is true of the situation in New York where sweeping changes are being instituted at the management level. While the line organizations have objected strenuously to some of these changes, they have not yet succeeded in stopping any of them. In a third city where the changes were largely in program style—the delivery of a new kind of law-enforcement service—the union has not been able to kill any programs, but it has managed to slow down implementation.

Two unions were quite active in opposing sweeping IACP recommendations for change in their departments and were at least partially successful in their attempts to frustrate change. The Pittsburgh FOP attempted to deprecate the IACP survey team's qualifications and engaged in several attempts to thwart proposals for changes such as merging traffic and patrol into one operations bureau, creation of a community-relations unit, creation of an inspection bureau with an internal-affairs division, the removal of vice control from detectives to inspection, and the creation of a master patrolman classification.[9] With the exception of the last, the city was able to implement each of the other changes over FOP objections. A West Coast union pursued much of the same tactics against an IACP report which called for nearly 600 changes. In this case, the union was able to frustrate both consolidation of precincts and the implementation of a master patrolman concept.

Summary

In this section, we have focused on the question "to what extent has the union interfered with the ability of the [police] chief to allocate resources within the department?" Our data on the issues of bargaining suggest several tentative conclusions. First, the demands of police unions seem to be consistent with the traditional demands of trade unions representing other production and maintenance workers with respect to wages, hours, and conditions of work. For all their talk of professionalization, the police are conceptually indistinguishable from steelworkers or auto workers in their on-the-job concerns, a finding consistent with Kleingartner's analysis of the unionization of professional employees in bureaucratic organizations generally.[10] We would argue from this that the real impact of the union has been to force shared decision-making in the allocation of resources, whether the resources discussed are monetary (more wages and fringe benefits instead of using those same dollars for new programs or equipment) or human resources (all of the hours provisions and working conditions which impinge on the chief's absolute freedom to assign men as he sees fit).

A second pattern that emerges is the importance of distinguishing what the union says it is going to do from what it actually does; of distinguishing what the union attempts from what the union accomplishes; and of distinguishing the anticipated effect of a union-induced change from the actual impact of that change. The union may demand 100 percent enforcement of the law, but the men faced with department sanctions do not respond to the union's call; the union may oppose sewn on name tags, but they are placed on the uniforms anyhow; the union may win a seniority clause, but the actual effect is negligible relative to the image of chaos anticipated prior to the change. This analysis is not to suggest that union threats and demands may not delay change or even frustrate change from being proposed; our study design did not allow us to develop accurate data on these types of situations. However, this analysis does suggest that there is some position between hysteria (resulting from a failure to distinguish accomplishment from attempt) and whitewash (refusing to consider the frustrating impact of strong unions on inexperienced management) which represents a realistic appraisal of the union's impact.

This leads to our third and fourth points. Much of the negative impact of unions has occurred because of union exploitation of the multilateral bargaining opportunities in the public sector and the failure of management to rationalize the process by limiting the arena for gains to the bargaining table. Numerous examples were found where the union was able to whipsaw management by moving from the bargaining table to the city council to the state legislature and back again. Finally, there must be a strong management across the bargaining table from the union demanding *quid pro quo,* seeking innovative solutions to mutual problems, and opposing demands which would impose intolerable burdens. We found no evidence of this kind of two-party bargaining on any broad scale; rather we found only selected cases in selected relationships where this degree of sophistication had been achieved.

We spoke earlier of the primary impact of unions as forcing joint decision-making particularly in the traditional areas of wages, overtime, protection against call-in, call-back, standby, and abuse of court-time requirements. Whatever the short-run consequences of higher costs and less flexibility may be, we see the long-run impact of this shared decision-making as forcing management to come to grips with the fact that the human resources of the department are not a free commodity but rather a scarce commodity, and as forcing management to deal with the managerial problem of allocating these scarce resources among competing ends. We cited examples where men are called out less frequently or hours assigned more rationally or court time scheduled more rationally only after overtime, call-in, call-back, and court time were paid at an overtime rate in cash. As long as overtime was straight-time compensatory time off there was little incentive for management to treat the human resources of the department as anything but a relatively free commodity.[11] We see this change in the economics of the situation as the major long-run impact of the union on the chief's ability to manage.

There were several examples where the union was able to frustrate management goals by resort to the referendum and legislative and elective politics over issues as varied as wages, the introduction of a fourth shift, unbalanced shifts, new shift hours, name tags, and departmental reorganization. However, where there was some rationalization of the bargaining process and a reasonably sophisticated management bargaining team, the bargaining process was used to generate mutually satisfactory or integrative bargains: the trade-off in one city of union cooperation in establishing a fourth shift in exchange for the implementation of eight-hour shifts; the trade-off between a shorter workweek and the right to use civilian employees in jobs previously performed by sworn personnel; and the cooperation of union and management in one midwestern city where detective tenure was exchanged for the new specialist rating and one-man cars were instituted along with a new communications system allowing the man to be in constant contact with headquarters.[12]

The Brookings Studies

Any discussion of the impact of unions on the ability of management to manage must acknowledge an intellectual debt to Slichter, Healy, and Livernash's 1960 study, *The Impact of Collective Bargaining on Management* (ICBM). Looking at the collective-bargaining landscape some fifteen to twenty years after the turbulent labor relations decade of the late 1930s and the early 1940s, those authors attempted to relate what had occurred to some of the dire projections that had grown out of the unrest surrounding the birth of industrial unionism. More recently, another Brookings study has attempted to replicate this effort in the public sector. David Stanley looks at the impact of unions during the period that they are in the process of organizing and attempts to place their impact in some kind of perspective vis-a-vis the criteria established a decade earlier by Slichter, Healy and Livernash.[13] We conclude this chapter with a brief review of the findings in each of these studies so that the reader may judge for himself the extent to which the findings of this and other studies are consistent.

Unions in the private sector, the authors of ICBM found, have narrowed the scope of management discretion, fostered the development of management by policy, and necessitated organizational changes whose net effect

464

was to centralize labor relations policy-making. The narrowing of management discretion has come about through contract language, contract administration and grievance arbitration as in the establishment of rules for lay off, transfer, promotion; through requirements that management be fair or reasonable or act with just cause; and sometimes through language prohibiting certain types of conduct such as excessive overtime.[14] The trend toward development of management by policy is largely a function of the costs imposed by the union on *ad hoc* decision-making in personnel matters—lost arbitration cases, whipsawing, and so forth:

> *If one single statement were sought to describe the effect of unions on policy-making, it would be: "They have encouraged investigation and reflection." Some unions are in fact only a slight check on management; other unions run the shop. But whether the union influence is weak or strong, it always tends to force management to consider the probable consequences of its proposed decisions and to adjust those decisions accordingly.*[15]

To carry out this "investigation and reflection," management developed labor-relations staffs and organizations to coordinate their activities. While the authors found a great deal of variance with respect to the focus of decision-making in multiplant firms, the net impact of unions was to centralize decision-making on policy matters in industrial relations.[16]

With respect to the nature of the relationship, Slichter, Healy, and Livernash found that as of 1960 there was a limited but significant growth of formal cooperation, a decline in the number of relationships with intense conflict, and a growing adjustment of the parties to the new relationship. The authors also noted an increase in management willingness to take a strike to eliminate inefficiencies brought on by earlier excessive yielding to union pressures (however, hindsight has shown us that this is a cyclical phenomenon related to management's ability to pass on costs).[17]

Compare these 1960 findings in the private sector with the following conclusions reached by Stanley after studying nineteen relationships in the public sector in the late 1960s. In response to the rhetorical question, "What is happening to government achievements under union pressures?" Stanley answers "Not much." For example, he says on the one hand "unions can impair efficiency in a strongly unionized department if they accelerate cost increases and if they insist on work rules and conditions that hinder the flexible use of management techniques. On the other hand, unions may improve program effectiveness by demanding that the organization be adequately staffed, by pressing for equal levels of service throughout the city or by insisting on a sound safety program."[18]

> *Mainly "what is happening" to local government is that both legislative bodies and chief executives are* more preoccupied with union matters *and are* more limited in their discretion to manage.[19]

In support of decreased discretion, Stanley cites the fact that unions now engage in bilateral decision-making on budgets, that unions have a voice in grievance procedures and the administration of grievances, and that unions become involved in job classification, work assignments, program policies, and to a limited extent the tenure of public officials.[20] In general, however,

> recent history suggests that the [financial] gains of the unions have not been excessive. There will be efforts in the future to get more, and both the political and procedural restraints will be burdened, but disastrous outcomes are hardly likely.[21]

The unions, says Stanley, do not want to take over management completely, rather they want an adversary against whom they can press demands: "Management needs to show strength."[22] He points out that management must organize and staff itself to deal with employee relations and do everything possible to maintain fundamental management prerogatives.[23] "Public officials often miss opportunities to bargain hard and merely use a defensive strategy of responding to union demands. In some units they could bargain for increased productivity, improved work quality, or work rules conducive to efficiency."[24] Stanley concludes:

> The increase of unionism in local governments has helped employees to keep up with the rest of the economy and has added to their protection against arbitrary or inconsistent treatment. They have clearly won the right to organize, to negotiate, and to secure structured consideration of grievances and they undoubtedly have the right to strike, de facto. But there seems to be little prospect that the transaction will become overbalanced against management, given the continued functioning of the American political system and the exercise by management officials of a reasonable mix of resolution, ability to listen, decisiveness, labor relations knowledge, and good will.[25]

We feel that our findings and the findings of these two studies are consistent on the following points: the unions have narrowed management discretion, they have fostered the development of management by policy, they have protected employees against arbitrary or inconsistent treatment, and they have shown that management had better begin diverting greater intellectual and organizational resources toward dealing with this new power center in its midst. Like Slichter, Healy, and Livernash, we too found the beginnings of cooperative relationships and a decline in the number of relationships with intense conflict. In this next section we look at the impact of unions on the formulation of law-enforcement policy in the community.

Footnotes

1. See the *New Haven Register,* 14, 15, and 18 May 1969.
2. Consider the implications of having the least seasoned men on the street during the most demanding time period.
3. See the section below on night-shift differentials for a more comprehensive account of this situation.
4. See the *Buffalo Evening News,* 26 September and 11 October 1968.
5. Kelling and Kleismet refer to this in their article ("Resistance to Professionalization," *Police Chief,* May 1971) when they discuss the police officer as the one

interested party to a criminal matter not considered when scheduling, continuances, and so forth are being discussed.

6. The union filed an interesting grievance challenging a management interpretation of this clause: the city was not including the shift premium in the checks of men injured or on sick leave. The union said they deserved the money because it was part of their regular pay. The arbitrator agreed.

7. This section contains a shortened version of the authors' findings excluding primarily their discussion of police grievance procedures, discipline and selected aspects of personnel administration. Interested readers should consult the original source for this material [editors].

8. See the *Boston Globe*, 14 April, 16, 18, 19, and 20 June 1969.

9. See the *Pittsburgh Press*, 6 December 1966.

10. Archie Kleingartner, *Professionalism and Salaried Worker Organization* (Madison, Wisconsin: Industrial Relations Research Institute, University of Wisconsin, 1967).

11. For example, a managerial interviewee in one large eastern city admitted that when overtime was costless the department regularly "overpoliced" parades and political demonstrations, and on occasion small demonstrations had more police than participants.

12. We know too little about the change process generally and almost nothing about change in police agencies. See Robert B. Duncan, "The Climate for Change in Three Police Departments: Some Implications for Action," *Fourth National Symposium on Law Enforcement Science and Technology* (Washington, D.C., May 2, 1972).

13. David T. Stanley, with the assistance of Carole L. Cooper, *Managing Local Government Under Union Pressure* (Washington, D.C.: The Brookings Institution, 1972).

14. Sumner Slichter, James J. Healy, and E. Robert Livernash, *The Impact of Collective Bargaining on Management* (Washington, D.C.: Brookings Institution, 1960), pp. 947-51.

15. *Ibid.*, p. 952.

16. *Ibid.*, pp. 952-54.

17. *Ibid.*, pp. 957-60.

18. Stanley, *Managing Local Government*, pp. 138-39.

19. *Ibid.*, p. 139.

20. *Ibid.*, p. 140.

21. *Ibid.*, p. 145.

22. *Ibid.*, p. 145.

23. *Ibid.*, pp. 148-49.

24. *Ibid.*, pp. 150-51.

25. *Ibid.*, pp. 151-52.

Police Union Impact on the Formulation of Law-Enforcement Policy

Hervey Juris and Peter Feuille*

What constitutes the formulation of law-enforcement policy can be a difficult question. A department has many policies: a policy concerning prostitution; a policy concerning the use of sick leave; even a policy concerning the frequency with which squad cars will be washed. In this list it is easy to distinguish the first, which is a law enforcement policy issue, from the other two, which are administrative policies. However, how does one classify policies coming under the broad rubric of "manning?" We discussed "manning" under the heading "ability to manage," but the use of civilians, the number of men in a squad car, and the number of cars on the street are also an important part of law-enforcement policy. Conversely, the question of the type and number of weapons carried by policemen and the conditions under which they may be used are discussed under "law enforcement policy" but they are clearly germane to the chief's ability to manage.

Other law-enforcement policy issues are not as easily discerned because they are discussed in contexts which draw attention away from the underlying law-enforcement policy implications. Thus earlier we discussed the question of entry standards and minority recruitment in the context of the professionalization issue. We might also have discussed these in the context of their impact on law enforcement policy—the extent to which the minority community perceives efforts to exclude blacks from the department as an unobtrusive measure of the department's hostility toward them. In short, while public attention is focused on particular disputes, each of which involves some aspect of control and authority, the broader policy issues tend not to get raised. In this next section we attempt to point up some of these broader policy questions.

Law-Enforcement Policy Issues[1]

How will the law be enforced. Police services are delivered within the context of broad policy guidelines. The precise policies to be followed are subject to a great deal of discretion. The basic thrust of union efforts has been to place limits on managerial discretion.

In the case of civil disturbances, for example, management may choose to follow a policy of containment rather than risking life on both sides by attempting to extinguish the disturbance. In several cities where this policy was pursued the unions objected strenuously. In New York City PBA President John Cassesse's call for "100 percent enforcement of the law" in August 1968 was issued in the context of police dissatisfaction with the containment policies of city officials established during the Martin Luther

---

*Reprinted from Hervey Juris and Peter Feuille, *Police Unionism* (Lexington, Mass.: D.C. Heath and Co., 1973), pp. 151-63.

King riots in April 1968 and continued into the following summer,[2] as was a similar statement by former Boston Police Patrolmen's Association President Richard MacEachern a few days later.[3] Similarly, a group of Baltimore policemen, through a publicized letter to their AFSCME local, criticized the department's preparedness for, and handling of, the King riots,[4] and during the riots the Police Wives Association publicly castigated the "weak-kneed" policy used in containing the disturbances.

The most explicit union activity in this area occurred in Pittsburgh where the Fraternal Order of Police (FOP) lodge published formal investigatory reports after two civil disturbances. The first followed the King riot, and strongly criticized the department's lack of preparedness and the containment nature of the city's response.[5] The second report dealt with a June 1970 disturbance which followed the slaying of a black youth by an elderly white woman. In this report the union severely criticized the city's permissiveness and appeasement of the "hoodlum element."[6]

Sometimes law-enforcement policy can be affected by benefits secured strictly for "bread and butter" reasons. In the previous chapter, for example, we mentioned that unions in many cities have secured financial compensation for off-duty court appearances, some of it at premium rates. Thus, at the time of our field visit, Boston patrolmen earned approximately $22.50 for each off-duty court appearance (time-and-one-half pay with a three-hour minimum). One conceivable law-enforcement impact of this benefit is that officers, especially those on evening and night duty, may see a financial incentive to make arrests which necessitate a court appearance the next day. This phenomenon has been given a name—"bounty hunting," making arrests primarily to increase earnings. We pursued this issue in three cities, where management interviewees admitted that when premium pay for court appearances was first established there may have been a few bounty hunters but that such men were transferred to other positions. Management interviewees minimized the phenomenon, saying that aggregate arrest figures (which we did not examine) showed no significant increase in arrests after court-time premium pay was established. However, street patrolmen in two of the cities were emphatic that bounty hunters did exist.

Another factor that can be quite important is the union's stance on residency. The question of whether a police officer need reside in the city of his employment is an important law-enforcement policy issue with emotional overtones. The men argue that given their middle-income economic status they should be free to live in the suburbs where the streets are safe and the schools sound. Cities, on the other hand, argue that residing implies a commitment to the city and to its improvement, that public employees should reside in the tax district, and that the men should be available for call-in, call-back, and standby. Norton Long raises another interesting perspective: with the center-city population becoming more dependent over time, the nonresident police, teachers, and other civil servants come to represent emissaries from the mother country to the colony or from the government to the Indians on the reservation.[7] This latter perspective is often overlooked.

Whenever the residency issue arose in our sample, it was usually because of union attempts to eliminate it. For example, the New York City PBA has lobbied extensively in Albany for the right to live outside the city, and successive pieces of state legislation now give city policemen the right to live in several suburban counties. Cleveland officers removed the residency requirement through a charter amendment. In contrast, unions in several other cities were unsuccessful in attempts to eliminate residency requirements. Police organizations in Chicago lost a lawsuit, and the Milwaukee union failed with a law suit and at the bargaining table. Cincinnati tried a city-council resolution and a lawsuit and lost both times.[8] In Detroit the patrolmen's union fought a lengthy court battle against the requirement but lost. The Seattle union objected to the mayor's decree that new policemen must live within the city limits (though those already on the force could maintain their suburban residency), but at the time of our visit had not been able to change the situation. In one city the union actually did oppose the elimination of a residency requirement.[9]

In summary, a few unions have been able to eliminate residency require-ments, and a few unions may have contributed to the phenomenon of bounty hunting through securing a premium for off-duty court appearances. Several unions have objected to management's containment policies for handling civil disturbances, but nowhere did we find that management had changed its riot policies in response to union criticisms. However, these union demands for a "hard line" are a clear statement to the community of how the rank-and-file views its law-enforcement duties, and they are a clear statement to police and city officials who may be considering adopting other policies or techniques which de-emphasize the use of force.

The use of force. The armament carried by officers and the conditions under which weapons or physical force is used are an important element of the law-enforcement policy of the community and, like the issue of how the law is to be enforced, has an impact on the way in which the community perceives the department's intentions toward them. Among the issues raised are the number of weapons carried, the use of private weapons, the presence of long guns, the conditions under which an officer may fire his weapon, and whether the rifles and shotguns should be carried in the trunk, in the front of the car, or taken from the car routinely.

Consistent with their "hard line" on the handling of civil disorders, police unions have pressed for heavy armaments and minimal restrictions on the police right to use force, especially fatal force. In seven cities in this sample the use of force was an overt issue, usually with the police unions opposing actual or proposed restrictions on their coercive license. The Cleveland unions, for example, were successful after the 1968 Glenville shootout in pressuring the department for new armaments. Interviewees in two other midwestern cities told of men on patrol carrying unauthorized long guns in addition to their authorized sidearms. In Hartford, the union's hard bargaining (not to be confused with collective bargaining), lobbying, and display of public support was instrumental in persuading the city council to vote against the adoption of gun-use restrictions. The San Francisco union was able to persuade the chief and the police commission to change a proposed set of gun guidelines so that an officer involved in an on-duty

470

homicide is not automatically suspended pending an investigation.[10] In Seattle the union negotiated a contract clause providing that no officer can be required over his objection to work without a gun.

In contrast the Oakland union has protested in vain against the chief's gun-use restrictions (which are much tighter than the "fleeing felon" standard in the state law). A union in a western city pressed unsuccessfully for the right of each officer to carry the weapon of his choice. In an eastern city the union lobbied the city council for the right to carry shotguns in squad cars, but the chief was able to muster sufficient opposition to have the union voted down. In a midwestern city the union unsuccessfully made public demands for, and lobbied with the chief for, a shotgun for each man in a squad car (instead of the existing one per car) and for the reinstitution of a formerly eliminated dog patrol. Finally, after the 1971 murders of two New York City patrolmen the PBA called for shotguns in every patrol car. Though this demand was rejected, the department did begin training in shotgun handling for many members of the force. The union again raised the issue in 1973.[11]

Many of the police demands for increased armaments and the authority to use them can be traced to their belief that patrol conditions in many central cities are tantamount to wartime. Support for this belief comes from the increasing rate of assaults on police officers and the increasing numbers of policemen killed during the 1960s and early 1970s. For instance, in 1960 28 police officers were killed in the line of duty as a result of felonious assault; in 1970, 100 officers were killed; and in 1971 the figure increased to 126.[12] Many of the rank and file see the use of heavier force as a self-protection issue.

The direct impact of union efforts in some departments has been to minimize the restrictions placed on an officer's use of firearms and to help obtain increased armaments. In other departments the unions have pushed in the same directions but have no observable impact. Successful or not, the union's demands for heavier armaments and minimal restrictions on their use are additional statements to the community, especially the minority segments of the community, of police intentions toward them.

Civilian review of police behavior. The topic that has attracted the most publicity in the area of law-enforcement policy is union opposition to civilian review of citizen complaints against individual officers or groups of officers. The most celebrated instances are the Philadelphia and New York cases: in both cities the unions successfully thwarted civilian review. In New York City the defeat of Mayor Lindsay's proposal came as a result of a referendum in which the union succeeded in killing civilian review but actually increased the volume of complaints to the departmental review board as a result of its publicity campaign broadcasting the existence of such a board. In Philadelphia the civilian review board was dropped by the mayor even after a favorable state supreme court verdict reversing two lower courts who had sustained a union challenge to the legitimacy of the board. The Rochester union's court battle against the review board in that city contributed to the board's demise.

471

In Boston in 1968 the patrolmen's union worked with several city-council members to scrap the police portion of Mayor Kevin White's proposed Model Cities program, including a civilian complaint board. In Buffalo the union lobbied vigorously against a proposal before the city council to give that city's Commission on Human Relations subpoena power when investigating charges of police misconduct, and the council defeated the proposal. In Baltimore in 1970 the two unions campaigned vigorously against a Baltimore Urban Coalition proposal for a civilian review board, and the issue was abandoned by its proponents in the face of this opposition.[13] After the Pittsburgh Commission on Human Relations investigated and recommended that several policemen be disciplined for their behavior in a series of incidents, the Pittsburgh FOP lodge castigated the commission, announced that policemen would refuse to cooperate with it, and asked the mayor to investigate it.[14]

The direct impact of union activities in many of these cities seems clear: civilian review boards that existed have been defeated, and new proposals to establish review boards have been stopped before they were implemented. In other cities the impact may have been more indirect. Union condemnation of human relations and civil rights commissions may not have produced any structural changes, but the expressions of police opposition to any kind of civilian review of police behavior have informed community leaders of the difficulties of instituting formalized review procedures. In all, civilian review was an issue in eleven of our twenty-two cities.

Citizen complaints and the identification of police officers. Like civilian review of complaints against officer behavior, facilitation of complaints and identification are a manifestation of an adversary relationship between police and the community.[15] The policy issue raised is the extent to which the department will facilitate the taking of complaints and the identification of officers.

In an eastern city the union objected to a department plan to have officers earn community goodwill by interviewing five citizens each week, with a key portion of the interview consisting of the officer explaining to the citizen how to file a complaint against the police. The union dropped its objection when the interview program produced evidence of substantial public support for the police. In Omaha the union criticized the department's new citizen complaint procedure, which the chief said was adopted at the request of a local citizen's committee. The union objected to the fact that complaints could be made by telephone, saying that all complaints should be made in person and the officer being complained about should have the opportunity to confront the citizen as he made the complaint.[16]

In Boston, Detroit, and Seattle the identification question surfaced as a name-tag issue. In Seattle the union agreed to name tags on shirts and identifying numbers on riot helmets and overalls, the latter after many citizens complained of police brutality and the inability to identify police offenders during campus and antigovernment demonstrations. The Detroit patrolmen's union used the grievance-arbitration procedure to stall but not prevent the introduction of name tags, and the Boston patrolmen's union was able to prevent name tags via the judicious combination of picketing police headquarters, using the grievance-arbitration procedure, lobbying with the state legislature and governor's office, and lobbying with the city council.

In Buffalo the identification issue surfaced as an identification lineup of all the police on a particular shift in order that the black victims of alleged excessive police zeal be afforded an opportunity to identify the assailants. The unions used a federal court suit to delay for more than a year the implementation of the lineups, thus reducing the chances for accurate identification.

These specific issues again point up the distinction between the direct and indirect impact of union efforts. Only in Boston did the union score a total victory, though in Buffalo and Detroit the unions were able to delay implementation of identification mechanisms. However, the union position in these cases conveyed to the community a clear picture of rank-and-file police attitudes toward the handling of citizen complaints and identification of police misconduct.

The functioning of the criminal justice system. In theory the various aspects of the criminal justice system function independently: the police effect arrests, the prosecutor decides if a formal charge is warranted and prosecutes the case, the judge presides over the trial and passes sentence, the legislature defines criminal activity and determines a range of penalties, and a parole board may determine what portion of a particular sentence will actually be served. While in practice these are not necessarily independent events, still the question arises as to whether such interdependence as does exist should be formalized through police union activities such as court-watching, union endorsements in campaigns for prosecutor and judge, or union endorsements in campaigns for mayor and governor where the candidates go on record as to the types of individuals who will be nominated to civilian review boards, parole boards, and other agencies having jurisdiction in the criminal justice area.

Police unions in our sample were quite concerned about judicial handling and disposition of criminal cases. Police unions in five cities threatened to engage in court-watching (stationing an observer in court to record the disposition of criminal cases), and these statements were invariably couched in coercive language castigating judicial leniency. The Detroit patrolmen's union, through its wives' auxiliary, actually engaged in court-watching for six months. The Seattle union publicly threatened to implement a court-watching program but backed off after receiving substantial adverse criticism. One midwestern union collected data for six months but never used it. The Seattle and Baltimore unions endorsed judicial candidates because of their ideological sympathy with the police.[17] In Pittsburgh the police delayed the appointment of a black magistrate in whom the union had taken a vote of no-confidence, and the union publicly castigated some magistrates for releasing on own recognizance and nominal bonds certain categories of criminal suspects. The union president warned that the union will watch all magistrates to see if they follow the magisterial code section on bail-setting and will charge them with misconduct if they violate the code.[18]

Union spokesmen in four cities said their organizations have lobbied to influence the substance of criminal statutes or changes in the penal code. For example, the Baltimore unions successfully lobbied against a city proposal to increase the upper age limit for juvenile offenders from sixteen to eighteen. The former president of the union in another city said he actively lobbied on behalf of certain criminal statutes in the state capitol. Electoral processes may also be used to influence law-enforcement matters. The California Supreme Court declared the state's death penalty unconstitutional in early 1972; the response among several police groups (and others) was to launch an initiative effort which resulted in a death penalty constitutional amendment on the November 1972 ballot. In Pittsburgh in 1971 a "law and order" district attorney who enjoyed good relations with the police and who was up for reelection refused to prosecute thirty-four policemen who fraudulently collected $41,000 in witness fees.[19] In an example from outside our sample, the Eugene (Oregon) Police Patrolmen's Association endorsed and gave a large contribution to the successful challenger to the incumbent district attorney in the November 1972 election.

It is difficult to pinpoint any direct impact of union efforts to influence the operation of the criminal justice system. One may feel, as we do, that the independence of the components of the criminal justice system is reduced when judges and district attorneys are elected with the aid of police-union support or when the police lobby to influence criminal statutes, but we cannot accurately describe the effects of this alleged reduced independence upon the handling and disposition of criminal cases. Similarly, several police unions have made threatening noises about "judicial leniency," but it is difficult to show how these union statements and activities have affected judicial handling of criminal cases.

In contrast, we can discern some indirect impact. By their statements and activities, the police organizations have informed the community that the police favor strict bonding, prosecuting, and sentencing practices and in general a "get tough" approach to the handling of criminal cases. On the one hand, these postures are supported by those segments of the community who are concerned about "law and order" and "crime in the streets." On the other hand, other segments of the community may see these police postures as being directed against them.

Other issues. We encountered a host of other law-enforcement-related issues and police-union involvement in them. In New York City the PBA opposed the creation, funding, and subpoena powers of the Knapp Commission and its investigations into police corruption. In Seattle the union went to court to block a new chief's use of polygraphs (lie detectors) in internal investigations of police corruption. The Seattle union also informally negotiated changes in the coroner's inquest system used when a civilian is killed by a police officer. The Boston patrolmen's union lobbied in the city council and state legislature to block a mayoral proposal to give traffic control duties to civilians, and the Buffalo union was instrumental in convincing city officials to abandon a 1968 plan to upgrade 475 civil defense auxiliary policemen to limited duty status (i.e., they would carry radios and nightsticks but would not have firearms or arrest powers).[20] The Buffalo union also opposed the establishment of minority-oriented, community-

474

peace-officer plan and stalled (but did not prevent) the introduction of a program whereby 61 officers would have off-duty use of squad cars in exchange for answering calls in their vicinity. In Rochester the union established a "truth squad" to monitor police-related news in the city papers (this effort was abandoned after one month),[21] attempted unsuccessfully to convince the state conference of police unions that officers should stop informing arrestees of their Miranda rights,[22] and attempted unsuccessfully to have a children's book that pictured police officers as pigs in blue uniforms removed from the public library.[23]

Police unions have also engaged directly in electoral politics on behalf of local candidates whom they perceived as ideologically compatible with rank-and-file law-enforcement interests. Some of the more publicized examples include police-union endorsement of or sympathy with such mayoral candidates as Sam Yorty in Los Angeles, Charles Stenvig in Minneapolis, Roman Gibbs in Detroit, Frank Rizzo in Philadelphia, and Louise Day Hicks in Boston. Police unions have also opposed candidates from whom they felt ideologically estranged: in Cleveland the unions were bitterly opposed to Mayor Carl Stokes; the New York City PBA was one of the few municipal unions that did not support Mayor John Lindsay's reelection efforts in 1969. Police unions have also supported city councilmen with whom they are ideologically compatible, including former police-union president Wayne Larkin's successful bid for a seat on the Seattle City Council. It is difficult to discern any direct impacts of these union electoral involvements, but an important indirect impact has been to increase the saliency of the "law and order" issue.

Summary

Because the individual issues over which conflict occurs in the area of law-enforcement policy tend to be viewed in isolation as single occurrences, often the underlying issues of control and authority are not articulated. In this section, we have attempted to relate the specific incidents to the larger policy context in which they might be viewed. Two major themes have emerged from this investigation. First, while the unions may not have been particularly successful in their frontal attacks on various aspects of law-enforcement policy, we should not overlook the impact of their actions on the minority communities and on the willingness of political officials to act in future situations. Second, as the reader reviews in his mind the types of actions undertaken by the unions, it becomes obvious that it was not the collective-bargaining process but rather the political arena which the unions exploited in their attempts to influence law-enforcement policy. We consider each of these themes briefly.

Direct vs. indirect impact. As one considers the direct victories by unions in the law-enforcement policy area, one is struck by the fact that they revolve around either one issue (civilian review) or two cities (Seattle and Boston). The list of unsuccessful efforts is much more impressive: the handling of civil disturbances, the judicial disposition of criminal cases, greater armament and more freedom to use it, the election of "law and order" politicians on any grand scale, influence on hiring standards, and so forth. For example, consider the efforts of the Detroit patrolmen's union: through its wives auxiliary it engaged in court-watching for six months; it attempted but failed to impeach a local black judge; it stalled the introduction of name tags (and flap holsters) until arbitrators ruled in support of the city's right to require them; it filed a lawsuit against a civil rights commission to force it to change its method of operation involving citizen complaints against the police; it spoke out against civilian review, including political candidates who supported the concept; it pressed for heavier armaments for street patrolmen; and it repeatedly espoused a "hard line" on law-enforcement issues. While the union scored no direct victories, the totality of its statements and actions created a clear picture about where it stood on civilian control, citizen identification, judicial disposition of criminal cases, and the use of force. Similar examples could be cited from other cities.

It is the overall impression left by the union's totality of behavior from which we draw our concern about the indirect impact of the union's efforts to influence the formulation of law-enforcement policy. While we cannot measure these results, we are concerned with the potential impact of overall union activity in causing city and police executives not to undertake certain programs and policies in anticipation of the union's reaction and the political costs attendant to the struggle—even if management believes it will ultimately prevail.

Secondly, we are concerned with the impact of the union's totality of behavior on police-community relations. Union positions on law-enforcement policy issues are frequently "hard line" or "get tough"—remove restrictions on the use of force, crack down on offenders, extinguish riots rather than contain them—and oriented toward maximizing rank-and-file discretion in the performance of their duties and insulating on-the-job behavior from civilian review, complaint systems, and identification.[24] While unions may have valid reasons for opposing civilian review and while each officer accused of a departmental or civilian indiscretion deserves a vigorous defense, the fact is that these union positions are perceived as hostile signs in the black community. Although the measurement of citizen attitudes toward police-union law-enforcement efforts was not within the scope of this study, our data (newspaper files and interview comments, especially from black officer association representatives) suggest that these union efforts had some negative impact on police minority-community relations in at least eleven cities: Boston, Buffalo, Cleveland, Detroit, Hartford, New York City, Omaha, Philadelphia, Pittsburgh, Rochester, and Seattle.

We caution strongly against ignoring these secondary consequences of union actions in the policy area, and we especially caution against underestimating the impact of a union on law-enforcement policy because the union has had few direct successes.

Collective bargaining and political action. Police union concern with proposals for civilian review boards and gun guidelines, with citizen complaint procedures and identification lineups, with judicial disposition of criminal cases, with managerial handling of civil disturbances, and with investigations of police corruption reflects very real rank-and-file police concern with actual or proposed changes in police working conditions. However, this concern usually cannot be translated into specific bargaining demands because these issues are not decided at the bargaining table. In contrast to the issues examined elsewhere in this study, most of which were resolved at the bargaining table, the resolution of the issues discussed here will remain political issues to be fought out in various political arenas.

In fact, the major factor that distinguishes the impact of police unions on law-enforcement policy formulation from their impact on the ability to manage is that the former would have occurred in the absence of collective-bargaining rights whereas much of the latter would not. Moreover, the changing constitutional climate with respect to the First Amendment rights of public employees, including free speech and participation in elective politics, has created an environment in which the already politicized police employee organizations have extended the range of their activities.[25]

Thus the testimonial dinner for a criminal court judge in Milwaukee, the New York City campaign against the civilian review board, and the visit of Vice-President Agnew to the prayer breakfast of a New York City police employee organization to praise the police and condemn opponents of law and order all would have occurred in the absence of collective bargaining. Similarly the activities of the line organizations in New York City in their attempts to block the Knapp Commission hearings into corruption (the attempts to block creation, funding, and subpoena power) all took place in the courts and the press outside the context of collective bargaining.

Public policy with respect to free speech and political action is unclear. For years, the celebrated dictum of Mr. Justice Holmes had been predominant: "The petitioner may have a constitutional right to talk politics, but he has no constitutional right to be a policeman."[26] This has been interpreted as limiting the rights of police officers to make critical public statements on policy issues and as limiting their participation in elective politics—the latter because of possible misuse of their unique power and station in the society. However, this position has recently been modified with respect to public-policy statements.

The ambivalence of public policy with respect to political participation is best seen in the sometimes tacit, sometimes overt encouragement by police executives of participation by employee organizations in legislative and elective political activity concerning larger appropriations for city government, salaries, retirement systems, and welfare benefits. Given this unofficial sanction and a functioning political organization, and given the leverage inherent in the public concern with law and order, it is not surprising that police employee organizations took advantage of their new constituency to move into elective political action and public statements on issues of law-enforcement policy even though local regulations may have prohibited both.

This expanded activity with respect to public statements was reinforced by the changing constitutional climate during the 1960s. In a line of cases from *New York Times Co. v. Sullivan* [376 U.S. 254 (1964)], through *Pickering v. Board of Education* [88 S.Ct. 1731 (1968)], the Court moved from a virtual prohibition of public employee rights to the exercise of critical speech to a standard which has been interpreted as allowing critical statements so long as they do not include knowing falsity, disclosure of confidential information, falsehood which would impair the operation of the agency, destruction of an effective superior-subordinate relationship, or adversely affect work relationships in the agency.[27]

An example of the extent to which we have moved from the Holmes' statement can be seen in the Maryland case, *Eugene C. Brukiewa v. Police Commissioner of Baltimore City* [257 Maryland 36, 263 A. 2d 210 (1970)]. Brukiewa, the president of the Baltimore police union, had made comments critical of the department and the commissioner on a local television program. He was suspended by the department's disciplinary board, which ruled that he had violated two departmental regulations relating to discussion of departmental business in public and criticism of superiors. A Baltimore City Court upheld the suspension on the grounds that the regulations cited were clear and unambiguous. The state appeals court overruled the city court on the grounds that the state did not show that the appellant's statements hurt or imperiled the discipline or operation of the police department and were, therefore, within his right to make under the First Amendment and the decisions of the Supreme Court.

Most of the activities we have discussed were a function of the unions' exercise of their political prerogatives. Whether these activities were legal or illegal is irrelevant; the fact that the unions are free to engage in such activities and the concomitant lack of official sanctions levied against them must be viewed as tacit approval consistent with the evolving climate just discussed. Finally, because of the numerous actors who participate in law-enforcement policy debates and the formulation of policy (judges, prosecutors, human-rights commissions, leaders from various segments of the community, elected officials, police management, police rank and file, etc.) and the fact that law-enforcement issues are decided in a variety of forums (the state legislature, the city council, the mayor's office, courtrooms and judicial chambers, the prosecutor's office, the station house, etc.), we suggest that most of the issues discussed in this section will remain political issues to be fought out in the political arena and are not likely to become included within the scope of collective bargaining in the short run.

Footnotes

1. We are indebted to Herman Goldstein for his discussions with us on policy generally and especially for his comments on earlier drafts of this chapter.
2. *New York Times*, 13 August 1968, p. 1. It also represented an attempt by Cassesse to co-opt the conservative dissatisfaction in the PBA.
3. *Boston Globe*, 15 August 1968.
4. *Baltimore Sun*, 17 April 1968.
5. The union was bitterly critical of city officials' use of "red vest" patrols of ghetto youths used to help calm the situation, for the police maintained that many of these youths also engaged in lawless behavior.
6. Fraternal Order of Police, Fort Pitt Lodge No. 1, *A Report: The Manchester Incident, June 21, 1970* (Pittsburgh: Fraternal Order of Police, 1970), esp. pp. 86-91.
7. Norton Long, "The City as Reservation," *The Public Interest* (Fall 1971), pp. 22-38.

8. The court found in favor of the police officer who resided outside the city but decided the case on such narrow grounds that it did not establish a precedent.
9. This occurred in Pittsburgh in 1968 when the city was having some difficulty finding qualified applicants. The union president proposed raising policy pay instead. See *Pittsburgh Press,* 5 June 1968. A union leader in another city, which had a residency requirement but which interviewees said was about to be eliminated, was ambivalent about the requirement's expected demise. On the one hand, his members are strongly in favor of its elimination, so he was not in a position to push for its retention. On the other hand, he believed the union would have reduced municipal political clout if substantial numbers of policemen moved out of the city, thus making his job more difficult.
10. See the *San Francisco Chronicle,* 6 January 1972, p. 1.
11. For a presentation of the PBA's position, see the statement by PBA President Robert McKiernan on the "op-ed" page of the *New York Times,* 7 February 1973, p. 39.
12. Figures on the assaults on police officers and the number of officers killed are available in the annual Federal Bureau of Investigation, *Crime in the United States, Uniform Crime Reports* (Washington, D.C.: United States Government Printing Office).
13. For a more detailed account of union efforts in Buffalo, Baltimore, and Philadelphia, see Stephen Halpern, "The Role of Police Employee Organizations in the Determination of Police Accountability Procedures in Baltimore, Philadelphia, and Buffalo," mimeo, State University of New York at Buffalo, 1972.
14. See the *Pittsburgh Press,* 6, 10, 11 June 1969.
15. For two examinations of relations between the police and the civilian community, see Skolnick, *Justice without Trial,* ch. 3; and Reiss, *The Police and the Public.*
16. *Omaha World-Herald,* 25 July 1971.
17. In 1970 the Seattle union endorsed a state supreme court candidate and a local superior court candidate, and in 1970 the Baltimore AFSCME local endorsed a municipal court candidate. Of these three, only the Seattle superior court candidate won at the polls.
18. Descriptions of these Pittsburgh efforts can be found in Ralph Hallow, "The Mayor is 'Nobody's Boy' " *Nation,* April 19, 1971, pp. 492-96; *Pittsburgh Post-Gazette,* 1, 22, and 26 October 1970.
19. See the *Pittsburgh Post-Gazette,* 13 March and 22 September 1971. These policemen were disciplined by departmental trial boards for receiving the money.
20. *Buffalo Evening News,* 6 January and 19 February 1968.
21. *Rochester Democrat and Chronicle,* 12 September 1970.
22. *Rochester Democrat and Chronicle,* 18 April 1968.
23. *Rochester Democrat and Chronicle,* 18 January and 28 May 1971. The book in question was *Sylvester and the Magic Pebble* by William Steig.
24. What we referred to earlier as the quest for professional status.
25. For a discussion of the political activites of social and fraternal organizations who were the predecessors of the current employee organizations, see Chapter 2 of the authors' original work [editors].
26. *McAuliffe v. City of New Bedford,* 155 Mass. 216, 220, 29 N.E. 519 (1892).
27. From a legal point of view: "The First Amendment and Public Employees: *Time* Marches On," 57 *Georgetown Law Review* 134 (1968). From an operational point of view: Anthony Mondello, "The Federal Employee's Right to Speak," *Civil Service Journal* (January-March, 1970), pp. 16-21.

Change and Continuity: The Role of a Labor-Management Committee in Facilitating Work Force Change During Retrenchment

Robert B. McKersie, Leonard Greenhalgh, and Todd Jick*

The tension between change and continuity is likely to be the central dilemma in labor-managment relations in the 1980s. Change is required if organizations are to prosper in increasingly competitive world markets, take advantage of new technology, or streamline operations in a declining niche. At the same time, continuity of employment is a goal that workers and their union representatives are embracing with increasing vigor: the old maxim that job loss is "one of the breaks of the game" is no longer acceptable (McKersie, Greenhalgh and Jick, 1980).

The purpose of this paper is to outline the experience of one program that reconciled the tension so that change and continuity could occur in a mutually reinforcing way. The change occurred as the State of New York phased out some of its programs and in response to fiscal constraints, cut back some others. As a result of these changes, continuity of employment was at stake for the state's more than 150,000 workers. The reconciliation was accomplished through the innovative work of a joint labor-management committee. The committee conducted research to assess impacts, needs, and pilot programs; developed and implemented reemployment programs for workers displaced prior to formation of the committee; and evolved policies and procedures for handling program shifts in ways that avoid the dysfunctions that arise when employment changes are poorly executed.

Origin of the Committee

The State of New York had been a stable employer from the 1930s through the 1960s. The early 1970s, however, saw a reversal of this trend whereby more than 10,000 employees had been laid off by 1976. The history of stability was a double-edged sword. First, the cuts suddenly and dramatically violated expectations of job security held by state workers, many of whom had self-selected into state employment because of the security it traditionally offered (Hall and Schneider, 1972; Hanlon, 1979; Schuster, 1974). Second, the years of stability had provided state decisionmakers with little experience in reducing its work force, so that when the cuts came, they were handled with little consideration of the impact on employees.

As a result of these factors, membership pressure on the unions grew dramatically. The major public sector union, the Civil Service Employees Association (CSEA)[1] entered the 1976 negotiations willing to fight hard for a

---

*Sloan School of Management, MIT: Amos Tuck School of Business, Dartmouth College and Faculty of Administrative Studies, York University, respectively. Reprinted from *Industrial Relations*, Vol. 20 (1981).

prohibition of future layoffs.[2] The chief negotiator for the state, Donald Wollett, was familiar with the work of the Armour Automation Committee which had experienced some success in cushioning the impact of major change in the meat packing industry (see Schultz and Weber, 1966). He advanced a counter proposal involving six months advance notice and establishment of a Continuity of Employment Committee, to which the union eventually agreed. The committee's three-year mandate, provided in the 1976 contract, was to:

(a) Study worker displacement problems arising from economy RIFs, programmatic reductions and curtailments, closedowns, relocations, consolidations, technological changes, and contracting out; and

(b) Make recommendations for the solution of these problems, including but not limited to the use of normal and induced attrition (e.g., early retirements), sharing of available State job opportunities (e.g., transfers), indemnification (e.g., severance pay), and transition to work in the labor market beyond State employment (e.g., retraining).

To indicate that it meant business, the state agreed to appropriate $1 million for the work of the committee. As will be seen below this money became a key factor for success, for it enabled the committee to buy its way into demonstration projects and provided seed money for the establishment of special programs within existing agencies. Since the rank and file quickly dubbed the committee "the million dollar operation," the money also put pressure on the committee to develop programs that would benefit workers who had been on layoff and to initiate visible preventative programs for those who might be subject to layoff in the future.

Formation of the Committee

The committee began operations in the fall of 1976, with the appointment of representatives. The president of CSEA nominated five vice presidents, representing different regions. These individuals brought status from the union side as well as an independence, since each of them was an elected official in his region. Management representatives were drawn from the middle ranks: the civil service department, the office of employee relations, the division of the budget, one of the mental health agencies, and the department of education.[3]

Early in its operation, the committee agreed upon a number of ground rules, which stood the test of time over the three-year period. First, all decisions would be taken only after full discussion and consensus by all members of the committee. This meant that each member was in a position to stop a decision until the individual felt comfortable with the proposal. Second, the work of the committee was viewed as parallel to the adversary process of collective bargaining. Recommendations were to be submitted to the principals, that is, the director of the office of employee relations and the president of the CSEA, and through their roles brought to the bargaining table or implemented by executive orders.

The most important ground rule involved what the committee members came to call the "black box" understanding; namely, the committee would concern itself with the impact of a specific program change on workers and not with the rationale for the program change itself. For example, the union strongly opposed the state's deinstitutionalization program[4] in other forums— yet, the committee agreed that the union's concern with the policy itself would not affect the design and implementation of contingent programs to help mental health care workers who would be displaced by deinstitutionalization. At times it became difficult to hold to this separation of the policy rationale from the consequences of the policy, since by dealing with the consequences it appeared to some rank and file that the committee was assenting to the policy itself. Nevertheless, this principle made it possible for the committee to move ahead with its program of assistance and protection and shielded it from the conflict that would have been inherent in discussing the appropriateness of the changes sought by the state.

Finally, the committee agreed that it would try to utilize existing state agencies and incorporate its ideas and programs within the existing agencies of the state rather than using its funds to establish a new and separate office.

Impact of Layoffs

The first task undertaken by the committee's research staff was an analysis of the layoffs that had occurred over the preceding six years to determine the extent and nature of needs to be addressed. The general picture that emerged indicated that about 10,000 individuals had been laid off with heavy concentrations occurring in the drug abuse agency and in the several mental health agencies. The heaviest hit area of the state was New York City. Females were underrepresented in the layoff group; whereas they comprised 44 percent of state employment, they accounted for 32 percent of those laid off. The reverse was true of minorities; whereas they represented approximately 10 percent of state employment, they accounted for almost 20 percent of those laid off. This pattern is explained largely by the sharp cutback in the state's drug abuse program; drug abuse officers were predominantly minority males.

For individual workers, the severity of the layoff experience ranged over the spectrum. Approximately 35 percent of those affected experienced a "technical layoff" that involved virtually no unemployment; these employees left one agency or title of work to be quickly reemployed by the state in another position. Another 45 percent were soon recalled to state employment, usually to the same or better pay grade than they had prior to the layoff. The remaining 20 percent were unemployed for an average of 24 weeks.

The research work also assessed noneconomic consequences of layoff for state workers. Through questionnaires and a large number of face-to-face interviews, it became clear that many individuals had experienced considerable stress as a result of the layoff experience. Particularly hard hit was a group of semi-professional employees in the drug abuse agency. This agency had come into being in the 1960s and had expanded rapidly, making it possible for individuals with associate degrees in counseling and narcotic control to advance rapidly into important positions of responsibility. Many of these individuals had salaries in the range of $15-20,000 and had bought homes and had been enjoying the other appurtenances of middle-class living when the cutbacks occurred. Having assumed—like so many state employees—that their jobs were secure, they were unprepared for the shock of job loss and the ensuing uncertainty of finding alternative employment. The result was widespread stress-induced illness (Greenhalgh and Jick, 1978) and alcohol abuse; two suicides also occurred.

State agencies as well as individuals experienced adverse effects arising from layoffs—specifically, in the form of impaired organizational effectiveness. This phenomenon occurred with sufficient regularity that the general pattern can be described as follows. The shock of actual or rumored layoffs generates a ripple effect that diffuses throughout the organization. Insecure employees react by engaging in dysfunctional behaviors. For example, there is a rise in the turnover rate that is correlated with impaired job security. Worse, it is the higher-quality and harder-to-replace workers who are the first to leave (Greenhalgh and Jick, 1979). Subsequent understaffing leads to greater costs of overtime and disrupted teamwork. Those that remain behind are often withdrawn and demoralized, and tend to put in the least effort that is acceptable.

The prospect of reduced effectiveness of state service delivery was recognized by the committee and its staff as a persuasive point, one that could be used in overcoming the resistance of the state system to adopting the committee's policies and programs. More specifically, since initial field research suggested that layoffs created costs for the state that might offset much of the presumed savings, systematic research was undertaken to estimate these costs (see Greenhalgh, 1978; Greenhalgh and McKersie, in press). The research was designed to enable state decisionmakers to draw conclusions about the relative cost effectiveness of the two principal alternatives for reducing a work force—layoff versus attrition.

As a result, it was ascertained that attrition could be a practical alternative to layoff. Since the typical layoff had involved only a small reduction relative to the size of the work force in a particular agency, an attrition program—for example, imposing a selective hiring freeze—could accomplish the same overall reduction after a transition period of less than a year in all but a few cases. Beyond the transition period, the savings from the reduced payroll size would be equal whichever strategy is chosen.

There are several costs that arise when the layoff strategy is chosen over the attrition strategy. The layoff strategy incurs the substantial costs of unemployment insurance chargebacks. These do not accrue to an employer using the attrition approach, wherein workers leave voluntarily; the costs accrue only when workers are laid off. Other incremental costs of the layoff strategy result from the effects of job insecurity that pervades an organization for a long time following the first rumors of layoffs. The drop in productivity noted earlier can be measured in cost terms, as can increased turnover and its multiple consequences. Furthermore, agencies experience increased alcoholism, grievances, and law suits contesting layoffs. Perhaps worst of all, job insecurity can engender resistance to change; thus ironically, the planned reorganizations that gave rise to the layoffs become much more difficult to introduce successfully.

When dollar amounts are attached to these factors, the cost effectiveness of layoff and attrition can be compared. For the typical work force reduction situation, layoffs do not prove to be cost effective. In fact, there is a difference in favor of attrition sufficiently large to justify an investment of almost $1,000 per surplus worker for programs to induce redeployment through retraining and relocation. In sum, the cost effectiveness study indicated a need for the committee to develop policies, guidelines and legislation so that the layoff strategy would be used as a last resort rather than as standard operating procedure.

Readjustment Programs

The research had identified a group of 1200 individuals as potentially in need of the committee's assistance. Approximately 500 (i.e., 5 percent of the total) had been laid off in the early 1970s and never recalled to state service. The other 700 had regained employment, but at lower salary levels. This combined group became a target clientele for the development of a number of readjustment programs operated by the committee during the first year of its work.

The first step was establishment of a special Continuity of Employment Center to provide counselling and referral services to the target group. Most laid off employees had expressed a strong desire to return to work with the state (primarily because of fringe benefits, especially pensions) — thus, it was natural to locate the center in the state's civil service department which had the best information about employment opportunities throughout the state system.

Next, all members of the target group were contacted and asked to complete a skills inventory profile. The existing civil service recall procedure had used only past state job titles to determine skills to be matched to openings. The profile was designed to broaden possibilities for matching by considering skills acquired through training programs and non-state jobs.

Members of the target group were then contacted by circulars when openings developed, and many came to the center to be interviewed and counselled about opportunities for reinstatement. In addition, several retraining programs were instituted to allow for reemployment into new careers. To give one example, with funds from the committee, a training program was established to retrain a group of laid-off meat inspectors to become fruit inspectors. Half a dozen such programs serving about 100 individuals were implemented on a pilot basis by the center, with development, funding and evaluation provided by the committee and its staff.

The committee also instituted, in cooperation with the state department of labor, an outplacement program, which sought to open up opportunities in the private sector for those still unemployed. Money was allocated on a pilot basis to enable individuals to enroll in training programs, to search for employment elsewhere within or even outside of the state, and to subsidize private industry for wages paid during the break-in period for the new workers. Only a handful availed themselves of the program, however, confirming the point revealed in interviews that very few individuals were interested in working in the private sector. Indeed, out of the original 10,000 affected, only about 5 per cent moved to employment in the private sector.

484

On the basis of this experience, the efforts of the readjustment center were subsequently refocused almost exclusively on finding employment for the job losers within the state system.

Overall, the work of the center and the readjustment activities more generally must be viewed as only minimally effective. Only about 10 percent of the target group benefited in any measurable way. One reason for the low yield involved the fact that the target group, after all, was "residual" in the sense that they had been passed up by potential state hiring agencies because of their unwanted skills or perhaps marginal performance records.

Policy Development and Recommendations

Having gone about as far as it could in reemploying those who continued to be disadvantaged as a result of layoffs, the committee turned its attention to formulating proposals for achieving program changes without layoffs. The union representatives on the committee advocated a guarantee of no layoffs for state employees, but the management representatives resisted it, knowing that such a policy would not be acceptable to top state officials since it would be too constraining in certain situations.

The compromise that developed involved the principle of "one employment alternative." The concept involved offering each surplus employee a reasonable alternative for remaining employed with the state. An alternative would be reasonable if it were in the same general pay range and commuting area. Access to a retraining program would constitute an offer. The worker would be free to refuse the offer and be laid off without losing any of the layoff/recall rights provided by state law, and without prejudicing eligibility to draw unemployment compensation.

Since the fall of 1978, when the committee submitted its unanimous recommendation for the avoidance of layoffs through the employment alternative concept, the state has laid off only a handful of employees on an involuntary basis. While the state has not adopted the policy in any formal sense (the executive branch has said that it did not want to tie its hands to the commitment of providing an employment alternative in all cases) this guideline has nevertheless been followed in the closing down of a number of programs and establishments involving several thousand workers.

The committee also advanced several accompanying recommendations that would be needed in the successful implementation of an employment alternative program. First, it would be essential for work force planning to take place on a centralized basis so that workers who were scheduled for displacement could be matched to openings that were available or projected. Consequently, the committee recommended that human resource planning be institutionalized in parallel with financial and program planning conducted by the division of the budget.

Another recommendation involved the provision of lead time. Based on several research studies the committee recommended that the state provide advance notice of three months before individuals would be displaced. Three months would allow sufficient time for arranging the employment alternative but would not be excessively long, as was the case with the six months' advance notice. The latter had been instituted for a one year experimental period, and then not renewed. It had been found that six months notice created so much slack that pilferage and other counter-productive behavior developed.

The Gouverneur Demonstration Project

The committee had made the case that the layoff strategy was not cost effective and that an array of viable techniques was available for managing work force reductions. A task remaining was to show by a demonstration project that with sufficient lead time, cooperation of the potential employing agencies, and resolution of local labor-management conflict, it should be possible to close down a facility and redeploy all the workers involved to other positions within state employment. The site that was chosen for the test was the Gouverneur Unit, operated by the Office of Mental Retardation in Lower Manhattan. This small facility had been slated to close for some time: as part of the overall program of deinstitutionalization, the state desired to move the patients to other care arrangements; furthermore, the building has been condemned. However, the union, opposed in principle to deinstitutionalization, had publicly indicated that it would fight the decision to close the facility with every means at its disposal. Into this bitter conflict walked the committee.

Starting first at the level of the state-wide committee, meetings were held with key representatives from the agency, the governor's office, the top staff of CSEA, and the Division of the Budget. A document was prepared by the committee that oulined the principles mentioned above for continuity of employment and commitment was secured that the various parties would cooperate with the demonstration project. For the Division of the Budget this meant agreeing to a phase-out timetable that would incur additional labor (i.e., "holding") costs. For the Office of Mental Retardation it meant exerting influence on the administrators of other units within the agency to accept displaced employees on a transfer basis. For the union, it meant "holding its fire" on the short-term question of deinstitutionalization and giving the project a chance—in order to see if it would be possible for the workers involved to continue employment without being subjected to layoff, thus providing potential long-term benefits for union members.

To summarize a complex stream of events, the project succeeded. All 300 workers were redeployed, many of them to other units in Manhattan operated by the Office of Mental Retardation. A local-level labor-management committee functioned very effectively in settling individual problems that inevitably arise in establishing seniority lists and transfer opportunities. A staff member from the state-wide committee chaired the local committee and provided the impetus for moving the project ahead.

Two previously laid-off employees, who had worked as counselors for the drug abuse agency, were recalled to serve as counselors for the project. In effect, they were the outreach arm for the Continuity of Employment Center. They performed the invaluable function of meeting regularly with the displaced workers, outlining options and helping them make intelligent choices.

In an effort to evaluate the effectiveness of the Gouverneur redeployment program, the staff conducted research to determine whether the

486

program had successfully avoided the dysfunctional consequences of job insecurity that had been measured at agencies where the layoff strategy had been used. The results were very encouraging. Job security itself was significantly higher among Gouverneur employees who were provided opportunities for continued employment. In addition, their productivity was higher and their propensity to quit the organization lower. Since the effects on productivity and turnover were the major costs associated with layoff-induced job insecurity, the Governeur redeployment program was judged a success (see Greenhalgh, 1980).

Work Force Planning

Although the Gouverneur demonstration project showed that a workable technology did exist for achieving a work force reduction without layoffs, it involved the closing of only a small organizational subunit. A question remained as to the applicability of this approach to large-scale program change. Thus the committee welcomed the opportunity that arose with a request from the state legislature to examine work force changes in the mental health agencies of the state. At this point in the history of deinstitutionalization, CSEA found itself ready to modify its opposition if it could be assured that program changes would take place without forcing its members out of the state system. The study, therefore, was undertaken by the committee's staff.

The study concluded that over a projected five-year period, depending on the rate at which deinstitutionalization took place, anywhere from 5,000 to 15,000 state workers might be displaced. However, by instituting an attrition program, the number of workers who would be in excess could be reduced to well under 1,000, and if a geographical transfer program were utilized, all displaced workers could be accommodated. While the overall conclusion was encouraging, a number of practical problems remained. For example, attrition rates in the Adirondack counties were far lower than those in the New York City Metropolitan area. Consequently, to achieve overall system balance it would be necessary to induce some employees from upstate counties to transfer to downstate counties, which would meet with resistance. Further, the attrition program with its attendant hiring freeze would have to be modified for some occupations where turnover would be higher than required and where it would be impossible to retrain people within the system to fill these openings: doctors and other high-demand occupations would be the examples. While a number of ramifications remained to be worked out in implementing program changes without layoffs, the work force planning exercise demonstrated to the legislature and to the executive branch that, with sufficient lead time and with proper staff work, it should be possible to achieve even major program changes as well as a successful redeployment of the personnel involved.

Overall Results

From the inception of the committee in 1976 through the end of its first phase of work in the summer of 1979, no massive layoffs of New York State employees took place. Moreover, the state subsequently adopted attrition programs as standard operating procedure for work force reductions.[5] Thus, in a very important sense, the work and thinking of the committee had been adopted by the decision makers within the executive branch of the state.

At the level of individual agencies, the concept of bringing about change without layoff had also been institutionalized to some extent. For example, during the summer of 1979, the remaining institutions of the drug abuse agency were phased out with virtually no involuntary layoffs. Moreover, this redeployment of personnel took place under the auspices of the industrial relations personnel in the agency, without the assistance of the committee. The transition program did not run as smoothly as Gouverneur, where a local labor-management committee solved implementation issues. Nevertheless, the agency did consult with the representatives of the union, and the handling of the phaseout emphasized a concern for the job security of the workers involved that was far different from that present in the early and mid 1970s.

During the period 1976-1979, at least half a dozen other program changes took place within state agencies that involved the redeployment of several hundred personnel. For most of these program changes the Continuity of Employment Center within the civil service department provided important support services. Staff counselors were dispatched to the sites to assist in the readjustment efforts. In addition, the data bank capabilities of the central office in Albany were utilized to help match individuals to openings in other state agencies.

In the longer run, the center will house two separate functional units.[6] First, intraorganizational transfer will be facilitated by a computerized information system programmed to match available personnel to position openings. Second, an expanded range of services will be provided. These services will include: employee assessment assistance in the form of career counselling, resume preparation, and development of interview skills; increased employability through retraining, job search grants, relocation allowances, on-the-job training wage reimbursement; and outplacement assistance with public and private sector employers. In practice, these units will be tightly integrated so as to facilitate the systematic progression of employees toward reemployment.

Lessons from the Continuity of Employment Committee

Several points stand out in retrospect. First, it is extremely important in bringing about a fundamental change in the thinking and approach of any large organization for the intervention entity to have "buying power." Part of this was supplied by the $1 million allocation, which enabled the committee to encourage agencies to undertake new functions by supplementing budgets with seed money. All changes require start-up funds, and the presumption was that after the test period the agency would be able to carry forward on its own out of existing funds or seek additional funds from the legislature for new levels of activity.

Support from the executive branch also became extremely important in securing the cooperation of agencies with a program of employment continuity for state workers. This was illustrated during the Gouverneur project, when it became necessary to invoke the prestige of the Governor's Office to encourage various agencies to accept displaced employees.

Another lesson learned was that civil service departments do not think of themselves as personnel agencies—on the contrary, they emphasize almost exclusively the standard functions of classification and appeal. Hence, it took considerable time and effort to reorient the thinking of key people in the state to the need for a "hands on" personnel function that would view the work force as more than a static factor, i.e., would view it as a human resource to be developed and effectively redeployed.

Finally, this project illustrates the important positive interaction between labor-management cooperation, demonstration projects, research analyses, policy recommendations and basic changes in the thinking and practice of governmental agencies.

Footnotes

1. At the time of the 1976 negotiations, CSEA was an independent union. In April 1978 it affiliated with the American Federation of State, County and Municipal Employees Union (AFSCME).
2. A minority of the state's work force was represented by AFSCME during this period, but no arrangement similar to the State-CSEA Continuity of Employment Committee existed for those workers.
3. The first author of this article was selected as neutral chairman of the committee. The other two authors directed the committee's fulltime professional staff.
4. The deinstitutionalization program involved a change in patient care from residential, institution-based to outpatient, community-based services.
5. The state experienced some operational difficulties in its early experience with attrition programs. In some cases, the result of a straight hiring freeze resulted in the work force shrinking faster than was projected. Some administrators compensated for this with overtime, which was costly and further increased the attrition rate.

References

DeAngelo, Charles. *Developing an Employment Readjustment System in Response to Layoffs in New York State Government: A Case Study*. Unpublished M.S. thesis, Cornell University, 1978.

Greenhalgh, Leonard, *A Cost-Benefit Balance Sheet for Evaluating Layoffs as a Policy Strategy*. Ithaca, N.Y.: New York State School of Industrial and Labor Relations, Cornell University, 1978.

Greenhalgh, Leonard. "Maintaining Organizational Effectiveness During Organizational Retrenchment." Working paper, Amos Tuck School of Business Administration, Dartmouth College, 1980.

Greenhalgh, Leonard, and Todd Jick. "The Relationship Between Job Security and Turnover, and Its Differential Effect on Employee Quality Level." Paper presented at the annual meeting of the Academy of Management, Atlanta, August 1979.

Greenhalgh, Leonard, and Todd Jick. *The Closing of Urban State Agencies: Impact on Employee Attitudes*. Ithaca, N.Y.: Continuity of Employment Research, New York State School of Industrial and Labor Relations, Cornell University, 1978.

Greenhalgh, Leonard, and Robert McKersie. "Cost Effectiveness of Alternative Strategies for Cutback Management." *Public Administration Review*, in press.

Hall, Douglas, and Benjamin Schneider. "Correlates of Organizational Identification as a Function of Career Pattern and Organizational Type." *Administrative Science Quarterly*, XVII (September, 1972), 340-350.

Hanlon, Martin, *Primary Groups and Unemployment.* Unpublished Ph.D. dissertation, Columbia University, 1979.

McKersie, Robert, Leonard Greenhalgh, and Todd Jick. "Economic Progress and Economic Dislocation." Working paper, Sloan School of Management, M.I.T., 1980.

Schultz, George, and Arnold Weber, *Strategies for Displaced Workers.* New York Harper & Row, 1966.

Schuster, Jay. "Management-Compensation Policy and the Public Interest." *Public Personnel Management,* III (November-December, 1974), 510-523.

The Boston Teachers Union and the Desegregation Process

Harry C. Katz*

Introduction

Extensive steps were taken in the 1970s in an effort to desegregate the nation's public school systems.[1] In contrast to early efforts at desegregation, in the 1970s desegregation occurred when most public school teachers were members of well established unions. Consequently, an understanding of the desegregation experience in the 1970s must consider how teacher union policies responded to and, in turn, affected the desegregation process.

This paper traces the interaction between the policies of the Boston Teachers Union (BTU) and the desegregation of the Boston public schools.[2] This case study illustrates how the process of pursuing the social objective of desegregation affects (and is affected by) a number of key aspects of the labor-management relationship such as (1) recruitment and hiring policies; (2) layoff and transfer policies; (3) the role of seniority versus affirmative action; (4) internal union politics; and (5) the relationships between the union, the courts, the school department, and various community groups. Events in Boston take place within the context of fiscal austerity and declining school enrollments. Therefore, the issue of job security looms behind the entire process. Since these pressures and problems are common to many urban school districts, the experiences in Boston to date are likely to be indicative of what other parties are confronting or will confront in the years ahead.

---

*Sloan School of Management and Department of Economics, Massachusetts Institute of Technology. The author gratefully acknowledges helpful comments on earlier drafts of this paper from Henry Farber, Robert McKersie, Charles Myers, Paul Osterman, Peter Temin and Thomas Kochan. This paper was written especially for this volume.

The Court Ordered Desegregation Plan

On June 21, 1974, Judge W. Arthur Garrity, Jr. of the First Circuit Court of Appeals found that the Boston School Committee had unconstitutionally fostered and maintained a segregated public school system.[3] That court decision arose out of a suit filed by the NAACP on behalf of black school children and followed investigations by the Federal Department of Health, Education and Welfare. Judge Garrity concluded that through an array of policies the Boston School Committee had fostered segregation and had actively worked to avoid enforcement of the Racial Imbalance Act of the State of Massachusetts. Through feeder patterns, and enrollment and transfer policies two subsystems had been created in the Boston schools. One subsystem was 71% non-white and the other 76% white. The very existence of such subsystems made voluntary desegregation efforts difficult. In addition, the court concluded that the use and location of school facilities were designed to promote segregation.

Faced with the complicated task of implementing desegregation, the court found it necessary to order a remedial desegregation plan that involved three phases. In the face of the short period of time that remained between the court's initial June ruling and the start of the upcoming school year in September, the court ordered that the first phase of desegregation (to take effect in September 1974) involve the implementation of an existing state "redistricting" plan originally designed to bring Boston schools in compliance with the state's Racial Imbalance Act. Judge Garrity then ordered the Boston School Committee to develop a full plan to desegregate the Boston schools. The School Committee failed to submit to the court a comprehensive desegregation plan and thereby thrust the design of desegregation back into the hands of the Federal Court. Judge Garrity, with the guidance of an appointed panel of experts, designed an extensive desegregation plan (Phase II) to be implemented starting in the fall of 1975. In the spring of 1976 the desegregation plan was modified further by the court in what came to be known as the third phase (Phase II-B) of the desegregation effort.

The complete desegregation plan included new community school districts, citywide magnet schools, and the busing of school children. In addition, various councils of parents, teachers, and school officials were established by the court to monitor compliance with the court orders and facilitate community involvement in the desegregation process. At times throughout the desegregation process, these various councils clashed with one another or with other participants within the school systems. Later, we discuss a recent dispute that emerged between parents and teachers. Although Judge Garrity has suggested that he would like to completely return administrative responsibility to the Boston School Committee, as of the winter of 1981 the court was still continuously involved in insuring compliance with its orders.

The BTU was not pleased with the desegregation effort. Early on the BTU had expressed its opposition to the state "redistricting plan" which had been designed to bring Boston schools in conformance with the 1965 State Racial Imbalance Act (that redistricting plan was later implemented as Phase I of Judge Garrity's desegregation order). The union, like many teachers in the school system, was unsympathetic to charges that the school system was blatantly discriminatory and required major restructuring to set it right. In addition, the BTU argued that reorganization of the school system would be "too educationally disruptive."[4] Instead, the union favored an expanded program of magnet schools and voluntary transfers.

The BTU was particularly upset about the large number of teacher transfers and reassignments that were produced by desegregation. These transfers and reassignments followed the creation of new schools, the closing of a number of schools, and large scale reorganizations of within-school programs which were all part of the desegregation plan. The Boston Teachers Union estimates that from one to two-thousand teachers were transferred as part of desegregation. To facilitate those transfers, the court felt it necessary to overrule existing language in the collective bargaining agreement between the Boston School Committee and the teachers' union which regulated transfer rights. The court argued that both the speed and the magnitude of the transfers precluded the use of the elaborate bidding and rating transfer procedures outlined in the collective bargaining agreement.

Once court-ordered desegregation had begun the BTU repeatedly petitioned Judge Garrity for relief from extensive teacher transfers and reassignments.[5] The teachers' union protested that mandatory transfers violated the placement rights teachers had accumulated through years of service. The union also petitioned for a delay in the implementation of the additional phases of Judge Garrity's desegregation plan.

The union's complaint against the desegregation plan involved procedural as well as substantive issues. The BTU adamantly protested the process by which the court overruled parts of the existing collective bargaining agreement between the union and the School Committee. The union had another procedural complaint as well, namely, the union's limited involvement in the *design* of the desegregation plan. Having grown accustomed to negotiating with the School Committee over policy changes that affected personnel, the union was upset by the court's control of decision-making authority. Of course, the union's procedural and substantive complaints were interrelated. The union wanted a more active voice in desegregation so as to influence the decisions being made.

By the fall of 1977, the bulk of the restructuring of school programs and boundaries initiated by Judge Garrity's orders had been completed. From that point on, the aspect of the desegregation process which precipitated the most heated response from the BTU was Judge Garrity's effort to provide greater racial balance in the teaching staff of the Boston school system. To induce change in the racial composition of the faculty, Judge Garrity issued a number of "hiring orders." Judge Garrity's hiring orders initially may have appeared to be only an incidental part of his complete desegregation orders. Yet, those orders have had important consequences for the teachers' union and the school system as a whole. A review of the history of those hiring orders, to which we now turn, will provide a background for our analysis of the union's response to those orders.

Judge Garrity's initial hiring order of July 31, 1974 included a number of components. The order set out as a goal that black teachers comprise 20% of all teachers in the Boston public school system.[6] In the 1973-74 school year black teachers made up 7.1% of the total. To attain the 20% figure, Judge Garrity ordered that the school system hire one black teacher for each new white teacher hired, to the extent that qualified black candidates were available. In addition, Judge Garrity ordered the immediate hiring of 280 new permanent black teachers. Implementation of that part of the order alone increased the percentage of black teachers in the system from 7.1% to 10.7%.

The judge also outlined procedures the school department should follow in order to recruit additional black faculty (such as appointing three black recruiters). To assist in monitoring compliance with its orders, the court required the preparation of long range recruitment plans and periodic reports describing recruitment efforts and hiring figures.

The School Department's Response

The school department complied with Judge Garrity's order to hire 280 new permanent black teachers for the 1974-75 school year, but then proceeded to dramatically alter its hiring policies. From September 1975 on, the Boston school department continued to hire a number of new teachers, but only hired new teachers on a *provisional* basis (one year contracts) and discontinued the hiring of teachers on a *permanent* contractual basis.[7]

The motives behind this switch in hiring policy are not clear. A substantial degree of uncertainty surrounded enrollment levels and the future course of court mandates. In the face of that uncertainty, the school department may have looked to the employment of provisional teachers as a device to deal with uncertain and changing manning requirements. In addition, school officials may have turned to provisional teachers as a cost-cutting device. Provisional teachers enter at lower salary levels and receive fewer fringe benefits than permanent hires.[8] In this way, the hiring of provisional teachers may reflect the "price responsiveness" of school officials who look to provisional teachers as a cheaper source of labor than permanent teachers whose price (wage) had been raised by gains won in collective bargaining.[9] But, the school department rehired many of the provisional teachers year after year and lost some of these economic benefits when an arbitrator ruled that in conformance with state law a provisional teacher (like a permanent teacher) acquires tenure and many of its accompanying benefits after working in the system for three consecutive years.

An alternative motive for the school department's policy may have been that it provided a way in which the school department could avoid the hiring of blacks. In his January 28, 1975 hiring order Judge Garrity included a provision that allowed the school department to rehire any provisional teacher employed the year before and not be bound in such rehiring by the one black for each white requirement. The Judge later lamented the consequences of the exception and subsequently amended his hiring order as the school department continually hired white provisional teachers. In the interim, that rehiring policy and the difficulties the school department allegedly encountered in recruiting qualified blacks led to slow progress in meeting the court's goal of a 20% black teacher workforce. As of the 1975-76 school year the percentage of black teachers stood at 11.4% (it was 10.4% in 1974-75) and rose to 15.6% by 1978-79.[10]

Table 1 reports the racial composition and the date of hire of the provisional teachers employed in the 1978-79 school year. These figures illustrate that it was not until 1977-78 that the school department actually attained the spirit of Judge Garrity's one for one hiring rule. It is also important to note the sizeable number of provisional teachers that were hired from 1975 on. Remember, this hiring occurred when the school department was no longer hiring new permanent teachers and the number of permanent teachers in the school system steadily declined through attrition. The total number of teachers in the Boston system has declined from 5443 in the 1975-76 school year to 5187 in 1978-79.[11]

Whatever the motives for the school department's shift to the hiring of provisional rather than permanent teachers, the *exclusive* hiring of new teachers on a provisional basis could not have helped the school department's efforts to recruit black teachers. Much of this recruitment activity involved trying to encourage black teachers to shift into the Boston system from other school systems in the Boston metropolitan area or from school systems in more distant locations. The absence of new *permanent* teacher contracts must have made this already difficult task more difficult.

Frustrated by the school system's slow progress in increasing the number of black teachers, Judge Garrity modified his hiring orders further on July 5, 1978. The new orders mandated that except for the rehiring of third year provisional teachers, all hiring and rehiring of teachers be done on a basis of one black for one white until in each school year there is a 1½% increase in the percentage of black teachers in the school system. The court thereby blocked the school department's policy of continually rehiring a dispro-portionate number of white provisional teachers.

With system-wide black employment at 15.5% of the total employment in the 1978-79 school year, if the school system only met the 1½% per year minimum, it would take three years until the court's goal of 20% black employment was attained. In its new orders the court rejected motions entered by the plaintiffs in the desegregation case to either grant existing

TABLE 1
Breakdown of White, Black and Other Minority Provisional Teachers Employed in 1978-79

Year First Hired	Black	White	Other Minority	Total
1978-79	207	61	66	334
1977-78	75	72	31	178
1976-77	58	138	49	245
1975-76*	81	185	36	302
Totals	421	456	182	1059

*Provisional teachers with more than three years of continuous service acquire permanent status and tenure.

From "Report of the Numbers of White, Black, and Other Minority Permanent and Acting Administrators," School Committee of Boston, March 14, 1979, Table ii.

black provisional teachers "super-seniority" in future hiring decisions or mandate the immediate awarding of tenure to black provisional teachers who had completed at least one year's teaching experience in the Boston system.[12]

Judge Garrity's refusal to grant black teachers "super-seniority" is consistent with some court decisions in related cases. For example, adhering to a seniority clause, in 1976, the city of Cincinnati laid off newly hired black firemen. A federal court then upheld those layoffs even though the layoffs jeopardized satisfaction of a consent decree which included minority employment goals for Cincinnati's fire department.[13]

The BTU's Response

As an interested party, the Boston Teachers Union submitted a response to the plaintiff's motion which preceded Judge Garrity's revised hiring order of July 5, 1978.[14] In that response the union adamantly expressed its opposition to "any order which gives preferential treatment to black provisional teachers."[15] Instead, the union recommended strict adherence to the seniority principle as the guideline for appointments and layoffs.

In the face of increased minority representation among teachers, the BTU's attitudes toward Judge Garrity's hiring orders did not go unchallenged within the union. After hearing a report concerning the plaintiff's motion and the official union response to that motion, in a general meeting union members voted to establish a special committee to formulate a positive BTU position on minority hiring to be submitted to a later meeting of the membership.[16] The special committee later met and formulated a list of proposals which included support for the goal of a 20% or more black teaching staff and encouraged the adoption of measures to increase minority recruitment. The BTU executive board then strongly voted down those proposals and after intense debate at a subsequent general membership meeting, the proposals were tabled. The union's general opposition to the court's hiring goals continued.

The dispute over the racial composition of teachers in the Boston school system has introduced a choice between seniority or affirmative action. In this way, the dispute has become a classic example of the dilemma which has plagued courts and unions throughout the United States in recent years. In this case, the union has unequivocally sided for the preservation of seniority. That choice can, in part, be explained by the fact that the strict preservation of seniority rights serves the interests of the older, white, permanent teachers—the politically powerful component of the BTU's membership.[17] In addition, the BTU, like most other unions, finds it extremely difficult to contemplate the abandonment of the seniority principle which has served as one of the basic tenets of the American collective bargaining system.

The preservation of seniority rights is now particularly important to the BTU because of the threat of teacher layoffs in the Boston school system. That threat is a consequence of the massive enrollment declines that have occurred in the Boston school system in the 1970s. In 1965 total enrollment in the school system stood at 94,035. Enrollment climbed to 97,344 in 1970 and then declined to 84,988 in 1975 and by the end of the 1979-80 school year stood at 67,527.[18] If class size was kept constant at the level of 25 students per class and teacher workloads remained constant, the drop in enrollment of 29,817 which occurred between 1970 and 1980 would facilitate a potential reduction of 1193 teachers (or 23% of the total number of teachers in 1973-74.)[19]

As in the seniority-affirmative action dispute, the hiring of provisional teachers created a situation in which the BTU has chosen to side with the interests of its traditional membership. When reviewing the course of relations in the 1970s between the BTU and the school department it might at first seem surprising to learn that the BTU did not adamantly resist the increased hiring of *provisional* teachers and the halt in the hiring of new *permanent* teachers. No union likes the wage and benefit reductions that accompanies the shift from permanent to provisional contracts and one might have expected the BTU to firmly resist the change in the school department's hiring policy. Yet, the BTU appears to have acquiesced rather passively to that new hiring policy.

In fact, it can be argued that the BTU took a number of steps to exacerbate the differences in the status of permanent and provisional teachers. One such step was the union's negotiation of a job security agreement (a school department promise not to lay off) covering only permanent teachers in the 1975 contract settlement. Union actions concerning job security continued to protect only permanent teachers when the "excess" procedure regulating seniority and bumping rights negotiated in the fall of 1978 excluded teachers on provisional status.

The BTU's actions, as in the seniority vs. affirmative action dispute, can be explained as part of the union's efforts to protect the interests of the traditional and politically dominant component of the union's membership, namely, the older permanent teachers. There was an ever-present possibility that the School Committee would respond to declining enrollments by laying-off teachers. The existence of a separate class of teachers with provisional status provided some assurance to permanent teachers that any layoffs that did occur would not spread into their own ranks. Steps such as limiting the coverage of the excess procedure served to insulate further permanent teachers from the threat of layoff.

When responding to a layoff threat by acquiescing in the creation of a "protected" and "unprotected" class of workers, the BTU was following a road previously travelled by a number of other unions. For example, in the 1950s in the West coast longshoring industry, containerization brought the threat of workforce reductions. The longshoremens' union responded by creating a similar two-class system—one class of protected senior workers who received job security and another class of unprotected junior workers who were without similar job security.[20]

Internal Union Politics

BTU policies which exacerbated the differentiation between permanent and provisional teachers did create some internal political problems within the union. Provisional teachers, as an increasing fraction of the teacher workforce, struggled to redirect the policies of the BTU. It is important to note that tensions were increased between these teacher groups because of the large minority representation among provisional teachers.[21] Provisional teachers were also, on average, a much younger workforce than the permanent teaching staff. Both the youthfulness and the racial composition of the provisional workforce led them to oppose the BTU's long-standing opposition to desegregation and the union's preference for more modest minority hiring goals. Furthermore, provisional teachers demanded that the BTU more aggressively push their particular interests, such as increased salaries, benefits, and job security for provisional teachers, in contract negotiations with the School Committee.

Many of the complaints against traditional BTU policies expressed by restive provisional and minority teachers had the support of teacher aides, another increasingly important fraction of the BTU's membership. By 1978-79 there were approximately 1500 aides in the school system.[22] And, like provisional teachers, a large fraction of the aides were either black or some other minority. In the 1975-76 school year, 43.4% of all aides were black and 10.6% were other nonwhite minorities.[23]

Dissension within the ranks of the BTU led to the creation of a slate of candidates (the New Unity Coalition) which ran for positions on the union's executive board in elections in the spring of 1978.[24] That slate was comprised heavily of minorities, provisional teachers and aides, and supported policies that would have promoted the interests of all three of those groups. Although the slate failed to elect anyone to the executive board, its strength in a primary election signalled the presence of significant dissension within the union.

One can speculate as to how the union's internal political balance will respond to these new claims. A possible course is for union policies to *gradually* shift so as to accommodate the desires of the newer members. Alternatively, the union's leadership and policies may continue to be dominated by the traditional membership—the older, predominantly white, permanent teachers. Following this latter scenario, at some point in time an explosive struggle for control of the union may occur between the traditional groups in the union and a coalition of minority and provisional teachers and aides.

Shifting Coalitions: The Union, The Court, and Community Groups

As well as struggling over its internal political alignment, the BTU is faced with the task of directing its relationship with external parties such as the court and the Boston community. As discussed earlier, the BTU has generally been opposed to the thrust of Judge Garrity's desegregation and hiring orders. And yet, as the desegregation process has continued, the BTU has at times found that there are advantages to court involvement in the school system. For example, until the spring of 1980, in fights over the extent of school closings, the BTU frequently found itself on the same side as Judge Garrity in opposition to cutbacks proposed by Mayor White or the School Committee. Teachers wanted to stop school closings in order to protect their jobs while Judge Garrity acted to protect the desegregation effort. The BTU has also supported steps taken by Judge Garrity which insured the fiscal solvency of the school system. In the spring of 1976, the union supported an order issued by Judge Garrity that forced Mayor White to fund a full school term even though the School Committee had accumulated a large deficit. Ironically, if at some point in the future the School Committee decides to impose substantial layoffs of teachers, the BTU may very well find itself arguing before Judge Garrity that teacher layoffs should be stopped because they threaten the court's minority hiring targets.

The BTU's relationship with community groups and parents is marked with the same ambivalence that characterizes the union's relationship with the court. As a public sector union, the BTU is dependent upon parents and the wider community for support of its bargaining demands with the School Committee. Without that support, the bargaining power of the BTU would be severely weakened.

Teachers and parents have found a commonality of interests on a number of issues. Teachers and parents have frequently joined together in support of expanded school programs and in opposition to school closings. Yet, as part of the desegregation process, a number of disputes have arisen in which the BTU and parents stood on opposing sides. For example, to monitor desegregation, the court created various parent and "citizen advisory" groups. A clash occurred in the fall of 1979 when parents entered the classroom as part of their efforts to monitor compliance with the desegregation order. Teachers and the BTU resented the intrusion of parents into the classroom, fearing that it might lead to parental involvement in evaluations of teacher performance. The union petitioned the court to stop the practice. Judge Garrity then upheld the rights of parents to enter the classroom as a legitimate aspect of their monitoring responsibilities. Other union policies which favored permanent teachers put the union in alliance with some parental groups and in opposition to other parents who supported the claims of minority and provisional teachers. One consequence of the latter is that the union's internal politics became intertwined with the union's "external" relationship with parents and community groups.

Conclusion

The early stages of school desegregation in Boston were marked by a series of court orders which set out to reshape the educational process. Over time, the desegregation effort has generated a host of labor-management issues and taken on the character of a complex bargaining process. For example, as the case study illustrates, the early court orders that sought changes in the racial composition of the faculty led to counterproposals, delays and countermoves by the school department and the BTU. The steps taken by the BTU in turn initiated both political conflict within the union and interactions between the union and community groups. Desegregation of the Boston public schools has thereby come to involve the same shifting political coalitions and competing demands that now so commonly arise in urban America.

Footnotes

1. Court actions in desegregation cases throughout the country are surveyed in, "Supplement to School Desegregation: A Report of State and Federal Judicial

and Administrative Activity," National Institute of Education, Washington, D.C., December 1978.

2. The Boston Teachers Union, Local 66 of the American Federation of Teachers, has represented and negotiated collective bargaining agreements for public school teachers in Boston since 1965.

3. The Boston desegregation case is discussed in, "A Citizen s Guide to School Desegregation Law," National Institute of Education, Washington, D.C., July 1978, pp. 39-41, and *Desegregating the Boston Public Schools: A Crisis in Civic Responsibility,* U.S. Commission on Civil Rights, Washington, D.C., 1975. Judge Garrity's desegregation plan is reported in "Memorandum of Decision and Remedial Orders," U.S. District Court of Massachusetts, Civil Action No. 72-911-G, Morgan V. Hennigan, D. Mass., June 5, 1974, 379 F. Supp. 410, 482. Also see "The Boston Case" by Ralph R. Smith in *Limits of Justice: The Court's Role in School Desegregation,* H. Kalodner and J. Fishman, eds., Ballinger Press, Cambridge, Massachusetts, 1978.

4. See the desegregation story in *The Boston Union Teacher,* March 1974, p. 1.

5. See stories on desegregation in *The Boston Union Teacher,* October 1974 and March 1975.

6. See "Order on Hiring," July 31, 1974, U.S. District Court ot Massachusetts. The 20% figure was equal to the fraction of the total population of Boston that was black according to the 1970 census. In this and later hiring orders the court stipulated that in meeting the one black for each white requirement, the hiring of other minorities would not count as the hiring of either a black or a white.

7. The number of provisional teachers was 698 (1973-74), 714 (1974-75), 947 (1975-76), 1050 (1976-77), 857 (1977-78), 1059 (1978-79). These figures are from "City Defendant's Report on Reassignments and Hiring of Teachers," various dates, submitted to U.S. District Court of Massachusetts.

8. The 1978-80 collective bargaining agreement between the BTU and the School Committee states that regarding provisional teachers, ". . . in no event shall they be placed on a step higher than the third step of the bachelor's salary schedule." See the "Contract Between the Boston Teachers Union and the School Committee of the City of Boston," September 1, 1978, Article 2, Section A-11(a), p. 9. Traditionally, provisional teachers had been hired by the school department to temporarily fill vacancies created by teachers on leave or sabbatical.

9. For evidence of price responsiveness in the municipal budgetary process see, Harry C. Katz, "The Municipal Budgetary Response to Changing Labor Costs: The Case of San Francisco," *Industrial and Labor Relations Review,* July 1979, vol. 32, no. 4, pp. 506-519.

10. These figures are from the "Report of the Numbers of White, Black and Other Minority Permanent and Acting Administrators," School Committee of Boston, March 14, 1979, Table i.

11. Provisional teachers made up 17.4% and 20.4% of total teachers, respectively, in 1975-76 and 1978-79. The number of total teachers used in these calculations and cited in the text is taken from *ibid.*

12. "Plaintiffs' Motion for Further Relief and Supplementary Orders Enforcing the January 28, 1975 Orders on Faculty Recruiting and Hiring," March 31, 1978, submitted to U.S. District Court of Massachusetts.

13. See "Government Employee Relations Report," BNA, No. 744, p. 12, January 30, 1978. Also see, "Affirmative Action Versus Seniority—Is Conflict Inevitable?", Bonnie G. Cebulski, Calif. Pub. Emp. Rels. Monograph Series, 1977. In a recent decision a federal judge nullified a seniority layoff procedure arguing that it contradicted desegregation goals. See, *Daily Labor Reports,* No. 199, October 10, 1980, p. A-10, B.N.A.

14. "Boston Teacher Union's Response to 'Plaintiffs' Motion," April 18, 1978, submitted to U.S. District Court of Massachusetts.
15. *Ibid.*, p. 2.
16. See the June 8, 1978 letter of the AFT Caucus on Desegregation and Equality in Education to the general BTU membership.
17. A reading of old union newspapers suggests that there has never been an executive officer of the union who was either black or a provisional teacher.
18. Enrollment (membership) figures for the years 1965 through 1975 are available in, "Annual Statistics of the Boston Public Schools," Boston School Committee, various years. Figures for the 1979-80 school year come from "Analysis of Students by Race by Grade 1979-80," June 15, 1980, Information and Statistics Section, Boston School Department.
19. There were 5,214 teachers in the school system in the year 1973-74. This figure is from "City Defendant's Report on Reassignment and Hiring of Teachers," U.S. District Court of Massachusetts, September 27, 1974, p. 6. Unfortunately, consistent numbers of teachers in the system prior to 1973 are not available.
20. This two-class system is described in Paul T. Hartman, *Collective Bargaining and Mechanization,* University of California Press, Berkeley, 1973.
21. See Table 1.
22. Aides were included in the BTU as of 1973 and the collective bargaining agreement between the BTU and the School Committee included separate provisions covering aides as of 1974.
23. See "Summary of Total Staff by Assignment, Sex, and Race," in "Selected Annual Statistics of the Boston Public Schools 1975-76," Boston School Committee, Table 46, p. 63.
24. The campaign planks of the New Unity Coalition and election results are reported in *The Boston Union Teacher,* May 1979, June 1979, and July 1979. In a primary election nine candidates from the New Unity Coalition running for spots on the executive board qualified for the final ballot.

8
Conclusions and Future Issues

It is customary for authors of a book such as this to use the final chapter to speculate about the course of future events. Since one of the arguments made throughout this book is that predictions about the future ought to be based less on armchair prognostication and more on empirically grounded understanding of past and present events, we will follow a somewhat cautious course. Indeed, in closing our first edition of this book we refrained from such a foolish venture altogether and instead outlined a number of research questions which needed answering before informed conclusions could be reached or empirically grounded predictions offered.

We still believe much more research needs to be done and we fully recognize the hazards of making statements about the future in environments as dynamic and diverse as the ones in which public sector bargaining operates. We also believe, however, that it is time to make some summary statements about what has been learned from completed research and what unanswered questions or practical problems are likely to pose the greatest challenges to professionals in this field in the years immediately ahead.

The reader should, however, be cognizant of the dubious track record of industrial relations researchers as crystal ball gazers. Suffice it to say that nobody we know of writing in this field in the 1950s predicted or anticipated the sudden rise of public sector bargaining in the 1960s. It is not surprising, therefore, that one of the more articulate and honest practitioners in the field for years published a monthly newsletter entitled "The Cloudy Crystal Ball."[1]

CONCLUSIONS AND PROJECTIONS

What have we learned from the accumulated research and experiences of the past two decades? We will organize our summary comments according to the framework used throughout the book, that is, by beginning with a discussion of the environment and working our way through to the outcomes and impacts of bargaining during the first and early stages of its second generation in the public sector.

The Environmental Contexts

Much of the early debate over the long run consequences of unionism and collective bargaining in the public sector was predicated on some assumptions about the nature of economic and political environments in which bargaining takes place. Those who initially opposed providing bargaining rights and/or the right to strike to public employees assumed that the absence of clear market constraints and the presumed vulnerability of elected officials to citizen pressure to avoid disruption in services would provide undue power to employees. It is clear that these early predictions underestimated (1) the diversity of the economic and political environments in which bargaining takes place, and (2) the changes experienced in bargaining environments in response to economic and political developments. The evidence to date simply does not support the hypothesis that collective bargaining inevitably and permanently alters the balance of power in favor of public employees. Instead, public employees gained an initial bargaining advantage in those environments where the economy was strong and the political context was supportive of labor. As the economic constraints tightened, however, the political climate turned against public employees, the backs of management stiffened, and the economic and substantive bargaining gains of employees moderated.

Still, however, there is no doubt some validity to the essence of the argument advanced by Wellington and Winter, namely, that the nature of the political process is altered through collective bargaining. What they failed to anticipate, though, is that not only would unions become more politically active and astute at the local level, but that collective bargaining would also stimulate the formation of more active school boards and school board associations, parent associations, taxpayer groups, management labor relations professional groups, and so forth. Whether an "appropriate" balance of power among these interested parties has evolved is still an open question and one worth constant attention and analysis in the years ahead. We have to wonder, however, whether the clash between taxpayers who call for tax relief and more responsive government, on the one hand, and the mounting relative and real wage losses suffered by public employees in recent years, on the other hand, does not portend a period of heightened interest group conflict in public sector labor relations.

It is clear that the boom years for collective bargaining legislation at the state level have been over since the mid 1970s, if not earlier. Unless political conditions change considerably, there is little prospect for the passage of new public sector bargaining laws in those states that have not yet enacted initial laws. Furthermore, the pace of amendments to laws in states that acted earlier also appears to have slowed somewhat in recent years. This leads to the logical question of whether the diversity of laws that, because of its "experimental" value, has been judged a virtue by most observers in the past will continue to be interpreted in this light. Alternatively, will concerns be raised that the end result of such state experimentation is an uneven distribution of employee and employer rights and responsibilities? Will the 1980s be a decade in which collective bargaining rights are brought to public employees in the South? Or have the pressures for legislation been relieved by the bargaining that currently goes on without statewide legislation in those large southern cities where public employees are strongest and the organizing potential is greatest? Because most of our research to date has focused on bargaining in those states with laws, we know very little about the conditions of employment, employee organizations and employer practices in the unorganized public sector. Whether or not the political climate portends change in policies in this latter group of states, we need to shift our attention to this environment if we are to understand the effects of an absence of public sector laws in environments not normally conducive to unionism.

The Structure of Bargaining

Despite periodic calls for greater consolidation of bargaining units and structures, the decentralized and relatively narrow structure of bargaining units has continued in most public sector jurisdictions. The main exceptions to this characterization are to be found in some state governments and very large cities, where unit consolidation and experiments in coalition bargaining have taken place. The latter experiments have occurred mainly in response to severe financial crises, such as in New York City.

There are two primary reasons why public sector bargaining has remained decentralized—one economic, the other political. The economic reason is that tax and revenue generation and allocation decisions are still made primarily at the local level. Although large cities are becoming increasingly dependent on state and federal sources for revenue, external funding agents have not attempted to constrain the wages paid to public employees (including in New York City and just recently in the Boston area transit system) where fiscal adversity has reached severe proportions. The political reason for this is that local authorities judiciously guard their autonomy on all issues, including decision making over collective bargaining. Thus, they are unlikely to be receptive to arrangements which require the sharing of authority or the coordination of decisions and policies with other political units. The same is true on the union side. Consolidation of units or more temporary experiments in coalition bargaining require union leaders to overcome traditional rivalries and to coordinate decision making across two or more independent constituencies. For these reasons, bargaining has remained quite decentralized in local governments and school districts. There is little reason to expect this to change, unless state and federal authorities choose to exert greater control over personnel expenditures that are funded with state and federal dollars.

The Bargaining Process

Has the process of negotiation settled more firmly into a bilateral pattern over time? Has collective bargaining blocked other groups from participating in the political process on issues where their vital interests are at stake? We have no clear empirical benchmarks to use in answering these questions. It does appear that the "routine" types of negotiations that are settled short of a visible impasse have taken on more of the characteristics of bilateral negotiations in many settings. However, divergent political officials and interest groups have found ways to make their voices felt when issues of major importance arise or where bargaining reaches the crisis stage. This is demonstrated by recent bargaining disputes in several major cities—e.g., Boston, Cleveland, New York, Chicago, Milwaukee—where in one way or another diverse political bodies and groups became involved in public sector labor negotiations. Thus, where the stakes are high and the political interests divergent, multilateralism appears to have endured.

Strikes and Dispute Resolution

No set of issues has provided more controversy and research than the role of the strike and alternative dispute resolution procedures. These issues, more than most others, have provided us with a laboratory for experimentation and research. Do we have some concrete conclusions and advice to give policymakers in return for these laboratory conditions? We think we do, even though each of us has been critical of the quality of research done on these topics.

The data from the recent Olson, Stern, Najita, and Weisberger study of strikes and penalties reinforce some earlier findings and conclusions reached on much sketchier data and shake us loose from a number of sacred shiboleths offered by various interest groups.[2] Based on the accumulated evidence to date, we believe it is safe to offer the following conclusions regarding public sector strikes during the first and the initial years of the second generation of public sector bargaining in the United States:

1. The average duration of strikes is considerably less in the public sector than in the private sector;
2. New York's Taylor Law, with its strong strike penalties and established impasse procedures, has lowered the number of strikes that occurred relative to what would have been expected in that state in the absence of the procedures and penalties built into the law;
3. Strikes by teachers in New York under that state's procedures and penalties were less frequent than (a) in states such as Pennsylvania, where the right to strike exists, (b) in states where bargaining takes place in the absence of a specific bargaining law or impasse procedures, and perhaps (c) in states such as Michigan, where a bargaining law exists and strikes are illegal, but penalties for striking are weak and uncertain;
4. The number of strikes by units of essential service employees has been lower under arbitration than in cases where these units bargain under a factfinding procedure or without a law. This effect has been stronger for firefighters than for police.

Even these statements should be interpreted and used with caution. Recall that we are only reporting on the experiences under laws passed in American states during the 1960-75 period. Whether states in different environments with different bargaining histories will experience these effects by passing laws similar to any one of those discussed above is an open question. Again, we are more proficient in interpreting past experiences than in projecting them into the future.

What can we say about performance of alternative impasse procedures? The best thing that can be said is a comment about the growing sophistication among researchers themselves. There are fewer evangelical zealots who still believe that there is "one best way" to resolve all public sector bargaining disputes. We seem to have gone beyond the stage of arguing for a single fixed system for all employees in all circumstances and at all times. Instead there is a growing recognition that a wide range of workable options are available to policymakers, depending on what weights they put on alternative policy objectives.

For example, if the most important objective is to avoid public employee strikes, some form of arbitration appears to be the preferred option. If the objectives of avoiding both strikes and dependence on arbitration are given heavy weight, a form of final offer arbitration or perhaps a tripartite mediation and screening committee prior to invoking arbitration are options that, to date, have proven most likely to serve these goals. If the main concern is to limit the discretion of the arbitrator and maintain as much control in the hands of the parties, then a tripartite arbitration structure may be built into the dispute resolution system. For those willing to relax somewhat their concern with avoiding strikes, a wide range of additional options is available, ranging from the choice of procedures (e.g., the right to strike or arbitration) to the right to strike itself. Those who remain philosophically opposed to both the right to strike and to arbitration can turn to factfinding with recommendations. The number of strikes that will actually occur under these alternative systems appears to turn on the severity and certainty of the strike penalties built into the law, the political contexts of the negotiations and the militancy of experts. Note again, however, that the validity of these predictions depends on the extent to which past experience serves as a guide to future events.

The Outcomes and Impacts of Bargaining

The more the results and impacts of public sector bargaining are examined, the more they appear to parallel the effects of unions and bargaining in the private sector. Unions have had a positive impact on wages in the public sector. The magnitude appears to fall in the range of between 5 and 15 percent—or not very different from private sector estimates. The meager evidence available to date, along with our general suspicions, suggest that public sector unions have had a somewhat larger impact on fringe benefit expenditures than on wages, again paralleling the experience in the private sector. Finally, there is even some qualitative evidence suggesting that public sector unions have exerted a "shock effect" on public sector management—forcing managers to formalize policies, professionalize their service delivery and administration, and search for ways to recoup increases in labor costs.

Within these general "average" statements we are continuously impressed by the diversity of union effects across bargaining units and organizations. Indeed, both in research and practice, the next step regarding the effects of public sector bargaining is to examine variations in the impacts of collective bargaining on the key economic and behavioral goals of individual workers, employers and public policy objectives and to use these variations to point out ways that managers and unions can improve the effectiveness of their bargaining relationships by making them more responsive to these diverse needs and goals. We expect that the pressures from the taxpaying public and from other sources external to the parties to public sector negotiations will mean that more will be demanded *from* collective bargaining in the years ahead, just as more is being demanded from all of our governmental institutions. Thus we need to shift the attention of both researchers and practitioners from their traditional focus on procedural and institutional aspects of the bargaining relationship as ends in themselves to the question of how we can use and/or adapt these structures, policies, procedures, and practices in ways that will improve the performance of the bargaining relationship. In operational terms, this implies giving greater attention to the administration of the bargaining relationship during the life of a contract and experimenting with and improving the performance of joint labor-management structures to address problems of productivity, safety and health, equal employment opportunity, quality of service, quality of working life, and so on. We know that these experiments do not always work and are not suited to all bargaining relationships. However, we need to break out of the inertia that characterizes bargaining relationships—relationships that are constantly preoccupied with questions of procedure and process at the expense of analysis of the substantive impacts on the constituents they serve.

A FINAL ILLUSTRATION: THE U.S. POSTAL SERVICE[3]

We end our discussion by presenting our nominee for the arena holding perhaps the greatest promise of chaos in public sector bargaining in the years ahead and, therefore, our candidate for the sector to watch most closely if the goal is to learn the most about collective bargaining in the shortest amount of time.

The U.S. Postal Service has been and promises to continue to be one of the most interesting and difficult bargaining environments in the public sector. The U.S. is clearly not alone in this regard—a look to our neighbors from the north indicates that Canadians are similarly entertained periodically by the labor relations events in their postal service. There is no simple explanation of why this is the case. Indeed, the range of pressures on the U.S. Postal Service run the entire gamut of the framework used in this book to analyze public sector collective bargaining. The Postal Service continues to run deficits and is entering an age of more severe competition from private letter and parcel carriers and from other advanced forms of communication. Its quasi-independent organizational status vis-a-vis the Congress and the Executive Branch combined with its need for a federal subsidy make its political environment complex. Since 1970, it has enjoyed its own separate collective bargaining law (actually, Postal Service bargaining is covered by the National Labor Relations Act), which extends bargaining rights over the full menu of wages, hours, and working conditions—a treat that is still the dream of other federal sector unions. While the right to strike is withheld, binding interest arbitration is present.

The structure of the postal unions and the structure of bargaining in the Postal Service are highly complex. Bargaining is done centrally at a national level with several craft and one quasi-industrial union, sometimes in a coalition arrangement (with each union having separate agreement ratification rights). There is a history of rivalry among the unions and a highly politicized and vocal membership within each of the unions. Postal employees have demonstrated their willingness and ability to engage in strikes, job actions and other forms of militancy. This was best illustrated in the 1978 Postal negotiations over a national agreement when, in the face of rank and file pressures, a threat of a national strike, some local strike activity, and pressures from federal political officials, it proved necessary to make several creative adaptations to the formal arbitration procedures in order to arrive at an agreement.[4]

The parties' problems also go well beyond these complex political and organizational pressures and extend to the substantive outcomes and impacts of their relationship. No other public sector area or entity has been undergoing a faster rate of technological change than the Postal Service. The potential for utilizing additional new technology, and thereby further reducing the workforce, is at least equally as great. This has produced the predictable problem of managing the tradeoff between, on the one hand, enhancing productivity and, on the other, preserving job security. Other substantive outcomes are also problematic. The Postal Service has been under considerable pressure from the Congress, the Occupational Safety and Health Administration and the unions to improve safety and health conditions. Here again, the complex union structure and the unique history of labor-management relations have made it difficult for the parties to make joint progress toward addressing health and safety concerns.

Hopefully, these examples are sufficient to show why we view the Postal Service as an intriguing arena in which a number of unmet challenges require the attention of researchers, policymakers, and practitioners—and why we commend it to your attention in the years ahead.

WILL THE "PUBLIC" SECTOR SURVIVE?

Perhaps we should not make our final point for fear of obviating the need for a third edition of this book. Indeed, it could be argued that a book such as this would not be needed if the character of "public" sector bargaining is not sufficiently distinctive as to warrant separate consideration from bargaining in the "private" sector. Yet the line of demarcation between these two sectors is increasingly becoming blurred. As a consequence, the types of problems and issues which are confronted in public and private sector bargaining may likewise be converging. Consider, for example, the differences in bargaining that occur among private, city, state, and federal hospitals or educational institutions. The organizational structures, financial problems and bargaining issues in these varied contexts are rather similar. Or consider the range of working arrangements that are funded, contracted, subcontracted, and often directly managed by the Federal Departments of Defense, Transportation, and Energy. Often private and government employees work side by side in the same installations, but are covered by different laws, rights, and responsibilities. Or consider the plight of the Long Island Railroad.

As of this writing, the courts are trying to decide whether its employees are to be considered "public" employees and, therefore, covered under the provisions of New York's Taylor Law, or "private" employees covered under the Railway Labor Act. The final disposition of this case will determine whether a strike by employees of the Long Island Railroad that took place early in 1980 was legal or illegal! The point of this final note, therefore, is to emphasize that it is less important to ask what "sector" a bargaining relationship is in than to analyze the environments, structures, processes and outcomes that characterize an employment relationship if an understanding of collective bargaining is to be achieved.[5]

FOOTNOTES

1. "Harold Newman's Cloudy Crystal Ball," *PERB Bulletin* (A monthly newsletter for mediators and factfinders published by the New York State Public Employment Relations Board.)
2. Craig A. Olson, James L. Stern, Joyce Najita and June Weisberger, "Public Sector Strikes and Strike Penalties," unpublished report to the U.S. Department of Labor, Labor-Management Services Administration, 1981.
3. For a comprehensive analysis of collective bargaining in the Postal Service see J. Joseph Loewenberg, "The Postal Service," in Gerald G. Somers, ed., *Collective Bargaining: Contemporary American Experience* (Madison, Wis.: Industrial Relations Research Association, 1980), pp. 435-86.
4. Other conflicts have occurred over the years in postal service bargaining. See, for example, Stephen C. Shannon, "Work Stoppage in Government: The Postal Strike of 1970," *Monthly Labor Review,* Vol. 101 (July, 1978), 14-22.
5. This theme was sounded and is further developed in David Lewin, "Public Employment Relations: Confronting the Issues," *Industrial Relations,* Vol. 12 (October, 1973), 309-321.

PART IV
COLLECTIVE BARGAINING EXERCISES

INTRODUCTION

The following exercises were prepared for use as learning experiences in a public sector labor relations course. They are included in this volume because they have been useful teaching tools and have elicited highly favorable student reactions. In particular, students participating in these exercises have enthusiastically involved themselves in their negotiation roles and have commented favorably on what they perceive as the realism of their experience. The teacher bargaining exercise has been added to this second edition to meet a wider range of student interests.

Each case is best used toward the end of the semester to give the students the opportunity to use the substantive knowledge they have acquired during the term. The negotiation portion of each exercise can profitably occupy four class meetings of 1½ hours' duration, but the number of meetings can be changed to suit the length of the term, the length of class periods, and instructor or student preferences. Four students per bargaining team is preferable in order to give each student the opportunity to participate fully, but the number can be varied to accommodate class size constraints. To save time and minimize arguments, the instructor may assign students to various negotiating roles (i.e., chief negotiator, attorney, etc.). Also to save time, union and management initial demands are specified in each case. The ideal physical location of each negotiation arena (one union and one management team) is a seminar room with a table that will accommodate at least four persons on each side, but changes can easily be made to conform to available settings. During the negotiating sessions, the instructor ought to be available nearby to handle any procedural questions and requests for case information.

Each exercise is largely self-contained, with relevant background information, a set of union initial demands, a set of employer initial demands and a current contract. The students are responsible for the actual conduct of the negotiation and impasse resolution processes, and their goal is to secure a new contract on favorable terms (which terms are defined by each bargaining team). Securing a new contract is easy; securing favorable terms is somewhat more difficult. There should be no bargaining outside of the official negotiation sessions, though individual team preparation meetings outside of class hours will be necessary. To increase each team's negotiating incentives, the instructor might establish and use a contest in which prizes are awarded to the teams which bargain the best management contract and/or the best union contract. A particularly valued prize is money, which may be contributed by each student (in the $5-10 range) and then distributed to the winning team or teams.

From an equity standpoint it is very difficult to grade the students' participation in these exercises. If a grade is deemed necessary, perhaps the most useful and equitable assignment is a post-exercise paper in which each student analyzes (rather than merely narrates) the negotiation experience along several dimensions: how and why the team developed issue priorities, how and why the team resolved internal conflicts, what criteria were used in making bargaining table trade-offs, what kinds of attitudinal structuring activities took place across the table, what forces pushed the participants toward agreement or kept them in a state of disagreement (with a special focus on the role of the arbitration procedures), and so forth.

The instructor may want or need to make a few changes in the setting and substance of the cases. For example, in the police case the New York location was used to increase the interest of the students in the course where the case was developed, and to utilize these students' knowledge of New York's Taylor Law and New York Public Employment Relations Board and court decisions interpreting the Taylor Law. The instructor may find it useful to substitute the body of relevant public sector legislation and case decisions from his or her own state. Similarly, pensions were not included as an issue in this case because the New York legislature had removed them from the scope of bargaining. The instructor may want to include a pension demand to make the exercise conform more closely to local practice. The teacher case was set in Illinois to meet the interest of students where this case was first developed, and to give students some experience in collective bargaining in a state with no public sector bargaining or impasse resolution legislation. In addition, each year the dates and salary figures in each exercise will need to be changed. Finally, if time constraints are tight the number of issues can be reduced.

Exercise I
QUEEN CITY, NEW YORK
and the
QUEEN CITY POLICE ASSOCIATION (Ind.)

I. Background

Queen City is an aging central city of 385,000 people (1980 Census) located in upstate New York, and is the center of a Standard Metropolitan Statistical Area of more than one million people. The city's main job base is in heavy manufacturing, but over the years the area has become steadily less attractive to employers because of obsolete plant and equipment, high taxes, high labor costs, etc. As a result many of them have moved away, taking thousands of jobs with them. This job decline is reflected in the SMSA's very high (10.0 percent in 1981) unemployment rate, and the hardest hit part of the area has been Queen City itself. The city has been losing population for years (in 1950 it had 560,000 residents), and it is no secret that most of the city's emigrants are middle class whites fleeing what they perceive as unsafe streets, poor schools, and high taxes. Over the past two decades, there has been a small influx of blacks and Puerto Ricans to the point where blacks currently comprise about 25 percent of the city's population and Hispanics about 5 percent. Many members of these two groups are indigent and, consequently, welfare costs have increased significantly over the past several years. One result of these population changes is a depletion of the city's tax rolls. In short, Queen City is a classic example of the stagnation and subsequent decline of central cities in the northeastern United States.

The city government is organized on a strong-mayor basis (meaning the mayor has appointive, budgetary, and veto powers over the city council), with the city council consisting of 15 seats elected on a ward basis. The mayor and the council members serve four-year terms, with half of the council up for election every two years. The elections are partisan, and the city is solidly Democratic (i.e., the mayor and 13 of the 15 council incumbents). The mayor is not only the dominant elected official, he is also the local strongman in the Democratic party and is the closest thing Queen City has to a "political boss." As a result, the council tends to pass what the mayor wants and rejects what he doesn't want, and the annual budget approval process provides the best example of the mayor's hegemony.

City finances strongly reflect the city's dismal economic situation. The 1981 city budget totals $228 million (the city school district has its own budget and the school district has been similarly hit by stagnating revenues and increasing costs), and the city expects that its 1982 budget will require even more money. The current budget includes about $98 million in county and state collected revenues of various kinds and about $27 million in federal revenue sharing, so the city has become the fiscal handmaiden of higher level governments. City officials have been hit with stagnating and even declining local revenues and rapidly increasing costs, and each year is a struggle to break even. 1982 promises to be a tough year because of the state's own financial problems and proclaimed inability to increase the amount of aid to local governments. City officials are constantly trying to persuade the county to assume various city functions (and, of course, the associated costs), but given that county government is largely Republican, the usual response is negative. The city has reached the constitutional ceiling on its property tax (taxes equal to 2 percent of the full value of city property), which means that in coming years only minimal additional revenues can be derived from this source. Because of very strong voter resistance to higher taxes (New York citizens on a per capita basis pay among the highest state and local taxes in the nation), city officials are reluctant to increase property taxes and do not dare institute a city sales or income tax (the latter two taxes would need enabling legislation from Albany). For 1982, the city's best estimate is that it will have 5 percent more money to spend on services and functions that it now provides. Labor costs account for about 70 percent of the city budget.

The city government employs about 5,500 people (down from 6,500 fifteen years ago), most of whom are in one of five bargaining units. The independent Queen City Police Association represents the patrol officers and communications operators in the Police Department; the International Association of Fire Fighters Local 754, AFL-CIO, represents the uniformed, nonsupervisory employees in the Fire Department; the American Federation of State, County, and Municipal Employees Local 610, AFL-CIO, represents most of the city's blue-collar employees (the majority of whom are in the Public Works and Parks Departments); the independent Queen City Civil Service Association represents most of the city's white-collar employees (who are scattered across virtually all city departments); and the Queen City Building and Construction Trades Council, AFL-CIO, represents the various craft classifications (electrician, carpenter, plumber, etc.). The city has a reputation as a "union town" due to the high incidence of unionization in the private sector. While this union influence contributed to the early and solid organization of the city's employees, and while some private sector union officials play important roles in local politics, it is not entirely clear how this union context has directly resulted in tangible benefits for city employees. Except for special cases, the city has not done any general hiring in the past few years and municipal employee ranks have been thinned by attrition. This year city officials are contemplating actual layoffs.

The city's Director of Labor Relations (DLR) heads the city's Office of Labor Relations, and is responsible for the negotiation and administration of contracts with all the city unions. He is appointed by and serves at the pleasure of the mayor, and currently enjoys the mayor's complete confidence. He receives policy (i.e., maximum dollar limit) guidance from the mayor, and has been able to convince the mayor and the council to shut off union

512

end runs on matters within the scope of bargaining. The DLR also maintains good relations with city department heads and works closely with them on contract language questions so that city labor contracts will not unduly limit managerial prerogatives. The city's collective bargaining takes place under the aegis of New York's Taylor Law (except as expressly modified for the purposes of this case), and the state Public Employment Relations Board's (PERB) decisions regarding the interpretation of the Taylor Law.

The Queen City Police Department is one of the most important of the city's departments. The police budget for 1981 totals about $45 million, of which about 80 percent goes for labor costs (including fringes, which average about 50 percent of payroll). The average 1981 salary (excluding fringes) in the department is about $20,000 and the department consists of about 1050 sworn officers and about 150 civilians, with the civilians employed in a wide variety of jobs. The police bargaining unit consists of 800 patrol officers (including detectives) and 50 communications operators (COs). The COs are civilians, but they wear uniforms and some of them eventually become patrol officers. The department is directed by the police commissioner, who is appointed by and serves at the pleasure of the mayor. The department is divided into a dozen police precincts, each with its own station house. Patrol officers assigned to regular patrol duty work out of the various station houses. Most patrol officers and CO's work rotating shifts (the shifts rotate every three months). The police department has the usual big city problems of crime, police-minority group friction, and political decision-making criteria.

The police union consists of two occupational groups, the patrol officers and the CO's. The patrol officers naturally look down upon the CO's because of the latter's civilian status—meaning they have no arrest powers and carry no weapons. The CO's are in the unit, though, because there is some measurable "community of interest" across the two groups and because the union leadership want them there in case of a strike—the police communications processes will be disrupted and there will be fewer personnel available for management to use during the stoppage. The union's membership (which includes 98 percent of the eligibles) is divided along the usual lines: age and seniority (the older officers are interested in pensions, the younger ones in wages and, more recently, job security), duties (the street patrol officers—the "combatants"—sneer at the desk jockeys or "noncombatants" in headquarters), etc. There is—for a police union—the usual rank-and-file militance to get "more" and get it yesterday.

An arbitrator awarded 7.1 percent and 5 percent pay increases in the current two-year contract, and because these pay raises lagged behind the double digit inflation of 1980-81 the union and its members are looking for a nice "catch-up" increase. In addition, there is substantial concern among the younger and shorter service officers over possible layoffs. They know the city is having fiscal problems, and they also know what happened to the ranks of New York City police when the financial crunch hit that municipality in 1975. Consequently, they are looking for job security protection in this year's contract as well as the usual bundle of cash and other benefits.

Currently there is police and fire pay parity—not contractually, but as a result of a long-standing political custom.

II. Union Demands

After careful evaluation of membership desires, the police union leadership has formulated the following package of contract demands to be submitted to management. They are listed in no particular order of importance, though the weights attached to them ought to reflect the facts of the case. Background information is provided for some of these demands to facilitate cost calculations.

TABLE 1
1981 Queen City Budget

	Revenues	
Local:		
	Property taxes	$93,018,000
	Licenses and permits	1,502,000
	Parking meters	1,350,000
	Fines and forfeitures	1,900,000
	Interest	1,420,000
	Other local	2,200,000
County and state distributions:		
	Sales taxes	70,205,000
	Gasoline taxes	5,315,000
	State aid	23,500,000
Federal revenues:		
	Shared revenue	8,600,000
	CETA	7,210,000
	Housing and urban renewal	10,880,000
	Other federal	1,465,000
Total revenues		$228,655,000
	Appropriations	
Police department		$45,150,000
Fire department		28,620,000
Public works department		44,873,000
Parks and recreation department		8,755,000
Finance and accounting department		3,220,000
City auditor		1,015,000
	Total departments	$131,633,000
City's share of special districts:		
	School	5,025,000
	Sewers	4,365,000
	Public health	4,815,000
	Public housing	32,030,000
General administration		50,122,000
Reserve		665,000
	Total appropriations	$228,655,000

TABLE 2
1980 Police Salary Comparisons (annual)

City	Minimum	Maximum	Years to Maximum
Chicago	$16,524	$25,440	30
Detroit	19,041	24,153	4
New York	15,247	19,741	3
Philadelphia	16,666	18,952	2
Boston	14,741	19,574	2
Cleveland	16,450	17,950	1
Columbus	10,836	18,740	2½
Cincinnati	17,068	19,005	3
Milwaukee	18,390	20,705	4
Syracuse	13,612	17,738	5
Yonkers	13,798	19,000	3
Queen View	15,000	17,400	3
Queen Woods	15,240	18,000	3
Queen Falls	14,400	16,800	3
Queen City	16,200	18,000	3

Note: Over the years the City and the Association have used these police salaries for comparison purposes. Queen View, Queen Woods, and Queen Falls are suburbs of Queen City, and all are in the 50,000-100,000 population category. Naturally, the Association likes to use the larger central cities for comparison purposes, while the City prefers upstate New York cities and its own suburbs.

TABLE 3
Queen City Police Salary History (monthly)

Year	Step D Patrol Officer	Step D Communications Operator
1976	$1176	$ 921
1977	1236	971
1978	1325	1025
1979	1400	1075
1980	1500*	1150*
1981	1575*	1225*

*Salaries set by an arbitrator; salaries in other years determined in collective bargaining. The City and the Association negotiated one-year contracts in 1976 and in 1977, and a two-year contract for 1978-79. The arbitrator awarded a two-year contract for 1980-81.

TABLE 4
Police Bargaining Unit Seniority Distribution

Years of Service	Number of Employees
25 or more	30
20-24	80
15-19	190
10-14	310
5-9	200
4	15
3	12
2	8
1	5
Probationary	0

Note: Within each years of service category employees are distributed on a linear basis.

1. In light of recent increases in the Consumer Price Index, the union wants a 20 percent pay increase at all steps for patrol officers and communications operators.

2. The city will pay the entire cost of the family Blue Cross-Blue Shield-Major Medical coverage. The city already pays the employees' premium and part of the family premium. The current employee-only premium is $600 per year; the current family premium is $1200 per year ($600 additional). Blue Cross benefits are the same across all city groups. Premiums have increased about 10 percent annually during the past three years. About 80 percent of the members have family coverage and about 20 percent have single coverage.

3. The city will pay the entire cost of the life insurance premium. Premiums are $50 annually for each employee. Firefighters and police receive this benefit but other city employees do not.

4. The city will provide a dental insurance plan covering each employee and his/her family; premiums are $75 per year for single coverage and $200 per year ($125 additional) for family coverage. No other city group has dental insurance.

5. A 10 percent shift premium for all hours worked between the hours of six p.m. and six a.m. No other city group receives such a premium. Approximately 50 percent of all police hours are worked between six p.m. and six a.m.

6. A $500 annual longevity pay increase for all patrolmen and CO's with 10 or more years of service. No other city employees receive longevity pay.

7. An increase in six leave accrual to 18 days per year of service (or 1½ days per month), including the first year, with the maximum accrual increased to 300 days. Whenever an employee is terminated for any reason, the employee shall receive a cash payment equal to the value of one-half of all accrued sick leave.

516

8. An increase in the uniform allowance to $350 for patrol officers and $175 for CO's.

9. Four more paid holidays (Washington's birthday, Lincoln's birthday, the day after Thanksgiving, and a floating holiday). Other city employees receive the same number of holidays the police presently receive. All officers are given one day's pay for each holiday. Officers who work on a holiday receive one day's holiday pay plus time-and-one-half for working on that day.

10. An increase in vacation time: three weeks after 5 years, four weeks after 10 years, and five weeks after 15 years. All city employees, including police, presently receive the same amount of vacation.

11. An increase in the standby pay rate as follows: 60 percent of the employee's straight time hourly pay rate for the first eight hours; $25.00 for each 12 hour period (or fraction) thereafter. In an average week approximately 20 officers will be required to stand by for one shift (8 hours) each.

12. A requirement that all squad cars used on regular or special patrol duty (not including detective or special unit duty) be manned by two officers. Currently, about two-thirds of the cars on patrol duty are manned by two officers. During 1980 patrol officers suffered four serious on the job injuries inflicted by hostile civilians, but no such fatalities. Two cases involved officers patrolling with two officers in a car, and two cases with one officer in each car.

13. A requirement that on the afternoon (4 p.m.-midnight) and night (midnight-8 a.m.) shifts, at least 50 percent plus one of all the squad cars assigned to a particular precinct be staffed and be on the street during those shifts (even if officers must be called in on overtime to staff them). Although on a few occasions in particular precincts there have been few cars on duty because of illness, holidays, vacations, etc., on average about 90 percent of the time there are at least 50 percent plus one of the cars in each precinct on the street during these shifts.

14. A new Section 2.3 be added to Article II which will establish an agency shop. About 98 percent of the unit already belong to the union, but union leaders believe that everybody should help pay for the costs of collective bargaining services.

15. Section 5.6 (Civil Service) be deleted and replaced by a new section: "*Just Cause*. No disciplinary action shall be taken against any member of the bargaining unit except for just cause." In 1980, seven major disciplinary cases were processed and discipline levied by the Police Commissioner according to departmental and civil service regulations. Two of these cases involved discharges (for on the job misconduct), and both cases have been appealed to court (with the Association's assistance).

16. A no layoff clause.

17. A requirement that seniority be the determining factor in layoffs, work assignments, transfers, vacation selection, and holiday scheduling. Seniority is presently used on a de facto basis for vacation selection and holiday scheduling, but this is a result of long-standing custom, not contractual requirement. As in any large city police department, there is the usual griping that many personnel decisions are made according to favoritism and

political criteria. Also as usual, there is little hard evidence to support these complaints.

18. A one-year contract expiring on December 31, 1982.

Again, these demands are not listed in any particular order of importance beyond the facts presented in the case. It is the responsibility of the union bargaining team to gather supporting evidence, to put priorities or weights on various items, to develop specific contract language to implement various proposals, to develop justifications for its demands, to decide what compromises to make, and to decide what a minimum acceptable agreement shall be. The city currently is negotiating with all the other unions and each is jockeying for position while keeping an eye on what is going on with the other groups. The current contract is enclosed.

Although the number of students to be assigned to each bargaining team will be constrained by the size of the class, experience has suggested that four students per team is preferable. The roles on the union bargaining committee include: the union president and chief negotiator, the union attorney, the union secretary-treasurer, and a communications operator. Other roles can be added, if necessary.

III. Employer Demands

In collective bargaining the employer typically spends much time responding to union demands. However, as a result of problems which have arisen during the life of the existing contract and because of the city's fiscal constraints, the city has formulated the following demands:

1. No increase in pay or in any monetary fringe benefit during 1982, a 5 percent salary increase on January 1, 1983, and other 5 percent on January 1, 1984.

2. A reduction in the off-duty court appearance pay minimum guarantee to one hour. About 100 officers per week make off-duty court appearances, and the city estimates that about 40 percent of them complete their appearances in less than three hours.

3. Sick leave accrual to remain the same; however, there shall be no payment to terminated or retired officers.

4. The definition of a grievance be changed such that everything beyond the comma in Section 5.1 is deleted. During 1980, about 300 step one grievances were filed, and five of these went all the way to arbitration. The Association won three cases (overtime pay, court appearance pay, and standby pay), and the city won two (sick leave pay at termination, Association representation at a step one grievance meeting). All five of the arbitration cases involved contractual interpretation disputes, but about one fourth of the step one grievances did not. The city does not want to process city or department rules complaints through the grievance procedure, and it notes that these matters can be processed through the existing Civil Service appeals procedure.

5. Deletion of the phrase "or at least reasonably close to those time limits" in the second sentence of Section 5.4.

6. Insertion of the following sentence into Article VI such that it is the second sentence in that Article: "The Association agrees that if any such

activity occurs the Association and its officers and agents shall work as speedily and diligently as possible for the complete cessation of any such activity." There have been no strikes in the department's history, but at contract negotiation time there are periodic rumblings from some officers about "showing the city we mean business."

7. The elimination of communications operators from the bargaining unit so that the unit will be limited to police patrol officers.

8. A three-year contract expiring on December 31, 1984.

These demands are not presented in any particular order of importance. It is the responsibility of the management bargaining team to gather supporting evidence, to put priorities or weights on various items, to develop specific contract language to implement various proposals, to develop justifications for its proposals, to respond to union demands, to decide what compromises to make, and to decide what a minimum acceptable agreement shall be. The city currently is negotiating with all the other unions and each is jockeying for position while keeping an eye on what is going on at the other bargaining tables. The current contract is enclosed.

Again, four-member student teams are recommended. The roles on the management bargaining team include the director of labor relations and chief negotiator, an assistant city attorney, an assistant budget director, and a deputy police commissioner. More roles may be added if necessary.

IV. Impasse Resolution

If no agreement is reached by the end of time set aside for direct negotiations, there are a variety of methods by which the impasse may be resolved: mediation, fact finding, some form of arbitration, or strike. In light of the increasing use of compulsory arbitration to resolve police and firefighter bargaining impasses, it would be useful and instructive to have any impasses in this case be resolved by the following arbitration procedures. If two or more negotiation arenas exist, it may be particularly instructive to use two or three of the following methods in order to see what impact the different procedures have on the bargaining process.

A. Final Offer Arbitration with Package Selection

If the two sides do not reach full and complete agreement by the end of the time set aside for negotiations, then all unresolved items shall be submitted directly to final offer arbitration. Specifically, at the next class session, each party shall submit to the arbitrator (the instructor or the instructor's designee) and to the other party a written list of all unresolved items and its final offer on each of those items. Each party shall concurrently submit a list of all items, if any, which have been agreed upon in direct negotiations. The arbitration hearing shall commence promptly at the beginning of the class period and shall be heard by the single arbitrator with full powers to issue a binding decision. Each side shall have 15 minutes to present its case and an addition 5 minutes for rebuttal, and each side shall be responsible for developing and presenting justifications of its final offer. The arbitrator's decision shall be final and binding upon the parties. The decision, together with accompanying explanation, shall be delivered orally to the parties before the end of the class period.

The arbitrator shall be limited in his decision to choosing the most reasonable final offer. The arbitrator shall not compromise or alter *in any way* the final offer he selects. The arbitrator shall make his selection decision on an entire package basis (i.e., he shall *not* make separate selection decisions on each issue), and his selection, together with any previously agreed-upon items, shall constitute the new collective bargaining agreement between the parties. In making his determination of the most reasonable offer, the arbitrator shall be guided by the arbitration criteria listed at the end of this section.

Nothing in the above shall preclude the parties from requesting a recess during the arbitration hearing in order to resume direct negotiations, nor shall it preclude the arbitrator from recessing the hearing and ordering the parties to resume direct negotiations if the arbitrator believes that such resumption of negotiations may be helpful in resolving the impasse. Similarly, nothing in the above shall limit the arbitrator from rendering any mediation assistance to the parties if the arbitrator believes such assistance will be helpful in resolving the impasse. (However, time constraints will limit the amount of additional negotiation or mediation activities during the arbitration session.)

B. Final Offer Arbitration with Issue Selection

Everything is the same as stated in the preceding section, with the important exception that the arbitrator will make a separate "most reasonable" selection decision on each issue in dispute.

C. Conventional Arbitration

Many of the details are the same as stated in the first section, with the important exception that the arbitrator can fashion the award he deems appropriate and hence is not limited to selecting either party's final offer.

D. Arbitration Criteria

In reaching a decision, the arbitrator shall take into consideration the following:

1. Comparison of the wages, hours, and conditions of employment of the employees involved in the arbitration proceeding with the wages, hours, and conditions of employment of other employees performing similar services or requiring similar skills under similar working conditions in public employment in comparable communities.
2. The interests and welfare of the public and the financial ability of the public employer to pay.
3. The average consumer prices for goods and services in the area, commonly known as the cost of living.

4. The overall compensation presently received by the employees, including direct wages, vacations, holidays and other excused time, insurance and pensions, medical and hospitalization benefits, the continuity and stability of employment, and all other benefits received.
5. Changes in any of the foregoing circumstances during the preceding negotiations or during the arbitration proceedings.

V. Post-Exercise Analysis

The instructor and the students will find it profitable to spend all or most of a class period analyzing the negotiation and impasse resolution experiences of the various bargaining teams (whether or not they go to arbitration). The students probably will have numerous questions about various facets of the negotiation and impasse processes, and the instructor ought to have a variety of constructively critical comments to make about how the students tried to obtain a favorable contract.

AGREEMENT

Between

QUEEN CITY, NEW YORK

And

QUEEN CITY POLICE ASSOCIATION

January 1, 1980
Through
December 31, 1981

AGREEMENT

This Agreement is entered into by and between Queen City, New York (hereinafter called the "City"), and the Queen City Police Association (hereinafter called the "Association").

ARTICLE I
Recognition and Representation

The City recognizes the Association as the sole and exclusive bargaining agent with respect to wages, hours, and other conditions of employment for employees classified as Police Patrol Officers and Communications Operator.

ARTICLE II
Check-off

Section 2.1. Check-off Association Dues. Upon receipt of a signed authorization from an employee in the form set forth by the City, the City agrees for the duration of this Agreement to deduct from such employee's pay uniform monthly Association dues. The Association will notify the City in writing of the amount of the uniform dues to be deducted. Deductions shall be made on the second City payday of each month and shall be remitted, together with an itemized statement, to the Treasurer of the Association by the 15th day of the month following the month in which the deduction is made.

Section 2.2. Indemnification. The Association shall indemnify the City and hold it harmless against any and all claims, demands, suits, or other forms of liability that may arise out of, or by reason of, any action taken by the City for the purpose of complying with the provisions of this Article.

ARTICLE III
No Discrimination

Section 3.1. General. Neither the City nor the Association shall discriminate against any employee because of race, creed, color, national origin, sex or Association activity.

Section 3.2. Job Transfers. The City will not use job transfers as a form of disciplinary action. Violations of this Section will be subject to the grievance procedure.

ARTICLE IV
Management Rights

The City shall retain the sole right and authority to operate and direct the affairs of the City and the Police Department in all its various aspects, including, but not limited to, all rights and authority exercised by the City prior to the execution of this Agreement. Among the rights retained is the City's right to determine its mission and set standards of service offered to the public; to direct the working forces; to plan, direct, control and determine the operations or services to be conducted in or at the Police Department or by employees of the City; to assign or transfer employees; to hire, promote, demote, suspend, discipline or discharge for cause, or relieve employees due to lack of work or for other legitimate reasons; to make and enforce reasonable rules and regulations; to change methods, equipment, or facilities; provided, however, that the exercise of any of the above rights shall not conflict with any of the provisions of this Agreement.

ARTICLE V
Grievance Procedures

Section 5.1. *Definition of Grievance.* A grievance is a difference of opinion between an employee or the Association and the City with respect to the meaning or application of the express terms of this Agreement, or with respect to inequitable application of the Personnel Rules of the City or with respect to inequitable application of the Rules of the Police Department.

Section 5.2. Association Representation. The Association shall appoint an Employee Committee of not more than three members to attend grievance meetings scheduled pursuant to Steps 3 and 4. The Association may appoint three Stewards, one from each shift (who may be the same persons selected for the Employee Committee), to participate in the grievance procedure to the extent set forth in Step 1 and Step 2 of the grievance procedure. The Association shall notify the Direct of Labor Relations in writing of the names of employees serving on the Employee Committee and as Stewards. One representative of the Executive Board of the Association and/or the Association's legal counsel shall have the right to participate in Steps 3, 4, and 5 of the grievance procedure.

Section 5.3. Grievance Procedure. Recognizing that grievances should be raised and settled promptly, a grievance must be raised within seven calendar days of the occurrence of the event giving rise to the grievance. A grievance shall be processed as follows:

STEP 1: *Verbal to Immediate Supervisor.* By discussion between the employee, accompanied by his Steward, if he so desires, and his immediate supervisor. The immediate supervisor shall answer verbally within seven calendar days of this discussion.

STEP 2: *Appeal to Captain.* If the grievance is not settled in Step 1, the Association may, within seven calendar days following receipt of the immediate supervisor's answer, file a written grievance signed by the employee and his Steward on a form provided by the City setting forth the nature of the grievance and the contract provision(s) involved. The Captain shall give a written answer in seven calendar days after receipt of the written grievance.

STEP 3: *Appeal to Police Commissioner.* If the grievance is not settled in Step 2 and the Association decides to appeal, the Association shall, within seven calendar days from receipt of the Step 2 answer, appeal in writing to the Police Commissioner. The Employee Committee and the Commissioner will discuss the grievance at a mutually agreeable time. If no agreement is reached in such discussion, the Commissioner will give his answer in writing within seven days of the discussion. The City may join the Step 3 and Step 4 meetings if it so desires, by having in attendance both the Commissioner and the Director of Labor Relations or his designee.

STEP 4: *Appeal to Director of Labor Relations.* If the grievance is not settled in Step 3 and the Association decides to appeal, the Association shall, within seven calendar days after receipt of the Step 3 answer, file a written appeal to the Director of Labor Relations. A meeting between the Director, or his designee, and the Employee Committee will be held at a mutually agreeable time. If no settlement is reached at such meeting, the Director, or his designee, shall give his answer in writing within ten calendar days of the meeting.

STEP 5: *Arbitration.* If the grievance is not settled in accordance with the foregoing procedure, the Association may refer the grievance to arbitration by giving written notice to the Director of Labor Relations within twenty-one (21) calendar days after receipt of the City's answer in Step 4. The parties shall attempt to agree upon an arbitrator promptly. In the event the parties are unable to agree upon an arbitrator, they shall jointly request the Federal Mediation and Conciliation Service to submit a panel of five arbitrators. The Assocition shall strike one name and the City shall strike one name; then the Association shall strike another name, and the City shall strike another name, and the person whose name remains shall be the arbitrator; provided, that either party, before striking any names, shall have the right to reject one panel of arbitrators. The arbitrator shall be notified of his selection by a joint letter from the City and the Association requesting that he set a time and a place for hearing, subject to the availability of the City and Association representatives. The arbitrator shall have no right to amend, modify, nullify, ignore, add to, or subtract from the provisions of this Agreement. He shall consider and decide only the specific issue submitted to him, and his decision shall be based solely upon his interpretation of the meaning or application of the terms of this Agreement to the facts of the grievance presented. The decision of the arbitrator shall be final and binding. The costs of the arbitration, including the fee and expenses of the arbitrator, shall be divided equally between the City and the Association.

Section 5.4. Time Limits. No grievance shall be entertained or processed unless it is filed within the time limits set forth in Section 5.3. If a grievance is not appealed within the time limits for appeal set forth above, or at least reasonably close to the time limits, it shall be deemed settled on the basis of the last answer of the City, provided that the parties may agree to extend any time limits. If the City fails to provide an answer within the time limits so provided, the Association may immediately appeal to the next Step.

Section 5.5. Investigation and Discussion. All grievance discussions and investigations shall take place in a manner which does not interfere with City operations.

Section 5.6. Civil Service. It is understood that matters subject to Civil Service such as promotion, discharge, or disciplinary suspension of seven days or more are not subject to this grievance procedure. However, in the event a permanent employee is discharged or suspended for seven days or more, the Association may request a meeting to discuss said discharge or suspension prior to institution of a Civil Service appeal. Upon receipt of such request, the City will meet promptly at Step 3 or Step 4 for this purpose.

ARTICLE VI
No Strikes—No Lockouts

The Association, its officers and agents, and the employees covered by this Agreement agree not to instigate, promote, sponsor, engage in, or condone any strike, slow-down, concerted stoppage of work, or any other intentional interruption of operations. Any or all employees who violate any of the provisions of this Article may be discharged or otherwise disciplined by the City. The City will not lock out any employees during the term of this Agreement as a result of a labor dispute with the Association.

ARTICLE VII
Wages and Benefits

Section 7.1. Salary Schedules. The salary schedule effective from January 1, 1980, through December 31, 1980, and from January 1, 1981, through December 31, 1981, is attached hereto.

Section 7.2. Fringe Benefits. The fringe benefits in effect during the term of this Agreement shall be as follows:

(a) Holidays shall be as follows:

New Year's Day   Thanksgiving
Good Friday   Christmas Eve
Memorial Day   Christmas
Fourth of July
Labor Day

(b) *Vacation* shall be accrued at the following rates:

Recruitment through 6th year   2 weeks
Seventh through 14th year   3 weeks
Fifteenth and later years   4 weeks

(e) *Uniform Allowance.* The City shall provide annual uniform allowances as follows:

Patrol officers: $250
Communications Operators: $125

In the administration of the foregoing uniform allowance, the City will not set any dollar limit on any authorized item.

(d) *Group Insurance.* The City's term life insurance program ($20,000 coverage per employee) shall be continued in effect for the term of this Agreement and the City's 50 percent contribution shall continue. The City's Blue Cross-Blue Shield-Major Medical program (single and family coverage) shall be continued in effect for the term of this Agreement. As of January 1, 1980, and for the term of this Agreement, the City shall pay the entire cost of "employee only" Blue Cross-Blue Shield-Major Medical coverage. As of January 1, 1980, the employee's monthly contribution for "family" Blue Cross-Blue Shield-Major Medical coverage shall be $10.00; effective January 1, 1981, said monthly contribution shall be reduced to $8.00.

(e) *Retiree Blue Cross-Blue Shield-Major Medical Coverage.* An employee who retires on or after January 1, 1980, and is eligible for an immediate pension under the New York Police Pension fund, may elect "employee only" or "family" coverage under the City's Blue Cross-Blue Shield-Major Medical program by paying the entire group premium cost, which may increase from time to time, by means of deduction from the pensioner's pension check.

(f) *Sick Leave.* The City's sick leave plan shall be continued in effect for the term of this Agreement (accrual of six days for the first full year of employment and 12 days for subsequent full years of employment), with the maximum accrual increased to 150 days. Whenever an employee with ten years or more of service is terminated for any reason, the employee shall receive one of the following, whichever is greater: (1) payment of all sick days accrued in excess of fifty days (to a maximum of 25 days' pay), or (2) the current four-week special retirement allowance for employees who retire with eligibility for current pension benefits.

Section 7.3. Overtime Pay for Emergency Duty. A Patrol Officer shall receive time and one-half his regular straight-time hourly rate when ordered to report for overtime emergency duty or when ordered to remain on the job for overtime emergency duty. A Patrol Officer will not receive overtime pay for any work during his regular working hours.

Section 7.4. Off-Duty Court Appearance Pay. A Patrol Officer shall receive time and one-half his regular straight-time hourly rate for required court appearances during his off-duty hours. Patrol Officers shall be guaranteed three hours at the time and one-half rate for each separate off-duty court appearance or actual time spent, whichever is greater.

Section 7.5. Emergency Standby Pay. Whenever the City places an employee on emergency standby, the employee shall receive standby pay as follows: (1) for the first four hours, 30 percent of the employee's straight-time hourly rate, and (2) for each 12 hour period thereafter, or fraction thereof, $10.00.

ARTICLE VIII
Termination and Legality Clauses

Section 8.1. Savings. If any provision of this Agreement is subsequently declared by legislative or judicial authority to be unlawful, unenforceable, or not in accordance with applicable statutes or ordinances, all other provisions of this Agreement shall remain in full force and effect for the duration of this Agreement.

Section 8.2. Entire Agreement. This Agreement constitutes the entire agreement between the parties and concludes collective bargaining on any subject, whether included in this Agreement or not, for the term of this Agreement.

Section 8.3. Term. This Agreement shall become effective January 1, 1980, and shall terminate at 11:59 p.m. on December 31, 1981. Not earlier than July 1, 1981, and not later than August 1, 1981, either the City or the Association may give written notice to the other party by registered or certified mail of its desire to negotiate modifications to this Agreement, said modifications to be effective January 1, 1982.

Queen City   Queen City Police Association

APPENDIX
Queen City, New York

Salary Schedule
Effective January 1, 1980 through December 31, 1980
(monthly salaries)

Step	Patrol Officer	Communications Operator
A (Probationary)	$1350	$1000
B	1400	1050
C	1450	1100
D	1500	1150

Salary Schedule
Effective January 1, 1981 through December 31, 1981
(monthly salaries)

Step	Patrol Officer	Communications Operator
A (Probationary)	$1395	$1075
B	1455	1125
C	1515	1175
D	1575	1225

On the annual anniversary date of his/her employment, each employee shall advance one step until Step D is reached.

Exercise II

RIVER CITY, ILLINOIS, SCHOOL DISTRICT
and the
RIVER CITY EDUCATION ASSOCIATION, IEA-NEA

I. Background

River City is a downstate Illinois city of 50,000 population (1980 Census), which serves as the commercial center of Hamilton County, which is primarily a farming area. There is also some light manufacturing and warehousing activity located in River City due to the town's location near the intersection of two interstate highways. In addition, many of the town's citizens are employed as faculty or staff members at Central Illinois University, a large public university located in the adjacent city of Urbanity. River City's population has grown slightly during the past ten years (in 1970 it had 48,000 residents), but during the last few years, however, the city's population appears to have stabilized, and this stability will probably continue during the 1980s. The prevalence of farming and government employment (primarily the university) in Hamilton County has meant a stable and reasonably prosperous economy for the area, as seen in the fact that the area's unemployment rate is usually about one point below the national average.

The River City School District encompasses all of River City plus some of the unincorporated areas adjacent to the city (with about 2,000 population). The District educates about 9,000 students in two senior high schools (grades 9-12), three junior high or middle schools (grades 6-8), and nine elementary schools (grades K-5). The school population expanded slightly during the early and middle 1970s, stabilized during the late 1970s, and now has started to decline (i.e., there were about 100 fewer students enrolled during 1980-81 than during 1979-80). The district (and the teachers) expect larger declines in enrollments during the next few years due to the stability of River City's population and the trend toward smaller families. The District has forecasted enrollment declines of at least 3 percent per year for each year through 1985-86, after which enrollments are expected to increase slightly. No school district employees have ever been laid off, but district employees are well aware of the layoffs in other districts which have been caused by substantial declines in enrollments.

The district employs about 900 people, of whom about 575 are certificated employees. About 500 regular and special classroom teachers, resource specialists, librarians, guidance counselors, and school nurses are in the teacher collective bargaining unit, and it is this group that is represented by

528

the River City Education Association, an affiliate of the Illinois Education Association and the National Education Association. The 75 certificated non-unit employees work in a variety of managerial or administrative positions (e.g., superintendent, principal, assistant principal, curriculum coordinator, department head, etc.), and the 325 noncertificated employees work in a variety of support positions (e.g., business affairs, data processor, secretary, custodian, groundskeeper, building maintenance, crossing guard, bus driver, food service employee, etc.). The chief executive officer is the superintendent, who serves at the pleasure of the River City School Board. The seven-member school board is elected to four-year terms on a nonpartisan, at-large basis, with either three or four seats becoming vacant every two years (i.e., board member terms are staggered). The current relations between the superintendent and the board are good (which was not always true with previous boards and superintendents), but this superintendent has been in the job less than two years.

Board members represent a wide variety of views (mainly they appear to advocate the interests of their own neighborhoods), and sometimes it is difficult for the board to achieve consensus. Perhaps the best example is the current desegregation debate. River City is about 18 percent black, and the school population is about 25 percent black. Most black families are concentrated in one part of town, and as a result two elementary schools and one junior high school have a majority of black students while two elementary schools and one middle school are overwhelmingly white (the remaining schools are reasonably well integrated). As a result, any desegregation plan will involve the redrawing of some elementary and middle school attendance boundaries and some crosstown busing. An additional possibility is the potential closing of the smallest (and oldest) elementary school, which is located in a white neighborhood. Naturally, the parents are more upset about these desegregation efforts than the children, and the common theme in most of the city's areas (especially the white ones) is the importance of neighborhood schools (i.e., "bus somebody else's children, not mine"). The board has not adopted any official plan yet, but it must do so well before the start of the 1982-83 school year if it does not wish to lose some of its state and federal aid. As would be expected, the teachers are following this desegregation debate quite closely, for any such plan may have substantial impacts upon the nature and location of their jobs.

Another example of the board's difficulty in achieving consensus is the two-week teacher strike in September 1980 which resulted primarily from the board's attempt to "hold the line" on salary increases. The board responded to the popular pressure for no tax increases by offering (through its chief negotiator) pay increases (7 percent per year) which the teachers felt were woefully inadequate in an era of double-digit inflation. The board eventually ended the strike by offering enough additional money to produce the current 1980-82 contract, and the amount offered was more than what the board originally characterized as its "final offer." In addition, it was apparent during the two-week strike (in which 85 percent of the teachers struck and the schools closed) that there were sharp differences of opinion among board members and among citizens about the wisdom of the board's action. There was also some anger directed at the teachers, most of it from working parents of the younger school-age children who faced a daily struggle to arrange for child care. However, once the strike was settled the administrators, board members, teachers, parents, and children rather quickly returned to their normal duties and there appears to be little, if any, lingering bitterness from the strike. The students and the teachers made up eight of the ten strike days by reducing some vacation periods and not using any "snow days."

The River City teachers have been unionized since 1968, when they persuaded the school board to conduct a representation election which the River City Education Association won by a 70 percent to 30 percent margin (with 95 percent of the teachers participating). Since then, the district and the association have bargained a series of one-year and, more recently, two-year contracts (a total of nine contracts in all), and all of these contracts except the current one were negotiated without strikes (though in some years only a last-minute settlement prior to the start-of-school strike deadline avoided a walkout). With few exceptions (usually at contract negotiation time), relations between the district and the RCEA have been good. Over time the RCEA has convinced most of the teachers that it is effectively representing their interests, and today about 85 percent of the eligible teachers are members of the association. No other school district employees are unionized, though periodically there are rumblings from some of these employees that they should organize and bargain collectively. The lack of unionization among the nonteaching employees can be attributed primarily to the board's willingness to provide them with most of the economic benefits that the teachers have negotiated for themselves (though the average nonteacher's salary is far below the average teacher's salary). Most of River City's rank and file employees are unionized (there are separate units for police, fire, blue-collar, and white-collar employees), but because the city government and school district are two entirely separate entitites, and because teachers naturally compare themselves to other teachers rather than to municipal employees, city labor relations have little apparent impact on school district labor relations.

The school district's personnel director (who also carries the title of associate superintendent) is responsible for all personnel and administration and labor relations matters in the school district, including the negotiation and administration of teacher contracts. He receives policy guidance from the superintendent and the school board, and he currently enjoys the support of both. The personnel director also maintains good relations with the building principals and works closely with them so that the teachers contract will not unduly restrict managerial prerogatives. He has convinced the school board and the superintendent to shut off union end runs on matters within the scope of bargaining. He was the district's chief negotiator during the 1980 strike, and while he did not personally approve of the board's strategy he attempted to implement it as best he could. He believes that the district would like to avoid a strike during the 1982 bargaining.

The River City School District's finances are in both good and bad shape. On the positive side of the ledger, the district has received enough money from local property taxes, state payments, federal special education funds. and other sources that it has been able to operate the school district without laying off any employees or eroding its relative salary position (i.e., River City pays the highest teacher salaries in Hamilton County). On the negative side, however, the coming declines in enrollment mean a slowdown in the growth of state aid, for such aid is the result of a relatively straightforward formula of X dollars (determined each year by the state legislature) per student multiplied by the number of students in the district. Further, the board is extremely reluctant to ask the district's voters for an increase in the local property tax rate, for such an increase would almost certainly be voted down (i.e., River City already has the highest school tax rate in the county). As a result, property tax revenues seem likely to increase only at the rate of increase in assessed valuation. In addition, during 1979-80 and 1980-81 the district had extremely small general fund surpluses, and the district has forecasted more than a $100,000 deficit by the time the 1981-82 year is completed. Accordingly, the district plans to speed up its recently begun policy of reducing the number of employees (certificated and noncertificated) by attrition. The district is also worried about cuts in federal aid.

Illinois has no public sector collective bargaining law, and consequently the relations between the district and the RCEA are subject to a minimum of statutory regulation. There are a variety of education laws on the books which regulate the operation of school districts (e.g., financial affairs, school district elections, reporting requirements, etc.), a union-lobbied teacher minimum salary law which establishes a statewide minimum teacher salary (which is significantly below the River City minimum), a teacher tenure law which provides teachers with tenure after three years of satisfactory service, and a union-lobbied teacher termination law which provides for a formal hearing before a state-appointed adjudicator (i.e., arbitrator) for any tenured teacher who is terminated involuntarily (if the teacher desires such a hearing). While these laws establish some constraints around teacher-district relations, the bargaining relationship is largely unregulated. This means, for instance, that the scope of bargaining theoretically can include almost anything the two sides wish to negotiate, though as a practical matter both sides are aware of the need to confine bargaining to the important aspects of the employer-employee relationship. Similarly, there is no statutory regulation of negotiating impasses, which means that the two sides are basically left to their own devices when it is necessary to break a negotiating deadlock. For negotiating pressure, the union has relied on strike threats and, in 1980, a strike. Teacher strike behavior is comparatively frequent in Illinois, an unsurprising result considering the absence of a statutory strike prohibition and the concomitant difficulty of securing strike injunctions on a timely basis (although there are a series of Illinois court decisions which clearly state that teacher strikes are illegal). For its negotiating pressure, the district has relied on the knowledge that it is free from third-party determination of impasse issues, the knowledge that the teachers will strike only on the most important issues, and in 1980 on its willingness to take a strike.

II. Union Demands

After careful evaluation of membership desires, the teachers' union leadership has formulated the following package of contract demands to be submitted

531

to the board. They are listed in no particular order of importance, though the weights attached to them ought to reflect the facts of the case. Background information is provided for some of these demands to facilitate cost calculations.

1. In light of recent increases in the Consumer Price Index, the teachers want a 16 percent increase (exclusive of increments) in the salary schedule.

2. To reward the long and faithful service of those teachers at the highest salary step in each salary column, the teachers want one new step added to each column. At least three-fourths of the teachers at each of these highest steps will move to any new steps. These top step teachers have been

TABLE 1
General Fund Expenditures 1979-82

	1979-80	1980-81	1981-82 (Est.)
Instruction—Regular Programs	$7,892,505	$8,563,071	$9,414,617
Instruction—Special Programs	259,048	278,284	287,741
Instruction—Summer School	196,372	213,966	254,427
Support Services—Pupils	297,845	369,561	420,034
Support Services—Instruction Staff	617,382	608,435	640,696
Support Services—General Administration	127,989	159,987	178,946
Support Services—School Administration	521,698	560,706	604,504
Support Services—Business	2,274,751	2,306,576	2,396,809
Support Services—Central	343,830	359,400	366,500
Non-programmed Charges	159,350	185,545	193,545
Total General Fund	$12,690,770	$13,605,531	$14,757,819

Note: Capital and transportation funds are separate.

TABLE 2
Revenues 1979-82

	1979-80	1980-81	1981-82 (Est.)
Basic Grant (State Aid)	$7,601,136	$7,964,231	$8,439,150
Summer School	48,648	44,000	41,000
Voc. Ed. Reimbursement	12,839	18,500	22,150
Special Education Programs	245,500	257,000	273,400
Transfer Tuition (Welfare & Military)	7,399	6,500	6,000
Private Transfer Tuition	3,432	2,035	2,035
Rent	28,702	32,100	34,000
Fees	66,165	68,500	71,265
Interest	28,438	42,300	34,175
Local Property Tax	4,638,947	5,174,028	5,702,928
Other	19,451	14,375	15,000
Total revenues	$12,700,657	$13,623,569	$14,641,103

pressuring the union leaders for years for additional steps, and as this top step group has grown over time this pressure has become louder and more insistent.

3. To encourage additional education for those teachers with bachelors degrees, the teachers want a new B.A. + 30 hours salary column established in the salary schedule, with the dollar amounts in this column to be at the midpoint of the difference between the B.A. and M.A. columns. Both sides estimate that about 30 percent of the teachers in the B.A. column will qualify immediately for placement in a new B.A. + 30 column, and both sides also expect that the existence of any such new column will cause the other B.A. teachers to take graduate courses at a faster rate so that they may qualify for higher salaries. The B.A. teachers have long been unhappy with the Board's policy of structuring the salary schedule to favor the M.A. teachers, and both sides are aware that at least 80 percent of Illinois school districts with teacher salary schedules have at least one salary column (e.g., B.A. + 15, B.A. + 30) between the B.A. and M.A. columns.

4. The teachers want a 16 percent increase in all the extracurricular activity salaries listed in Appendix C.

5. The teachers want new language in Article XIX that the board shall pay "the entire cost" of the family hospitalization and medical insurance coverage. The board now pays the employee's premium and half the family premium. The current single premium is $600 per year; the current family premium is $1200 per year ($600 additional). Premiums have increased about 10 percent annually during the past three years. About 40 percent of the unit members have family coverage and about 60 percent have single coverage. The new language will require the board to absorb any future cost increases.

6. The board shall provide and pay for the entire cost of family dental insurance coverage. Family coverage premiums are $150 per year over and above the single premium of $83 per year. Almost 100 percent of the employees are enrolled under single coverage, and about 70 percent of the employees would enroll their families under family coverage if it were provided.

TABLE 3
River City Teacher Salary History

Year	BA			MA			MA + 30		
	Min.	(Steps)	Max.	Min.	(Steps)	Max.	Min.	(Steps)	Max.
1975-76	8,300	(13)	11,600	8,800	(20)	14,760	9,200	(20)	15,160
1976-77	8,700	(13)	12,000	9,250	(20)	15,710	9,650	(20)	16,110
1977-78	9,150	(13)	12,450	9,750	(20)	16,500	10,150	(20)	16,900
1978-79	9,900	(13)	13,100	10,600	(20)	17,650	11,000	(20)	18,200
1979-80	10,750	(13)	13,750	11,650	(20)	19,275	12,050	(20)	19,675
1980-81	11,664	(13)	14,918	12,640	(20)	20,968	13,074	(20)	21,402
1981-82	12,714	(13)	16,261	13,778	(20)	22,855	14,250	(20)	23,328

TABLE 4
Hamilton County Teacher Salary Comparisons

District (Population)	BA					MA				
	Min.	1980-81 (Steps)	Max.	1981-82 Min.	Max.	Min.	1980-81 (Steps)	Max.	1981-82 Min.	Max.
Westfield (6,200)	10.500	(10)	13,750	11.300	14,800	11.100	(14)	17.000	12.100	18.100
Noblesville (11,300)	11.300	(10)	14.100	12.300	14,550	11.900	(16)	18.950	13.000	20.750
Marion (22,000)	11.450	(12)	14,575	12.550	16,000	12.200	(17)	19.500	13.400	21.450
Centerville (7,500)	10.850	(10)	13,900	11.500	14,750	11.400	(15)	18.450	12.085	19.550
Greenwood (18,000)	11.400	(10)	14.450	12.425	15,750	12.225	(17)	19.400	13.325	21.150
Urbanity (42,000)	11.600	(14)	15,100	12.650	16,459	12.500	(20)	19.850	13.625	21.636
River City (50,000)	11.664	(13)	14,918	12.714	16,261	12.640	(20)	20.968	13.778	22.855
River City's rank in Hamilton County	1		2	1	2	1		1	1	1

Note: Westfield has a BA + 15 salary column; Noblesville has BA + 15 and MA + 15 columns; Marion has BA + 15 and MA + 15 columns; Centerville has a BA + 20 column; Greenwood has a BA + 30 column; and Urbanity has BA + 30 and MA + 30 columns.

TABLE 5
River City School Enrollments 1975-1982

Grades	1975-76	1976-77	1977-78	1978-79	1979-80	1980-81	1981-82
K-5	3515	3605	3642	3645	3610	3503	3435
6-8	2210	2247	2275	2308	2280	2255	2221
9-12	3003	3080	3087	3126	3174	3198	3150
Total	8728	8932	9004	9079	9064	8956	8806

Note: (1) All figures are the official enrollment figures taken in September of each school year, and they include all special education students.

(2) In 1981-82, there are 438 regular and special classroom teachers: 142 at the high schools, 108 at the middle schools, and 188 at the elementary schools. In addition, there are 50 certificated employees in the bargaining unit who are librarians, guidance counselors, resource specialists, and so forth.

7. The mileage reimbursement figure in Article XX shall be increased to 25 cents per mile. Unit members collectively drive their personal cars about 5000 miles per year on a required and approved basis.

8. Personal illness leave shall be increased to 12 days per year for each year, and shall accumulate to a maximum of 200 days. Each year several (i.e., 5-10) teachers will use more than 8 days personal illness leave. Also, the higher entitlement rate and the larger accumulation amount will enable retiring teachers to earn somewhat larger severance compensation under Article X.

9. A new article on employee hours which states the following: "The regular in-school workday shall consist of not more than eight (8) consecutive hours High School; seven and one-half (7½) consecutive hours Middle School; and seven and one-quarter (7¼) hours Elementary. Employees may be required to remain after the end of the regular workday, without additional compensation, for the purpose of attending faculty meetings one day each month. Such meetings shall begin no later than fifteen (15) minutes after the student dismissal time and shall run for no more than 45 minutes. Meetings shall not be called on Fridays or on any afternoon preceding any holiday." The workday length figures are what teachers are currently required to work, but the teachers would like to incorporate these figures into the contract in order to prevent any future increases in their workday. The teachers want the restrictions on after school meetings because of the propensity of two or three elementary school principals to schedule rather frequent after school meetings (in one case as often as once a week). The teachers in these schools believe that most of these meetings are unnecessary.

10. A new provision (perhaps as part of the previous article) which guarantees each teacher a duty-free preparation period: "Each High School and Middle School teacher shall receive at least one fifty-five (55) minute duty-free period each workday for preparation purposes, and each Elementary School teacher shall receive fifty-five duty-free minutes each day for preparation purposes." The high school and middle school teachers already receive a duty-free preparation period, and the elementary teachers receive about

535

TABLE 6
Teacher Salary Placement 1981-82

Step	BA	MA	MA + 30		Nurses	
0	19	5	0		0	
1	18	10	0		0	
2	19	22	0		2	
3	21	24	0		1	
4	15	28	0		1	
5	8	27	2		0	
6	10	14	0		1	
7	9	19	1		0	
8	5	12	3		1	
9	4	20	1		0	
10	6	13	1			
11	12	16	1			
12	27	8	2			
13		4	2			
14		7	1			
15		9	3			
16		10	4			
17		4	1			
18		8	1			
19	—	25	7		—	
Totals:	173	285	30	(488)	6	(494)
1980-81 totals:	176	288	31	(495)	6	(501)
1979-80 totals:	175	290	31	(496)	6	(502)

Note. (1) Teachers who remain in the district from one year to the next automatically advance one step in their salary column. These salary step increments range from 1.8 percent to 3.3 percent, depending upon each teacher's salary placement, and the average cost of these increments for the entire bargaining unit is about 2.5 percent.

(2) Each year about 20-30 new teachers are hired to replace incumbent teachers who depart for one reason or another, except that for the 1981-82 year only 15 new teachers were hired (the district eliminated seven positions by attrition). Often these new hires are cheaper than the departing teachers because of placement at lower steps on the salary schedule. The district and the Association estimate that each new hire saves the district an average of $500 (compared to the salary paid to the departing teacher).

(3) Each year about 3-4 teachers will receive their master's degree and move from the BA column to the MA column, and once every two or three years a teacher will move from the MA column to the MA + 30 column.

TABLE 7
Assessed Valuation 1975-81

	1975-76	1976-77	1977-78	1978-79	1979-80	1980-81
River City	$118,978,000	$127,895,000	$135,635,000	$146,550,000	$158,700,000	$168,153,000
River City Per Pupil	13,631	14,318	15,063	16,141	17,508	18,775
Hamilton County	340,155,000	356,505,000	378,825,000	396,118,000	422,833,000	456,380,000
Hamilton County Per Pupil	12,991	13,304	14,024	14,495	15,550	16,986

Note: The 1980-81 assessed valuation figures are the latest ones available from the county assessor's office.

537

50 minutes before and after school. However, the elementary teachers complain that they must spend most of that time supervising children before and after school, and thus they cannot use that time for preparation purposes.

11. A new article which limits class size: "Except as agreed to otherwise, regular Elementary School classes shall contain no more than twenty-five (25) students, regular Middle School classes shall contain no more than twenty-eight (28) students, and regular High School classes shall contain no more than thirty (30) students. These limitations shall not apply to physical education, vocational arts, or home room classes, nor to special events. Other exceptions may be mutually agreed to by Board and Association representatives." This language would have little immediate impact, for almost all regular education classes are within these limits (and special education classes usually are considerably smaller). However, the teachers are worried that the board may be forced to increase class size as an economy measure (even though the board is on record as favoring smaller rather than larger classes), and consequently they want to protect against larger workloads.

12. A new article which establishes staff reduction (i.e., layoff) and recall rights with seniority being the dominant criterion (with the precise language to be drafted by the teacher bargaining team). The teachers are aware that no layoffs have occurred in the district, but they are worried that the coming declines in enrollment may result in layoffs (as have occurred in other school districts), and consequently they are very eager to be protected by an orderly and fair staff reduction procedure which will recognize length of service.

13. A new article which establishes voluntary transfer rights within the district (with the precise language to be drafted by the teacher bargaining team). The teachers want to ensure that the voluntary transfer procedures now being used (and which are reasonably satisfactory) are contractually guaranteed (i.e., posting of vacancy notices, bidding rights for vacancies, right to be interviewed for a vacancy, seniority as the tie-breaker when employees compete for the same vacancy and their qualifications are equal, etc.). The teachers believe that this language will be necessary if a desegregation plan is adopted.

14. A new article which establishes involuntary transfer rights within the district (with the precise language to be drafted by the teacher bargaining team). The Association recognizes the district's right to transfer teachers on an involuntary basis, but teachers want to have some restrictions imposed on the involuntary transfer process (i.e., no involuntary transfers if there are qualified volunteers available, the right to a meeting with the superintendent (or his designee) prior to such a transfer, the use of seniority in the selection of teachers to be transferred if more than one person is qualified, etc.). Again, the teachers believe this language will be necessary if a desegregation plan is adopted.

15. A one-year contract expiring on June 30, 1983.

Again, these demands are not presented in any particular order of importance beyond the facts presented in the case. It is the responsibility of the union bargaining team to gather supporting evidence, to put priorities or weights on various items, to develop specific contract language to implement

538

various proposals, to develop justifications for its demands, to decide what compromises to make, and to decide what a minimum acceptable agreement shall be. The current contract is enclosed.

Although the number of students to be assigned to each bargaining team will be constrained by the size of the class, experience has suggested that four students per team is desirable. The roles on the teacher bargaining committee include: the Association president and chief negotiator, the Association attorney, the Association secretary-treasurer, and the Association grievance committee chairperson.

III. Employer Demands

In collective bargaining the employer typically spends much time responding to union demands. However, as a result of perceived problems which have arisen during the life of the existing contract and because of the district's fiscal constraints, the board has formulated the following demands:

1. An increase of 3 percent in the salary schedule for 1982-83 and another 3 percent in 1983-84, to produce a total average increase (schedule plus increments) of 5.5 percent for bargaining unit members in each of the next two years. The board expects that the state aid formula will not increase as rapidly as it has in past years, and when combined with declining enrollments, the formula should produce a sharp slowdown in the growth of state aid. Similarly, the board does not believe it can convince the voters to approve an increase in the school tax rate, and thus local property taxes will increase only at the rate of increase in assessed valuation (the board estimates about 7-8 percent per year growth in property taxes).

2. No new steps, columns, or any other structural modifications of the salary schedule. The board has long followed a policy of encouraging teachers to earn masters degrees and paying them for doing so, and it sees no reason to depart from that policy now. Similarly, the board has rewarded longevity by agreeing to larger step increments for the longer service teachers in the M.A. columns. In short, the board likes the shape of the current schedule and notes that teachers agreed to it in past negotiations.

3. An increase of 4 percent in the extracurricular activity payment schedule in each of the next two years.

4. No increase in any monetary fringe benefit during the next two years. Teacher monetary fringes (retirement, social security, insurance, sick leave, other leaves) currently cost the board about 23 percent of salaries, and there may be state-mandated increases in retirement contributions and federally mandated increases in social security contributions even without any negotiated increases.

5. No changes in the noneconomic provisions in the contract. The board and the administration value the managerial discretion they possess under the current contract and they do not want this discretion curtailed. To date this board has traded off high wages and fringes for the preservation of managerial prerogatives, and the board has complemented this policy by insisting that the administration be consistent and equitable in its handling of all staff personnel issues.

6. A two-year contract expiring on June 30, 1984.

These demands are not presented in any particular order of importance beyond the information presented in the case. It is the responsibility of the management bargaining team to gather supporting evidence, to attach priorities to various items, to develop specific contract language, to implement various proposals, to develop justifications for various proposals, to decide what compromises to make, and to decide what a minimum acceptable agreement shall be. The current contract is enclosed.

The roles on the management bargaining team include the director of personnel and chief negotiator, the business manager, a middle school principal, and a board member.

IV. Impasse Resolution

If no agreement is reached by the end of the time set aside for direct negotiations, there are a variety of methods by which the impasse may be resolved: mediation, factfinding, some form of arbitration, or strike. For example, the instructor may decide to use one of the arbitration methods specified a few pages earlier at the end of the police bargaining exercise. As another example, the instructor may prefer to use the statutory impasse procedure which applies to teachers in the state or city where this exercise is being used. As a third option, the instructor may use a strike as the impasse resolution process. In Illinois and several other states, teacher strikes are comparatively frequent, and it may be informative for the students to cope with the stresses and strains associated with a strike situation. If this option is used, the instructor should devise a penalty schedule which will make the participants aware of the increasing costs of any such strike as time passes.

V. Post-Exercise Analysis

The instructor and the students will find it profitable to spend all or most of a class period analyzing the negotiation and impasse resolution experiences of the various bargaining teams (no matter in what manner the bargaining is resolved). The students probably will have numerous questions about various facets of the negotiation and impasse processes, and the instructor ought to have a variety of constructively critical comments to make about how the students tried to obtain a favorable contract.

CONTRACT

Between

THE BOARD OF EDUCATION
of the
RIVER CITY SCHOOL DISTRICT
and the
RIVER CITY EDUCATION ASSOCIATION,
an affiliate of the
ILLINOIS EDUCATION ASSOCIATION
and the
NATIONAL EDUCATION ASSOCIATION

COLLECTIVE BARGAINING AGREEMENT

This Agreement is entered into this 18th day of September, 1980, by and between the Board of Education of River City School District of Hamilton County, Illinois, hereinafter called the "Board," and the River City Education Association, an affiliate of the Illinois Education Association and the National Education Association, hereinafter called the "Association."

In consideration of the mutual covenants hereinafter contained, the parties hereto agree as follows:

ARTICLE I
Recognition

For the term of this Agreement, the Association is recognized by the Board as the exclusive representative of the following described school employees of the Board as set forth in the following appropriate unit:

Included: All certificated employees of River City Schools of Hamilton County, Illinois, including regular and special education teachers, librarians, guidance counselors, resource specialists, and school nurses.

Excluded: Superintendent, assistant superintendents, directors and supervisors with school corporation-wide responsibilities, principals, vice-principals, administrative assistants, deans, athletic directors, director of student affairs, department heads who have the responsibility for evaluating teachers, director of the special education cooperative, confidential employees, and employees performing security work.

ARTICLE II
Contract Procedures

This Agreement shall constitute the full and complete commitments between both parties and may be altered, changed, added to, deleted from or modified only through the voluntary mutual consent of the parties in a written and signed agreement.

ARTICLE III
Rights, Responsibility and Authority of Board of Education

The Association recognizes that the Board has the responsibility and authority to manage and direct in behalf of the public all of the operations and activities of the school district to the full extent authorized by law. The exercise of these powers, rights, authority, duties, and responsibilities by the Board and the adoption of such rules, regulations, and policies shall include but not be limited to the right of the school employer to:

A. Direct the work of its employees in the best interest of the community; establish policies in areas of pupil evaluation, reporting to parents, curricula, special programs and methods of instruction; athletic, recreational and social events for students, all as deemed necessary or advisable by the Board.
B. Manage and control the school properties and facilities.
C. Determine the qualifications for employment, promotion, demotion, transfer, assignments, and retention of employees.
D. Suspend or discharge its employees in accordance with applicable law.
E. Maintain the efficiency of the school operation.
F. Relieve its employees from duties because of lack of work or other legitimate reason.
G. Take actions necessary to carry out the mission of the public schools as provided by law.

ARTICLE IV
Association and Teacher Rights

A. The Board hereby agrees that every certificated employee within the Bargaining Unit shall have the right to organize, join, and support the Association for the purpose of engaging in negotiations for mutual aid and protection.
B. The Board further agrees that it will not encourage nor discourage any teacher in the enjoyment of any rights conferred by this contract or the laws and Constitutions of the United States and Illinois.
C. The Board will not discriminate against any teacher because of membership or non-membership in the Association.
D. Nothing contained herein shall be construed to deny or restrict to any teacher rights he/she may have under the Illinois General School Laws or other applicable laws and regulations.
E. The Association shall have the right to use school buildings, facilities, and equipment by following the established Board procedure. If materials and supplies are required, the Association shall reimburse the Board at cost.
F. The Association may use the bulletin board in the faculty lounge in each building; nothing religious or obscene in nature shall be posted. All materials must be identified as to source.

G. The Association shall be permitted to use the teacher mailboxes and inter-school mail service. All materials must be identified as to the source.

H. Each teacher shall have the right, upon request, to review the contents of his/her own personal file as maintained by the Director of Personnel and/or building principal, in the presence of a representative of the administration. A representative of the Association may accompany the teacher in such reviews when requested by the teacher.

I. Any member or representative of the Association who visits a school for the purpose of conducting Association business shall make known his/her presence in the building to the building principal or designee should the principal not be available.

J. The administration shall provide a copy of the printed agenda and all other public materials to the Association President or designee at the time materials are provided to the Board members.

ARTICLE V
Payroll Deductions

A. The Association shall deliver to the business office the names and authorization of teachers who request payroll deductions of membership dues of the Association no later than October 15. The authorization for payroll deduction of Association membership dues may be either for one (1) year or on a continuing basis unless revoked, in writing, by the teacher through the Association during the month of September. The Association will provide all forms for such notification which shall be available from each Faculty Representative.

B. The Board shall deduct such authorized sum in eighteen (18) equal continuous pay periods beginning with the first pay period in November. The deductions shall be remitted in nine (9) installments once each month to the Association treasurer.

ARTICLE VI
Length of School Year

The school year shall consist of one hundred eighty-eight (188) teacher contract days.

ARTICLE VII
Salary Adjustments

All adjustments to salary as a result of additional college or university training shall be effective at the beginning of the semester succeeding the completion of such training provided the teacher has notified the Director of Personnel at least thirty (30) days prior to the beginning of that semester. An official transcript verifying additional training shall be filed with the Director of Personnel within sixty (60) days of completion of such training.

ARTICLE VIII
Pay Periods

The number of pay periods shall be at least twenty-six (26) and shall be due every other Friday.

ARTICLE IX
Experience Credit

A. Teacher Experience Credit
  1. Credit shall be granted toward salary and retirement for each verified full year of public school experience in an approved accredited elementary or secondary public school in the United States, its territories or official overseas divisions.
  2. Credit will be granted for each full year of nonpublic school experience in the United States and its territories, with such credit not to exceed eight (8) years. For such nonpublic school experience to be credited, it shall be necessary that said experience shall be in a school accredited by a State Department of Public Instruction.
  3. One (1) full year of experience credit shall be allowed toward salary, retirement, and tenure for any teacher who has:
     a. Ninety-five (95) or more actual teaching days in one (1) school year in the River City School System, July 1 to June 30.
     b. One hundred twenty (120) or more actual teaching days in one (1) school year in any school system outside the River City schools July 1 to June 30 in addition to 1 and 2 above.
B. Temporary Contracts
  Any teacher hired to replace a teacher on leave should be placed on a temporary contract which shall specify the name of the teacher being replaced. All other teachers shall be placed on regular contract.
C. Salary Schedule Placement
  Each teacher shall be placed on the salary schedule in the appropriate educational column and at the appropriate experience step and shall be paid the appropriate salary specified in Appendix A for the 1980-81 year and in Appendix B for the 1981-82 year.

ARTICLE X
Severance Compensation

A. All teachers who have acquired twenty (20) or more years of experience and have been employed by River City Schools for the complete preceding ten (10) consecutive years, as recognized by the Illinois State Teachers Retirement Fund Board at the time of their retirement, will be eligible for additional compensation according to the following schedule
  20-24 year's experience—30% of the accumulated total of the teacher's sick leave.
  25-29 years' experience—55% of the accumulated total of the teacher's sick leave.
  30-plus years' experience—80% of the accumulated total of the teacher's sick leave.

The additional compensation is to be equivalent in an amount to the retiring teacher's accumulated sick leave according to the above schedule, but is not to exceed one hundred (100) days. The compensation will be calculated by the following formula: Teacher's daily salary times one hundred (100) days or the appropriate categorical per cent of accumulated sick leave, whichever is lesser.

B. To be eligible for severance compensation, a teacher must:
    1. Have applied for and be eligible to receive appropriate benefits under the provisions of the Illinois State Teachers Retirement Fund.
    2. Notify the Superintendent in writing not later than January 1, of his/her last contract school year, of his/her intention to retire. In the event poor health necessitates a teacher's retirement without such notification having been made by the required time period, such retirement will be granted provided an examination by a physician agreeable to the Board verifies the necessity of retirement.

ARTICLE XI
Personal Illness Leave

A. Each teacher shall be entitled to be absent from work without loss of compensation on account of personal illness, injury, or quarantine as follows:
    1. Ten (10) days the first (1st) year and eight (8) days each year thereafter.
    2. Each unused personal illness day shall accumulate to a maximum of one hundred seventy (170) days. Any accumulated days may be used in subsequent years.
B. Illness days may be taken in half day segments; one-half (½) day shall be deducted when a teacher is absent for three and one-half (3½) hours or less.
C. Teachers on summer teaching employment shall be eligible to use illness leave on the same basis as is used during the regular school year; that is, a teaching day in summer school is equal to a regular school teaching day.
D. In the event of catastrophic illness or injury to a faculty member causing him/her to be out of school more days than his or her accumulated Personal Illness Leave, other teachers may voluntarily transfer unused portions of their accumulated illness leave to that teacher, with the following provisions:
    1. No faculty member may contribute more than one (1) day per year.
    2. No teacher may receive more than eighty-eight (88) days by voluntary transfer in any school year.
    3. Extended illness must be verified by a physician.

ARTICLE XII
Personal Business/Family Illness Leave

A. Each faculty member shall be entitled to four (4) days for the transaction of personal business, civic affairs and/or family illness during each year of employment without loss of compensation for such absence. A written statement shall be submitted to the Superintendent, setting forth the reason and necessity which shall be the cause of such absence.

B. Any unused days will be added to the accumulation of personal illness leave, at the end of each school year.

C. These days may be taken in half (½) day amounts.

D. Teachers on summer teaching employment shall be eligible to use personal/family illness leave on the same basis as is used during the regular school year; that is, a teaching day in summer school is equal to a regular school teaching day. No additional personal/family illness days shall be granted for summer school.

E. A teacher shall be granted leave for illness in the immediate family. Those considered immediate family would be: mother, father, brother, sister, wife, husband, children, or any relative living in the household of the teacher. The above leave shall also be granted for mother-in-law, father-in-law, brother-in-law, sister-in-law, son-in-law, daughter-in-law in the event of the hospitalization of any of these persons for illness, surgery, or accident. The Superintendent may require proof of hospitalization for in-laws, when he feels misuse of the leave by the teacher has been made.

F. Each faculty member will be highly ethical in choosing to take a personal/family leave day. It is the intent that personal/family leave days are not to be used for the sole purpose of extending a holiday or school recess period.

ARTICLE XIII
Bereavement

A. For death in the immediate family a period extending not more than five (5) consecutive calendar days, beginning the day such leave is requested by the teacher but not later than the day following the death, shall be granted. Immediate family is interpreted as wife, husband, father, mother, brother, sister, children, father-in-law, mother-in-law, brother-in-law, sister-in-law, son-in-law, daughter-in-law, grandchild, or any person who at the time of death has been living as a member of the teacher's household for at leave five (5) years, has established the teacher's home as his/her permanent residence, and has named the teacher administrator or executor for his/her estate.

B. In case of death of a grandparent, uncle, aunt, first cousin, niece, nephew or any person who at the time of death had been living as a member of the teacher's household for at least five (5) years and had established the teacher's home as his/her permanent residence, the teacher is entitled to be absent one (1) day without loss of compensation.

ARTICLE XIV
Maternity Leave

A. Any teacher who is pregnant is entitled to a leave of absence any time between the commencement of her pregnancy and one (1) year following

546

the birth of the child, if, except in a medical emergency, she notifies the Superintendent at least thirty (30) days before the date on which she desires to start her leave. She shall also notify the Superintendent of the expected length of this leave, including with this notice either a physician's statement certifying her pregnancy or a copy of the birth certificate of the newborn, whichever is applicable. In case of a medical emergency caused by pregnancy, the teacher shall be granted a leave, as otherwise provided in this section, immediately upon her request and certification of the emergency from an attending physician.

B. All or any portion of leave taken by a teacher because of a temporary disability caused by pregnancy may be charged, at her discretion, to her available sick leave. After her available sick leave has been used, the teacher may be absent without pay, subject to Section (A) of this Article. This leave may be taken without jeopardy to reemployment, retirement and salary benefits, tenure, and seniority rights.

ARTICLE XV
Adoption Leave

A. A teacher shall receive adoption leave, without pay, for a period not to exceed one (1) year, provided a written request has been submitted to the Director of Personnel thirty (30) days prior to leave. In the event the adoption agency fails to provide the applicant with sufficient advance notice, the thirty (30) day notice may be waived.

B. This leave may be taken without jeopardy to re-employment, retirement, salary and fringe benefits, tenure, and seniority rights.

ARTICLE XVI
Jury Duty

A. A teacher may serve as a member of a jury in response to a summons for jury duty. A teacher so serving shall pay all jury earnings to the school corporation within ninety (90) days of the completion of said service. Parking fees, room, meals, and the school approved mileage may be deducted from these earnings upon the filing of a signed statement of actual expense. Anyone serving on jury duty is not eligible for summer pay until all jury duty earnings have been returned to the school corporation. At no time shall any teacher receive more than his/her regular contracted daily rate of pay.

B. A faculty member, employed in summer school, shall be compensated the same as in (A) above for the performance of duties described.

ARTICLE XVII
Lunch Period

Teachers shall have a duty-free lunch period of at least thirty (30) continuous minutes each school day. Teachers may leave the building without seeking permission during their designated lunch period by signing out prior to departure and signing in upon return. Such forms will be provided in the office.

ARTICLE XVIII
Grievance Procedure

A. *Definitions*
  1. A "grievance" is a claim by one (1) or more teachers of a violation, a mis-application, or a misinterpretation of this Contract.
  2. "Grievant" shall be defined as the school employee as defined in this Agreement directly affected by the alleged violation making the claim.
  3. "Days" shall be defined as school contract days. During the summer recess, days shall be defined as week days.
B. *Structure*
  The grievant may be represented by any person(s) of his/her own choosing at all levels of the Procedure.
C. *Procedure*
  1. The number of days indicated at each level should be considered as maximum.

    a. *Informal Grievance*
      Within twenty (20) days of the time the grievant first knew of the act or condition upon which it is based, the grievant must present the grievance to his principal or immediate supervisor or his designee by meeting with him in an informal manner. Failure to so meet and discuss said alleged grievance as provided herein shall prevent the grievant from filing said alleged grievance at any formal grievance level(s). Failure on the part of the principal, supervisor or his designee to meet and discuss with the grievant will automatically move the grievance to the next step. Within ten (10) days after presentation of the grievance, the principal or immediate supervisor or his designee shall give his answer orally to the grievant.
    b. *Formal Grievance*
      (1) *Level One*
        (1a) Within five (5) days of the expiration of the ten (10) days provided for the answer in the informal procedure, if the grievance is not resolved, it must be filed by the grievant with the principal or immediate supervisor or his designee in writing, signed by the grievant, on the appropriate grievance form. The written grievance shall name the school employee involved, shall state the facts giving rise to the grievance, shall identify what has been violated, and shall indicate the specific relief requested.
        (1b) Within ten (10) days after receiving the written grievance, the principal or supervisor or his designee shall communicate his answer in writing to the grievant.

548

(2) *Level Two*

    (2a) In the event that the grievance is not resolved at Level One, the grievant may appeal the decision to Level Two provided said appeal is filed with the Superintendent within ten (10) days after the expiration of the ten (10) days provided for the answer in Level One utilizing the appropriate form.

    (2b) The Superintendent shall hold an informal hearing within ten (10) days after the appeal has been filed. Evidence and materials may be presented at this informal hearing. Within ten (10) days after informal hearing, the Superintendent shall communicate his written decision to the grievant.

(3) *Level Three*

    (3a) If the grievance remains unresolved at the completion of Level Two, the Association shall have ten (10) days to submit to the Superintendent a written request to enter into arbitration. Upon receipt of such request, the Superintendent or his designee and the Association shall have ten (10) school days to agree upon a mutually acceptable arbitrator and obtain a commitment from said arbitrator to serve. If the parties are unable to agree upon an arbitrator or to obtain such a commitment within these ten (10) school days, a written request for a list of arbitrators shall be made to the appropriate regional office of the American Arbitration Association by either party. The list shall consist of seven (7) potential arbitrators and the parties shall determine by lot which party shall have the right to remove the first name from the list. The party having the right to remove the first name shall do so within two (2) school days. Then the parties shall have one (1) school day alternately to remove until only one (1) name remains, and the person whose name remains shall be the arbitrator.

    (3b) The arbitrator so selected shall confer with the Superintendent or his designee and the Association and hold hearings promptly and shall issue his decision not later than thirty (30) school days from the date of the close of the hearing, or if oral hearings have been waived, then from the date the final statements and proofs on the issues are received by him. The arbitrator's decision shall be in writing and shall set forth his findings of fact, reasoning, and conclusions on the issues submitted. The arbitrator shall have no power to alter, add to, or detract from the specific provisions of this agreement. The decision of the arbitrator shall be submitted to the Superintendent or his designee and the Association and shall be final and binding upon the parties.

(3c) The fees and the expenses of the arbitrator shall be shared equally by the Board and the Association.

ARTICLE XIX
Group Insurance Program

A *Group Hospital and Medical Insurance*
The Board shall pay the amounts below for employee coverage to the group insurance carrier for hospital and medical insurance coverage pursuant to the group insurance policy purchased for the River City Schools by the Board.
Up to $900.00 for those employees who elect family plan coverage.
Up to $600.00 for those employees who elect single plan coverage.
The premium amount may not be received in lieu of enrollment in the group medical plan.

B. *Dental Insurance*
The Board shall pay up to $83.00 per year for employee coverage to the group insurance carrier for Dental Insurance coverage pursuant to the group insurance policy purchased for the River City Schools by the Board. The premium amount may not be received in lieu of enrollment in the group dental insurance plan.

C. *Income Protection*
The Board shall pay up to $50.00 per year for employee coverage to the group insurance carrier for Income Protection Insurance coverage pursuant to the group insurance policy purchased for the River City Schools by the Board which shall include a 90 calendar day waiting period; 66-2/3% of salary to age 65 for disability due to illness or life if disability is due to accident, and waiver of premium clause. The premium amount may not be received in lieu of enrollment in the group income protection insurance plan.

D. *Group Life Insurance*
Fifteen thousand dollars ($15,000.00) Group Life Insurance will be provided for each teacher employed by the River City Schools.

ARTICLE XX
Automobile Travel Expense

A. A teacher required in the course of his/her work to drive a personal automobile shall receive a travel reimbursement. The Board agrees to reimburse the teacher at the rate of twenty (20) cents per mile as required and approved for professional business and/or fulfillment of contractual obligations.

B. The Board shall examine and determine the maximum amount necessary for the teacher to fulfill his/her assignment.

C. Any travel reimbursement in excess of the contractual amount must have prior approval of the immediate supervisor and the Personnel Director.

ARTICLE XXI
Severability Clause

Should any Article, Section, or Clause of this Agreement be declared illegal by a court of competent jurisdiction, said Article, Section, or Clause, as the case may be, shall be automatically deleted from this Agreement to the extent that it violated the law; but the remaining Articles, Sections, and Clauses shall remain in full force and effect for the duration of the Agreement if not affected by the deleted Article, Section, or Clause.

ARTICLE XXII
Effective Date and Term of Agreement

This Agreement shall be effective July 1, 1980 and shall continue in effect through June 30, 1982.

In Witness Whereof, the parties hereto have duly executed this Agreement this 18th day of September, 1980.

Board of Education of   River City Education Association
River City Schools of
Hamilton County

APPENDIX A
1980-81
River City Schools
Salary Schedule

Experience	BA	MA	MA + 30
0	11,664	12,640	13,074
1	11,935	12,939	13,373
2	12,206	13,237	13,671
3	12,478	13,535	13,969
4	12,749	13,834	14,268
5	13,020	14,132	14,566
6	13,291	14,566	15,000
7	13,563	15,000	15,434
8	13,834	15,434	15,868
9	14,105	15,868	16,302
10	14,376	16,302	16,736
11	14,647	16,736	17,170
12	14,918	17,170	17,604
13		17,604	18,038
14		18,038	18,472
15		18,472	18,906
16		19,096	19,530
17		19,720	20,154
18		20,344	20,778
19		20,968	21,402

School Nurses shall receive seventy-five percent (.75) of the appropriate BA column salary.

APPENDIX B
1981-82
River City Schools
Salary Schedule

Experience	BA	MA	MA + 30
0	12,714	13,778	14,250
1	13,009	14,103	14,576
2	13,304	14,428	14,901
3	13,601	14,753	15,226
4	13,896	15,079	15,552
5	14,192	15,404	15,877
6	14,487	15,877	16,350
7	14,783	16,350	16,823
8	15,079	16,823	17,296
9	15,374	17,296	17,769
10	15,670	17,769	18,242
11	15,965	18,242	18,715
12	16,261	18,715	19,188
13		19,188	19,661
14		19,661	20,134
15		20,134	20,607
16		20,815	21,288
17		21,495	21,968
18		22,175	22,648
19		22,855	23,328

School Nurses shall receive seventy-five percent (.75) of the appropriate BA column salary.

APPENDIX C
Extracurricular Payment Schedule

The extracurricular activities schedule shall be as follows:

	Schedule	
Position	1980-81	1981-82
High School:		
Head Football	2000	2200
Assistant Football	1600	1760
Head Baseball	1600	1760
Assistant Baseball	1000	1100
Head Track	1600	1760
Assistant Track	1000	1100
Head Basketball	1800	1980
Assistant Basketball	1400	1540
Head Cross Country	1300	1430
Assistant Cross Country	800	880
Head Tennis	1200	1320
Assistant Tennis	750	825
Head Wrestling	1700	1870

| | Schedule | |
Position	1980-81	1981-82
Assistant Wrestling	1000	1100
Head Swimming	1500	1650
Assistant Swimming	900	990
Head Golf	1200	1320
Assistant Golf	750	825
Cheerblock	400	440
Yearbook	800	880
Class Sponsor	600	660
Intramurals	1000	1100
Assistant Intramurals	600	660
Dramatics	800	880
School Paper	700	770
Debate	800	880
Volleyball	1000	1100
Gymnastics	1000	1100
Cheerleader Sponsor	600	660
Honor Society	550	605
Middle School:		
Football	1500	1650
Assistant Football	1000	1100
Basketball	1200	1320
Assistant Basketball	800	880
Tennis	500	550
Track	900	990
Assistant Track	600	660
Cross Country	800	880
Assistant Cross Country	500	550
Wrestling	1100	1210
Assistant Wrestling	800	880
Baseball	900	990
Assistant Baseball	600	660
Volleyball	600	660
Assistant Volleyball	400	440
School Paper	600	660
Intramurals	700	770
Cheerleader Sponsor	500	550
Dramatics	500	550
Gymnastics	600	660